Caesars Palace
Grand Prix

Caesars Palace Grand Prix

*Las Vegas, Organized Crime
and the Pinnacle of Motorsport*

RANDALL CANNON

McFarland & Company, Inc., Publishers
Jefferson, North Carolina

Library of Congress Cataloguing-in-Publication Data

Names: Cannon, Randall, 1956– author.
Title: Caesars Palace Grand Prix : Las Vegas, organized crime
and the pinnacle of motorsport / Randall Cannon.
Description: Jefferson, North Carolina : McFarland & Company, Inc., Publishers, 2021
Includes bibliographical references and index.
Identifiers: LCCN 2021032518 | ISBN 9781476683775 (paperback : acid free paper) ∞
ISBN 9781476642826 (ebook)
Subjects: LCSH: Caesars Palace Grand Prix (Automobile race) | Gambling—Nevada—
Las Vegas. | Organized crime—Nevada—Las Vegas. | Automobile racing—
Nevada—Las Vegas. | BISAC: SPORTS & RECREATION / Motor Sports / General |
HISTORY / United States / State & Local / West (AK, CA, CO, HI, ID, MT, NV, UT, WY)
Classification: LCC GV1033.5.C34 C36 2021 | DDC 796.7209793/135—dc23
LC record available at https://lccn.loc.gov/2021032518

British Library cataloguing data are available

ISBN (print) 978-1-4766-8377-5
ISBN (ebook) 978-1-4766-4282-6

Front cover: The Formula One field of the Caesars Palace Grand Prix takes
the green flag at the start of the race on October 17, 1981, in Las Vegas, Nevada
(William D. Weinberger Collection)

Printed in the United States of America

*McFarland & Company, Inc., Publishers
Box 611, Jefferson, North Carolina 28640
www.mcfarlandpub.com*

To Jimmy, Spunki,
and Reina

Table of Contents

Acknowledgments

The Caesars Palace Grand Prix presented a fascinating opportunity to study two parallel threads of history, the progression of Formula One motorsport through America and forward *to* Caesars Palace, alongside the influences of the national crime syndicate and the development and operational plan *for* Caesars Palace. As such, the body of research traverses several decades. This is a story, then, that could not have been told without the willing recollections of the participants and observers populating both paths through the past. Photographic contributions, as well, brought the story to a vivid reality. The author acknowledges the contributions of the following for the generosity of their time, their remembrances, and their resources, with deepest gratitude.

Most of all, I express my heartfelt appreciation to my patient, supportive, loving wife Julie. Further, this work would not be possible without the constant encouragement and wisdom of our children, Courtney, Camille, and Clark.

Former Caesars Palace Vice President of Casino Marketing William D. Weinberger provided invaluable insight into the origins of the Caesars Palace Grand Prix as well as a peek inside the Palace of Caesar. Mr. Weinberger also provided several images from his personal collection.

Former Caesars World, Inc. legal counsel and Caesars Palace Vice President Bruce Aguilera steered the Caesars Palace Grand Prix storyline through the transition from Formula One to the CART IndyCar series, as well as provided background on the Caesars Palace chief executive and later Formula One efforts in Las Vegas. Mr. Aguilera also facilitated access to Caesars Palace Grand Prix press materials, race programs, and race posters.

Friends and colleagues who contributed selflessly to the success of the project: Josh Ashby/International Motor Racing Research Center, Mike Follmer, Rick Lake, Tony Landis, Scott Liles, Mike Machat, Marc Nelson, Ernie Ohlson, and Pete Ward.

The racers, journalists, broadcasters, archivists, historians, photographers, and other contributors to the history of the Caesars Palace Grand Prix, Caesars Palace, Formula One in America, and this story, in alphabetical order: Jenny Ambrose/International Motor Racing Research Center, Mario Andretti, Duke Argetsinger/International Motor Racing Research Center, Allen Brown/Oldracingcars.com, Jeff Burbank, Su Kim Chung, Ph.D./University of Nevada–Las Vegas, Allan Coy/California Sports Car Club, Wally Dallenbach, Jr., Jay Dalton, Tom Daniel, Gary Gerould, Bill Green/International Motor Racing Research Center, Michael Green, Ph.D./

University of Nevada–Las Vegas, Mike Henle, Bethany Khan/Culinary Workers Union Local 226, Las Vegas News Bureau, Jack Long, Pete Lyons, Jane Tyler Maners/Caesars Entertainment, Anthony Marnell/Marnell Companies, Brent Martin, Jim Michaelian/Grand Prix Association of Long Beach, Robin Miller/Racer.com, Jeff Motley/Las Vegas Motor Speedway, Mary Lou Pernicano/Penske Corporation, Chris Pook, Revs Institute for Automotive Research, Lyn St. James, Jay Sarno, Jr., David G. Schwartz, Ph.D./University of Nevada–Las Vegas, Tony Scodwell, Jeffrey A. Silver/Dickinson-Wright, John L. Smith, Stuart Sobek/Las Vegas Concours de Elegance, Sir Jackie Stewart, John Surtees, Jeff Teasley/HistoricAerials.com, Rick Titus, Al Unser, Bobby Unser, Tina Van Curen/Autobooks-Aerobooks.com.

Preface

FORMULA ONE—the undisputed pinnacle of professional motorsport. For more than 70 years, Formula One has represented the highest level of technology, achievement, and spectacle in motor racing. The Formula One World Drivers Championship was first awarded in 1950. Luminary international names such as Juan Manuel Fangio, Alberto Ascari, Jack Brabham, Jimmy Clark, Graham Hill, John Surtees, Jackie Stewart, Nelson Piquet, Alain Prost, Ayrton Senna, Sebastian Vettel, Lewis Hamilton, and the incomparable Michael Schumacher have made their indelible mark on the championship. America, too, has produced Formula One champions, Phil Hill in 1961 and Mario Andretti in 1978.

Formula One has also forged a reputation of political maneuvering, incessant meddling, and extreme profiteering. The premier event of the Formula One series is certainly the Grand Prix of Monaco, renowned for its stunning display of wealth, celebrity, and high-stakes gambling. Formula One, however, also counts its casualties; 47 sobering fatalities have been recorded among its combatants. With its contrast, then, of Monaco and mortality, Formula One could be regarded as the ultimate game of chance. It might also be inevitable, then, that Formula One would develop a special relationship with Las Vegas, the undisputed gambling, hospitality, and entertainment capital of the world.

Formula One first sampled American soil in 1959 at Sebring, Florida, and in 1960 at Riverside International Raceway. The international racing series then found long-term American homes at Watkins Glen, New York, and Long Beach, California. The path to the Caesars Palace Grand Prix, however, would run through the American power-centers of organized crime, shadowy dealings, and political intrigues. In that regard, Formula One may have found the perfect partner in Las Vegas and Caesars Palace, each entity steeped in secrets to present its own lavishly constructed image.

In 1981, the Formula One series forever departed the time-honored U.S. Grand Prix at Watkins Glen. Instead, Formula One traveled to the luxury-branded Caesars Palace resort on the world-famous Las Vegas Strip. The brainchild of Formula One Constructors Association supreme Bernie Ecclestone and Caesars Palace executive William D. Weinberger, the Caesars Palace Grand Prix would bring the glamor and panache of Formula One to the self-proclaimed "Palace of Pleasure." The pinnacle of global motorsport was also put to speed on a tight, twisting, truncated circuit, constructed over an existing parking lot and a vacant dirt lot north of the Las Vegas resort. Much like the Caesars Palace circuit, the path of Formula One to the United States and, in turn, Las Vegas would be tortuous.

Oddly, though, research in Watkins Glen, Riverside, and Long Beach provided some rare public glimpses into the structure of American organized crime, concurrent with the development of Grand Prix racing at those venues. In fact, events near the village of Watkins Glen in upstate New York forever altered the American understanding of La Cosa Nostra—the Mafia. The Long Beach overlaps were subtle, perhaps a simple matter of timing, yet connected directly to Caesars Palace in Las Vegas. One of the owners of Riverside International Raceway, on the other hand, would drive a tap directly into the Teamsters and their Central States Pension Fund, along with deep organized crime entanglements and further Caesars Palace connections.

The Caesars Palace Grand Prix also presented a public-facing contrast in motorsports disciplines. The Grand Prix races of 1981 and 1982 were international Formula One events, while the 1983 and 1984 editions were stops on the domestic PPG CART IndyCar series. The four Caesars Palace events were also presented amid protracted disputes between their respective sanctioning bodies and team organizations. Formula One was mired in a struggle between the venerable Fédération Internationale de l'Automobile—along with its sporting arm FISA—and FOCA, the Formula One Constructors Association controlled by Brabham team owner Bernie Ecclestone. Stateside, the soul of American IndyCar racing was being torn asunder by a pitched battle between USAC, the United States Auto Club, and the breakaway CART, Championship Auto Racing Teams.

Further, the Caesars Palace Grand Prix would spell transition for the existing United States Grand Prix events at Watkins Glen and Long Beach. Bernie Ecclestone's rendezvous with Caesars Palace may not have been the underlying reason for the termination of Formula One at Watkins Glen in 1981, but the Las Vegas opportunity certainly hastened the New York demise. Across the country, the Long Beach organizers became foundational forces in the production of the Caesars Palace race events. Members of the Caesars Palace Grand Prix team also moved on to undertake Formula One promotions beyond Las Vegas.

Finally, though, the four events of the Caesars Palace Grand Prix would stand as a testament to the racing resolve of Mario Andretti, the great American race car driver. Called upon by the public to stand *for* Watkins Glen and *against* Las Vegas, Andretti was the only racer to compete in the premier class of all four Caesars Palace Grands Prix. Mario Andretti drove for the Alfa Romeo and Ferrari teams at the Formula One events. Andretti then won the 1983 CART IndyCar Caesars Palace Grand Prix III. In 1984, Mario Andretti finished second in Las Vegas to clinch the 1984 CART IndyCar championship.

This is the story of a glimpse in history, and the trajectories launched decades earlier toward its existence, an unholy alliance of the desert Palace of Caesar, the shadows of the American organized crime syndicate, and the international czar of Formula One.

I

Neighbors Upstate

*Grand Prix Racing and La Cosa Nostra
Are Awakened in Upstate New York*

Here lies the east; doth not the day break here? (*Julius Caesar* 2.1.111)

The end of World War II in 1945 brought closure to hostilities that had plagued the global population for nearly 10 years. In Europe, America, and around the globe, conflict and killing slowly receded to restoration and repatriation. Cities were rebuilt, industries rebooted, economies revitalized, and—for the fortunate—loved ones returned. The end of World War II was a planetary pivot of unprecedented scale. Indeed, much of modern history can rightfully trace its origin to events occurring either during or immediately after the war.

For some, World War II created opportunities of profit and position. Pre-war, the vast American organized crime syndicate experienced significant growth during the Great Depression, leveraging Prohibition and illegal gambling to secure its foothold in American society and the national economic engine. During the war, however, organized crime further explored legitimate industries as a means to enhance its wartime balance sheet, as well as to cheat the proverbial taxman. In post-war restoration, organized crime found a virtually unlimited landscape in which to plant new seeds of opportunity.

The transition from global war to Cold War brought defense industrialization for new technologies, businesses in which organized crime would also find a margin. When post-war suburbanization created a new lust for land and construction capacity, the organized crime syndicate would become an early control-group investor. Across the country, the syndicate was prepared to penetrate the *pro forma*, provide the institutional financing, control the service providers, and force a fee on the back end. Illegal gambling too—a time-honored syndicate profit center—would continue unabated in post-war America and Europe. In fact, the convergence of the American peacetime dividend and western suburbanization would present a new frontier for the organized crime syndicate, legalized gambling in the sunbelt southwest. Las Vegas, Nevada, would become the syndicate's primary resort destination development horizon.

American folklore casts Benjamin "Bugsy" Siegel as the progenitor of Las Vegas resort gambling. The Fabulous Flamingo Hotel with which Siegel is credited was certainly not the first Las Vegas resort when it opened in December of 1946. Nor did Ben Siegel originate the Flamingo concept. Rather, Siegel was more of a traveling advance man for a new syndicate sales territory and—for purposes of construction—remote project manager for the organized crime syndicate cast in their role as the take-over developer.

Whether folk tale or fact, Benjamin Siegel and his handlers in the Midwest and East Coast syndicate offices imprinted their strategic plan on Las Vegas gambling institutions for the next four decades. Those who study the subject would argue that syndicate control over legalized gambling operations continues to this day. "Nothing changed when the big gambling corporations like Caesars World and some of the others went public," wrote Robert W. Greene in *The Sting Man*. "The wise guys simply had banks, corporations, and other nominees hold their stock. And they still got their points of the skim."[1]

The financing, fees, and free cashflow of legalized gambling and its underlying property development needs were simply too important to the economic engine of the syndicate, fueling its cor-

Meyer Lansky was the longtime financial wizard of American organized crime, generally believed to rank number three in the vast organized crime syndicate behind Charles "Lucky" Luciano and Vito Genovese. Lansky was extremely influential in the financial structure of early Las Vegas casino operations, including—it is widely believed—Caesars Palace. Meyer Lansky was also alleged to mentor an heir-apparent, Alvin Malnik of Miami. The banner signage of the Caesars Pocono Resorts owned by Malnik would be displayed at the Caesars Palace Grand Prix (Library of Congress).

porate expansion curve. And with the Fabulous Flamingo Hotel as the prototype, the syndicate organizational chart was plotted for the Las Vegas construction program to follow. The second phase of that development program would include the Caesars Palace luxury resort hotel. In the organizational pyramid of the post-war syndicate, the names of Meyer Lansky and Vito Genovese were somewhere near the top. Quite simply, the foot soldiers of mob kingpins Lansky and Genovese would be hidden influencers in the development, management, and early operation of Caesars Palace.

Just as Las Vegas gambling development flourished in the post-war period, so did society make its return to other forms of recreation and sport. As league play in professional sports returned, so did illegal sports betting, always a stalwart of the crime syndicate calculus. And where there was illegal sports betting, there was always the potential for a fixed outcome. In fact, two of the most infamous sports fixing scandals in history occurred closely following World Wars I and II, the Chicago

Benjamin "Bugsy" Siegel (left) opened the Fabulous Flamingo Hotel in Las Vegas, Nevada, in January 1947. Siegel was murdered in Beverly Hills, California, on June 20, 1947. Siegel colleague Meyer Lansky approved the hit. Actor George Raft (right) was a social acquaintance of Siegel. In the 1960s, George Raft was a casino front man for Meyer Lansky in London's Mayfair gambling district. Formula One czar Bernie Ecclestone was known to gamble frequently in Mayfair establishments (Library of Congress).

Black Sox scandal of 1919[2] and the National Football Championship game of 1946.[3] Remarkably, both national sports-fixing scandals arc forward to the early management of Caesars Palace.

Auto racing, as well, resumed in the post-war period. High performance racing automobiles were in effect a beneficiary of trickle-down war technologies. Sports racing cars would soon be outfitted with superchargers, fuel injection, lightened structures, and exotic metals that had been integral to the war effort. The emerging European sports racing scene would also bring new competitors and competition disciplines. The European sanctioning organization, Fédération Internationale de l'Automobile (FIA), developed numeric rules formulae for the new racing series. The preeminent, most powerful formula was "Formula One." A World Drivers Championship was organized in 1947 while a Formula One World Championship was launched in 1950. The Formula One World Championship would be contested in a series of *Grand Prix* events, French for "great prize" or "grand prize." Thirty-one years later, the Formula One World Championship would be decided in the parking lot of

Caesars Palace, notably about a hundred yards from the Caesars Palace sports betting parlor.

While the sanctioning and stewardship of Formula One motorsport belonged to the FIA, much of its legacy has been crafted by one person, Bernard "Bernie" Ecclestone, who was born in England in 1930. Young Bernie Ecclestone's life would steer toward motorcycle and automotive sales, trade, and repair. Ecclestone had a natural affinity for a profitable transaction, especially if it involved loss to another. The transition to adulthood then introduced Ecclestone to another profit and loss proposition, gambling. Quite aptly, well before the debut of the Caesars Palace Grand Prix in 1981, Ecclestone would effectively control the contracts, the commercial rights, and the cash pay zone of the Formula One series.

As racing rebooted in Europe, so did organized competition among its American counterparts. The American post-war sports racing scene would be dominated by European imports. Nameplates such as Alfa Romeo, Maserati, Mercedes-Benz, and Vauxhall found early American road racing success. Some American sports racing enthusiasts would also create their own adaptations of the import platforms, the hand-built sports racer forming a boutique after-market. As with the predominant European marques, American sports racers also sought to emulate the stage play of European Formula racing. Post-war American sports racing would be popularly contested hill-and-dale on country roads and municipal thoroughfares. One of the most notable venues was located in upstate New York, in and around the village of Watkins Glen. In 1980 and 1981, the fate of the Watkins Glen venue would be associated with Caesars Palace. As American promoters and competitors favored the European style of road racing, so would they appropriate the European lexicon for their American variety of sports road racing. Organized road racing contests in the United States would thus be christened—*Grand Prix*.

***

In April 1948, one year after the formation of the World Drivers Championship in Europe, efforts began in Watkins Glen, New York, to develop a counterpart event in the United States. "Directors of the Chamber of Commerce are endeavoring to attract the most unusual convention in America to this village," ran the upstate reports. "They hope to hold a meet in July or August of the Sports Car Club of America."[4] The Sports Car Club of America (SCCA) was another example of the post-war reboot. With its predecessor organization dissolved at the onset of World War II, the reformed SCCA was organized in 1944 for sports car enthusiasts and for amateurs-only competition. "Both foreign and American automobiles are well represented in the [SCCA] membership, the newer models of the sports cars being all European makes," continued the coverage. "Watkins Glen may originate the only 'American Grand Prix.' Such an event would draw tremendous crowds, it is believed."[5] SCCA member Cameron Argetsinger would then be credited with the concept of the Watkins Glen event.

Two months later, the United Press International pushed out the formal announcement, "European style road races across open county roads will make their debut here at the first American Grand Prix, Oct. 2 and 3."[6] The inaugural Grand

Prix was organized with four different classifications competing on a 6.6-mile course around the village of Watkins Glen. The United Press also passed along the company tease of the SCCA, "Grand Prix races have been held in England, Belgium, Italy, and from other countries. A team from London and another from Melbourne, Australia may be invited to take part in the event here."[7] Following the announcements, SCCA member Cameron Argetsinger conducted a survey to finalize the details of the layout, as well as the staging areas for the inspection paddock and pit area.

Thirty-five classified sports racers were presented for the inaugural American Grand Prix. Entrants included Sam and Miles Collier, principals in the pre-war American sports car organization. The Collier brothers were entered in supercharged MG machines. Well-known cartoonist Charles Addams would compete in a Mercedes-Benz SS, an interesting mount only three years removed from World War II. Seminal American sports racer Briggs Cunningham was also entered, driving a pre-war

Cameron Argetsinger is regarded as the originator of Grand Prix racing at Watkins Glen, New York. Argetsinger is pictured here at the inaugural 1948 American Grand Prix on the original village circuit in Watkins Glen. Argetsinger was later the executive director of SCCA. Cameron Argetsinger was thus credited with both terminating the original Can-Am series and delivering the Long Beach Grand Prix proposal to the FIA (courtesy International Motor Racing Research Center).

Buick Century shrouded in Mercedes SSK donor sheet metal, the *Bu-Merc*. Pre-race notes included mention of Frank Griswold and his Alfa-Romeo 2900, "The Italian automobile concern only made 50 cars such as Mr. Griswold has entered."[8] Alfa Romeo was described as the fastest passenger car in the world, "capable of 150 miles per hour."[9] Alec Ulmann of the SCCA was posted as the Watkins Glen race steward.

Pre-race descriptions of the Grand Prix captured the bucolic tree-lined upstate setting, "practically every road hazard imaginable. Curves, bridges, and railroad crossings, as well as macadam, concrete, brick, and dirt roads will test the skill and daring of the drivers."[10] The course would be primitive at best; over 75 percent of the circuit consisted of unpaved roads. Dirt sections were salted as a dust palliative.

The starting grid rolls off for the inaugural 1948 American Grand Prix in the village of Watkins Glen, New York: (1) Mike Vaughn in a Lagonda Rapide, (2) Dud Wilson in a Stutz Blackhawk Boat Tail Speedster, (3) syndicated cartoonist Charles S. Addams in a Mercedes-Benz SS, (4) Frank Griswold in an Alfa Romeo 8C 2900B, (5) George Weaver in an R1 Maserati, (6) Briggs Cunningham in a custom Bu-Merc (beyond man in light shirt), (7) Ken Hill in a Merlin Special (beyond Cunningham). All of the vehicles were generally derived from pre–World War II automobiles. The event was won by Frank Griswold. Briggs Cunningham was second. Cameron Argetsinger finished ninth (courtesy International Motor Racing Research Center).

Despite the marginal surfaces, the objective was not endurance or derring-do. High speed would be the order of the competition, and vehicles were expected to approach 100 mph on race day.

The debut of the American Grand Prix opened to a chilly Watkins Glen morning with temperatures near freezing at sunrise. The skies, however, were clear; the Grand Prix would roll off as scheduled. At 12:01 p.m. the course roads were closed off by local police. "Mayor Allan D. Earway was visited every resident along the route," ran the local daily, "and requests have been made that during the race dogs of the area not be allowed to run at large."[11] Children of the Watkins Glen village apparently received fair warning as well.

At the start of the feature, Briggs Cunningham and Frank Griswold quickly controlled the front of the field. "The race apparently was between Griswold and Briggs Cunningham," according to the local account. "Once [Cunningham] was ahead of his opponent from the Keystone State but the Bu-Merc could not keep up with the Alpha-Romeo [sic]."[12] After eight grueling laps on the makeshift racing course, Frank

Griswold won the first American Grand Prix in his 2.9-liter Alfa Romeo coupe. Griswold's time for the eight-lap feature was 49:24.60, an average speed of nearly 64 mph. Frank Griswold reported hitting 102 mph in his Alfa. Second was Briggs Cunningham in his American-German combination, some 10 seconds behind Griswold. The Collier brothers were recorded in fourth and fifth positions. Cameron Argetsinger— effectively the founder of the American Grand Prix—trailed ninth in an MG, some six minutes behind Griswold.

The inaugural American Grand Prix was an unqualified success. With a crowd estimated at 10,000, there were no serious incidents or reported injuries, not to dogs, children, or livestock alike. A group of 400 racers, local dignitaries, politicians, and press attended an awards banquet that evening at the host Seneca Lodge. Cameron Argetsinger was appropriately recognized for his contributions to the event. Three weeks later, the Watkins Glen Chamber of Commerce met to discuss the outcomes of the inaugural event as well as plans for a 1949 Grand Prix. The gathering of prominent local businesspeople also considered the potential liabilities. "Another resolution carried was that the Grand Prix not be held," reported the Elmira, New York, *Star-Gazette*, "unless the Chamber of Commerce is incorporated."[13]

One month after the Watkins Glen report, there was news on the sports fixing scandal involving the 1946 NFL championship game. Jerome Zarowitz of New York was released from prison after serving nearly two years of a three-year maximum. Zarowitz had been convicted in 1947 along with three others of conspiring to bribe two New York Giants players to influence the game. At the time of his arrest in December of 1946, Zarowitz was linked with Arnold Rothstein of 1919 Chicago Black Sox infamy. "Zarowitz, whose connections stem indirectly back to that master fixer, Arnold Rothstein," reported the major dailies, "is believed to be the Jerry whose voice was tapped in a gambling conversation."[14] Jerome Zarowitz was only six years old when the 1919 World Series scandal broke, but it should be reassuring to know that he was mentored well.

After release, the New York authorities did not wait for Jerome Zarowitz to get comfortable, "Zarowitz was immediately arraigned in Felony Court on a charge of being a fugitive from justice."[15] Zarowitz's latest charges arose from a grand jury indictment involving a 1946 bookmaking operation in New Jersey. It would not be Jerome Zarowitz's last brush with the law nor with high-profile gambling. To wit, in 1966 Jerome Zarowitz would be installed as the casino executive of Caesars Palace in Las Vegas.

***

The American Grand Prix in Watkins Glen continued with its public road format until 1955. In 1949, the spectator count reportedly grew to over 30,000 while car count grew to 52. Entrants included Briggs Cunningham and the Collier Brothers. The distinction was further enhanced by the entry of radio and TV personality Dave Garroway. Zora Arkus-Duntov, later to become the father of the performance Corvette, joined in 1949 as well. The Watkins Glen Grand Prix was a place to see and be seen for the one-percenters of of the northeast parading their post-war panache, an upper crust sporting event for lawyers, bankers, doctors, industrialists and—over

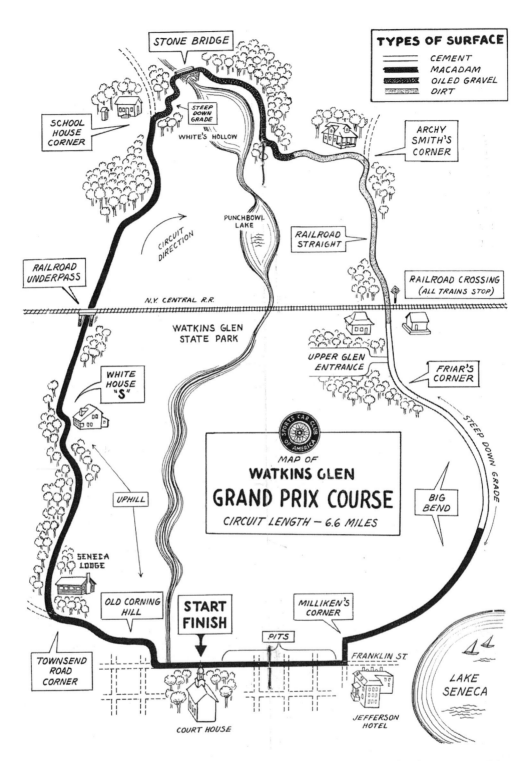

Track map of the original Watkins Glen village road circuit as prepared for the program of the September 23, 1950, American Grand Prix. The course was run counterclockwise. Competitor Sam Collier was killed during the 1950 event at the railroad underpass. Four spectators were injured in a separate incident in 1950. In 1952, a child was killed and 12 others injured when a vehicle left the roadway on the start/finish Franklin Street straightway at bottom (courtesy International Motor Racing Research Center).

time—their hired gun drivers, all presented at the multi-hued splendor of the autumnal equinox.

Tragedy struck in 1950, however, with the rollover death of SCCA progenitor Sam Collier. Four spectators were also injured after being struck by a competitor in a separate incident. Walt Hansgen would then enter the Watkins Glen Grand Prix in 1952. Hansgen was an American sports racing name that would continue well into the 1960s. The 1952 event, however, would be remembered for another fatality, this time involving the gallery. With a crowd estimated at over 100,000 huddled around the track, an incident involving Briggs Cunningham, teammate John Fitch, and SCCA president Fred Wacker claimed the life of a seven-year-old child and injured 12 other spectators.

Amid the horrible loss and the public outcry, Watkins Grand Prix organizers had reason to doubt that there would be a 1953 edition. "Most officials agree chances of getting state approval again for the sports car chase were slim."[16] Legal claims by the family of the deceased child and those injured were made against the Village of Watkins Glen, the Watkins Glen Chamber of Commerce, the SCCA, and the three drivers. Damage claims eventually totaled over $300,000. On the other hand, some of the individual claims were less than the drivers paid for their race cars.

The tragedy also drove the creation of the Watkins Glen Grand Prix Corporation, a single-purpose entity behind which to somewhat shield individuals from race-related liabilities. The push was also on for a new Watkins Glen race course that would provide a higher level of safety control over the original circuit. The 1953 event would be run on a new 4.6-mile country road layout, farther from the population and with increased separation for spectators. Inevitable amid the legal actions, the 1953 Grand Prix would not include the SCCA nor drivers Briggs Cunningham, John Fitch, and Fred Wacker.

The increased demand for public safety would also elevate Charles Kress in the functions of the Grand Prix. Kress, a safety volunteer for each of the preceding Watkins Glen events, was a Watkins Glen native. With a background in law enforcement, Charles Kress was appointed as security and safety director of the Watkins Gen Grand Prix Corporation. "I knew Charlie Kress when I was a teenager," recalled Watkins Glen historian Bill Green. "He was the former mayor of Binghamton and the former sheriff of Broome County. Charlie was also involved with the Kefauver Committee."[17] Indeed, Charles Kress was an investigator for the organized crime committee hearings of Senator Estes Kefauver from 1950 to 1951.

The selection of Charles Kress, the former law enforcement official and senate investigator, as the Watkins Glen security director was instructive. Indeed, crowd control issues at the upstate New York race venue would force a virtual police state in the years ahead. Cameron Argetsinger, Henry Valent, and Charles Kress all continued in Watkins Glen Grand Prix stewardship into the 1960s. In fact, Henry Valent would remain with the Watkins Glen Grand Prix Corporation all the way through to the 1980s and the standoff with the Caesars Palace Grand Prix.

In 1956, the Watkins Glen Grand Prix Corporation moved further from their village origins with construction of their own purpose-built race course, a 2.3-mile course constructed with funds raised by selling debentures against the corporation.

The construction undertaking also underscored a history of corporate debt, another driver of the Caesars Palace debates to come 25 years hence. As well, the SCCA would not be the sanctioning body for the 1956 Grand Prix. "The local committee could not accept the SCCA sanction," it was reported, "because of four monetary demands made by the sports car club which would amount to paying $6,000 to $10,000 for the sanction."[18] Again, the sanctioning fees were less than the cost of a proper imported race car. On the other hand, it was more than Jerome Zarowitz paid to bail himself out of jail after he was released from prison and rearrested in 1948. The disagreement with the sanctioning body also set the tone for the sanctioning wars of the 1980s, the effects of which were on display in the parking lot Grand Prix events of Caesars Palace.

The 1956 event also tested the mettle of Watkins Glen safety director Charles Kress in the wake of the SCCA sanctioning issues. "Each event had been halved because of hazardous track conditions on the tricky asphalt circuit, completed only hours before the start," was the race report. "It was admitted by all that the new $150,000 circuit was not satisfactory because of loose gravel, pit-holes, and slick spots. Rigid safety measures were ordered."[19]

The organizational postscript for Charles Kress and the Watkins Glen Grand Prix Corporation was rather mixed headed into 1957. Further, in upstate New York, the first centurion formation of Caesar was soon to be revealed. Charles Kress—former investigator for the United States Senate Special Committee to Investigate Crime in Interstate Commerce—would be acutely aware of the perils.

***

Despite the accumulated safety concerns, tensions between the Watkins Glen Grand Prix Corporation and the SCCA would subside in 1957. "All unreasonable hazards have been removed," declared the sports car sanctioning body, "and the Watkins Glen circuit now qualifies as a first-rate course."[20] The popular Walt Hansgen won the September 22, 1957, feature race around the 2.3-mile purpose-built course before a crowd estimated at over 30,000.

By October 1957, though, the Watkins Glen Grand Prix Corporation was reporting grim financial results through 11 racing events in multiple disciplines at the one-year-old facility. With $190,000 in debts against $21,000 cash on hand, the financial future was bleak. "Will the holders of the notes allow their interest to accrue another year?" the local *Star-Gazette* reported. "Will the creditors forbear and affirm their faith in this community value?"[21] On November 15, 1957, though, the attentions of the *Star-Gazette* reporters were drawn 50 miles away to an imposing hilltop estate in Apalachin, New York. In fact, the entire nation was paying attention.

"65 Hoodlums Seized in a Raid," opened the coverage of the *New York Times* on November 15, 1957, "And Run out of Upstate Village."[22] Similar reports splashed the front pages of major dailies across the country. "It looked like a meeting of George Rafts," stated New York State Detective Sergeant Edgar Croswell, a reference to the typecast film noir Hollywood actor.[23] Notably, it was Sergeant Croswell who had cracked the Apalachin gangster gathering. The George Raft reference, however, would later inform gambling dens in the Mayfair district of London, a casino haven

Walt Hansgen won the September 22, 1957, Watkins Glen Grand Prix in a D-type Jaguar for Briggs Cunningham. Hansgen later attended the September 21, 1965, ribbon cutting ceremony of Stardust International Raceway in Las Vegas, Nevada. Hansgen toured Irwin Molasky, Las Vegas developer and Stardust Raceway constructor, around the circuit in a Shelby Ford GT-350 Mustang. Cleveland racketeer and Molasky business partner Moe Dalitz was the president of Stardust International Raceway (courtesy International Motor Racing Research Center).

frequented by Bernie Ecclestone of Formula One, with George Raft himself standing at the door of one of the more popular nightspots.

The upstate meeting in New York was a who's-who of known or suspected national organized crime figures. One official described the hoodlum meeting as "the hierarchy of the Eastern Seaboard criminal world."[24] Although the names predominantly ran through New England, attendees provided the state police with addresses literally from coast-to-coast, the Midwest, California, Texas, Cuba, even the Cleveland suburb of Shaker Heights, Ohio. "[Croswell] said police did not know," continued the reporting, "if the men were members of the Mafia, an organization of criminals."[25]

The *Star Gazette* near Watkins Glen described "a convention held by mobster Vito Genovese."[26] The newspaper also named the location: "The meeting … was held at a stone mansion owned by Joseph Barbara, who runs a bottling works in nearby Endicott."[27] Charles Kress of the Watkins Glen Grand Prix Corporation immediately recognized the name of Joseph Barbara, not to be confused with the well-known television cartoonist Joseph Barbera. While Sheriff of Broome County, Kress investigated the gruesome 1934 murder of Joseph Morreale of Endicott, New York. Charles Kress' prime suspect was none other than Joseph Barbara. Born Giuseppe Maria Barbara in Sicily in 1905, he would carve out a career as a bootlegger, mob assassin, racketeer, and—eventually—the proud owner of a Canada Dry bottling plant. Further, the transition of Joseph Barbara from Mob to Main Street informed the play to come of Jerome Zarowitz at Caesars Palace.

As the news of the 1957 Apalachin crime retreat spread out, Charles Kress went in. "Working with state police, we questioned … Joseph Barbara at length," Kress stated to New York governor Averill Harriman. "A material witness changed her story and then disappeared. A number of years later another very material witness, possibly even a suspect, mysteriously disappeared."[28] Charles Kress pushed Governor Harriman for a new investigation into the case, centering on Joseph Barbara. Kress also pushed for legislative reforms to better track organized crime figures and to limit criminal possession of firearms.

Sixty-five members of the American Mafia, *La Cosa Nostra*, convened on November 13, 1957, at the home of mobster Joseph Barbara (pictured) in Apalachin, New York, some 50 miles from Watkins Glen, New York. Former law enforcement officer Charles Kress, security director of the Watkins Glen Grand Prix Corporation, investigated Joseph Barbara for murder in 1934 (Library of Congress).

The underlying purpose of the Apalachin crime conference dominated the police blotter and national media for weeks. The U.S. Senate probe of labor racketeering and the October 25, 1957, murder of mob boss and former Murder Inc. leader Albert Anastasia the month prior were at the top of the list. Both subjects were of extreme importance to Vito Genovese. Indeed, Anastasia and Genovese had wrestled over control of New York rackets prior to the murder of Anastasia. Albert Anastasia had also reportedly attempted an incursion into gambling operations in Cuba. The Cuban gambling houses, however, were controlled by Meyer Lansky, under direct contract with Cuban dictator Fulgencio Batista.

As Fidel Castro's revolutionary army moved closer to the Batista strongholds and Havana, the gambling operators had every reason to be concerned for their investments, and the massive daily cash take. The Cuban revolution elevated the Apalachin discourse, as well as the potential need to reposition the investment of organized crime toward the Las Vegas gambling market. For his part, Apalachin host Joseph Barbara was not talking. In fact, other than to lament that his friends might not visit him again, Joseph Barbara was silent. After being compelled to testify to a State investigation about the Apalachin meeting, Joseph Barbara was stricken with an apparent heart attack on May 24, 1959. Barbara passed on three weeks later: "Joseph

Barbara, Sr. died tonight with the secret of the underworld convention at his home in Apalachin still intact."[29]

Coined as the "prime catch"[30] of the Apalachin roundup, "king of the rackets"[31] Vito "Don Vitone" Genovese would move on from the Apalachin summit to consolidate his power in the national organized crime syndicate. In term of mob-lore name recognition, Vito Genovese was positioned number-two, right after Lucky Luciano, just before Meyer Lansky. Further, the Vito Genovese crime family would become linked with any number of Las Vegas gambling operators including—according to a leaked report of a Scotland Yard investigation—Steve Wynn, the father of modern Las Vegas.[32] In particular, Genovese crime family connections would be linked to the development and hidden ownership of Caesars Palace.

On the same day that news broke of the Apalachin organized crime convention, the same dailies reported from a Senate chamber investigating organized labor, the United States Senate Select Committee on Improper Activities in Labor and Management. Informally the "Rackets Committee," a team of Senate investigators spearheaded by Robert F. Ken-

Mob boss Albert Anastasia was murdered in New York City on October 25, 1957, just three weeks before the organized crime conclave. At the time of his death, Anastasia was believed to be infiltrating gambling operations controlled by Meyer Lansky in Cuba (Library of Congress).

nedy pondered the potential connections. "We know there is a lot of corruption and racketeering in the Teamsters," stated committee vice-chair Irving Ives of New York, "and I think we ought to find out how much the Mafia is represented."[33]

"We've got to determine if the government is bigger than hoodlums and crooks," said chairman John McClellan of Arkansas, "or if they are running this

Vito Genovese, a long-time organized crime associate of Charles "Lucky" Luciano. Genovese was believed to have ordered the murder of Albert Anastasia, as well as the Mafia meeting on November 13, 1957, at the home of Joseph Barbara in Apalachin, New York. Anthony Salerno, an underboss in the Genovese crime family, allegedly held hidden ownership interests in Caesars Palace in Las Vegas, Nevada (Library of Congress).

country."[34] Senator McClellan's query was a time-honored and worthwhile question. It also brings inquiry that persists to this day.

The Apalachin summit and its aftermath would ignite the furor of Robert F. Kennedy and the Rackets Committee. In the six years since the close of Senator Estes Kefauver's post-war organized crime hearings, a national naiveté had persisted about the scale of what was rightly described as "the interwoven mobs which make up the national crime syndicate."[35] Post-Apalachin, there could be no more public apathy about the existence of the Mafia, of *La Cosa Nostra*. Nor could J. Edgar Hoover and the Department of Justice sit idle on investigation and prosecution of national organized crime members. In the decade ahead, organized crime would drive Hoover, the FBI, Robert Kennedy, and the Department of Justice on an agenda straight to Las Vegas. That mission would, in turn, force the subject of organized crime right through the August 5, 1966, grand opening of Caesars Palace.

It should be noted that both the Apalachin and McClellan stories also ran on November 15, 1957, in Las Vegas; both made the front page of the largest Las Vegas daily. The Apalachin story, though, was tucked away discreetly at the bottom right-hand corner. Conversely, the McLellan Committee investigation of the relationship between Teamsters and Mafia was above the fold.[36] Notable as well, Las Vegas racket elements were already feeding at the Teamsters trough. To wit, a loan from the Teamsters Central States Pension Fund was being used by Moe Dalitz, Irwin Molasky, and

James Riddle "Jimmy" Hoffa was the longtime president of the International Brotherhood of Teamsters and a trustee of the Teamsters Central States Pension Fund. The Teamsters pension fund bankrolled much of the early resort development in Las Vegas, Nevada, including Caesars Palace (Library of Congress).

Merv Adelson to complete the construction of Sunrise Hospital in Las Vegas. Thus opened a thinly veiled tradition of the Teamsters in mid-century Las Vegas development, the favored source of venture capital that also drove the storyline of Caesars Palace.

***

The Watkins Glen Grand Prix Corporation was eager to build its racing program after development of the purpose-built facility, debt issues notwithstanding. The corporation was also eager to play its part in elevating American race craft, to pull alongside and then become part of the international fold. In 1958, a professional event was introduced to the former amateur-only venue. The new format was dubbed *Formula Libre*, the free Formula. The race would be open to both closed-wheel sports racers and open-wheel Formula-type vehicles. It was the first event at Watkins Glen to carry the sanction of the Federation Internationale de l'Automobile (FIA). The race also paid a purse, which would force the SCCA amateurs to stay home.

The United States Auto Club (USAC) stepped in to provide domestic sanction for the Watkins Glen Formula Libre Grand Prix. USAC was formed in the wake of the tragedy at the 1955 24 Hours of Le Mans, a horrific competition accident in which 83 spectators and a driver were killed and 180 injured. USAC, in fact, had just completed the running of its third Indianapolis 500. USAC had also organized a sports racing

Joakim Bonnier of Sweden driving a Maserati 250F leads American Phil Hill in a Ferrari 412 during the Watkins Glen Formula Libre Grand Prix. Formula Libre combined open-wheel vehicles and sports cars in a single format. Bonnier won the event while Hill dropped out 11 laps from the finish. American Dan Gurney was second in a Ferrari. American Bruce Kessler was fourth (courtesy International Motor Racing Research Center).

division. The Watkins Glen event would thus be one of four road races in the 1958 USAC road racing championship.

The September 28, 1958, Formula Libre event, billed as the first of its type in the United States, was to run 300 kilometers, 187 miles and 81 laps around the Watkins Glen circuit. Event press pushed out extensive mention of the first sports racing purse at Watkins Glen. "The lucrative event … was expected to lure a starting field of 20 to 25 drivers Sunday to compete for a $5,000 guaranteed purse," posted one account. "Top Prize is $2,000."[37] The Formula Libre field would be drawn from a solid mix of domestic road racing talent as well as some international flair.

Phil Hill led off for the Americans. Hill was already a winner at Le Mans and was newly entered in the international Formula One series. Twenty-seven-year-old Dan Gurney from California would also contest the event. Bob Said of New York, father of modern driver Boris Said, was entered. Bruce Kessler of Beverly Hills was also entered at Watkins Glen. Kessler was notably an entrant for Bernie Ecclestone in the 1958 Monaco Grand Prix. The American drivers were joined by Joakim Bonnier from Sweden. Bonnier started the 1958 Formula One series for Maserati and had recently transitioned to the British BRM team.

Race day reality, however, would trail off considerably from the promotional build-up. Only 15 cars made the start and only 5,000 spectators attended. Perhaps spelling good fortune for things to come, though, Jo Bonnier won the Watkins Glen Formula Libre event in his open-wheel Formula Maserati. "A goateed Swedish driver and his two Italian mechanics," read the jargon of the time, "rode their opposition into the ground with a searing pace that won this country's first big professional road race in 21 years."[38] Reporting also noted the pre-war Vanderbilt Cup races of 1936–1937.

Bonnier's average speed was 97.40 mph, a considerable bump over Walt Hansgen's 84.70 mph sports car speed in 1957. Dan Gurney was second in a 3.5-liter Ferrari. Bruce Kessler of Beverly Hills was third. Neither Phil Hill nor Bob Said would make it to the finish. "I never felt sure about victory," remarked Bonnier, "until I was signaled that Hill was out."[39] Bruce Kessler—reportedly the last person to speak to James Dean before Dean's fatal September 30, 1955, dinner run to Paso Robles, California—went on to direct episodes of *The Monkees*, *McCloud*, and *MacGyver*, as well as dozens of other TV programs. Phil Hill and Jo Bonnier departed Watkins Glen to compete in the 1958 Moroccan Grand Prix in Casablanca where they finished third and fourth, respectively. The Moroccan Grand Prix was won by Stirling Moss. Dan Gurney, who did not win a single event of the 1958 USAC road racing series, nonetheless claimed the 1958 championship.

Across the country, a Palace for Caesar was being penciled for consideration. The vast American organized crime syndicate was moving on from Apalachin and their power-centers around the country to implement their next 10-year Las Vegas strategic plan. The desert march of organized crime to Caesars Palace would also be their new definable, measurable strategic goal. For Watkins Glen, Las Vegas and the Caesars Palace Grand Prix would spell the death knell for the upstate New York facility. Finally, Bernie Ecclestone—Bruce Kessler's 1958 Monaco car owner—would arrive in Las Vegas in 1981 for the first Caesars Palace Grand Prix, not only as owner of a race team, but also in control of the relationship between the Formula One teams and the sporting arm of the FIA. Ecclestone, an unrepentant gambler, would also close the deal for the Caesars Palace Grand Prix in the bunker board room of the resort that traced its origins to Meyer Lansky—allegedly.

***

The continued Senate investigation of organized labor and its relationship with organized crime would inevitably draw back the curtain on the Teamsters' greatest financial resource, the huge Central States Pension Fund. As Senate rackets committee chairman John McClellan, committee member John F. Kennedy, and chief counsel Robert F. Kennedy went to war in-chambers with Jimmy Hoffa, the lending practices of the fund bore certain scrutiny. That scrutiny also made the newspapers. Throughout the country, the Central States Pension fund was extending credit to horse tracks, shopping malls, hospitals, suburban housing, lodging, raw land, golf courses and Las Vegas casinos. Further, the relationship of the borrowers to lender would always be a distinct curiosity. Teamsters loans to Las Vegas interests often begat a foregone inquisition. Many loans were simply excused away as a sound business deal at a fair interest rate. One loan though—to a hospitality start-up in the deep South—was worth a deeper look. That loan would also point the way to Caesars Palace.

"A five-story motor hotel, costing $3,000,000, will be built on the southwest corner of Peachtree and Seventh streets, NE," announced the *Atlanta Constitution* on June 5, 1957. "To be called the Atlanta Cabana, the building will have 200 guest units and parking facilities for 200 cars. The developers of the hotel are Jay J. Sarno and Stanley A. Mallin and Associates."[40] In 1965, the same Jay Sarno and Stanley Mallin would indeed be posted in front of the Caesars Palace hotel-casino development.

The Atlanta Cabana was the second publicly-announced development by Sarno and Mallin. Both men were partners in a 36-unit Atlanta apartment complex underwritten by a $136,000 FHA-guaranteed loan. With a $3 million budget, though, the Atlanta Cabana was exponentially larger and a much more complex undertaking. The Atlanta Cabana development would also publicly introduce Jay Sarno to law enforcement. Indeed, going forward, Jay Sarno was never far from the reaches of the law, whether local, the FBI, the SEC, or the IRS. Similarly, Stan Mallin would merit audiences with the FBI and the IRS. For purposes of their Las Vegas destination, the Atlanta Cabana also forged the relationship of Jay Sarno and Stanley Mallin with Jimmy Hoffa, the Teamsters Central States Pension Fund, and Allen Dorfman.

Constructed just blocks away from Grant Field, home of the Georgia Bulldogs football team, the lavish, rococo-style Atlanta Cabana opened on October 15, 1958, to much local fanfare. Within two weeks, however, Jay Sarno was indicted by the Fulton Grand Jury, "on charges of stealing guest reservation records valued at $10,000 from a plush downtown Atlanta motel."[41] Sarno's alleged accomplice was a poached former employee of the competing downtown hotel. Three months after the grand opening of the Atlanta Cabana, though, the stakes would be raised considerably for Jay Sarno and Stanley Mallin, and this public mention would make the front page.

"James R. Hoffa's Teamsters Union will own one of the nation's most luxurious

Jay Sarno and Stanley Mallin developed the Atlanta Cabana in 1958 with a mortgage loan from the Teamsters Central States Pension Fund. With Teamsters financing, Sarno and Mallin were also the public fronts of the Caesars Palace hotel-casino in Las Vegas which opened in 1966. The Atlanta Cabana concept provided design cues that were later used at Caesars Palace (author's collection).

motels—the Atlanta Cabana Motor Hotel—in 15 years," reported the *Atlanta Constitution* on January 22, 1959. "They'll get ownership after they are repaid the money they lent to help build it."[42] The Teamsters loan was reported at $1,800,000 of the total budget.

"It's an unusual deal," Jay Sarno commented. "It's unusual in any language."[43] Of the union officials, Sarno would joke, "They're tough lenders. We ought to know … we're professional borrowers."[44]

News of the Teamsters loan broke amid withering daily dispatches from Senate chambers regarding the investigations of the Rackets Committee. The financing disclosure also arose as Hoffa was involved in multiple legal actions brought by the Rackets Committee. Two days after the loan broke, though, Jimmy Hoffa was installed as the leader of the International Brotherhood of Teamsters, the most powerful trade union in the country, along with its $250 million pension fund. Apalachin host Joseph Barbara had passed of his apparent heart attack only three months before. Within five years, then, the strategic plan for Caesars Palace in Las Vegas, Nevada, would be fully deployed.

***

The 1958 Formula Libre event at Watkins Glen appeared to clear a path for the proper American debut of the international Formula One series. It was certainly the intention of the Grand Prix Corporation of Watkins Glen that they host the first American Formula One event as well. In a bizarre turn, though, Alec Ulmann— SCCA race steward for the inaugural 1948 American Grand Prix at Watkins Glen— would steal away the Watkins Glen Grand Prix Corporation's show.

"The Sebring will be the scene March 22 of the first European-type grand prix auto race ever held in the United States," it was reported from Florida. "The Grand Prix of the United States has been officially approved and listed on the international calendar by the FIA."[45] Alec Ulmann's press wording was strikingly similar to the advance for the 1958 Watkins Glen Formula Libre. The Sebring event, though, would count where it mattered most: "drivers will be competing for the coveted world championship points."[46] In one of the symmetries of history, the Sebring announcement sounded on January 22, 1959, the same day that the Teamsters loan for the Atlanta Cabana went public.

The Sebring Grand Prix of the United States would ultimately be delayed until December 12, 1959, the final event of the Formula One season. The Sebring event, though, was also set to decide the Formula One world championship. In the meantime, the Watkins Glen Grand Prix Corporation promoted another edition of the Formula Libre on October 18, 1959. The Watkins Glen event touted the entry of England's Stirling Moss, a 1959 Formula One championship contender. Notably, Roger Penske of Pennsylvania also entered the event. Penske, however, was lapping some 8 mph slower than Moss in time trials. Joakim Bonnier, winner of the 1958 Formula Libre event, was entered but did not compete. Unfortunately for the cachet of the Watkins Glen Formula Libre show, the balance of the entrants were domestic racers.

The rain-hampered race then belonged to Stirling Moss in a Formula One Cooper-Climax, winning by nine laps over Indy 500 veteran Eddie Johnson in an Offenhauser-powered midget. Cameron Argetsinger of the Grand Prix Corporation remarked that the Watkins Glen circuit was committed for a true Formula One event in October of 1960. "Confirmation was given after today's event," it was reported, "and the race may offer points as a world championship event."[47] Unfortunately for Argetsinger and the corporation, Alec Ulmann had stolen the Watkins Glen talking points—and then improved upon them—some seven months earlier.

The entry list for the Sebring Grand Prix of the United States would far surpass that of the Watkins Glen Formula Libre. The event also returned Stirling Moss to the U.S., still in mathematical contention for the Formula One championship. Further, the Sebring Formula One Grand Prix counted points leader Jack Brabham of Australia, Tony Brooks, Graham Hill, and Innes Ireland of England, Bruce McLaren of New Zealand, as well as Phil Hill, Masten Gregory, and Jim Rathmann of the United States. Another notable American entry was the 1959 winner of the Indianapolis 500, Rodger Ward of Speedway, Indiana. Ward was set to contest the first Grand Prix of the United States in an upright Kurtis-Kraft-Offenhauser roadster, a marked contrast to the low-slung Formula racers.

Although Jack Brabham led most of the way, 22-year-old Bruce McLaren would win the first Grand Prix of the United States. McLaren passed Brabham with the

Stirling Moss of England won the October 18, 1959, Watkins Glen Formula Libre Grand Prix in a Cooper-Climax. Moss was credited with the design of racketeer Moe Dalitz's Stardust International Raceway in Las Vegas, Nevada. Stirling Moss would also attend the 1981 Caesars Palace Grand Prix. American midget and champ car racer Eddie Johnson finished second in the 1959 Formula Libre in an upright Offenhauser-powered midget. Johnson was nine laps behind Moss at the finish of the 100-lap event (courtesy International Motor Racing Research Center).

checkered flag in sight as the points leader pushed his broken Cooper-Climax to the finish. "It was a weird finish as the crowd of 15,000 ignored McLaren and cheered wildly for Brabham as he struggled slowly toward the line," ran the trackside report. "Soon after he made it, the Australian dropped to the track from exhaustion."[48]

Nonetheless, Jack Brabham broke through for the 1959 Formula One title, the first of his storied career. Tony Banks finished third in a Ferrari and claimed second in the points. Stirling Moss was out on lap five and denied the championship, a resultant third in the points standings. Harry Blanchard of Connecticut finished ninth in a Porsche, the lone American across the line.

The Grand Prix fates of 1959 also created the template for the 1960 season, no shortage of speculative press, the holdout of Formula One hope for Watkins Glen, and—eventually—a somewhat compromised Grand Prix of the United States. Notable as well, the Havana sports car Grand Prix in Cuba was canceled in 1959 due to the revolutionary march of Fidel Castro into the gambling capital of the island nation. The Havana sports car Grand Prix would return in 1960, though, as the provisional Cuban government stabilized the nation in the exile of Fulgencio Batista. Gambling operations in Havana, however, were soon to be nationalized, and the take of organized crime from the Havana tables would be lost forever. Two decades hence, the public motorsports path to the Caesars Palace Grand Prix thus somewhat replicated the fate of Watkins Glen, a horizon of hope for a Formula One Grand Prix, astride

Bruce McLaren of New Zealand driving a Cooper-Climax won the first United States Grand Prix on December 12, 1959. McLaren was 22 years old. The event was held at Sebring, Florida. Jack Brabham of Australia finished fourth and won the 1959 Formula One world drivers championship. American Rodger Ward was classified 10th in a Kurtis-Kraft Offenhauser-powered midget. Martini & Rossi banner beyond is noteworthy. Martini & Rossi also sponsored Mario Andretti and Lotus in 1979. Martini & Rossi bridge also adorned the iconic spectator bridge at Stardust International Raceway (Tom Burnside Photographic Collection, The Revs Institute).

a multitude of obstacles along the way. As in Havana, though, the Caesars Palace Grand Prix would also reunite gambling, motorsports, and the shadows of organized crime.

***

Two weeks after the Apalachin crime convention made headlines, another faction of the American organized crime syndicate would seize the front page, and the operational rotation of Caesars Palace would begin to take shape. In fact, just as Jay Sarno and Stan Mallin were opening their loan documents for the Atlanta Cabana, some 500 miles away, the eyes of the nation were being drawn to Terre Haute, Indiana. "T-Men Study Raid Evidence" was the top-billed trumpet of the trusted *Terre Haute Tribune*, "Sports Wagering Ring Smashed by Revenue Agents."[49]

The federal raid in Terre Haute, Indiana, closed an illegal sports bookmaking and wagering operation that was estimated to churn $1 million per month. The scale was such that IRS agents speculated the Terre Haute boiler room was connected to "international gambling operations."[50] Eight men were arrested in the IRS raid. Two of those arrested provided Las Vegas addresses. Charges were initially limited to simple failure to possess a $50 state gambling stamp. As with Al Capone, however, there was the inevitable matter of income taxes on ill-gotten gains. Further, the Terre Haute gambling case unfolded to reveal the testimony of 180 witnesses from across the country, including future Caesars Palace executives, names that would circle the fates of the chief executive of Caesars Palace during the inaugural Caesars Palace Grand Prix.

On August 18, 1958, former professional basketball player Irving "Ash" Resnick testified before the federal grand jury in Indianapolis investigating the Terre Haute operation. Resnick, naturally, denied any illegal betting. Ash Resnick would later be named as a Caesars Palace executive and investor. Ruby Lazarus, a Miami bookmaker, was also subpoenaed. Lazarus would figure in a 1965 meeting in Palm Springs, dubbed a *Little* Apalachin, that allegedly involved the distribution of hidden shares in Caesars Palace ownership and, in turn, the rights to the count room skim.

Former professional basketball player Irving "Ash" Resnick was a longtime gambler, bookmaker and—according to the FBI—swindler. In 1958, Resnick was questioned by a federal grand jury about a massive gambling syndicate in Terre Haute, Indiana. Resnick was later a licensed owner of Caesars Palace in Las Vegas, Nevada (author's collection).

The next day, Eugene Koren—nominally from Springfield, Illinois—stepped forward to testify, as well as to make public comment. "Business is dead," remarked Koren to gathered media. "People stopped [making bets] with all this publicity."[51] Seven years later, using a Las Vegas address, Eugene Koren was revealed publicly as an investor in Caesars Palace right alongside Jay Sarno and Stanley Mallin. Along with Koren, Elliot Paul Price—reportedly from Brookline, Massachusetts—was subpoenaed. Within the decade, Price was also posted to an executive position at Caesars Palace.

By August 20, 1958, the federal jurists were knee deep in current and future Las Vegas gambling executives. Jerome Zarowitz—convicted felon in the 1946 NFL title game case—was subpoenaed in the Terre Haute probe. Zarowitz sought the protection of the Fifth Amendment throughout his Indiana testimony. Zarowitz, though, would also be installed as the casino executive and vice president of Caesars Palace. The specter of Jerome Zarowitz was also a catalyst to regime change at Caesars Palace after the 1981 Caesars Palace Grand Prix.

Chester Simms of Las Vegas, "manager of the Flamingo Hotel," also provided testimony in the Terre Haute case.[52] Chester Simms was later involved in a Flamingo skimming case with Meyer Lansky and Sam Cohen, a case that also bore on the fates of Caesars Palace.

The Terre Haute case would then drag on for another three years, eventually proceeding all the way to the U.S. Supreme Court. The defendants were represented through much of their proceedings by Morris Shenker, sometime counsel for Jimmy Hoffa and later, organized crime investor in Las Vegas gambling resorts. Notably, Morris Shenker was also the majority owner of the Dunes hotel-casino when the former chief executive of Caesars Palace sought to purchase the aging Las Vegas resort in 1983.

The original Terre Haute arrestees served prison time for conspiracy to evade income taxes and failure to register as a federally-taxed gambling syndicate. Upon their release from prison in 1964, the IRS filed tax liens against the convicts for over $11.5 million. In fact, pursuit of payment by the IRS lasted well into the 1970s.

Notably, none of the Terre Haute gamblers later connected with Caesars Palace went to trial, all remaining free to steward the hidden ownerships of Caesar just a few years hence. In fact, within two years of the Terre Haute convictions, the connections of the bookmaking, gambling, and *moxie* ranks of the American organized crime syndicate would begin to close ranks with their counterparts in the mobility, muscle, and murder ranks of La Cosa Nostra, while the sentries and centurions of Caesar would herald the collective desert march to their new Las Vegas battleground.

***

Press notes from the 1959 Sebring Grand Prix of the United States were still rattling when motorsports pundits began to predict the demise of Sebring as the 1960 venue for a U.S. round of the Formula One world championship. "This obsolete World War II airstrip has outgrown its usefulness and should be abandoned," read one of the blasts from the West Coast. "Located in the middle of the Florida swamp lands, Sebring's obsolescence has reached the point of no return."[53] The pundits also leaned in on Alec Ulmann, the Sebring promoter: "Last December's U.S. Grand Prix, when only a handful of spectators showed up," continued the opinion piece, "should have proved to promoter Alec Ulmann that his track has had it."[54]

Some 70 years of road racing events at Sebring might prove the opinion writer wrong, but the swamp land reference was strong. The swamp land refrain would also be leveled against a Florida land company once headed by the first chairman of Caesars Palace, wherein unwitting purchasers bought undevelopable "swamp and wilderness lots and acreage from land peddlers."[55]

Attendance for the 1959 Sebring Grand Prix of the United States had been announced at 15,000. By contrast, Sebring was pulling a reported 40,000 spectators for its spring 12-Hour endurance race. Certainly, Alec Ulmann had hoped for a similar number for the Formula One Grand Prix. Famed Grand Prix driving star Stirling Moss, however, offered his own pointed opinion. "Sebring cut its own throat on the Grand Prix and unless the attitude of people there change, it might lose the 12-Hour Endurance Race in March too," Moss said. "They stung us like mad on motel prices and everything else. They tried to make a killing on the one shot."[56]

Stirling Moss was also being teased in a new car for the 1960 Grand Prix of the United States. The mystery vehicle was soon revealed to be a rear-engine Lotus designed by Colin Chapman. "There is every reason to believe," reported the London *Observer*, "that the Formula One Lotus could prove to be the fastest car on all but the really high-speed circuits."[57]

Soon after the March 26, 1960, Sebring 12-Hour event, Alec Ulmann confirmed the departure of the United States Grand Prix from Sebring. In a piece by *Miami News* sports editor Howard Kleinberg, Ulmann was quoted as saying, "I am not ready to say where I will hold the race ... but it will not be in Sebring. Southern California appears the logical spot for it."[58] Speculation, and then confirmation, would obviously run through Riverside International Raceway.

By June of 1960, the Riverside Grand Prix of the United States began to take form. Still, though, the Sebring barbs were being thrown: "about as much to offer as Stanleyville, Belgian Congo, and is not nearly so accessible."[59] As the Grand Prix moved from Sebring, Alec Ulmann also appeared to be highly taken with the Riverside team. "I'm bringing this great race west," Ulmann was quoted as saying by Joe Scalzo, "because I'm impressed with the way that Roy G. Lewis, owner of Riverside Raceway, has been handling the plant."[60]

Hollywood automobile dealer Roy G. Lewis acquired majority ownership of the Riverside motorsports facility in early 1960 from the original track developers. Lewis then hired Paul Schissler away from the *Los Angeles Times* as general manager and vice president in charge of promotions. Schissler immediately announced expansion plans for Riverside "to develop the 600 acres around the track into a multimillion dollar sports, shopping, and housing area."[61] In one of those twists of history, however, Roy G. Lewis would also have his own connections with Nevada gambling, connections that also engaged the Teamsters and the centurions of Caesars Palace.

The apparent long game of Lewis and his partners deployed organized crime elements from coast to coast. The Lewis play also drew in such disparate entries as Robert Petersen, publisher of *Hot Rod Magazine*, and the Pacific Bridge company, one of the builders of Hoover Dam and the Golden Gate Bridge. Before the decade was out, the fallout from Roy Lewis' relationship with the Teamsters would also find him under federal investigation, an investigation that resulted in a prison sentence for the one-time owner of Riverside International Raceway.

In the build-up of the U.S. racing season to the Riverside Formula One Grand Prix finale, Augie Pabst of Milwaukee, Wisconsin, won the September 24, 1960, Watkins Glen Grand Prix for sports cars. Pabst took the Watkins Glen event in a Lance Reventlow "Scarab." A reported 30,000 spectators also watched Pabst set a new single-lap sports car record of 1:30.30. Roger Penske finished second at Watkins Glen in a Porsche. Walt Hansgen led much of the event in a "birdcage" Maserati before blowing the engine.

On October 9, 1960, Stirling Moss then claimed his second International Formula Libre event at Watkins Glen. Moss' Formula One Lotus-Climax finished seven seconds clear of World Formula One champion Jack Brabham in his Cooper-Climax. Moss, too, set a new lap record for the Formula Libre event, a 1:16.00 time set near the halfway point of the race. Roy Salvadori finished third in a Cooper-Monaco. Joakim Bonnier of Sweden, winner of the inaugural 1958 Watkins Glen Formula

Stirling Moss won the October 10, 1969, Formula Libre event at Watkins Glen driving a Lotus-Climax. World champion Jack Brabham finished second in a Cooper-Climax. Roy Salvadori of England finished third in a Cooper-Monaco. Salvadori was an early consort of Bernie Ecclestone (courtesy International Motor Racing Research Center).

Libre, finished fourth. "A crowd estimated at 16,000 by Henry Valent, Grand Prix Corp. president," it was reported, "turned out for the contest in bright Indian summer weather."[62] The Watkins Glen throng also watched the vastly superior performance of the Formula One cars over the sports racers of just 1 month before. With all but the U.S. round of the Formula One season wrapped, Stirling Moss would have the momentum headed to Riverside International Raceway. Once again, however, Jack Brabham held the points lead.

Press notes in the week after the Watkins Glen event then picked up the entries for the Riverside Formula One field. "[Alec] Ulmann said he signed world defending champion Jack Brabham of Australia, runner-up Bruce MacLaren [*sic*] of New Zealand, Graham Hill and Stirling Moss of England," reported the UPI, "as well as American stars Phil Hill, Dan Gurney, Masten Gregory, and Lance Reventlow."[63] One week later, American sports car drivers Bob Drake and Jim Hall of the U.S. were announced. Formula One competitors Tony Brooks, Innes Ireland, John Surtees, Jim Clark, and Joakim Bonnier then rounded the field for the November 20, 1960, event.

On Saturday, Stirling Moss in his new Lotus scorched the two-year-old Riverside track record of 2:04.30 set by Chuck Daigh in a Scarab. Moss' quick qualifying lap of 1:54.40 again pointed up the performance disparity of the best sports racers in America, against the pinnacle of the open-wheel Formula One vehicles. In fact, two thirds of the Formula One entries qualified quicker than the former lap record. Jack Brabham—already a clinch for the championship—qualified second in a Cooper while

FIRST TIME IN CALIFORNIA!

THE ONLY UNITED STATES WORLD CHAMPIONSHIP GRAND PRIX

For SINGLE SEATER RACING CARS
(FORMULA ONE)
NOVEMBER 19th & 20th
RIVERSIDE INTERNATIONAL RACEWAY
RIVERSIDE, CALIF.
The finest racing motor-cars in the world
in their first appearance on the West Coast!

WORLD CHAMPIONSHIP DRIVERS
include Jack Brabham • Bruce McLaren • Stirling Moss
Tony Brooks • Olivier Gendebien • John Surtees • Roy Salvadori
Jo Bonnier • Dan Gurney • Ken Miles • Maurice Trintignant
Walt Hansgen • Pete Lovely and many others!

GENERAL AND RESERVED SEATS
Seats On Sale Now-Boxoffice & Mail Orders
RIVERSIDE RACEWAY OFFICE, 1617 No. El Centro Hollywood 28 · HO. 7-5128

SATURDAY
—NOON—
Formula Jr.
International
Race for the
Count Lurani
Cup·
Presented by
Count Lurani

—2 P.M.—
Final Qualifying
for the
GRAND PRIX
of the U.S.

SUNDAY
—NOON—
International
Compact Car Race

—2 P.M.—
The GRAND PRIX

GRAHAM HILL
2 LITRE B.R.M.
FORMULA ONE

TICKETS AVAILABLE ALSO AT	• MUTUAL TICKET AGENCIES, 737 So. Hill St., Los Angeles 14
	• Humphrey's Music Co., 130 Pine Ave., Long Beach • Caravan Inn, 1860 8th St., Riverside
	• Harris Dep't. Store "On the Plaza" Riverside • Econo Motors, 5th & Main, Riverside
	• Berry and Grassmuek, 925 E. Colorado, Pasadena

Print ad for the November 20, 1960, United States Riverside Grand Prix appeared one week before the event. Event promoter Alec Ulmann got what he paid for. A three-column ad that ran for a single weekday during football season resulted in a crowd turnout one third the size of his pre-race projections. The event was the second Formula One Grand Prix held in the United States, the first on the West Coast until the inception of the Long Beach Grand Prix in 1976 (author's collection).

Dan Gurney in a BRM represented the front of the field for the Americans, only two tenths back of Brabham.

A reported 25,000 fans enjoyed brilliant weather for the Riverside Grand Prix of America. Dan Gurney, from his third qualifying position, led the drag race into the first turn. Jack Brabham then passed Gurney while Stirling Moss would do the same by the end of the first lap. Innes Ireland slotted fourth in a BRM followed by John Surtees driving a Lotus. By lap three, Joakim Bonnier in another BRM moved up to fourth behind Gurney.

Jack Brabham pitted from second on the fifth lap to diagnose an apparent fire. He then returned to the pits on lap 10 for the same issue, putting the World Champion a lap down. Five laps later, Stirling Moss was leading Dan Gurney by six seconds with Bonnier directly behind. Gurney, though, was overheating. The southern California hope retired three laps later with a terminal water leak.

Jack Brabham (#2) in a Cooper-Climax leads the Grand Prix of the United States at Riverside International Raceway on November 20, 1960. Brabham is followed by Jimmy Clark (#5) of Scotland in a Lotus-Climax, Wolfgang von Trips (#16) of Germany in a Cooper-Maserati, and American Chuck Daigh (#18) driving a Scarab for Lance Reventlow. Hollywood automobile dealer and Los Angeles public official Roy Gene Lewis was then an owner of Riverside Raceway. Lewis was sentenced to prison in 1973 for his role in a Santa Monica property development that involved the Teamsters Central States Pension Fund and connections to the American organized crime syndicate (William Hewitt Photograph Collection, The Revs Institute).

Jack Brabham was then on a march through the field, consistently moving back up to reclaim positions through brilliant overtaking and attrition. By lap 67, Brabham passed Jim Hall for the fourth position. Stirling Moss, though, was unchallenged the rest of the way, crossing the finish line first by over one-half lap ahead of Innes Ireland. Moss' average speed was 99 mph. Innes Ireland was followed by Bruce McLaren in third, the inspired recovery of Jack Brabham in fourth, and Joakim Bonnier in fifth. The first American was Phil Hill in a Cooper, nearly two laps down to Moss. Jim Hall in a Lotus followed Phil Hill.

Stirling Moss played both confident and comic from the victory celebration. "I never really did push the car," Moss was quoted as saying by Bob Thomas for the *Los Angeles Times*. "Once Jack [Brabham] went out, I didn't have to drive all out."[64]

"By the way, what happened to Brabham when I flipped that match at him?" poked Moss afterward. "I noticed his car was on fire."[65] Stirling Moss could joke, but Jack Brabham was now a two-time Formula One world champion, with both of his international championships celebrated at an American Formula One event.

Stirling Moss certainly preferred the Riverside Formula One venue in 1960 to the Sebring course in 1959. After the Riverside victory, though, Moss quipped about the pending reduction in Formula One engine size, from 2.5 to 1.5 liters. "I hope we come next year," Moss stated, "racing the same size cars in a new special class."[66] Technical and sporting divisions were forming in the Formula One series. Those divisions would seal a time-honored and tripartite power struggle in the years ahead between the FIA, the teams, and the drivers. It was also a bickering and back-biting that continued through to the Caesars Palace Grand Prix.

The Riverside wrap reports then speculated about the future of a 1961 U.S. Grand Prix at Riverside. "Promoter Alec Ulmann … hasn't said yet," reported Thomas for the *Times*. "He had visions of a turnout of around 70,000. And he hadn't gotten over the shock of the crowd of 25,000."[67]

Just as Stirling Moss scorched qualifying, promoter Alec Ulmann then scorched the southern California media. "I am afraid there will have to be a change of attitude on the part of the local press," Ulmann said, emulating Moss' comments about Sebring, "before I or any other organization would bring big time racing in [Southern California] again."[68] Ulmann's lament placed blame with the *Los Angeles Times* for a lack of promotion, in apparent competition with the *Times* sponsorship of the preceding Riverside sports car Grand Prix.

Competing newspapers in the Los Angeles market were quick to push back. "They bounced in with the missionary attitude so typical of New York types arriving on these shores," wrote one pundit of the Ulmann promotion, "that they were the big town bringing light and urbanity to the grateful provincials."[69] Alec Ulmann was

The promotion of the November 20, 1960, United States Grand Prix at Riverside International Raceway involved several different badges. The Automobile Racing Club of California was a construct of event promoter Alec Ulmann. The California Sports Car Club (second logo from left) was aligned with the Sports Car Club of America at the time of the event (William Hewitt Photograph Collection, The Revs Institute).

thus dispatched from Riverside, California, back to Sebring, Florida, to commence promotions for the 1961 Sebring 12-Hour endurance event. Ulmann would soon also announce a 20 percent reduction in Sebring ticket prices.

For those same New York types, news soon broke of a potential new venue for the 1961 American Formula One Grand Prix. "A road racing event of highest international standing," read a January 9, 1961, dateline from upstate New York, "will be held Oct. 8 [1961] on the Watkins Glen International Grand Prix Road Race Course."[70] The news from Watkins Glen, New York, also visited Stirling Moss' comments about engine displacement for 1961. "Atty. Cameron R. Argetsinger, Watkins Glen Grand Prix Corp. executive director, announced Sunday," continued the presser, "that the Glen has been awarded the 1961 Intercontinental Formula Championship points for the United States."[71]

Intercontinental was drafted as a new six-race series classifying race cars with engine sizes between two liters and three liters in a separate championship from the new 1.5-liter Formula One. The Watkins Glen announcement pointed up the disagreement of the proposed engine changes as much as it did Alec Ulmann's deteriorated relationship with Riverside, California. Despite the post–Riverside unpleasantries, Alec Ulmann was still the *de facto* stateside promoter of Formula One headed into 1961. As with many pre-season declarations to come in American Formula One, though, the actual race season unfolded far differently. Events heading into the inaugural Caesars Palace Grand Prix certainly fit the pattern.

Formula One would soon, however, find a long-term American home at Watkins Glen, dubbed simply the *United States Grand Prix*. Watkins Glen, in turn, paved the way 15 years later for the Long Beach Formula One Grand Prix. The Long Beach Formula One Grand Prix would be titled the United States Grand Prix *West*. Both Watkins Glen and Long Beach, in turn, pointed to the unique luxury resort-branded Caesars Palace Grand Prix. Caesars Palace, however, also marked the end of both Watkins Glen and Long Beach as Formula One venues. Bernie Ecclestone then chased deep-pocket American promotional dollars from Las Vegas (1981–1982), to Detroit (1982–1988), to Dallas (1984), and to Phoenix (1989–1991). To that list of major media markets—not to mention organized crime power centers—were added unproductive Formula One overtures in San Francisco (1985) and New York (1983–1985).

Similarly, the upstate New York Apalachin crime convention in 1957—less than a pleasant one-hour drive on country roads from Watkins Glen—catalyzed the vast American organized crime syndicate around the value of real property, and the liquid cash opportunities to be derived from a stake in land ownership and financing. With Nevada gambling opportunities discussed at the Apalachin meeting, the development model for Caesars Palace would thus be born. In turn, the nexus of gamblers exposed in Terre Haute, Indiana, formed the core of the Caesars Palace operational apparatus, to preside over the various stakes of the organized crime syndicate and its constituents in the Caesars Palace allegedly skim.

In September of 1961, new president John F. Kennedy signed three bills into law, all of them directed at illegal gambling, one of which "made it a federal crime to transmit gambling information between states."[72] The following month—just 1 week after the Formula One Grand Prix at Watkins Glen—Attorney General Robert F. Kennedy returned from a whirlwind cross-country tour, meeting federal agents in prominent illegal gambling havens around the country. "At most of these cities," proclaimed Robert Kennedy, "we discussed individuals in whom we are interested and situations we are investigating."[73] Las Vegas press reported that Kennedy described such persons as "kingpins of organized crime."[74]

On the same day that Las Vegas media reported front-page on the Kennedy developments, hometown press also covered the departure of Jimmy Hoffa and the International Brotherhood of Teamsters from their annual conference in Las Vegas. Hoffa took leave of Las Vegas for his own whirlwind tour of prominent American cities, gambling havens, organized crime power centers, and otherwise. As Jimmy Hoffa flew from McCarran Field on October 17, 1961, and into the skies toward Los Angeles, the race to Caesars Palace—and the luxury brand of the Caesars Palace Grand Prix—was officially on.

II

Parallel Paths

*The Path of Formula One in America
and the Path of Caesar to Las Vegas*

Therefore let our alliance be combined. (*Julius Caesar* 4.1.47)

The dawn of the 1960s presaged a period of profound change for America. John F. Kennedy moved over from the U.S. Senate and the McClellan Committee to the White House. Brother Robert F. Kennedy then joined the new administration as Attorney General. The younger Kennedy would also add his contribution to the great American history with his takeaway piece from the McClellan Committee, *The Enemy Within: The McClellan Committee's Crusade Against Jimmy Hoffa and Corrupt Labor Unions*. Robert Kennedy's book entrenched the vitriol between his work for the committee, and with Jimmy Hoffa, Allen Dorfman, and the International Brotherhood of Teamsters. The Teamsters and their massive Central States Pension Fund, on the other hand, were already hard at work perfecting their great American property development template, and Caesars Palace in Las Vegas would appear near the top of a very top-secret *pro forma*.

Fidel Castro and the Cuban Revolution had now driven dictator Fulgencio

In January of 1961, John F. Kennedy was inaugurated as the President of the United States. Brother Robert F. Kennedy (pictured) soon joined the new administration as attorney general. Robert Kennedy thus moved on from Senate investigations of organized labor and organized crime to vigorous prosecution of them. The Department of Justice successfully pursued prosecutions of Teamsters president Jimmy Hoffa and Miami contractor Calvin Kovens. Kennedy's DOJ also opened an illegal wiretap program that would lead to Las Vegas, Alvin Malnik, Edward Levinson, Moe Dalitz, and the centurions of Caesars Palace (Library of Congress).

Batista from power. The revolutionary wave through the island also drove the American organized crime syndicate to safe haven, abandoning their multi-million-dollar gambling resort investments to languish in the capital city of Havana. As overlord Meyer Lansky, host George Raft, operator Dino Cellini, and investors such as Santo Trafficante and Charles "The Blade" Tourine departed their casino operations and returned stateside, they inevitably gathered the attentions of American law enforcement. In fact, some faced continued investigations about the October 25, 1957, murder of Albert Anastasia, as well as the Apalachin crime convention on November 14, 1957, at the home of Joseph Barbara near Watkins Glen. Notably, the casino refugees formed their new power center in Miami, Florida.

Miami would then become ground-zero for clandestine American campaigns to upend Fidel Castro, the product of the operations think-tank of the Central Intelligence Agency. Others would be spearheaded by the American organized crime syndicate and their exiled casino investors. At times, the operations of the CIA and the syndicate joined in their mutual agenda to remove Fidel Castro's communist cabal. Some of those efforts engaged the facilities of the aviation-themed Skyways Motel at the gateway to the Miami Airport.[1] In the years ahead, the Skyways would be a noted gathering spot for Meyer Lansky, Santo Trafficante, and others, typically under the watchful eye of the FBI.[2] The Skyways Motel would also be a stopover on the career path of Murray Gennis, a future casino executive at Caesars Palace in Las Vegas, a resume entry that would be rather difficult to embrace as a simple matter of coincidence.[3]

By 1960, international Grand Prix racing also departed Cuba. The Havana Grand Prix—*Gran Premio Libertad*—was originally conceived by the Batista regime as a tourism companion piece to legalized gambling operations in Cuba. The final Havana Grand Prix on February 28, 1960, placed Stirling Moss on the top of the podium, followed by Pedro Rodriguez and Masten Gregory. The history of Grand Prix should be thankful that the three racing stars were not detained by Castro rebels before they could escape the island. The stars of international Grand Prix racing would be wagered, however, amid the discontent following the 1960 Riverside Formula One Grand Prix. Indeed, a suitable venue for the 1961 American Formula One event would take months to sort.

The 1960s would be a decade rich in events with global implications. The year 1961 then played its part. Eight days after his inauguration on January 20, 1961, President John F. Kennedy was briefed on executive-action tactics for the Bay of Pigs invasion into Cuba. Two months later, the CIA recruited Cuban exiles into the newly-minted Cuban Revolutionary Council, notably from the grounds of the Skyways Motel.[4] Concurrently, casino gambling was legalized in Great Britain, and Meyer Lansky and Dino Cellini would take notice. Thirty-year-old Bernie Ecclestone—the future czar of Formula One—was paying attention as well.

***

The announcement on October 8, 1960, that an Intercontinental Formula Championship event would run at Watkins Glen in 1961 did little to settle the status of premier-level Formula One competition in the United States. Moreover, the

The Cuban Grand Prix was organized by the regime of Cuban dictator Fulgencio Batista as a companion piece to the tourism gambling economy managed by mob financial overseer Meyer Lansky. The Hotel Nacional of Havana in the right background was renowned for its Lansky-operated casino. Las Vegas resort owner Moe Dalitz was also an owner of the Nacional casino. On the grid of the 1957 Cuban Grand Prix is the #2 Maserati 300S driven by winner Juan Manuel Fangio. Fangio is just left of the car while mechanic Guerino Bertocchi is at the right of the vehicle. The 1958 Cuban Grand Prix was notable for the kidnapping of reigning Formula One world champion Fangio by Cuban rebels. Juan Manual Fangio later presided as grand marshal over the 1966 Stardust Can-Am Grand Prix in Las Vegas, Nevada. Nineteen-sixty was the final year of the Havana Grand Prix amid the rise of Fidel Castro. Castro drove out the gambling operations of Meyer Lansky as well. The government presence on the starting grid is noteworthy. Others in the image are not identified (Tom Burnside Photograph Collection, The Revs Institute).

Intercontinental Formula was a stopgap, derived to address driver concerns about the reduction in Formula One engine displacement. Whereas the FIA desired a smaller engine displacement as a cost-management measure, British drivers in particular were keen to race on in the larger displacement compromise.

The Intercontinental Formula, however, ran almost immediately into conflicts over driver availability and purse strings. Further, the new Formula was competing in dated chassis technology, effectively diminishing the attraction of the series. Finally, the Intercontinental series was effectively a direct competitor to the established Formula One series, a competitive threat that did not survive past August of 1961, well short of the announced October 8, 1961, Watkins Glen Intercontinental date.

The effects of the 1960 Riverside Grand Prix of the United States continued to gust as well, especially in the person of promoter and FIA licensee Alec Ulmann. "As long as the public are content with their sports car races," Ulmann would complain to the media after the Riverside Formula One Grand Prix, "why cast pearls before swine?"[5] One might then detect the burning of rubber out of the Los Angeles market. As Alec Ulmann analogized his Formula One promotion with the *Los Angeles Times*-sponsored Riverside Grand Prix for sports cars, he also went in on newspaper placements produced by the *Times*. "As a World Champion event it was played down until the last few days," continued the promoter, "and the advertising we could buy … looked like nothing after what the public had become used to expecting from events organized by the local papers."[6] It is highly unlikely that Riverside International Raceway and regional Los Angeles media conspired to downplay such a prominent international event. Much more so, it is probable that Alec Ulmann planted—and then presided over—his own laments. As one California writer diplomatically painted Ulmann, "he may be a hard man to do business with in the future."[7]

The fortunes of Riverside International Raceway were then fortified in early 1961 by the announcement of a new hire. "Football star Les Richter, outstanding linebacker of the Los Angeles Rams," pitched Paul Schissler of Riverside Raceway, "has been appointed assistant manager of Riverside International Raceway."[8] The tenure of Les Richter proved a stabilizing force at Riverside, shepherding the racing facility through numerous guard changes, including a near-terminal affiliation with Lawrence LoPatin of American Raceways, Inc. Richter was also involved in early race course development in Las Vegas, as well as in the formative structure of the Long Beach Grand Prix. Les Richter, however, would prove a prickly presence in the creation of the Caesars Palace Grand Prix.

News out of Miami in March of 1961 then confirmed the departure of Alec Ulmann and the United States Grand Prix from California. "They refused to co-operate with us," announced Alec Ulmann. "We couldn't get any publicity in the papers and we weren't allowed to sell tickets much in advance because other promoters there were trying to protect themselves first."[9] Ulmann noted that other venues under review for the 1961 Formula One event were his somewhat-captive Sebring facility, Miami, Florida, Bartow, Florida, or the Bahamas. Promoter Ulmann further noted that his production of the United States Grand Prix required a sponsor's guarantee with a check for $150,000. To that demand should have been added the requisite approval of the FIA for the race venue. The SCCA apparently then lobbied to stage the United States Formula One event at Laguna Seca Raceway on the Monterey Peninsula in California. As the weather warmed into spring, however, the trail of the 1961 United States Grand Prix went cold.

The Formula One odyssey of Alec Ulmann then wound its way through Miami city government and, eventually, to the newly-opened high banks of Daytona Speedway. Both Florida coast efforts, however, were also rejected for the 1961 Formula One race. "[Alec] Ullman, who holds the right to the date for the international race," reported the *Miami News* on July 9, 1961, "has indicated it now will not be possible to hold the event in the United States."[10] Headed into the penultimate Grand Prix of the Formula One season, however, an American was in contention for the World Championship. With the Italian Grand Prix yet to go, Phil Hill of the United States trailed Wolfgang von Trips of Germany in the Formula One standings, 29 points to 33. Alec Ulmann had failed in his stewardship of the Grand Prix of the United States, but the hopes of the United States would be high for its first-ever Formula One World Champion.

American Phil Hill won the 1961 Formula One championship driving for Ferrari. Hill was withdrawn from the first U.S. Grand Prix at Watkins Glen, New York, due to the death of teammate Wolfgang von Trips at the preceding Italian Grand Prix. Phil Hill also raced in the 1966 Can-Am series, including the season finale at Stardust International Raceway in Las Vegas, Nevada (Lothar Spurzem/Wikimedia Commons).

The Italian Grand Prix was scheduled to run on September 10, 1961. Both Wolfgang von Trips and Phil Hill had a chance to take advantage in the Formula One championship. The Italian Grand Prix would indeed mark the destinies of the championship contenders, as well as the future of the United States Grand Prix.

∗∗∗

Just as Alec Ulmann steered the early path of Formula One in the United States, so too did organized crime stamp the blueprint for the development of Caesars Palace in the mid–1960s. In fact, the plans for Caesars Palace were already informed by events revealed publicly in the late 1950s. The 1957 Apalachin crime convention in upstate New York would point up the consolidation of power by Vito Genovese. The Teamsters loan taken in 1957 by future Caesars Palace principals Jay Sarno and Stanley Mallin marked them as patrons of organized crime, likely an indelible mark made for life. Further, the 1958 investigation of the Terra Haute gambling syndicate united the names of Ruby Lazarus, Eugene Koren, Ash Resnick, Elliott Paul Price, and Jerome Zarowitz under a single umbrella, an umbrella soon to be the Greco-Roman canopies of Caesars Palace.

To the early Caesars Palace control group were then added three more names, compliments of the FBI. "ANTHONY SALERNO aka Fat Tony," had a burgeoning FBI file by 1961.[11] "[Salerno] has been described as a 'caporegime' [captain]," read one

FBI report, "in the VITO GENOVESE family."[12] The FBI tracked Salerno from Harlem to Miami and later, to Palm Springs and his hidden interests in Las Vegas. At 5' 7", 250 pounds, and typically chomping a cigar, Salerno was believed by the FBI to be the chief executive of a massive numbers racket in Harlem, while also serving the policy gambling proclivities of his constituents in Miami. Further, loan sharking, bookmaking, counterfeiting, and sports-rigging investigations were conducted against Salerno by the FBI, always with the tag "ARMED AND DANGEROUS."[13] Anthony Salerno would ascend to the upper echelon of the Vito Genovese crime family and its hidden influence in the affairs of the Teamsters union and its pension fund loans. The FBI also documented the secret investment gambit of Anthony Salerno at Caesars Palace, reportedly worth "millions of dollars."[14]

By 1961, the FBI also noted the connections of Anthony Salerno to both Ruby Lazarus and Vincent "Jimmy Blue Eyes" Alo.[15] Ruby Lazarus was reportedly tasked to "take care of all the syndicate betting business for SALERNO," and further, "LAZARUS is SALERNO'S right hand man."[16] Ruby Lazarus had also been splayed rather publicly in the Terre Haute gambling case. Vincent Alo, though, generally stayed clear of national headlines. Nonetheless, Vincent "Jimmy Blue Eyes" Alo was linked to a homicide case in 1947 with Meyer Lansky, "the blood-flecked names of ... veteran hoods."[17]

Vincent "Jimmy Blue Eyes" Alo was a high-ranking member of the Genovese crime family. Alo acted as liaison between the Genovese family and the criminal syndicate apparatus of Meyer Lansky, including matters involving casino operations. Alo was present with Anthony "Fat Tony" Salerno at a "Little Apalachin" meeting in September 1965 to sort concealed stakes in Caesars Palace, then under construction in Las Vegas (Library of Congress).

During the construction of Caesars Palace, Anthony Salerno, Vincent Alo, Jerome Zarowitz, Elliott Paul Price, and Ruby Lazarus would then all be linked together, placed at a meeting in Palm Springs, California, to sort Caesars Palace ownership, and the skim from its Las Vegas gambling take.

The FBI also established some otherwise obscured relationships during their investigation of Anthony Salerno. "Cal Kovens Construction Company," read another FBI report, "advised ANTHONY SALERNO was unknown to him until he walked into his place of business."[18] As Cal Kovens described the happenstance, Anthony Salerno then engaged Kovens' construction business for home renovation work on a newly-acquired property in Miami, a room addition and swimming pool for which Salerno paid $15,000 in cash, or about $131,000 in 2021 dollars. Calvin Kovens, though, was already deeply involved with Jimmy Hoffa and Allen Dorfman in Teamster loans and the related cash culling opportunities.

Indeed, in 1964, Cal Kovens would be convicted with Hoffa on charges of wire fraud, mail fraud, and conspiracy to commit fraud, all in connection with loans from the Teamsters Central States Pension Fund. A close and collegial relationship between Anthony Salerno and Cal Kovens might thus be presumed. Further, the brother of Calvin Kovens was Irving Kovens. Irving Kovens, a hard-nosed Maryland political and financial operator, also testified at the trial of Jimmy Hoffa, Allen Dorfman, and brother Calvin. Irving Kovens notably "invoked the fifth amendment seven times in five minutes." [19] Irving Kovens also refused to identify Calvin Kovens to the court as his own brother. In 1966, Irv Kovens would then be publicly revealed as a licensed owner in Caesars Palace.

The bench of the secret Caesars Palace squad would thus run deep, a veritable wrecking crew of bookmaking, numbers, policy, and strong-arm syndicate racketeers and mobsters, along with their political patrons and apparent legitimate business partners. Further names will be added—some ensconced even more deeply in the massive labyrinth of the American organized crime syndicate—and their intrigues would shadow the podium celebration of the inaugural Caesars Palace Grand Prix.

***

"It's official. The Grand Prix of the United States has been firmed for Watkins Glen, Oct. 8." [20] The punch piece from motorsports columnist Jerry Diamond ran on September 6, 1961. It also ran from the West Coast. Diamond, who had updated the Formula One misadventures of promoter Alec Ulmann for much of the year, was also among the first to laud the official new home of the United States Grand Prix. In the wake of Ulmann's failures to launch the 1961 Formula One event at Sebring, Miami and Daytona, Jerry Diamond also leaned in a bit on the rumblings. "The volatile auto racing entrepreneur was set to give it one more shot at Miami this fall," offered Diamond of Ulmann, "but factory pressure due to slow pay last season forced FIA to look elsewhere." [21]

The prospects of Alec Ulmann sputtered through the summer of 1961. As the Formula Intercontinental series waned, Cameron Argetsinger and the Grand Prix Corporation of Watkins Glen seized opportunity and applied to the FIA for the Formula One event. In fact, less than three weeks after Ulmann's Miami venture was pulled off the table, the Watkins Glen group submitted their petition to the stateside delegate-body of the FIA, the Automobile Competition Committee of the United States (ACCUS). Cameron Argetsinger then served the press notes on the Watkins Glen application, while he also recognized the positioning of Alec Ullman. "Dissatisfied with the poor financial showing for the U.S. Grand Prix last year at Riverside," ran one New York account, "the American committee of FIA in effect pulled the race ... and assigned it to [Watkins Glen]." [22] While acknowledging the role of Alec Ulmann in the origins of the Watkins Glen Grand Prix, the coverage also alleged that Ulmann had attempted to lease the Watkins Glen facility for the 1961 U.S. Grand Prix. The apparent discontent of both ACCUS and the FIA, coupled with the aspirations of the Watkins Glen Grand Prix Corporation, scuttled the final overture of Ullman.

As Watkins Glen became a staple of American road racing in the years ahead, it is important to consider the tenuous nature of the 1961 United States Grand Prix. "The population of the town itself would scarcely fill a good sized grandstand," continued Jerry Diamond from the Bay Area, "and Watkins Glen is located as far from a major metropolis as a community in an eastern State can be."[23] Such concerns— as well as payment issues—would also factor in the 1981 withdrawal of Formula One from Watkins Glen as the Caesars Palace Grand Prix then appeared center-stage. Commentary from the East Coast, though, ran somewhat counter, citing Watkins Glen's "nearness to metropolitan centers."[24] Watkins Glen was notably close to Apalachin as well.

Ultimately, the New York notes pitched the emerging attraction of the United States market to the otherwise European-based championship, "the need of staging the scheduled American race this year as part of the world circuit."[25] The United States Grand Prix at Watkins Glen was then placed in the balance. "If Watkins Glen fails," wrote Diamond, "the Formula One clash may be labeled a white elephant with no future prospective buyers."[26] The angle of Jerry Diamond's piece read as if released on the world-famous Las Vegas Strip the day before the inaugural 1981 Caesars Palace Grand Prix.

***

The confirmation of the U.S. Grand Prix at Watkins Glen came just days before the Italian Grand Prix at Monza, the penultimate race of the Formula One season. The Watkins Glen round thus protracted a program that was otherwise prepared to declare its champion. Through the preceding event at the Nürburgring, Germany's Wolfgang von Trips led the championship points over American Phil Hill, 33 to 29 on a best-five-finishes-to-date basis. Both von Trips and Hill also drove for the vaunted Scuderia Ferrari, the Ferrari works racing division that had won four-of-11 championships since the 1950 formulation, more than any other constructor. The Ferrari duo in their flaming red shark-nosed 156 chassis did, however, have a challenger. Stirling Moss of Britain, the perennial contender, stood at 21 points with two Formula One race victories. If Stirling Moss won out, and locked both von Trips and Hill out of the points, the Lotus-Climax driver for Rob Walker claimed his first World Drivers Championship. Moss, however, was otherwise on a disappointing 6-year run of second and third-place disappointments.

On the Friday before the September 10, 1961, Italian Grand Prix, Shell Oil placed a full-page ad in major U.S. newspapers to stake their position in the fortunes of the championship leaders. "The man out front in this year-long competition is a steel-nerved, 32-year-old Count named Wolfgang von Trips," ran the copy. "His closest rival is Phil Hill, 34, a quiet, determined Californian who still stands a chance of becoming the first American to win the world race-drivers' championship."[27] The storylines were thus set for Sunday, a championship for Ferrari nearly assured, Wolfgang von Trips, Phil Hill, contender Stirling Moss, and the rest. The storyline, unfortunately, would become one of profound tragedy.

Leading from the pole, Count von Trips appeared to block Jimmy Clark in a Lotus on the second lap, fast approaching from seventh place on the grid. "Von Trips and I were racing along the straightaway. Von Trips was running close to the inside of the track. I was closely following him keeping near the outside," recalled the 25-year-old Jimmy Clark afterward. "Von Trips shifted sideways so that my front wheels collided with his back wheels. It was the fatal moment."[28] Count von Trips' Ferrari careened wildly and "hurtled into a crowd packed elbow to elbow."[29] Count Wolfgang von Trips perished along with 11 spectators. Dozens more were injured. Five more spectator deaths were later reported.

The Italian Grand Prix then continued to its somber conclusion, drivers racing "past the bodies of the dead strewn over the grass and covered with newspapers."[30] Phil Hill in a companion Ferrari to that of von Trips claimed the win of the Italian Grand Prix and clinched the World Drivers Championship. Hill was followed across the finish by compatriot Dan Gurney in a Porsche and New Zealand's Bruce McLaren in a Cooper-Climax. Although modern records vary, the 1961 Italian Grand Prix appears second only to the horrific 1955 24 Hours of Le Mans in total number of spectator casualties.

Afterward, the new world champion was contemplative. "I lost more than a teammate," offered a very subdued Phil Hill. "I lost a brother."[31] In the days ahead—just as after the 1955 Le Mans tragedy—newspapers around the globe unified in a call to abolish the sport of auto racing. "The gladiator games also were a gruesome and risky affair," read an edition from Milan, "but mankind decided to stop them."[32] As oft-championship contender Stirling Moss checked out of his Monza hotel, he simply "drove off in a Maserati telling no one of his itinerary."[33] Such was the sad and stunned state of Formula One as it journeyed across the Atlantic for the first United States Grand Prix to be held at Watkins Glen.

Stirling Moss—now locked out of the World Drivers Championship for seven years running—would make the long trip to New York. The podium finishers of the Italian Grand Prix, Phil Hill, Dan Gurney, and Bruce McLaren, traveled to Watkins Glen as well. New championship constructor Scuderia Ferrari, however, stayed behind. Nor did new champion Phil Hill compete in the finale. The 20-year run of the United States Grand Prix at Watkins Glen would thus have its origins, and the decades in upstate New York would then deliver the gladiator games and the *Circus Maximus* of Formula One directly to Caesars Palace in Las Vegas.

***

One week after the 1961 United States Grand Prix at Watkins Glen, the U.S. Department of Justice (DOJ)—led by new Attorney General Robert F. Kennedy—reported on progress in its fight against the curse of illegal gambling across the country. "Several major gambling information services have gone out of business," read the *Las Vegas Review-Journal*, "since President [John F.] Kennedy signed tough anticrime laws five weeks ago."[34]

The DOJ was also pleased to report that it had shuttered illegal gambling operations in New Orleans, Little Rock, Chicago, and Minneapolis. Conspicuously without mention, though, was Miami, Florida, the logistical launch point for the Meyer Lansky–led gambling operations in Cuba and most recently the failed launch point for the CIA's Bay of Pigs invasion. Rather, the exodus of the Lansky gambling operatives from Cuba had rendered Miami as the *de facto* power-center of illegal gambling in the nation. In turn, as the FBI focused new attention on the Miami money market, the trumpeted closures of "gambling information services" across the country led to a migration in-force of organized crime gambling operators to the legal havens of Las Vegas and the Bahamas.

Simultaneously, the pre-election inquiries of the McClellan Committee into racketeering activities of organized labor led to continued post-election investigations into Teamster financing of property development, notably with a similar movement into the western states. Further, the investigations drilled into the influences lurking *behind* the approval of loans, as well as the strong-arm strings attached to the front, side, and back doors of the deals. In early 1961 then, both a federal grand jury—and the FBI—called upon the future developers of Caesars Palace for some Q-and-A on both subjects.

"U.S. Jury Here Probes Teamsters Motel Loans" was the front-page report on March 6, 1962, from the *Atlanta Constitution*.[35] Federal investigators were being sworn in by a federal judge to investigate records related to the Atlanta Cabana and Dallas Cabana projects developed by Jay Sarno and Stanley Mallin. The investigators derived their authority from the DOJ "to assist in the trial of a case or cases in which the government is interested."[36] Although not publicly disclosed, those cases would engage numerous actions being brought by the DOJ against Jimmy Hoffa, including those involving contractor Calvin Kovens and pension fund administrator Allen Dorfman. The potential legal violations, however, *were* cited, most notably "employers

The exodus of Meyer Lansky and his gambling operations from Cuba consolidated a power base of organized crime players in the Miami, Florida, area. Miami was then the launch point for expanded gambling development in Las Vegas, Nevada. Caesars Palace would be the beachhead. Las Vegas and Miami figured in the fortunes of open-wheel racing in America as well (Library of Congress).

paying or giving anything of value to representatives of their employes [*sic*]."[37] The practical implication was thus bribes paid to union officials by Sarno and Mallin as the employer. Other subjects being considered by the federal jurists were violations involving "mail fraud and the use of fictitious names and addresses."[38]

Behind the headlines, the FBI was plying Jay Sarno and Stanley Mallin for any peripheral entanglements related to their Teamster financing. "Reports have been received that Allen Dorfman ... with no apparent effort [has] obtained the insurance and bonding business connected with hotels, motels, and other businesses which have recipients of loans from the Central States Southeast and Southwest Areas Pension Fund," read a 1962 DOJ memorandum. "Allegedly, the insurance is going through the local agencies but the Dorfman group is receiving the commissions."[39] The Central States Pension Fund thus appeared to function as the venture capital bank of Jimmy Hoffa, Allen Dorfman, et al., "one of the very largest private sources of real-estate investment capital in the world."[40]

"Stanley Mallin of the Atlanta Cabana Motor Hotel ... said Dorfman got the insurance business through Haas and Dodd Co. of Atlanta," continued the DOJ document, "that Haas invested $20,000 in the Atlanta Cabana and in return wrote a $500,000 policy on Mallin and Jay Sarno."[41] According to the DOJ, the underwriter notified Elliot Haas that Haas and Dodd would be splitting the commissions with Cambridge Insurance Agency, an intermediary agent for the underwriter. Cambridge Insurance, however, was owned by Allen Dorfman, the insurance administrator for the Teamsters Pension Fund making the Cabana Motel loans. The FBI then documented nearly *fifty* apparently "fictitious names and addresses" of entities in which Allen Dorfman held a controlling interest.[42] Over one half of the enterprises were listed as insurance companies.

Just three years hence, Jay Sarno, Stanley Mallin, and fellow investor Nathan Jacobson would secure over $10 million in institutional financing from the Teamsters Central States Pension Fund for the development of Caesars Palace. Sarno, Mallin, and Jacobson—at least as the propped public personalities of the Caesars enterprise—also sought to downplay the involvement of the Teamsters Pension Fund in their new venture. Allen Dorfman, though, already held the life policies on Jay Sarno and Stan Mallin. To Sarno and Mallin, Dorfman soon added the Caesars-derived business opportunities of Nathan Jacobson, himself a Baltimore insurance agent. It is also worth noting those in position to benefit in the event of an unfortunate passing of Jay Sarno and Stanley Mallin. "Beneficiary on each policy," confirmed an FBI report, "listed as Central States and Southwest Areas I.B.T. [Teamsters] Pension Fund, Chicago Illinois."[43] Indeed, Jimmy Hoffa and Allen Dorfman held the life *markers* on Jay Sarno and Stanley Mallin.

***

The Formula One flotilla labored across the Atlantic Ocean to Watkins Glen after the tragic 1961 Italian Grand Prix. Early press notes counted the entries of Roy Salvadori and John Surtees in Cooper-Climax machines. Other Formula One regulars included Jack Brabham and Bruce McLaren, confirmed in Cooper mounts with Climax engines. Stirling Moss and Jim Clark would represent Colin Chapman's Lotus

From left, Walt Hansgen, Stirling Moss and Roger Penske all competed in the inaugural U.S. Grand Prix at Watkins Glen, New York, on October 8, 1961. Moss drove a Lotus-Climax while Hansgen and Penske drove Cooper-Climax machinery. Roger Penske finished eighth, four laps down to winner Innes Ireland. Moss and Hansgen retired with mechanical issues. Twenty years later, Roger Penske was on the NBC broadcast team for the inaugural Caesars Palace Grand Prix (Albert R. Bochroch Photograph Collection, The Revs Institute).

design. Graham Hill was entered in a BRM-Climax while Joakim Bonnier was driving a Porsche. Stateside entrants included Dan Gurney in a Porsche, Roger Penske in a Cooper-Climax, Hap Sharp and Walt Hansgen also in Cooper machines, and Jim Hall, Lloyd Ruby and Masten Gregory in Lotus-Climax racers. With American Phil Hill secure in the World Championship, and the departed Count Wolfgang von Trips second, the stricken Scuderia Ferrari works team remained behind in Maranello. "It was reported … that Enzo Ferrari of the automotive firm," press confirmed, "has decided not to enter his cars in the race."[44] Malcolm Currie of the Watkins Glen Grand Prix Corporation further confirmed that Phil Hill would not compete.

Stirling Moss was certainly the press pick headed into the first U.S. Grand Prix at Watkins Glen, Moss also had little to lose, shut out of the championship but with third place nearly assured. Stirling Moss would nonetheless enjoy a well-paid appearance. Pre-race notes also trumpeted Roger Penske's new Watkins Glen sports car lap record of 1:28.80, a 93.24 mph average set on September 24, 1961, around the 2.3-mile circuit. Race fans would then see that mark obliterated by the much quicker Formula One machinery.

Jack Brabham in the factory Cooper claimed the Saturday pole with a 1:17.00, one second slower than Stirling Moss' outright lap record set the year before for the larger displacement Formula Libre event. Brabham was joined on the front row by Graham Hill with Moss and Bruce McLaren slotted behind. Tony Brooks of England

Stirling Moss stands (third from right) just beyond his #7 Lotus-Climax on the starting grid of the first Formula One Grand Prix held at Watkins Glen, New York. Moss qualified third behind Jack Brabham and Graham Hill. Moss retired just past the halfway point with engine issues. The event was won by Innes Ireland. Bruce McLaren sits in his #2 Cooper-Climax in the background. McLaren qualified third and finished fourth. Crew members are not identified. The armed police sergeant at right of image is noteworthy (courtesy International Motor Racing Research Center).

and Scotland's Jimmy Clark rounded the third row. The starting field for the 1961 United States Grand Prix was then anchored by the Americans. Walt Hansgen would start 14th, Roger Penske 16th, Hap Sharp and Jim Hall from Texas 17th and 18th on the grid, and Lloyd Ruby from the USAC championship trail rolled off from 19th and last. Only Dan Gurney broke the top-10 in qualifying for the United States contingent, starting 10th in his factory Porsche next to John Surtees.

At the start, Jack Brabham from pole and Stirling Moss from the second row set a torrid opening pace. Innes Ireland moved smartly from eighth on the grid to third on the first lap. Ireland also briefly passed Jack Brabham before Brabham returned the favor on lap two. "Moss and Brabham tossed the lead back and forth like a hot potato," ran the report. "They exchanged first place 11 times."[45] The bumper-to-bumper battle between Brabham, the deposed champion, and Moss, the perennial contender, continued even as they started to encounter lapped traffic. At the 100-mile mark, "Brabham pulled into the pits with an engine that was losing water ... because of its high operating temperature."[46]

Jack Brabham rejoined the race but was nearly a lap behind Stirling Moss. Brabham then soldiered on for another 14 laps before the Climax engine gave up. Moss, not content to steady the pace with Brabham off, continued at speed until his own engine expired on lap 60. Innes Ireland then inherited the lead and would not be challenged, rolling to the checkered flag some 40 laps later. Ireland's factory Lotus was followed five seconds behind by American Dan Gurney in second, Tony Brooks third in a BRM, and Bruce McLaren fourth in a Cooper. Graham Hill was fifth in another BRM entry. Jim Clark was seventh while Roger Penske trailed in eighth. Canadian Peter Ryan followed ninth and Hap Sharp was 10th.

Innes Ireland—in the only Formula One Grand Prix victory of his career— took the $5,000 first-place check and another $2,800 in appearance money. "I never expected to win and it's pretty hard to believe," remarked Ireland from the victory celebration, "even though I know I've won it."[47] A reported 28,000 paid spectators watched Innes Ireland claim the popular win; over 20,000 more watched the event from the hill-and-dale of upstate New York. Only 12 of the 19 starters finished the event, only three of them on the same lap with Ireland. Dan Gurney scored the only Formula One points by an American on the day. Stirling Moss returned to Great Britain with third place in the World Drivers Championship secured. New World Champion Phil Hill, withdrawn by Scuderia Ferrari, watched the first U.S. Grand Prix at Watkins Glen from the sidelines. Finally, the day ended with Roy Salvadori as the new darling of the fans, pushing his Cooper across the finish line after it expired four laps from the finish while running in second behind Ireland.

In the days ahead, Henry Valent of the Watkins Glen Grand Prix Corporation announced that interest was to be paid on debentures sold for the 1956 construction of the original 2.3-mile facility. "This has been our most successful financial season since the Grand Prix Corporation was started," declared Valent. "All accrued interest … will be paid as soon as bookkeeping computations have been completed."[48]

Charley Lytle, course marshal of the 1961 U.S. Grand Prix, weighed in as well. "There just isn't enough interest generally," offered Lytle, "to permit anyone to promote big racing of this type in this country on a steady diet."[49] "It costs $100,000 to bring the cars and crews here," continued Lytle. "One rainy day with the fans at home watching television and you're murdered."[50] The well-dressed, gun-toting guests at Joseph Barbara's home in Apalachin on November 14, 1957, would have enthusiastically agreed.

References aside to the decisive solution of organized crime to difficult financial matters, Charley Lytle struck two chords that would resonate in the decades ahead with Formula One supreme Bernie Ecclestone. Bernard C. Ecclestone would drive the hard-negotiated cost for the Formula One show to appear, and then derive the related cash opportunity of fans watching television. In 1981, the Caesars Palace Grand Prix would then sing the full tune.

***

As the gambling operators of organized crime decamped from Cuba into their resettlement lifestyles of Miami, so they began to fan out anew, across the United States and the Caribbean. New gambling operations also further defined the Caesars Palace playbook to come, the X's and O's of syndicate racketeers and their opposite numbers in La Cosa Nostra. The emerging structural relationships also informed, to some extent, who owned what or, rather, who owned *whom*. That exertion of total control by organized crime over *individuals*—their names, histories, reputations, likenesses, and finances—also instructs the success of the vast American organized crime syndicate in its Las Vegas strategic plan. Whether it was a business-leader, a politician, a bookie, a gambler on the hook, a pawn, or a patsy, the tentacles of the organized crime business model would construct Caesars Palace. Further, the bunker they built would be the signing table for the Caesars Palace Grand Prix.

The multiple investigations of Jimmy Hoffa would ultimately lead to convictions, but not before Hoffa sat as an honored guest at the grand opening of Caesars Palace, while the public faces of the resort attempted to downplay the subject of Teamsters financing. In fact, James Riddle Hoffa reported to prison less than seven months after he dined at the feast of Caesar, in the Roman temple of the Teamsters.

To underscore the organizational chart and the effect of its momentum, an FBI memorandum to J. Edgar Hoover on April 2, 1962, documented the somewhat resurfaced bookmaking activities of Jerome Zarowitz. "ZAROWITZ ... telephonically contacted DAVE GEIGER ... and that subsequently," ran the FBI document, "GEIGER ... RUBY LAZARUS, ANTHONY SALERNO ... bet heavily."[51] Oddly, the FBI entry was catalogued in the John F. Kennedy Assassination file system of the Bureau.

At stake was the outcome of the March 24, 1962, National Basketball Association contest between the Boston Celtics and the Philadelphia Warriors. Boston, a 10-point favorite, matched up Bill Russell against Wilt Chamberlain and the Warriors. The Celtics and Bill Russell then crushed the Warriors, Wilt Chamberlain, *and* the spread, 117 points to 89. The Zarowitz group placed bets on Boston in the tens of thousands and won accordingly. The FBI source, however, "could not learn to whom or how the bets were placed."[52] Of note, Dave Geiger was a trusted floor veteran of Meyer Lansky's Cuban gambling operations and was later posted to the Bahamas.

In a tangent, the FBI also documented their belief that Wilt Chamberlain was betting on his own games with Ash Resnick, associated with Caesars Palace.[53] Again, Jerome Zarowitz, Ruby Lazarus, and Anthony Salerno would all figure in the development and operation of Caesars Palace.

At the same time, the FBI documented the orbit of Jerome Zarowitz with the infamous Frank "Lefty" Rosenthal. Frank Rosenthal was another of the national bookies, gamblers, and sports wagering influencers of the period. Rosenthal was also one of the more animated Fifth Amendment claimants before the McClellan rackets committee. In September of 1962, Frank Rosenthal spoke to Howard Kleinberg, sports editor of the *Miami News*, the same Howard Kleinberg who had reported so diligently about the U.S. Grand Prix efforts of Alec Ullman. "So what if I'm a gambler?" Rosenthal proclaimed to Kleinberg. "There's no law against that. There's a law against bookmaking, but I'm not a bookmaker. I'm a professional handicapper ... or rather, I was."[54] Frank Rosenthal was then effectively driven from Florida—and straight to Las Vegas.

In 1970, Rosenthal was also arrested with Caesars Palace executives Jerome Zarowitz and Elliott Paul Price on suspicion of holding "undisclosed interests indicating ownership" of a local betting parlor.[55] In 1981, during the Caesars Palace Grand Prix, Frank Rosenthal was front-and-center as the Mob's man in the operations of the Stardust Hotel & Casino. Frank Rosenthal was also a role played to perfection by actor Robert De Niro as the renamed "Ace Rothstein" in the movie *Casino*.

To the burgeoning Caesars Palace advance team, the FBI then added one more name, and this name emerged from the darkest shadows of the alleged American organized crime underworld. Once again, the name was catalogued in the JFK Assassination System. "ALVIN I. MALNIK—MALNIK is an attorney; represents JIMMY HOFFA and a number of other racket figures in whom the bureau is interested, including GIL BECKLEY and AL MONES..." read the September 28, 1962, FBI report to J. Edgar Hoover. "Permission has been granted by the Bureau to recontact MALNIK in connection with this program, but efforts to contact him again in Miami have not yet met with success."[56]

According to the FBI report, Alvin Malnik contacted an FBI agent with whom he was acquainted in his youth and provided general information about some of his clients. Alvin Malnik was then catalogued accordingly by the FBI. Perhaps more likely, though, is that Alvin Malnik—as alleged functionary of Meyer Lansky—simply hustled the Bureau for an intelligence gathering opportunity of his own. The FBI would find Mr. Malnik to be an extremely elusive interview in the decades ahead. In fact, they still do.

The infamous Frank "Lefty" Rosenthal testified before a McClellan Senate investigations subcommittee in 1961 and invoked the Fifth Amendment 37 times. Rosenthal was well-connected with the national criminal gambling syndicate, including Jerome Zarowitz and Elliott Paul Price of Caesars Palace. Rosenthal was portrayed by actor Robert De Niro in the Martin Scorsese movie *Casino* (Special Collections and Archives, University of Nevada at Las Vegas).

In 1975, a former member of the Raymond Patriarca crime family put a fine point on the role of Alvin Malnik as heir-designate to Meyer Lansky's position as chairman of the organized crime board. "It is an understanding in the Mafia that Malnik is Lansky," stated the informer, "and all dealings with Malnik must be cleared by the top people in each Mafia family."[57] The cloaked presence of Alvin Malnik ultimately became an indelible stain on the throne of Caesar and, later, provided a glimpse behind the curtain of the entire Caesars Palace throne room—allegedly.

The names of Gil Beckley and Al Mones in the FBI's Malnik entry were instructive as well. Gil "The Brain" Beckley was one of the most infamous of the nationally-staked gamblers and bookies, "reportedly the biggest bookie in the Midwest."[58] Beckley was also in league with Anthony Salerno, Frank Rosenthal, and Jerome

Zarowitz. Al Mones, another Miami-based gambler and bookie, was described else-where as "an old-time crook who'd worked for [Meyer] Lansky."[59] The FBI's 1962 shortlist of Alvin Malnik's clientele and company was telling, and the lineup pointed up the legal attentions of organized crime after-care. At the top of the list, though, the name of Jimmy Hoffa required no introduction whatsoever.

As the multiple investigations of Jimmy Hoffa wound through the DOJ, the loans of the Hoffa-controlled Teamsters Central States Pension Fund continued to make national headlines. In late 1962, those headlines engaged Hollywood, and one of America's sweethearts: "Doris Day in Teamsters Investigations."[60] "Miss Day is a major investor in a nationwide chain of luxury motels," reported the *Los Angeles Times*, "to which the Teamsters fund has loaned $1.8 million and committed an additional $5 million."[61]

The cited "luxury motels" were the Atlanta Cabana and the Dallas Cabana motor hotel resorts, developed by future-Caesars Palace front men Jay Sarno and Stanley Mallin. A Cabana resort in Palo Alto, California, was also under development by the partners. "The motel investments are known to be under investigation by the federal grand jury," continued the *Times*.[62] The *Times* further reported that co-investors with Miss Day were husband and producer Martin Melcher, Clifford Heinz, Jr., "scion of the pickle family," and Jerome Rosenthal, an attorney from Beverly Hills.[63]

Jimmy Hoffa went on trial on October 22, 1962, in a federal court in Nashville, Tennessee, on charges of unfair labor practices and fraud in obtaining a $1 million Teamster loan through a dummy corporation. Hoffa and Miami contractor Calvin Kovens were convicted in 1964. Both men were deeply connected to Caesars Palace and the national crime syndicate (Library of Congress).

Notably, it was Jerome Rosenthal who negotiated Doris Day's divorce in 1949 from saxophonist George Weidler. Unmentioned in the 1962 reporting, however, was that Jerome Rosenthal also represented Sarno and Mallin separately in their operating agreement for a "Birmingham Cabana" motor-hotel.[64]

On the same day that Doris Day and the Teamsters made the front page in Los Angeles, Jimmy Hoffa went on trial in federal court in Nashville, "charged with conspiring to violate the Taft-Hartley act [against unfair labor practices] and unlawfully obtaining $1,000,000 through a dummy corporation."[65] Amid the glare of the Hoffa-fueled press, Doris Day's husband Marty Melcher found himself on the defensive. "We are only passive partners," Melcher said while deflecting specific questions to attorney Jerome Rosenthal. "The corporation just borrowed the money. The details I don't know."[66]

The organized power players of the syndicate, La Cosa Nostra, and the Teamsters then looked toward Las Vegas and their majestic master development plan. On May 10, 1963, a small piece in the hometown *Las Vegas Review-Journal* tipped their collective hand. "Jay Sarno, [president] of the Cabana Motor Hotel chain," rolled the *Review-Journal*, "wants to build one here in the Best City Of Them All [Las Vegas]. Doris Day and hubby Marty Melcher would have a financial interest in it."[67] The Cabana properties of Jay Sarno, Stanley Mallin, and—by extension—Doris Day, were each designed in Greco-Roman gaudery. Sarno's *Desert Cabana* in Las Vegas would be the codex of Caesars Palace, a luxury-branded design manual that would dramatically elevate the themed Cabana concept. Three weeks after the veiled Caesars Palace announcement in Las Vegas press, Jimmy Hoffa, Calvin Kovens, and six others were indicted by a federal grand jury in Chicago on charges of fraudulently obtaining $20 million in loans from the Teamsters Central States Pension Fund.

***

As the influences of Formula One in America consolidated their base at Watkins Glen, New York, so too was Watkins Glen the embarkation point of Formula One to the western United States. The geographic proximity of Watkins Glen in upstate New York to the organized crime power-meeting in Apalachin also echoed the confluence of the Sebring 12-Hour race to illegal gambling operators in Miami, the Havana Grand Prix and Meyer Lansky's Cuban gambling empire, and the Nassau Speed Weeks with Lansky's subsequent casino beachhead in the Bahamas.

Whether coincidence or consequence, the accumulated juxtapositions lend intrigue and encourage inquiry. The ownership of the vaunted Riverside International Raceway would also engage in an intimate—though cloistered—relationship with gambling and the organized crime syndicate. In 1965, Stardust International Raceway in Las Vegas then directly advanced the notion of motorsports facilities developed and owned by a syndicate racketeer. Later, just as Caesars Palace elevated the themed resort gambling experience in Las Vegas, the Caesars Palace Grand Prix—with an FIA-approved racing circuit immediately behind the curb-line of the Las Vegas Strip—then appeared to perfect the concept. At Caesars Palace, coincidence and consequence would be overtaken by convergence and consolidation, unlimited gambling and entertainment, the influences of organized crime, and premier level motorsports under a luxury-branded resort *destination* umbrella.

The timeline of Formula One in America was also parallel to that of Caesars Palace; the forces of each thread would be crystallized in the early 1960s, stabilized in the mid–1960s, and maximized by the *late* 1960s. Both, however, would also be *destabilized* in the mid–1970s, Watkins Glen by the development of the Long Beach Grand Prix, Caesars Palace by the inevitable revelations of hidden ownership. Formula One at Watkins Glen also marked the transition from the old-guard race drivers of the 1950s to the youth movement of the 1960s. International stalwarts Juan Manuel Fangio, Stirling Moss, Roy Salvadori, and Joakim Bonnier—as well as American Phil Hill—were giving way to twenty-somethings, Bruce McLaren, Jimmy Clark, Denny Hulme, and John Surtees. That transition was also pointed up by the horrific career-ending crash of Stirling Moss on April 23, 1962, at Goodwood in England. So, too, the Formula One U.S. Grand Prix at Watkins Glen played its part in the pedigree of racing drivers who later competed in the Caesars Palace Grand Prix.

The 1962 U.S. Grand Prix would find Scotland's star Jimmy Clark and his Lotus-Climax in the winner's circle. Just 26 years old in his first winning Grand Prix season, Clark figured prominently in the box score of the early U.S. Grand Prix events. Despite the drawdown of the more seasoned competitors, 33-year-old Graham Hill of England followed Jimmy Clark into second at Watkins Glen. Hill also took track notes that served him and his BRM machines well for the next 3 years running. Standing across the Watkins Glen podium from Graham Hill, 25-year-old Bruce McLaren of New Zealand finished third in a Copper-Climax. McLaren, winner of the first U.S. Grand Prix at Sebring, added his Watkins Glen points to also finish behind Graham Hill and Jimmy Clark in the 1962 Formula One World Championship. The former British Empire was thus well-represented in American Formula One, just as they would be with Bernie Ecclestone for the contract signing of the Caesars Palace Grand Prix.

Nineteen sixty-three marked the beginning of Graham Hill's remarkable victory

From left, Graham Hill, Pedro Rodriguez, and Dan Gurney competed in the 1963 U.S. Grand Prix at Watkins Glen, New York. Hill was entered in a BRM, Rodriguez in a Lotus-Climax, and Gurney in a Brabham-Climax. Graham Hill won the 110-lap event. Pedro Rodriguez retired on lap 36 while Dan Gurney retired in lap 42. Graham Hill went on to win the two successive U.S. Grand Prix events. American drivers Phil Hill, Jim Hall, Hap Sharp, Rodger Ward, and Masten Gregory also competed. Crew members beyond are not identified (courtesy International Motor Racing Research Center).

run in the U.S. Grand Prix at Watkins Glen. Hill and his BRM won the U.S. Grand Prix three years in a row from 1963 to 1965. It was the only standing three-peat of the U.S. Grand Prix until Michael Schumacher extended the United States record to four-in-a-row starting in 2003 on the Formula One circuit at Indianapolis Motor Speedway. In 1963 at Watkins Glen, Graham Hill was followed by American Richie Ginther in another BRM. The Watkins Glen round of the 1963 Formula One series also brought a robust American contingent, albeit driving in a string of broken cars; Jim Hall, Rodger Ward, Dan Gurney, Masten Gregory, Hap Sharp, Phil Hill, and Walt Hansgen all failed to finish. Jimmy Clark rounded the 1963 Watkins Glen podium in a Lotus-Climax. Clark also broke through to claim the 1963 World Drivers Championship, winning out in Mexico and South Africa after the Watkins Glen round.

Graham Hill was followed in the 1964 Watkins Glen finishing order by another British driver soon to make his mark in American motorsports. Former Fédération Internationale de Motocyclisme (FIM) world champion John Surtees campaigned the Formula One championship in 1963 and 1964 for Scuderia Ferrari. Surtees, only four years removed from his final FIM championship, added his second place at the U.S. Grand Prix to wins in Germany and Italy to take the 1964 World Drivers Championship. In two years, John Surtees would return to America to contest the inaugural Canadian-American Challenge Cup, the Can-Am series, once again with winning results. In fact, two of John Surtees' Can-Am wins were notched at Stardust International Raceway in Las Vegas, just 6 miles from Caesars Palace.

Third at Watkins Glen was Jo Siffert of Sweden, racing a Brabham for Rob Walker. Richie Ginther was the top American driver in fourth, contesting the entire season as a BRM teammate to Graham Hill. In the American order, Ginther was followed by Walt Hansgen in fifth driving a Lotus-Climax, improved from 17th on the starting grid and taking two championship points. Further back, Dan Gurney, Hap Sharp, Ronnie Bucknum, and Phil Hill also carried the banner for the United States.

In 1965 Graham Hill then completed his personal trifecta with wins in three successive U.S. Grand Prix competitions. Hill also lowered the Watkins Glen qualifying record to 1:11.25, nearly 5 seconds quicker than Jimmy Clark's lap record of 1962. Dan Gurney recorded a fine second place finish in a Brabham-Climax for team owner Jack Brabham. Thirty-nine-year-old Jack Brabham then completed the podium in his own eponymous machine, the only other car on the lead lap with Hill and Gurney. Dan Gurney's fellow American racers Richie Ginther, Bob Bondurant, and Ronnie Bucknum then contributed to the flag waving. Notably, Bob Bondurant was then training actor James Garner for his driving role in the 1966 movie *Grand Prix*. Graham Hill, Jack Brabham, Richie Ginther and Bruce McLaren, 1965 U.S. Grand Prix contestants, also had roles in the film which included location filming at Watkins Glen. Jimmy Clark, 1963 Formula One world champion, retired from the Watkins Glen round as well as Mexico to follow. Nonetheless, Clark's preceding six wins on the season propelled him to the 1965 championship over Graham Hill and Jackie Stewart.

*** *

Through the 1960s, the United States Grand Prix anchored Formula One to the multi-hued autumn grandeur of upstate New York, just a bit down the road from the organized crime retreat of Joseph Barbara. Many of the stars of Formula One, though, picked up swing shifts for the springtime 12 Hours of Sebring in Florida. Some drivers also found part-time employment during the month of May at Indianapolis Motor Speedway. Other of the international stars found their side-hustle on the opposite coast, specifically a cross-country road trip following the Watkins Glen round to Riverside International Raceway for the Los Angeles Times Grand Prix.

Some of the Formula One race drivers already knew the route to southern California by way of Alec Ullman's 1960 Riverside Grand Prix of the United States. From that 1960 Riverside Formula One field, international regulars Stirling Moss, Jack Brabham, and Bruce McLaren would also take in the 1961 Riverside USAC sports car Grand Prix. In fact, Brabham would win the event over McLaren.

Notably, at Riverside in 1961, Stirling Moss and Jack Brabham encountered Las Vegas gambling owner—and sports racing enthusiast—Richard Levinson. Richard Levinson was the son of Edward Levinson, conduit through which much of the Las Vegas–based racket action flowed in the early 1960s, including the due to Meyer

For benefit of the camera, Jack Brabham and Stirling Moss ponder the race poster for the October 28–29, 1961, Las Vegas Speed Week sports car races. The two drivers were entered in the Riverside three-hour endurance race at Riverside Raceway on October 14, 1961. Brabham and Moss finished fourth in the Riverside race driving a Sunbeam Alpine. The October 28–29, 1961, Las Vegas event was promoted by the downtown Horseshoe hotel-casino owned by Edward Levinson. Edward Levinson was connected with Alvin Malnik in business interests, as well as FBI wiretaps. Son Richard Levinson (hand at left) was a minority Horseshoe owner as well as a sports car racing enthusiast. The hands of international Grand Prix racing embraced those of Las Vegas gambling interests long before the Caesars Palace Grand Prix. Stirling Moss also attended the 1965 groundbreaking of racketeer Moe Dalitz's Stardust International Raceway in Las Vegas, Nevada (image from the Collections of The Henry Ford).

Lansky. Concurrently, Ed Levinson was an investment associate of Alvin Malnik,[68] later alleged as heir-apparent to Lansky. From his Miami Beach cover, Alvin Malnik appeared to author much of the deeply-coded backstory of Caesars Palace, a cloud that cloaked the inaugural Caesars Palace Grand Prix.

For 1963, the Los Angeles Times Riverside Grand Prix was conducted under sanction of the SCCA. The USAC versus SCCA sports car wars were then sorted and the professional sports racing crowd enjoyed the top cover of ACCUS. The Times event included Formula One drivers Jimmy Clark, Pedro Rodriguez, John Surtees, Roy Salvadori, Graham Hill, Dan Gurney, Richie Ginther, and Ronnie Bucknum. The field was also stacked with Formula One domestics, Roger Penske, Bob Bondurant, Walt Hansgen, Lloyd Ruby, Jim Hall, and Rodger Ward. A.J. Foyt also made the Riverside show in a Scarab for John Mecom, Jr. Although career records do not document a foray into Formula One, A.J. Foyt's remarkable career does nonetheless arc forward to the final Caesars Palace Grand Prix.

The 1965 Los Angeles Times Grand Prix was held on October 31 at Riverside International Raceway, four weeks after the Formula One Grand Prix at Watkins Glen. From the Formula One round, eight drivers then traveled to California for the Riverside sports car event. U.S. Grand Prix contestants Jimmy Clark, Bruce McLaren, Graham Hill, and Jackie Stewart were joined by Americans Ronnie Bucknum, Dan Gurney, Richie Ginther, and Bob Bondurant. The 1965 Riverside Grand Prix, though, was won by Hap Sharp in a Chaparral 2A, constructed by his Chaparral Cars partnership with Jim Hall. Hap Sharp followed his Riverside win two weeks later at the professional opener of racketeer Moe Dalitz's Stardust International Raceway in Las Vegas. Jim Clark finished second at Riverside in a Lotus 40 while Bruce McLaren followed in a McLaren M1B, effectively the first generation of the McLaren-designed and branded sports racers.

In the week before the 1965 Riverside Grand Prix, the *San Bernardino County Sun* published an article trumpeting the extensive improvements at the Riverside plant. The *Sun* article also lauded the rigorous development efforts of the well-regarded Riverside general manager, former Los Angeles Rams football great Les Richter. "The Inland Empire can be justly proud of the accomplishments at Riverside Raceway," sang the *Sun* on October 28, 1965. "We, of this area, have a first class auto racing facility which is rapidly approaching the status of one of the finest in the world."[69] Riverside International Raceway, however, was also rapidly approaching its own higher-use development into strip centers and suburbia. In the midst of the Riverside hurrah, it bears mention that Les Richter was also advising construction manager Leo Margolian in the development of Stardust International Raceway.

The *San Bernardino County Sun* article went on to extol the governance of Riverside Raceway: "The raceway board of directors includes many prominent Southern Californians."[70] Indeed, the Riverside board was served by oil barons, a prominent publisher, sportsmen, industrialists, and some high-profile entertainment. The requisite fields of law and politics also appeared to be represented. Notable, as well, was Hollywood Mercedes dealer Roy G. Lewis, "the No. 1 Mercedes-Benz dealer in America."[71]

Roy G. Lewis ascended to prominence at Riverside International Raceway in the purchase transition from the original track ownership. Roy Lewis, described in 1960 as "owner of Riverside Raceway"[72] and "president of Riverside Raceway,"[73] certainly cut the image of a respectable southern California businessman. In addition to the Mercedes line, Roy Lewis carried Auto-Union, DKW, and—if one desired it—the latest from the Studebaker-Packard offerings. Lewis also made marks as a member of the Los Angeles Municipal Arts Commission. Roy G. Lewis was later appointed by Mayor Sam Yorty to the Los Angeles Building and Safety Commission. In 1963, Yorty named Lewis to the Forward Los Angeles Committee, a task force effort led by Robert E. Petersen, publisher of *Hot Rod Magazine*.

From the high-speed back straight of Riverside International Raceway—site of the second Formula One Grand Prix of the United States—the Riverside line then veered hard left, through a tight carousel turn toward Nevada gambling, racketeering, and the Teamsters Central States Pension Fund. It was a hard pull that would also include a direct connection to Jimmy Hoffa and Caesars Palace.

***

"Three California men have applied to the State Gaming Commission," reported Nevada press in early 1965, "for authority to establish a gambling casino at the Sierra Tahoe Hotel … on the north end of Lake Tahoe."[74] "Partners are Harold K. Riel of Studio City, Calif., president of an automotive parts firm in Burbank," continued the statement, "and Roy G. Lewis, Playa del Ray, a businessman."[75] The Nevada report also identified the third partner: "Norman Tyrone of Pacific Palisades … mortgage broker and banker and a partner in one venture with Elliott Roosevelt."[76]

Roy G. Lewis of Riverside International Raceway and Harold Riel, Los Angeles-area parts man and chrome plating magnate, were teaming with Norman Tyrone to acquire the lodging-only Sierra Tahoe establishment. The Southern California investors also sought to add a casino, "50 slot machines" as well as "three 21 games, a crap table and roulette."[77] The Sierra move appeared as an extremely odd play for Roy Lewis, prominent Mercedes-Benz dealer and a driving force at Riverside.

Notable as well, the proposed purchase of the Sierra Tahoe by Lewis, Riel, and Tyrone received very limited press in California. Further, the alignment of Roy G. Lewis and Howard Riel with Norman Tyrone was curious. Norman Tyrone—variously known as "Norman Thirion," "Norman Bernard Thirion," "Bernard Thirion," and the apparently ceremonial "Doctor Thirion"—played the lead role in frauds over the next two decades, from Lake Tahoe, to Los Angeles, to Miami, to London, to the apparent end of the racket-riddled road, Sioux Falls, South Dakota.

Prior to the Lake Tahoe gambling proposal, Norman Tyrone and Elliott Roosevelt—son of Franklin Delano Roosevelt—also appeared to lead afoul the well-regarded Robert Petersen of Los Angeles. Bob Petersen—publisher of *Hot Rod Magazine*—then returned fire on Roosevelt and Tyrone with a $1.5 million lawsuit. Unlike the relative quiet of the Lake Tahoe casino deal, the Petersen lawsuit splashed the Los Angeles newspapers. "The suit alleges that in September of 1964, when Petersen was planning to buy the Pacific Plaza in nearby Santa Monica," ran one California report, "Roosevelt told [Petersen] that he could arrange a $7.5 million loan from the Teamsters Union pension fund."[78] "For arranging the loan," continued the piece, "Roosevelt was to receive $150,000 and a Mercedes Benz automobile."[79]

The Pacific Plaza shopping center project in Santa Monica, California, involved Robert Petersen, publisher of *Hot Rod Magazine*, Roy Gene Lewis of Riverside International Raceway, Norman Tyrone, and Elliott Roosevelt. Petersen allegedly paid a $75,000 finder's fee to Roosevelt in exchange for a financing commitment from the Teamsters Central States Pension Fund. With the finder's fee gone and loan proceeds diverted, Robert Petersen sued Roosevelt and Tyrone for $1.5 million (author's collection).

Bob Petersen's lawsuit alleged that a $75,000 advance was made to Roosevelt on promise of the loan commitment. When the Teamsters pension fund loan failed to materialize, Elliott Roosevelt apparently refused to return the deposit. Petersen also sought $1 million in damages, $500,000 in lost profits, and $45,000 already invested in pursuit of the Pacific Plaza shopping center project. As Norman Tyrone responded to the Petersen lawsuit, he claimed he received approval for a Teamsters loan—for the same Pacific Plaza property—in the names of Harold Riel and Riverside president Roy G. Lewis. Perhaps as a matter of dignity, "[Tyrone] denied the part about the Mercedes."[80] Remarkably, at the time of Bob Petersen's lawsuit, Elliott Roosevelt was the mayor of Miami Beach, Florida, base of operations for Alvin Malnik. "The mob doesn't run this town," Elliott Roosevelt said. "It owns it."[81] As mayor of Miami Beach—and as an accused swindler—Roosevelt might have had some insight.

Norman Tyrone's London and South Dakota hustles ran similarly. Each exercise involved eager investors, chameleon identities, and the disappearance of other people's money. In fact, the London play in 1982 would drag *Grand Prix* star James Garner though the Tyrone mire.[82] Despite the extensive travels of Norman Tyrone, though, the Lake Tahoe proposal appeared as the plum. The Lake Tahoe property also deployed the deepest connections. Further, the Lake Tahoe venture propelled Roy G. Lewis—Mercedes man, Riverside International Raceway president, and host of the first Formula One Grand Prix in the western states—all the way to power, patronage, and prison.

On September 25, 1964, the same day that Elliott Roosevelt was allegedly meeting the Teamsters to close Robert Petersen's loan, Norman Tyrone met with William Swigert and attorney Frank Farella of Pacific Bridge and Associates. Pacific Bridge was a legend in heavy construction projects in the western states, the highly-respected builder of the San Francisco Bay Bridge, one of the Six Companies conglomerate that constructed Hoover Dam near Las Vegas, Nevada. Pacific Bridge also owned 28 acres in north Lake Tahoe and was seeking financing from the Teamsters to further develop the property. As Elliott Roosevelt apparently hustled Robert Petersen, so to did Norman Tyrone play William Swigert and Pacific Bridge.

During the fictitious loan closing in Chicago, Norman Tyrone surprised Swigert and Farella with a loan demand to a Bahamian financial company controlled by Roosevelt and Tyrone. Financial records and a receipt, however, would not be forthcoming. "To Swigert and Farella in the hotel suite," ran one report, "the Bahamian loan had an immediate and unmistakable stench."[83]

Despite dismissing Norman Tyrone and withdrawing the loan application, William Swigert received a conditional letter of funding approval from the Teamsters four days later on September 29, 1964. The letter was signed by Francis Murtha, executive director of the Teamsters Central States Pension Fund.

Within months, William Swigert was contacted by a pair of buyers interested in the Sierra Tahoe hotel property, Roy G. Lewis of Riverside International Raceway and Harold Riel. Just prior to the property closing, William Swigert was informed that there was a third investor, none other than Norman Tyrone. Further, the institutional financing of the trio was familiar. "Swigert, bolstered by Murtha's letter of September 29," it was reported, "believes it was his loan."[84]

As Roy G. Lewis, Norman Tyrone, and Harold Riel acquired the Sierra Tahoe and commenced casino development, they also experienced construction and cost setbacks. "Cal Kovens, a Miami contractor convicted with Jimmy Hoffa ... of mail and wire fraud and a long-time Teamsters courtier," continued the report, "showed up and said he was representing the Teamsters as an 'expeditor.'"[85] With Lewis, Tyrone, and Riel steering toward property foreclosure, Calvin Kovens then acquired the ground lease from Pacific Bridge.

The presence of Calvin Kovens drew the inevitable attention of the Nevada Gaming Control Board (GCB). Indeed, the GCB went on the offensive, making clear to convicted felon Calvin Kovens that he was not suitable for a gambling license. Calvin Kovens also made for a troubling landlord. Another Miamian, Albert Kroll, then presented an offer to inject funding into the gambling operation of Lewis, Tyrone, and Riel. Kroll was then granted a probationary license to operate the resort.

As the spring of 1966 broke in the Sierra, however, the GCB learned that Alvin Kroll was the brother-in-law of Calvin Kovens, thereby denying Kroll an extension of his gambling license. Two months after the expulsion of Alvin Kroll by the GCB, the same board announced that Calvin Kovens' brother Irving Kovens was approved for a gambling license as an investor in Caesars Palace. Three years later, the troubled Sierra Tahoe resort was acquired by former Caesars Palace

CAL KOVENS CONSTRUCTION CORP.

GENERAL CONTRACTOR

BUILDINGS - ADDITIONS - REMODELS

1657 West Avenue   **Calvin Kovens - President**
Miami Beach, Florida   **Irving Kovens - Treasurer**

Miami building contractor Calvin Kovens was convicted of fraud in 1964 with Jimmy Hoffa of the Teamsters union. Both men were sentenced to prison. Brother Irving Kovens was an original investor in Caesars Palace. Calvin Kovens also formed a back-channel power circuit, a continuous current running through the Teamsters, Roy Gene Lewis of Riverside International Raceway, Anthony "Fat Tony" Salerno of the Genovese crime family, Alvin Malnik, Allen Dorfman, Caesars Palace, and the podium celebration of the 1981 Caesars Palace Grand Prix (author's collection).

chairman Nathan Jacobson—with financing from the Teamster Central States Pension Fund.

The Nevada gambling adventure of Riverside International Raceway president Roy G. Lewis would thus conclude. The connection of Roy Lewis with the Teamsters and Calvin Kovens, however, would continue in the years ahead. In one of the first cases involving the Racketeer Influenced and Corrupt Organizations Act—the RICO Act—Lewis found himself under federal investigation with a cast including Calvin Kovens and Allen Dorfman as well as Leonard Bursten, Irving Davidson, and Hyman Green, "close friends of imprisoned Teamsters union chief James R. Hoffa."[86]

"Beverly Ridge, a now defunct country club subdivision in the Santa Monica Mountains," ran a 1970 investigative report, "was financed with $13.5 million in loans from the [Teamsters] Central Sates Fund."[87] Notably, the failed country club listed Frank Sinatra and Dean Martin as directors. The federal investigation revealed multiple massive frauds, improper benefits, and financial kickbacks. Several government officials were ensnared, including Roy G. Lewis, "member of the Los Angeles Building and Safety Commission, who voted on Beverly Ridge matters ... at the same time he was ... a director of one of the project's ancillary corporations."[88] Roy G. Lewis even made the hallowed pages of the *Congressional Record*. "While [Lewis] was doing this," documented the *Record*, "he was also identified as having a financial interest in the project."[89]

Three years later, Roy Gene Lewis—*former* president of Riverside International Raceway—received the gavel, six months in federal prison for "perjury involving a $200,000 finder's fee ... in connection with a Teamsters Union loan to the Beverly Ridge project."[90] In 1986, the federal government finally caught up to Norman Tyrone, then in operation as Norman Bernard Thirion. Norman Bernard Thirion pulled a five-year sentence in federal court in Sioux Falls, South Dakota, perhaps one year for each of his rotating identities. Tyrone's final play was the defrauding of 35 midwest farmers out of finder's fees for loans they never received.

As Roy G. Lewis of Riverside International Raceway helped steer the course of Formula One in the United States, so too did his racketeering actions illuminate the funding mechanisms and the intricate connections involved in the development of Caesars Palace to come. The coalition of organized crime, ready racketeers, Teamsters financing, and varied business interests would soon deploy the development plan for Caesars Palace. Across the Atlantic, Bernie Ecclestone would deploy his own development plan for control of Formula One. And in the next decade, both Formula One and Bernie Ecclestone would return to the West Coast—on their parallel path to the Caesars Palace Grand Prix.

III

Developments and Dictators

Caesar Constructs a Palace in Las Vegas,
While Formula One Constructs a Czar

To give this day a crown to mighty Caesar. (*Julius Caesar* 2.2.99)

"Plan[s] for construction of the $20 million 'Caesar's Palace,'" proclaimed national dailies from coast to coast on January 28, 1965, "first major hotel to be built on the Las Vegas strip in the last eight years, were disclosed yesterday by Desert Palace Inc."[1] Indeed, the development of Caesars Palace was the first significant movement of dirt on U.S. Route 91 since Moe Dalitz's Cleveland Syndicate opened the Stardust Hotel and Casino in the summer of 1958.

National beats reported a 700-room resort, 300 guest rooms in a 14-story tower with another 400 rooms situated in low-rise buildings around the pool garden. Despite trailing Dalitz's Stardust opening room count by over 300 units, Caesars Palace was touted as "the largest multi-story hotel ever designed as a complete unit for the strip."[2] The "strip," of course, was the world-famous Las Vegas Strip. News of the day also tipped the consortium of promoters out in front of the Caesars development: "Principal owners will be Jay J. Sarno, Atlanta hotelman; Nathan S. Jacobson, Baltimore, vice president-secretary; Stanley A. Mallin, Atlanta, vice president, and Harry L. Lewis, Miami, treasurer."[3]

Jay Sarno, by now the well-documented and oft-investigated primary of the Teamsters-financed Atlanta, Palo Alto, and Dallas Cabana properties, was teaming with business partner Stanley Mallin for the new Las Vegas resort. Jay Sarno also planted himself in Las Vegas with a large appetite for consumption, perhaps insatiably so. Whether food, beverage, women, Cadillacs, golf, or gambling, Sarno maximized his indulgence in Las Vegas. Of his proclivity for gambling, a biographer described Sarno as a "gambling degenerate."[4]

In contrast to the wanderlust of Jay Sarno, Stanley Mallin appeared to sample the Las Vegas offerings in moderation. By most accounts a staid businessman, Stan Mallin was nonetheless inexorably attached to Jay Sarno in numerous ventures that left a troubled trail, including a burgeoning portfolio of Teamsters loans, and the apparently requisite Allen Dorfman insurance policies. Caesars Palace was simply the latest outing for the two. Amid their subsequent Circus-Circus hotel-casino endeavors—another of Sarno's vision boards fleshed from a dubious financial palette—both

The development fronts of Caesars Palace were Jay Sarno, right, and Nathan Jacobson, center. Partner Stanley Mallin is not pictured. At left is project manager Harry Wald. In this 1965 publicity image, Sarno, Jacobson, and Wald stand adjacent to the basement rooms of Caesars Palace. The basement of Caesars Palace included the underground count room from which the skim flowed to the power centers of organized crime. It was also the location of the contract signing for the Caesars Palace Grand Prix. On October 17, 1981, Harry Wald stood on the victory podium to celebrate Alan Jones, winner of the inaugural Grand Prix event. The image looks roughly south, across Dunes Road, to the low-rise hotel rooms of the Dunes hotel-casino (courtesy LVCVA News Bureau).

Sarno and Mallin would be tried on "federal charges of conspiracy and bribery in connection with the alleged payment of $64,000 in bribes to Internal Revenue Service agents."[5] It might be fairly said that Stanley Mallin's greatest excess was Jay Sarno himself.

After Sarno and Mallin, Nathan Jacobson appeared publicly as a wild card in the Caesars lineup. Stanley Mallin later recalled the origins of the relationship with

This image of the Dunes hotel-casino looks north across Dunes Road toward the property on which Caesars Palace was constructed in 1965 and 1966. The Caesars Palace parcel was owned by Kirk Kerkorian. The Dunes was opened in 1955 while the 24-story hotel tower followed in 1961. The Dunes had a troubling relationship with organized crime interests throughout its existence. Kirk Kerkorian was licensed as a minority shareholder of the Dunes hotel-casino in 1955 (author's collection).

Jacobson. "So we went around the country and a guy told us about a fellow in Baltimore named Nate Jacobson; we should go see him," Mallin was quoted in 2015 as saying. "He was in the insurance business, but he knew a lot of people and he loved the idea. He took over raising all the money for the project."[6]

Less than two years after the opening of Caesars Palace, Nathan Jacobson offered his own origin story. "One of our associates thought about putting a hotel up here," Jacobson said as quoted in the *Baltimore Sun*. "He had the idea but he didn't have the money."[7] The relegated "associate" of Nathan Jacobson was Jay Sarno. "Jacobson did [have the money]," continued the *Sun*, "or at least he could raise it."[8] Like Sarno, Jacobson too was a fast talker. Nate Jacobson was also a gambler, with "a gambling problem almost as big as Sarno's."[9]

Nate Jacobson, as well, counted a relationship with Irv Kovens. Far from Las Vegas, both Jacobson and Kovens were past-principals of Florida's Gulf American Land Corporation.[10] Despite boasts of massive profits and a board peppered with prominent personalities, by 1968 Gulf American was mired in claims of land fraud,

an alleged billion-dollar swindle later described as "over a million land buyers …
buying swamp and wilderness lots and acreage from land peddlers."[11]

Like Nathan Jacobson of Baltimore, Harry Lewis of Miami appeared at a glance
as something of a geographical oddity. Well known in Miami financial and development circles, Harry L. Lewis was a "certified public accountant and tax consultant …
a business advisor in real estate, construction, and investment activities."[12] Lewis, by
day, was the respected "president of Cedars of Lebanon Hospital [Miami]."[13]

Harry Lewis, however, was also connected with the controversial—and convicted—Saul Silberman, owner of the Tropical Park thoroughbred race track in
Miami. Silberman was found guilty in 1957 of using the Tropical Park facilities for
illegal telephone transmission of racing information.[14] Notably, Silberman acquired
the race track in 1953 from a group headed by Nathan Herzfeld, later involved in the
racketeered pump-and-dump Parvin-Dohrmann Corporation ownership of the Stardust Hotel & Casino and Stardust International Raceway.[15]

Other reports drilled slightly deeper into the frontline public structure of Caesars Palace. "Members of the board of directors include Jud McIntosh of Atlanta,
Edward Jacobson of Baltimore, and Kirk Kerkorian of Las Vegas," read another dispatch. "Kerkorian, a former stockholder
of The Dunes Hotel, owns the land
for 'Caesar's Palace.'"[16] While Edward
Jacobson was the son of Nathan Jacobson—and certainly benefited from his
top-cover—both Jud McIntosh and Kirk
Kerkorian merit special mention.

Jud McIntosh was previously involved with Jay Sarno and Stanley Mallin in Atlanta real estate and development. McIntosh then followed Sarno
and Mallin from Caesars Palace into an
ownership position on the Circus-Circus
casino project in Las Vegas. Post-Cae-
sars, Jud McIntosh engaged with Nathan
Jacobson in the King's Castle Hotel &
Casino in Lake Tahoe. The Kings Castle
property was redeveloped from the troubled former Sierra Tahoe resort owned
variously by Pacific Bridge, Calvin Kovens, Norman Tyrone, and Roy G. Lewis
of Riverside International Raceway,
among others. Notably, Jud McIntosh
also defaulted on his Kings Castle obligations to the Teamsters Central States
Pension Fund, obligations that originated with the purchase of the Sierra
Tahoe property by Lewis and Tyrone.

**Property development and Hollywood mag-
nate Kirk Kerkorian owned the vacant parcel on which Caesars Palace was constructed.
Kirk Kerkorian was also licensed with an
interest in Caesars Palace alongside Jay
Sarno, Stanley Mallin, and Nathan Jacobson. Kerkorian also developed the International, MGM, MGM Grand, and City Center
hotel-casino resort properties in Las Vegas
(courtesy LVCVA News Bureau).**

Despite the modern-day heft of his name, Kirk Kerkorian was a much less known air charter operator and sometime land speculator in early 1965. In 1962, Kerkorian acquired the parcel on which Caesars Palace would break ground. Caesars principals Jay Sarno and Stanley Mallin then entered into a ground lease with Kerkorian. Notably in 1955, Kirk Kerkorian invested $144,000 for a 3 percent stake in the notoriously mob-controlled Dunes Hotel & Casino, directly south of the new Caesars Palace site. Indeed, over a life spanning 98 years, Kerkorian would shake many a soiled hand, yet always emerged unscathed, his public reputation as a daring deal-maker relatively intact.

In 1965 Kirk Kerkorian also started an air taxi operation operating a Learjet between Las Vegas and southern California, "an executive type charter service" to include service to "off-line points," sometimes "simply for prestige purposes."[17] Within months after launch of the air operation, though, the FBI called upon Kirk Kerkorian as they investigated events behind the cloak of Caesars Palace. "[Kerkorian] has been cooperative," read an FBI dispatch to J. Edgar Hoover in early 1966, "and has stated that … he would be more than willing to furnish copies of and all contracts, agreements, etc. he has entered into with the individuals building the hotel."[18] The FBI would also appear interested in the manifest of Kerkorian's discreet charter flights during the Caesars development. In the Caesars Palace arrangement, Kirk Kerkorian thus played landlord, gambling licensee, and perhaps, the air taxi of hidden interests—allegedly.

To the starting seven of Sarno, Mallin, Jacobson, Lewis, McIntosh, Jacobson, and Kerkorian were then added another 44 names, all of them licensed by the State of Nevada for a gambling stake in the name of Caesar. Ed Olson, chairman of the Nevada Gaming Control Board, boasted of the magnitude and depth of the accumulated licensing inquiry, "the largest investigation into the backgrounds of proposed hotel-casino stockholders in Nevada history."[19] "[Olson] said it took six months, more than 50 pounds of paperwork," continued the report, "and cost the prospective licensees $10,000."[20]

Despite the crack detective work of the Nevada investigators, the Caesars Palace license group presented the proverbial rogue's gallery; the brother of a convicted Hoffa crony, a sports bribery convict, a suspect in the 1957 Terre Haute gambling ring, a person alleged to be connected to the New Jersey head of the Genovese crime family, a stockholder in the Cleveland Indians, two gamblers previously rejected by the Nevada Gaming Commission due to unsatisfactory background, and two others later indicted for income tax evasion.[21]

Three of the licensees also refused to testify to the Securities and Exchange Commission in 1971 when questioned about apparent hidden ownership interests amid the sale of Caesars Palace in 1969. From its deep heritage of such nobility, Caesars Palace then delivered the Caesars Palace Grand Prix to Las Vegas.

Behind the vigorously investigated luminaries of the public license group of Caesars Palace, the Federal Bureau of Investigation would make note in 1965 of the apparent players involved in the *hidden* ownership of Caesars Palace. The FBI also appeared to crack the public facade of the front line, Jay Sarno, Stanley Mallin, and Nathan Jacobson. Those players behind the block of Jay Sarno formed their roots in the vast American organized crime syndicate, Miami, Terre Haute, Harlem, even palatial Apalachin in upstate New York. They were also connected to Meyer Lansky.

At the same time, across the Atlantic Ocean, the soldiers of Meyer Lansky were infiltrating the gambling houses of London, the casinos where Bernie Ecclestone—the future czar of Formula One—loved to play. Formula One, in turn, made its annual pilgrimage back across the ocean to Watkins Glen in upstate New York.

***

The U.S. Grand Prix on October 2, 1966, marked the end of the winning Watkins Glen run for Graham Hill; the U.S. round was one of three retirements in a row to close the season for the reigning winner. Hill, however, had already set a new American mark, winning the 1966 Indianapolis 500 on May 30, 1966, in a Lola-Ford for John Mecom, Jr. Jimmy Clark then returned to the Watkins Glen winner's circle in 1966, lapping the entire field in his Lotus-BRM over Jochen Rindt and John Surtees in Cooper-Maserati machines.

As the 1966 U.S. Grand Prix wrapped, so did production on the James Garner MGM star vehicle, *Grand Prix*. Garner and fellow cast actors Jessica Walter and Toshiro Mifune joined the reported 100,000 spectators for the event. "I may be hooked on this darn racing bit," proclaimed Garner to the local press. "Once you get used to 120 miles an hour around tipped, sharp curves at these courses. It's thrilling."[22] James Garner would move on from his motorsports baptism as both a competitor and a race team owner. Fifteen years later, fellow actor Paul Newman took the same mantle as grand marshal of the 1981 Caesars Palace Grand Prix and as a competitor in the 1983 Trans-Am support class.

Fast qualifier for the 1966 U.S. Grand Prix was then-40-year-old Jack Brabham, again in a race car of his own design and construction. Prior to the start of the Grand Prix, Brabham also did hot laps in a specially outfitted Shelby Cobra GT film car for *Grand Prix* producer John Frankenheimer. Starting the race from pole, though, Jack Brabham fell out on lap 55 of 108 with an engine failure. On the strength of four wins on the season, however—as well as second place in Mexico following Watkins Glen—Jack Brabham won both the 1966 Formula One Drivers Championship *and* the Formula One Manufacturers Championship, a feat never since repeated.

The appearance of Jochen Rindt and John Surtees on the 1966 Watkins Glen podium also marked transition in the sport. Rindt joined the Cooper Formula One team in 1965 alongside Bruce McLaren, winner of the first-ever U.S. Grand Prix at Sebring, Florida. In 1966, Bruce McLaren departed Cooper to form his own racing enterprise. Jochen Rindt was then joined by John Surtees, the brilliant former motorcycle road racing champion and 1964 Formula One champion. Under the team management of former race driver Roy Salvadori, Surtees and Rindt combined to finish second and third for Cooper in the Formula One championship behind Jack Brabham. Roy Salvadori—notably a competitor at both the 1959 and 1960 U.S. Grand Prix events promoted by Alec Ullman—would introduce Jochen Rindt to Bernie Ecclestone, a former car dealing colleague of Salvadori.

John Surtees then commenced his own foray into team ownership. Team Surtees fielded a Lola T70 in the inaugural season of the Canadian-American Challenge

Nineteen sixty-four Formula One world champion John Surtees qualified his Cooper fourth and finished third at the October 2, 1966, U.S. Grand Prix at Watkins Glen. One month later, Surtees was in Las Vegas, Nevada, for the 1966 Stardust Can-Am Grand Prix at Stardust International Raceway. John Surtees won the 1966 Can-Am season finale at Stardust and clinched the inaugural Canadian-American Challenge Cup (courtesy International Motor Racing Research Center).

Cup series, the Can-Am. Surtees claimed the 1966 Can-Am championship with a win at the series finale on November 13, 1966, at Stardust International Raceway in Las Vegas. It was a race that introduced John Surtees and several other of the Formula One echelon to Las Vegas. Joining Surtees at the Las Vegas Can-Am round were Formula One competitors Bruce McLaren, Jackie Stewart, Dan Gurney, Masten Gregory, Paul Hawkins, and Chris Amon. Mario Andretti, future Formula One world champion, made his first Las Vegas racing visit for the 1966 Can-Am finale as well.

John Surtees spoke years later of the world travelers and their stopover in Las Vegas. "One is always partly forewarned about Las Vegas because of all the publicity it gets," recalled John Surtees. "It was an *experience*. In fact, I enjoyed it."[23]

Jackie Stewart—driving a Lola T70 in Las Vegas for John Mecom, Jr.—then stayed as a guest at the newly-opened Caesars Palace. "I remember staying on the 13th floor," reminisced the knighted three-time Formula One world champion. "That was unusual because in Britain, thirteen is a rather unlucky number. I was surprised that in a *casino*, there was a 13th floor."[24] Jackie Stewart did not, however, try his luck at the Caesars tables. "I'm not a gambling man. I once gambled in Monte

Carlo, $100 and that was it," lamented Sir Jackie. "No I didn't win, a real Scottish story."[25] Jackie Stewart's later remarks regarding the Caesars Palace Grand Prix events, though, were rather pointed, offered in a terse Scottish brogue.

Finally, the 1966 season also reset the power balance in Formula One, returning to a larger engine displacement, a full three liters or 183 cubic inches for normally aspirated engines. With the few V-12 power plants then competing, the three-liter displacement resulted in pistons no larger than a small cup of coffee. This element of the Formula One power structure then remained through to the Formula One Caesars Palace Grands Prix, in 1981 the V-12 Alfa Romeo 179D of Mario Andretti touring alongside the Las Vegas Strip—*Café Americano* for 12.

***

The public-facing gambling license consortium of Caesars Palace was informed, to a great extent, through investigations conducted by the FBI and the U.S. Senate. Indeed, the names of Jay Sarno, Stanley Mallin, Irv Kovens, and Kirk Kerkorian all leapt from the files of government inquiries. Conversely, the backfield of Caesars Palace—those allegedly assigned to the investments of the national crime syndicate in the Las Vegas resort—would spring from the front page of a newspaper, some 2,500 miles away.

"Following up sensational new disclosures of national crime operations," reported the *Miami News*. "Mayor Robert King High today released the names and addresses of 67 'hoodlums' who have settled in the Miami area."[26] Mayor King's list was a solid roster of frontline mid-century national organized crime talent. Among those named were Charles "The Blade" Tourine and Santo Trafficante, formerly of Meyer Lansky's Havana gambling operations. Al Mones made the cut, a client of Alvin Malnik and runner for Meyer Lansky. Murray Humphreys, connected to Moe Dalitz of the Stardust Hotel and Stardust International Raceway, was on the list. Marvin Krause booked his own double, granted a Nevada gambling license for Caesars Palace *after* appearing on the hoodlum list of the Miami mayor.

As the list continued, some of the *secret* centurions of Caesars Palace came into view. Ruby Lazarus, Anthony Salerno's "right hand man," was calling Miami home. About two miles away from Ruby Lazarus was "Fat Tony" Salerno himself, living on Biscayne Island in a home remodeled by Calvin Kovens. Three miles up Venetian Way from the home of "Fat Tony" was Jerome Zarowitz, pinned to the Miami hoodlum lineup directly across the street from the fourth hole at Bayshore Golf Club, well known to the FBI as "a hoodlum hangout."[27]

Another name of note on the Miami card was Dino Cellini, calling the Keystone Islands home at the north end of Biscayne Bay. Cellini, a product of the Steubenville, Ohio, gambling rackets, was the table game *maestro* of Meyer Lansky in the gambling properties of Cuba, the Bahamas, and London. Of note, Dino Cellini trained the croupiers in the Colony Sports Club and nearby Crockfords, situated blocks from each other in the affluent Mayfair district of London. Both of the London gambling houses also held their legends, Hollywood actor George Raft as the front man for organized crime in the Colony Sports Club, while Crockfords was the favored haunt of Formula One monarch Bernie Ecclestone.

Notably missing from the Miami depth chart, however, were Vincent "Jimmy Blue Eyes" Alo and Meyer Lansky, that duo of "blood-flecked names of … veteran hoods."[28] Vincent Alo and Meyer Lansky apparently had the good sense to reside slightly up-coast from the reform-minded Miami Mayor High, a short drive north to Hollywood and Hallandale, respectively. Missing also was Alvin Malnik, the alleged financial protégé of Meyer Lansky. Malnik, despite living in the recently completed Hampshire Towers of Miami Beach—right alongside three other members of the hoodlum set—managed to evade the radar of Miami Mayor High.[29]

The FBI, though, was slightly more skeptical of the young Miami attorney. To wit, concurrent with the release of the Miami hoodlum list, the FBI was bugging the Miami law office of Alvin Malnik, convinced that the criminal lawyer was "connected with the Las Vegas group."[30] Concurrently, the Bureau was tapping offices in Las Vegas, including the executive office of Edward Levinson. The wiretaps and the frailty of their legal basis also became a powder keg of national proportion.

Three months after the Miami hoodlum article, the Special Agent in Charge of the Miami field office of the FBI noted that Jerome Zarowitz was on the move to Las Vegas.[31] Zarowitz was indeed on his way, leaving behind the relative luxury of the Bayshore Golf Club to live in an apartment one block east of the Las Vegas Strip, behind the modern shadow of the MGM Grand developed by Kirk Kerkorian. Zarowitz's Las Vegas apartment also offered a view of the construction site for Caesars Palace off to the northwest, on the property owned by Kirk Kerkorian.

One month later, the Miami Special Agent for the FBI reported that Jerome Zarowitz and Anthony Salerno were hidden investors in the Lucayan Beach Casino in Freeport, Grand Bahama Islands, an operation later peeled back under the control of Meyer Lansky.[32] Again, Dino Cellini was involved. "CELLINI … operated the school in London, England," continued the FBI, "where gambling instructions were issued to prospective employees."[33]

London casinos learned from Meyer Lansky's Bahamanian base as well. "Crockford's sent a team to the Bahamas," described one account, "to study the syndicate's Lucayan operations."[34] A London to Las Vegas field trip for the Crockfords crew, though, was apparently off the table.

On the ground in Las Vegas, Jerome Zarowitz—the convicted sports-fixer—exercised the familiar play of gangsters and gamblers preceding him like Joseph Barbara, Moe Dalitz, Morris Kleinman, Ruby Kolod, and so many others "to penetrate, assimilate, and eventually, to become legitimate—allegedly."[35] It was a time-honored play, one that would regularly leave Nevada gambling regulators flat-footed. Indeed, less than two months after the FBI report to J. Edgar Hoover that Miami hoodlum Jerome Zarowitz was dispatched westward, newly-minted Las Vegas family man Jerome Zarowitz attended a meeting with his wife at the newly-formed Las Vegas Hadassah Chapter. The luncheon was held at the Sands Hotel and Casino of "Rat Pack" fame, Frank, Dean, Sammy, and the boys.[36]

Undeterred by Jerome Zarowitz's evolving appearance of civic duty, the FBI field offices stayed on his Las Vegas trail. Later that same year, a confidential informant for the New York Field Office of the FBI went in on Zarowitz, invoking the location of the Hadassah meeting. "ZAROWITZ has been brought into the operation of the Sands

```
11/12/63

TO:        DIRECTOR, FBI   (62-9-29)

FROM:      SAC, MIAMI   (92-515)

SUBJECT:   CRIMINAL INTELLIGENCE PROGRAM
           MIAMI DIVISION


                   WEEKLY SUMMARY

        MM 509-C-TE advised there are indications that
JERRY ZAROWITZ (MM 165-256) has moved to Las Vegas, Nev.
```

FROM THE DESK OF

JEROME ZAROWITZ

EXECUTIVE VICE PRESIDENT

From the attempted fix of the 1946 NFL championship game, to the 1957 Terre Haute gambling syndicate, to the 1963 Miami hoodlums list, Jerome Zarowitz was never far from the police blotter nor from the inbox on J. Edgar Hoover's desk. In 1965, Zarowitz was installed as the casino executive of Caesars Palace while the hotel-casino was still under construction. By 1968, the oft-investigated, never-licensed Jerome Zarowitz was promoted to executive vice-president of the luxury-branded Las Vegas resort (top, Federal Bureau of Investigation; bottom, author's collection).

Casino," read the FBI letter, "to protect the interest of 'BIG TONY' from Miami (possibly TONY SALERNO)."[37] The Sands in Las Vegas was yet one more casino property where "the shots were called by Meyer Lansky."[38]

By late 1965, the sanitized image of Jerome Zarowitz was nearly perfected. In the buildup to the November 22, 1965, WBC heavyweight title bout between Floyd Patterson and Cassius Clay, Zarowitz was quoted on the matchup: "Jerry Zarowitz, an executive at Caesars Palace, now under construction," wrote a columnist for the *Las Vegas Sun*, "thinks it 'might be a hell of a fight.'"[39]

"Patterson is fast, quick with his hands, and he's got a chance," claimed Zarowitz.

"After all, who has Clay beaten that had any class?"[40] It should be noted that five years earlier, Jerome Zarowitz's colleague Anthony Salerno was the obscured underwriter of the title fight between Floyd Patterson and Ingemar Johansson. "Zarowitz," closed the columnist, "has an opinion to be respected."[41]

Two weeks after the emerged Muhammad Ali defeated Floyd Patterson by TKO at the Las Vegas Convention Center, Jerome Zarowitz was named as an associate chairman for the Las Vegas Chapter of the State of Israel Bonds.[42] Zarowitz's fellow chairmen of the bond chapter also merit attention.

Associate bonds chairman Edward Levinson was the primary owner of the Lansky-connected Fremont Hotel, as well as investment partner with Alvin Malnik in an apparently spurious venture.[43] Jerome Mack was a partner in the Fremont Hotel with Levinson and a partner with E. Parry Thomas in Bank of Las Vegas, conduit of so many Teamsters loans to Las Vegas resort properties. Along with Levinson, Jerome Mack would also be a shareholder in the corrupt Parvin-Dohrmann corporation that later owned the Stardust Hotel and Stardust International Raceway. Al Benedict was an officer of the Stardust Hotel and Casino, long connected with the Chicago Outfit. Benedict was also one of the incorporators of the Stardust Racing Association, original ownership entity of Stardust International Raceway under Moe Dalitz. Milton Jaffe was a partner in the Cleveland syndicate led by Moe Dalitz, owners of the Desert Inn and Stardust Hotel-Casinos. Another associate chairman, Charles "Kewpie" Rich, was a longtime bookmaker and gambler from St. Louis, also a partner with Sid Wyman and criminal lawyer Morris Shenker in the notoriously racketed Dunes Hotel. In 1977, Rich partner Sid Wyman was the last person to talk to Culinary Union leader Al Bramlet before Bramlet was found dead in the Nevada desert. The apparently condemned Al Bramlet—later shot six times and dumped in the Nevada desert—was *also* an associate chairman of the Las Vegas Chapter of the State of Israel Bonds.

The bond list continued with several other associate chairmen of similar backgrounds, holding similar positions in Las Vegas gambling operations. By all appearances, "the members of the interwoven mobs which make up the national crime syndicate"[44] were well-represented in Las Vegas, and the legitimatized public-facing image of Jerome Zarowitz was well-constructed. Unreported in Las Vegas press, however, was a conclave held in Palm Springs just two months before the bond drive, a secretive meeting attended by Jerome Zarowitz, Vincent "Jimmy Blue Eyes" Alo, Anthony Salerno, Ruby Lazarus, and Elliott Paul Price. The FBI covered that story first, and federal agents documented for J. Edgar Hoover the conversations about who *really* owned Caesars Palace.

***

The 1966 U.S. Grand Prix at Watkins Glen and the 1966 debut of the Can-Am series created a double-pronged influence of international racing stars in America. Combined with the influx of Formula One-derived rear-engine race vehicles at the Indianapolis 500—and the Formula One stars who would drive them—the balance of the decade witnessed a spectacular growth of American immersion in European-style motorsports. In fact, the rise in motorsports popularity paralleled the 1960s

British invasion of rock music, mod Carnaby Street-influenced fashion, and the rapid evolution of related popular culture. It was a sea change that also foretold the vertical synthesis of motorsports, celebrity, entertainment, hospitality, and gambling modeled by the Caesars Palace Grand Prix.

When the movie *Grand Prix* was released on December 22, 1966, the attraction to American motorsports enthusiasts—and movie goers—was sealed. "The Grand Illusion that is the motion picture," gushed the *Los Angeles Times*, "probably comes as close to fruition as it ever will in MGM's 'Grand Prix,' the new, definitive, great film about auto racing."[45] The Academy of Motion Picture Arts and Sciences agreed, awarding three Oscars to *Grand Prix* for technical merits. The John Frankenheimer film was shot with extensive wide angle 70 mm footage from the 1966 Monaco Grand Prix and 1966 U.S. Grand Prix at Watkins Glen. The footage included virtually every driver in the Formula One field, including the Watkins Glen podium of Jimmy Clark, Jochen Rindt, and John Surtees. "[Bernie Ecclestone] was most impressed with the final product," according to an Ecclestone biographer, "which even now he occasionally watches on video."[46]

The 1966 Formula One season also sealed the relationship between Jochen Rindt and Bernie Ecclestone. "During endless low-stakes games of gin rummy and backgammon," wrote another of Ecclestone. "Ecclestone and Rindt had become close friends."[47] By season's end, Bernie Ecclestone would formally join Jochen Rindt as manager and business advisor. United by the thrill of auto racing, the culture of the Formula One paddock, marathon gambling, common business interests, and even Carnaby Street fashion, Rindt and Ecclestone were effectively each other's mirror and muse. Although Rindt was committed to Cooper for the 1967 season, the 25-year-old from Austria would be looking elsewhere for 1968, and Bernie Ecclestone would provide the introductions.

Meanwhile, Bernie Ecclestone's return to the Formula One paddock—as well as the *zeitgeist* of the 1960s—stoked his proclivity for gambling. With a personal style that straddled Carnaby Street and Savile Row, Ecclestone did enjoy his grand evening arrival at Crockfords. "Gambling became Ecclestone's passion, not because he was compulsive or addicted," offered one assessment of Bernie Ecclestone, "but because chance, risk, and weighing the odds matched his philosophy of life."[48]

For himself, Bernie Ecclestone was thus inclined to treat gambling as an even proposition. Meyer Lansky, though, sensed a whale with an impulse *before* they entered one of his joints. Further, the rise of Bernie Ecclestone in London, and his newly activated engagement in Formula One, paralleled the infiltration of the Lansky apparatus in London casinos, including Crockfords. "He understood the fundamental psychology of gambling from a professional point of view," it was written of Lansky. "He knew high rollers wanted to gamble big and always, *always*, he had provided the opportunity in an environment that would play to their sense of entitlement."[49]

Entitlement, ego, unmitigated arrogance; all would be said of Bernie Ecclestone in 4 decades as the iron-fisted ruler of Formula One. With Bernie Ecclestone at 5' 3" and Meyer Lansky at 5' 0", the diminutive dictators were nonetheless giants of their respectively vast industrial complexes, each of them underwritten by contests of chance. Had Ecclestone and Lansky crossed paths—and it is *not* improbable that they did—each would have no doubt regarded the other, a mutual respect bestowed of position, power, privilege, and an absolute dearth of penance. They would also have found common ground in their regard for Caesars Palace.

***

The ground-breaking ceremony for Caesars Palace was held on January 26, 1965. The obligatory photo-op for the local dailies depicted president Jay Sarno, vice-president and secretary Nathan Jacobson, treasurer Harry L. Lewis, landlord Kirk Kerkorian, and contractor Robb Johnson atop a massive Caterpillar earth-scraper. The roadside billboard behind the construction equipment touted, "Opening Here in March 1966." A construction schedule of 13 months for a multi-story project on the scale of Caesars Palace was incredibly ambitious. That bold statement cast the mold for the many spins of Caesar to follow, some superlative, others straight-up subterfuge.

Robb Johnson was a former employee of Taylor Construction of Miami, the builder of such mob haunts as the Eden Roc and Fontainebleau hotels in Miami. In Las Vegas, Taylor Construction also logged the very well-connected Riviera and Tropicana hotel-casinos on its construction resume. Robb Johnson, of note, was the project manager for Taylor on the Las Vegas Riviera and Tropicana projects. The Lucayan Beach Casino in Freeport, Grand Bahama Islands—with alleged hidden investments of Jerome Zarowitz and Anthony Salerno—was yet another Taylor Construction project. It could be fairly said that the alleged underwritings of Meyer Lansky were a common thread through early Taylor Construction undertakings.

Although Robb Johnson remained in Las Vegas to start his own company after the completion of the Tropicana Hotel & Casino in 1957, the Caesars Palace project reunited the project manager with his former employer. "When the Caesars Palace opportunity came up—I'm not sure how my dad met Jay Sarno," recalled Stuart Mason, son of Taylor Construction founder Morry Mason. "My dad … contacted Rob [sic] Johnson … and a joint venture was formed between Rob Johnson and Taylor to build Caesars Palace."[50] "And in '64," continued Mason, "I moved out here to build Caesars Palace."[51]

Stuart Mason's move from the sugar sand beaches of southern Florida placed him in the desert scrub of Las Vegas before the ink was dry on the parchment of Caesar. Indeed, the articles of incorporation for Desert Palace, Inc., the first corporate parent of Caesars Palace, were dated December 2, 1964.[52] Mason's Las Vegas landing was also early in the corporate timeline of Robb Johnson. Available records indicate that R.C. Johnson Construction Co., Inc., did not incorporate until November of 1964,[53] immediately prior to the Desert Palace incorporation and the national announcements in January 1965 about the Caesars Palace development.

A national account of the construction arrangements, however, failed to acknowledge the attributed role of Taylor Construction. "Crane Construction company [of Chicago] has become a partner with R.C. Johnson & Associates," reported the Chicago Tribune in early 1965, "in construction of a $20 million dollar [sic] hotel to be built on the Las Vegas 'strip.' The hotel will be called Caesar's [sic] Palace."[54] The respective power centers of Miami and Chicago certainly lend intrigue to the

The groundbreaking ceremony for Caesars Palace on January 26, 1965, featured a timeless lineup. From left, Robb Johnson, Jay Sarno, Kirk Kerkorian, Harry Lewis, and Nathan Jacobson. Robb Johnson was president of R.C. Johnson Construction. Johnson was involved in the construction of a number of mob-tainted resorts. Harry Lewis was a licensed shareholder of Caesars Palace and the president of Cedars of Lebanon Hospital in Miami, Florida. Lewis was also documented to have connections to illegal gambling interests in Florida (courtesy LVCVA News Bureau).

movement of Teamsters construction funding to the Caesars Palace project in Las Vegas. With R.C. Johnson of Las Vegas, Taylor Construction of Miami, and Crane Construction of Chicago, though, Caesar may have simply preferred seating for three.

"The job started slowly," wrote a Sarno biographer of Caesars Palace, "with grading, digging, and foundation work."[55] The excavation and underground work also involved the original underground casino count room, the secure compartmented income facility where the take from the tables, slots, and card rooms would be aggregated, tallied, and then skimmed—allegedly. It was also where Bernie Ecclestone would sign the agreement for the Caesars Palace Grand Prix. "The gambling

Mecca made no secret of its mobster foundations," read an account of the transaction, "which Bernie found intriguing."[56]

As the larger-than-life Jay Sarno led the figurative block behind which hidden runners followed, so too did Jay Sarno form one of the most iconic elements of the exterior architecture of Caesars Palace, literally the "Sarno block."[57] The distinctive open lattice block formed a floor-to-roof shade screen across the guest room faces of the new hotel. The see-through cement block was also integral to the design of the preceding Atlanta, Dallas, and Palo Alto Cabana properties. At Caesars Palace though, the effect was perfected, a continuous vertical plane of Las Vegas light and underworld shadow, stretching 14 stories into the sky from its "mobster foundations."

For the extensive masonry and Sarno block requirements of Caesars Palace, the construction team turned to John E Yoxen Masonry of Las Vegas. John Yoxen was a long-standing Las Vegas community builder of schools, commercial buildings, and gambling properties. John Yoxen, though, also became directly connected with an extremely interesting land transaction after the completion of Caesars Palace. It was a land transaction that engaged Howard Hughes, Hughes' minion Robert Maheu, and—by all appearances—illegal campaign contributions to the 1968 presidential election, "a Las Vegas real estate deal in which Maheu admittedly invested no money but realized a $73,950 cash profit."[58] Notably, the real estate was part of an original land package upon which the Stardust International Raceway property of Moe Dalitz was constructed. Like Caesars Palace, Stardust International Raceway commenced construction in 1965.

Of further curiosity, then, were the hands through which the Teamsters dollars flowed to Caesars Palace, the monthly progress payment from Desert Palace, Inc. to the joint venture and, in turn, into the hands of subcontractors like John Yoxen. Perhaps unsurprisingly, the construction funds were designated to flow through a Miami bank. "First National Bank of Miami," reported the *Miami News*, "has been named disbursing agent for all construction funds."[59]

The actual escrow agreement for the Teamsters construction funds is lost to history. In its absence, the proper name of the bank is at question. It also, though, becomes a point of inquiry. According to author Hank Messick, U.S. senator from Florida "Gorgeous George" Smathers held "a large interest" in "First National Bank of Miami."[60] George Smathers also held a connection with Calvin Kovens, convicted crony of the Teamsters' Jimmy Hoffa and brother of Caesars Palace investor Irving Kovens. In fact, seeking an early release for Kovens' conviction, George Smathers "acted as Kovens lawyer before the US Parole Board."[61] Smathers also counted a relationship with Bebe Rebozo, personal friend of Richard Nixon and proxy through whom illegal campaign cash flowed. Further, George Smathers was connected with Bobby Baker, consort of President Lyndon Johnson. Baker was notably caught up in a national scandal involving the FBI Las Vegas wiretaps of Edward Levinson.

Connected as well in Teamsters affairs, though, was the similarly-named Miami National Bank. In 1962, Lou Poller, then-president of Miami National Bank, was called to testify in the trial of Jimmy Hoffa and Calvin Kovens, testimony that included the prior Teamsters financing of the Taylor-constructed Fontainebleau in Miami. Poller resigned from the bank on the heels of his testimony, yet the Teamsters investment in Miami National Bank remained. In early 1966, concurrent with the Caesars Palace construction project, Miami investor and developer Sam Cohen then acquired Miami National Bank.[62] At the time of the Cohen purchase, the Teamsters held greater than a 50 percent interest in the institution. Sam Cohen was then also an owner of the Flamingo hotel-casino in Las Vegas, a property soon to be acquired by Kirk Kerkorian.

Five years later, Meyer Lansky, Sam Cohen, and then-Caesars Palace employee Jerry Gordon were indicted on charges of skimming from the Flamingo. The same Lou Poller, formerly of Miami National Bank, was named as an unindicted co-conspirator in the Flamingo skim. "Certain Miami banks have long been popular with organized crime money managers," it was reported, "and FBI wiretaps have picked up more than one revealing conversation about the attractiveness."[63] The staggering series of connections inform and instruct the apparatus of Meyer Lansky, a vast complex of moving parts, pieces, people, properties and, sometimes, projectiles. "The solution, [Lansky] decided," also wrote Hank Messick, "was to own people, not property."[64]

The till and the take of the Teamsters Central States Pension Fund was thus an integral part of the Meyer Lansky property development machinery. For Lansky, a dollar shilled for every three tilled. Meyer Lansky's empire of shills thus pledged their fealty, the centurion swords of Caesar outstretched to Miami and—of course— nearby Hallandale. In 1981, Bernie Ecclestone would then bring his own battalion to the Palace for the Caesars Palace Grand Prix. Ecclestone was now in league with the chairman of the board of the host resort, one of Meyer Lansky's shills—allegedly. It is *truly* a tangled tale.

***

The 1967 Formula One season would be a miserable campaign for Jochen Rindt. Rindt was paired in the Cooper-Maserati team with Pedro Rodriguez following the departure of John Surtees to the Honda works effort. Rodriguez launched his season with a win for Cooper at the opening South African Grand Prix. Jochen Rindt's similar Cooper, however, expired before the halfway point of the event. The failure of the Cooper racer set a tone. Of 10 Grand Prix rounds contested in 1967, Jochen Rindt failed to see the finish of eight, salvaging only a pair of fourth-place finishes in Belgium and Italy. The U.S. Grand Prix at Watkins Glen was no different, an engine failure long before the halfway mark of the event. Rindt's fine second place at the 1966 U.S. Grand Prix was followed by a disappointing unclassified 15th in 1967. Further, Jochen Rindt's third place in the 1966 championship—in only his second Formula One season—was gutted by finishing 13th in the points tally for 1967. Jackie Stewart *never* finished 13th in the Formula One world drivers' championship.

The 1967 U.S. Grand Prix would, though, be another triumph for Jimmy Clark. Clark, the 1965 Indianapolis 500 winner, engaged in a thrilling duel at Watkins Glen with 1966 Indy 500 winner Graham Hill, along with Denny Hulme and Chris Amon. Jimmy Clark then won out in his Lotus for Colin Chapman, claiming the Mexican Grand Prix to close the campaign with four wins total. Denny Hulme, however, claimed the 1967 Formula One championship ahead of team owner Jack Brabham.

Jimmy Clark finished third in the championship behind Brabham. One month after the Formula One closer in Mexico, Denny Hulme was back in the United States, finishing second in the Can-Am championship at Stardust International Raceway in Las Vegas. Notably, John Surtees repeated as the Stardust winner over a dejected Mark Donohue driving for Roger Penske. At Stardust, Bruce McLaren would take the Can-Am championship in the second year of that overlapping North American racing series.

Eager to advance his craft, Jochen Rindt then stood at the crossroads of his concluded 1967 season. Constrained by the financial wherewithal of the Cooper effort—and encouraged by financial advisor Bernie Ecclestone—Rindt signed on with Jack Brabham's Motor Racing Developments

Jimmy Clark won the 1967 U.S. Grand Prix at Watkins Glen, New York. Clark was driving a Lotus-Ford for Colin Chapman. Graham Hill was second, followed by Denny Hulme. Jochen Rindt, driving for Cooper, dropped out on the 33rd lap of his third U.S. Grand Prix event. Rindt had also enlisted Bernie Ecclestone as business advisor, a relationship that steered both of their careers to the Brabham works (courtesy International Motor Racing Research Center).

going into 1968. Rindt was teamed with the founder and namesake, Jack Brabham, after Denny Hulme moved over to contest Formula One for Bruce McLaren. The team of Brabham and Rindt were buoyed at the opening South African round by strong qualifying times in their Brabham-Repco mounts, fourth and fifth, respectively. Jochen Rindt then finished third to Jim Clark and Graham Hill, both in Lotus-Ford machines for Colin Chapman. Jack Brabham, though, was out early with a failure of the Repco engine. Again, it would set a tone.

Before the next round in Spain, inconsolable tragedy struck the Formula One circuit. On April 7, 1968, Jimmy Clark was killed. During a Formula Two event in Germany during the layoff between South Africa and Spain, Clark's Lotus veered wildly on a high-speed straightaway and careened into the woods lining the track. "Clark died instantly," ran one report, "of a broken neck and multiple skull fractures."[65] Twice World Driving Champion, Indianapolis 500 winner, and a three-time winner of the U.S. Grand Prix at Watkins Glen, 32-year-old Jimmy Clark was destined for further greatness. The fates, though, determined otherwise.

"Fear is a constant in this sport. I've always recognized and respected my own safety margins, for myself and for the others," Clark said of risk and chance. "I'd rather lose a race than exceed the capabilities of myself or my car."[66] The death of Jimmy Clark called into question the reliability of Colin Chapman's Lotus racers. In the short term, though, Jimmy Clark's sentiments may have passed along with him.

The 1968 Formula One chase resumed in Spain after the passing of Clark. The Brabham team rather picked up where they left off in South Africa—poorly. Jochen Rindt was ninth quickest on the Spanish grid while Jack Brabham struggled in qualifying and did not make the start. Rindt was then off on the 10th lap with issues in the Repco powerplant. Chris Amon scored a fine pole in his Ferrari but was out past halfway. The 1968 Spanish Grand Prix was won by Graham Hill, scoring a redemption win for Lotus in the famous Gold Leaf livery of Imperial Tobacco. It was an auspicious debut for the first fully-realized tobacco sponsorship in Formula One. Tobacco also seeded nearly half the field at the 1981 Caesars Palace Grand Prix.

Jack Brabham and Jochen Rindt then thrashed their way through the balance of a dismal season. Brabham was shut out of points except for a fifth place in Germany. Jack Brabham's junior colleague was little better. Jochen Rindt took a solitary pole position in his Brabham-Repco at the French Grand Prix, a solid 1.20 seconds quicker than Jackie Stewart in the Matra-Ford. Rindt's pole, however, was discarded with another failure in the race, his sixth retirement in a row. Another third place in Germany was little consolation for a season shown promise at the direction of Bernie Ecclestone. Jochen Rindt then added four more failures to close the season, including at the U.S. Grand Prix in Watkins Glen, from a solid sixth starting position on the grid.

Another competitor, though, would make his Formula One race debut at the 1968 U.S. Grand Prix at Watkins Glen, the penultimate round of the season. Mario Andretti, the 1966 and 1967 USAC IndyCar national driving champion, was entered in a Lotus-Ford for Colin Chapman. In a 1968 race season which included dirt ovals, paved ovals, road courses, endurance racing, NASCAR, the Pikes Peak hill climb, and *drag racing*, Mario Andretti's 1968 portfolio was without peer. Mario would then build his Formula One portfolio all the way to the 1982 Caesars Palace Grand Prix, his final starting grid at the pinnacle of motorsport. Andretti also sat on pole for his inaugural Formula One start at Watkins Glen, nudging Jackie Stewart and Graham Hill by .07 seconds and .08 seconds, respectively. Chris Amon qualified fourth in a Ferrari followed by Denny Hulme in a McLaren-Ford. Notably, Dan Gurney was seventh on the grid in a companion machine provided by Bruce McLaren.

Dropped at the start of the 1968 U.S. Grand Prix by Jackie Stewart, Mario Andretti nonetheless proved game, chasing hard in second place until a Lotus bodywork failure removed him from contention. Stewart was then unrivaled in his Matra-Ford, continuing to a resounding win, over 24 seconds ahead of Graham Hill in a Lotus. It was Stewart's third win of the season. Graham Hill, however, went on to win the finale of the Formula One season, the Mexican Grand Prix.

Mario Andretti made his Formula One competition debut driving a tobacco-sponsored Lotus for Colin Chapman at the 1968 U.S. Grand Prix in Watkins Glen, New York. Andretti put the Lotus on pole in his first start but retired on lap 32. A decade later, Mario Andretti claimed the Formula One championship driving a tobacco-sponsored Lotus for Colin Chapman. Andretti was also the only driver to contest the four premier class events of the Caesars Palace Grand Prix (author's collection).

Graham Hill also seized the World Driver Championship over Jackie Stewart. The 1968 crown was Hill's last championship in Formula One. Denny Hulme was third in championship points with two wins, a remarkable debut year with Team McLaren. Bruce McLaren also registered a win at the Belgian Grand Prix and claimed fourth in points. John Surtees followed seventh in points in a disappointing campaign for the Honda squad. Chris Amon slotted 10th for the Scuderia Ferrari. Jochen Rindt trailed further, 12th in championship points in the Brabham. One position ahead of Rindt—by virtue of nine points scored for the win of the season-opening South African Grand Prix—was the departed Jimmy Clark.

One week after the Mexican Grand Prix, several of the competitors of the U.S. Grand Prix were back on American soil. Bruce McLaren, Denny Hulme, Dan Gurney and Mario Andretti returned to Stardust International Raceway in Las Vegas for the finale of the 1968 Can-Am season. Chris Amon landed in Las Vegas as well, making the debut of the heralded Ferrari 612P, a purpose-built Can-Am racer entered by northern Nevada gambling mogul William Harrah. The five gathered competitors from the U.S. Grand Prix figured in the storyline of the Can-Am finale, as well as of the championship.

Qualifying first and second, Bruce McLaren and Denny Hulme dominated the pre-race punditry. At the start, though, Mario Andretti pushed forward from the

Jackie Stewart of Scotland won the 1968 U.S. Grand Prix in Watkins Glen driving a Matra-Ford for team principal Ken Tyrell. Stewart finished second in the 1968 Formula One championship to Graham Hill. Jackie Stewart said of the Caesars Palace Grand Prix, "You can't hold a Grand Prix in a bloody car park" (*Las Vegas Review-Journal*, December 8, 2017). Official at right is identified as Bill Bell, regional SCCA member and, apparently, sometime Formula One event announcer (courtesy International Motor Racing Research Center).

third row and shunted Bruce McLaren in the first turn. The incident then collected Chris Amon, ending his race almost before it started. Denny Hulme would take the lead while Dan Gurney circulated in second place. Hulme then took off, taking the Stardust victory and the Can-Am championship.

After Stardust, Mario Andretti returned to the 1968 USAC IndyCar championship trail, taking the fight to Bobby Unser all the way to the IndyCar finale at Riverside International Raceway. Dan Gurney won the Riverside closer while Bobby Unser finished second. Mario Andretti sputtered to an 18th place finish. Bobby Unser prevailed in the 1968 IndyCar championship over Mario Andretti by 11 points; it was the closest points finish in the IndyCar points system of the time. Sixteen years later, Mario Andretti would win the 1984 IndyCar championship over Tom Sneva, a championship clinched at the 1984 Caesars Palace Grand Prix.

***

"I, Caesar, invite you," read the late–July tease in national dailies, "to an orgy of excitement!"[67] As if written by Jay Sarno himself, the cross-country come-on led

The tease for the August 5, 1966, grand opening of Caesars Palace ran from coast to coast. The gala celebration was notably attended by Jimmy Hoffa, the convicted leader of the International Brotherhood of Teamsters. Caesars Palace opened amid national reports of hidden ownership interests in the glamorous Las Vegas resort. The reports—as well as the alleged hidden interests—also ran from coast to coast (author's collection).

the lurid and lascivious to indulge Caesar's own "Palace of Pleasure."[68] The three-day grand opening of Caesars Palace checked the customary low-level assortment of flesh-pressing pols with ribbon and scissors and, instead, turned up with an army of centurions, a bevy of Greco-Roman goddesses, colossal headline entertainment, endless food and libation, the governor of Nevada, and—seated near the stage—Jimmy Hoffa. As Jay Sarno placed his mark on the many excesses of Caesars Palace, so would the celebration follow. "Sarno estimated the opening party would cost the hotel $1 million," it was reported, "one of the most lavish openings in history."[69]

One day before the August 5, 1966, opening, though, national press drilled in on Caesars Palace, this time with allegations of hidden ownership. "Caesars Palace, a swank new $25 million gambling hotel on the Las Vegas strip, opens Friday," reported the *Los Angeles Times*, "amid charges that top gangsters own secret interests in the casino."[70] Picking up a report from Sandy Smith of the *Chicago Sun-Times*, the Los Angeles story dropped the names of Sam Giancana, boss of the Chicago Outfit;

Raymond Patriarca of the New England rackets; and Gerardo Catena of the New Jersey crime family, noting that "each holds a 10% hidden interest in Caesars Palace."[71] Also mentioned was "Anthony (Fat Tony) Salerno."[72] The names of Patriarca, Catena, and Salerno fit neatly under the criminal umbrella of the imprisoned Vito Genovese, the "boss of bosses,"[73] alleged as the party planner for the November 1957 criminal conclave at the Apalachin home of Joseph Barbara near Watkins Glen. Further mentioned in the structure of hidden Las Vegas interests was Vincent "Jimmy Blue Eyes" Alo, at that point a secret handshake away from the secret ledger system of the secretive Meyer Lansky.

"The charges [were] vehemently denied by the hotel president, Nathan S. Jacobson," continued the *Los Angeles Times* report. "He demanded a retraction but it was not forthcoming."[74] The originating *Sun-Times* piece also alleged political payoffs, "from $200,000 for a former governor to $200 to a Clark County Justice of the peace."[75] Governor Grant Sawyer demanded that the Nevada Gaming Commission convene an investigation to question Las Vegas gambling owners about the alleged criminal interests standing behind them. First though, Governor Sawyer would attend the opening night romp of Jay Sarno and Nathan Jacobson at Caesars Palace. "The closed door inquiry," stated the *Times*, "will open Tuesday in Las Vegas."[76] The governor of the great State of Nevada thus had an opportunity to return his tuxedo on Monday.

The appearance of convicted felon Jimmy Hoffa—president of the International Brotherhood of Teamsters—at the August 5, 1966, grand opening of Caesars Palace in Las Vegas, Nevada, should have been instructive. At the same time, the owner fronts of Caesars Palace downplayed the Teamsters financing for construction of the lavish Las Vegas resort. With bribery and fraud convictions then under appeal, Hoffa reported to prison seven months after Caesars Palace opened (author's collection).

The appearance of Jimmy Hoffa at the grand opening of Caesars Palace also became a lightning rod for the new operation, a nettlesome subject to be explained away at every turn. "Financing was a tremendous problem with the tight money market," Nathan Jacobson said. "Conservative lending institutions are not interested in Las Vegas because of its image. Most won't even write insurance here."[77] The Teamsters, however, would provide both by way of Allen Dorfman, a primary influencer of pension fund loan approvals as well as the Teamsters insurance administrator. The due of Allen

Dorfman, though, appeared to require that the life beneficiary designations follow suit. National news stories then drilled in on the magnitude of Teamsters loans in the Las Vegas valley, by then approaching $50 million of development underwritten by the Central States Pension Fund.

As the Nevada Gaming Commission hearings entered their second week, the Caesars Palace crew would get their turn in the chair. "The commission said it would call four representatives of the newly-opened Caesars Palace on the Las Vegas Strip," it was reported from Binghamton, New York, near Watkins Glen. "They included Nathan Jacobson, president of the hotel, Jay Sarno, vice-president; and two employees, Jerry Zarowitz and Elliott P. Price."[78] It was as close as the Nevada Gaming Commission would ever get to Jerome Zarowitz and Elliott Paul Price.

Nathan Jacobson led off for Caesars, reportedly on the hot seat for two hours before the commission chairman emerged for his mid-day briefing. "He claims he has no knowledge of these allegations," stated Nevada regulator Milton Keefer of Jacobson. "He says the first he heard of them was in a newspaper."[79]

Jay Sarno sought to distance his awareness of the operation, stating he "was only involved in the design of the hotel-casino complex."[80] Sarno also apparently played the clown: "Asked how the winnings are tabulated, Sarno replied, 'We just take it out of the boxes and count it.'"[81] Elliott Paul Price kept it even closer, refusing to identify his executive position at Caesars Palace.

As Jerome Zarowitz approached the Nevada commission hearings, national media dusted off reports of his conviction for attempting to fix the 1946 NFL championship game. Asked if the gaming commission was aware of Zarowitz's unsavory backstory, Milton Keefer sidestepped the conviction altogether: "Many licenses are granted to people in bookmaking."[82] Confronted by reporters, Jerome Zarowitz offered no comment. Keefer's apparent subterfuge was also telling; Jerome Zarowitz was neither a licensed owner nor licensed key employee of Caesars Palace. The outward cover of Zarowitz by the gaming official was overlooked. The role of Jerome Zarowitz in the Caesars operation, though, was to unfold in the months ahead.

Three weeks after the Caesars Palace representatives appeared for the hearings in Las Vegas, the Nevada Gaming Commission issued its conclusion. "In a report highly critical of the Federal Government and Robert F. Kennedy, as Attorney General," posted the *Baltimore Sun*, "the Nevada Gaming Commission denied any substantial rake-offs in Nevada casinos."[83] On the strength of uninspired denials by a reported 26 gambling owners, "the investigation produced no evidence of any undisclosed ownership of any licensed Nevada gambling establishment."[84]

The Department of Justice and the agents of the FBI, however, were much better informed. Notably, though, a request by the Nevada Gaming Commission to interview FBI agents was rejected. At stake for the feds was their most reliable source of organized crime intelligence, the massive wiretapping operation that had overheard the gamblers of Las Vegas in the first place—and Alvin Malnik.

Two days after the release of the Nevada Gaming Commission report, Nevada press published a story about five additional investors seeking gambling licenses for Caesars Palace. Leading the list was "Irving (Ash) Resnick, a Las Vegas gambler."[85] Concurrent with the Nevada inquiry, national press was also picking up reports from

London. "Reports have reached Scotland Yard," read one account, "that the Lansky-schemed skimming racket already is working in a number of London casinos."[86] Meyer Lansky would thus be smiling on both sides of the Atlantic Ocean. Bernie Ecclestone soon would as well.

***

Jochen Rindt was burdened by the back-to-back disappointments of 1966 and 1967. From fifth place and 22 points in the 1966 Formula One championship, to a combined total of 14 points spread across the following two dismal years. Rindt's final year with Cooper was an abject letdown. Shepherded by manager Bernie Ecclestone, the sojourn of Jochen Rindt with Jack Brabham produced little more, sullied even further by the tragic loss of Jimmy Clark driving for Lotus. The year 1969 thus somewhat split the vote of the two.

"I told Jochen that the Lotus was not as safe as the Brabham," Ecclestone said, "but could win the world championship."[87] Rindt was thus poached away from Jack Brabham by Colin Chapman, fitted for a racing seat in a Gold Leaf Lotus at the behest of Ecclestone. Bernie Ecclestone, conversely, considered the performance misfortunes of Brabham's Motor Racing Developments, now compounded by the loss of the world champion-in-waiting. Bernie Ecclestone would later be fitted for a seat at the Brabham table.

Jochen Rindt's 1969 Formula One season started slowly, accompanied with some measure of irony. Rindt qualified well in the South African opener, second in his Lotus-Ford. Pole, however was taken by Jack Brabham in the new Ford-powered Brabham. Rindt's Lotus then fell out just past halfway with a mechanical issue. Jackie Stewart, driving a Matra-Ford for Ken Tyrell, won the opening round over Graham Hill, the reigning world champion and still the ostensible Lotus leader.

The following Spanish Grand Prix produced a similar result for Jochen Rindt. Despite starting from pole, Rindt was off the track at lap 19 in a frightening crash that brought him to rest on the crumpled Lotus of Graham Hill. Notably, the Lotus mounts of Hill and Rindt had both suffered an aerodynamic failure. "Here was exacting proof that the rear wing," according to one account, "was a disaster."[88] Jackie Stewart then prevailed in Spain as well, this time over Bruce McLaren in his works McLaren-Ford racer.

Jochen Rindt's head injuries in Spain removed him from the following round, the celebrated Monaco Grand Prix. Graham Hill triumphed in Monaco, his fifth win in the principality but the last Formula One victory of his career. Rindt then returned for the swing through the Netherlands and France. Jochen Rindt scored pole for the Dutch Grand Prix and qualified third in France. Unfortunately, the strong qualifying efforts were squandered with another pair of retirements.

Jackie Stewart took a resounding fifth win of the season at the following round in Britain. Jochen Rindt once again qualified on pole and took a commendable fourth, his first points of the season. Once again, though, Rindt experienced a wing issue, this time while dicing with Jackie Stewart. So dominant was Stewart, however, that he lapped the field, including second and third on the podium, Jacki Ickx in a Brabham and Bruce McLaren. Jochen Rindt followed with a pole at the Italian Grand

Brothers Clifford Perlman and Stuart Perlman built their Lum's regional fast food restaurant chain into a national brand in the 1960s. A public offering of Lum's in 1969 provided the liquidity and positioning for their purchase of Caesars Palace in Las Vegas, Nevada. The 13-year run of Clifford Perlman at Caesars Palace was riddled with investigations, accusations, and allegations of connections to organized crime. According to the storyline of the 2019 Martin Scorsese movie *The Irishman*, Lum's was a favorite of Pennsylvania mob boss Russell Bufalino (author's collection).

Prix and finished a very strong second to winner Jackie Stewart, only eight seconds adrift.

The Canadian Grand Prix at Mosport then showed another strong result for Jochen Rindt, once again with a taste of irony. Rindt qualified third on the grid, well ahead of Lotus team leader Graham Hill. Rindt was beaten to pole, however, by Jacky Ickx for the Brabham team Rindt had departed. Jochen Rindt powered through a solid race as well, third at the line but led there, unfortunately, by the Brabham-Ford machines of Ickx, and Rindt's former employer Jack Brabham.

From the London gambling houses, to the time-honored *tifosi* of the Italian Grand Prix, across the Atlantic Ocean to Canada, Jochen Rindt, Bernie Ecclestone, and the sport of Formula One then traveled around Lake Ontario to Watkins Glen, New York, for the 1969 United States Grand Prix. As the news reports of Formula

One still circulated in Canada, the Securities and Exchange Commission circulated news of their own. "Lum's, Inc.... Miami, Fla," read the SEC report, "filed a registration statement with the SEC on September 17 seeking registration of $27,200,000 of ... debentures, due 1989."[89] Lum's Inc., the original beer-brined hot dog restaurant chain of Miami, was making a large national play. "$20,000,000 will be used to pay a portion of the purchase price of all interests in ... Caesars Palace, a Las Vegas hotel and casino," the report continued. "Stuart Perlman is president and Clifford Perlman board chairman."[90] With mention of Clifford Perlman, the presiding placeholder on the podium celebration of the 1981 Caesars Palace Grand Prix had just come into view.

***

The final report of the Nevada Gaming Commission quieted the subject of hidden interests in Las Vegas casinos, certainly to the benefit of the newly-opened Caesars Palace. The federal government, however, remained pitched in disagreement with Nevada regulators about mob money investments in Nevada gambling establishments. The FBI knew better but was scrambling themselves to control the damage about whether their widespread wiretapping program was legally authorized. The quiet on the street, however, was about to be pierced.

"A little 'Apalachin' meeting reportedly held in Palm Springs and attended by five notorious gambling figures—some with ties to the nationwide crime syndicate," reported the *Los Angeles Times*, " is under investigation here."[91] The invocation of "Apalachin," the site of the infamous November 1957 crime conference near Watkins Glen, was instructive. Nine years removed, the term was no longer ascribed to the idyll in upstate New York. Rather, Apalachin was now coded for any meeting of two or more members of the national crime syndicate, typically when gathered in the name of Meyer Lansky.

"Two alleged participants in the meeting were Vincent (Jimmy Blue Eyes) Alo and Anthony (Fat Tony) Salerno," continued the *Times*, "alleged New York members of the Cosa Nostra family headed by Vito Genovese."[92] The report noted that Vito Genovese was a high-level delegate at the November 1957 meeting at Joseph Barbara's home in Apalachin, New York. "Others who reportedly attended the Palm Springs session," the report stated, "were Jerome (Jerry) Zarowitz and Elliott Paul Price, both associated with Caesars Palace, and Ruby Lazarus, a Miami Beach bookmaker."[93]

The news of the days-long Palm Springs meeting then streaked across the national wires, coast-to-coast. The coverage in Las Vegas, however, was somewhat muted. National stories also confirmed the positions of Jerome Zarowitz and Elliott Paul Price in Caesars Palace, Zarowitz, the "credit manager," and Price "a host at the club."[94] What was not known, though, is what was discussed by the Palm Springs attendees. One writer dismissed the gathering as "small scale villainy,"[95] perhaps a boys-will-be-boys bender of booze, betting, and bookmaking. The FBI, however, soon refined their own reporting of the Palm Springs "Apalachin."

In a subsequent report from the Los Angeles FBI Field Office to J. Edgar Hoover, the female companion of Jerome Zarowitz was specific. "The meeting in Palm Springs concerned financial difficulties of Caesar's [sic] Palace," read the dispatch to Hoover.

"JAY SARNO and NATE JACOBSON, owners of record, had not made *any* financial investment [italics added]."[96] The FBI intelligence would have been shocking, particularly given the grand public narrative of Caesars Palace. "ZAROWITZ contacted ALO and SALERNO who came to Palm Springs," continued the FBI, "and … put in 'millions of dollars.'"[97] As to the level of "villainy," the report continued to state, "gambling at Palm Springs was only incidental."[98]

Sensed as the weakest link, Ruby Lazarus was issued an order of immunity. The evasive testimony of Ruby Lazarus before the grand jury, though, was determined false. Amid the ensuing trial for perjury, excerpts of the Lazarus testimony made the press. Questioned about discussions of gambling at the Palm Springs retreat, Ruby Lazarus offered, "No sir, except for the fact that Mr. Zarowitz was interested in Caesars Palace and the conversation might have led to Las Vegas, and that was all."[99]

A former U.S. Attorney, testifying at the Lazarus trial, left little margin as to what investigators knew. "[W]e had information that in Palm Springs, California … there was a meeting at a certain residence there," stated the agent, "which involved people who were reputedly very much up in the Mafia organized crime syndicate in this country."[100]

The "Mafia" characterization may have been narrow, but the context was crystallized. The meeting was a reunion of the Miami hoodlum list perfected, and once again Nevada gaming regulators were flat footed. Back home in Las Vegas, the tawdry subject of female companions might also have tarnished the presentation of Mrs. Zarowitz at Hadassah. A pall was certainly cast over the grandeur of Caesars Palace, and the public-facing Nevada-licensed "owners of record" would find the Department of Justice at their palace door. As Jay Sarno was coy for the Nevada Gaming Commission hearings, so too would the apparently nominal "owners" play their hand carefully going forward.

The recollections of partner Stanley Mallin then traced from the original nationwide capital drive of Nathan Jacobson, and potential investor Saul Silberman. "He was going to put in two hundred and fifty thousand dollars … if we would hire a certain guy to run the casino from the Sands," stated Mallin, "a guy named Jerry Zarowitz."[101] Stanley Mallin also invoked the narrow subject of the Mafia, perhaps conveniently. "We didn't know," Mallin added. "I particularly didn't know any of these ins and outs of the Mafia."[102]

Again, behind the public block from scrimmage by Jay Sarno, Jerome Zarowitz apparently handled the ball at Caesars. "He was under Tony Salerno," confirmed Stan Mallin. "A very bright guy this Zarowitz. After a while we found out that every month he was sending substantial amounts of money to New York, to the Mafia."[103] "We never heard of them," continued Mallin. "Well, we heard of the Mafia, but we never associated with them."[104]

Again, was the context of the "Mafia" conveniently narrowed? The public owners *were* associated with the national crime syndicate, a veritable extension of their core business model. That coalition of La Cosa Nostra, syndicate racketeers, and the Teamsters formed a treacherous synthesis of power and pressure. The background of their benefactors simply could not have been overlooked or ignored by the astute businessmen from Baltimore, Miami, and Atlanta.

The pressure of organized crime may have been plied directly against the obvious proclivities of Jay Sarno and Nathan Jacobson, namely their gambling habits. The hook of organized crime for Stanley Mallin was less clear, save perhaps for his own attachment to Sarno. One account of Jay Sarno did not mince words. "FBI memos asserted, Jay Sarno, the ostensible boss at Caesar's [*sic*] Palace," wrote Steven Brill, "was a front."[105]

With intensified scrutiny from the Department of Justice, the pressure was then on Nathan Jacobson, Jay Sarno, Stanley Mallin, and Harry Lewis to peddle Caesar's own Palace of Pleasure. "So the Justice Department, according to our lawyer, said, 'We've got to get out of it,'" said Mallin. "You guys are going to jail."[106]

***

While the Justice Department focused on Caesars Palace, the board of Desert Palace, Inc. announced its first shakeup of corporate management. Notably, Nathan Jacobson of Baltimore would step down as president in favor of William S. Weinberger of Cleveland. Bill Weinberger, an original Caesars Palace investor, was announced to the press on June 23, 1968.[107] "Billy Weinberger had a restaurant in Cleveland ... a real high class restaurant," recalled a former Caesars Palace employee, also from Cleveland. "A lot of the mob used to hang out there."[108]

As the Desert Palace board voted in William S. Weinberger, they also named other officers. Jay Sarno continued at the Palace as vice president and executive manager. Stanley Mallin remained as a vice president. Harry Wald, active during the Caesars construction project, was named as vice president and corporate secretary. Jerry Gordon, formerly of Sam Cohen's Flamingo, was named as vice president and director of hotel operations. Finally, in the midst of the federal investigations, Jerome Zarowitz was confirmed as executive vice president.[109] It is instructive that, of those named to executive positions, Jerome Zarowitz was the only casino officer *not* licensed by Nevada regulators as an owner-of-record or key employee of Caesars Palace.

Two weeks after the appointment of William S. Weinberger, the new president was called to quell rumors of a pending sale. "No deal is pending with Walter Kidde Co., Inc."[110] Sale rumors involving Walter Kidde continued to circulate for two months, at which point APL Corporation, a plastic bottle manufacturer, entered the public discourse. "We've taken it off the market," announced Jay Sarno. "There has not been a formal offer offer ... nothing in writing."[111] At the same time, Caesars Palace doubled down, acquiring the land upon which the resort was built, a purchase from Kirk Kerkorian for a reported $5 million. "Caesars management has announced plans," continued the report, "to expand the facility into a $100 million 'recreation complex.'"[112]

By year's end, Harold Butler of Denny's jumped in, offering a reported $101 million in stock for Caesars Palace, including the land package.[113] Two weeks later, though, the negotiations with Denny's were terminated.[114] Purchase explorations were also conducted with Aero-Chatillon Corp. and Vernitron Corp., both manufacturing concerns.[115] At that point, one might sense Meyer Lansky in the Miami background, vetting the mettle of the various national players while, in Las Vegas, Caesars

Six lanes of Las Vegas Boulevard—the world-famous Las Vegas Strip—curve along their northerly path toward downtown Las Vegas. The towering signage of the newly opened Caesars Palace hotel-casino resort is at lower left of the image. The Castaways Casino is visible beyond the Caesars Palace property. Howard Hughes acquired the Castaways operation in 1967. Beyond the Caesars Palace sign are Shell, Standard, and Mobil gas stations. The three stations were still in place when the circuit of the Caesars Palace Grand Prix was developed in 1981. Directly across the Strip from Caesars Palace is the Capri Motel. The Capri property was acquired in the 1970s by Ralph Engelstad. Engelstad was also a developer of Las Vegas Motor Speedway in the 1990s (author's collection).

Palace tested the patience of the Department of Justice. Notably, five months after the termination of the Denny's deal with Caesars Palace, Harold Butler and Denny's purchased a large block of Parvin-Dohrmann stock, then owners of the Stardust hotel-casino and Stardust International Raceway.

Finally, after a tense weekend turn of investment speculation, a sale proposal was confirmed. "In the announcement by Clifford Perlman of Lum's and William S. Weinberger of Caesars Palace," came the news from Miami, "it was disclosed the contract is contingent on the hotel-casino reporting minimum pre-tax earnings of $5.8 million for the fiscal year ended April 30."[116] Clifford Perlman further confirmed that Lum's was committed to an all-cash purchase and placed $2 million in escrow to secure the contract. "Perlman … said it was buying Caesars Palace because the company," continued the Miami report, "has considered entering into the field of recreation and leisure-time activities."[117]

"This is our first step in that direction," confirmed Clifford Perlman.[118] "We intend to keep the present Caesar's [*sic*] Palace management," added Perlman, "which has made this one of the world's most famous hotel-casinos."[119] Clifford Perlman's comment was certain to please the old guard, as well as the hidden investors among the national organized crime syndicate—allegedly.

On the surface, the announcements further calmed the concerns of the federal government and of Nevada regulators about the basement rooms and the balance sheet of Caesars Palace. The acquisition by Clifford and Stuart Perlman, though, would eventually expand the scope of investigations as never before, perhaps unlike any Las Vegas resort had ever experienced. Clifford and Stuart Perlman—as well as their own unsavory connections—later drew the scrutiny of New Jersey regulators into their Nevada operations. Nonetheless, with the land package in the Caesars portfolio, the path to the Caesars Palace Grand Prix was now cleared. In 1981, Bernie Ecclestone and Clifford Perlman then consummated the Grand Prix, their own *great prize*.

It was said of Bernie Ecclestone early in 1982 that the Formula One *supremo* was "behaving like a Mafia Don, spreading the message that anyone who got the better of him was 'dead' while schemers were destined to become 'history.'"[120]

Five years earlier, it was stated of Clifford Perlman with attendant aplomb, "Clifford Perlman, Mr. Lansky owns lock, stock, and barrel." "He put him in business," read the transcript from the secret tape. "Do you think that Cliff goes to the fuckin' bathroom without talking to Malnik?"[121]

The threads of Grand Prix, of Caesars Palace, and of organized crime would now draw even and they would draw near. Further, their parallel paths would soon be overlain on the great and glorious battlefield of a mighty new Caesar.

IV

Traditions and Transitions

*Watkins Glen Faces New Challenges
and the Empire Has a New Caesar*

Indeed, it is a strange disposed time. (*Julius Caesar* 1.3.33)

The 1969 United States Grand Prix at Watkins Glen, New York, was the 10th anniversary of the inaugural American Formula One event in Sebring, Florida. After a one-off at Sebring in 1959 promoter Alec Ullmann decamped to Riverside, California, for another one-and-done United States edition of the pinnacle of motorsport. Eight subsequent Grand Prix events were conducted at Watkins Glen, the top of the podium in every single year taken by a driver from the United Kingdom. In his only Formula One triumph, Innes Ireland won the 1961 U.S. Grand Prix. Jimmy Clark followed in 1962 and then took back-to-back wins in 1966 and 1967. Graham Hill, though, was the first three-time winner, taking three straight from 1963 to 1965, the same year that scenes for the movie *Grand Prix* were shot on location. Finally, Jackie Stewart—knighted by the Empire in 2001—won the 1968 U.S. Grand Prix in dominant fashion. *Sir* Jackie Stewart it is then.

History also records that, when Graham Hill of Britain wasn't winning the U.S. Grand Prix at Watkins Glen, he was likely second. Indeed, Graham Hill also logged three fine runner-up finishes in the U.S. Grand Prix. John Surtees of England claimed second place in 1964. Americans then started to populate the next tier, Dan Gurney with second-place finishes in 1961 and 1965, Richie Ginther second in 1963. The only driver to break the U.S. versus UK deadlock on the top two tiers through 1968 was Jochen Rindt of Austria, second place in a Cooper-Climax at the 1966 U.S. Grand Prix in only his second year of Formula One competition. In fact, Rindt's finish behind Jimmy Clark at the 1966 U.S. Grand Prix was the high watermark of his last three seasons. Three seasons in at Cooper, Jochen Rindt was a strong third in points in 1966 but otherwise logged two years in 13th, no relief from superstition in a sport with such a razor-thin margin between chance and championship.

Moving to Jack Brabham's Motor Racing Developments concern for 1968, Jochen Rindt followed the lead of Bernie Ecclestone, his appointed personal advisor. Under the Brabham umbrella, it was a lost season of only two points-paying finishes and a string of 10 retirements. Steered once again by Bernie Ecclestone, Jochen Rindt departed Brabham to join Colin Chapman at Team Lotus. Chapman's Lotus machines powered Jimmy Clark to his three wins at Watkins Glen as well as Graham Hill's second-place finishes in 1967 and 1968. Lotus racers were thus proven winners of both races and championships. They were lightweight pieces of iron and aerodynamically advanced as well. Convergence of the Lotus around those two axes could loom lethal. Lotus racers were indeed both fast and fragile.

Aerodynamics and adhesion were also the most visible manifestations of Formula One development in the 1960s. From 1961 to 1968, tire width increased by a factor of three, while the body profile evolved from that of a World War II drop tank to that of a low-slung jet fighter fuselage. Further, although the Formula One machine of 1961 was designed to slip though the oncoming wall of air, there were no spoilers, foils, or wings of any type affixed to the vehicle. By 1968, the entire Formula One field was experimenting with mounted airflow-management devices at both ends of the racer, all the better to plant the fully-maximized rubber width to the racing surface.

Watkins Glen in upstate New York, too, had evolved. In 1961, race day attendance was reported at 50,000. It was nearly double the previous attendance record for a Watkins Glen race event. Moreover, it was a huge number for such a sparsely-populated hamlet; in 2010 the population of Watkins Glen was still less than 2,000. By 1968, race attendance had nearly doubled again. A throng of 93,000 race fans, hangers-on, and party-goers pushed through the gates and over the fences to watch Mario Andretti make his Formula One debut. Less than 10 years into its own existence, the U.S. Grand Prix was being overtaken by *festivalization*, "the audience's desire to be plunged into a multi-day spectacular."[1]

Even before the 1969 Woodstock festival in nearby Bethel, New York, motorsports pundit Bob Cochnar pondered the crowd-spectacle of Watkins Glen. "At Watkins Glen ... outhouse burning is a popular sport," mused Cochnar. "All-night parties in the in-field areas run a close second."[2] "Lodging is practically unavailable," continued the piece. "Young sports invade the infield with tents, trailers, and sleeping bags."[3] Cochnar caustically dubbed the Watkins Glen infield as the "Animal Farm," a nod to George Orwell's metaphoric short wherein it all goes somewhat badly for the humans. Others simply termed it "The Bog."

For Watkins Glen, the issues of available lodging and crowd control proved pervasive over the next decade, so much so that the local constabulary posted a field court at the U.S. Grand Prix, reportedly adjudicating hundreds of onsite offenses from the sod. Despite the myriad efforts of the Watkins Glen Grand Prix Corporation to develop manageable workarounds, the underlying issues—as well as finances—foretold the end. Further, the issues of Watkins Glen created opportunities elsewhere, at Long Beach, California, and—eventually—Caesars Palace in Las Vegas.

***

"The first $200,000 purse in the history of road racing," read the deck of the local *Star-Gazette*, "will be awarded at the Formula 1 Grand Prix of the United States at Watkins Glen Sunday."[4] The "road racing" qualifier was noteworthy. Indeed, this was not Indy money. With the most recent Indianapolis 500 as contrast, Mario Andretti collected a reported $206,000 for his win at the 1969 Indianapolis 500, from a total purse of $800,000. The Watkins Glen purse, however, was a dramatic increase from

1968, truly the richest on the international Formula One tour. Jackie Stewart collected a cool $20,000 for his win of the 1968 event, then a record for a Formula One payday. The 1969 winner would then place his palms around the proverbial plum, $50,000 on offer for the first to the flag.

"The $50,000 reserved for the winner," announced Cameron Argetsinger, executive director of the Watkins Glen Grand Prix Corporation, "should create the keenest competition among drivers, mechanics, and team managers of any road race ever staged."[5] Team managers were intensely interested in the potential windfall, none more so than Colin Chapman. Chapman's Lotus effort paired reigning world champion Graham Hill with the rising Jochen Rindt. The Team Lotus duo was joined by Mario Andretti, at that point winner of the richest purse in motorsports history, the 1969 Indianapolis 500 victory with Andy Granatelli.

Jochen Rindt showed the way in qualifying, as he had already done four times in 1969. Rindt's pole of 1:03.62 took well over a second out of Mario Andretti's 1968 mark. Denny Hulme followed second on the grid in his McLaren, mere hundredths behind. Jackie Stewart slotted third in the Matra-Ford. Jackie Stewart, however, had already clinched the 1969 championship for the Ken Tyrell–led team. Rindt teammate Graham Hill started fourth. Berthed in eight through 10th at the start were the Brabhams of Jacky Ickx, Piers Courage, and Jack Brabham. Mario Andretti was set to roll off 13th.

With the urging of Bernie Ecclestone, Jochen Rindt (#2) joined Colin Chapman's Lotus team for the 1969 Formula One season. Rindt perished in a Lotus the following year. Jochen Rindt took pole and the win of the 1969 U.S. Grand Prix at Watkins Glen, New York. Colin Chapman stands to the right of the race car. Motorsports journalist and broadcaster Chris Economaki is to the right of Chapman, facing slightly away. Others are not identified (courtesy International Motor Racing Research Center).

Jochen Rindt led from pole chased by Jackie Stewart, while Denny Hulme fell back. Rindt and Stewart then pulled away from the field, while Jochen Rindt tried to shut out the distractions of a season amiss. The Lotus of Rindt and the Matra of Stewart would then duel, often side-by-side, through the autumn of upstate New York. Rindt focused further as Stewart started to slow at the quarter-mark, his wounded Matra losing oil pressure. By the one-third mark, the fate of Jackie Stewart's race was sealed, retired to the pits with an engine failure.

Jochen Rindt then raced on, building his lead over the field, "as he lowered the single lap record several times."[6] The Brabham machines of Courage, Ickx, and Brabham then closed ranks, jostling with each other for some 40 laps before Jacky Ickx retired on lap 77. When Jack Brabham later pitted for fuel, the battle of the Brabham brand went to Piers Courage.

Five years into his Formula One career, Jochen Rindt would not be denied. The accumulated inventory of engine failures, squandered qualifying efforts, and lost opportunities stowed, Jochen Rindt crossed the finish line after 108 laps of the 1969 U.S. Grand Prix as a first-time Formula One winner. Piers Courage trailed over 40 seconds in arrears. So compelling was Rindt's performance that the third-place competitor was two laps down, John Surtees completing the podium in a BRM.

Sadly, though, Jochen Rindt's Lotus teammate Graham Hill suffered a horrific crash on lap 90, an end-over-end accident at over 100 mph. Spun-off and stalled on lap 88, the world champion push-started his car and rejoined somewhat askance. "When Graham got back in," remarked Hill's wife Bette, "he didn't have time to fasten his seat belt."[7] Two laps later, a tire let go on the Lotus, launching Graham Hill out of control. "When the car went over Graham held on as long as he could," continued Mrs. Hill, "Then when he saw a good chance to get out he let go."[8] The reigning Formula One champion suffered severe injuries to both legs in the accident, injuries that compromised his career going forward.

Playing to a crowd of over 100,000, the victory stand was swarmed, "by autograph-seekers, well-wishers, and adoring female fans."[9] "You said you wanted a victory," quipped Chris Economaki from the microphone, "now you'll have to pay the price."[10] Jochen Rindt could also well afford it, his $50,000 payday the richest in Formula One history. The combination of America and record-setting cash also appealed to his personal manager, Bernie Ecclestone. Further, Rindt's win and Hill's misfortune created its own opportunity. "Ecclestone knew that this was the moment," wrote Tom Bower, "to negotiate Rindt's new contract with Chapman."[11]

***

Two weeks after the 1969 U.S. Grand Prix, news from Florida once again took aim at Meyer Lansky. In a series of lawsuits filed by the Florida Attorney General, state government attempted to bring pressure on Lansky's apparent stranglehold on Miami Beach lodging properties. "Mr. Lansky was been widely heralded as the financial wizard of organized crime," blasted AG Earl Faircloth. "He is a genius at infiltrating legitimate business."[12] It was a flattering description of the underworld supreme, one that Bernie Ecclestone might have admired.

Two days later, however, Meyer Lansky saw his name splashed on the front page of national dailies from coast to coast. "Mobster's Deal Paid for Douglas" ran one headline.[13] From coast to coast, such was also the common theme. The emerging national scandal linked Meyer Lansky, Las Vegas casino owner Albert Parvin, and U.S. Supreme Court Justice William O. Douglas. Justice Douglas was disclosed as the paid president of the Albert Parvin Foundation. The Parvin foundation, however, was underwritten by the first mortgage on the Flamingo Hotel & Casino. The Flamingo sale was facilitated in 1960 by Meyer Lansky between seller—and Lansky associate—Albert Parvin, to buyers—and Lansky associates—Sam Cohen, Morris Lansburgh, and Daniel Lifter, all of Miami. It was a transaction for which Meyer Lansky then received a $200,000 fee. Notably, the Albert Parvin Foundation held as its major asset a block in the racketeered Parvin-Dohrmann Corporation, owners of the Stardust Hotel and Stardust International Raceway.

In 1969, the name Meyer Lansky was connected with U.S. Supreme Court Justice William Douglas. While sitting on the bench, Justice Douglas was the paid president of the Albert Parvin Foundation. The primary asset of the Parvin Foundation, however, was the mortgage on the Flamingo hotel-casino. Meyer Lansky received a $200,000 finder's fee for the sale of the Flamingo Hotel & Casino in Las Vegas from Albert Parvin to Sam Cohen, Morris Lansburgh, and Daniel Lifter of Miami. The four principals in the Flamingo transaction were all associated with Lansky. In 1969, the Parvin-Dohrmann Corporation was the owner of Stardust International Raceway. Sam Cohen was later involved in Florida property development with Alvin Malnik and Clifford Perlman of Caesars Palace (Library of Congress).

Criminal attorney Alvin Malnik found himself in the news as well, indicted by a federal grand jury for filing false tax returns in 1962 and 1963. As with Jerome Zarowitz and Elliott Paul Price before the Nevada Gaming Commission, it was the closest the federal government would ever get to Alvin Malnik. With a case ostensibly derived from the 1963 wiretaps in Malnik's Miami law office, federal prosecutors put on a case riddled with compromised and collateral information that was unconvincing to the court. "The jury," reported the *Miami News* on March 26, 1970, "found Alvin Malnik not guilty of falsifying his 1962 income tax report."[14] Two weeks later, the presiding judge issued a directed acquittal for the 1963 charge.

News surrounding the trial, however, illuminated the various business ventures of Alvin Malnik. One report named Malnik as "mortgagor for a development known as the Sky Lake Country Club,"[15] a property developed with a loan from the Teamsters Central States Pension Fund. Malnik was also named as the owner of the Old Forge Restaurant in Miami. According to son Mark "Shareef" Malnik, ownership was transferred from father to son 30 years later.[16]

Another report named some of the dignitary residents of the Canongate

Apartments immediately adjacent to Sky Lake; Frank Fitzsimmons—named by Jimmy Hoffa to lead the Teamsters during Hoffa's stint in federal prison, Jackie Presser—Teamsters boss in Ohio, Allen Dorfman—insurance administrator of the pension fund, and the notorious Paul "Red" Dorfman—stepfather of Allen.[17] Further, the Canongate apartment tower was constructed by Calvin Kovens. Finally, Alvin Malnik's partner in the Sky Lake Country Club was Sam Cohen. Sky Lake was an apparently tight, cozy community.

While Meyer Lansky and Alvin Malnik garnered their share of newsprint, the sale of Caesars Palace from the Jay Sarno group to Lum's Inc. proceeded through the investigative processes of the intrepid Nevada gambling regulators. The investigation, however, was nearly over before it started.

"The Nevada Gaming Control Board … asked for a fine of up to $100,000 against a Las Vegas Strip hotel," it was reported, "that hosted 12 men 'associated with members of organized crime in the Kansas City area.'"[18] The Las Vegas Strip hotel at issue was, of course, Caesars Palace. The bombshell announcement also hit less than six weeks after the purchase announcement by Clifford Perlman and William S. Weinberger. "They were wined and dined and given free rooms," read the *Independent* from Long Beach, California, "on order of Jay Sarno, managing director and vice president of Caesars."[19] News reports crafted a troubling mention of Sarno. It was also not the last time that the major Long Beach daily weighed in directly on the public-facing front man of Caesars Palace.

The Lum's, Inc. corporation of Clifford Perlman (pictured here) and brother Stuart Perlman acquired Caesars Palace in 1969 from the ownership group of Jay Sarno, Nathan Jacobson, and Stanley Mallin. The Caesar-reign of Clifford Perlman would be highly controversial and contentious throughout its history. Investigations by the SEC and DOJ were underscored by the New Jersey Casino Control Commission. The multiple investigations were also punctuated by Perlman's personage being identified on the infamous Abscam tapes, "Mr. Lansky owns [Perlman] lock, stock, and barrel" (Greene, *Sting Man*, 221). Clifford Perlman would preside over the Caesars Palace Grand Prix just two years after the Abscam recordings (Bruce Aguilera collection).

Harry Wald was tied in as well. Wald was the signer of Caesars Palace letters carried by Carl Caruso of Kansas City, "identified … as the casino's representative there for forming junkets."[20] Carl Caruso, however was later named by the FBI as a carrier of skimmed funds from Las Vegas casinos to the Kansas City mob.[21] Further, eight of the 12 men hosted by Sarno and Wald were subpoenaed just three months earlier by a Miami grand jury "investigating a meeting reportedly held to select a successor to Cosa Nostra chief Vito Genovese."[22] That meeting, held after Vito Genovese died in prison early in 1969, was inevitably dubbed an "Apalachin." Also subpoenaed by the same Miami Grand jury were Meyer Lansky and Vincent Alo.[23] Especially notable among those hosted by Jay Sarno and Harry Wald at Caesars was Anthony Civella, nephew of Nicholas Civella, then head of the Kansas City mob.[24]

Two months after Nevada regulators initiated the disciplinary action against Caesars Palace, the charges involving the Kansas City hoodlums were inexplicably dropped.[25] One day later, Clifford and Stuart Perlman received their long-awaited news. "The Nevada Gaming Control Board," read the Nevada report, "gave preliminary approval … to Lum's Inc. of Florida to buy the Caesars Palace hotel-casino on the Las Vegas Strip."[26]

One week later, the Nevada Gaming Commission moved forward with final approval of the recommendation by the investigative board. "The conditions include immediate licensing of officers and casino personnel," reported Nevada press, "who are not licensed to be active in Nevada gaming."[27] The conditions also pointed up the transition of Caesars Palace from the privately held Desert Palace, Inc. to the publicly traded Lum's Inc. Clifford Perlman and Stuart Perlman thus submitted to the Nevada Gaming Control Board for licensing investigations. Lum's directors Jay Leshaw and William McElnea submitted their applications as well. Melvin Chasen, a vice president and director of Lum's, would also be active in Caesars gambling operations. "We intend to continue this operation as well," remarked Chasen of the approval, "and as profitably as in the past."[28]

Looking back, though, Melvin Chasen's remarks may have betrayed a tell. To wit—apparently lost in the hullabaloo of the purchase—was that Jerome Zarowitz and Elliott Paul Price were still on the Caesars Palace premises of Clifford Perlman and Lum's. Indeed, as the centurions proclaimed the battlefield triumph of the new Caesar, it was the clarion call of Jerome Zarowitz that was still ringing amid the 1981 Caesars Palace Grand Prix.

***

Jackie Stewart's failure to finish the 1969 U.S. Grand Prix did not deter his lock on the World Drivers Championship. With six race wins and a total of 69 points, Stewart claimed the 1969 Formula One crown with a huge margin over his closest competitor, Jacky Ickx driving for Jack Brabham. Bruce McLaren was then third in the 1969 championship in his works McLaren racer. When Jochen Rindt won the U.S. Grand Prix at Watkins Glen, he was elevated to fourth in the championship standings, a significant improvement over three seasons outside the top 10.

After the 1969 U.S. Grand Prix at Watkins Glen wrapped, several of the Formula One competitors resumed play in the North American Can-Am series. Bruce McLaren, Denny Hulme, Chris Amon, Mario Andretti, Jackie Oliver and Jo Siffert all traveled cross-country to contest the Los Angeles Times Grand Prix at Riverside International Raceway, an event won by Hulme. Jack Brabham then joined the Can-Am tour as the series doubled back to Texas for the finale of the 1969 season.

The Texas round of the Can-Am series was delegated from the shuttered Stardust International Raceway in Las Vegas, after the Parvin Dohrmann Corporation acquired the Las Vegas racing property. Bruce McLaren in his high-winged McLaren M8B was victorious in the Can-Am closer, the Texas International Grand Prix, at the newly opened Texas International Speedway. Bruce McLaren also won the 1969 Can-Am championship over Denny Hulme. It would be the last championship, however, for the 32-year-old designer, racer, and constructor from New Zealand.

Notably absent from the 1969 Can-Am results, however, was Jochen Rindt. Rather, Rindt and manager Bernie Ecclestone were consumed with their prospects for 1970 at the pinnacle of motorsport. Their combined goal was the singular pursuit of the Formula One world championship. "For Jochen and Bernie the 1970 Formula 1 racing season began," wrote an Ecclestone biographer, "with the conviction that the World Championship would soon be theirs."[29]

As the 1970 racing season opened, though, the ownership interests of Texas International Speedway, Riverside International Raceway, and Stardust International Raceway were somewhat intertwined, certainly behind the veil. Texas International Speedway was opened by controversial Michigan developer Lawrence Lopatin. The Texas facility was constructed by Leo Margolian, former general manager of Stardust Raceway as well as the original construction manager of the Las Vegas motorsports property. Lopatin also held a significant stake in Riverside International Raceway, under umbrella of his publicly-traded parent American Raceways, Inc.

As the fortunes of Lawrence Lopatin turned downward in early 1970, he sought an institutional bridge from Morris Karp of First National Realty. Morris Karp, in turn, was connected with investor Philip Levin of Transnation, one of the several extremely interesting investors in the Parvin-Dohrmann Corporation, then owners of the Stardust hotel-casino and Stardust International Raceway. Notably, Stardust International Raceway was originally developed by Cleveland racketeer Moe Dalitz and sold in 1969 to the Parvin-Dohrmann Corporation as part of the Stardust hotel package.

In 1970, the Illinois Bureau of Investigation placed Philip Levin of Transnation in meetings at the infamous Acapulco Towers in Mexico, along with Moe Dalitz, notorious criminal attorney Sidney Korshak, and Dean Shendal, a licensed owner-employee of Caesars Palace. At Caesars Palace, Shendal notably reported to Jerome Zarowitz.[30] The presiding deity of the Acapulco Towers meetings, though, was Meyer Lansky. Spirited off the grid from Acapulco to Mexico City, "the Mafia chieftain flew openly from there to his home in Miami."[31] Described as "a sunny place for shady people,"[32] the Acapulco Towers meetings might thus appear to involve the acreage and development potential of at least three very prominent motorsports complexes, Texas, Stardust, and Riverside.

From Riverside International Raceway and Roy G. Lewis, to Stardust International Raceway and Moe Dalitz, to Texas International Speedway and Lawrence Lopatin, all of them were perhaps placeholder entries in the intricate playbook of Meyer Lansky. From Apalachin to Acapulco—allegedly.

✳✳✳

The 1970 Formula One season for Jochen Rindt and manager Bernie Ecclestone did not start where the 1969 season ended, victorious in the penultimate round at Watkins Glen. Rather, it started where the 1969 season *began*, out of the points with a dreaded 13th place finish at the South African Grand Prix. Perhaps worse, the 1970 South African Grand Prix was won by 44-year-old Jack Brabham, the team that Ecclestone had advised Rindt against joining for the 1969 campaign.

Jochen Rindt's third-place starting position on the grid of the following Spanish Grand Prix was then squandered with an ignition failure. Rindt, however, was reportedly also disappointed with the form of Colin Chapman's new mount for the 1970 season. Further, the Spanish round was won by world champion Jackie Stewart, driving an interim March-Ford for Ken Tyrell, pending development of Tyrell's eponymous racer. Bruce McLaren followed Stewart into second while Mario Andretti came third in another March. Jochen Rindt and Bernie Ecclestone then set their sights on the glamorous Monaco Grand Prix, set in the principality for May 10, 1970.

Two weeks before the Monaco round, however, a small entry in the California press would portend a new foothold in American Formula One history. Further, this next step was far west of Watkins Glen in update New York. "Sears Point Raceway will officially present its application," read the deck on April 24, 1970, "for a world championship grand prix race."[33] The proposed race in the Sonoma, California, wine country would be "a pot of gold worth $200,000 for the Sonoma road course."[34]

The Sears Point proposal was presented to ACCUS, the Automobile Competition Committee of the Unites States. ACCUS, with a board comprised of representatives from USAC, SCCA, NASCAR, and the NHRA, was the American delegation to the FIA, the Fédération Internationale de l'Automobile. FIA was also the sanctioning body of Formula One.

The Sears Point announcement then drew even with a competing overture from Ontario Motor Speedway, a new California motorsports super-complex scheduled to open in August of 1970. The Ontario proposal, spearheaded by the SCCA, then won out in the ACCUS board room in New York, to be formally considered, in turn, by the FIA. Ontario Motor Speedway and the SCCA also tied their own knot. "David B. Lockton, president … announced that OMS and SCCA," read another California report, "had entered into a five-year agreement for SCCA sanction of an unprecedented second U.S. Grand Prix."[35]

A second round of Formula One in a single country was extraordinary. Further, a decade had passed since Formula One had last visited California for the 1960 round at Riverside. "It was a financial fiasco," wrote Shav Glick of the 1960 American Grand Prix, "and never returned West."[36] The new Ontario round would also be scheduled in the early spring, "in March or April each year, beginning in 1971."[37]

Amid the new Formula One proposals, Cameron Argetsinger departed the Watkins Glen Grand Prix Corporation, replaced as executive director by Malcolm Currie. Preparing his exit, Cameron Argetsinger also announced an increase in the purse for the 1970 Watkins Glen Grand Prix, a new record of $250,000. "Watkins Glen feels an intense obligation to the growth of Formula One racing," Argetsinger emphasized. "The Glen has pioneered and will continue to innovate in staging the ultimate drama of pure road racing for the American public."[38] The parting comment by Cameron Argetsinger may have been a jab at Ontario's infield road course, circled by its massive Indy-style oval. Deflecting the punch, Ontario Motor Speedway stepped up with its own reported $250,000 match of the Watkins Glen purse.

In a two-week turn, the Sears Point and Ontario promoters—as well as their USAC and SCCA counterparts—had stolen thunder from the build-up to the Monaco Grand Prix, the most storied Formula One event of the season. The Formula One regulars, however, would not be distracted. American audiences, too, would revel at the spectacle of the 1970 Monaco event.

Qualified eighth at Monaco in a 1969 Lotus, Jochen Rindt had a marginal view of Jackie Stewart and Chris Amon on the all-March front row. Rindt's prospects for success were considered marginal as well. Stewart led out until the one-third mark when his March-Ford slowed and pitted with engine issues. Jack Brabham than took over the lead from his fourth qualifying position, followed by Chris Amon, Denny Hulme, and Jochen Rindt. Hulme then slowed and moved Rindt to third. Chris Amon retired at lap 62, moving Jochen Rindt and the year-old Lotus up to second. Rindt, though, trailed Jack Brabham by nearly 10 seconds. Further, the Monaco street circuit was notoriously difficult on which to make a pass.

Jochen Rindt, however, closed the gap to Jack Brabham to less than one second as the laps wound down. On the last turn of the last lap, reportedly navigating a lapped car, Jack Brabham slipped off and into the protective barriers. Jochen Rindt and the aging Lotus moved smoothly past Jack Brabham to take the lead and win the 1970 Monaco Grand Prix. Jack Brabham then recovered his machine from the run-off and soldiered through for second place.

"It was," wrote an author of Rindt, "one of the most outstanding drives of his career."[39] The Monaco win moved Jochen Rindt to third in the championship standings behind Jack Brabham and Jackie Stewart. The Team Lotus ship of Colin Chapman was righted as well. "The Monaco Grand Prix was a thriller down to the wire," wrote a California pundit, "and points out the reason why some smart race drivers never give up."[40] Bernie Ecclestone was further buoyed, while he also paid rapt attention to the team business model of Chapman.

On May 11, 1970, the Monday after the Monaco Grand Prix, Sears Point Raceway in Sonoma, California, was closed. The Formula One challenger of just the month before was a financial casualty, "reported losses coming to $300,000 since its opening."[41] After the loss of the USAC-backed Formula One effort, Sears Point had implemented cost savings measures, "staff reductions, stop in track construction, and attempt to finish 1970 on an austerity program."[42] Rather, the track was shuttered with immediate effect.

Two weeks later, the news in the Formula One paddock turned from track closure to tragedy. Bruce McLaren was killed on June 2, 1970, in England while testing the McLaren team's new machine for the 1970 Can-Am season. Three weeks later at the Dutch Grand Prix, Piers Courage died in a fiery crash while driving a new De Tomaso-Ford for Frank Williams. Jochen Rindt won the Dutch Grand Prix by 30 seconds over Jackie Stewart. Rindt also moved to second place in the Formula One points standings. Jochen Rindt, however, was subdued. "He would never again feel the same desperate enthusiasm for motor racing."[43]

Formula One, the pinnacle of motorsport, moved on in mourning to the next round of the championship, just as it had with 30 fatalities before. American prospects for a second U.S. Grand Prix in the western states simply moved on in a muddle.

***

On the same day that Sears Point announced its failed Formula One bid, news also broke in Las Vegas. Jerome Zarowitz, embattled executive vice president of Caesars Palace, was on the move. Zarowitz would take his leave of Caesars Palace and head off to California, "off to a life of ease in a new Palm Springs pad."[44] Jerome Zarowitz was to be replaced at Caesars Palace by Sanford Waterman, formerly of Frank Sinatra's Cal-Neva Lodge at Lake Tahoe.

"Zarowitz, one of the most popular gaming figures in the history of this town," wrote Ralph Pearl in the Las Vegas Sun, "will be sorely missed because of his gaming know-how."[45] It was an interesting send-off from Pearl, the veteran Las Vegas entertainment editor. The agents of the FBI, NYPD, Miami Mayor High, and that federal grand jury in Terre Haute would have taken issue with Zarowitz's public popularity. They would nod in agreement, however, with the gambling genius of the departing Caesars Palace executive.

The notorious Frank "Lefty" Rosenthal was also a Jerome Zarowitz fan. "Jerry Z was the top gun at the Palace, a solid operator, a great sports handicapper, brilliant," later wrote Rosenthal, "and very influential through the gaming industry."[46] The FBI, certainly no fan of Frank Rosenthal, kept an eye on the movements of both Zarowitz and Rosenthal in Miami before "Jerry Z" moved west to Las Vegas. The FBI also arrested Frank Rosenthal in Miami in late 1965 during a gambling sting, another of the countless national investigations involving "interstate transmission of gambling information."[47] That investigation also tied in Jerome Zarowitz and Elliott Paul Price, both as line customers of the gambling information allegedly provided by Rosenthal. Further, the Miami investigation appeared to be ignored by the Nevada Gaming Commission as they pondered the employment of Zarowitz and Price in 1966 at Caesars Palace.

The departure of Jerome Zarowitz did, however, appear to tidy up the conditions of the Nevada Gaming Commission upon Clifford Perlman and Lum's Inc., specifically, "immediate licensing of officers and casino personnel."[48] Sanford Waterman was previously licensed by the Nevada Gaming Commission at Sinatra's Cal-Neva Lodge. Waterman was also licensed with a minority interest at the Sands hotel-casino owned by Sam Cohen and later, Kirk Kerkorian. Sanford Waterman, however, was at the Sands in the same period that the FBI reported the hidden involvement of Jerome Zarowitz, reportedly posted to oversee the concealed interests of Anthony Salerno at the Sands.

The announcement of Jerome Zarowitz's departure from Caesars Palace came nearly one year-to-the-day after Clifford Perlman and William Weinberger announced the purchase of the resort, over 8 months after the Nevada Gaming Commission approved the purchase and stipulated its conditions. It should also be instructive that Sanford Waterman was posted to Caesars Palace at the *request* of Jerome Zarowitz.[49]

As Clifford Perlman settled into his new Caesars Palace role in 1970, the financial results of the purchase settlement period came into view. From May 1, 1969, to September 30, 1969, Caesars Palace posted a pre-tax loss of $932,266. For the same period in the year prior to the purchase, Caesars Palace booked a pre-tax *profit* of $2,230,014, over a $3 million swing in the waning months of Jerome Zarowitz's stewardship. "Losses during the settlement period were due to patron win at the baccarat tables," Zarowitz reportedly explained to Clifford Perlman, "and, generally, to the fortunes of gaming."[50]

According to New Jersey gambling regulators, Clifford Perlman accepted the explanation without inquiry, while Jerome Zarowitz was rewarded with the farewell gift of a complimentary suite and a secure lockbox. Seven years later, Alvin Malnik appeared to illuminate the parting play of Jerome Zarowitz at Caesars Palace. "Malnik talked on about his group's ability to make or break almost any casino," wrote author Robert W. Greene, "through control of key employees."[51] Greene's comment appears to describe Jerome Zarowitz with precision. Alvin Malnik then punctuated with authority. "Just like poor credit, we take a joint that's making ten million dollars a year," Alvin Malnik was recorded saying, "and turn it into a loser of ten million dollars a year."[52] The context of Alvin Malnik's comments was specific, Caesars Palace and the role of the Meyer Lansky–led national crime syndicate in Las Vegas resort gambling.

The vagaries and vice of Las Vegas gamblers notwithstanding, William D. Weinberger—son of William S. Weinberger—would take down the wildcard loss explanation of Jerome Zarowitz. "Putting on a race is a gamble, we know that. But nearly everything we do at Caesars Palace is a gamble," the younger Weinberger commented before the 1981 Caesars Palace Grand Prix. "Except the casino. That's where we know the outcome down to the last percentage point."[53]

* * *

The sport of Formula One picked up after the tragic losses of Bruce McLaren and Piers Courage, traveling some 1,500 miles south to the French Grand Prix two weeks later. Jacky Ickx took the French pole, now driving for the Scuderia Ferrari. Ickx was followed to the grid by Jean-Pierre Beltoise, Chris Amon, Jackie Stewart, and Jack Brabham. Jochen Rindt was qualified sixth, one place ahead of the grieving Denny Hulme, teammate of the departed Bruce McLaren.

Jochen Rindt then went on to take the French event over Chris Amon, his second triumph of the season. With Jack Brabham finishing third and Jackie Stewart nearly a lap down in ninth, Rindt also ascended to the top of the standings in the Formula One world drivers' championship, his first time in the rarified air atop the points standings.

Jochen Rindt repeated two weeks later at the British Grand Prix, this time with the pole position and a dominant 30-second lead over Jack Brabham. Denny Hulme was a competitive third in the McLaren. Jackie Stewart, though, dropped out just past halfway and was out of the points. Notably, Emerson Fittipaldi of Brazil joined the Formula One tour in Britain, finishing eighth, two positions behind the Lotus of Graham Hill. Fittipaldi would also figure as a team owner in the Caesars Palace Formula One events and as a competitor in the 1984 CART IndyCar edition.

Rindt than backed his British win with a victory at the German Grand Prix on August 2, 1970. Jacky Ickx was second in Germany over Denny Hulme. Notably, Emerson Fittipaldi was a strong fourth while teammate Graham Hill failed to finish. Championship contenders Jackie Stewart, Chris Amon, and Jack Brabham were well down the order, out of the points. Jochen Rindt thus extended his points total to a full two-race lead over Brabham.

The following Austrian Grand Prix—Jochen Rindt's home event—was another letdown for the Lotus driver. Starting from pole, Rindt was out on the 21st lap with an engine failure. Jacky Ickx and Clay Regazzoni placed one-two for the Scuderia Ferrari. Along with Rindt, Jack Brabham and Jackie Stewart were again out of the points-paying positions. The championship points order of Rindt, Brabham, and Stewart thus remained intact. Further, the championship points lead of Jochen Rindt would not be relinquished. The Austrian Grand Prix, however, was also the last Formula One start of Jochen Rindt's young career.

The 10th round of the 1970 Formula One season was held at Monza, Italy, on September 6, 1970. The 1970 Italian Grand Prix would not be well-remembered. During the Saturday qualifying session, Jochen Rindt went out in the Lotus 72, notably shorn of its rear wing for increased speed on the fast Monza circuit. As Rindt braked hard into the *Curva Parabolica*, the Lotus wiggled out of control and struck the end post of the Armco barrier system in a horrific crash. "He died," wrote Susan Watkins, "within fifteen to thirty seconds of the accident."[54]

Colin Chapman and Jackie Stewart both described the loss of their best friend. Bernie Ecclestone too lost his best friend, his business partner, his gambling consort, and his muse. "What happened has had a profound effect on me, my attitude, and my feelings for motor racing," Stewart wrote in his post-race diary, "perhaps forever."[55] As a throng gathered at the infield hospital to await word on Rindt's condition, the seconds ticked away on the timed qualifying session. "I knew there was nothing I could do to stop the crying," wrote a shaken Stewart, "so I went out."[56]

As with the passing of Bruce McLaren and Piers Courage earlier in 1970, Formula One regrouped and moved on. Jacky Ickx, who had come into contention after his win in Austria, followed with another win in Canada. Ickx then finished fourth in the U.S. Grand Prix at Watkins Glen as 120,000 fans watched Emerson Fittipaldi take his first Grand Prix victory. Jacky Ickx closed the 1970 Formula One season with a win in Mexico. Jochen Rindt, the beloved Austrian, however, became the only posthumous champion in the history of the sport, his 45-point total after the British round holding firm for the final five events. The fast-closing Jacky Ickx trailed with 40 points in the championship.

Bereft in his grief, Bernie Ecclestone now faced another crossroads in life and career. As with high-stakes gambling, though, high stakes motorsport was in Ecclestone's blood. A keen business admirer now of the Cooper works, Brabham's Motor Racing Developments, and Colin Chapman's Team Lotus, Bernie Ecclestone assembled his own strategic plan to conquer Formula One. "His vehicle would be Brabham," wrote Tom Bower, "the team that Rindt had abandoned."[57] Ecclestone would then spell the fates of the U.S. Grand Prix at Watkins Glen, the early efforts at a western states Grand Prix, and the Long Beach Grand Prix itself. His was a series

Emerson Fittipaldi won the October 4, 1970, U.S. Grand Prix at Watkins Glen in a Lotus-Ford for Colin Chapman. It was Fittipaldi's first season at the pinnacle of motorsport. Tragically, teammate Jochen Rindt was killed in a Lotus team machine just four weeks before at Monza, Italy. Emerson Fittipaldi's career took him to two world driving championships, 14 Formula One wins, and—in his rookie season of CART IndyCar competition—the Caesars Palace Grand Prix IV (courtesy International Motor Racing Research Center).

of high-stakes wagers, bold all-in gambits that Ecclestone would take all the way to Las Vegas, and to Clifford Perlman and William D. Weinberger in the underground board room of Caesars Palace.

***

The relative calm at Caesars Palace after the departure of Jerome Zarowitz to Palm Springs in June of 1970 was to be short-lived. The high-profile Zarowitz—despite being unlicensed—carried a lengthy reputation and cast a long shadow. Frank Rosenthal described Jerry Z as "the top gun at the Palace." With Sanford Waterman now in charge of dispensing—or *withholding*—casino credit, that calm was nearly pierced with a bang.

"Frank Sinatra stormed out of Caesars Palace Hotel-Casino," read the September 7, 1970, headline, "after a quarrel during a card game that ended when a casino executive pulled a gun."[58] In an argument reportedly involving credit in the baccarat room, Sanford Waterman drew down on a drunk, belligerent Sinatra. Sanford Waterman—on the job for four months at Caesars Palace—was packing, clearly the new "top gun at the Palace."

"The mob," one account quoted Sinatra, "will take care of you!"[59] Waterman was arrested for assault with a deadly weapon, although charges were later dropped when it became apparent that Frank Sinatra, the Chairman of the Board, had put his hands around Waterman's neck.

Frank Sinatra later offered his own spin of events. "I wasn't in the baccarat game," he protested. "I just sat down at the blackjack table and hadn't even placed a bet."[60] "Waterman came over to the dealer and said, 'Don't deal to this man,'" Sinatra insisted. "I just got up and said, 'Put your name on the marquee and I'll come to see what kind of business you do.' And walked away."[61] An investigation by the Clark County Liquor and Gaming License Board naturally produced no further action.

Two weeks after Frank Sinatra posted his comments in the press, Cliff Perlman cleared his next hurdle with Nevada gambling regulators. "Clifford S. Perlman, chairman of the board of Lum's Inc.," reported the Nevada press on November 13, 1970, "was recommended for approval as chairman of the board of Desert Palace, Inc., the operating company of Caesars Palace, Las Vegas."[62]

The approval by Nevada authorities created the public appearance of business as usual at the Las Vegas resort, an appearance that was absolutely essential to the underlying premise of Caesars Palace. The Palace sought routine even more so after the Sinatra versus Waterman incident with mentions splashed across the country of "mob" and gun play. Lum's Inc., however, had just inherited the Teamster's due, and Lum's publicly traded structure would bring new scrutiny to the cash-laden treasury of Caesar. Indeed, the Securities and Exchange Commission was about to make a call. From the podium of the 1981 Caesars Palace Grand Prix, Clifford Perlman might have looked back on November 13, 1970, as the high point of his rule over the empire, the lofty perch from which his Caesar reign then retreated into resignation.

∗∗∗

"The SEC announced today the filing of a complaint in Federal court in New York," trumpeted the *SEC Digest* on December 3, 1970, "seeking to enjoin violations of the…. Federals securities laws by Lum's, Inc."[63] Named in the SEC action were Melvin Chasen, vice president and director of Lum's, as well as Lehman Brothers, the brokerage house. "The complaint charged that Melvin Chasen, chief operating officer of Lum's, told Benjamin Simon, a Chicago salesman for Lehman Bros," read one news account, "about disappointing earnings by the firm."[64] "While the stock brought $17.50 per share in the morning of January 9 [1969]," continued the report, "it closed at $14.50 a share in January 12, the day that trading resumed."[65]

Indeed, over 83,000 shares of Lum's Inc.—parent of Caesars Palace—were transacted in morning trading on January 9, 1969, prior to the release of the quarterly earnings report. In fact, Lum's trading led all other activity that day on the New York Stock Exchange. Notably, the earnings report followed the $3 million swing in casino performance under the stewardship of Jerome Zarowitz. The January 12, 1970, share price also marked a sharp decline from the end-of-year close only two weeks before at $20, nearly a 30 percent loss in value. On the news of the SEC action, the Lum's stock plummeted, closing on December 31, 1970, at 5⅞.

Lum's, however, was no stranger to the attention of the SEC. In January of 1965, the SEC suspended an initial public offering of Lum's shares. Named in the suspension were stockholders Clifford Perlman, Stuart Perlman, and Aetna Securities. "The

The Securities and Exchange Commission filed a complaint against Lum's, Inc. and brothers Clifford Perlman and Stuart Perlman in December 1970, less than two years after they acquired Caesars Palace. The SEC action also included former licensed owners Jay Sarno, Nathan Jacobson, Stanley Mallin, and William S. Weinberger. SEC filings folded unlicensed ownership interest Jerome Zarowitz into the case. Seven years later, William D. Weinberger—son of William S.—attended the 1977 Long Beach Grand Prix, shaping the path to the Caesars Palace Grand Prix (author's collection).

acts of Lum's and the selling stockholders," charged the SEC, "operated as a fraud and as a deceit upon purchasers of the stock."[66] Perhaps not coincidentally, the 1965 SEC suspension of Clifford Perlman and Lum's Inc. occurred two days prior to the grand public announcement of the Caesars Palace development by Jay Sarno, Stanley Mallin, and Nathan Jacobson. Further, the suspension of the Lum's stock offering did not appear to deter Nevada regulators as they pondered the sale of Caesars Palace to Lum's Inc. in 1969.

Amid the most recent SEC charges and the resultant news cycle, Melvin Chasen was forced to spin more unpleasantries; the purchase of Caesars Palace was no longer an all-cash proposition. Installment payments to the Sarno group were reduced to one-third, interest was reduced by nearly 30 percent, and Lum's stock was offered in exchange for debt to the former owners. "We had to do something," offered Chasen, "to assure that we would be in business."[67]

Years later, former Caesars Palace owner Stanley Mallin recalled the renegotiation behind the headlines. "[Lum's] gave the third down," according to Mallin. "They couldn't come up with the rest." "We have a lien on the hotel," continued Jay Sarno's former partner. "We should take the hotel back."[68] Attorney Mickey Rudin, however, rebuffed Mallin and Sarno. "Well, the government isn't going to let you," recalled Mallin of Rudin. "Lum's is a public company."[69] Attorney Milton "Mickey" Rudin presented an interesting turn, as well as a conflict. To wit, Mickey Rudin was best known as legal counsel and business advisor to Frank Sinatra, then under contract *with* Caesars Palace while also pitched in dispute with Sanford Waterman.

"See, that's where we made a terrible mistake, meaning some of us," surmised Stanley Mallin. "We agreed to what [Rudin] said. But in retrospect, we should have bought out Zarowitz and the Mafia group and we should have told him, 'We're not doing it.'"[70] Instead, the former Caesars Palace core of Jay Sarno, Stanley Mallin, and Nathan Jacobson took the extension, as well as the attendant haircut.

On the heels of the extension, the investing public also learned about the effects to the corporate balance sheet of over-extended casino credit. "Lum's doubts that $4.9 million, or 34 percent of the firm's $14.3 million in accounts receivable," offered one Wall Street pundit, "will be paid."[71]

Asked about the aging of Caesars Palace receivables, Melvin Chasen was dismissive. "We don't rank high on their list of creditors," quipped Chasen of the accumulated gambling markers.[72] Chasen's comment was also another tell of the gambler. Conversely, collection of marker debt was extremely high on the priority list of the Caesars Palace operation. To wit, an overseas collection mission occurring after the 1981 Caesars Palace Grand Prix would make international news, while a Caesars Palace executive would also be arrested and jailed.

As Melvin Chasen attempted to quell the concerns along Wall Street in the week after the SEC complaint—and while Clifford Perlman kept his head down—the Department of Justice was preparing a weekend raid in 26 cities from coast to coast, attention-getters like Las Vegas, Miami, New York, Detroit, Cleveland, Atlanta, Palm Springs, and Steubenville, Ohio. The resultant headlines were much more difficult for Caesars Palace to quiet. The news splash also returned Jerome Zarowitz front and center.

***

The competing overtures for a second U.S. Formula One Grand Prix in the western United States stilled as the 1970 Formula One season marched on. Sears Point Raceway sputtered to a halt after their USAC-backed venture was rejected. Ontario Motor Speedway, however, aligned with the SCCA and received the nod from ACCUS along with the parent FIA. When Ontario Motor Speedway opened its sprawling campus on August 8, 1970, discussions were renewed about the prospects for Formula One in California. The discourse would also be spirited.

"Of necessity, the 3-plus-mile road course is set out in the lake lined interior of the huge oval," wrote one California motorsports pundit. "It's almost pool table flat—it lacks 'definition.'"[73] The bulk of the road course turns are "far, FAR away from the stands," continued the piece. "It's almost like watching a parade of ants perform through the wrong end of the telescope."[74] The pointed remarks went on to describe the mammoth Ontario facility precisely. "A U.S. Grand Prix or a Can-Am would draw the first time around, if only for the novelty," as the writer leaned in, "but because of the poor road course positioning, this one could fall on evil times later on."[75] It was not a good sign. Ontario Motor Speedway had been open for exactly one week, yet to turn the wheels of a single professional motorsports event.

On September 15, 1970, Ontario Motor Speedway then held its opener, the USAC IndyCar California 500. The California 500 was run, however, one day after the tragic death of Jochen Rindt in Italy. Nonetheless, over 180,000 fans crowded the new racing plant to see Jim McElreath win by two seconds over Art Pollard. In a race of mechanical attrition, only seven of 33 starters finished the event. Notably, Mario Andretti, Al Unser, Bobby Unser, Mark Donohue, and A.J. Foyt all retired from the race. Jim McElreath collected a reported $146,850 from the total purse of $727,500.[76] The payday of the California 500 certainly grabbed attention. Again, it wasn't Indy money, but it was close. Further, the spectator draw from the huge Los Angeles population center would be of interest to the gathering prospects of a western states U.S. Grand Prix. As the thousands returned home on Sunday evening to their newspapers and television reports, many learned of the passing of Jochen Rindt. Others would simply read of Sanford Waterman pulling a gun on Frank Sinatra at Caesars Palace.

While the premier international and domestic racing series sorted to their championship conclusions in 1970, news was also renewed of a pending Formula One Grand Prix at Ontario Motor Speedway. "Ontario Motor Speedway will shortly announce that it is going to hold an International Grand Prix," reported the *San Francisco Examiner* on November 29, 1970. "The date is March 28, 1971."[77] The report continued to confirm that the FIA had approved the event, "the first such race held on the Coast in more than a decade."[78]

The report however, then took a hard left turn, perhaps directly toward the vast Ontario oval. "The Ontario affair, however, is strictly invitational," continued the *Examiner.* "It looks like several…. Formula 5000 cars will run … along with the traditional Formula 1 Grand Prix machines."[79] The time-honored traditions of Formula One had, perhaps, turned to folly. "The official United States Grand Prix is still to be conducted in the Fall," claimed the report, "at Watkins Glen in New York."[80]

As the California event began to take shape, the pressures of the competing Ontario and Watkins Glen interests in the ACCUS and FIA board rooms would be intense. The crisp suits and ties of the corporate racing world, however, would be no match for the open shirts, flashy jewelry, and tennis whites in the Caesars Palace bunker board room, as news of the raid by federal agents splashed from coast to coast.

***

"Sanford Waterman, executive vice president of Caesars Palace, was arrested at the casino," read a report from Florida. "Elliott Paul Price, casino executive host, was arrested in his car."[81] The news gathered, grew, and then took the nation by storm.

Although Caesars Palace was a focal point, the raids by the Department of Justice were conducted from coast to coast, "the largest, coordinated antigambling raids ever."[82] "Conviction of those arrested," Attorney General John Mitchell said, "would 'severely damage the financial apparatus which bankrolls organized crime.'"[83] Mitchell's bluster was soon tempered, though, as the Nixon White House and Watergate conspirators worked to secure early parole for the convicted Calvin Kovens.

The arrests of Sanford Waterman and Elliott Paul Price also tied in three Las Vegas sports books. The Caesars Palace executives were "in effect acting as illegal underwriters to the nation's top bookmakers."[84] Frank "Lefty" Rosenthal, then of the Rose Bowl Sports Book in Las Vegas, was among the book operators arrested.

After the arrest reports, the news cycle then consolidated around the search warrants at Caesars Palace. "More than $1.5 million in cash was seized from lock boxes at the plush Caesars Palace gambling casino," read the reports. "Most of the money—$1,120,000—was found in boxes maintained by Jerome (Jerry) Zarowitz, onetime credit manager of Caesars Palace."[85] Unlike Sanford Waterman and Elliott Paul Price, Jerome Zarowitz was arrested in Palm Springs.

News reports inevitably turned to the 1965 Palm Springs "Apalachin" of Jerome Zarowitz, Elliott Paul Price, Anthony "Fat Tony" Salerno, Vincent "Jimmy Blue Eyes" Alo, and Ruby Lazarus. Criminal records and indictments were splashed as well, including the sports bribery felony conviction of Zarowitz. The gentle touch of Nevada gambling regulation was also tipped. "[Zarowitz] operated as a sports bookmaker in Miami, according to files of the Nevada Gaming Commission."[86]

The raids and arrests struck directly at the propensity of Nevada casinos to engage the most sullied and studied of the nation's illegal gamblers and bookmakers, in the privileged business of legal gambling in Nevada. Such was the time-honored tradition of Nevada licensing, the so-called "Grandfather Clause," whereby illegal operators across the country planted legal roots in Las Vegas—from notorious hoodlum one day, to civic-minded family man the next. This case, though, also struck directly at the operation of the Palace of Caesar.

Days later, the Clark County Liquor and Gaming Licensing Board considered the magnitude of the Caesars case. In the short term, though, their concerns went nowhere, "an effort to close Caesars Palace casino ... failed to get off the ground."[87] Sanford Waterman and Elliott Paul Price, however, were suspended from their executive positions. Notably, when Jerome Zarowitz, Sanford Waterman, and Elliott Paul Price were arrested, they were released on a $5,000 bond each, each of them free to return to a newly-opened bank of tip-line telephones elsewhere.

Just as with Alvin Malnik and his tax evasion trial, FBI wiretaps came into play. "The FBI said its evidence was largely based on telephone calls to Zarowitz at his home in Palm Springs, Calif., from Waterman, Price, and employees of the Rose Bowl," read a Nevada report. "The calls were secretly recorded by the FBI."[88] Once again, the Department of Justice would shepherd a compromised case, and the FBI wiretaps would become the primary defense target. The federal investigation and the national news influenced the word along Wall Street as well. "Speculative shares," wrote one analyst, "are unappealing at this time."[89] As the shares of Lum's Inc. closed at 5⅞ on December 31, 1970—a drop-off of nearly 75 percent in 12 months—the SEC redoubled their scrutiny of Caesars Palace, and the involvement of Jerome Zarowitz on both sides of the sale.

***

"It's official now," once again trumpeted the *San Francisco Examiner*. "Ontario Motor Speedway president David Lockton announced today that the track would hold the world's richest road race on March 28."[90] A premier road racing event at the new California complex had been tagged and teased for much of the last year. "Apparently it took this long to line up a sponsor," continued the *Examiner*, "to pick up most of the astounding $250,000 purse posted for the event."[91] "The benefactor is the Questor Corp.," continued the announcement, "which makes everything from mufflers to baby bottles."[92]

The purse had been pitched since early in the promotion, apparently under-written by little more than hyperbole. Rather than "richest" or "astounding," the announced purse merely drew even with the $250,000 paid at the 1970 U.S. Grand Prix in Watkins Glen, New York. Call it the double-play of effective promotion.

The press teased the invitations of the domestic race drivers, all scheduled to compete in five-liter, V-8 powered, Formula 5000 machinery. Mark Donohue, Bobby Unser, Al Unser, George Follmer, John Cannon, Peter Revson, Swede Savage, and A.J. Foyt were all expected to represent the domestic road racing series. Splitting the six-week gap between the South African and Spanish Grand Prix events, the Questor Grand Prix was anticipated to draw international Formula One regulars as well, Jackie Stewart, John Surtees, Jacki Ickx, Jackie Oliver, Denny Hulme, Emerson Fitti-paldi, Pedro Rodriguez, and Jean-Pierre Beltoise.

The press also lamented that the Questor-sponsored event at Ontario would not be a points-paying round of the Formula One championship. "Ontario had originally

Mario Andretti on the way to winning his first Formula One event on March 6, 1971, driving a Ferrari 312B at the Kyalami circuit in South Africa. Three weeks later, Andretti drove the same machine at the Questor Grand Prix at Ontario Motor Speedway in California. In 1982, Mario Andretti made the last Formula One start of his storied driving career at the Caesars Palace Grand Prix driving a Ferrari (Toronto Star Archives, Toronto Public Library).

sought to hold a second U.S. Grand Prix," noted Shav Glick for the *Los Angeles Times*, "but was rejected by the FIA."[93]

Dan Gurney, though, was glib about the mixed non-championship program. "The race will be better than a second U.S. Grand Prix," suggested Gurney. "It shapes up as a perfect Europe vs. U.S. match, although I don't know what we'll do about Mario Andretti."[94] Mario Andretti, fresh from a win in the season-opening South African Grand Prix, would play his Ontario hand in the same Formula One Ferrari 312 that he campaigned across the Atlantic.

One week before the Questor event, the Formula One forecast shifted yet again. "The United States was awarded … a second race on the world Grand Prix circuit," rang the update. "The second race … will be held at the new $30 million racing facility at Ontario, Calif., on April 9, 1972."[95] The post also confirmed the name of the event, "the Western U.S. Grand Prix."[96] As with Watkins Glen and the pending Questor event, the purse was announced at $250,000. Formula One was thus to be restored to the California race calendar, if only in the motorsports op-eds.

The Questor Grand Prix was split into two 100-mile heats, with points then combined to determine the overall winner. Before the start, pundits locked onto the power advantage of the Formula 5000 vehicles down the long Ontario straightway. Purists countered with the handling, weight, and throttle response advantages of the Formula One machines. Denny Hulme, entered in a McLaren M19A for the McLaren

Mark Donohue leads Mario Andretti in the first heat of the Questor Grand Prix at Ontario Motor Speedway on March 28, 1971. Donohue was driving a Formula 5000 Lola T192 for Roger Penske. Andretti brought his familiar Ferrari 312B from the Formula One series. Mario Andretti overtook Donohue for the heat win and also claimed the main event (author's collection).

works, called his shot. "The top American finisher," according to Hulme, "will be about sixth."[97]

Jackie Stewart in his Tyrell-Ford claimed the pole for the Questor Grand Prix. Stewart was followed to the grid by Chris Amon, Jacky Ickx, and Denny Hulme. Bolstering Denny Hulme's pre-race claim, Mark Donohue was the top Formula 5000 qualifier in seventh. Mario Andretti, qualifying late on Saturday after flying from a USAC race in Phoenix, was set to roll off from 12th.

Mario Andretti and Ferrari battled Mark Donohue and Lola in the first heat while Jackie Stewart led up front. "I had quite a time getting by Donohue. He was driving a brilliant race," Andretti remarked. "Once I got by Donohue, I knew my car was running well."[98] Setting after Jackie Stewart, Mario Andretti took aim on the last lap and drafted past Stewart's Tyrell to win the heat. In the second heat, Jackie Stewart led Mario Andretti for 10 laps. Andretti then moved past Stewart and had no challengers to the finish. Jackie Stewart scored second in the Questor finish standings, followed by Denny Hulme and Chris Amon.

Notably, Tim Schenken was recorded fifth in a Brabham for new team owner Bernie Ecclestone. "Owning Brabham," noted author Tom Bower, "automatically made Ecclestone a member of the Formula One Constructors Association."[99] FOCA, the Formula One Constructors Association, would then become the primary wealth-building vehicle for Bernie Ecclestone. Shrouded in secrecy under the iron rule of Bernie Ecclestone, the enterprise was not entirely unlike the national crime syndicate of Meyer Lansky, La Cosa Nostra, and the Teamsters.

Graham Hill, effectively discharged from Lotus after his leg injuries, joined Ecclestone and Brabham for the Questor event as well. Down the finishing order, Denny Hulme's prognostication would not be denied. In seventh place overall—and first American in a Formula 5000 racer—was Mark Donohue driving for Roger Penske.

In the post-race presentation, Mario Andretti played both to the crowd, and to his craft. "The U.S. vs. Europe promotion was unfair to our boys," Andretti commented. "They never had a chance."[100] On his own performance preferences, Andretti similarly played down the middle, "I just like to race," deferred Andretti. "You really can't compare the two types of cars anyway. So as long as I have a ride in a car I feel I can win in, I'm happy."[101]

Finally, though, the 31-year-old Mario Andretti had an opportunity to ponder the potential for a second U.S. Grand Prix in 1972. "The people like Jackie Stewart, Jacky Ickx, and Chris Amon," proclaimed the Questor winner, "won't just be names people read about in the papers. They will get a chance to see them race, just as they did at Ontario in the Questor."[102]

Despite the appearance of Jackie Stewart, Chris Amon, and Jacky Ickx in the domestic Can-Am series—including stops by Stewart and Amon in Las Vegas— Mario Andretti was quite correct. Indeed, the same name-awareness issue drifted over the Caesars Palace Grand Prix. In fact, other than for Mario Andretti, the backgrounds of the other competitors at the Caesars Palace Formula One events were somewhat lost on the Las Vegas audience. On the Questor event and a second U.S. Grand Prix in 1972, however, Mario Andretti—the great American race car driver— would be wrong.

One month after the event concluded, the president of Questor punctuated the entire exercise. President P.M. "Sandy" Grieve, asked about the role of Questor in the future of auto racing, stated that he "couldn't care less."[103] Despite the origins of Questor as an automotive parts supplier, Grieve was focused at the bottom line. "I'll consider this a failure," continued the Questor industrialist, "if it doesn't get Questor better known in the financial community."[104]

Questor, however, was already well known to the *dark* side of American finance, purchasing nearly $6 million of stock in 1964 from Charles Bluhdorn of Gulf and Western Industries.[105] Bluhdorn's Gulf and Western company, too, was built on auto parts, "manufacturing and engaging largely in wholesale distribution of automotive parts."[106] The Bluhdorn connection, though, also opens a financial gate that leads to the Illinois Bureau of Investigation, Philip Levin, Transnation, and Acapulco Towers, "a hotel partially owned by Gulf and Western."[107] It is also a dark portal that leads to Caesars Palace and Meyer Lansky.

Mario Andretti won the Questor Grand Prix on March 28, 1971, at Ontario Motor Speedway. Andretti collected nearly $40,000 for the win. Driving a Formula One Ferrari 312B, Mario Andretti led Jackie Stewart, Denny Hulme, and Chris Amin across the finish line. Neither the Questor Grand Prix nor the combined race formula were ever repeated. Nonetheless, William D. Weinberger attempted a combined Formula One—CART IndyCar event at the Caesars Palace Grand Prix. Others are not identified (GP Library Limited / Alamy Stock Photo).

***

During the build-up to the Questor Grand Prix, news once again out of Miami rocked the already unstable foundations of Las Vegas gambling, as well as striking another blow at Caesars Palace. "Meyer Lansky, the reputed financial brain behind the Mafia," read the report, "was indicted … on charges of illegal gambling activities in connection with the Flamingo Hotel in Las Vegas, Nev."[108] The "illegal gambling activities" of note translated to an efficient, extremely well-organized count room skim conspiracy. News reports involving Meyer Lansky and the Flamingo had circulated for the better part of the last year, certainly since the front-page reveal involving Supreme Court Justice Douglas, Albert Parvin, Morris Lansburgh, and Sam Cohen.

By the time of the indictment, however, Meyer Lansky had departed Hallandale, Florida, and was seeking return-citizenship in Tel Aviv, Israel. Refusing to return to the U.S. upon subpoena, Lansky was indicted separately for contempt of court. U.S. Attorney General John Mitchell declared that bond for Lansky was to be set at $200,000. Curiously, the bond demand was the same amount that Meyer Lansky collected as a finder's fee when the Flamingo was sold by Al Parvin to Sam Cohen and Morris Lansburgh in 1960.

Indicted with Meyer Lansky on the skimming charges were Sam Cohen, Morris Lansburgh, and Jerry Gordon. Gordon, notably, was then vice president and director of hotel operations for Caesars Palace, moving over from the Flamingo when Kirk Kerkorian acquired the resort from Cohen and Lansburgh. Named as an unindicted co-conspirator was Lou Poller, formerly of the Miami National Bank, believed to be the construction funding escrow for Caesars Palace.

One week later, Jerry Gordon resigned from his executive post from Caesars Palace. Concurrent with the Gordon resigna-

The March 28, 1971, Questor Grand Prix was one of the most innovative motorsports events ever undertaken. The Questor corporation, however, had an odd connection to the shadowy world of American back-channel business interests. It was a channel that connected further to the Meyer Lansky syndicate apparatus and Caesars Palace. The program cover graphically depicts the confluence of the Questor concept, although somewhat in the abstract. Clay Regazzoni in his 1970 #4 Ferrari 312B is at the point but did not compete in the Questor Grand Prix. Trailing appears to be the distinctive livery of John Cannon's 1970 Formula 5000 McLaren M10B. Cannon typically carried #2 during the 1970 season, but did run #25 at the Questor event (author's collection).

tion, Caesars Palace executive Irving "Ash" Resnick was under investigation by the FBI. In an investigation involving Resnick's attempt to cash $50,000 in collateral trust notes, the issuer notified the FBI that the notes were reported "lost, strayed, or stolen."[109]

Resnick stated to the FBI that the notes had been offered as collateral for credit but were not retrieved. "[Resnick] said that these securities were held by him in a safe deposit box," documented the FBI, "until he decided to determine whether or not they were saleable."[110] Once again, a Caesars Palace lock box contained third-party secrets. "The facts as they concerned RESNICK," continued the FBI, "merited prosecutive action."[111] The resignation of Jerry Gordon, as well as the investigation of Ash Resnick, brought to five the number of Caesars Palace praetorians that were now under stain of the federal microscope.

The federal government also *re-indicted* Meyer Lansky, Sam Cohen, Morris Lansburgh, and Jerry Gordon. The refined indictment charged the conspirators with skimming $36 million from the Flamingo over the full eight years of the Cohen-led ownership, "to conceal and distribute through the facilities of interstate and foreign commerce…. Florida, New York, Switzerland, and elsewhere."[112] The group was further charged with income tax evasion and preparation of false tax returns.

Three days before the Questor Grand Prix, Meyer Lansky was indicted on charges of skimming millions out of the Flamingo Hotel and Casino in Las Vegas. His co-conspirators included Flamingo owners Sam Cohen and Morris Lansburgh of Miami. Jerry Gordon, an executive at Caesars Palace, was also indicted. Sam Cohen was later a business partner in a Miami property development with Clifford Perlman of Caesars Palace (Everett Collection Historical / Alamy Stock Photo).

Less than two months later, the Securities and Exchange Commission would pay a visit to the corporation. "The commission … announced the filing of a complaint in the Federal District Court of New York," read the SEC report, "to enjoin Lum's Inc. Desert Palace, Inc., … from engaging in violations … of the Securities and Exchange act."[113] Also named in the action were Nathan Jacobson, Jay Sarno, Stanley Mallin, William S. Weinberger, Harry Wald, and Jerome Zarowitz. The mention of Weinberger and Zarowitz was certainly curious. William S. Weinberger was an original investor and licensee in Caesars Palace and remained after the sale to Lum's, Inc. Jerome Zarowitz, however, was neither a Caesars licensed employee nor a recorded investor.

The charges filed by the SEC were troublesome. The SEC listed unaudited, false, and misleading financial statements. Further charged was a failure to disclose material facts to Lum's shareholders about the wild $3 million swing in gambling profits during the settlement period. Finally, the SEC took a swing directly at Jerome Zarowitz. "Jerome Zarowitz received about $3.5-million in two lump sum payments from Lum's," reported the *New York Times*, "although he was not recorded as an owner of the casino."[114] Ten days after the charges were filed, Lum's Inc. changed the name of the corporation to Caesars World, Inc.

Again, a subsequent perspective described the apparent culture of corporate gambling ownership. "Nothing changed when the big gambling corporations like Caesars World and some of the others went public," wrote author Robert W. Greene.

"The wise guys simply had banks, corporations, and other nominees hold their stock. And they still got their points of the skim."[115] Stanley Mallin later described the analogous roster of the Zarowitz-controlled Caesars Palace casino as "all kinds of guys, dems-and-doughs guys."[116]

The SEC case against Caesars World and corporate officers on both sides of the sale would take nearly four years to resolve. The case was eventually settled down to simple enjoinment, more rigorous accounting procedures, and a $1.1 million set-aside fund as a hedge against private lawsuits. Despite the apparent skim during the settlement period, and the secret payments to Jerome Zarowitz, the charges produced no grand jury indictments, nor were they adjudicated further in federal court.

Conversely, Sam Cohen and Morris Lansburgh were convicted in 1973 in the Flamingo skimming case and sentenced to one year in federal prison. Charges against Jerry Gordon were dropped one month later. Meyer Lansky, then purged from Israel and back in Miami, received a hall pass amid his claims of chronic ill health and the ensuing legal wrangles. "The [Lansky] case would lie dormant until either the defendant dies," ruled U.S. District Court Judge Roger Foley, "or the government acts responsibly and dismisses the indictment."[117]

The indictment of Meyer Lansky for the Las Vegas skim thus faded from the headlines. Meyer Lansky, though, was very much alive and engaged. So, too, were crony Sam Cohen and alleged Lansky heir-apparent Alvin Malnik. In fact, the names of all three would be recorded on tape in a forthcoming investigation of congressmen, gambling, and bribes. The name of Clifford Perlman of Caesars Palace would be heard on tape as well.

* * *

News of a "Western U.S. Grand Prix" picked up after the conclusion of the 1971 U.S. Grand Prix at Watkins. Celebrating its 10th anniversary, the Watkins Glen Grand Prix Corporation once again upped the purse to a record of $267,000. Francois Cevert collected $50,000 for the first—and only—win of his Formula One career.

On the west coast, however, all was not well in Ontario. Further, the promised $250,000 purse had not been funded. "Ontario management balked at paying $75,000 to transport the cars from Europe," came the reports, "and no agreement was reached."[118] The implacable stand-off between promoters and FOCA thus became the enduring hallmark of Bernie Ecclestone. "By the autumn of 1971," noted one author, "Ecclestone had negotiated improved terms with the circuits and the freight contractors."[119]

David Lockton of Ontario Motor Speedway then apparently sought to reschedule the event to the fall. Calendar alignment with the Watkins Glen date would indeed mitigate the cost of race transportation. A fall date, however, would also conflict with the Los Angeles Times Grand Prix at Riverside International Raceway, a long-standing promotion sanctioned by the SCCA. The SCCA then broke their five-year agreement with Ontario and turned to a known commodity for the western U.S. Grand Prix promotion. "The SCCA," continued the explanation, "hammered out a deal with Riverside president Les Richter."[120]

"Riverside's biggest problem now," the report concluded, "is to locate a sponsor to pick up all or part of the close to $300,000 in prize money and expenses."[121] Indeed, there was no Questor Corporation to underwrite the Western U.S. Grand Prix. In fact, the first corporate branding of a Formula One event would be the 1981 Caesars Palace Grand Prix.

The Marlboro cigarette brand then briefly jumped into the discourse, already sponsoring eight cars in the Formula One series. "I have talked to several others," Les Richter said, "but Marlboro is the best hope at this stage."[122] On the street, Riverside International Raceway was also in peril, caught up in the financial woes of Lawrence Lopatin and American Raceways, Inc. "Riverside, also in financial trouble," ran the talk, "is expected to drop the race any day now."[123] As the rumors swirled, Road Atlanta stepped in to request the second U.S. Grand Prix event, a notion that also sputtered.

Finally, less than two months before the scheduled date of the Western U.S. Grand Prix, former Los Angeles Rams great Les Richter retreated to the sidelines. "Everybody is anxious for a second Grand Prix event in the U.S.," Richer acknowledged, "but there was not enough time to put together a financial package."[124] On February 20, 1972, the Western U.S. Grand prix was officially canceled. "Time, or timing," wrote one columnist, "was the major factor in Grand Prix West's short history."[125] Indeed, it was a history that existed only on paper.

Formula One then returned to its fall destination in upstate New York for the 1972 U.S. Grand Prix. Jackie Stewart dominated the event for Ken Tyrell, leading a one-two podium punch with teammate Francois Cevert. Denny Hulme completed

Mario Andretti continued with the Scuderia Ferrari Formula One team in 1972 on a limited schedule. Andretti finished sixth in a Ferrari 312B2 in the U.S. Grand Prix at Watkins Glen on October 8, 1972. Mario Andretti made his final Formula One start a decade later driving a Ferrari 312B2 at the Caesars Palace Grand Prix (courtesy International Motor Racing Research Center).

Jackie Stewart won the October 8, 1972, U.S. Grand Prix at Watkins Glen driving a Tyrell-Ford. Stewart was followed by Tyrell teammate Francois Cevert and Denny Hulme driving a McLaren. Jackie Stewart won his second Formula One world championship the following year—and retired (courtesy International Motor Racing Research Center).

the podium for the McLaren works. Mario Andretti, running Formula One on a limited basis in 1972 for Ferrari, qualified 10th and finished sixth. Notably, Emerson Fittipaldi retired early in the 1972 U.S. Grand Prix. On the strength of five race wins and an insurmountable point lead, though, Fittipaldi claimed the 1972 Formula One world championship for Colin Chapman. Of further note, the 1972 U.S. Grand Prix built on its burgeoning tradition of hooliganism. "The Glen's a hard thing to explain," commented one young rowdy, "but I'll probably keep coming back for the rest of my life. You explain it."[126] In the years ahead, Bernie Ecclestone would press for an explanation as well.

Eight years after the cancellation of the Western U.S. Grand Prix, Dan Lufkin—investor and board chairman of Ontario Motor Speedway—acquired a controlling interest in the Questor Corporation. Lufkin also held a large stake in Columbia Pictures. One month after the Questor investment, Kirk Kerkorian—former landlord and licensee of Caesars Palace in Las Vegas—sued Columbia Pictures and Dan Lufkin for $10 million in damages, "charging the company's management with ignoring stockholders' interest to preserve their control."[127]

The connections among the players as well as the lawsuit inform the great financial adventures of the international super-wealthy, as well as the collateral pursuits that serve their whims, sometimes even auto racing. The entitlements of the global 1 percent are also indulged in extreme exclusivity. Further, Kirk Kerkorian's contentions against Columbia echoed the 1971 complaint by the SEC against Lum's, Caesars

Palace, and the corrupt interests straddling the transaction.

One year after the cancellation of the Western U.S. Grand Prix, "Western Promotions & Marketing, Inc," registered a name statement for a Long Beach travel services company with the County Clerk of Los Angeles County. The president of the company was listed as "Christopher R. Pook."[128] Chris Pook would soon make an improbable pitch to the Long Beach City Council, a fantastic promotion to be named "the American Grand Prix at Long Beach."[129] Somewhat poetically, Cameron Argetsinger—former executive director of the Watkins Glen Grand Prix Corporation—would present the Long Beach proposal to ACCUS for subsequent consideration by the FIA and Bernie Ecclestone of FOCA.

73-17927
FICTITIOUS BUSINESS NAME STATEMENT

The following corporation is doing business as:

AMERICAN AVIATION TRAVEL SERVICES at 555. E. Ocean Blvd., Long Beach, California 90802.

Western Promotions & Marketing, Inc. 3250 Wilshire Blvd., Los Angeles, California 90010

This business is conducted by a corporation.

Western Promotions & Marketing, Inc.
CHRISTOPHER R. POOK, Pres.

This statement was filed with the County Clerk of Los Angeles County on July 10, 1973.

Pub. July 16, 23, 30, Aug. 6, 1973.

Chris Pook filed a name statement on July 10, 1973, for a travel services business in Long Beach, California. One year later, Chris Pook and attorney Don Dyer pitched the Long Beach City Council on the concept for the Long Beach Grand Prix. In 1981, Chris Pook and the Long Beach Grand Prix Association would produce the inaugural of the Caesars Palace Grand Prix (author's collection).

Christopher R. Pook would also make an appearance in Las Vegas, to produce the show for Clifford Perlman, Harry Wald, and William D. Weinberger at the 1981 Caesars Palace Grand Prix.

V

Crossed Paths

*Long Beach Launches a Formula One
Foray While the Centurions of Caesar
Launch a Foray to Long Beach*

That methinks is strange. (*Julius Caesar* 4.3.212)

The failure of the 1972 Western U.S. Grand Prix would strike professional American road racing at its own emerging points of weakness. The Canadian-American Challenge Cup Series and the Formula 5000 series—both sanctioned by the SCCA—raced into the 1970s as the premier forms of road racing in the United States. Despite the introduction of additional road races to the Indy 500-based USAC championship trail, the purist road racers made their home under the SCCA banner. Both SCCA series also found their niche with few restrictions on chassis and unlimited power, generally derived from American V-8 powerplants.

The Can-Am series was dominated by Team McLaren from 1967 to 1971. In fact, Bruce McLaren and Denny Hulme sealed their consecutive 1967 and 1968 championships at the former Stardust International Raceway in Las Vegas. After the death of team owner Bruce McLaren in 1970, Denny Hulme went on to win the Can-Am championship in 1970, followed by Peter Revson in 1971. So frustrated was Roger Penske by the march of McLaren through the series that he unleashed the fearsome Porsche 917/10 and 917/30 twin-turbo racers on the competition. Belching over 1,500 horsepower, the Porsche 917/30 was the most powerful sports racer ever built. George Follmer and Mark Donohue unbridled their respective Porsche behemoths to capture the 1972 and 1973 Can-Am championships, taking 12 of the 17 events in those two years.

Formula 5000 also enjoyed its own heyday in the early 1970s. With a purse underwritten by tobacco brand L&M, both accomplished domestic and international road racers competed in the series. Formula 5000 also attracted USAC crossovers like Mario Andretti, Al Unser, and Bobby Unser. Further, Formula 5000 counted among its champions such brand names as John Cannon, David Hobbs, Jody Scheckter and Brian Redman. Finally, the series boasted Mario Andretti and Mark Donohue among its race winners.

On October 17, 1973, however, the oil embargo of Middle East oil producers rendered all forms of petroleum-consuming motorsports vulnerable. Sandwiched between the finale events of the Formula 5000 and Can-Am seasons, the oil embargo hovered over the 1973 Los Angeles Times Grand Prix at Riverside International Raceway like an acrid cloud. Indeed, the October 28, 1973, Times event won by Mark Donohue in the Sunoco-sponsored Porsche 917/30 was the swan song for both. "I don't think at this stage," remarked Mark Donohue from the Riverside post-race presser, "I'm getting any better."[1]

When the SCCA then reduced in-race fuel allotments, Penske and Porsche pulled the plug on the thirsty 917/30 in Can-Am competition. "We put in an awful lot of energy to make [the 917/30] the best in the business," Roger Penske commented. "Nobody says we have to run it in a race."[2]

The FIA, championship parent of the SCCA Can-Am series, then ordered a 25 percent reduction in fuel usage in its governed racing series in 1974. The cut, however, was not directed at fuel *efficiency*. Rather, like a war-footing maneuver, the FIA order was an emergency conservation measure. The Formula One series of the FIA, though, was also beset with another fatality.

Francois Cevert, winner of the 1971 U.S. Grand Prix at Watkins Glen, died during practice for the 1973 edition of the fall classic. Devastated by the loss of another close friend and his Tyrell teammate, Jackie Stewart announced his retirement. "I have been racing since 1961 and I haven't a mark on my body to tell me," Stewart noted. "I am proud of this."[3] Jackie Stewart had also just won his third World Drivers Championship for team owner Ken Tyrell. Tyrell—bereft after the loss of Cevert—was then faced with a dilemma, a world championship race team with no drivers. For 1973, Ken Tyrell signed on Jody Scheckter, the reigning U.S. Formula 5000 champion.

Racing on without Mark Donohue or the full Penske effort, the 1974 Can-Am season was the last of the original run. The 1974 Can-Am season was also truncated. After teasing a championship of seven rounds, Laguna Seca withdrew from the original SCCA Can-Am lineup. The SCCA then moved forward with a formal schedule of six events. Following round five in Edmonton, the scheduled Can-Am closer at Riverside was canceled. "We regret to cancel the Can-Am," Riverside president Les Richter was quoted as saying tersely in the *Los Angeles Times*, "but the costs involved simply aren't justified by the competition being offered."[4] Sports racers, the bulwark of the Los Angeles Times Grand Prix since 1958, were indeed scrubbed. Further, Les Richter's comments resonated at SCCA headquarters.

The Formula 5000 series was compromised in 1974 as well. After the loss of title sponsor L&M, the Formula 5000 competitors raced in 1974 as a joint USAC-SCCA championship. The combination would have simply been unthinkable during the USAC and SCCA sports car professional sanctioning battles of little over a decade before. Nonetheless, in a seven-event championship, the 1974 Formula 5000 season made it all the way to Riverside. Brian Redman claimed the championship in a tight point battle with Mario Andretti. The series also introduced American race fans to James Hunt, the 1976 Formula One champion.

The Can-Am series then attempted to soldier on with a new engine-rules package for 1975. With only three tracks committed, though, the season was canceled in its entirety. In an announcement that reverberates to this day among sports racing

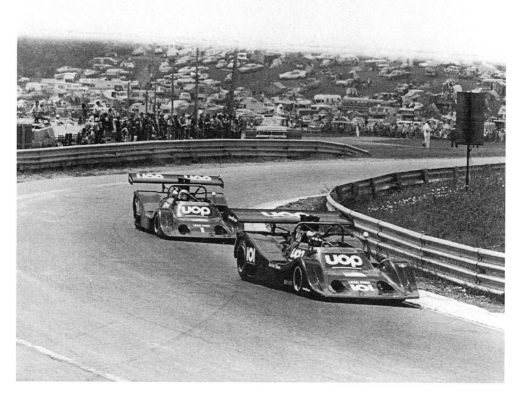

Jackie Oliver (#101) and George Follmer (#1) finished one-two at the July 14, 1974, Can-Am event at Watkins Glen, New York. Oliver and Follmer were both driving Shadow DN4 machines for Don Nichols. Oliver and Follmer also finished one-two in the 1974 Can-Am championship, the final year of the original Can-Am series. Follmer previously won the 1971 Can-Am championship driving a Porsche 917/10 for Roger Penske. George Follmer competed in the 1975 Long Beach Grand Prix for Formula 5000 machines. Follmer also competed in the Trans-Am class at the 1983 Caesars Palace Grand Prix (author's collection).

enthusiasts, the news was delivered by Cameron Argetsinger. "After nine years as North America's premier road racing series," lamented Argetsinger, "the high cost of Can-Am participation brought about the need for change."[5] Certainly after 1966— for those not named "McLaren" or "Penske"—that might be reasonably interpreted to mean "the high cost of Can-Am *domination*." Further, with the progressive reactions of the SCCA to technical innovations borne *by* the original unlimited formula, one pundit described the end of the Can-Am series. "The Can-Am," blasted the opinion, "was murdered by its creator—the SCCA."[6] It was a fair assessment.

As the SCCA Can-Am series found its end, though, the SCCA Formula 5000 found some relief, particularly after the loss of the L&M tobacco money. "The SCCA's Formula 5000 series may benefit from the discontinuation of the Can-Am program," read one report. "Several promoters expressed interest in staging a second F-5000 race on their circuit to fill an open date caused by the loss of a Can-Am event."[7] This apparent *plus-three* for Formula 5000 would then be bolstered even further.

On November 20, 1974, the same date on which the demise of the Can-Am circulated, a motorsports tremor of some magnitude was felt in Southern California. "A Grand Prix for Formula 1 cars, which would be held in April of 1976," reported the *Independent*, "was approved in principle … by a unanimous vote of the Long Beach City Council."[8] "A race on the same circuit will be held in September of 1975," continued the report, "for the slightly smaller Formula 5000 cars."[9] The SCCA Formula 5000 series was now, apparently, *plus-four*.

It was thus time for transition, the beginning of a sea-change that impacted professional American motorsports for decades to come. Cameron Argetsinger—progenitor of the bucolic Watkins Glen Grand Prix in 1948—presided over the initial transition as he carried the Long Beach Formula One package to ACCUS and the FIA. Pitched battles between sanctioning bodies and owner groups then drove the transitions home, the business-politic of professional motorsports steering a course all the way through the parking lot of the Caesars Palace Grand Prix and well beyond.

Amid the Formula One approval in Long Beach, however, another report broke on the same day in Southern California, and it involved the same public chambers and power corridors of the Long Beach City Council. "A sweeping investigation into allegations of fraud and corruption in Long Beach city government is being pursued by federal authorities," announced the *Los Angeles Times*. "The allegations involve bribery, gambling, conspiracy, and money-laundering operations."[10] The FBI was on the ground in Long Beach, and one of the names in their dossier was from Las Vegas, someone with an extremely deep connection to Caesars Palace.

***

President Richard M. Nixon could do little to effectively manage the oil crisis after Libya first announced the oil embargo on October 19, 1973. The embargo arose directly from the commitment of U.S. military aid to Israel during the Yom Kippur War. Saudi Arabia and Algeria followed the Libyan lead one day later.

The Nixon White House, however, had started to unravel over a year before. On June 17, 1972, five men reporting to operatives of the Nixon administration broke into the Democratic National Committee offices at the Watergate office campus in Washington, D.C. The ensuing cover-up, scandal, and Congressional investigation would lead the U.S. to constitutional crisis. To wit, on the same Saturday that Saudi Arabia joined the oil embargo, President Richard M. Nixon fired Archibald Cox, the special prosecutor appointed to oversee the Watergate investigation. At issue was some matter of taped conversations in the Oval Office and the President's refusal to honor the subpoena from Archibald Cox for same.

In the course of the Watergate investigation, collateral subjects inevitably arose, including over $1 million in secret cash donations to the 1972 reelection campaign for Nixon. One of those slipping the secreted cash to Nixon's handlers was Calvin Kovens, convicted in 1964 with Jimmy Hoffa and paroled early after vigorous lobbying on his behalf. Cal Kovens, notably, was the brother of Irving Kovens, original investor and licensee in Caesars Palace. A powerful political operator from Baltimore, Maryland, Irving Kovens also held his own relationship with Richard Nixon's

Teamsters president Frank Fitzsimmons (pictured) and Allen Dorfman hosted former president Richard Nixon on October 9, 1975, at the Teamsters golf tournament at La Costa Country
Club near Carlsbad, California. Nixon's first public appearance since leaving office occurred
less than three months after the disappearance of former Teamsters president Jimmy Hoffa.
Jimmy Hoffa received a pardon from President Richard Nixon on December 23, 1971, and was
released from federal prison for his conviction on bribery and fraud charges. Miami contractor Calvin Kovens, convicted along with Hoffa in 1964, was also released by the Nixon administration. Jimmy Hoffa disappeared on July 30, 1975. La Costa was notably developed by Moe
Dalitz, Allard Roen, Merv Adelson, and Irwin Molasky of Las Vegas. Molasky was also the constructor of Stardust International Raceway in Las Vegas, while Dalitz and Roen were president
and treasurer respectively of the motorsports facility (Toronto Star Archives, Toronto Public
Library).

vice president, Spiro T. Agnew, later to become another convicted felon like Calvin
Kovens and Jimmy Hoffa.

On December 23, 1971, President Nixon commuted the sentence of convicted
Teamsters president Jimmy Hoffa to time served. Released from prison, Hoffa then
steered the nearly unprecedented support of the Teamsters union to the Republican
incumbent Nixon in the 1972 general election. It was certainly newsworthy; organized labor was never a favorite cause of the Grand Old Party. Jimmy Hoffa, too, still
had a special relationship with Caesars Palace. To wit, the Teamsters Central States
Pension Fund still held the first mortgage on the Las Vegas resort.

Four months after the flow of oil resumed from the Middle East, the U.S. Congress assembled the necessary votes for impeachment of the President. On August 8,
1974, Richard M. Nixon then resigned the presidency, returning with wife Patricia to
his California home, the former western White House in San Clemente. It is worth

noting that citizen-Nixon's first public outing after resignation was the Frank E. Fitz-simmons Invitational Golf Tournament at the nearby La Costa Country Club.

Richard Nixon also played with the tournament's namesake, a team of five that included Teamsters president Frank Fitzsimmons and three others of the Teamsters brass. "Prominent also on Nixon's big day," noted one reporter, "was Allen Dorf-man."[11] Noticeably missing from the Teamsters golf tournament, however, was the *former* boss of the Teamsters. Indeed, unlike the lavish grand opening of Caesars Palace nine years earlier, past-president Jimmy Hoffa simply could not be found.

The press would have a field day with the Nixon appearance. For Richard Nixon, golf with the Teamsters at La Costa after the disappearance of Hoffa was somewhat analogous to Supreme Court Justice Douglas presiding over the Albert Parvin Foundation. To those curiosities, we will add Clifford Perlman on the victory podium of the 1981 Caesars Palace Grand Prix. Three impossibly captivating scenarios, each of them also a secret hand shake away from Meyer Lansky—allegedly.

***

The 1974 Formula One season would bring several milestones to the pinnacle of motorsport. With the retirement of Jackie Stewart after winning the 1973 championship, there was no reigning world champion on the circuit. Both Parnelli Jones and Roger Penske fielded their own start-up teams, joining late in the season with the Canadian and United States Grands Prix. Notably, Roger Penske would coax Mark Donohue out of retirement for the Formula One effort. Mario Andretti took up the Formula One cause for Parnelli Jones, after a rather dismal season for Parnelli on the USAC IndyCar trail. French driver Jacques Lafitte marked his debut in Formula One, driving for Frank Williams. The perennial Chris Amon also attempted to enter an eponymous Formula One effort, with results no better than his first-turn retirement in the Ferrari 612P at the 1968 Stardust Can-Am Grand Prix in Las Vegas.

The 1974 season also had its constants. Bernie Ecclestone continued as owner of Motor Racing Developments and the Brabham race team. Brabham's primary driver was once again Carlos Reutemann, returning for his third year with Bernie Ecclestone. John Player Team Lotus of Colin Chapman, Ken Tyrell's Elf squad, Team McLaren, and March Engineering all returned to the fold, all sporting Ford power as did Brabham. Tragedy, too, would be at constant. Peter Revson, driving for the UOP Shadow team, was yet another victim of the dreaded Armco barrier system during a test session prior to the South African Grand Prix.

The resumed flow of oil from the Middle East also somewhat calmed concerns about the visibility—*and viability*—of Formula One motorsport. The resignation of President Richard M. Nixon then eased the searing national debate about what would come next in Washington, D.C. The judicial fallout from Watergate was then to be discharged among the White House minions while Nixon—as the metaphoric Nero—later golfed with the Teamsters at La Costa.

In 1974, Formula One competition enjoyed some balance as well. "Why is it in our present era, so bedeviled with new concern about energy, environment, and economy," wrote motorsports historian Pete Lyons, "Grand Prix racing is growing in prestige?"[12] After the championship runaways of Jackie Stewart, Emerson Fittipaldi, and—to some extent—the late Jochen Rindt, the 1974 campaign saw seven differ-ent drivers and five different constructors take wins. In fact, five drivers took multi-ple wins.

As the 1974 Formula One campaign departed Italy and headed to North Amer-ica, Clay Regazzoni led the points standings for Ferrari, followed closely by Jody Scheckter for Tyrell and Emerson Fittipaldi in a McLaren. When Emerson Fittipaldi won the Canadian Grand Prix over Regazzoni, the points were then tied. Jody Sheck-ter stood seven points in arrears, likely an insurmountable deficit unless Fittipaldi and Regazzoni fell out in the final race. The finale of the season was the 13th edition of the U.S. Grand Prix at Watkins Glen. The U.S. Grand Prix was thus Emerson Fitti-paldi versus Clay Regazzoni, and McLaren versus Ferrari.

Carlos Reutemann in the Brabham qualified first at Watkins Glen followed by James Hunt for Hesketh. Mario Andretti was a stellar third on the grid in only the second outing of the Parnelli-Ford. Emerson Fittipaldi and Clay Regazzoni were paired in the order, eighth and ninth, respectively. Mark Donohue in the

Carlos Reutemann (#7) won the October 6, 1974, U.S. Grand Prix at Watkins Glen. Reutemann was driving a Brabham BT44 for Bernie Ecclestone. Emerson Fittipaldi claimed his second Formula One championship in 1974. Reutemann finished sixth in the final points standings. Carlos Reutemann also figured in the Formula One championship battle at the 1981 Caesars Palace Grand Prix. Brabham owner Bernie Ecclestone signed the contract between FOCA and Caesars Palace with Clifford Perlman and William D. Weinberger in an underground board room (courtesy International Motor Racing Research Center).

Penske-Ford was slotted a miserable 16th on the grid, nearly two seconds off the pole.

Reutemann and Hunt would lead out from the start. Mario Andretti, however, was black-flagged after a balky ignition forced a push start from the grid. "Would you believe it?" Andretti said wryly. "The little things always seem to happen to me."[13]

Mario Andretti, the great American race car driver, offered that statement 25 times at the Indianapolis 500 alone. Andretti thus moved off. Emerson Fittipaldi and Clay Regazzoni, however, moved in opposite directions as the laps ensued. Fittipaldi advanced into the points positions, while Clay Regazzoni went backward with suspension issues. Mark Donohue dropped out at the halfway point, also with suspension issues.

Carlos Reutemann then claimed the 1974 U.S. Grand Prix by some 10 seconds over young Brabham teammate Carlos Pace. James Hunt was another minute back, followed by Emerson Fittipaldi in fourth. Clay Regazzoni soldiered home four laps down in 11th place, out of the points. For Emerson Fittipaldi, it was a triumphant second Formula One world championship. The year of 1974 was also the apogee of Fittipaldi's Formula One career, a slow decline into team ownership and diminished results that would culminate with retirement in 1980, and a move to the CART Indy-Car series in 1981. Second in the championship was as close as Clay Regazzoni would ever get. Regazzoni, too, departed Formula One in 1980.

Tragedy also remained in constant at the 1974 U.S. Grand Prix at Watkins Glen. In only his second Formula One start, 25-year-old Austrian driver Helmuth Koinigg driving for John Surtees was killed at turn seven. Like Francois Cevert the year before, Koinigg was thus one more victim of the Armco barrier. Once again, as well, the U.S. Grand Prix was blemished by arrests. "Property theft, drug possession, driving while intoxicated, and criminal trespass," according to the local sheriff, "all typical of a Grand Prix weekend."[14] A series of car fires—including a Greyhound bus—then made the Watkins Glen party complete. The autumn idyll of upstate New York was also becoming increasingly tedious for Bernie Ecclestone.

One month after the 1974 U.S. Grand Prix at Watkins Glen, the Long Beach City Council considered the concept for Chris Pook's Long Beach Grand Prix in California. Bernie Ecclestone's quest for destination-city experiential entertainment would soon be fulfilled, while Las Vegas and Caesars Palace waited in the wings. In fact, seven years to the day after the first appearance of Jacques Lafitte at the 1974 U.S. Grand Prix, then-veteran driver Jacques Lafitte compared the Caesars Palace Grand Prix circuit to a "Go-Kart" track. "How could Lafitte judge on the Las Vegas track?" Mario Andretti clapped back. "He's never seen it!"[15]

∗∗∗

On the same day that President Nixon was rehearsing his resignation from the Oval Office, far across the nation, Christopher R. Pook and attorney Don Dyer were meeting with Allen Wolfe of the Long Beach *Independent-Press Telegram*. Pook and Dyer were prepared to push a point, and their point of reference was the Monaco Grand Prix, "a single bastion against the so-called progress of 'text book race tracks.'"[16]

The concept of Chris Pook for the Long Beach Grand Prix was approved by the Long Beach city council in November 1974. The race was routed through downtown Long Beach and on roadways developed on the tidelands fill in the center of the image. Federal investigators swarmed Long Beach city offices during the same week that the Grand Prix was approved. One of the names the investigators uncovered in Long Beach was Jay Sarno of Las Vegas, former public front of Caesars Palace. The THUMS oil drilling island in the foreground is manmade. THUMS was an acronym of Texaco, Humble, Union, Mobil, and Standard oil companies. The facade and landscaping of the island were designed by Joseph Linesch, one of the original Disneyland landscape architects. The *Queen Mary* ocean liner would berth at the left of the image when it arrived in Long Beach harbor in December 1967. Organized crime connections arrived in Long Beach along with the storied vessel (Rick Lake collection).

Chris Pook and Don Dyer envisioned just such a race on the downtown and tideland waterfront streets of Long Beach. Pook and Dyer were joined in their vision by racing legend Dan Gurney. Remarkably, Les Richter, would-be promoter of the failed Western U.S. Grand Prix, joined the formative promotion as well. "The American Grand Prix at Long Beach, a fully sanctioned international Formula 1 Grand Prix," wrote Allen Wolfe for the *Independent*, "is the ultimate goal of race organizers."[17]

By 1974, both Chris Pook and Don Dyer had immersed themselves in the civic affairs of Long Beach. Rotary Club, Lions Club, and the Long Beach State football boosters, all were lavished and leveraged in the advance of the Grand Prix pitch. The municipal engagement of the pair was not entirely unlike the play of East Coast gamblers upon their remote postings to Las Vegas. Pook from England and Dyer from Idaho, however, likely did not cast the same shadow as the hoodlum list from Miami.

The addition of Gurney and Richter thus lent the requisite air of legitimacy to their Long Beach profile.

"There were two major considerations that prompted me to get into this," Pook explained. "First, within the last year the FIA was reassessed their position ... of the United States holding more than one Formula 1 race."[18] The FIA, in fact, had taken this pitch nearly three years before, granting a second U.S. Formula One date before the 1971 Questor Grand Prix was run. "I can only think," Pook continued, "that they saw the obvious merit of tapping the rich Los Angeles market."[19] Here too, though, was a play the FIA had already run, sanctioning the 1960 U.S. Grand Prix at Riverside Raceway.

"Can you imagine ABC Wide World of Sport televising it," Pook wondered, "to 80 million people around the world with the International Towers, the Pacific Ocean and the Queen Mary in the background?"[20] The imagery offered by the promotions and travel man suggested that a glossy travel brochure was not far behind. To the credit of Chris Pook, broadcast contracts and global audiences were also the real marketplace, where the *real* money was to be made. The television pitch might further suggest that Bernard C. Ecclestone was already whispering in the ear of Christopher R. Pook.

Mention of the *Queen Mary* restoration project was instructive. A civic undertaking of massive scale, the *Queen Mary* would draw the ranks of the organized crime syndicate and their apparent proxies. The *Queen Mary* and the Long Beach Grand Prix would then take turns in the Southern California headlines, one seeming constantly to either be dragging or drafting the other.

Chris Pook also touted the motorsports credentials of Dan Gurney and Les Richter. "We have two of the most respected men in the motorsports field helping us," offered Pook, "and they would not jeopardize their good standing with fly-by-night, ill-conceived venture."[21] Dan Gurney would be a fixture in the organizational structure of the Long Beach Grand Prix. Les Richter, on the other hand, later jabbed at Chris Pook's assessment of the effort.

Inevitably, Chris Pook invoked City Hall as well. "Now all we have to do," furthered Pook, "is get the support of the community, City Manager John Mansell's office, and the City Council for the project to become a reality."[22] Indeed, the Long Beach Grand Prix project followed closely behind the *Queen Mary* project. With cost overruns publicized in the tens of millions, the *Queen Mary* restoration and redevelopment project was regarded as a classic municipal boondoggle, a civic standard-bearer of waste and mismanagement. Further, allegations of fraud, sweetheart contracts, bribery, and the infiltration of organized crime further stained the undertaking.

Perhaps unavoidably, allegations of illegal gambling and money laundering also entered the public discourse. "During the last few years," reported the *Los Angeles Times*, "Long Beach has been under continual investigation by the FBI, district attorney, and the federal Strike Force on Organized Crime."[23] The ensuing federal investigations would consume City Manager John Mansell *and* the City Council, all of whom presided over the *Queen Mary* debacle, all of whom also voted unanimously for the Long Beach Grand Prix.

Finally, attorney Don Dyer summarized the essential pitch point. "Everybody knows about the Queen Mary, but they still don't know where Long Beach is," Dyer said, tossing the gauntlet: "I flat guarantee this race will put Long Beach on the map."[24] Attorney Dyer hammered the argument for benefit of the press. Don Dyer, however, was also mistaken. The national crime syndicate knew exactly where Long Beach was, and dispatched Sidney Korshak—the notorious and enigmatic Chicago syndicate attorney—to mediate the stakeholders on the *Queen Mary* project. As the *Queen Mary* project pillaged the public coffers, so too would similar appearances be created by the Long Beach Grand Prix, the effect of persistently alleged multi-level looting. The Long Beach playbook also bore the marks of Allen Dorfman of the Teamsters Central States Pension Fund and Jay Sarno, the development impresario of Caesars Palace.

***

The cumulative costs of the *Queen Mary* and Long Beach Grand Prix projects churned over $100 million in redevelopment activity through the waterfront and downtown of the California port city. Ancillary development would drive that figure much higher. Both endeavors were loosely-structured public-private partnerships. The rather open structures of the consecutive redevelopment efforts also made them ripe for plunder. Further, it was also the sort of civic spending that grabbed the attention of the national crime syndicate.

The development of Caesars Palace some 10 years earlier was a much smaller capital project of some $25 million. The casino of Caesars Palace, however, held the advantage on the back end, while Long Beach was the richer of the short-term burns. The federal investigation in Southern California then drew parallel with the *Queen Mary* fallout and the emerging Long Beach Grand Prix. The probe and its various elements consumed the city for years, while the publicly-funded infrastructure costs of the Long Beach Grand Prix—and allegations of favors to public officials—made for withering headlines.

"[Long Beach] leaders called in crime probe" was the November 15, 1974, blast in the local. "Subpoenas were issued ... to more than a dozen high-ranking Long Beach officials—including a majority of the City Council," read the deck, "ordering them to appear before a ... federal grand jury looking into organized crime's influence on city government."[25]

"Areas of investigation are expected to include gambling and amusement operations, real estate attractions, the financing of the city's purchase of the Queen Mary," read one account, "and alleged bribery and solicitation of payoffs."[26] "Leads are coming in so damn fast," one FBI official said, "that we're having trouble keeping up with them."[27] Indictments in Los Angeles then revealed a vast criminal network with known Mafia members as well as known syndicate racketeers, some with connections dating back to Meyer "Mickey" Cohen and Benjamin "Bugsy" Siegel in the 1940s.[28]

Gambling arrests then followed in Long Beach, an illegal "gambling operation involving dice and card games."[29] Separate arrests were conducted to shut down an apparent game-of-chance in the Long Beach city amusement zone. The Long Beach gambling investigation then steered straight to city council, and the role of council in licensing the operation of the shuttered game. Robert Crow, former city council member and vice mayor, offered damning testimony to the Grand Jury. "Every member of the City Council was offered a certain percentage of the take," Crow stated, "if we would help secure a permit for the game to operate."[30] The Long Beach game operation also included connections to Las Vegas gambling, "Edward Hagen (aka Edward Avakian), former operator of the 'Saratoga,'" a race and sports book in downtown Las Vegas.[31]

It is important to note that the federal investigation into Long Beach was directly alongside the presentation of the Long Beach Grand Prix by Chris Pook and Don Dyer to Long Beach city manager John Mansell and members of the city council. In fact, as the grand jury subpoenas were delivered to city hall on November 14, 1974, by an army of FBI agents, City Manager John Mansell and the Long Beach city council were pondering their votes to move forward with the Grand Prix project.[32] On November 19, 1974, the Long Beach Grand Prix proposal then carried unanimously, "by a 7–0 vote."[33]

The headline news in Long Beach of grand jury, federal agents, and subpoenas then sorted, and another Las Vegas name joined the news reports. "Also currently under question are leases aboard the Queen [Mary]," read the Long Beach daily, "and a possible tie-in between Queen leaseholders and Las Vegas gambling figures."[34] "The probe into the Las Vegas–*Queen Mary* connection appears to have resulted," continued the report, "from … attempts by Las Vegas kingpin Jay Sarno to get a lucrative lease aboard the ship."[35]

Jay Sarno, the deposed emperor of Caesars Palace, was apparently looking for an angle in Long Beach. The name of Sarno's new promotion also had a motorsports ring, the perfect tie-in to the newly-approved Long Beach Grand Prix. Jay Sarno dubbed his venture "Le Mans Speedway."[36] Remarkably, Allen Dorfman of the Teamsters Central States Pension Fund joined Sarno on the board of directors of the coin-operated game company.[37] Amid the long arm of the federal task force, however, Long Beach city officials were concerned that Jay Sarno's new coin arcade business aboard the *Queen Mary* might provide "a front for legitimatizing crime syndicate money."[38]

***

The approval of the Long Beach Grand Prix by city council engaged a new—and certainly unique—development project for the California port city. Despite the magnitude of the *Queen Mary* project, the conversion of the ocean liner required what were otherwise fairly common maritime and commercial construction trades. Labor strife between those two trade groups, however, appeared to open the door for a push by organized crime into the project. The prospect of race vehicles traveling 160 mph on city streets designed for 40 mph, though, brought an entirely new vocation—and vernacular—to the city of Long Beach.

"The Long Beach Grand Prix-United States West," trumpeted the Long Beach daily on December 17, 1974, "took a significant step … when the proposed 2.23 mile course … was formally approved by the Fédération Internationale de l'Automobile

(FIA)."[39] Industrialist Tom Binford of USAC and the Indianapolis 500 carried the proposal to the FIA on recommendation of ACCUS. The proposed course was enthusiastically supported by the FIA safety committee. In fact, a member of the FIA committee personally toured the street layout with Chris Pook two weeks before FBI agents stormed city hall. "This was one of the major obstacles we had to deal with," Pook said. "If we had been denied approval, that in all probability would have been the end."[40]

The Long Beach street circuit also received the blessing of the Grand Prix Drivers Association and the Grand Prix track promoters. Notably missing from the list, however, was FOCA, the constructor's association of Brabham owner Bernie Ecclestone. Indeed, Ecclestone and his syndicate of Formula One platform builders would determine whether there would be a Formula One race in Long Beach at all, just as his iron fist was felt before the proposed "Western U.S. Grand Prix" at Ontario. Despite Chris Pook's typical volubility, Bernie Ecclestone and FOCA appeared to be one subject that the promotions man played close. "There are so many details to be worked out," Pook remarked before the first Formula One event, "that it would be ridiculous to discuss the matter until after Bernie and I have our talk."[41]

Whether domestic Formula 5000 or international Formula One, the Long Beach street circuit faced safety challenges otherwise unique to the Monaco Grand Prix, and the first post-war Grand Prix events in the village of Watkins Glen. "Along the entire length of the circuit will be the latest safety innovations," continued the Long Beach report. "These include escape roads, spin-out areas, the latest design in three-tiered crash barricades, and specially-formulated catch fences."[42] Further, as the Armco post-and-rail crash barrier system was falling out of favor, the Long Beach Grand Prix was a pioneer in a soft-barrier system of tire walls.

One week after the FIA announcement, Bobby Unser drove a Gurney-Eagle Formula 5000 race car down the newly-opened Shoreline Drive. Unser also cut the ceremonial ribbon. Bobby Unser's appearance in the powder-blue Dan Gurney-built race car was fortuitous. Bobby Unser would later win the 1975 Indianapolis 500 in a Gurney-Eagle, as well as drive an updated Gurney-Eagle in the Formula 5000 Long Beach Grand Prix to follow.

Dan Gurney also weighed in on the FIA approval and prognosis for the race event in Long Beach. "I think the city of Long Beach should be commended for its foresight and courage in undertaking an event like this," the American Formula One winner said. "There aren't many cities that would even take a second look at such a project, let alone support it the way Long Beach has."[43]

With the recently-finished *Queen Mary* project, and redevelopment efforts underway along the waterfront and urban core, Long Beach established a track record of supporting innovative city renewal. According to the FBI, though, that track record appeared to be dependent on the extent to which the projects *also* supported the city council—allegedly.

***

The path of Jay Sarno and Las Vegas interests to Long Beach was likely laid some seven years before, quite literally as the *Queen Mary* steamed across the Atlantic

Ocean in 1967 to a dry dock destination at the Long Beach piers. After purchase of the ocean liner by the city of Long Beach, William D. Fugazy was engaged by the city to charter the *Queen Mary* from Cunard Lines in 1967 for its final 39-day voyage from Southampton, south around Cape Horn, and then north to the port of Long Beach. "Two international firms—Diners Club and Fugazy Travel Bureau will be hired," reported the Long Beach daily, "for the final, delivery voyage of the Queen Mary."[44] In fact, Long Beach City Manager John Mansell was quoted on the expertise of Fugazy, saying it was "one of the three top travel agencies in the world, and has been most successful in developing, promoting and sponsoring ocean cruises."[45]

With the *Queen Mary* staged in Southampton, if the reader believes that there are no such things as happy coincidences, that at least a few good conspiracy theories are probably true, and that there really is a national organized crime syndicate, this is as good a place as any to drill in. From the nexus of William Fugazy, the connections to the underworld of organized crime would uncoil like tentacles. Those connections would also extend laterally to Caesars Palace.

In 1960, William Fugazy partnered with the contemptible Roy Cohn in Feature Sports, Inc. to promote the heavyweight boxing rematch between Floyd Patterson and Ingemar Johansson at the Polo Grounds in New York City. "Both Bill and Roy," read one report, "are well connected financially and socially."[46] That title fight, however, was bankrolled by Anthony Salerno of the Genovese crime family. Anthony Salerno was also documented as a hidden investor in Caesars Palace, his points—and the attendant skim—allegedly managed by Jerome Zarowitz.

Four years later, William Fugazy and Roy Cohn found themselves in opposite corners of a federal courtroom. In Cohn's 1964 perjury trial involving the United Dye and Chemical Corp. stock swindle, Fugazy testified for the prosecution against his former business partner. "William D. Fugazy ... testified that Cohn coached him to lie in a 1959 grand jury investigating a stock fraud case," was the news from the trial. "He gave wrong answers ... because he felt sorry for Cohn, 'who was once my friend.'"[47] Further, William Fugazy testified that Roy Cohn sent him as a messenger to Moe Dalitz, Allard Roen, and Sam Garfield of the Desert Inn and Stardust hotel-casinos in Las Vegas, the three men also involved in the United Dye fraud. Notably, Moe Dalitz and Allard Roen were officers in Stardust International Raceway.

As the *Queen Mary* dry-docked, it transitioned from maritime vessel to land-borne construction project. Concurrent with the dry-docking of the ship, Diner's Club was announced as the primary 25-year lessee for the commercial development project. Once again, the lease selection was approved by the Long Beach City Council.[48] One month later, William Fugazy was named as the president of Diners Club by Diner's chairman Alfred Bloomingdale.[49]

Commencement of the *Queen Mary* conversion and construction project did, however, bring labor unrest. While union bosses consulted their work rules, government agencies made efforts to determine just what the *Queen Mary* now *was*, and how codes and standards should apply to the former liner. Amid the disputes, William Fugazy and Alfred Bloomingdale brought in Sidney Korshak. Syndicate attorney Korshak, oft-described as "the most important link between organized crime and legitimate business,"[50] was also a longtime attorney for Diners Club.

Established 1870
FUGAZY TRAVEL BUREAU Inc.
A Division of
THE DINERS CLUB Inc.

OFFERS

The R. M. S.

Queen Mary

ON A

FINAL FABULOUS CRUISE

AROUND SOUTH AFRICA
AND CAPE HORN

Sponsored by

The City of LONG BEACH, CALIFORNIA
U. S. A.

Sailing From

SOUTHHAMPTION, ENGLAND

Embarkation OCT. 30, 1967

William Fugazy of Fugazy Travel Bureau, Inc., provided backstory in both Long Beach and Las Vegas. As the president of Diners Club, Fugazy charted the *Queen Mary* ocean liner for her final voyage to Long Beach, California. Diners Club and Fugazy then managed the *Queen Mary* conversion project and the tens of millions in cost overruns, a municipal debacle that appeared to engage the reach of organized crime. To some extent, the *Queen Mary* project in Long Beach also cemented the tenuous foundations of city government involving the Long Beach Grand Prix. As the majority partner in Feature Sports, Inc, William Fugazy promoted the heavyweight boxing match between Floyd Paterson and Ingemar Johansson. The Patterson-Johansson fight was notably bankrolled by Anthony "Fat Tony" Salerno of the Genovese crime family. Salerno was also an alleged secret owner of Caesars Palace in Las Vegas (author's collection).

"Korshak had been paid $25,000," wrote author Gus Russo, "to help his ... friend Alfred Bloomingdale [chairman of Diners Club] secure a labor contract with the mob-infested Hotel and Restaurant Culinary union."[51] A 1971 audit by the City of Long Beach also confirmed the $25,000 payment by Diners to Korshak.[52]

The famed hotel operation of the *Queen Mary* was yet another port of entry for Sidney Korshak. "Long-standing Korshak client Hyatt, which was to operate a four-hundred-room hotel on board," wrote Russo, "was to join Diners as the principal commercial lessee of the Queen Mary."[53] Indeed, by the time of the 1975 Long Beach Formula 5000 event, the *Queen Mary* lodging operation sailed under flag of Abram Pritzker's Hyatt Hotel chain.

It is also worth mention that, when former Caesars Palace president Nathan Jacobson and investor Judd McIntosh defaulted on the Teamsters mortgage for Kings Castle in Lake Tahoe, the mountain gambling resort was acquired by Abram

Pritzker and Hyatt Hotels. Further, Sidney Korshak reportedly had his own hand in Caesars Palace. Again, according to Russo, "after Hoffa proceeded with the Caesars loan, Korshak … became its labor advisor."[54]

The presence of the Pritzker family of Chicago in the musical chairs of development deals is, perhaps, instructive in itself. Their presence in the *Queen Mary* project also tips the much larger organizational backstory of such elaborately structured undertakings as Caesars Palace. Of the Pritzkers and their super-wealthy cohort, one insider made comment. "There is a network in this country," the insider suggested, "that people come to for deals."[55] Sidney Korshak—also of Chicago—was then often in position to navigate such complex deals between the hidden shadow figures, their public proxies, sources of development funding, and those extorting hidden fees for approval of the funding.

Infamous Chicago syndicate attorney Sidney Korshak brokered labor deals for the beleaguered *Queen Mary* conversion project in Long Beach. Korshak was reportedly also a labor consultant for Caesars Palace in Las Vegas (author's collection).

Finally, it should be noted that William Fugazy also counted a relationship with Elliott Roosevelt—the mayor of Miami Beach—in an effort to acquire the *Queen Elizabeth* ocean liner for Port Everglades, Fort Lauderdale, and Hollywood, Florida.[56] Recall also that Elliott Roosevelt was involved in the bizarre Teamsters loan swindle—with Roy Gene Lewis of Riverside International Raceway and hustler Norman Tyrone—for the Sierra Lake Tahoe, a property that was later developed by Nathan Jacobson as Kings Castle. Again, "there is a network in this country."[57]

It is perhaps fair to say that, when the *Queen Mary* pulled up to the Long Beach pier the fix was in, just as with the Patterson-Johansson bout promoted by William Fugazy and backed by Anthony "Fat Tony" Salerno. Facilitated by William Fugazy, Sidney Korshak, and countless others, the Long Beach treasury would then be plundered—likely for tens of millions of dollars—and apparently rubber-stamped "approved" by John Mansell and the Long Beach City Council. It is remarkable, then, that the lease overture of Jay Sarno was rejected.

The lease application of Jay Sarno, however, was submitted to Long Beach city officials in the midst of the intensified investigations by the FBI and the federal Strike Force on Organized Crime. Further, Allen Dorfman, Sarno's partner in the gaming company, was indicted in February 1974 for fraud related to Teamsters loan approvals. Jay Sarno, too, was in the middle of legal woes, indicted along with Stanley Mallin one month after Dorfman for attempting to bribe an IRS official. In 1974, both Dorfman and Mallin thus would have been glaring signatures on the radar screen of the federal Strike Force.

In a lawsuit arising from newspaper stories involving the Sarno lease, Long Beach Assistant City Manager William Talley noted his apprehensions. "Talley testified … that the Intelligence Division of the Long Beach Police Department," reported the Long Beach daily, "said 'there were possibilities of organized crime figures involved in these leases.'"[58] "Talley said he recommended to…. John Mansell," continued the report, "that the leases be rejected, and they were."[59] William Talley also related the appearance of a Chicago man at City Hall, "to 'find out why they were turning down the leases.'"[60] The visitor from Chicago was not identified in testimony but was likely Allen Dorfman himself, certainly no stranger to Southern California. Notably, Allen Dorfman and Frank Fitzsimmons were also acquainted with William Fugazy.[61]

Jay Sarno's Las Vegas vision was equal parts hubris, hedonism, and hospitality. This image captures the first Caesar of the Palace in his executive suite, the library of the great masters in the left background, Picasso, Renoir, and Van Gogh. Jay Sarno's play with Allen Dorfman for the gaming concessions aboard the *Queen Mary* in Long Beach, though, appeared to be pure master racketeering (author's collection).

Prior to the departure of the *Queen Mary* from Southampton, William Fugazy waxed ebullient about the prospects for the legendary liner in Long Beach. "Long Beach is going to spend $142 million to build a port around the ship," Fugazy said from New York. "They may bring golf tournaments there."[62] Fugazy may then have set the price tag for the syndicate before the 14,500-mile final play of the *Queen Mary* was even run. Further, the City of Long Beach would also bring a Grand Prix event running clockwise circles around the convention core along with a paddock next to the *Queen Mary*.

From the *Queen Mary* project with William Fugazy, to the Long Beach Grand Prix with Chris Pook, the oft-investigated John Mansell and the Long Beach City Council would give their many blessings. As the Long Beach–*Queen Mary* debacle connected at multiple points to the investment interests in Caesars, so too did Chris Pook and the Long Beach Grand Prix arch forward to the parking lot race course of the Caesars Palace Grand Prix.

***

The resolution of the charges by the Securities and Exchange Commission in 1975 against Lum's Inc., Desert Palace, Inc. and individuals on both sides of the Caesars Palace sale represented a significant bullet dodging for the conglomerate. "Without admitting or denying any of the allegations of the Commission's complaint,"[63] the defendants consented to enjoinment, loosely translated as a promise not to do it again. Notably, the SEC did not require that Jerome Zarowitz forfeit the $3.5 million he received in proceeds from the sale of Caesars Palace, nor was there any apparent legal action to resolve income taxes on the windfall.

Against a Teamsters mortgage of $20 million and another $5 million of alleged original shareholder equity, the $60 million sale price of Caesars Palace calculated to approximately $35 million of profit against equity, a 700 percent return in three years. The $3.5 million collected by Jerome Zarowitz thus appeared to represent a 10 percent equity position by unknown and unlicensed interests. Further, the dubious cross section of *known* licensees cast doubt on whether they were legitimate stand-alone investors or whether, they too, were simply nominees for a broad-base syndicate investment.

The SEC action was also to be a bellwether for regime change at the corporate parent, the former Lum's Inc., now renamed Caesars World, Inc. In fact, regime change away from Miami hot dog stands and Las Vegas hucksters, toward mainstream corporate America had already begun. With the apparent exposure of Melvin Chasen during the SEC disclosures, Clifford Perlman and Caesars World made a change at the top.

"William H. McElnea … will resign as a partner of the investment banking house of Van Alstyne, Noel, & Co.," reported the *Miami News*, "and take over the president's chair."[64] McElnea was already well-acquainted with the financial profile of Caesars World, serving as an outside director of Lum's while still posted at Val Alstyne. William McElnea was also integral to the Lum's stock offering in 1969, the financing vehicle for the purchase of Caesars Palace. Further, McElnea had avoided mention during the SEC action, and the stain of insider trading that had sullied Melvin Chasen. Finally, Bill McElnea was also involved in the early discussions involving the Caesars Palace Grand Prix.

Two years later, Clifford Perlman signed another skilled player for the Caesars organization. William D. "Bill" Weinberger, son of William S. Weinberger, joined Caesars World in 1974. The younger Weinberger would also report to William McElnea, the new corporate president. "When Cliff Perlman, my father and I were having breakfast at Caesars Palace the morning he told me to contact Bill McElnea," recalled Bill Weinberger, "Cliff was sitting between my father and me. While Cliff was telling me about the job my father was, unseen by Cliff, shaking his head 'No.'"[65]

The admonition by the senior Weinberger, an investor in the original Caesars Palace consortium, certainly raised alarm. "Later when I asked my father why, he explained Caesars World (CWI) was on the brink of bankruptcy, there was a contentious lawsuit in progress between CWI and the sellers of Caesars Palace (of which my father was a party) due to the fact that CWI had reneged on the original deal," continued Bill Weinberger, "[and] there was a Justice Department investigation going on regarding the terms of the sale and Caesars Palace's financial performance during the

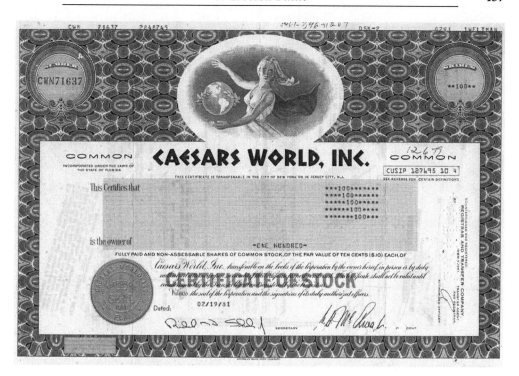

Lum's, Inc. was renamed Caesars World, Inc. after the Securities and Exchange Commission filed action in 1971 against the ownership group of Caesars Palace. William McElnea joined Caesars World in 1972. The facsimile signature of McElnea as president of Caesars World endorses this stock certificate. Richard Sheehan, Jr., signs as corporate secretary. In a split decision, William McElnea survived the license hearings of the new Jersey Casino Control Commission in 1981. McElnea was also involved in the early planning of the Caesars Palace Grand Prix with William D. Weinberger (author's collection).

transition."[66] The younger Weinberger, already a successful investment baking partner at McDonald and Co. in Cleveland, was forced to confront the continued financial turmoil, as well as a 50 percent pay cut.

Indeed, as William D. Weinberger pondered his career move to Caesars World, the sins of the consortium yet hung over the corporation. Caesars World shares were still in steep decline, trading below $5, a virtual junk stock. Meanwhile, the former public faces of Caesars Palace sought to collect their due, while they also confronted their separate financial and legal troubles. Nathan Jacobson was mired in Kings Castle debt and a troubled Teamsters mortgage. Jay Sarno and Stanley Mallin, on the other hand, were under indictment in the IRS bribery case. Amid the widespread financial questions of the Caesars deal partners, Nevada gambling regulators threw a lifeline. "The Nevada Gaming Commission has approved plans by Caesars World, Inc.," reported Nevada press, "to turn over one million shares of stock to former owners of Caesars Palace."[67]

Despite the uncertainties at Caesars World, Inc., William D. Weinberger took the cut in compensation to join Clifford Perlman, William McElnea, and the beleaguered parent corporation in Los Angeles. "I paid no attention to what today looks like sound advice and made the move anyway," recalls Bill Weinberger. "I'm not sorry

I did."[68] The career move placed father and son under the same corporate umbrella, although William S. Weinberger was posted separately at Caesars Palace in Las Vegas. It was a career transition that later positioned the younger Weinberger in charge of sports promotions at Caesars Palace. In 1981, William D. "Bill" Weinberger then went on to assemble his own consortium, Chris Pook and Jack Long from the Long Beach Grand Prix among them. Bill Weinberger, representing Caesar, would also negotiate for the new consortium with Bernie Ecclestone, the recognized czar of Formula One. The new sports promotion was, of course, the Caesars Palace Grand Prix.

New frontline hires notwithstanding, board chairman Clifford Perlman remained in charge at Caesars World, Inc. and by extension, Caesars Palace. Indeed, Clifford Perlman was present to preside from on high over the 1981 Caesars Palace Grand Prix. In fact, other than for troubling national headlines, the 1981 Caesars Palace Grand Prix was one of the final public appearances in the reign of Clifford Perlman as Caesar of the Palace. Clifford Perlman was soon operating inexplicably with Alvin Malnik, while the publicly-traded Caesars World, Inc., was once again left in the dark. The bizarre dealings with Alvin Malnik, though, also gathered the dark clouds from which Clifford Perlman would ultimately depart Caesars Palace.

William D. Weinberger of Cleveland joined the Los Angeles offices of Caesars World, Inc. in 1974. William D. Weinberger was the son of William S. Weinberger, one of the original 1966 gambling licensees of Caesars Palace. In 1974, the senior William S. Weinberger was president of the Caesars Palace resort. William D. Weinberger attended the Long Beach Grand Prix in 1977 and joined Caesars Palace later that year as father William S. moved on to Atlantic City gambling. With the blessing of Clifford Perlman and William McElnea, William D. "Bill" Weinberger then developed the Caesars Palace Grand Prix (Bill Weinberger collection).

***

The approval of the Long Beach street circuit by the FIA was an incremental step on the journey toward Formula One. In March of 1975, as the FIA finalized the 1976 race calendar, the news that Chris Pook so eagerly awaited finally came through. "The Long Beach Grand Prix-United States West," reported the Long Beach daily, "was granted final approval at a meeting of the Fédération Internationale de l'Automobile (FIA) executive committee."[69] Approval by the FIA for the Formula One event was the last piece of the international sanctioning puzzle for the California race event. The announcement by the FIA was also timely. To wit, the Long

Beach City Council had finalized their own contract with Chris Pook one month before.[70]

Despite the approvals of city government and the FIA, however, neither the Formula 5000 event nor the 1976 Formula One event could turn a wheel without the approval of the California Coastal Commission. Governing 1,100 miles of California coastline, the Coastal Commission had only been in existence since 1972. Nonetheless, the Commission controlled the use of much of the industrial and urban areas of Long Beach, including the entire Grand Prix circuit on tidelands fill. The review process by the state agency consumed a full seven months after the Long Beach city council first approved Chris Pook's concept. The high-level state review of the low-altitude Long Beach program then produced a single outcome. Promoter Pook was directed to offer away-excursions for those neighboring residents who simply did not want to be bothered by the noise of the race events. The review by commission was also echoed by the Caesars Palace Grand Prix, as county government attempted to leverage a desirable property grant completely unrelated to the race circuit adjacent to the Las Vegas Strip.

Approval by the Coastal Commission then cleared the way for a full summer build-up to the Long Beach Formula 5000 Grand Prix. The build-up also made great news fodder, while it further tipped the backstory. "Pook said he conceived the idea two years ago after a luncheon with Bob Lichtenham and Paul Baessler," reported the *Los Angeles Times*, "managers of the Long Beach convention and news bureau."[71]

"Ten days later I came up with the idea for the Grand prix," Chris Pook said. "Auto racing … is recognized around the world and would present an opportunity to gain overnight international recognition for the city."[72] That close connection with the convention authority—as well as the harbor commission—would be illuminated going forward. Further, a new convention center was deed-obligated to reimburse state funding for the completed *Queen Mary* project. The many relationships In Long Beach were thus convoluted, while contentiousness and controversy would often follow.

Amid the build-up, Chris Pook had to acknowledge the obvious, the failure of the 1972 Formula One Grand Prix at Ontario and, in turn, Riverside. "It was tough talking to the FIA," Pook said. "They were a little miffed about the Ontario thing and I can't blame them."[73] Pook also had to address the 81,000-ton pachyderm at the pier. "It certainly hurt us," Chris Pook stated of the *Queen Mary*, "and I think the judgement of the city fathers is being questioned again—'Are you giving us another Queen Mary?'—which is a shame."[74] By 1975, the term "*Queen Mary*" might have been co-opted as a euphemism, unpleasant and—at the same time—rather painful.

Pre-race press also noted the involvement of the Long Beach general fund in the motorsports promotion. "Long Beach city officials agreed to advance $400,000 that was already scheduled in the master plan," reported the *Los Angeles Times*, "and to pay another $101,500 for special reinforcing, pavement, curbs, and safety barriers that will be paid back by the race promoters."[75] Amid the federal investigation and the increased scrutiny at City Hall, the public investment in the otherwise private *for-profit* promotion would become a flashpoint. "The city is being paid for *extraordinary costs* [italics added], such as extra police" was the terminology offered to the public.[76]

The *Los Angeles Times* also touted the investment and financing of the Long

The inaugural Long Beach Grand Prix brought the cars of the 1975 SCCA Formula 5000 series to the California port city. Paddock facilities also offered overlap with the troubled Long Beach *Queen Mary* project. In 1975, the *Queen Mary* lodging operation was notably flying the flag of Abram Pritzker's Hyatt Hotels. The same year, Hyatt Hotels acquired the troubled Lake Tahoe resort that had been variously stained by Roy Gene Lewis of Riverside International Raceway, Elliott Roosevelt, Norman Tyrone, Calvin Kovens, and Nathan Jacobson. The Lola T332 of Tuck Thomas is in the foreground. The hauler of Don Nichols's UOP Shadow team is in the right background. The THUMS oil island is in left background (Rick Lake collection).

Beach Grand Prix Association itself. Building on a $40,000 start-up investment by Chris Pook and his partners, "additional funding is being arranged through a special intrastate public offering to raise from $950,000 to $1,575,000 for operational and organizational expenses."[77] As late as six weeks before the Long Beach Formula 5000 event, though, the take from the public offering was still locked in escrow by the California Corporations Commission. "Now we can get down to the business of putting on a race," Chris Pook commented in Long Beach. "With the funds released, we can accomplish what we said we would do."[78]

Two days after the splash in the *Los Angeles Times*, Les Richter of Riverside International Raceway resigned from the Long Beach Grand Prix Association. Logically, Richter was somewhat competing with himself, spread between two separate Southern California auto racing promotions. The very public loss of Les Richter, though, would sting the Long Beach effort. Richter's public comments after the 1976 Long Beach Formula One Grand Prix would sting even worse.

On the heels of Les Richter's departure, the Formula One series was rocked, and Bernie Ecclestone's FOCA was front-and-center. "The Formula One Constructors Association, in a financial dispute with race organizers," it was reported across North America, "announced it has withdrawn from [the] Canadian Grand Prix."[79] At issue—as with the "Western U.S. Grand Prix" at Ontario—was the cost of transportation. Despite agreements with the FIA, the Canadian organizers had not agreed with the demands of Bernie Ecclestone for a transportation premium. Absent the payment of an additional $65,000, FOCA and their member teams refused to appear. Representing nearly every Formula One chassis constructor, Ecclestone promised the organizers a cancellation, and then delivered. "When I say I'll do something," Ecclestone said, "I do it."[80]

With Bernie Ecclestone at the nexus, pundits inevitably played the gambling angle. "He was only playing the first ace of a loaded hand," ran an opinion from Canada, "Next season, any of the other hidden aces will be played."[81] "[FOCA] is gearing up for next year ... when the already sizable stakes are to be increased enormously," continued the op-ed, "and those that don't wish to waltz—well, many new partners are waiting in the wings."[82] "Next season," naturally, included the Long Beach Grand Prix. Headed into their Formula 5000 event, Chris Pook, Don Dyer, and Dan Gurney had cause to pay heed. Indeed, a similar breakdown between Chris Pook and Bernie Ecclestone would eventually spell the end of Formula One in Long Beach.

The termination of the 1975 Canadian Grand Prix was also fair warning to the upstate New York hamlet of Watkins Glen and Malcolm Currie of the Grand Prix Corporation. Further, William D. "Bill" Weinberger would soon be in the wings at Caesars Palace in Las Vegas, and the invitation to the Formula One circus would shortly come.

***

"Caesars World, Inc., owner of the sumptuous Caesars Palace hotel-casino on the Las Vegas strip," trumpeted the *Los Angeles Times*, "is under investigation by Nevada gaming authorities because of a multi-million-dollar transaction early this year with Alvin Ira Malnik."[83] The blast in the *Los Angeles Times* seeded similar headlines across the country, from Las Vegas, Nevada, all the way to Miami, Florida. Further, the news came less than 6 months after the final disposition of the Securities and Exchange Commission action against Caesars World and the former partners in Caesars Palace.

"Malnik is a Miami Beach lawyer," the *Times* leaned in, "long associated in business with organized crime figures."[84] Alvin Malnik was only 32 years old; his national profile was already well-established. Whispers of his being the heir-apparent to Meyer Lansky had turned to shouts as the FBI tapped the Malnik law office in the early 1960s. Further, Alvin Malnik's property deals in Miami with Sam Cohen were well-documented. Cohen, the convicted Flamingo skim felon and indicted co-conspirator with Meyer Lansky, was indeed a visible partner with Malnik in the Sky Lake development in Miami.

"Nevada investigators learned some weeks ago of Malnik's role in a partnership that bought two 'honeymoon resorts' in Pennsylvania ... from Caesars World," continued the *Times*, "and then immediately leased the properties back to the company for $42.6 million on a 20-year lease."[85] The sale of Cove Haven was publicized regionally in February of 1975.[86] Conspicuously omitted from regional coverage, though, were the names of the purchase partners, Alvin Malnik and Sam Cohen.

Further at issue with Nevada regulators—and also inexplicable—was an investment by Caesars World, Inc. in the Sky Lake development of Alvin Malnik and San Cohen. Here too, the Sky Lake purchase was previously publicized. Incredibly, the Sky Lake purchase occurred during the multiple investigations involving the purchase of Caesars Palace by Lum's, Inc. from Jay Sarno, Stanley Mallin, and Nathan Jacobson.

"Lum's, Inc. announced an agreement … to lease and acquire a property in North Miami Beach," read a Las Vegas newspaper report in late 1971. "The property includes the Sky Lake Country Club … and approximate three-hundred acres of developable real estate."[87] The report further described the transaction as a long-term lease with purchase option. Notably, the Sky Lake announcement included the names of the sellers. "Lum's has the option to purchase in 1974 or 1975 all the stock … from its present owners," continued the article, "Alvin Malnick [sic], Samuel Cohen, and members of the Cohen family."[88]

Reporting in early 1974 then confirmed that the renamed Caesars World, Inc. had completed the land purchases and continued with a long-term lease for the Sky Lake Country Club.[89] To some extent, the Sky Lake and Cove Haven transactions between Caesars World and Alvin Malnik pointed up the effect of the corporate veil in ancillary dealings involving Nevada gambling licensees. In the financial priorities of Caesars World, Inc.—publicly traded on the New York Stock Exchange—the corporation answered first to Wall Street, then to shareholders, and finally, to the Nevada Gaming Commission. It is worth mention that the various Sky Lake reporting did not list its high-profile country club apartment residents, Frank Fitzsimmons, Jackie Presser, and Allen Dorfman, nor one of the builders, Cal Kovens.

Shortly after the Sky Lake announcement, Caesars World further expanded its gambling portfolio with the $13.5 million acquisition of the Thunderbird hotel-casino from Del Webb. The Thunderbird, originally opened in 1948, was acquired by Del Webb in 1964 from Joe Wells, former operator of Thunderbird Speedway in Henderson, Nevada. Like the Flamingo, the Thunderbird was yet another Meyer Lansky-tainted resort upon which Las Vegas pinned its early foundations.[90]

Caesars World then announced an ambitious plan to develop a $150 million hotel and shopping complex on the site of the Thunderbird, a 2,000-room behemoth to be called the "Mark Anthony." An obvious abstract of "Mark Antony," the new resort would have been a bookend piece to Caesars Palace, the tragedy of Julius Caesar thus anchoring both ends of the famed Las Vegas Strip. The luxury shopping component would also presage the Forum Shops at Caesars Palace, developed over the former Caesars Palace north parking lot after cancellation of the Caesars Palace Grand Prix.

Four months after the Caesars World, Inc. sale of Cove Haven to Alvin Malnik, the Mark Anthony plans were cancelled. "We can't raise the financing," William D. Weinberger said. "We searched worldwide for the money and we were unable to secure it."[91] Notably, only two years after the Middle East oil embargo, the Mark Anthony project reportedly included efforts "to attract Arabian petrodollars."[92]

The Cove Haven purchase by Alvin Malnik purportedly involved 100 percent financing from the Teamsters; neither Malnik nor Cohen thus had cash in the deal.[93]

More so—nearly 10 years on from Jimmy Hoffa's much-publicized grand opening appearance in the Caesars Palace *Circus Maximus* showroom—Caesars World, Inc. had tied itself to yet another Teamsters mortgage.

Corporate president William McElnea was quoted on the longer-term Cove Haven prospects, ostensibly concocted to infuse short-term cash into Caesars World. "We think," offered McElnea, "that we made one hell of a deal."[94] The "we," however, included Alvin Malnik, while the operative word in McElnea's exclamation may thus have been "Hell." Further, the Cove Haven sale stood at odds with the extended Sky Lake investments and the concurrent purchase of the Thunderbird Hotel.

Once more, only six months removed from the SEC enjoinment, Caesars World found itself in the crosshairs of the commission. "The Securities & Exchange Commission," continued the *Times* reporting, "is investigating the adequacy of the disclosures relating to this transaction."[95] Reporting described the shareholder disclosures simply as "sketchy."[96]

One day after the extensive *Los Angeles Times* report, the news for Caesars World got worse, and rather weird. "Jeff Silver, a member of the Nevada Gaming Control Board," opened a Las Vegas dateline, "asserts that the Thunderbird Hotel … received $2 million for working capital from the Teamsters Pension Fund through a middle man, Alvin Ira Malnik of Miami Beach."[97] The Thunderbird item was scarcely reported, yet involved Alvin Malnik effectively investing in a Las Vegas casino. The $2 million loan also recalled the origins of the Thunderbird hotel-casino itself wherein Jake Lansky—brother of Meyer—made loans to Thunderbird owners Marion Hicks and Nevada Lt. Governor Clifford Jones.

The Thunderbird affair was also believed by Nevada regulators to be tied to the Cove Haven sale, and was thus incorporated into the investigation. Once again, from a rather flat footing, the Nevada Gaming Commission imposed a ruling directly against Caesars World, Inc., requiring that the publicly-traded corporate parent abide by Nevada gaming regulations otherwise imposed only on the gambling operating company, Desert Palace, Inc.

In the course of the reporting, it was also revealed that Clifford Perlman was cautioned in 1972 by Nevada regulators about further dealings with Alvin Malnik. Throwing such caution to the desert wind, Clifford Perlman and Caesars World then engaged further with Alvin Malnik in Sky Lake properties, the Sky Lake country club itself, and sale-leaseback of Cove Haven in the Poconos. Clifford Perlman also invested personally in the Cricket Club in Miami, a development of which Alvin Malnik was president. The contractor for the Cricket Club was, of course, Calvin Kovens.

Peter Echeverria, chairman of the Nevada Gaming Commission, was quoted on the relationship between Caesars World, Clifford Perlman, and Alvin Malnik. The investigation of Malnik, stated Echeverria, "caused us to think he's closer to Meyer Lansky than we had been led to believe."[98]

Clifford Perlman was asked in late 1975 by investors if Caesars World shareholders should be concerned about the fallout of the Nevada investigation. Perlman apparently played it straight from ego. "No," remarked Perlman, "I don't think so."[99] Caesars World stock then closed out 1975 at 3⅛, down another 25 percent from the announcement of the 1970 SEC action against Lum's Inc.

The Securities and Exchange Commission investigation of Caesars World and the Cove Haven sale then continued. As Caesars World sought to expand into Atlantic City gambling, the New Jersey Casino Control Commission overlapped the SEC, and picked up the twisted trail of Clifford Perlman and Alvin Malnik. The ego of Perlman would not, however, play well with New Jersey investigators. Secret recordings in the Abscam case then further connected Clifford Perlman and Alvin Malnik, as well as connected Malnik to Caesars Palace. Standing later as a testament to their well-forged relationship, in 1981 the signage of "Caesars Pocono Resorts"—still owned by Alvin Malnik—would be displayed proudly at the Caesars Palace Grand Prix.

***

News banners during the week before the 1975 Long Beach Formula 5000 Grand Prix brought firsthand ride-along reports of the new street circuit. Reporters lauded the unique safety features of the downtown street circuit. As well, the daily dispatches introduced names that would converge 6 years ahead in the parking lot of the Caesars Palace Grand Prix.

IndyCar veteran Al Unser, back-to-back winner of the 1970 and 1971 Indianapolis 500, provided the media ride-alongs in the sponsoring Toyota Celica GT. "This is the greatest thing to ever happen to racing in America," Unser offered. "For years, we've been waiting for some city to have the guts to put a course like this together. Now that it's happening, I think a dozen cities will follow the leader."[100] Al Unser may not have been privy to the backroom negotiations with City Manager John Mansell, but Unser's notion of follow-on urban Formula One events would bear out. Further, in the never-ending battle of

Al Unser competed in the inaugural 1975 Long Beach Grand Prix driving a Lola T332 for the Vel's–Parnelli Jones team. Unser qualified second, won his heat race, and led the main event into the first turn. At the 1984 Caesars Palace Grand Prix IV, Al Unser raced hard with Tom Sneva for the win (Rick Lake collection).

the import tuner coupes, Al Unser also provided the media ride-alongs for the sponsoring Datsun 280ZX at the 1981 Caesars Palace Grand Prix.

Marketing man Jack Long of Long Enterprises was introduced by the Long Beach Grand Prix Association, tasked with selling sponsorships for the inaugural event. Long was credited with landing the Toyota partnership, as well as a CBS highlight telecast of the race. Jack Long was also hired later as the vice president of marketing for the Caesars Palace Grand Prix, a post he held under the Caesars umbrella until the final Caesars IndyCar Grand Prix in 1984. Further, Jack Long and William D. Weinberger of Caesars Palace partnered later in their own motorsport promotions company, organizing the productions of the 1984 Detroit and Dallas Formula One Grand Prix events.

Safety features around the Long Beach street circuit were a noticeable point of departure from the Watkins Glen race course. Armco barriers—culprits in the death of two Formula One drivers at the U.S. Grand Prix in two years—were not part of the Long Beach plan. "Many recent deaths to race drivers can be attributed to cars wedging underneath, or between, Armco-like barriers," stated safety director Peter Talbot. "By using tires and oil drums, we eliminate the hazard."[101] Indeed, some 25,000 rubber tires were lashed together to provide an energy-absorbing barrier in the event race cars left the circuit. Another 50 feet of separation was then laid out to further isolate the limits of the course from spectator areas. Concrete rails and chain-link catch fences were also strategically located to confine the action.

The run-up to race day also invited inevitable logistical comparisons to the time-honored Watkins Glen Grand Prix course, by then 25 years removed from competition on the Glen's village streets. "There are plenty of problems [Long Beach] will face which the Watkins Glen Grand Prix Corporation never has to consider," ran one opinion piece from upstate New York. "Housing, food, sanitary facilities—where is it all going to come from?"[102] The upstate New York hamlet of 2,000 thus dropped the gauntlet—on the Southern California city of some quarter-million.

***

The race weekend for the 1975 Long Beach Formula 5000 Grand Prix opened to sunny California skies, temperatures in the seventies, and a pleasant offshore breeze. California weather was yet one more point of comparison between Long Beach and Watkins Glen. Indeed, three of the five remaining U.S. Grand Prix events at Watkins Glen were to be affected by rain.

"With a cloud of blue smoke and a thunderous roar," opened the race day story in the local daily, "the Long Beach Grand Prix will finally become a racing reality today."[103] The long-awaited west coast racing event and strong Long Beach crowd had already been warmed up by the opening acts, Friday practice and Saturday qualifying sessions featuring the stars of the USAC-SCCA Formula 5000 series, some Formula One transplants, IndyCar crossovers, and the also-rans.

A reported 25,000 spectators swarmed the Long Beach stands and sidelines on Saturday to see American favorites Mario Andretti, Al Unser, Danny Ongais, Gordon Johncock, and Brett Lunger join international names Chris Amon, Jody Scheckter, Jackie Oliver, Brian Redman, Tony Brice, David Hobbs, and Tom Pryce. Can-Am

Mario Andretti was paired with Al Unser on the 1975 Vel's–Parnelli Jones Formula 5000 team. Andretti set the first lap record during qualifying for the new Long Beach Grand Prix circuit. Mario Andretti also won his heat and started the Formula 5000 main event on pole. In 1983, Andretti would win the CART IndyCar Caesars Palace Grand Prix III (Rick Lake collection).

champion in 1972, George Follmer joined the Long Beach show as did Can-Am veteran John Cannon. The Long Beach Grand Prix thus sported two race winners of premier events at the former Stardust International Raceway in Las Vegas, John Cannon at the 1966 SCCA U.S. Road Racing Championship and Danny Ongais in the funny car class at the 1969 NHRA National Open.

To the delight of the partisan crowd, Mario Andretti and his Vel's-Parnelli Jones Viceroy Lola T332 set the first lap record of the Long Beach Grand Prix circuit, qualifying on pole with a time of 1:21.297 around the 2.02-mile course. Andretti's resultant speed average of 89.45 mph was 5 mph faster than Niki Lauda's qualifying speed for the 1975 Monaco Grand Prix, certainly a consideration for a close-quarters street contest. Nonetheless, top racers were approaching 170 mph on the sweeping Shoreline Drive straight. Mario Andretti was understandably upbeat after his qualifying performance. "I never thought it would happen in America," Andretti exulted. "It's here, though, and it can be nothing but good."[104]

Andretti's teammate Al Unser was next on the time sheets with a lap of 1:21.94. Oval veteran Unser was a road racing revelation to both the Formula drivers and the Long Beach audience. "The Pikes Peak hill climb is how the Unser brothers learned how to do road racing way before the other drivers did," recalled Bobby Unser of the familial right-turn prowess, "No one should ever think that Pikes Peak was a straight road. 160 turns, half of them to the left ... but half of them to the right."[105]

Andretti and Unser were followed in qualifying by the internationals, Tony Brise, Jackie Oliver, Tom Pryce, and Brian Redman. Redman was also the Formula

5000 points leader in his Carl Haas Lola. Notably, Vern Schuppan qualified seventh in a Dan Gurney-prepared Jorgensen-Eagle. Formula One driver Jody Scheckter slotted tenth in a Lola. Danny Ongais was down the time sheets in 20th while George Follmer trailed in 24th. Formula One and Can-Am regular Chris Amon qualified 26th in a Talon-Chevrolet, nearly 6 seconds off of Andretti's pole.

The qualifying order was then split by alternating times into a pair of 12-lap heats. The first 12 finishers in each heat then advanced to the starting grid for the Formula 5000 final. Four additional drivers were also added at the promoters' option. Fast qualifier Mario Andretti started on pole for the first heat. Andretti led into turn one before he overcooked it, nearly ending his day in the tire barriers. Tony Brise, Tom Pryce, and Vern Schuppan slipped past the faltering Andretti. Mario Andretti gave chase, picking off Schuppan and Price and then setting after Tony Brise. Andretti also uncorked a race lap that was faster than his qualifying effort, gaining on Brise by two seconds per lap. At the finish, though, it was Tony Brise over Mario Andretti by 0.017 seconds, only a tire diameter separating them across the Long Beach finish line.

Second qualifier Al Unser in the companion Vel's–Parnelli Lola then led off in heat two. Unser, though, gapped Brian Redman by nearly a second a lap to take his 12-lap heat win convincingly. Formula One convert Jackie Oliver, however, spun off in his UOP Shadow and could not return. Brian Redman was followed through by Jody Scheckter, David Hobbs, Eppie Weitzes, Chris Amon, and John Cannon.

The qualifying and the heats of the Long Beach Grand Prix put a premium on handling and speed. The rough paving, surface transitions, and the Shoreline Drive hairpins then tested both driver and drivetrain in the afternoon final. "This course is going to be extremely hard on equipment," noted Mario Andretti. "It puts a big demand on transmission and brakes. Just surviving … will be a major accomplishment."[106] Andretti would take the same lament to the Caesars Palace Formula One Grand Prix.

Heat winners Al Unser and Tony Brise lined up on the front row for the 50-lap main event of the Long Beach Formula 5000 Grand Prix, followed by their respective runners-up, Brian Redman and Mario Andretti. "Due to constant delays in the program," it was reported, "the feature race did not get underway until 5:10 p.m."[107]

Al Unser would then lead the pack into the first turn of the final, holding point to complete the first lap on the Long Beach street circuit over Brise, Andretti, and Redman. Tony Brise, though, soon passed Unser and took off, gapping the field until lap 15 when he spun. Brise rejoined but Andretti and Unser moved by. The Long Beach crowd cheered as the two Americans commanded the front. Al Unser then clipped one of the concrete barriers on lap 17 and retired. Mario Andretti continued at the point, followed by Tony Brise and a trailing Brian Redman.

Tony Brise then chased Mario Andretti for nine laps, finally out-braking Andretti into a turn and making it stick. On lap 23, though, Mario Andretti slowed. Andretti then pulled off on Shoreline Drive, the prophetic victim of a broken drivetrain. Tony Brise, unchallenged, survived for only one more lap before he too was off with drive issues. Well past halfway, Brian Redman then advanced—from a presumptive third at best—to the lead of the race. Brian Redman held the point for another 16 circuits, crossing the finish line on Ocean Boulevard in his Carl Haas

The starting field of the inaugural 1975 Long Beach Grand Prix prepares for 50 laps of combat through the streets of the California port city. Identified from front to back, right to left, Al Unser (#51), Tony Brise (#64), Mario Andretti (#5), Tom Pryce (#00), Jody Scheckter (#3), David Hobbs (#10), Vern Schuppan (#48), Eppie Weitzes (#94), Chris Amon (#2). Unser, Andretti, and Hobbs went on to race in various disciplines at the Caesars Palace Grand Prix (Rick Lake collection).

Lola-Chevrolet amid very long shadows to win the inaugural Long Beach Grand Prix.

"I don't like to win in this fashion. I'll be the first to admit that I backed into it," remarked Brian Redman from the twilight victory celebration. "But winning is always nice, no matter how one attains it."[108] The Formula 5000 regular competing against IndyCar and Formula One standouts was astute, although history certainly records no asterisks. With the Laguna Seca and Riverside rounds yet to go, Brian Redman also clinched his second USAC-SCCA Formula 5000 championship.

Brian Redman was followed to the finish by Vern Schuppan, some 30 seconds back in the Gurney-Eagle, a fine second place recorded for Dan Gurney as an officer of the Long Beach Grand Prix Association. Eppie Weitzes was third, the only other car on the lead lap. Chris Amon advanced nicely to finish fourth, from 12th on the grid and a dismal 26th on the time sheets. Notably, only 11 drivers made it to the finish. Tony Brise and Mario Andretti were credited with 12th and 13th, respectively. George Follmer, dominant in the Can-Am series for Roger Penske only three years before, was last.

Chris Pook reported that paid attendance was 46,500, a solid number through the turnstiles of a downtown festival. Over 15,000 more were estimated to watch the race from rooftops and balconies outside the event perimeter. Paid attendance, however, was well short of projections. Nonetheless, the post-race was positive. "I would think," Pook judged, "one would say it was a success."[109] Further, Chris Pook was forging his reputation as someone who could assemble an internationally-flavored motorsport competition as an urban festival, no matter what it took. It was a skillset he also deployed at the Caesars Palace Grand Prix along the Las Vegas strip.

Long Beach city government, integral to the Long Beach Grand Prix project—as well as the federal organized crime investigation—weighed in as well. "I was naturally concerned," City Manager John Mansell offered after the race. "Long Beach had a lot at stake but my reaction after three days is one of elation. I couldn't be more delighted."[110]

Amid the teardown of the 1975 Long Beach Grand Prix festival, the Formula One regulars headed across the country to upstate New York for the 1975 U.S. Grand Prix. Mario Andretti, Jody Scheckter, Tony Brice, Tom Pryce, and Brett Lunger all competed at Watkins Glen, an event won by Niki Lauda over Emerson Fittipaldi and Jochen Mass. Tragically, Mark Donohue would not make it to Watkins Glen. Soldiering through a difficult Formula One season for Roger Penske, Donohue went off course at high speed during the final morning practice at the Austrian Grand Prix on August 17, 1975. Mark Donohue died two days later of a cerebral hemorrhage.

Chris Pook, too, was on the move, attending the U.S. Grand Prix at Watkins

John Watson and the Penske Cars Formula One team pressed on to the 1975 U.S. Grand Prix at Watkins Glen after the tragic death of Mark Donohue two rounds prior in Austria. Niki Lauda won the Watkins Glen event. Watson qualified 13th and finished eighth, four laps down to Lauda. The Penske team withdrew from Formula One competition at the end of the 1976 season. First National City Travelers Checks would sponsor the 1977 Long Beach Grand Prix. John Watson figured in the Formula One championship points standings at the 1982 Caesars Palace Grand Prix (author's collection).

Glen, on a "fact finding mission."[111] Pook then traveled to Paris for a meeting of the Commission Sportive Internationale (CSI), the motorsport directorate of the FIA. Chris Pook also met with Bernie Ecclestone to hammer the financial demands of FOCA for the 1976 Long Beach Formula One Grand Prix. "I'm not going to comment further," said Pook, cutting off a Long Beach reporter. "This will all come out when Bernie and I sit down at the negotiating table and begin talking pence and sterling."[112] Pook's "this" would ultimately involve several hundred thousand dollars' worth of "pence and sterling."

As the post-race of the 1975 Long Beach Grand Prix turned to post-*script*, the harbor fog seemed to roll in across the *Queen Mary*. "We probably lost money," Chris Pook said, "because of heavy expenses over the last few days."[113] Extensive spending by the City of Long Beach in support of the Grand Prix also came under scrutiny, as did alleged inside favors. Private relationships between Long Beach city council and the Long Beach Grand Prix Association would be bared, while the Association sought to delay their fee payments and reimbursements to the City.

Amid a reported financial loss of over $300,000 on the 1975 Grand Prix—*prior* to settlement with the city—Long Beach government appeared once again to be astride a white elephant. The financial report of the Association, prepared by an outside auditor, was troubling. "They owe us money," City Manager John Mansell said, "and we are going to get the money they owe us."[114] "They [the Association] don't have much cash," added the city auditor, "and their only assets are a bunch of barriers."[115]

Rather like Caesars World with Cove Haven, the Grand Prix Association of Long Beach then sought to leverage their assets. "The association," noted the financial statement, "has entered into a sale and leaseback agreement of some of its fixed assets like fences and street barriers."[116] It was an ostensible short-term cash infusion, a financial arrangement of which Clifford Perlman and Alvin Malnik likely would have approved.

VI

Entanglement and Exaction

The Intertwined Formula One Fortunes
of Watkins Glen, Long Beach and Las Vegas

Take thou what course thou wilt. (*Julius Caesar* 3.3.276)

The 1975 Long Beach Formula 5000 Grand Prix marked the ascendance of the California street circuit as a viable premier-level motorsport venue. The Long Beach Grand Prix has flourished as a brand name racing program for nearly 45 years since. As 1975 marked the rise of Long Beach, so too did it mark the certain decline of the U.S. Grand Prix at Watkins Glen as a Formula One attraction. Nonetheless, as the California and New York venues charted their respective paths, their underlying finances charted their headlines, as well as their convergence on the battleground of Caesar.

The purse of the Watkins Glen Grand Prix had grown from $250,000 in 1970 to over $350,000. Legal actions by the organizers of the canceled Canadian Grand Prix, however, encumbered the 1975 Watkins Glen purse, "prize money totaling more than $350,000 will be held in escrow until a judgement can be made."[1] Further, the Watkins Glen Grand Prix Corporation was forced by the Commission Sportive Internationale (CSI) of the FIA to make additional safety improvements to the nearly 20-year-old circuit. "We knew we had to make some changes," remarked Malcolm Currie of the Grand Prix Corporation, "but we didn't know how long a period of time we had."[2]

Indeed, the Corporation was ordered to make the track changes before the 1975 event. FOCA, at the direction of Bernie Ecclestone, then demanded that Watkins Glen increase their investment in the absence of the Canadian Grand Prix, "an increase of about $85,000 in the purse and transportation and per diem expenses."[3] It was, effectively, a financial hardship from which Watkins Glen would never recover.

Rampant festivalization of the U.S. Grand Prix at Watkins Glen also impacted the continued viability of the location, particularly for the upscale penchants of the Formula One procession. Arrests by local constabulary at the 1975 U.S. Grand Prix numbered nearly 200. The list of charges filed were increasing in scope and severity as well. The simple mischief of the early 1960s was now displaced by weapons charges, distribution of controlled substances, burglary, arson, and "possession of explosives."[4] "They are factors," observed one writer, "which cannot be ignored."[5]

For Bernie Ecclestone, the grandeur of his evening arrivals at Crockford's in London would simply not be found at the "Animal Farm" of Watkins Glen.

As festivalization ran amok in Watkins Glen, so too did mounting debt for Chris Pook and the Grand Prix Association of Long Beach. An extended footnote by auditors in the financial report after the Formula 5000 event was both troubling and telling. The $300,000 loss of the 1975 event was to be carried as a deferred charge against the 1976 Long Beach Formula One Grand Prix. "The first race ... was needed to qualify the association to host a Formula One event. This qualification has been achieved," reported the Long Beach daily, "and therefore the entire net cost of the Formula 5000 event is considered to be the cost of qualifying for the Formula One event to be in March 1976."[6] The effect of the accounting was a creative break-even ledger for the 1975 Formula 5000 event. The due of the Long Beach Grand Prix Association to the City of Long Beach was then kicked forward to the fortunes of the 1976 Formula One race, an event now more encumbered than the 1975 U.S. Grand Prix at Watkins Glen.

***

The massive Formula One fleet arrived in California one week before the 1976 U.S. Grand Prix West. Greeted by a delegation from the Long Beach Grand Prix Association, a charter of 240 passengers touched down in Los Angeles, and traveled south on Interstate 405 to Long Beach for their extended stay. With over 1,000 rooms on offer, the 81,000-ton whale at the Long Beach pier would get the call. "The majority of the Grand Prix teams," it was reported, "will be staying aboard the Queen Mary."[7] The highly contentious cost, debt, and schedule issues which plagued the *Queen Mary* had also become highly litigious. "The city sued Diner's Club for $139 million," it was reported after the 1975 Formula 5000 event. "Diner's Club in turn sued for $41 million."[8]

The lodging aboard the beleaguered *Queen Mary* also set the opening tone for the 1976 U.S. Grand Prix West. Reporting that had lavished the Long Beach Grand Prix concept and the inaugural was noticeably tempered, if not terse. "The same confusion and disarray that plagued the September 1975 race," wrote Allen Wolfe for the Long Beach *Independent Press-Telegram*, "was evident ... on the opening day of practice and time trials for the United States Grand Prix West."[9]

Once on course, the Formula One drivers found the varied paving of the street circuit to be unusually rough. Further, rumble curbing added at the behest of the Commission Sportive Internationale slowed the lap times at the pinnacle of motorsport by nearly two seconds over Mario Andretti's qualifying mark at the 1975 event in Formula 5000 machinery. "It's a definite commitment now," remarked Mario Andretti of the curbs, some three seconds off his 1975 time. "We had more room to maneuver before."[10]

The appearance of homeland hero Mario Andretti in Long Beach during the Bicentennial year ignited the public, the press, and the paddock. "If we took the scene back about 2000 years," offered one piece on Andretti, "we might find someone who looked hauntingly familiar standing on the blood-soaked sands of the Coliseum of Imperial Rome, muscles sharply defined ... and short bladed sword at the ready. Mario Andretti is the best illustration you'll ever find of the racing driver as

Gladiator."[11] The graphic analogy also served as the perfect entrée to the stand of Mario Andretti in the premier class of four consecutive Caesars Palace Grand Prix events, the only race car driver to do so.

John Watson—driving for Roger Penske after the death of Mark Donohue—was quite vocal about the rigors of the Long Beach circuit on equipment. "The cars are taking quite a hammering through the gearbox," stated Watson, echoing Andretti the year prior. "This course is going to be murder on drive trains and transmissions."[12] Nonetheless, the two-mile Long Beach course was racy.

"It's a fun course to drive," commented Jochen Mass, driving for Marlboro Team McLaren, "It's not as sterile as the usual race tracks these days."[13] The personal life of Mass' McLaren teammate, James Hunt, was racy as well. Trading his former playboy image for public marital discord, James Hunt certainly made the headlines. Slotted in the Marlboro McLaren machine, James Hunt also figured into the early Formula One championship conversations.

Mario Andretti entered the 1976 Formula One season driving for Vel's–Parnelli Jones Racing. Andretti had competed in the USAC IndyCar series for Vel's since 1972. Despite the Bicentennial aspirations of the American race team, the Vel's operation missed the opening Formula One round in Brazil. The team was then shuttered after the third round in Long Beach. Mario Andretti would not be unemployed for long (Rick Lake collection).

The weather at the vernal equinox in Long Beach was a near repeat of the autumnal, high temperatures near 70 degrees, zero precipitation, and an offshore breeze from the west. Pre-race estimates put the potential crowd at 100,000 to 150,000. Despite the fair weather and the promise of a sellout crowd, Chris Pook led into the Long Beach weekend with as many questions as answers. A pitched debate involving crowd control and the net loss of the 1975 event crept into the dailies. The LBGPA now blamed the City of Long Beach squarely for the loss, claiming that officers should have staffed the gates when volunteer ticket-takers apparently deserted their stations and allowed non-paying spectators thought the gates. "We called the police and they

Jacques Lafitte driving a Ligier-Matra for Guy Ligier powers out of turn 12 in front of Rothbart's Long Beach Jewelry at 201 Pine Ave. Lafitte qualified 12th and improved to a remarkable fourth at the finish. The first Formula One event at Long Beach was won by Clay Regazzoni in a Ferrari. Downtown merchants had a very mixed response to the impacts of the Grand Prix events on their businesses. Manhole cover in the racing line at right is noteworthy (Rick Lake collection).

told us they weren't ticket takers," argued Don Dyer for the LBGPA, "and as a result we lost about $300,000."[14]

Chris Pook also had to dispel rumors of relocation, including wild cards from Miami Beach and Las Vegas. "We have been approached by Las Vegas interests … investigating the possibility of staging a Formula 5000 race," stated Pook. "They didn't want a world championship Formula One event, so the matter was dropped."[15] A proof-of-test event such as Formula 5000 presumably was a condition precedent to Formula One in Las Vegas. Nonetheless, the notion of "Las Vegas interests" certainly lent some backroom intrigue. Finally, though, Chris Pook paid patronage to the backroom of Long Beach. "Pook maintains … that he has received 'excellent cooperation,'" continued the local coverage, "from city manager John Mansell and the Long Beach City Council."[16]

Qualifying for the 1976 U.S. Grand Prix West was an all-contender lineup. Clay Regazzoni claimed pole with a 1:23.099 for the Scuderia Ferrari, still over a second off Andretti's 1975 time. Patrick Depailler followed for Tyrell. James Hunt would start third while championship leader Niki Lauda in a Ferrari was alongside in fourth. Notably, Tom Pryce—fifth in qualifying for UOP Shadow at the 1975 Formula 5000 event—returned for Shadow to slot fifth on the Formula One grid. John Watson qualified ninth for Roger Penske followed by Carlos Reutemann in a Brabham for Bernie

Chris Amon driving an Ensign-Ford exits turn three, "Penthouse Corner," at the 1976 Long Beach Grand Prix. The high-rise residences of Long Beach Towers and the International Towers beyond provided excellent spectator viewing. Multi-story buildings surrounding the circuit also cut into the paid gate of the Long Beach Grand Prix (Rick Lake collection).

Ecclestone. Mario Andretti in the Vel's–Parnelli Jones machine, though, was mired in 15th. Alan Jones—in his second year of Formula One—was deep as well, qualifying 19th for John Surtees.

Clay Regazzoni would then lead the 1976 U.S. Grand Prix West from pole. Patrick Depailler slotted second behind Regazzoni followed by James Hunt and Niki Lauda. Carlos Reutemann and the Brabham, however, were out in the first turn. On the fourth lap, though, Depailler appeared to block Hunt into the tire barriers. James Hunt also retired, while Depailler continued with minimal damage. "It was a blatant case of dangerous driving," claimed Hunt. "We can't have people running into each other like that."[17] Lauda moved into second and the order remained. From the midfield, Mario Andretti was the next retirement on lap 15. Regazzoni then went wire-to-wire to win, in a virtual "slot car performance."[18]

Niki Lauda finished second in his fading Ferrari some 42 seconds back, while also padding his championship points lead. Patrick Depailler followed third and moved to second in the points standings. From 12th on the grid, Jacques Lafitte advanced to finish fourth in a rather ungainly-looking Ligier-Matra. Alan Jones trailed by 10 laps to finish an unclassified 11th. John Watson followed behind for Roger Penske, the last car running at the finish. On the strength of a compelling win, Clay Regazzoni climbed to third in the points. "The win didn't surprise me," remarked Regazzoni from the top step of the podium, "but I did think the competition would be a little stronger."[19]

At center of image, the starting grid for the 1976 Long Beach Grand Prix forms on Ocean Boulevard between turn 13 at Pine Avenue and turn one at Linden Avenue, "Cook's Corner." The 1976 event marked the debut of Formula One on the port city street circuit. Clay Regazzoni started from pole and won the event in a Ferrari. Ferrari teammate Niki Lauda was second (Rick Lake collection).

While Clay Regazzoni celebrated, James Hunt still fumed. Hunt also confronted Patrick Depailler from the microphone. "The man's a lunatic," blasted the Briton. "He hit me into a wall."[20] James Hunt, however, forged his post-race fury to fuel a championship run, starting with a win at the following Spanish Grand Prix.

As the stands settled and the barriers came down, the post-script for the Grand Prix Association of Long Beach was once again one of fans and finances. "100,000 had been predicted ... but only an estimated 72,000 showed up," it was reported. "Although race organizers deny it, the future of the event appears to be in doubt."[21] Reports also indicated that the 1976 Formula One event was outdrawn by the 1975 Formula 5000 inaugural. Further, early loss estimates ranged from $400,000 to $500,000. Even worse, Bernie Ecclestone was reportedly shut out. "At the end of the race," read one account, "there was nothing left for Ecclestone."[22]

Chris Pook—the inveterate promoter—was predictably optimistic. "I think we're finally over the hump," proclaimed Pook. "I don't foresee any big changes next year."[23] Two weeks later, however, change was afoot. Further, those changes would involve "excellent cooperation" from Long Beach City Manager John Mansell, his assistant Randall Verrue, and the City Council.

"A plan calling for the city of Long Beach," reported the Long Beach daily, "to assume ownership of the United States Grand Prix West ... is to be presented to the

City Council."[24] The news was accompanied by a report that the 1976 U.S. Grand Prix West promotion was $237,000 in the red, while Chris Pook conversely claimed a profit of $20,000. Again, it was all apparently in the accounting.

Further, the take-over plan was to be presented to the Long Beach city council by City Manager John Mansell. Mansell—architect of the *Queen Mary* debacle and central to the strike force investigations—would take up the banner for the Grand Prix Association of Chris Pook and Don Dyer. It was also one of the last banners that John Mansell would unfurl in the city of Long Beach.

On the same date that news broke in Long Beach about the proposed Grand Prix bailout, a headline also broke in Nazareth, Pennsylvania, the hometown of Mario Andretti, "Mario Andretti Checking Drivers Wanted List."[25] Indeed, two weeks after the 1976 U.S. Grand Prix West in Long Beach, Mario Andretti—the great American race car driver—found himself on the dreaded mid-season unemployment line.

***

The simultaneous mentions of Las Vegas and Miami Beach in the pre-race press of the 1976 Long Beach Grand Prix were little more than clipboard curiosities from a roving reporter. Nonetheless, mention of the two cities also informed the forward path of international Grand Prix racing in America. Oddly, though, the Las Vegas and Miami Beach drops also informed both sides of the Sky Lake and Cove Haven deals, Clifford Perlman of Caesars World and Caesars Palace, along with Alvin Malnik of Miami Beach, alleged heir apparent to Meyer Lansky.

National news stories about the alleged nexus of Clifford Perlman, Caesars World, and Alvin Malnik would circulate unabated for the next three years. Peripheral entanglements would also arise. Inevitably, illegal gambling was at the core, the time-honored transaction guaranteed to slake the thirst of the national crime syndicate for off-grid liquidity. A Florida grand jury investigation into illegal gambling in May of 1976 then appeared to tidy a few more relationships.

"Jerry Catena, Vito Genovese's reputed successor as the organized crime lord of New Jersey," opened the headlines, "appeared … before a statewide grand jury investigating illegal gambling in Florida."[26] The appearance of Gerardo "Jerry" Catena occurred shortly after his release from prison for refusing to testify with immunity before the New Jersey State Commission of Investigation. The mentions also harkened back to the 1957 Apalachin crime conclave in upstate New York. Indeed, both Vito Genovese and Gerardo Catena were in attendance in Apalachin. Predictably, Catena offered few words to the 1976 Florida grand jury. Notably, Gerardo Catena was reputedly associated with original Caesars Palace investor Sam Kline of Cleveland.[27]

Others called to testify before the Florida grand jury further punctuated the subject of hidden investments in Caesars Palace, as well as the public Caesars World, Inc. dealings with Cove Associates. "Also on hand … were Anthony 'Fat Tony' Salerno and Alvin Malnik," continued the reports, "both identified as reputed South Florida crime figures."[28] Anthony Salerno and Alvin Malnik thus anchored the Caesars connections to the grand jury. Salerno and Malnik also counted connections to Vincent "Jimmy Blue Eyes" Alo, the mob whisperer to Meyer Lansky. The collective mention of Gerardo Catena and Anthony Salerno then further underscored the continuum of the Genovese crime family. The trio of Catena, Salerno, and Malnik cloistered in South Florida, however, simply begged for an update of the former Miami "Mayor's List of Hoodlums."[29]

***

In the same week that the three South Floridians appeared before the Florida grand jury, the politicians of Long Beach braced for their own grand jury subpoenas. The continuing federal strike force and Los Angeles county investigations in Long Beach netted the arrest of a Long Beach official, while the city manager and city council scurried in self-preservation. The concurrent debt issues of the Long Beach Grand Prix then paralyzed the city council, while the cozy relationships of the Long Beach Grand Prix Association (LBGPA) and government officials were then laid bare. Further, the arrest of the city official tied in with the Long Beach Grand Prix itself.

"City Oks move," read the banner headline on April 14, 1976, "to save Grand Prix."[30] The proposed plan involved a three-year incremental deferred payback of the amounts owed by the LBGPA to the city. Further, the proposal would engage the Long Beach Convention and News Bureau as the organizer of the event, while the LBGPA would produce the event as a contractor for the Bureau.

81,000 TONS OF FUN.

The Queen Mary! See her from bow to stern, bridge to engine room. A day of unique family adventure. Open daily at 9, at the end of the Long Beach Freeway. Plan to stay in Long Beach, the Southland's holiday spot!

QUEEN MARY LONG BEACH
Convention & News Bureau
555 Ocean Boulevard, Suite 718
Long Beach, California 90802

The Long Beach *Queen Mary* was the $100 million attraction that intertwined the fortunes of William Fugazy, the Long Beach Grand Prix, Jay Sarno of Caesars Palace fame, Allen Dorfman of the International Brotherhood of Teamsters, and the tentacles of organized crime. All it took was a final 14,000-mile final voyage to bring them all together under the umbrella of the Long Beach city council and scandalous civic spending. The Long Beach Convention & News Bureau at 555 Ocean Boulevard became the de facto organizer of the Long Beach Grand Prix in 1977. The travel services company of Chris Pook was also located at 555 Ocean Boulevard in Long Beach (author's collection).

The two-pronged initiative, "a complex series of financial and management arrangements,"[31] was immediately controversial, dividing the council. Despite significant dissent on record, the Long Beach city council voted to ratify the Long Beach Grand Prix proposal.

The Long Beach Convention and News Bureau—funded predominantly by a city-levied room tax—would thus ostensibly undertake a sports promotion, to then be produced by a separate sole-sourced for-profit enterprise. It did not go easily. Further unresolved were the cost overruns of the 1975 and 1976 Long Beach Grands Prix and the resultant unpaid debts to the private vendors of the LBGPA. "The past two races have been quite exciting for the city," observed one councilperson succinctly. "Nonetheless, there is a $500,000 debt."[32]

The rescue plan also stipulated that the LBGPA raise $400,000 from private sources to resolve its private debt. "All indications are positive," Chris Pook assured the city council, "that we can raise the $400,000."[33] City Manager John Mansell, the chief executive of Long Beach government, was adamant. "If the association fails to raise the $400,000," Mansell stated, "the city will abrogate its agreements."[34]

The contract between the LBGPA and the City of Long Beach—inked little over a year before—was thus ordered by the city council to be amended by the city attorney. The contract amendment also lingered as a particularly divisive subject. Councilperson Wallace Edgerton was notably vocal. "[Edgerton] … was not happy with the way the amended contract proposal was presented to the council," it was reported, "during what he called 'backroom discussions.'"[35] Again, dissent notwithstanding, the finalized contract amendment was approved by the city council. It is worth reinforcement that the highly controversial changes to the agreement between the LBGPA and the City of Long Beach, formed the underpinning that allowed the Long Beach Grand Prix to continue for 45 years.

Three weeks after the LBGPA contract amendment was approved, the city government of Long Beach would be further rendered. "Long Beach City Planning Director Ernest Mayer Jr.," reported the *Los Angeles Times* on May 14, 1976, "was arrested today just minutes after he allegedly accepted a $25,141 bribe paid in gold coins by two architects."[36] The arrest of Ernest Mayer involved solicitation and acceptance of bribes over a multi-year period, in exchange for favorable planning department actions on several shoreline development projects. Extortion, however, might have been the more appropriate term. Further, the bribery scandal formed a tangled backstory rivaling the development of Caesars Palace, albeit from sunny southern California.

Central to the arrest of Mayer and the gold coin bribe, was the development of the new headquarters of Harbor Bank, opened after the 1975 Long Beach Formula 5000 Grand Prix. In the reported bribery arrangements. Ernest Mayer received a kickback of 5 percent of the design fees collected by project architects James Coppedge and Claflin Balance. Coppedge and Balance, in turn, were equity partners in the new Harbor Bank building with William Dawson, a prominent Long Beach property developer.

Geographically, the new bank building was located immediately northwest of the turn-five hairpin at the top of the Long Beach Grand Prix circuit. Notably, Ernest

Mayer had also considered planning requirements of the Long Beach Grand Prix circuit.[37] Harbor Bank, in turn, was the official bank of the Long Beach Grand Prix.[38] Harbor Bank, however, also formed the certain turn that moved the Long Beach Grand Prix from the sports pages, to the desks of the investigative journalists.

As the bank building was then sold from the development partners to Harbor Bank, Ernest Mayer reportedly took another cut. Indeed, the bulk of the gold coin payoff was the split of the proceeds from sale of the development to Harbor Bank, one-third of the architect's share of the net with development partner William Dawson—transferred to Long Beach Planning Director Ernest Mayer in gold.

Recorded evidence in the Ernest Mayer bribery investigation involved discussions of Mayer's significant influence over the Long Beach City Council. Within days of Mayer's arrest, one city councilperson withdrew from a partnership with "stockbroker Stewart Elner, a partner in the Long Beach Grand Prix Association."[39]

Evidence then recovered in search warrants led to the subpoena of Harbor Bank co-developer William Dawson, as well as Harbor Bank director James Gray. Within weeks, City Manager John Mansell and virtually every member of the Long Beach City Council also testified under subpoena. The cumulative fallout also led to calls for the resignation of Mansell himself.[40]

News on June 17, 1976, then implicated Long Beach City Manager John Mansell directly in the unchecked malfeasance of Ernest Mayer. "Four years before his indictment on bribery charges," reported the *Los Angeles Times*, "Ernest Mayer Jr. was caught using city employees on city time in a private consulting business he ran out of City Hall."[41] The *Times* also reported that Long Beach city employees were used by Mayer on personal projects, "such as a desert retreat he was building near Palm Springs."[42] Ernest Mayer's partner in the Palm Springs home was none other than William Dawson. At trial, the judge hearing Mayer's bribery case argued that the Palm Springs venture was effectively a cover-up to transact illicit cash between the partners.[43]

The *Times* report also engaged William Talley, former Assistant City Manager to John Mansell. "Talley told The Times he asked Mansell to conduct an investigation," continued the report, "But no investigation was conducted."[44] Notably, it was William Talley who handled the *Queen Mary* leases involving Jay Sarno and Allen Dorfman.

One the same day that the *Los Angeles Times* published their story, Long Beach City Manager John Mansell submitted his resignation. "I have long been dismayed at the purchase, reconstruction, and horrendous public expense involved with the Queen Mary," one councilperson said upon Mansell's resignation. "I have watched the extremely questionable and startling decisions made in reference to the Grand Prix. The time has come to rearrange our civic affairs from the top down."[45]

The departure of John Mansell, though, did little to quiet the Long Beach headlines. Inevitably, the Los Angeles District Attorney investigated other Long Beach agreements in which Ernest Mayer and the departed John Mansell played a role. "Several other city contracts," it was reported, "including the Long Beach Grand Prix Association, are also being investigated."[46]

A separate federal grand jury probe then focused on Harbor Bank, and the ground lease between William Dawson and the City of Long Beach at 777 E. Ocean

Boulevard alongside the Grand Prix circuit. "It is believed to focus," reported the *Los Angeles Times*, "on whether there may have been any bribery, extortion, or racketeering in connection with the lease."[47] Indeed, the Feds were prepared to unleash the RICO act on the City of Long Beach.

As with other stops on this Grand Prix trail, the many juxtapositions lend significant intrigue and encourage further inquiry. To wit, James Gray—already a founder and director of Harbor Bank—was also "a director of the Long Beach Convention and News Bureau."[48] Notably, the Convention and News Bureau was approved by contract amendment to become the operator of the Long Beach Grand Prix just one month before Ernest Mayer's arrest. James Gray was also the president-elect of the Long Beach Area Chamber of Commerce, one of the first organizations to support the Grand Prix concept in 1974. "He can put a deal together," one local noted, "faster than anyone in town."[49]

James Gray, however, was involved on the executive committee of the Chamber-affiliated "Committee of 300," a booster group organized to provide the "extras" for attendees of the Long Beach Grand Prix, "the presentation of a positive community image."[50] Notably, one of James Gray's fellow Committee of 300 members was William Dawson. On August 7, 1976, amid the outcry of Ernest Mayer's arrest and John Mansell's resignation, James Gray was then announced as president of Harbor Bank, the William Dawson project at the center of the bribery scandal.

Three weeks after James Gray was elevated at Harbor Bank, the headlines turned worse for the Long Beach Grand Prix. "Long Beach city officials spent public funds to subsidize a private company that promoted two Grand Prix races," it was reported by the *Los Angeles Times*, "despite promising 'not to spend a dime of city money' on it."[51] Indeed, former Long Beach City Manager John Mansell assured City Hall repeatedly that the Grand Prix Association would pay their own way. "At least $190,000 in public funds was spent on race tickets and lavish parties for city officials and 'insiders,'" continued the report, "and for engineering, design, publicity, and other work, according to city records."[52] Remarkably, one such Grand Prix "insider" party was hosted by Ernest Mayer in the midst of the bribery investigation.

The *Los Angeles Times* also drew in Les Richter, general manager of Riverside International Raceway and the former race director of the Long Beach Grand Prix. "Pook said he had the votes before it ever went to City Council," Richter stated. "The investigation I made after being involved, I should have made before."[53] The comments by the venerable Richter were damning, particularly so in the wake of compelling debt issues, overstatements of attendance, and the Harbor Bank bribery scandal appearing to enfold elements and envoys of the Long Beach Grand Prix.

As the Long Beach Grand Prix was assailed on multiple fronts, Chris Pook then attempted to navigate the severe $400,000 debt to private, unsecured creditors. Pook's offer was dated June 29, 1976, a letter proposing 35 cents on the dollar in cash and 20 cents on the dollar in treasury stock of the Long Beach Grand Prix Association. Chris Pook's lament to creditors also appeared to leverage his control of the show. Apart from limited cash and stock, the only Association assets were "concrete barriers good only for operating a race, some old tires and steel drums, which have been drilled and cut to accommodate the guard rail, and (whose) only worth is as use for a street circuit in Long Beach."[54] Peter Talbot's pre-race genius had just been reduced to a junk yard bargaining chip. Further, post-resignation, John Mansell's tough talk of abrogation was silent.

Reports also involved Chris Pook's travel business receiving apparent insider treatment at City Hall, as well as favorable travel contracts with the Long Beach Convention and News Bureau and Long Beach Harbor Commission.[55] Further reporting described apparent unilateral, unsupported reductions by city staff in amounts owed by the Long Beach Grand Prix Association. The latter resulted in an audit of City billings to the Association, an audit that then generated its own thread of headlines. "The report listed a number of problems in connection with wording of the contract with LBGPA and with the city's method of determining its billable expenses," described the city auditor. "These problems made it impossible to conclude that expense billings for the two races were proper and correct."[56] The "wording" at issue was the descriptor "extraordinary costs," a tortured piece of terminology that hung over the financial relationship of Long Beach and the Long Beach Grand Prix into the foreseeable future.

On September 21, 1976, the Long Beach City Council approved the contract for the 1977 Long Beach Grand Prix, an event to be conducted under the organization of the Long Beach Convention and News Bureau. At the same time, the Long Beach council laid out additional measures to ensure payment for the accumulated debts of the 1975 and 1976 events, as well as to prevent a repeat of the race fees going unpaid to the city. "If we insisted on payment now, we'd probably get no more than $5,000, and we'd break the Grand Prix Association," offered one councilperson. "I think it's a good gamble to wait and try and get it all."[57]

In the final agenda item of the September 21, 1976, council meeting, James Gray was then approved as a member of the Long Beach Harbor Commission. Curiously, Gray was unanimously supported after the city council met privately the week prior to float his appointment. The appointment of James Gray thus positioned him to further influence the fortunes of the Long Beach Grand Prix, as well as the travel business of Chris Pook, perhaps wearing all hats at once from his president's office in the Harbor Bank building next to the turn five hairpin.

Walking back the bluster of one city councilperson, the time had thus apparently *not* come to rearrange the civic affairs of Long Beach from the top down. To wit, Mayor Thomas Clark had to explain away his shares in Harbor Bank.[58] Another Harbor commissioner was then revealed to own stock in the Grand Prix Association.[59] Nonetheless, the perilous path to the 1977 Long Beach Grand Prix had been approved. Bernie Ecclestone, of course, would be in attendance at Long Beach in 1977, representing both FOCA and Team Brabham. Further, William D. Weinberger of Caesars World—representing Clifford Perlman, William McElnea, and the gambling house of Caesar—would be there to meet him.

***

"Mario Andretti's dream of winning the world driving championship in an American-built car during the Bicentennial year," rang the headlines, "has collapsed."[60] Andretti's American dream was also an incredibly lofty goal, especially inasmuch as an American-built car had won only one modern Grand Prix event ever, Dan Gurney's inspirational win at the 1967 Belgian Grand Prix driving his Eagle-Weslake. "It just got too frustrating after a while," stated Andretti of his Vel's–Parnelli Jones team. "They'd let me down every race."[61]

Headed into 1976, Mario Andretti had spurned Formula One opportunities with Roger Penske and Don Nichols's Shadow team to remain in the Parnelli chassis. Foundering after the loss of Viceroy sponsorship, the team owned by Vel Miletich was at a financial crossroads, particularly after Andretti failed to finish in Long Beach. "I had to push for a decision," bemoaned Andretti. "I've already blown all the good deals I could have had, like Penske."[62]

Mario Andretti then flew to London two weeks after Long Beach for a non-championship Formula One event at Silverstone. Andretti's London itinerary included a visit to Colin Chapman, the legendary designer-owner of Team Lotus. "Lotus is a disaster right now," continued Andretti. "But I'm interested to see what they have in mind for the future. Colin Chapman is still a man to be reckoned with."[63]

Mario Andretti then competed at Silverstone for Frank Williams, new owner of the 1975 Lord Hesketh machines. Andretti's result was an encouraging seventh. Three weeks later, Andretti took the bit of Colin Chapman's John Player Lotus 77 at the Spanish Grand Prix. A ninth-place qualifying effort in the new machine, however, was followed with a mechanical failure, the result a disappointing 19th in the final order. Two weeks later, the Belgian Grand Prix produced another letdown, 11th on the grid and 20th in the closing tally.

During the month of May, Mario Andretti leveraged his open-market status stateside to drive for Roger Penske at the Indianapolis 500. Remarkably, the 1976 Indy stint was Andretti's first open-wheel foray with the Penske squad. Mario Andretti also leveraged a 19th place grid position in Penske's McLaren M16C-Offenhauser to an eighth-place finish, one lap down to winner Johnny Rutherford. The result also matched Andretti's best finish at the Speedway since 1970.

As Mario Andretti returned to Team Lotus for Formula One, results started to improve as well. A fine second-quick qualifying session at the Swedish Grand Prix was also accompanied by the fastest lap in the race. A solid fifth-place finish followed at Circuit Paul Ricard in the French Grand Prix. The points in France were Andretti's first in the championship since the second round in South Africa. Nonetheless, the season would ebb and flow for Andretti and Lotus. Andretti was third on the grid for the British Grand Prix but out on lap four with another failure. Two weeks later at the Nürburgring in Germany, Mario Andretti reverted to the middle of the pack. Andretti put the Lotus-Ford a miserable 12th on the grid, nearly 10 seconds off the pole pace of James Hunt in the McLaren and nine seconds adrift of Niki Lauda in the Ferrari. The German Grand Prix was also the event at which the championship prospects of Hunt and Lauda were immediately reversed, Hunt winning from pole while Niki Lauda was horribly burned in a near-fatal accident. Mario Andretti finished 12th, nearly five minutes arrears of Hunt. Niki Lauda, however, maintained the championship points lead from the hospital burn ward. With the win in Germany, James Hunt moved to within 14 points of Niki Lauda, a two-race deficit.

Mario Andretti, Colin Chapman, and Team Lotus then improved further,

Mario Andretti joined Colin Chapman and Team Lotus at the Spanish Grand Prix on May 2, 1976. The Lotus effort showed promise, particularly after the failure of the Vel's–Parnelli Jones Formula One team. Mario Andretti's 1976 run with Lotus produced five points-paying finishes, a victory at the miserable season-ending Japanese Grand Prix, and sixth place in championship points. The pairing of Andretti and Chapman launched a championship run for the Lotus works. Andretti's Formula One career was thus propelled forward to the Caesars Palace Grand Prix (courtesy International Motor Racing Research Center).

another fifth in Austria and then a highly encouraging third-place finish at the Dutch Grand Prix from sixth on the grid. The resurrected Canadian Grand Prix at Mosport would also see a balanced attack from Mario Andretti and Colin Chapman. Mario spread the performance of the updated Lotus 77 with a fifth-place slot on the grid, followed by another fine third place at the finish. Incredibly, Niki Lauda had returned to competition as well. Lauda missed the points positions in Canada, but still held the championship advantage over James Hunt with the second U.S. Grand Prix and the newly-added Japanese Grand Prix to go.

Headed into the penultimate round of the Formula One season at Watkins Glen, Mario Andretti—the great American race car driver—had climbed into the top-ten in the championship standings. Andretti was sufficiently impressed with the aerodynamic updates in the Lotus 77 that he also committed to a full season with Colin Chapman for 1977. The following campaign was thus Mario Andretti's first full effort toward the Formula One championship. "Track observers feel that if Mario Andretti would concentrate solely on Formula One racing," ran one opinion, "he would have an excellent chance at winning the world title."[64] Andretti was also set to return to the United States for Roger Penske to contest the three 500-mile USAC events.

As James Hunt and Niki Lauda squared their Formula One prospects headed into Watkins Glen, so too did the Watkins Glen Grand Prix Corporation (WGGPC) square off with Formula One itself. "I can't say we'll have Grand Prix racing here in the future," remarked Malcolm Currie of the WGGPC before the 15th anniversary U.S. Grand Prix. "We're only going to hold racing here if we can run it in the black, and last year, we didn't finish in the black."[65] Currie's comments were directed at the financial demands of the drivers, but the remarks also pointed up the arrayed interests engaged in Formula One. "Why can't the racing organizations like the Federation International Association (FIA)," continued Currie, "take this over and control the drivers?"[66]

Indeed, the Grand Prix Drivers Association was an autonomous group. Further separated was the Formula One Constructors Association controlled by Bernie Ecclestone. Grand Prix manufacturers such as Ferrari were organized distinctly from FOCA. The various factions and functions of the FIA then compounded the tangled bargain required to stage a Formula One event, while the domestic SCCA waited offstage for their own domestic sanctioning fees. Nevertheless, it was Ecclestone who held the power to negotiate for the majority of the teams, while the drivers were then beholden to the team owners. The failed Grand Prix events at Ontario in 1972 and Canada in 1975 were thus the Excalibur examples, the sword of Bernie Ecclestone fully capable of piercing public dissent and bending Formula One to his whim, with the FIA often reduced to little more than a logo on the program. Again, Meyer Lansky would have tipped his hat in respect.

"If the drivers want a $1 million guarantee in prize money three years from now," howled Malcolm Currie, "Watkins Glen can be expected to have the same adverse reaction as the other tracks."[67] Currie thus appeared to establish the timetable for the demise of the U.S. Grand Prix *East,* while he also marked the financial distress limits of the Watkins Glen Grand Prix Corporation. Finances of the Watkins Glen Grand Prix Corporation, in fact, would be a mounting issue in the years ahead, driven ostensibly by mounting costs and continuing track improvements necessary to retain the Formula One event. The balance sheet of the Grand Prix Corporation—a non-profit adjunct of the chamber of commerce—would also be held more closely going forward. "The [Watkins Glen] books have never been made public," suggested a report from New York in 1976, "and probably never will."[68]

Moving into the race weekend of the 1976 U.S. Grand Prix at Watkins Glen, the proposition lines were thus James Hunt minus-eight-points to Lauda, Mario Andretti and Formula One were plus-one, and the over-under of the U.S. Grand Prix East at Watkins Glen was sitting at three. Andretti also liked his chances on Sunday, "because I probably know the Glen a little better that any of the others."[69]

The U.S. Grand Prix East on October 10, 1976, then set up the potential championship closer for James Hunt, and the potential spoiler for the still-injured Niki Lauda. Rain and fog delayed the Friday practice qualifying sessions. A stationary, driving rainstorm then impacted the Saturday qualifying sessions, in marked contrast to sun-soaked Long Beach. On a drying track, Hunt and his McLaren qualified dominantly on pole followed by Jody Scheckter in a Tyrell-Ford. Niki Lauda then slotted fifth. John Watson in the lone Penske-Ford was eighth on the starting grid. Notably, the improved aerodynamic experiments of Colin Chapman pinned

Andretti's Lotus to the surface but came with a decided sacrifice in speed. Mario Andretti was bogged in 11th on the Watkins Glen time sheets.

Watkins Glen weather was then forced into further contrast with Long Beach when an overnight snow fell on the circuit. The open spectator areas were rendered a mud festival. A reported 125,000 fans, though, were on hand for a sunshine race day. Those prone to mischief, however, would cavort in the gunge, and their effects—once again—dominated the postscript.

The 59-lap Grand Prix unfolded as did the qualifying queue, James Hunt across the finish line first, followed by Jody Scheckter, some eight seconds back. Niki Lauda bravely improved on his starting grid position to the third step of the podium, just fractions of a second ahead of fast-closing Jochen Mass, James Hunt's McLaren teammate. John Watson soldiered across in sixth for Roger Penske, the last car on the lead lap. In the second United States Grand Prix of the bicentennial year, top American was Brett Lunger finishing 11th in a Surtees machine. Unfortunately, the maladies of Mario Andretti and Colin Chapman returned in full, Andretti's Lotus giving up the battle of 1976 before the halfway mark.

Great Britain and James Hunt thus prevailed in the Bicentennial matchup, moving to within three championship points of the remarkable Niki Lauda. Niki Lauda, gamely working to maintain the championship lead, was reduced to a final showdown with James Hunt in Japan. Mario Andretti closed his American campaign oh-for-two. Andretti, however, still clung to the top 10 in points. With a single point for sixth-place, John Watson held sixth in the championship points for Roger Penske.

Assaults on the sanctity of the U.S. Grand Prix at Watkins Glen continued unabated in the 15th anniversary. Car burnings had ascended as an inexorable rite of the three-day festival. Controlled substance arrests were pervasive. Revelers were also becoming more violent as local police attempted to quell behaviors run amok. The team areas were under siege as well, with thefts reported from the paddock. Even worse in 1976, the foul weather and the unruly crowd made the post-race grounds impassable.

"Tractors were busy Sunday night," reported an upstate newspaper, "pulling cars and campers out of the swamp-like conditions."[70] "Mal Currie, executive director of the Watkins Glen Grand Prix Corporation," continued the report, "said ground repairs would probably be made in the spring."[71] "There's no sense in doing it now" was Currie's opinion.[72]

Formula One and its constituent groups then flew from New York to the Japanese Grand Prix on October 24, 1976. Niki Lauda still led the championship by three points over James Hunt. Motorsports press had a field day with the various points possibilities and, in a rare season, the potential tie-breaker. Mario Andretti led the field in qualifying to take pole by just .030 seconds over James Hunt. Niki Lauda was third on the grid, just over three tenths back. John Watson was a strong fourth in the starting order driving the Penske-Ford. Jody Scheckter in a Tyrell and Carlos Pace driving a Brabham for Bernie Ecclestone rounded out the third row.

The promise of the Lauda versus Hunt showdown, however, was then overtaken by severe weather on the Mt. Fuji circuit. Despite debate and dissent about the safety of the conditions, the inaugural Japanese Grand Prix would go on. James Hunt led at the start over John Watson and Mario Andretti. Four drivers withdrew in the opening laps. Notably, Niki Lauda pulled off on lap two. The chastened Lauda would not compromise life and limb for the Formula One title in 1976. With Lauda off, James Hunt then appeared as an easy race winner and champion. Hunt fell back, however, as the track dried. Mario Andretti then took the lead from James Hunt on lap 62 while Hunt pitted for a change of tires.

James Hunt struggled to recover points positions as he returned to the circuit on slicks. Two laps from the end, Hunt managed past Clay Regazzoni and Alan Jones to finish third behind Patrick Depailler. Mario Andretti, though, was unchallenged the rest of the way, taking the win for Colin Chapman and Team Lotus. Andretti was the only car on the lead lap. The 1976 Japanese Grand Prix was the second win of Andretti's Formula One career. "I've done a lot of 24-hour races," remarked Mario Andretti after his victory, "but this had to be the longest race of my career."[73]

From third place, James Hunt also took the 1976 World Drivers Championship by a single point over Niki Lauda. "I felt very sorry for Niki," offered James Hunt afterward. "It wasn't fair that he should have to race in these conditions."[74] Enzo Ferrari, however, would not be so charitable, reportedly critical of Lauda's withdrawal from the event.[75]

Relegated to second-place in the championship from the relative calm of the paddock, Niki Lauda was both reflective and resolute. "I have had no change of mind," affirmed the season-long points leader, "I still think that the Grand Prix race in Fuji was madness."[76]

Mario Andretti's win in Japan moved him up to fifth in the final point standings, a remarkable climb from the *single* championship point he held at the halfway mark of the season. John Watson was two points behind Andretti in sixth position. Watson's effort at Mt. Fuji was also the last Formula One entry in Roger Penske's considerable portfolio as a team owner. "We are proud of our effort," offered Roger Penske of his Formula One departure, "highlighted by our victory at Austria."[77]

John Watson's win at the 1976 Austrian Grand Prix was, in fact, the only Formula One victory for Team Penske. Roger Penske's short foray into the pinnacle of motorsport, however, will always be punctuated by the tragic death of Mark Donohue in Austria one year before. The 1981 Caesars Palace Grand Prix was then Roger Penske's next official appearance at a Formula One event.

Committed to Colin Chapman's John Player Special Team Lotus for 1977, Mario Andretti also continued to drive select IndyCar events for Roger Penske through 1980. Andretti, in fact, won at Michigan International Speedway in 1980 in one of his last starts for Roger Penske. This 1977 pairing of proud Pennsylvanians, however, also stood in vivid contrast to their respective—and rather contrary—positions headed into the 1981 Caesars Palace Grand Prix.

From his home in Nazareth, Pennsylvania, Mario Andretti could then look forward to a competitive full-time opportunity in Formula One for 1977, the great American race car driver fully redeemed from the abject Bicentennial failure of the Vel's–Parnelli Jones team. Mario Andretti also looked forward to another opportunity at two home Grand Prix events in 1977.

***

Tobacco money had underwritten the Formula One *pro forma* since Colin Chapman adorned Graham Hill's 1968 Lotus with the Gold Leaf livery of Imperial Tobacco. By 1976, fully one-third of most Formula One starting grids were supported by a tobacco sponsorship, including world champion James Hunt in the Marlboro-McLaren. Moving forward to the Caesars Palace Grand Prix, the battalion of tobacco liveries would grow to over one-half of the field.

Headed into the 1977 Formula One season, however, tobacco-related interests would also strike organizational discord among the constituent groups. Theirs was an incursion that was also focused directly at Bernie Ecclestone. "The Formula One world championship," read the pre-season reports, "may succumb to racing politics and become a hollow holy grail."[78] Patrick Duffeler—European marketing man for Phillip-Morris and its Marlboro brand—was attempting to organize a new Grand Prix racing series, World Championship Racing (WCR).

More so, the efforts of Patrick Duffeler would effectively split the 16 Formula One circuits, sever the race constructors from the nameplate manufacturers, and further wedge FOCA and the FIA. The prospect of the upstart series also sent the national associations—such as the SCCA—scrambling to make sense of it all. The European circuits generally fell in with Duffeler and the WCR, while the offshore tracks such as Long Beach, Watkins Glen, and South Africa remained aligned with FOCA. Notably, Britain, Belgium, and Sweden were reported to remain in the FOCA fold by way of standing national association agreements.

"I went to Paris for a meeting," offered Malcolm Currie of the Watkins Glen Grand Prix Corporation, "Depending on who you talked to—the [FOCA] or WCR—the 16 circuits were all lined up with one group or another."[79] Malcolm Currie also had to acknowledge the isolation of the New World from the power brokers and decision makers of the European racing continent. "You have to remember that the European organizers are constantly meeting, talking, and coming up with new deals," continued Currie, "It's a long way across 3,000 miles of ocean."[80] Indeed, Patrick Duffeler's World Championship Racing series did nothing to clear the quagmire on the grounds of Watkins Glen at the hibernal solstice.

"Duffeler launched a media campaign to raise the stakes," wrote an Ecclestone biographer, "comparing Ecclestone's 'unscrupulous' tactics to the Mafia."[81] Patrick Duffeler's comments were a tidy analogy, a comparison from which Ecclestone did not shrink. "I know that in the past the constructors' association [FOCA] has been likened to the Mafia," Bernie Ecclestone was quoted as saying. "I wish I was a Godfather. They have millions of pounds, don't they?"[82]

Ultimately, the various constituents of the Formula One championship stepped back from the brink of mutually assured destruction; the 1977 season would race on. Bernie Ecclestone, though, emerged more hardened, determined to suffocate even mere whispers of dissent. The WCR skirmish also drew the battle lines for the clashes to come, including those on the battleground of Caesar.

The three opening rounds of the 1977 Formula season were then won respectively by Jody Scheckter, Carlos Reutemann, and Niki Lauda. Mario Andretti opened with a fifth at the Argentinian Grand Prix, two championship points with which to ante his 1977 season. In the next two rounds, however, Andretti's John Player Lotus

78 came up short. Headed to the fourth round at Long Beach, Mario Andretti only had one more point on tally than in his truncated 1976 season with Parnelli Jones.

Tragedy, too, would strike in the early season. Tom Pryce, racing for Don Nichols's Shadow team, was killed in the South African Grand Prix when course marshal Jansen Van Vuuren ran across the track. Van Vuuren was killed instantly. Pryce was then struck by Van Vuuren's fire extinguisher, perishing in the cockpit of his Shadow-Ford. Two weeks later, Carlos Pace—Brabham driver for Bernie Ecclestone—was killed in the crash of a light aircraft in his hometown of Sao Paolo, Brazil.

The Formula One caravan was thus resigned to mourning once again, and the paddock of the U.S. Grand Prix West in Long Beach bore the effects. Nonetheless, Mario Andretti carried the American banner into California, on a mission for his first Grand Prix victory in home territory. From the plush offices of Caesars World in Los Angeles, Clifford Perlman and William McElnea would also send William D. "Bill" Weinberger on a mission, a fact-finding foray south from Los Angeles down Interstate 405 to Long Beach—and the 1977 U.S. Grand Prix West.

***

The path of Chris Pook and the Long Beach Grand Prix Association to the 1977 U.S. Grand Prix West was marked as was their ledger, a myriad of footnotes and asterisks. The SCCA stuck first, America's national oversight organization for Formula One declared, "all the prize money has to be in escrow before we can permit the race to be run again."[83] The City of Long Beach jumped in as well, flexing considerable council, managerial, and mayoral muscle to call for "sharper scrutiny" of the Long Beach Convention and News Bureau.[84]

Notably, the call for oversight of the Bureau came as the city council approved a new contract with the publicly-funded agency. The new agreement was marked by an increase of, "about $130,000,"[85] nearly a 20 percent bump over the prior year. "The council took no official action," it was reported, "save for approving the contract."[86] The contract also covered the Convention and News Bureau's new organizational role in the Long Beach Grand Prix.

As the relationship between the Long Beach Grand Prix and Long Beach Convention and News Bureau was borne of contention, so it continued. Indeed, the first official act of the Bureau toward the Grand Prix Association appeared as a handout of public funds, "a contract granting the Grand Prix Assn. $135,000 in exchange for the publicity and promotional value."[87] "The money comes not from tax funds," it was reported, "but from a room tax."[88] Such tortured logic was perhaps the semantics of "sharper scrutiny." Notably, Bob Lichtenham and Paul Baessler of the Convention and News Bureau were the voices in front of the $135,000 gift, the same lunch hour progenitors of the Grand Prix concept with Chris Pook some four years before.[89]

In a bow to the citizenry, the City of Long Beach did, however, attach the first $86,000 of agency ticket sales in effort to recover the accumulated "extraordinary costs" from the 1976 event.[90] The city also demanded a performance bond of $43,000 as a hedge against contemplated "extraordinary costs" for the 1977 event.[91] Further, the approvals by Long Beach city council enabled Chris Pook to seek expanded commercial sponsorship.

"[Pook] found a major one in First National City Travelers Checks," it was reported. "It is estimated that it put up more than $100,000 for the drivers to race for the Citicorp Cup."[92] Associate sponsorships then further bolstered the Citicorp number. "Before the race is even held we are $275,000 better off ... than we were last year," trumpeted Chris Pook, "and we have an additional $135,000 with our managerial contract with the Convention and News Bureau."[93] Notable amid the apparently fortified pre-race fortunes, the "old tires" of Chris Pook's June 29, 1976, debt settlement offer were now check-listed as "spherical elastic attenuators."[94]

By 1977, the First National City Travelers Checks branding of Citicorp adorned race vehicles from NASCAR to IndyCar to Formula One. Moving from the shuttered Roger Penske Formula One team of 1976, Citicorp famously appeared on the side pods of Ken Tyrell's radical new six-wheeled P34 racers. Headed into Long Beach, though, Tyrell drivers had five failures and a third-place finish at South Africa to show between them. The Long Beach fans, nonetheless, enjoyed their first glimpse of the revolutionary Citicorp-sponsored hexapods.

The motorsports presence of Citicorp also introduced William D. "Bill" Weinberger to the Long Beach Grand Prix. "I had called the SCCA to inquire about promoting an F1 race," recalled Weinberger, "They told me for only $50,000 they would sanction the race."[95] "I couldn't get the race as part of the World Championship unless they sanctioned it," continued Weinberger. "That was my first introduction to the convoluted structure of F1 racing."[96] The junior Weinberger, much more accustomed to the economic engine of the gambling-based Caesars World, received his motorsports baptism in 1977. "[SCCA] then suggested I contact a gentleman at [Citicorp] who was pouring money into auto racing as a way to advertise their travelers check program," Weinberger related. "[SCCA] thought they would be a natural source of sponsorship money and information."[97]

Moving forward from the building blocks of Caesars Palace—acronyms like DOJ, FBI, SEC, GCB, and the NGC—Bill Weinberger was required to navigate the convolution of SCCA, FIA, FOCA, CSI, CART, *and* the LBGPA on his path to the Caesars Palace Grand Prix. Soon, though, Bill Weinberger also added NJCCC—the New Jersey Casino Control Commission—to the daily discourse of the Caesars World digest.

***

"The beleaguered United States Grand Prix West will go off as scheduled," read the sports deck of the Las Vegas daily, "despite last minute financial complications, threats of loss of insurance, crowd control problems, and absent ticket takers."[98] The potential barriers to the 1977 U.S. Grand Prix West were onerous. They were also quite public. Most notably, headed into the race weekend, Chris Pook and the LBGPA were still $150,000 short in their race guarantee to FOCA.

"We knew about it before we left (England) to come over here," Bernie Ecclestone said. "There is no problem now. We will race on Sunday. What upsets me is that people want to hear bad news."[99] The quotes appeared as a rare act of magnanimity from the czar of Formula One, particularly after the financial shutout of the 1976 event. Long Beach, though, was rather accustomed to bad

The First National City Travelers Checks brand of banking giant Citicorp blanketed professional motorsports in the mid–1970s. First National City would underwrite the 1977 Long Beach Grand Prix as well as Ken Tyrell's revolutionary six-wheeled Formula One team. William D. Weinberger of Caesars World, Inc., attended the 1977 Long Beach Grand Prix at the invitation of Citicorp (Rick Lake collection).

From Formula One to USAC IndyCar to NASCAR, First National City Travelers Checks under-took a 200-mph commercial campaign in 1977. Johnny Rutherford took his Team McLaren M24 to the win of the Jimmy Bryan 150 at Phoenix International Raceway on March 27, 1977. Rutherford started 23rd in the 1983 CART IndyCar Caesars Palace Grand Prix and finished 24th (author's collection).

news. Further, it was significant that the Las Vegas sports beat was paying attention.

While pre-race press assailed the 1977 U.S. Grand Prix West on all fronts, Mario Andretti assailed the Friday time sheets. Andretti led all comers with a 1:22.067 tour of the 2.02-mile circuit. Mario Andretti's Lotus 78 took over a second out of Clay Regazzoni's 1976 Formula One lap record in Long Beach. Remarkably though, the pinnacle of motorsport was still nearly a second adrift of Andretti's qualifying time in 1975 with a stock-block Chevrolet engine, FIA-mandated rumble strips be damned.

"The improvements in tires," remarked Andretti, "have a great deal to do with it. But really, everyone is much better prepared for this particular circuit."[100] "We came here blind last year, not knowing what to expect," continued Andretti. "The circuit holds no secrets anymore."[101] In fact, eight other drivers practiced with times quicker than Clay Regazzoni's 1976 qualifying mark. Further, the practice order was separated by less than three seconds from top to bottom. Mario Andretti was followed on the Friday sheets by Jacques Lafitte in a Ligier, John Watson driving a Martini-Brabham for Bernie Ecclestone, and Carlos Reutemann in a Ferrari. World champion

James Hunt in a Marlboro-McLaren trailed Reutemann with Niki Lauda rounding out the quick-six for the Scuderia-Ferrari.

Saturday qualifying shaped up as a back-and-forth battle between Mario Andretti in the Lotus-Ford and Jody Scheckter in a Wolf Ford for much of the final session. With time running out, Mario Andretti was on top with a 1:21.868, just .019 seconds quicker than Jody Scheckter. While Andretti appeared as the presumptive pole sitter, Niki Lauda then took the track for one last timed run before the final horn. Lauda put together an amazing last lap in his Ferrari to emerge with the pole, a dominant 1:21.630 to push Andretti aside to second on the starting grid. Jody Scheckter then followed third quick with a 1:21.887. Mario Andretti, though, took the bump in stride. "I guess I just had one problem today," quipped Andretti. "Lauda."[102] Carlos Reutemann slotted fourth followed by Jacques Lafitte, John Watson, and Emerson Fittipaldi. Defending world champion James Hunt anchored the fourth row, nearly a second back of Lauda's pole.

As the qualifying parade settled to the paddock, though, more bad news then came from the perimeter. It was the sort of news that seemed inimitable to the Long Beach Grand Prix. "More than a score of souvenir vendors were complaining," reported the Long Beach daily, "of alleged threats and manhandling by what several private concessionaires called a 'goon squad.'"[103] The ugly dispute over merchandising rights arose between city-licensed vendors lining the circuit and Augie Speth, the contracted master concessionaire for the Long Beach Grand Prix Association. Speth and staff reportedly harassed the separate vendors, damaged their displays, and demanded some 65 percent of their sales. "It's like a syndicate shake-down out here," complained one vendor. "Who the hell is this guy?"[104]

Augie Speth was accompanied by merchandiser Joel Vest on their strong-arm rounds of the perimeter vendors. Notably, Joel Vest was another member of the Long Beach Grand Prix Committee of 300, along with William Dawson and James Gray. "As far as I'm concerned, this is a cheap muscle job," concluded one vendor. "Folks are pretty disappointed with this whole Grand Prix deal."[105] The contracting of concessions for the Long Beach Grand Prix became yet one more of the post-race asterisks.

Race day for the 1977 U.S. Grand Prix West dawned to another beautiful California setting. By comparison to the overnight at the 1976 U.S. Grand Prix in Watkins Glen, there was not a hint of snow in the forecast. Temperatures then settled in the mid–70s, winds were calm, with 15 miles of visibility out into the blue surf of the vast Pacific Ocean.

From third on the grid, Jody Scheckter took the lead at the start, racing past Niki Lauda and Mario Andretti on the inside line into turn one. Carlos Reutemann then attempted to follow Scheckter through the inside path of the collapsing queue. Reutemann, though, locked up and went straight at the hard right onto an escape road. Niki Lauda, Mario Andretti, and Jacque Lafitte managed to avoid the Reutemann trajectory and trailed Scheckter. Behind though, James Hunt's McLaren found the front wheel of John Watson's Brabham, launching Hunt airborne. Jochen Mass and Vittorio Brambilla then collided further back. James Hunt and Carlos Reutemann rejoined the race from the escape road. Jochen Mass was able to continue as well.

Jody Scheckter then led dominantly in his Wolf-Ford. "This was motor racing

Patrick Depailler qualified fourth for the 1977 Long Beach Grand Prix in his six-wheeled First National City Tyrell P34. Depailler also finished fourth, over a minute behind third-place Jody Scheckter in a Wolf. The 1977 Long Beach Grand Prix was won by Mario Andretti. The six-wheeled Tyrell design was scuttled at the end of the season. Patrick Depailler was killed on August 1, 1980, during testing prior to the German Grand Prix (Rick Lake collection).

with no let-up. Scheckter was driving extremely confidently," reported *Motorsport Magazine*, "hurling his Wolf round with a dash of opposite lock that let his two immediate pursuers know full-well that he wasn't to be trifled with on this particular day."[106] Inside 20 laps to go, however, Scheckter noticed his right front tire slowly going down, while Mario Andretti's Lotus filled the mirrors of the Wolf-Ford. Headed down Shoreline Drive with three laps to go, Mario Andretti ducked inside Scheckter and made it stick, emerging from the Queen's Corner hairpin with the lead of the race. Lauda then followed past Scheckter to take over second place.

Niki Lauda drew close to Andretti as the streaking pair opened the final lap. "With the crowd willing him on," continued *Motorsport*, "Andretti wasn't about to let a Ferrari stand between him and victory."[107] Mario Andretti then flashed under the checkered flag on the 80th lap to become the first American to win a Formula One race on American soil. Andretti's margin of victory over Lauda was .773 seconds.

"This is better than winning at Indianapolis," Mario Andretti gushed from the victory celebration. "It's the greatest point of my career."[108] Andretti praised the circuit, while he was also optimistic for the future of the Long Beach Grand Prix. "The drivers, the Europeans," continued Andretti, "enjoy coming here more than anything else."[109]

After the Ferrari of Niki Lauda, Jody Scheckter remarkably survived to take third-place nearly five seconds back. Patrick Depailler in the Tyrell P34 six-wheeler improved from 12th on the grid to come home fourth. Emerson Fittipaldi was next in fifth, the last car on the lead lap. Jean-Pierre Jarier finished sixth in John Watson's 1976 machine acquired from Roger Penske. Notably, James Hunt brought the

Mario Andretti won the 1977 Long Beach Grand Prix driving a Lotus-Ford for Colin Chapman. Andretti held off Niki Lauda in a Ferrari to claim an extremely popular Formula One victory by an American driver on American soil, an accomplishment that stands to this day. Mario Andretti was also the only driver to contest all four premier classes of the Caesars Palace Grand Prix. Niki Lauda competed at Caesars Palace in 1982. Toyota Celica safety car at back left is noteworthy (Rick Lake collection).

battle-damaged Marlboro-McLaren to a seventh-place finish, closing his Long Beach misadventure out of the points.

The much-maligned Chris Pook was allowed a brief moment to celebrate as well. "We couldn't have had a better guy win the race than Mario," Pook said. "I couldn't be more pleased."[110] By 1977, though, the pleasure bar for Chris Pook might have been set rather low. Further, Pook was still marked in Long Beach. "Pook stirs deep emotions. Opinions about him range from dynamic and brilliant," offered one post-race pundit, "to con man and thief."[111]

The Long Beach post-race reports then turned to finances, and a fraught future. Questioned afterward about whether the race could have gone forward pending the $150,000 infusion, Bernie Ecclestone was slightly more specific about the stakes involved. "No," confirmed Ecclestone. "We would not have moved an inch."[112] Bernie Ecclestone also provided the punchline, certainly as a point of contrast to Monaco. "After we raced here last year, somebody asked me how Long Beach was," Ecclestone quipped. "I said, 'I think it was closed when we were there.'"[113]

***

In the days after the 1977 Long Beach Grand Prix, contention and controversy again climbed above the front-page fold of the Long Beach daily. The dispute over concessions pitted Augie Speth and Joel Vest against any number of city-licensed vendors and storefront merchants lining the Grand Prix circuit. Once again, the agreement between the City of Long Beach and the LBGPA occupied the news stories. Once again, the two parties did not agree on its provisions, in this case the exclusivity of concessions on city streets. "It was expressly stated that concession rights granted were not to be exclusive," claimed a deputy city attorney. "They're reading something into the contract that simply isn't there."[114] On the heels of another financially and logistically troubled Grand Prix, both Chris Pook and Don Dyer chose circumspection in the media.

One week later, though, the City of Long Beach reported that the Long Beach Grand Prix Association was able to retire some of the accumulated debt from 1975 and 1976. Still due, however, was the city's share of the 1977 gate as well as the "extraordinary costs" arising from city staff and equipment in support of the 1977 Grand Prix. The Association also owed a flat fee for the city's share of unrealized profits from the first two races, part of the three-year deferral plan approved prior to the 1977 Grand Prix.

Amid the clashes over concessions and the apparent short-term financial improvements, however, news was scarce regarding a financial snapshot at the bottom line of the 1977 U.S. Grand Prix West. Finally, on June 10, 1977, it was reported that the Grand Prix Association earned a net profit of $25,000 on gross race event revenues of $1,571,000. News of the paltry 1.6 percent return on revenue was accompanied by mention of continued debts, "between $100,000 and $150,000."[115] The debt position of the Long Beach Grand Prix Association thus closely echoed the tack and tone of the Watkins Glen Grand Prix Corporation 20 years before.[116] Curiously, though, the financial information for the 1977 Grand Prix was disclosed not by Chris Pook, but by Randall Verrue of the City of Long Beach.

Randall Verrue—executive assistant to disgraced former City Manager John Mansell—was also a principal in the city's 1976 bailout plan of the Grand Prix. When Verrue reported the financial results of the 1977 Long Beach Grand Prix, he was also "a key figure in the pending negotiation of a controversial $200,000 service contract between the city's new Long Beach Promotion and Service Corp. and the Grand Prix Association."[117] The Promotion and Service Corporation, in turn, was a roll-up of the Convention and News Bureau and Queen Mary tourist operations under a single quasi-public umbrella.

As with its predecessor, the successor government services corporation overseeing the Grand Prix was funded largely by guest room taxes levied by the City of Long Beach, including the rooms on the Queen Mary. "I still feel it's illegal use of tax money to support a private, profit-making corporation (the Grand Prix Association)," stated city auditor Robert Fronke. "I told them it's almost unauditable. Who's going to be doing what?"[118] Further, the contract proposal was signed by Randall Verrue and Chris Pook in private, "without knowledge of the corporation's three-man board."[119] It is worth mention that Randall Verrue was also close to the lease arrangements for the controversial Harbor Bank building at 777 E. Ocean Drive, the project at the center of the Ernest Mayer bribery case.[120]

On the same date that Randall Verrue broke news of the 1977 Grand Prix finances, Ernest Mayer—former Long Beach Planning Director—was then sentenced in the Harbor Bank bribery case "1 to 14 years in state prison."[121] Mayer's Long Beach play was, according to the prosecutor, "the most aggravated bribery case we've tried in the County of Los Angeles in the past five years."[122] "This was," continued the district attorney, "a shakedown heavily proved."[123]

The Long Beach City Hall empire of dirt and deals would reverberate in Long Beach for years to come, despite the 1976 resignation of Long Beach City Manager John Mansell, and the 1977 conviction of Long Beach Planning Director Ernest Mayer. In fact, Caesars Palace development front Jay Sarno soon brought legal action against the Long Beach daily for their reporting of the attempted 1974 incursion by Allen Dorfman and him in the amusement concessions aboard the *Queen Mary*. Further, the actions of Randall Verrue and others more deeply entwined the Long Beach Grand Prix Corporation in the taxes and treasury of the city charter.

Whether "dynamic and brilliant" or "con man and thief,"[124] Christopher R. Pook had nonetheless demonstrated an uncanny ability to survive the apocalypse of backroom Long Beach politics, as well as to navigate the byzantine boardrooms of Bernie Ecclestone and Formula One race-making. Christopher R. Pook was now something of his own entity, able to represent combinations of "Long Beach" and "Formula One" to interested bidders across the country. Amid the continued decline of Watkins Glen as an international venue, Chris Pook would then assume the leading edge of Formula One in America, seated at the table among the most powerful racing operators in the country. "On top of the table is the sport," the great Enzo Ferrari said, "and underneath is the business."[125] "If you're not at the table," the notion is then furthered, "you become part of the menu."[126]

One month after the 1977 Long Beach Grand Prix, there was movement at Caesars Palace on the Las Vegas Strip. "Caesar's Palace president William S. Weinberger," reported Nevada press, "will soon be leaving the Las Vegas casino to head up a hotel-casino in Atlantic City, NJ."[127] The senior William Weinberger was indeed on the move, newly posted to Bally's Park Place casino in the newly-legalized New Jersey Boardwalk tourist gambling district.

One day after the Weinberger announcement from Las Vegas, Cameron Argetsinger announced that he was returning to upstate New York to rekindle his law practice. Argetsinger—seemingly forced from the SCCA after the marginalization of the SCCA Can-Am and Formula 5000 series—took the occasion to wax of the formative Grand Prix events at Watkins Glen. "We took some poetic license and called it the sports car Grand Prix," reminisced the former head of the Watkins Glen Grand Prix Corporation. "I think the name had a lot to do with capturing the imagination of the people."[128] Cameron Argetsinger was replaced at SCCA headquarters by Thomas Duval.[129]

The following week, the junior William D. Weinberger was also on the move, posted to a newly created executive position at Caesars Palace, moving over from the Caesars World corporate parent in Los Angeles. William D. "Bill" Weinberger would take the curated role of "Caesars Palace Vice President of Casino Marketing." Sports promotions were positioned under the Weinberger umbrella and would spring directly from his desk. One of Bill Weinberger's earliest such undertakings would be the development of the Caesars Palace Grand Prix. Clifford Perlman—still besieged by the Caesars Poconos and Sky Lake undertakings with Alvin Malnik—would preside over the inaugural. Springing forth from Long Beach, Chris Pook and his figurative formation of "spherical elastic attenuators," were soon also to be at the table of Caesar.

Advance signage for the new Caesars Palace hotel-casino braves the parched Las Vegas desert in early 1965. The paved road at right is Las Vegas Boulevard, the world-famous Las Vegas Strip. The Strip was designated Federal Route 91. The image looks north from the southwest corner of the Strip and Dunes Road (now Flamingo Road). Flamingo hotel-casino signage is visible at right. This marquee was at the north end of the Flamingo property. The marquee bills comedian Jack Carter and country music singer Molly Bee in the Flamingo showroom. Carter and Bee appeared at the Flamingo from December 14, 1964, to January 20, 1965 (*San Francisco Examiner*, January 3, 1965). Jerry Gordon, later indicted with Meyer Lansky, was the vice president of the Flamingo at the time. Beyond the Flamingo is the Capri Motel. The Capri property was later acquired by Ralph Engelstad, one of the developers of Las Vegas Motor Speedway. The Caesars Palace Grand Prix was held from 1981 to 1984 directly across the Strip from the Capri Motel property (courtesy Culinary Workers Union Local 226).

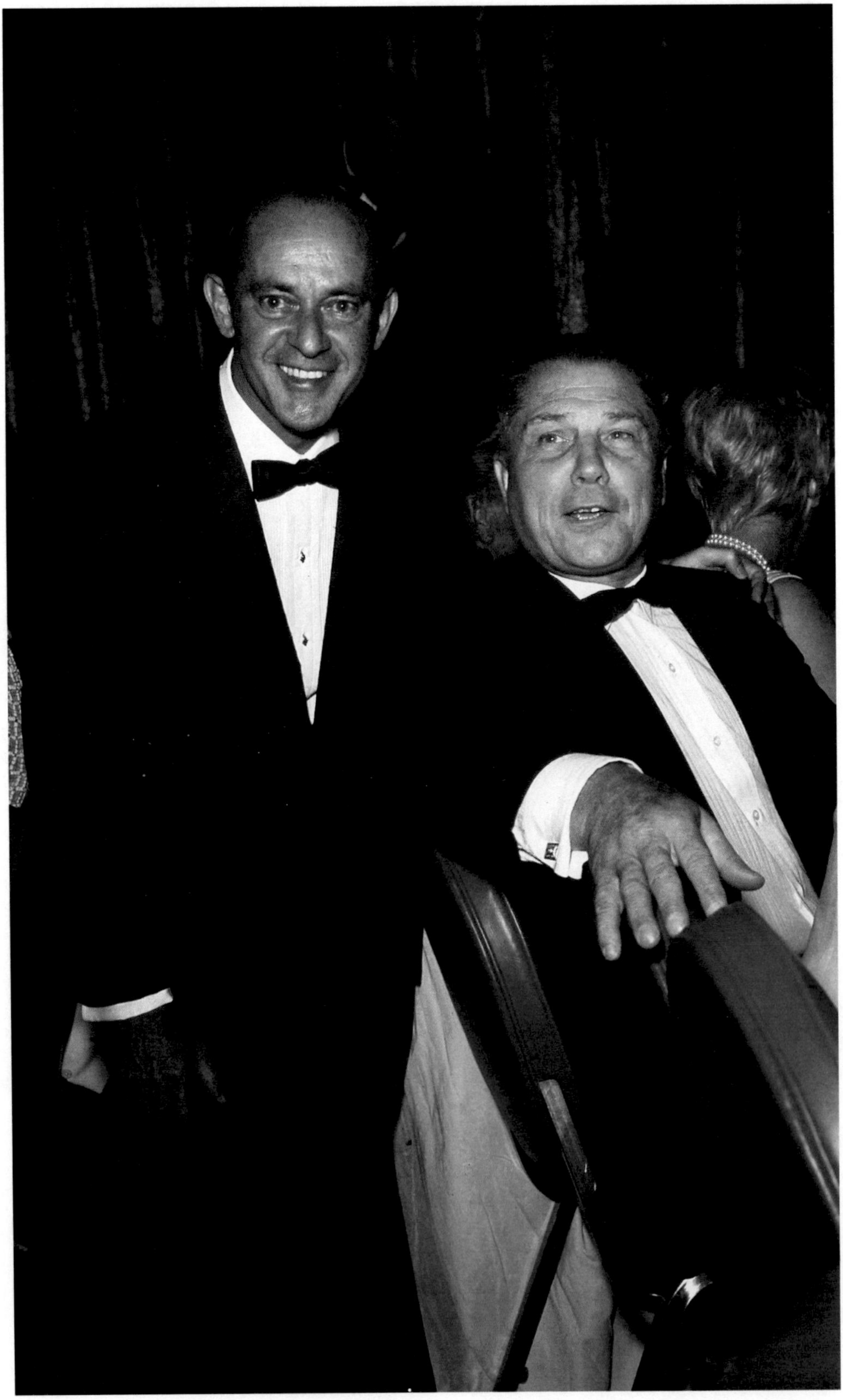

The multi-faceted Danny Ongais threads a multi-faceted storyline, from racketeers to race car drivers. Ongais won the funny car final for Mickey Thompson at the 1969 NHRA Stardust National Open at Stardust International Raceway, notably owned by Moe Dalitz of the Cleveland Syndicate. Ongais was in the Formula One field for the 1977 U.S. Grand Prix at Watkins Glen, a country drive from the 1958 La Cosa Nostra crime convention in Apalachin, New York. Finally, Danny Ongais raced in the final Caesars Palace Grand Prix, the 1984 season finale of the CART IndyCar series (courtesy International Motor Racing Research Center).

Opposite: Nathan Jacobson (left) of Caesars Palace requested this shot with Jimmy Hoffa at the August 5, 1966, grand opening of Caesars Palace in Las Vegas, Nevada. With convictions then under appeal, Hoffa would report to prison seven months after Caesars Palace opened. Jacobson later purchased the Sierra Tahoe property that was converted to a gambling casino by Roy Gene Lewis of Riverside International Raceway and Norman Tyrone. The Lake Tahoe resort was subsequently acquired by Abram Pritzker of Hyatt Hotels (courtesy LVCVA News Bureau).

Above: A Marlboro-sponsored McLaren streaks past the lens during the October 17, 1981, Caesars Palace Grand Prix and illustrates the convergence of Las Vegas, organized crime, and the pinnacle of motorsport. The world-famous Las Vegas Strip is at the left. The 27-story Caesars Palace Fantasy Tower looms to the south of the Formula One circuit, providing both unlimited viewing and the broadcast booth for NBC Sports. The domed structure in front of the tower is the Caesars Palace OmniMax theater. Kirk Kerkorian developed the MGM Grand hotel-casino in the left background of the image. Country singer Eddie Rabbitt appears on the MGM marquee. Kerkorian was also the original Caesars Palace landlord and an original gambling licensee of the Las Vegas resort. The tragic MGM fire which killed 87 people occurred one year before the inaugural Grand Prix event (photograph by Marc Nelson).

The race program for the October 14–17 inaugural Caesars Palace Grand prix featured a painting by modern impressionist Leroy Neiman. The #27 Ferrari of Gilles Villeneuve leads Carlos Reutemann (#2 Williams) and Alain Prost (#15 Renault) while the Palace of Caesar provides the backdrop. Neiman also painted the program art for the 1982 and 1983 Caesars Palace Grand Prix events (courtesy LVCVA News Bureau).

Opposite: The barren infield north of turn seven of the Caesars Palace Grand Prix circuit offers this 1981 view of the Rat Pack–era Sands Hotel and Casino at left, famous for the raucous late-night performances some 20 years earlier of Frank Sinatra, Dean Martin, and Sammy Davis, Jr. Notably, Rat Pack original Sammy Davis, Jr., smiled for the cameras on pit lane prior to the October 17, 1981, inaugural Caesars Palace Grand Prix (photograph by Marc Nelson).

Above: Al Holbert (#14 CAC-2) leads Teo Fabi (#6 March), Rocky Moran (#15 Frissbee), John Morton (#46 Frissbee), and Tom Klausler (#8 Frissbee-Prophet) down the back straightaway at the SCCA Can-Am event of the 1981 Caesars Palace Grand Prix. The drivers finished seventh, second, 17th, fifth, and sixth, respectively (Bill Weinberger collection).

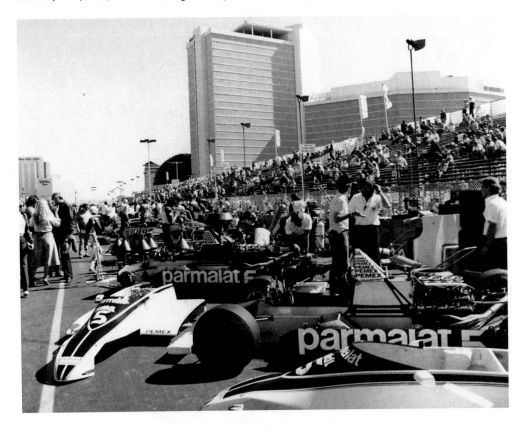

Bobby Rahal drove a Budweiser March 817 for owner Paul Newman at the October 16, 1981, SCCA Can-Am race at the Caesars Palace Grand Prix. Rahal qualified fourth and finished in the same position behind winner Danny Sullivan, teammate Teo Fabi, and Geoff Brabham. Rahal joined the CART IndyCar series the following season for Jim Trueman. The image looks across the Las Vegas Strip to the Imperial Palace of Ralph Engelstad beyond (photograph by Marc Nelson).

Opposite: Bernie Ecclestone of FOCA and the Brabham Formula One team was the primary motorsport influencer in the development of the Caesars Palace Grand Brix. Nelson Piquet finished fifth in his #5 Brabham BT49C to claim the 1981 Formula One world championship. Hector Rebaque and the #6 Brabham machine dropped out on lap 20. The imposing 27-story Caesars Palace Fantasy Tower provided the broadcast platform for NBC Sports. The domed structure is the Caesars Palace OmniMax Theater. The Asian-themed gable roof of Ralph Engelstad's Imperial Palace hotel-casino is visible across the Las Vegas Strip. Engelstad was later involved in the development of Las Vegas Motor Speedway (Bill Weinberger collection).

Above: Danny Sullivan at high speed in the west straightaway between turns 13 and 14 on the Caesars Palace Grand prix circuit. Sullivan won the October 16, 1981, SCCA Can-Am event at the Caesars Palace Grand Prix driving a Lola Frisbee for Garvin Brown Racing. Danny Sullivan drove briefly for Gerald Forsythe and Paul Newman in the 1982 CART IndyCar series. Sullivan also returned to the 1982 Caesars Palace Can-Am event driving for Paul Newman (photograph by Marc Nelson).

Mario Andretti in the #22 Marlboro Alfa Romeo at the October 17, 1981, Caesars Palace Grand Prix. Despite the highest of expectations going in, 1981 would be a miserable season for the Alfa squad. Indeed, Mario Andretti finished 17th in the Formula One points standings. According to Andretti, Marlboro would have supported him at either Alfa Romeo or McLaren for the 1981 Formula One season. "I could've gone with McLaren," reflected Mario Andretti years on, "and I probably should've" (Mario Andretti interview) (Bill Weinberger collection).

Opposite: American Eddie Cheever (#3 Tyrell) leads Eliseo Salazar (#14 Ensign) through the chute between turns nine and 10 at the 1981 Caesars Palace Grand Prix. In his third year of Formula One competition, Cheever qualified 19th for Ken Tyrell. Cheever dropped out with engine issues on lap 10. Salazar qualified 24th for Morris Nunn and finished 14th. The structures of the Interstate 15 freeway are visible in the background (Bill Weinberger collection).

Above: New Zealander Graham McRae picked up a lively pink and white Circus-Circus hotel-casino sponsorship for the final three races of the 1981 SCCA Can-Am season. McRae qualified eighth in his McRae GM9 for the October 16, 1981, Can-Am event at the Caesars Palace Grand Prix but retired on lap two. Nonetheless, the Circus-Circus sponsorship on the grounds of Caesars Palace linked the two Las Vegas properties developed by Jay Sarno, as well as the numerous federal investigations bearing the Sarno name (photograph by Mark Nelson).

Geoff Brabham—son of former Formula One champion Jack Brabham—arches the familial lineage forward from his father's gritty performance at the 1959 Grand Prix of the United States at Sebring, Florida, through to the presence of Brabham team owner Bernie Ecclestone at the 1981 Caesars Palace Grand Prix. Jack Brabham pushed his disabled Cooper fourth across the 1959 Sebring finish line and claimed the Formula One world championship. Son Geoff Brabham finished third in the SCCA Can-Am event at the 1981 Caesars Palace Grand Prix and won the Can-Am championship. Nelson Piquet, driving for Bernie Ecclestone, finished fifth in a Brabham at the 1981 Caesars Palace Grand Prix to win the Formula One world championship (photograph by Marc Nelson).

Opposite: Bruno Giacomelli (#23 Alfa Romeo) leads Mario Andretti (#22 Alfa Romeo) at the October 17, 1981, inaugural Caesars Palace Grand Prix. Giacomelli qualified eighth and finished third for the only podium of his Formula One career. Andretti qualified 10th but retired on lap 22 with a suspension failure. The Alfa Romeo drovers were disadvantaged throughout the season as Brabham developed a hydraulic system to cheat the ride height checkpoints on pit lane and other teams followed the Brabham lead (Bill Weinberger collection).

Above: Jacques Lafitte carried the familiar French cigarette brand Gitanes on the side pods of his #26 Ligier JS17 at the October 17, 1981, Caesars Palace Grand Prix. In the build-up to the event, Lafitte was also quoted in an Italian newspaper with disparaging comments, describing the Caesars Palace course as a "ridiculous go-kart track" (*Salina* [KS] *Journal*, October 15, 1981). The praetorians of the Palace responded with threat of a $10 million libel lawsuit against the paper, proclaiming that the resort would not have its "reputation tarnished by flimsy journalism." In other news from Caesar, Jacques Lafitte qualified 12th, finished sixth, and was fourth in the 1981 Formula One world championship (photograph by Marc Nelson).

John Watson (#7 McLaren) leads Eliseo Salazar (#14 Ensign) at the October 17, 1981, Caesars Palace Grand Prix. Watson qualified sixth and finished seventh for McLaren Racing. Salazar qualified down the order, 24th on the time sheets for Morris Nunn, but improved to a 14th place finish. Both drivers returned for the 1982 Caesars Palace event. The world-famous Las Vegas strip is just beyond the row of signage in the background. The Imperial Palace hotel-casino of Ralph Engelstad is across the Strip (photograph by Marc Nelson).

Opposite: Gilles Villeneuve powers his Ferrari F126 through the chute between turns three and four at the October 17, 1981, Caesars Palace Grand Prix. Villeneuve qualified a strong third in Las Vegas but retired on lap 22. Gilles Villeneuve was later disqualified for starting from the wrong grid position. Villeneuve was tragically killed at the Belgian Grand Prix on May 8, 1982, and would not make a Las Vegas return. Gilles Villeneuve was the father of 1995 Indianapolis 500 winner Jacques Villeneuve (photograph by Marc Nelson).

Above: The four-year run of competition at the Caesars Palace Grand Prix was remarkably safe, despite the proximity of high-speed race cars with unforgiving concrete barriers. Patrick Tambay endured the most spectacular shunt of the four premier-class races in his #25 Ligier JS-17. With the front end of the race car sheared and Tambay's legs exposed, the intrepid driver suffered no broken bones and was released after X-rays. Patrick Tambay returned for the 1982 Caesars Palace Grand Prix in the #27 Ferrari of the departed Gilles Villeneuve (photograph by Marc Nelson).

Enzo Ferrari put Mario Andretti in the #28 turbocharged Ferrari 126C2B of the injured Didier Pironi for the final two events of the 1982 Formula One season. Andretti qualified on pole and finished third at the penultimate Italian Grand prix. Pictured here at the September 25, 1982, Caesars Palace Grand Prix, Mario Andretti qualified seventh but dropped out with a rear wishbone failure on lap 26. Andretti was in an IndyCar the very next day on the high banks of Michigan International Speedway for CART IndyCar team owner Pat Patrick (John Blakemore Photograph Collection, The Revs Institute).

Opposite: This view of the Rat Pack–era Sands Hotel depicts the proximity of the world-famous Las Vegas Strip to the Caesars Palace Grand Prix circuit. The Sands was on the east side of the Strip beyond the grandstands while the race course was on the west. On track through turn 10, the McLaren of Andrea de Cesaris leads the Fittipaldi of Chico Serra. Mark Surer trails in a Theodore TR3 for owner Teddy Yip. The "spherical elastic attenuators" of the Long Beach Grand Prix Association abound on the run-offs (photograph by Marc Nelson).

Above: Michele Alboreto concluded his second season of Formula One with Team Tyrell at the September 25, 1982, Caesars Palace Grand Prix. After scoring no points in the 1981 campaign, Alboreto found consistency in 1982, with six points-paying finishes and one podium. In the 1982 season finale Michele Alboreto and Ken Tyrell put it all together. Alboreto qualified third in the Tyrell 011. On the 53rd lap of the race, Alboreto moved into the lead of a Formula One event for the first time in his career and held it to the finish, winning the 1982 Caesars Palace Grand Prix by 27 seconds over John Watson of McLaren. Sunrise and Frenchman mountains in the background form the east wall of the Las Vegas valley (John Blakemore Photograph Collection, The Revs Institute).

Teo Fabi (#33 March) leads John Paul, Jr. (#12 Penske), Derek Daly (#90 March), Mario Andretti (#3 Lola), and Pancho Carter (#21 March) down the front straight and into the formation lap of the October 8, 1983, CART IndyCar Caesars Palace Grand Prix III. The last IndyCar event in Las Vegas was 15 years before at the long-shuttered Stardust International Raceway some six miles in the distance. Spring Mountains in the background form the west wall of the Las Vegas valley (photograph by Ernie Ohlson).

Opposite: Formula One departed the luxury-branded trappings of the world-famous Las Vegas Strip with the conclusion of the 1982 Caesars Palace Grand Prix. Never since has the 12,000 RPM scream of the pinnacle of motorsport bounced among the high-rise hotels along the most recognized boulevard in the western United States. Arrayed from right are the MGM developed by Kirk Kerkorian, the Barbary Coast of Michael Gaughan, the Flamingo Hilton originally opened by Benjamin "Bugsy" Siegel, and the Imperial Palace developed by Ralph Engelstad, while a Marlboro McLaren screams in song through the north side of the Caesars Palace Grand Prix circuit (photograph by Marc Nelson).

The Caesars Palace Sports Pavilion provided covered paddock facilities for the Caesars Palace Grand Prix. In the foreground, Tom Sneva's crew conducts an inspection of the #4 Texaco Star March for car owner George Bignotti. Sneva, the defending winner of the Indianapolis 500, was slow in qualifying for the Caesars Palace Grand Prix III and was added to the rear of the field as a promoter's option. Sneva dropped out on lap 150 with a fire (photograph by Ernie Ohlson).

Rick Mears (left) of Team Penske stands on the pit wall during the 1983 Caesars Palace Grand Prix III. Mears qualified a rather lackluster 16th in his Penske PC-10B for team owner Roger Penske and was flagged in 13th position at the finish. Mears won the following 1984 Indianapolis 500 but was replaced for the 1984 Caesars Palace Grand Prix by Michael Thackwell due to injury. Penske crew member and firefighters are not identified (photograph by Ernie Ohlson).

Mario Andretti in his #3 Budweiser Newman-Haas Lola T800 leads the formation lap of the November 11, 1984, CART IndyCar Caesars Palace Grand Prix IV. Polesitter Danny Sullivan (#30 Lola) is at right as the field moves through turns three and four of the Caesars Palace roval. Bobby Rahal (#5 March) trails third followed by John Paul, Jr. (#17 March), Emerson Fittipaldi (#40 March), Tom Sneva (#4 March), Geoff Brabham (#18 March), and Al Unser (#1 March). The first four rows of the 1984 Caesars Palace event would eventually comprise nine Indianapolis 500 victories and three Formula One world championships (author's collection).

Above: Wally Dallenbach, Jr., contested the 1984 SCCA Trans-Am season in a family-run race team, the #98 Colorado Connection Camaro. Dallenbach, the son of CART IndyCar race steward Wally Dallenbach, Sr., put together a run of consistent top-10 finishes during the Trans-Am season. At the November 11, 1984, Trans-Am round at the Caesars Palace Grand Prix, Wally Dallenbach, Jr., raced for the lead and finished a strong second to race winner Tom Gloy. "Being able to race there and being able to walk to your hotel or walk to the casino. It was such a cool deal," recalled Dallenbach. "Those early years in Las Vegas were very special" (Wally Dallenbach interview). Others are not identified (photograph by Brent Martin).

The first four qualifiers of the November 11, 1984, SCCA Trans-Am race at the Caesars Palace Grand Prix hit the apex of turn one in the early laps. Tom Gloy (#7 Mercury Capri) chases Darin Brassfield (#3 Chevrolet Corvette), Dave Watson (#37 Chevrolet Camaro), and Richard Wall (#43 Chevrolet Camaro). Tom Gloy won the event over Wally Dallenbach, Jr. The "Caesars Palace Self Parking" sign at left of image indicates the site of the Grand Prix circuit. "Spherical elastic attenuators" of Chris Pook and the Long Beach Grand Prix Association line the run-off area of the turn. Signage panels beyond screen the sidewalk of the Las Vegas Strip from pedestrian onlookers. The Holiday Inn hotel-casino is directly across the Strip. The balcony spectators are noteworthy (photograph by Ernie Ohlson).

Opposite: The Coors Light Silver Bullet March 84C of Al Unser, Jr., in the infield gallery of the 1984 Caesars Palace Grand Prix IV. Unser qualified 16th for car owner Rick Galles and improved to fourth at the finish, having recorded his first IndyCar win at Portland earlier in the season. Unser and Galles went on together to win the 1992 Indianapolis 500. The 7-Eleven–sponsored March of Bobby Rahal is visible at right. Parking lot striping of the Caesars Palace infield is evident. The floral arrangement and Caesars Palace coin bucket at upper left are noteworthy (author's collection).

The venerable A.J. Foyt ran a limited ovals-only schedule during 1984 in his Gilmore March. Foyt was over five seconds off the pole in qualifying and was added to the show as a promoter's option. A.J. Foyt's March 84C is noticeably shorn of its right front wing from contact in the early laps. Foyt continued without a wing change but retired on lap 56 with a fire, posted 22nd in the final standings with $3,720 at the Caesars Palace pay window (author's collection).

The Robert Bosch Super-Vee open wheel series joined the CART IndyCar series at the 1984 Caesars Palace Grand Prix III. The 1984 Bosch contingent featured such rising stars as Arie Luyendyk, Roger Penske, Jr., Mike Follmer, Tommy Byrne, Dominic Dobson, Mike Groff, and Jeff Andretti. The event was won by Ludwig Heimrath, Jr. (#5 Ralt RT5) over Luyendyk and Penske (photograph by Ernie Ohlson).

Mario Andretti turns his Newman-Hass Lola T800 toward the apex of turn four at the November 11, 1984, Caesars Palace Grand Prix IV. Andretti finished second to Tom Sneva in the final race event on the Caesars Palace Grand Prix circuit. Mario Andretti also clinched the 1984 PPG CART IndyCar championship, his first national championship since 1969 when he also won the Indianapolis 500. The cast-off rubber "marbles" from race tires on outer fringes of asphalt are noteworthy (author's collection).

Nearly 40 years on, the Caesars Palace mega-resort in Las Vegas has long since built over its Grand Prix history, and its mobster foundations—allegedly. The world-famous Las Vegas Strip is at right bottom corner and angles away to the right. Flamingo Road angles from bottom right to mid-left. Turn one of the Caesars Palace Grand Prix circuit was roughly at mid-right, just left of the Strip. The Forum Shops at Caesars were developed over the former parking lot section of the Grand Prix course. The Mirage hotel-casino at upper right claimed the former Howard Hughes property on which the north section of the Grand Prix circuit was constructed. The Mirage was developed by Steve Wynn and opened in 1989. The Mirage notably hosts the hugely popular Cirque du Soleil show "The Beatles Love." The 27-story Caesars Palace Fantasy Tower (now the Forum Tower) still stands just right of center but is dwarfed by the later high-rise towers. At lower right are the shops of the Bellagio, also developed by Steve Wynn. The Bellagio was the host resort of a scuttled 1998 United States Grand Prix venture in Las Vegas discussed between Steve Wynn and Bernie Ecclestone (Creative Commons).

VII

Rumors and Rackets

The Emergence of the Caesars Palace Grand Prix,
the Exposure of the Emperor

I heard a bustling rumor like a fray. (*Julius Caesar* 2.4.21)

Recorded history is rich with the convergence of seemingly unrelated occurrences, neatly overlain yet disparate events that subsequently enmesh to produce a fully synthesized outcome. In that regard, on June 3, 1977, the same date that the Long Beach City Auditor decried the "illegal use of tax money to support a private, profit-making corporation (the Grand Prix Association),"[1] a singular event far across the country emerged to anchor the fates and fortunes of Caesars World, Inc. as well as its chairman, Clifford Perlman. The paired events, in turn, indelibly underscored the storyline of the Caesars Palace Grand Prix.

"Dream comes true for Atlantic City" was the blast from Hackensack, New Jersey. "Byrne signs casino law."[2] The celebration in the moribund beach resort city heralded hopes for a vigorous casino-anchored redevelopment of the historic Boardwalk and downtown core. As Governor Brendan Byrne signed the Casino Control Act into law, hope also rang that the dreams of the Monopoly city could be realized without the monopoly of the Mob. "Organized crime is not welcome in Atlantic City," proclaimed the New Jersey governor. "Keep your filthy hands out of Atlantic City."[3]

The Mob, though, was deeply entrenched in New Jersey and Atlantic City, marking territorial control dating back to the Depression. "Organized crime," remarked the Atlantic City police chief, "has been here for decades."[4] Indeed, the Mob had embedded influences in New Jersey labor unions, construction, vending, food provisioning, laundry services, and the time-honored waste management racket. Even more so, Atlantic City did not operate as an open, negotiated organized crime profit center like Las Vegas and Miami Beach. "The mob from New Jersey," suggested one informant. "These guys will kill you if you don't go along."[5]

Resorts International was first to the Atlantic City casino market and, in turn, the desks of the newly constituted New Jersey Casino Control Commission. Resorts International, however, immediately ran afoul of New Jersey regulators for the employ of Edward Cellini in their Bahamanian casino operations. Edward—like brother Dino Cellini—was a product of the Steubenville, Ohio, gambling rackets. Edward Cellini managed casinos in the notorious Newport, Kentucky, district in the

179

In May 1977, William S. Weinberger departed Caesars Palace in Las Vegas for a new post at the Bally's Park Place development in Atlantic City, New Jersey. Bally's would be constructed on the site of the former Marlborough-Blenheim Hotel. The historic structure was demolished in 1979. The site was at the high-rent intersection of Boardwalk and Park Place. Clifford Perlman and Caesars World, Inc., also pursued Atlantic City gambling development. The Atlantic City adventures of Caesars World, though, would cause Clifford Perlman to be severed from Caesars Palace—and shadowed the podium celebration of the 1981 Caesars Palace Grand Prix (Library of Congress).

1950s and "from there was a dealer in Havana casinos controlled by [Meyer] Lansky."[6] Resorts International, though, was further tainted by investment from the infamous Bernard Cornfeld's secretive mutual fund labyrinth, Investors Overseas Services.[7] Notably, in 1969, Cornfeld's mammoth investment apparatus also acquired stock in the racketed Parvin-Dohrmann Corporation, proud owners of the Stardust hotel-casino and Stardust International Raceway in Las Vegas.

    Also queuing up in Atlantic City was the Bally's Park Place casino venture headed by William S. Weinberger, formerly of Caesars Palace. Bally's then had to square their early relationship with Gerardo Catena of the Vito Genovese crime family. Bally's was also forced to part company with Sam Kline, due to his own alleged relationship with Catena. Notably, Sam Kline of Cleveland was an original investor in Caesars Palace with William S. Weinberger. Further, Bally's had a distributorship relationship with Dino Cellini, described by the New Jersey Casino Control Commission as an "associate of Meyer Lansky and a person of unsuitable character."[8] It was also Dino Cellini who provided the training structure for the London gambling establishments, including Crockford's where Bernie Ecclestone would ply his penchants. William T.

O'Donnell, central to the various "notorious and unsavory" partnerships, thus resigned as Bally's president and chairman of the board.[9]

Notably, both the Resorts International and Bally's ventures bore close to the apparent logistics leasing rackets of Eugene R. Boffa, Sr. Boffa was believed by federal investigators to have strong ties to the powers of tri-state organized crime, "ranging from upstate Pennsylvania mob boss Russell Bufalino and alleged Mafia member Anthony (Tony Pro) Provenzano."[10] Eugene Boffa reportedly negotiated his trucking agreements directly with another name of note, "Teamsters boss Frank Sheeran, who allegedly received kickbacks in exchange for his help in arranging the labor contracts."[11]

Caesars World and their own considerable coterie then traced Resorts International and Bally's into the emerging Atlantic City marketplace. Caesars World and Clifford Perlman also had to navigate a well-honed negative percep-

Infamous international financier Bernie Cornfeld epitomized the bull market run of the late 1960s. His Investors Overseas Services mutual fund complex, however, tainted the New Jersey gambling bid of Resorts International. Cornfeld's orbit also included connections to Meyer Lansky, Alvin Malnik, and Sidney Korshak. In 1969, the Cornfeld Fund-of-Funds even owned a slice of Stardust International Raceway in Las Vegas, Nevada (Toronto Star Photograph Archive, courtesy Toronto Public Library).

tion of their Miami dealings with Alvin Malnik and Sam Cohen. Indeed, the Securities and Exchange Commission continued to investigate the disclosure implications of the Sky Lake, Cove Haven, and Cricket Club arrangements. Nonetheless, Caesars World and officers Clifford Perlman and William McElnea applied for a temporary gambling permit for their Caesars Palace Boardwalk Regency property. "That will have no bearing, though," read one analysis, "on the commission's ultimate decision on a permanent license for Caesars."[12] The path of Caesars World, Inc. through the New Jersey Casino Control Commission, thus tracked simultaneously, with the path of Formula One from Long Beach and Watkins Glen—to the luxury-branded Caesars Palace in Las Vegas, Nevada.

***

The 1978 U.S. Grand Prix West opened as the 1977 edition closed; multiple controversies once again engulfed the motorsport enterprise of Chris Pook and the Long Beach Grand Prix Association (LBGPA). "Some city-watchers," reported the *Los Angeles Times*, "regard the race as an idea that has never been as good as promised, and never will be."[13] Although such city-watchers might find the word "performance" slotted somewhere between "politics" and "public funds," the pre-race of the 1978 Grand Prix added charges that sounded rather like "payola." Councilperson-elect Ed Tuttle was particularly vocal.

"Earlier this year, as a member of the quasi-public Long Beach Promotions and Service Corp. board," continued the *Times*, "Tuttle charged that the corporation was funneling 'hidden' money to the Grand Prix."[14] The incendiary allegation read as though crafted by the Nevada Gaming Control Board. Ed Tuttle's accusation also precipitated his ouster from the board of directors of the tax-funded municipal Long Beach Promotions and Service Corporation.

A report by the Long Beach city auditor then further clouded the operations of the Grand Prix Association. "Some provisions of the contracts with the Grand Prix," read the auditor's report, "are sufficiently broad that almost any expense connected with promoting the Grand Prix can be charged against the contract."[15] The reports further cited weak internal controls, "lack of support for some disbursements ... incomplete files on payroll, disbursements and contracts, [and] incomplete records on bank accounts."[16] Again, those bank accounts could likely be found at the Grand Prix branch of Harbor Bank at 777 E. Ocean Drive, just northwest of the turn-five hairpin. William F. Dawson, newly-appointed general manager of the Promotions and Service Corporation, then sought to downplay the report. "No one," claimed Dawson, "has run off with any money."[17]

"The heavy wagering on Mario Andretti's chances of repeating as winner," rang another lead-in, "is nothing compared to the bets placed a year ago on Chris Pook's chances of living through the weekend."[18] To the credit of Chris Pook and the LBGPA, however, the $762,000 advance payment for trans-Atlantic transportation, purse, and expenses to Bernie Ecclestone and FOCA was posted 2 weeks in advance of the Grand Prix, a considerable improvement over the washout for Ecclestone in 1976, and a $150,000 shortfall in the Ecclestone advance in 1977.

The resounding win by Mario Andretti in the 1977 U.S. Grand Prix West also provided significant stature with which to anchor the event, as well as public perception of its propriety. As testament to the appeal of the homeland hero, Abram Pritzker of Hyatt Hotels requested a hot lap in the pace car with the defending race-winner. Andretti then toured Pritzker around the street circuit for a three-lap elevator pitch. "When [Abram] Pritzker got out of the car," according to Chris Pook, "he ... said, 'If you guys have the guts to run a race here, I've got the guts to build you a hotel.'"[19]

With a win at the season-opening Argentinian Grand Prix, followed by fourth-place points in Brazil, Mario Andretti and John Player Team Lotus also came into Long Beach as the Formula One championship leader. Lotus teammate Ronnie Peterson, too, stood atop the victory podium at the South African Grand Prix preceding Long Beach. Carlos Reutemann was a race winner as well, taking the round in Brazil ahead of Emerson Fittipaldi, Niki Lauda, and Andretti.

The 1978 U.S. Grand Prix West in Long Beach, though, would not repeat for Mario Andretti. Carlos Reutemann grabbed pole for the 1978 U.S. Grand Prix West in Long Beach for the Scuderia Ferrari, setting a new Formula One lap record of 1:20.636. Reutemann also pulled a second out of Niki Lauda's 1977 mark. Gilles Villeneuve qualified second in a companion Ferrari. Niki Lauda claimed third on the grid in his new Parmalat-Brabham machine for Bernie Ecclestone. Mario Andretti, second on the 1977 grid behind Lauda, sat fourth in his Lotus-Ford alongside the Brabham. Mario Andretti's Ford Cosworth V-8 also spelled his fate, to the fortune of Carlos Reutemann's 12-cylinder Ferrari.

John Watson launched hard at the start from the third row to lead through the first turn. Watson's trajectory also forced Carlos Reutemann to take evasive action. "At the start I was in the lead," recalled Reutemann afterward, "I made the corner a little longer or [Watson] could have hit me hard."[20] Pinned in fifth position in the opening laps, Mario Andretti circulated behind Gilles Villeneuve, John Watson, Niki Lauda, and Carlos Reutemann. John Watson retired on lap nine, moving the order forward and Villeneuve to the point. Andretti, however, was overtaken by the Williams-Ford of Alan Jones on lap 19. Lauda and Villeneuve then retired, handing the race lead to pole-sitter Reutemann. As Jones' Williams-Ford began to sour, Mario Andretti regained position down Shoreline Drive on the 63rd lap, then trailing only Reutemann. Unchallenged the rest of the way, Carlos Reutemann raced under the checkered flag on lap 80 to take the 1978 edition of the Long Beach Grand Prix. Mario Andretti followed through in the John Player Team Lotus some 11 seconds back.

With nine-points for the victory, Carlos Reutemann also moved into a tie with Mario Andretti in the championship chase. "Before the race I felt out of place with an eight-cylinder engine with all those 12 cylinders buzzing on front of me," Andretti remarked afterward, "I had no chance with them on a straight line but the superior handling of my Lotus through the corners … gave me a chance."[21] Indeed, Mario Andretti was enjoying the early development of downforce-generating side skirts, devices that would exemplify the bitter feud between FISA and FOCA in 1980 and 1981.

As Carlos Reutemann savored the win—and Mario Andretti savored a solid six points for second—Chris Pook then declared the gate. "Pook announced that 75,000 tickets were sold," reported the *Los Angeles Times*, "more than the total viewers of the previous races."[22] Subsequent reports also indicated that the Grand Prix Association was able to retire one-half of the remaining debt to the City of Long Beach from the 1975 and 1976 events. "[Pook] gave no estimate," the reports continued, "of the Grand Prix Assn. profit."[23]

A piece of reporting in Las Vegas, however, then splashed to upend the postscript of the 1978 U.S. Grand Prix West. "[Bernie] Ecclestone, a Grand Prix spokesman," reported the *Las Vegas Review-Journal*, "said the race which has been held in Long Beach, Calif., the past three years may be moved to Las Vegas."[24] A Formula One event on the Las Vegas Strip had just peered from behind the veil of the Long Beach Promotions and Service Corporation, and the countdown to the Caesars Palace Grand Prix was a matter of written record.

***

Carlos Reutemann won the 1978 Long Beach Grand Prix driving a Ferrari 312T2. Mario finished second in a Lotus, 11 seconds back. Patrick Depailler completed the podium for Ken Tyrell. Reutemann and Andretti departed Long Beach tied on points in the Formula One world championship. Mario Andretti, however, would win five Grand Prix events before the series returned to America for the penultimate round at Watkins Glen (Rick Lake collection).

"You can't turn right or left in the Poconos," warned the Pennsylvania Crime Commission, "without bumping into gangsters."[25] The cautionary tale from Commission director Joan Weiner came just two weeks after the 1978 U.S. Grand Prix West in Long Beach. Further, the interim comments from the Pennsylvania Crime Commission drew directly on Caesars World, Inc. and their arrangements in the Poconos with Alvin Malnik. The Commission also charted the alleged nexus of Clifford Perlman, Alvin Malnik, Sam Cohen and Meyer Lansky.

"The mob's financial wizard," proclaimed the Commission of Lansky, was also "a pioneer in establishing mob-controlled gambling casinos in Las Vegas, Cuba, and the Bahamas."[26] Although an obvious awakening in Pennsylvania, the Commission nonetheless obtained a copy of the 1975 investigative report of Caesars World, Inc. by the Nevada Gaming Control Board. The Gaming Control Board report, virtually quashed in Las Vegas, revealed the depth and sources of their investigation.

"Al Malnik was an employee of Meyer Lansky," revealed Vincent "Fat Vinnie" Theresa, "and the purpose of his association with Meyer Lansky was that Al Malnik would convert illegal cash by laundering into various real estate ventures."[27] The Pennsylvania announcement also invited a rather hollow rebuttal from William McElnea, president of Caesars World.

"Any implication that Caesars World is involved with organized crime," insisted McElnea, "is totally untrue."[28] Mr. McElnea also stated that the Sky Lake land purchased just four years before from Malnik and Cohen was due to be liquidated, "a substantial drain on our earnings."[29] Notably, Caesars World—buoyed on speculation of Atlantic City gambling—was then trading above 10 dollars per share, a 300 percent improvement over the junk value at the end of 1975.

One month after the Pennsylvania Crime Commission blast, the House Select Committee on Assassinations (HSCA) added sidebar to the ongoing saga of Caesars Palace and Mob-control in Las Vegas gambling. In a digest of reports, the House Committee catalogued entries originating from the Chicago Police Department, offering gems involving Frank "Lefty" Rosenthal, Elliott Paul Price, Jerome Zarowitz, Dino Cellini, and Meyer Lansky.

The digest further cemented the bookmaking and illegal gambling connections of Rosenthal, Price, and Zarowitz. "Close with bookies and shylocks and professional jewel thieves," the report stated of Rosenthal. "He is a mathematical genius."[30] "[Rosenthal] is listed as top executive for Allen R. Glick, Nevada Casino owner financed by $100 million from Teamsters Central States Pension Fund," continued the reports. "[Rosenthal] has absolute control over Glick's gambling operations."[31]

The HSCA also noted Rosenthal's affinity for Caesars Palace. Notably, it was Jeff Silver—later to preside over the 1984 Caesars Palace Grand Prix—who was credited with "denying Frank Rosenthal a gambling license in the State of Nevada."

Of Dino Cellini and Meyer Lansky, the HSCA file appeared to summarize the global strategic plan of the organized crime syndicate. "Lansky and [Dino Cellini]," stated the report, "are kingpins of a gambling empire extending to every casino in the free world."[32] For benefit of Bernie Ecclestone, that global plan

Nineteen seventy-eight was a banner year for government publications exploring the alleged criminal associations of Meyer Lansky (pictured), Dino Cellini, Alvin Malnik, Sam Cohen, Jerome Zarowitz, Frank Rosenthal, Sidney Korshak, Edward Levinson, and Moe Dalitz. "Lansky and [Dino Cellini]," stated one government report, "are kingpins of a gambling empire extending to every casino in the free world" (House Select Committee on Assassinations, Chicago Police Department Files, May 22, 1978, 7). The Pennsylvania Crime Commission, House Select Committee on Assassinations, Senate Permanent Subcommittee on Investigations, and the California Organized Crime Control Commission all submitted their respective findings—while Clifford Perlman and the centurions of Caesars submitted their gambling license application to the New Jersey Casino Control Commission (Library of Congress).

logically extended to Crockford's in London and the Casino de Monte-Carlo in Monaco.

Simultaneously, the Senate Permanent Subcommittee on Investigations convened in 1978 to update the discourse on "Organized Criminal Activities," probing connections between Las Vegas casinos and Swiss bank accounts involving such old guard Mob figures as Meyer Lansky, Morris Lansburgh, Sam Cohen, and Edward Levinson. "The mob works in strange ways," offered one law enforcement witness. "It gets someone clean, surfaces them, puts them up front, then he operates, but what happens is the mob moves in ... and begins to place selected personnel," continued the investigator, "That same pattern is the pattern that you find in the casino industry."[33] At the same time, the Senate subcommittee pondered secreted meetings involving Meyer Lansky and young player Alvin Malnik at the Forge Restaurant in Miami Beach.[34]

Across the country, the California Organized Crime Control Commission resolved its own investigation, bringing sharp focus to Sidney Korshak, Edward Levinson, Moe Dalitz, and Jerome Zarowitz. "In 1965, [Zarowitz] met in Palm Springs with New York Mafia members Vincent Alo and Anthony Salerno to discuss the division of ownership of Caesar's Palace in Las Vegas," concluded the California report. "Zarowitz was part of the management group that ran Caesar's during that time."[35]

The effect to Clifford Perlman and Caesars World headed into the New Jersey Casino Control Commission, however, was more of refresher than revelation. Indeed, Clifford Perlman had already accumulated a daunting dossier of GCB, DOJ, and SEC investigative materials before the Caesars Boardwalk Regency venture in Atlantic City. The accumulated reports might thus include some duplicates, as they also contributed to the overall heft of Perlman's stowage. Soon as well, the signage of Alvin Malnik's "Caesars Pocono Resorts" would be affixed to concrete track barriers in Las Vegas, pushed into place by Chris Pook and the Long Beach Grand Prix Association.

As the various government documents underscored the Caesars World licensing investigation in New Jersey, one of Caesars' centurions added his own organized crime-view to the proceedings. Attorney Mark Geller, "a suave young man ... in sculpted suits,"[36] was dispatched by Clifford Perlman and William McElnea from Los Angeles to oversee the Caesars Boardwalk Regency license application in Atlantic City. From the stump in New Jersey, Geller went on the offensive, decrying excessive government regulation and unfounded allegations of mob-control causing reluctance among financial institutions to invest in gaming. "Everybody knows," quipped Geller, "that there aren't gangsters in Las Vegas anymore."[37]

Geller's tell inadvertently traced the direct path of organized crime influences from Las Vegas to Atlantic City, while his own character and connections were his dispatch in early 1980 back to Los Angeles, courtesy of the New Jersey Division of Gaming Enforcement.

***

The Formula One caravan picked up after the U.S. Grand Prix West in Long Beach for the trans-Atlantic return to Europe. Following on the championship schedule was the prestigious Grand Prix de Monaco. Monaco, if anything, is the existential essence of Formula One, the *haute grandeur* presence at the pinnacle of everything. The *Great Prize* of the principality was also a hallowed tradition, the super-wealthy of the continent and abroad, rubbing shoulder-to-shoulder with the fast and famous of the Formula One Circuit. This was the favored ballroom of Bernie Ecclestone, to see and be seen from the mega-yachts in the Monaco harbor, to the luxury motor homes of the paddock, to the Hotel de Paris and the Casino de Monte-Carlo.

Headed into Monaco, Mario Andretti of John Player Team Lotus and Carlos Reutemann of the Scuderia Ferrari led the championship points battle with 18 points each. Andretti and Reutemann were followed by Ronnie Peterson for Lotus, Patrick Depailler for Tyrell, and Niki Lauda in Bernie Ecclestone's Brabham. The starting grid formed with Reutemann at the point followed by John Watson, Lauda, Andretti, and Depailler. Unfortunately for the championship leaders, the finishing order would be nearly the reverse. Patrick Depailler prevailed on the streets of Monaco by 20 seconds over Niki Lauda. It was the first Formula One victory of Depailler's driving career. John Watson trailed fourth at Monaco. Both Carlos Reutemann and Mario Andretti were out of the points, eighth and 11th, respectively. Depailler thus overtook Andretti and Reutemann for the championship points lead, out ahead with 23 markers.

Mario Andretti then went on a Formula One summer tour in 1978, taking the consecutive Belgian and Spanish Grands Prix, while Lotus teammate Ronnie Peterson stood second on both podiums. Andretti's debut of the Lotus 79 at the Belgian Grand prix also vaulted him once again to the top of the championship point standings. After Spain, teammate Peterson then moved up to a solid second in the tally. Andretti and Peterson added another one-two finish in France, while they claimed consecutive race wins at the German and Austrian Grands Prix. Further, after the

Patrick Depailler scored his first Formula One victory at the historic Monaco Grand Prix on May 7, 1978. Depailler drove the new Tyrell 008. Niki Lauda and Jody Scheckter completed the podium. Mario Andretti was classified 11th at the finish. The Tyrell team was staffed at the 1981 Caesars Palace Grand Prix by Eddie Cheever and Michele Alboreto (author's collection).

German round, Mario Andretti held a two-race advantage in points over Peterson. Peterson, though, clawed back to within a one-race deficit with his victory in Austria.

The side-skirted one-two punch of John Player Team Lotus became one of the enduring storylines of the 1978 season. "I hired Andretti and Peterson to do a job," remarked team owner Colin Chapman, "and they're both doing it well."[38] The points dominance of the Lotus duo also sparked rumors of team orders to see Mario Andretti through to the championship.

Andretti, however, was not interested in an administrative conclusion to his 1978 campaign. "I don't want anybody to give me anything. It's true that I'm the No. I driver at Lotus," proclaimed Mario Andretti. "But Ronnie hasn't been told to move over, at least not by me."[39]

Mario Andretti and Ronnie Peterson then finished one-two to dominate the podium at the Dutch Grand Prix. With three rounds remaining, Andretti led the Formula One championship over Peterson, 63 points to 51. The next closest challenger was Carlos Reutemann, 20 points back of Peterson, already eliminated from

Mario Andretti won the Belgian Grand Prix on May 21, 1978, driving a Lotus 79 for Colin Chapman. One week later, Andretti started last and finished 12th in the Indianapolis 500 driving this Penske PC-6 for Roger Penske. The following weekend, Mario Andretti was back in Europe, contesting the Formula One series in the Lotus 79. At the Spanish Grand Prix on June 4, 1978, Andretti started from pole, set the fastest lap of the race, and won the event over Jody Scheckter and Jacques Lafitte (author's collection).

championship contention. The Formula One caravan moved next to the Italian Grand Prix at the storied Monza circuit. Once again, the pre-race storyline involved the public pecking order of John Player Team Lotus, with Ronnie Peterson still in contention to spoil the championship march of Mario Andretti.

A poorly-formed grid flashed green for the start of Italian Grand Prix while the backmarkers were still rolling from the formation lap. Mario Andretti in the dominant Lotus 79 led into turn-one followed by Gilles Villeneuve in a Ferrari. Ronnie Peterson, however—qualified fifth in a backup Lotus 78—was clipped by James Hunt's McLaren after apparent contact from Riccardo Patrese in an Arrows, charging forward aggressively from the sixth row. The contact sent Ronnie Peterson hard into the guardrail, then to be speared by the Surtees-Ford of Vittorio Brambilla. Ronnie Peterson's Lotus broke up and erupted into flames while the badly injured driver sat crumpled in the cockpit. James Hunt and Clay Regazzoni departed their damaged vehicles and pulled Peterson from the shattered wreckage. Both Ronnie Peterson and Victor Brambilla were transported to the hospital where they were alert but reported in serious condition, Peterson with badly broken legs and Brambilla with head injuries.

On the long-delayed restart after the crash, Gilles Villeneuve and Mario Andretti led out once again with Niki Lauda in Bernie Ecclestone's Brabham in third. Once again, Riccardo Patrese attempted to force an advantage from the midfield headed into turn one. Andretti would overtake Villeneuve on the eighth lap and lead Villeneuve and Lauda across the line of the darkness-shortened event. Race marshals, however, determined that both Andretti and Villeneuve had jumped the restart. As both were assessed a one-minute penalty, Niki Lauda was declared the winner of the Italian Grand Prix, followed to the podium by John Watson and Carlos Reutemann. Mario Andretti and Gilles Villeneuve were thus relegated to sixth and seventh, respectively. Andretti also collected a single championship point.

With 64 points in the tally—against the apparent injuries to Ronnie Peterson— Mario Andretti was thus the presumptive World Driving Champion for 1978. Amid a tempered celebration, though, the news turned from triumph to tragedy the following day for Team Lotus. Ronnie Peterson died on September 11, 1978, from a fat embolism caused by his leg injuries. Ronnie Peterson was the 27th driver to perish at a Formula One championship event, the 41st to die at the wheel of a Formula One vehicle.

Just as with the passing of Tom Pryce before the 1977 U.S. Grand Prix West, the paddock of the 1978 U.S. Grand Prix East in Watkins Glen was draped in a pall. Further, while the Formula One drivers acknowledged the walk-off championship of Mario Andretti, their collective ire over the Italian Grand Prix would be directed squarely at Riccardo Patrese. The gathering concerns over the driving actions of Patrese in Italy also engaged the Watkins Glen Grand Prix Corporation.

"What began as a lesson in humility for Riccardo Patrese," read one report from upstate New York, "may finish as a course in American law for the Formula One Constructors Association."[40] Indeed, the stand-off headed to Watkins Glen pitted the most prominent of the Formula One drivers against Jackie Oliver's Arrows team and driver Patrese. Malcolm Currie of the Watkins Glen Grand Prix Corporation was then forced to reject the race entry of Riccardo Patrese. "Currie had little choice," continued the report. "[FOCA] indicated they might not race at Watkins Glen if Patrese was accepted."[41]

Bernie Ecclestone of FOCA and the Brabham works also weighed in on the controversial Riccardo Patrese. "It would be ridiculous to have everyone pull out," the Formula One czar remarked, "and leave Patrese alone on the track. Then the Watkins Glen people could sue us."[42]

As the stalemate between Jackie Oliver and the Grand Prix Corporation appeared headed to court, Mario Andretti was drawn into the debate. "We had a meeting to discuss [Riccardo Patrese's] driving before the race in Italy. Then comes the crash," offered Andretti. "Then comes the restart and.... Patrese tried the same maneuver. That's what set everybody off—including me."[43]

"He showed me he has no racing conscience," insisted the new Formula One champion. "He may be brave, but the brave ones usually cause the injuries and don't get injured themselves."[44] The safety concerns of Mario Andretti also joined the timeless voices of Jimmy Clark, Jackie Stewart, and Niki Lauda before him. Amid the growing chorus in Watkins Glen, Jackie Oliver and Arrows Racing Team accepted the one-race stand-down for Riccardo Patrese.

With the Formula One championship decided, the U.S. Grand Prix on October 1, 1978, in Watkins Glen thus set up as an American victory lap for Mario Andretti. For those notched below, the race was on for points toward the constructor's championship. For Niki Lauda and Carlos Reutemann, there remained a shot at second in the final points standings, however unpopular to unseat the departed Ronnie Peterson.

The Formula One drivers moved on from the Patrese refrain to complain anew about the condition of the aging and weather-impacted Watkins Glen circuit. Indeed, the preceding upstate winter had noticeably deteriorated the condition of the track base and racing surface. Mario Andretti, though, did his part for the American homecoming. taking a dominant pole for the U.S. Grand Prix, over a full second clear of Carlos Reutemann in a Ferrari. Alan Jones qualified third for Frank Williams followed by Gilles Villeneuve in another Ferrari. Niki Lauda's Brabham and James Hunt's McLaren occupied the third row.

A mammoth Watkins Glen crowd enjoyed rare pleasant fall weather in anticipation of a commanding Grand Prix performance by Mario Andretti. During the pre-race warm-up, however, Andretti crashed the lead Lotus 79 machine. Andretti then moved over to the companion Lotus of replacement driver Jean-Pierre Jarier, while Jarier reported to the grid in a Lotus team spare.

As the start lights went green, Mario Andretti and his substitute Lotus 79 led the drag race into the first turn of the 1978 U.S. Grand Prix at Watkins Glen. Andretti led the opening laps but was not sufficiently comfortable with the set-up of the replacement Lotus to push the lead. Carlos Reutemann and Gilles Villeneuve managed past while Andretti lost the pace of the leaders. On lap 27, the Ford Cosworth of Mario Andretti's John Player Special Lotus 79 let loose, retiring the American to the Watkins Glen pit lane. Carlos Reutemann in the Ferrari continued on to victory in the 1978 U.S. Grand Prix. Alan Jones finished second in the Williams, some 20 seconds back. Jody Scheckter was third, another 25 seconds adrift in a Wolf-Ford. Jean-Pierre

Mario Andretti commanded the championship points lead as Formula One returned to the U.S. Grand Prix on October 1, 1978. Andretti started on pole but went backward, retiring on lap 27 with engine issues. The 1978 U.S. Grand Prix was won by Carlos Reutemann. Watkins Glen, though, would be a victory lap for the first American Formula One champion since Phil Hill in 1961. Mario Andretti stayed with Lotus for two more seasons before joining the Alfa-Romeo team with Bruno Giacomelli (author's collection).

Jarier, Mario Andretti's interim teammate for Lotus, was credited with a 15th-place finish after running out of fuel on the 55th lap.

From the celebration, pundits duly noted the direction of Carlos Reutemann for the following Formula One season. "There was irony ... in the fact," read one report, "that [Reutemann] will be jumping to Lotus for the 1979 Grand Prix campaign."[45] Carlos Reutemann then took the momentum of the Watkins Glen—and the new Lotus contract—to close the season in Canada with a third-place effort. Reutemann also finished third in the final championship standings with 48 points.

Mario Andretti—scuttled from contention at Watkins Glen—nonetheless savored his world championship, a winning ride for Colin Chapman that started in 1976 with a mid-season gamble after Long Beach. "Colin's just a genius," proclaimed Andretti from Watkins Glen. "Colin has it designed so that the wind that comes underneath is funneled around and acts as a down force."[46] The candor of the new world champion ignited the technological development of the Formula One paddock. The rapid progress of Grand Prix aerodynamic science would also outpace Mario Andretti and his Alfa Romeo racer at the 1981 Caesars Palace Grand Prix. The 1978 World Driving Champion then traveled to Canada where he closed out the 1978 campaign with a forgettable 10th place finish. Andretti's single point at the tragic Italian Grand Prix was his last of the season.

Notably, Mario Andretti was joined at Watkins Glen by another American,

Bobby Rahal, driving for Walter Wolf Racing. Rahal then carried his own emerging driving career forward to Las Vegas, competing in the Can-Am event of the 1981 Caesars Palace Grand Prix. Rahal also competed against Mario Andretti in the 1983 and 1984 Caesars CART IndyCar Grand Prix events.

With 51 points accumulated before his tragic passing in Italy, Ronnie Peterson finished as the posthumous runner-up for John Player Team Lotus in the 1978 Formula One World Driving Championship. Riccardo Patrese—largely blamed for the horrible Peterson crash—continued driving for the Arrows Racing Team of Jackie Oliver. Patrese, in fact, would lead the Arrows effort at the 1981 Caesars Palace Grand Prix, where he once again lined up on the sixth row—directly behind Mario Andretti.

For Watkins Glen, the postscript was another tale of rampant criminal behavior, now 15 years of time-honored "violent and destructive traditions."[47] As before, alcohol consumption and drug use begat physical assaults and car burnings. "We're not just talking about bum kids," stated the Schuyler County sheriff.[48] Indeed, arrests included suits, school teachers, and grad students. The Watkins Glen Grand Prix Corporation, a function of the local chamber of commerce, was under attack as well. "The WGGP corporation may have forgotten," read the chamber comments, "the original auspices under which it was formed for the promotion and sponsorship of races."[49] Both entries were figurative notations for Bernie Ecclestone, tucked away in his burgeoning Watkins Glen dossier.

One month after the open-wheel international Formula One season wrapped, news from the vicinity of 16th and Georgetown in Indianapolis, Indiana, rocked the domestic open-wheel IndyCar series. "The Championship Auto Racing Teams and United States Auto Club collided at the crossroads," reported venerable IndyCar journalist Robin Miller, "and it appears there may only be one survivor."[50] The battle lines for the "Split" of premier-level American open-wheel racing were being drawn. The "Split" then broke wide open as an entrenched, decades-long, fiercely-contested war for the heart and soul of domestic open-wheel motorsport, the scars of which also appeared on the great battleground of Caesar in Las Vegas.

***

The Teamsters Central States Pension Fund would accrue a massive portfolio of rampant and reckless lending over a period of two decades. From the $1.8 million loan in 1958 to Jay Sarno for the Atlanta Cabana, to the $15 million loan in 1975 to Alvin Malnik for the Caesars Poconos Resorts, the entrusted treasury of interstate truckers consummated hundreds of loan packages across the country. The Teamsters loans were often in excess of valuation, woefully undercollateralized, and pegged to below-market interest rates. Troubled loans were also accompanied by fund trustees raking an advance fee on the front, organized crime interests muscling business opportunities on the back, and—of course—Allen Dorfman brokering the life insurance policies of the mortgagors.

"The Mob had control of one of the nation's major financial institutions," wrote Steven Brill, "and one of the very largest private sources of real estate investment capital in the world."[51] The unchecked racketeering of the Pension Fund and its trustees were thus the underwriters of the sun-state property development universe of Las

Vegas, Nevada, Los Angeles, California, and Miami Beach, Florida. In fact, nearly one-third of the Teamster billion-dollar mortgage portfolio was staked along the Las Vegas strip. Further, the Teamsters still held the mortgage on Abram Pritzker's Hyatt Lake Tahoe, the property successively sullied by Roy Gene Lewis of Riverside Raceway, Norman Tyrone, Elliott Roosevelt, Calvin Kovens, Nathan Jacobson, and Judd McIntosh. "Outfit funds and connections formed the foundation," according to author Gus Russo, "on which lawyer Abe Pritzker's family built the Hyatt hotel chain."[52]

Unscrupulous institutional lending from pension funds also led to enactment of a body of federal law that remains to this day, ERISA—the Employee Retirement Income Security Act of 1974. The watershed legal structure established minimum standards for disclosures to plan beneficiaries, codes of conduct for plan trustees, and legal remedies for beneficiaries. The existence of ERISA was also a directed strike at Jimmy Hoffa, Allen Dorman, Pension Fund trustees, and the organized crime connections of the trustees and their influencers. Perhaps as a matter of subtext, Jimmy Hoffa disappeared less than a year after ERISA was signed into law by President Gerald R. Ford, a disappearance for which Russell Bufalino remained a primary suspect.

ERISA also caused the constellation of storied Teamsters Pension Fund mortgagors to seek alternative sources for refinancing, as well as to sow new seeds of expansion capital. Not surprisingly, at the center of that constellation was Caesars Palace in Las Vegas. "Aetna Life Insurance Co. has entered into a $60 million mortgage agreement with Caesars Palace Hotel," read the reports in late 1978, "marking the first major long-term financing commitment by an insurance company to the Nevada gambling industry."[53] Harry Wald of Caesars Palace described the financing as a blend of expansion capital and a "restructuring of existing debt maturities."[54] While leaving some room in his comments, Harry Wald had just tipped the retirement of the 12-year-old Teamsters mortgages on the Caesars Palace resort. The 27-story Caesars Fantasy Tower, then under construction by Marnell Corrao Associates, was the first brick-and-mortar beneficiary of the financing package. The Fantasy Tower also loomed large over the Caesars Palace Grand Prix as the broadcast booth and observation deck.

"This is the first instance of a major insurance company ... providing loans ... for a Nevada casino," stated Jeff Silver of the Nevada Gaming Control Board. "The insurance companies, if you preclude union pension funds, represent the only other large source of funds available to Nevada."[55] The comments by Silver were an interesting piece of public posture, especially from the government body tasked with examining the flow of funds into and out of casinos. Jeff Silver's statement, however, overlooked investments in Nevada casinos by American National Insurance Company (ANICO) as early as 1963, rather secreted stakes in such properties as Joe Well's Thunderbird, Morris Shenker's Dunes, Jay Sarno and Stanley Mallin's Circus-Circus, as well as Williams Harrah's namesake in northern Nevada. ANICO also held a stake in the scandal-ridden Parvin-Dohrmann Corporation, owners of Stardust International Raceway. At each stop, the ANICO investments doubled as concealed, off-the-record ownership stakes for rogue ANICO executives Rollins Furbush and William Vogler.

"There is a rapidly growing public acceptance of gaming as a legitimate business operation as well as a legal enterprise," Caesars World president William McElnea said in reference to the Aetna financing. "The combination is creating a vast new market for our industry."[56] Public comments by McElnea, the former investment banker, certainly acknowledged the emerging New Jersey gambling market. The New Jersey investigations of Caesars World, however, were quite unkind to Clifford Perlman, investigators only slightly less so to William McElnea. The press of the Aetna financing also overlooked the original public offering of Lum's Inc. under the Aetna umbrella, an offering in which the Aetna business unit engaged in manipulative practices.

As the herald of the Caesars Palace financing circulated, the SEC continued to mull their latest action against Caesars World and Clifford Perlman, an action that arose from the successive Caesars Pocono Resorts, Sky Lake, and Cricket Club ventures with Alvin Malnik. Simultaneously, the New Jersey Casino Control Commission pondered the gambling license application of Clifford Perlman and William McElnea for the Caesars Boardwalk Regency property in Atlantic City. The State of New Jersey acted first, approving a temporary casino permit for the Caesars Boardwalk Regency on June 26, 1979.[57] Remarkably, though, the temporary gambling permit came at the temporary expense of Clifford Perlman, being "granted ... on the condition that Clifford S. Perlman ... take an unpaid leave of absence from Caesars World and its New Jersey subsidiaries."[58] The Emperor would thus have to forgo a ruler's wages, while the alleged back end of Meyer Lansky and Alvin Malnik might thus be a logical balance sheet beneficiary.

The New Jersey Division of Gaming Enforcement then moved forward to comprehensively investigate the centurions of Caesars World for full licensing. Less than a month later, however, the Securities and Exchange Commission filed injunctive

The path of Caesars World, Inc. chairman Clifford Perlman through the licensing investigations of the New Jersey Casino Control Commission would thread Meyer Lansky, Alvin Malnik, Sam Cohen, Jerome Zarowitz, Abscam, and the 1981 Caesars Palace Grand Prix (author's collection).

action against Caesars World Inc. (CWI) and Clifford Perlman, citing securities violations involving, "a series of real estate transactions with certain persons with whom Perlman concurrently had an undisclosed but substantial private business involvement."[59]

The SEC wordsmiths crisply averted mention of "Alvin Malnik" and "Sam Cohen" in their official digest, let alone the invocation of "Meyer Lansky." The SEC did, however, deliver a side-door swipe at the Nevada Gaming Commission, and their failure to do more than warn Caesars and Perlman as their deal-making with Alvin Malnik continued. "The Commission's complaint alleges that CWI and Perlman concealed material facts concerning those transactions," continued the SEC, "including certain actions taken by the gaming authorities of the State of Nevada."[60] Against the securities landscape of the time, Caesars World and Clifford Perlman essentially pled down, agreeing not to do it again—once again.

The Securities and Exchange Commission thus closed their case, just as the New Jersey Division of Gaming Enforcement ramped up their own investigations. On September 20, 1979, three months after the SEC ruling, an FBI operative would sit for dinner with Alvin Malnik at The Forge restaurant in Miami Beach. Although Caesars Palace was not the entrée, it would later be served up by Malnik as a savory side.

The overlapping investigations recalled the Caesars Palace investigations 10 years earlier by the FBI, SEC and the GCB, those various factions converging around Jerome Zarowitz. It was also an extremely off-balance war footing for Clifford Perlman and the centurions of Caesar, one that became an extended standoff with New Jersey regulators. Indeed, as Clifford Perlman presided over the podium celebration of the inaugural Caesars Palace Grand Prix, New Jersey continued their push to have Perlman severed as Caesar, while the Division of Gaming Enforcement argued that the centurions of Caesar were erecting a stone wall around the Palace.

***

As the winter solstice of 1978 brought a bitter cold to the relationship between CART and USAC, the vernal equinox of 1979 engaged FOCA and the FIA in a heated battle for control of Formula One. CART—the Championship Auto Racing Teams led by Roger Penske and Pat Patrick—would go their own way in 1979, launching an 11-event IndyCar championship series. The inaugural CART series was oddly sanctioned by the SCCA, an organizational strategy folding the new racing series under the governance of ACCUS, the domestic delegate to the FIA—the Federation Internationale de l'Automobile. Further odd was that USAC continued forward with their *own* 1979 championship, a seven-event shell of a program that sputtered to a halt in August.

In a remarkable turn, both the CART and USAC series featured the centerpiece of American motorsports on their 1979 calendar. Indeed, the venerable Indianapolis 500 would see both USAC regulars and CART rebels competing in a somewhat unified event at the Speedway. Both organizations also awarded championship points for Indianapolis 500 finishes, points awarded separately to the respective series loyalists.

When Rick Mears won the 1979 Indianapolis 500 for Roger Penske, he was awarded 1,000 points toward the CART championship, zero however for the USAC crown. A.J. Foyt finished second to Rick Mears at Indy and was awarded his rightful second-place points, 800 markers toward the separately contested *USAC* championship. The original finale of the USAC season was scheduled on September 2, 1979, as the California 500 at Ontario Motor Speedway. As open-wheel war waged in 1979, however, the California 500 moved over to become the eighth event of the CART series.

Whereas CART and USAC effected the first phase of the "Split" in their single premier-level form of open-wheel motorsport, Bernie Ecclestone's FOCA and the governing FIA each sought to control Formula One as their own rightful enterprise. Informed by the "World Championship Racing" incursion of Patrick Duffeler two years prior, even Bernie Ecclestone recognized that the FIA alone sanctioned the World Drivers Championship of Formula One. Nonetheless, Bernie Ecclestone would organize his own separatist movement two years hence, a singular salvo toward the FIA to open the 1981 season. Control of the show itself, however—and the peripheral commercial opportunities afforded thereby—were always regarded as open territory in the long game of Ecclestone, not entirely unlike the open structure of the Mob in Las Vegas.

As the only racer competing regularly in IndyCar and Formula One events, Mario Andretti was inevitably drawn into the FOCA versus FISA debate. "I think this battle is very bad for motor racing," Andretti objected. "Personally, I don't think either one of them is right."[61] "They have both made mistakes," continued the 1978 world driving champion, "and these mistakes could hurt Formula One. I hope they come to a compromise as soon as possible, otherwise it will be the USAC-CART battle all over again."[62]

The FIA then made significant organizational changes for 1979, a restructuring that functioned to entrench the battles as effectively as any plays run unilaterally by Bernie Ecclestone. The CSI—the Commission Sportive Internationale—of the FIA, was reformed as FISA—the Fédération Internationale du Sport Automobile. At the helm of FISA was the often-truculent Jean-Marie Balestre. Bernie Ecclestone and Jean-Marie Balestre then squared off, waging a protracted war of the four-letter international acronyms.

FOCA went forward holding the face cards of the teams. The FISA, however, controlled the aces of the championship, along with the wild cards of the procedural and technical regulations. The diminutive Ecclestone and the robust Balestre also appeared in dispute among the field at the 1981 Caesars Palace Grand Prix. Meanwhile, the respective disputes for control of domestic and international open-wheel racing became the lead-in for Chris Pook and the 1979 U.S. Grand Prix West at Long Beach.

"USAC must realize that it's in the entertainment business," Chris Pook said. "Championship racing isn't professional in settling problems. USAC doesn't realize that it's competing for the buck of the guy going to the movies or a ball game."[63] USAC may have been something of an easy mark for Formula One promoter Pook, by 1979 rather established as one of the reckoning voices in motorsport. Chris Pook, however, would serve as a similar stationary target in his own stormy tenure later at the helm of CART. Ironically, former Long Beach Grand Prix marketing man Jack Long was equally criticized for his leadership of the IRL—the Indy Racing League—formed to force the second phase of the American open-wheel "Split." It is of some further irony that the Long Beach alumni of Chris Pook and Jack Long would staff alongside each other at the first three editions of the Caesars Palace Grand Prix.

"Formula One has gone from total disarray," continued Chris Pook, "to what I consider the best show in town."[64] With Ontario Motor Speedway 1 year away from its demise—and Riverside International Raceway another 10—the Long Beach Grand Prix would eventually be the *only* show in the southland of California. Further, by 1983 Pook would walk it all back, calling upon CART and the IndyCar championship series to replace Formula One at the Long Beach Grand Prix venue. Remarkably then, a lawsuit by the Long Beach Grand Prix Association *against* CART and Caesars Palace over the rightful promotion of the 1984 Caesars Palace Grand Prix, according to Chris Pook, hovered over the first year of Long Beach as a CART event.

***

"Grand Prix Here to Stay, Finally."[65] The sports drop in the *Los Angeles Times* at the Ides of March 1979 was a marked contrast to the skepticism and strife in prior pre-race reporting of the Long Beach Grand Prix. Further, while the Long Beach daily had historically provided top-cover for the backroom deal-making of city politics, the *Los Angeles Times* often drilled in sideways, publishing several scathing pieces about Long Beach that dissected downtown development and named the attendant Long Beach names. The *Queen Mary*, William Fugazy, Sidney Korshak, John Mansell, Ernest Mayer, Harbor Bank, Chris Pook, and the Long Beach Grand Prix were all pierced by the pointy end of the *Times* quill. The *Los Angeles Times* had also duly noted, the federal investigations into fraud and corruption involving "bribery, gambling, conspiracy, and money-laundering"[66] in their southland stepchild of Long Beach—allegedly.

"It took three or four years to get accepted," Chris Pook was quoted as saying by the *Times*. "We've managed to hang on by our fingernails a couple of years and now we are established."[67] For the guile and—perhaps—the wile of Chris Pook, the Long Beach Grand Prix Association had managed to make the right deals, churn just enough money, and fortify their foundation. Further, the stabilizing effect of Mario Andretti's resounding win at the 1977 U.S. Grand Prix West simply cannot be over-estimated. Notably, new title sponsor "Lubri Lon" dispatched the full $875,000 fee to FOCA well in advance of the event.[68] It should also be noted that, on Monday following the race, Long Beach City Council was also prepared to collect the last of the Association's deferred debt from the 1975 Long Beach Formula 5000 Grand Prix.

For Mario Andretti, the 1978 Formula One champion, the U.S. Grand Prix West was a welcome homeland stop on the early-season race calendar. The Formula One campaign had started slowly for Andretti and the newly badged Martini Team Lotus 80, fully emblazoned with the well-deserved number-one on the bodywork. Through three events, Mario Andretti had scored only five championship points. New Lotus teammate Carlos Reutemann, the contracted number two to Andretti, held the team advantage with 12 markers. As Reutemann departed the Scuderia Ferrari for the Lotus squad in 1979, he was optimistic for his fortunes. "I was promoted from a No. 2

team," remarked Reutemann, "to a No. 1 team."[69] As the Formula One field caught—and then surpassed—the technical genius of Colin Chapman, though, the 1979 campaign would be difficult for both Mario Andretti and Carlos Reutemann. Reutemann would likely look back wistfully to the 1978 Ferrari ride in which he won four races. Reigning champion Mario Andretti was left to wonder where it all went wrong.

Qualifying for the U.S. Grand Prix West bore the trending fates of Ferrari and Lotus. In his third year of Formula One, Gilles Villeneuve put his Ferrari 312T4 on pole. Carlos Reutemann was alongside the red Ferrari in his Martini Lotus. Jody Scheckter qualified third in another Ferrari followed by Patrick Depailler and Jacque Lafitte in a pair of Ligier machines. Mario Andretti in the number one Lotus trailed sixth on the grid, over six-tenths back of Villeneuve. From the third row, Mario Andretti also understood his prospects. "On street courses like Long Beach or Monte Carlo," stated Andretti, "you have to be on the front row, or close to it, to have a chance."[70]

The 80-lap race through the streets of Long Beach then became a demonstration of emerging dominance for the Scuderia Ferrari. Gilles Villeneuve, Patrick Depailler, and Jody Scheckter led the early laps. Carlos Reutemann was shuffled back after starting from pit lane due to an electrical issue, and eventually retired at the one third point. Mario Andretti circulated in fourth place for much of the event and would finish on station, benefiting from Reutemann's retirement and transmission issues for Depailler. Gilles Villeneuve and Jody Scheckter, however, formed a powerful echelon for the Scuderia Ferrari. Villeneuve took the dramatic win of the 1979 U.S. Grand Prix West and the trifecta, consolidating his pole position and fastest race lap under his Long Beach laurels. Jody Scheckter trailed Villeneuve by nearly 30 seconds. Scheckter, a Formula 5000 competitor in Long Beach four years before, then opened a compelling 1979 Formula One campaign. The Ferrari duo of Scheckter and Villeneuve, in fact, combined for a formidable six race wins as the year progressed.

Alan Jones stood third on the podium with his FW06 Williams-Ford Cosworth. Jones claimed Formula One race victories in 1979 as well, advancing his racecraft along with the constructor fortunes of Frank Williams and designer Patrick Head. Just five years removed from the OPEC oil embargo, the Williams' livery was notably punctuated by a powerful Saudi conglomerate, "Albilad," as well as the Saudi national airline, "Saudia." "The Saudis had a lot of money arriving because they were increasing the oil prices," Frank Williams would later comment. "The younger groups of princes picked up the baton pretty enthusiastically."[71] Albilad, in fact, was one of the trading companies of the Saudi royal family. Saudi oil money and the FW07C Saudia-Albilad Williams of Alan Jones would lead the starting procession of the 1981 Caesars Palace Grand Prix. The lure of Middle East oil wealth would also underscore the conversations between Alvin Malnik and the FBI operative.

One step removed from the podium, Mario Andretti scored three championship points and lamented another U.S. Grand Prix lost. Andretti then rebounded slightly with a third-place finish in the following Spanish Grand Prix. The summer of 1979, however, was a stark departure from the dominant form of Andretti and Lotus in 1978. Mario Andretti and Colin Chapman's Martini Team Lotus scored a run of seven successive failures. Indeed, Andretti's podium in Spain was the high point of

Mario Andretti arrived for the 1979 Long Beach Grand Prix as the defending Formula One world champion. Andretti qualified sixth in the updated Lotus 79 and improved to fourth in the finishing order behind winner Gilles Villeneuve, Jody Scheckter, and Alan Jones. The Essex livery on the Lotus sidepod is noteworthy. In April 1981, Monaco-based Essex Overseas Petroleum owner David Thieme was arrested by Swiss police on charges of fraud (*Vancouver Sun* [Vancouver, British Columbia, Canada], April 14, 1981). The arrest came one month after the 1981 Long Beach Grand Prix. Further, the Lotus team bus was impounded by authorities (Rick Lake collection).

his efforts, scoring only two more championship points through the duration of the season. Mario Andretti even skipped the 1979 Indianapolis 500 in order to defend his world championship with an appearance at Monaco. Andretti's Monaco weekend was punctuated by a 13th place qualifying effort and another Lotus retirement. Conversely, Jody Scheckter won Monaco from pole, a portent for the balance of his Formula One campaign.

In contrast to events past, the postscript of the 1979 U.S. Grand Prix West in Long Beach was somewhat settled. It was reported, however, that the Long Beach Promotion and Service Corporation (LBPSC) exhausted its available room-tax funding after providing only one third of their promotional contract commitment to the Long Beach Grand Prix Association. Chris Pook and the Grand Prix Association (GPA) then negotiated with the LBPSC to terminate the contract, "in return for waiving the $81,000 the GPA owed the promotion group from last year's race."[72]

Amid the comparatively subdued controversy, Chris Pook, "estimated that he made a $400,000 profit on this year's race."[73] Although the term "illegal gift" was splashed, it would be the last such mention in Long Beach. City Councilperson Wallace Edgerton, a former critic of the Long Beach Grand Prix, then spun the subject into submission. "When you consider what the Grand Prix has done for the city …

Jody Scheckter (#11 Ferrari) leads Jean Pierre Jarier (#4 Tyrell) Mario Andretti (#1 Lotus, on outside), Riccardo Patrese (#29 Wolf, beyond fence line), Alan Jones (#27 Williams, on outside) into turn seven, "Queen's Hairpin," during the 1979 Long Beach Grand Prix. Scheckter's Ferrari teammate won the event, followed by Scheckter, Jones, and Andretti. George Follmer Porsche-Audi, Inc. banner at left is noteworthy. Follmer was the 1972 Can-Am champion driving for Roger Penske (Rick Lake collection).

it amounts to millions and millions and millions," proclaimed Edgerton. "The Grand Prix is a blessing."[74] The last substantive debate to follow the Long Beach Grand Prix thus closed with one more deal well-made, "millions and millions and millions" of dollars churned, and the foundation of the Long Beach Grand Prix firmly footed. Even Abram Pritzker's *Queen Mary* Hyatt Hotel was booked solid.[75]

True to his word in 1978 to Mario Andretti and Chris Pook, Abram Pritzker attended the groundbreaking for the Long Beach Hyatt Regency on June 16, 1981. "I'm not satisfied to build anything but the best," commented the 85-year-old Pritzker in Long Beach. "I promise you it (the hotel) will be first-class."[76] One month later, 116 people perished in the horrific walkway collapse of the Kansas City Hyatt Regency. The death toll in Kansas City exceeded the catastrophic fire at Kirk Kerkorian's MGM Grand in Las Vegas just seven months before. The Kansas City Hyatt tragedy then remained as the deadliest structural collapse in American history—until 9/11.

***

As the torturous early history of the Long Beach Grand Prix eventually led to a stabilized foundation, so too did the 1979 U.S. Grand Prix West serve as a foundational element for the Caesars Palace Grand Prix. Indeed, three months after Long Beach wrapped—and just one month after the last mention of "illegal gift"—Formula One news broke with a Las Vegas dateline. "International approval of a Formula

1 Grand Prix race in Las Vegas is being sought," trumpeted the *Associated Press*, "the Sports Car Club of America confirmed."[77] The quest for an unprecedented third U.S. Grand Prix was now officially sanctioned.

Tom Duval, executive director of the SCCA after the departed Cameron Argetsinger, fronted the announcements stateside. "We anticipate there will be some opposition," Duval stated to the AP. "There was some when we wanted a second grand prix race before Long Beach was approved, but I don't know where it might come from."[78] With Cameron Argetsinger returned to practice law in upstate New York, it bears mention that there was no shortage of opposition to Long Beach in 1975 from the vicinity of the Watkins Glen Grand Prix Corporation. In the tumult of the tides, Watkins Glen was also fighting for its continued existence on the Formula One calendar after the 1979 U.S. Grand Prix wrapped. Further, the proposed Las Vegas Grand Prix was tentatively scheduled for October of 1980, a potentially direct conflict with the long-standing Watkins Glen date.

"Duval said the Caesars Palace casino and hotel," continued the AP report, "would sponsor the proposed Las Vegas race."[79] Caesars Palace officials—specifically William McElnea and William D. "Bill" Weinberger—would not, however, be drawn into the opening announcement. Tom Duval, then, took the point to laud the professional boxing and tennis promotions of the Caesars Palace resort. "I'm sure sponsorship of a Grand Prix would enhance them," Duval continued, "and enhance the sport."[80] Corporate branded hosting of a Formula One Grand Prix was utterly without precedent, domestically and internationally. The corporate umbrella of Caesars also connected Alvin Malnik to the show, still the owner of the Caesars Pocono Resorts. Malnik's Pennsylvania properties would indeed be the beneficiaries of trackside Grand Prix signage.

A Formula One event sponsored by the gambling resort would also play to the proclivities of Bernie Ecclestone, the rich and famous joining in an immersion of unlimited gambling, world-class entertainment, luxury-branded hospitality, and Formula One, all on lavish display in a destination setting. "Bernie loves to play baccarat," Chris Pook confirmed of Ecclestone's later Las Vegas layovers, "and he did!"[81]

Chris Pook—progenitor of the Long Beach Grand Prix—was also, however, a probable obstruction in the path of progress to Caesars Palace. A strategy of opportunity and optimization by Caesars Palace then removed the potential competitive obstacle from play. "Pook, president of the organization which made a success of the 5-year-old Long Beach race after three years of financial difficulty," concluded the Associated Press, "said his staff would be involved in putting on the proposed Las Vegas race."[82]

By 1979, it was indisputable that Chris Pook and his Long Beach staff were fully capable of managing the logistics, construction, production, and dismantling of a temporary Formula One event. They were well versed in the movement of four-ton concrete barriers as well. The resultant consulting contract between the Long Beach Grand Prix Association and Caesars Palace would involve placement of the contentious Caesars Pocono Resorts signage. The four-year agreement might also afford Chris Pook the opportunity to fully amortize the Association's inventory of 25,000 "spherical elastic attenuators."[83]

Three days later, word from Paris on the proposed Las Vegas Grand Prix was mixed. "Chances of staging a third American Grand Prix … at Las Vegas next year are poor," reported the *United Press International*, "because the schedule for 1980 has already been arranged, officials at the International Automobile Federation (FISA) said."[84] The balk from FISA thus appeared to pit Jean-Marie Balestre squarely against a supportive Bernie Ecclestone, while the formative Caesars Palace Grand Prix waited in the wings.

Despite the varied reporting, conjecture was rampant that the prospect of a Caesars Palace Grand Prix imperiled the U.S. Grand Prix at Watkins Glen. Bob Kelly of the Watkins Glen Grand Prix Corporation was blunt. "This could be the end of the Watkins Glen Grand Prix."[85] "Money is no object in Vegas," continued Kelly, "and they could produce a purse of $1 million which we couldn't touch."[86] Clearly, the scales of Formula One held the balance, the time-honored Watkins Glen on one chain, and the well-connected Caesars Palace on the other, with a fulcrum perhaps comprised of equal parts FOCA and FISA, Bernie Ecclestone and Jean-Marie Balestre.

***

The meeting on September 20, 1979, at Alvin Malnik's Forge restaurant in Miami Beach with the FBI operative setting the Abscam snares tipped an interesting adjunct in the historic investigation and subsequent prosecutions. Indeed, Meyer Lansky was both alive and active, and Alvin Malnik spoke with apparent authority on behalf of the aging mastermind of mob money matters. The encounter at The Forge then produced a return engagement with Alvin Malnik at the luxury Hallandale, Florida, apartment of tri-state middleman, attorney Howard Criden. "What you have to do is what *we* did with Caesars Palace," suggested Alvin Malnik, captured for posterity by an FBI tape recorder, "*We* never made any money because we always put it back into the joint."[87]

The persistent use of "we" in Malnik's argot was the presumed nexus of Meyer Lansky, Alvin Malnik, and the financial apparatus of the national organized crime syndicate. Further, the mention of Caesars Palace did not appear to be invited by the FBI operative. Nonetheless, the palace of Caesar, its shadowy origins, and the tantalizing "*we*" were offered by Alvin Malnik with certain context as he floated a purchase offer to the FBI operative and non-existent Arab investors for the Aladdin hotel-casino in Las Vegas.

The Aladdin Hotel and Casino transitioned in 1971 from the ownership of Delbert Coleman's racketed Parvin-Dohrmann Corporation, former owners of the Stardust hotel-casino and Stardust International Raceway. The purchase group acquiring the Aladdin, however, was led by brand name fronts from St. Louis, while being underwritten by furtive organized crime figures from Detroit. Coleman and Nevada gambling figure Edward Torres held first options on a lifeline acquisition of the Aladdin, which had been closed by Nevada regulators in 1979 because of the concealed Detroit connections. As the FBI operative questioned the primary positions of Coleman and Torres, Alvin Malnik then underscored his close *personal* grasp of the subjects. "I'll arrange it," affirmed Malnik, "so they can't [exercise their option]."[88]

Alvin Malnik was insistent, however, that the potential Arab owners would

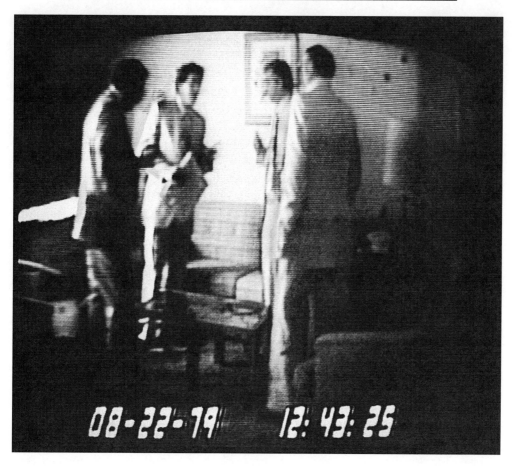

FBI surveillance footage from the Abscam operation taken on August 22, 1979, captures, from left, FBI agent Anthony Amoroso as a fictitious sheik representing the fictitious "Abdul Enterprises," Michael "Ozzie" Myers (New Jersey Congressman), Angelo Errichetti (mayor of Camden, New Jersey), and FBI operative Mel Weinberg. Myers has just accepted an envelope containing $50,000 from Amoroso. Angelo Errichetti also facilitated connections that introduced the FBI operation to Alvin Malnik. The FBI operative first met Malnik on September 20, 1979, at Malnik's Forge restaurant in Miami. One month later, FBI agent Amoroso and Weinberg met Alvin Malnik in Hallandale, Florida—and Malnik would invoke the name of Caesar (Federal Bureau of Investigation).

be required to retain Edward Torres under the Aladdin umbrella. "I'm not worried about his integrity," stated Malnik of Torres, "because he'll owe the integrity to me."[89] The offer of the Aladdin hotel-casino by Alvin Malnik—and his professed leverage over Delbert Coleman and Edward Torres—invoked the unmistakable structural control mechanisms of the mob. The mob had perfected the carefully concealed ownership of gambling resort assets and those strategically posted to oversee their operations—along with the attendant skim. Indeed, neither Meyer Lansky nor Alvin Malnik held any public presence or position with the Aladdin, pointing up a tightly-knit power center of apparent puppet-masters, and a vast array of dancing puppets. Further instructive, Malnik sought to package the Miami Beach Cricket Club development *with* the Aladdin, a component of the transaction that drew Clifford Perlman in directly. Mention of Clifford Perlman in the Abscam tapes also echoed those substantial pressures apparently exerted over Delbert Coleman and Edward Torres.

Howard Criden, the primary influence peddler of Abscam, was specific on the subservient relationship of Clifford Perlman with Meyer Lansky. "Mr. Lansky owns [Perlman] lock, stock, and barrel," confirmed Criden to the FBI operative. "He [Lansky] put him in business."[90] Criden also painted a compliant coziness between Clifford Perlman and Alvin Malnik. Further, it was offered in the explicit context of Malnik's relationship with Atlantic City gambling operators. "I know that as far as Cliff is concerned," continued Criden. "They're partners."[91]

The conjoined mention of Caesars Palace, Clifford Perlman, and the Cricket Club on the Abscam tapes—by recorded voice of Alvin Malnik—would then become a lightning rod issue for New Jersey gambling regulators. The business relationships between Perlman and Malnik—both the reported public and the reputed private—then hung as the death knell while regulators pondered permanent licensing for Caesars Boardwalk Regency in Atlantic City.

In the same week, though, that Alvin Malnik, Howard Criden, and the FBI operative discussed high-level Las Vegas deal making and hidden gambling interests, it was another Las Vegas engagement that grabbed the sports headlines, "Grand Prix race okayed for Vegas."[92]

***

The impending Caesars Palace Grand Prix in Las Vegas notwithstanding, lead-ins to the 1979 U.S. Grand Prix at Watkins Glen heralded a well-deserved clinch in the Formula One championship. Another Formula One champion, however, chose to retire his helmet, while defending champion Mario Andretti was left to bemoan a miserable title defense. Indeed, with three wins and 51 points, South African Jody Scheckter driving for the Scuderia Ferrari was already confirmed as the 1979 World Driving Champion. Further, teammate Gilles Villeneuve held a virtual lock on second in championship points.

With only four points accrued and 11 retirements, though, Niki Lauda was ready to call it a career. "I have realized that there are things in my life," reflected the two-time World Driving Champion, "which are more important than driving a car in a circle."[93] The courageous Lauda had proven himself on the track and in life, defying near-death with a resounding championship for Ferrari in 1977. Moving to Bernie Ecclestone's Brabham squad, though, the champion found himself in problematic machinery and diminished results; a 25 percent failure rate over two seasons was certainly an influence.

Brabham boss Bernie Ecclestone could not stand in the way of the determined Lauda. "That is a clever man," offered Ecclestone on Lauda's retirement. "He knows that one cannot enforce this sort of thing."[94] Further, as the boss of FOCA—and the *de facto* Formula One czar—Ecclestone might already have his eyes set on a date in Las Vegas while the racing star made his announcement.

Mario Andretti, only one year removed from his own walk-off win in the Formula One World Drivers Championship, had to ponder a season gone awry as he prepared for the U.S. Grand Prix. Andretti and Colin Chapman's evolving Lotus 79 marked their own 60 percent failure rate in the 1979 season, with only 14 points on tally and a paltry two points scored since the halfway mark. "I have two things I want to accomplish this weekend," offered a terse Andretti, "I want to win this race. And I want to get the season over with."[95] With a year remaining on his Lotus contract, Andretti also had to hope for an improvement at his homeland event. Hope, however, would not deliver for the departing world champion.

The frequent upstate New York rains once again dampened qualifying for the U.S. Grand Prix. Friday sessions resulted in lap times 20 seconds or more off of Mario Andretti's 1978 lap record of 1:38.114. As Saturday weather improved, so did the natural assault on Andretti's former mark. Alan Jones claimed a hard-earned pole with a 1:35.615 for Frank Williams. Nelson Piquet followed 1.299 seconds back of Jones. Gilles Villeneuve, dominant in the Friday wet sessions, was third on the grid, just .034 seconds off of Piquet. Struggling in the qualifying sessions, though, Mario Andretti found himself buried in 17th at the start, nearly five seconds back of Alan Jones pole, two seconds adrift of his own 1978 mark.

Race day of the 1979 U.S. Grand Prix then opened to freezing temperatures and a driving rain. Gilles Villeneuve and the wet-weather tires of his Ferrari streaked past Nelson Piquet on slicks at the start. Villeneuve then drove past Alan Jones into the first turn. From there, Gilles Villeneuve would have no challengers. Despite nursing his machine to the finish, Villeneuve finished 48 seconds clear of Rene Arnoux in a Renault. Didier Pironi driving a Tyrell-Ford was another five seconds back in third. Only seven cars survived to the finish.

The final curtain on Mario Andretti's championship defense was yet another mechanical failure, dropping out on lap 17 and logging an unclassified 20th in the order. "Andretti kept his frustrating record intact," read one report, "he has never won the U.S. Grand Prix at Watkins Glen."[96] Andretti also retired the prominent number one on the cowl of his Lotus 79 after nine retirements in 15 Grands Prix contested. Mario Andretti, unamused at the 1979 season lost, was understandably muted in the press.

One month after Gilles Villeneuve accepted the victor's laurels of the 1979 U.S. Grand Prix at Watkins Glen, whispers from Paris appeared to confirm the demise of the upstate New York classic. Rustlings from the international press corps about accommodations, then gave rise to a full-scale effort to scuttle the prospects of Formula One at Watkins Glen. Predictably, Bernie Ecclestone—head of the Formula One Commission of FISA—appeared to direct the chorus. Notably, the Formula One Commission did not include a representative from America. "Ecclestone … is using the glamor and glitter of Las Vegas," read one account from New York, "as a bargaining chip to lure drivers and other car builders to his side in the fight against Watkins Glen."[97]

Days later, William D. Weinberger of Caesars Palace confirmed the corporate commitment—as well as a $750,000 bond—for a Formula One event in Las Vegas. Weinberger, though, was also pressed for comment on the fate of Watkins Glen. "The story is that the FISA has scratched that race," offered Weinberger. "It's something over which I have no control or knowledge."[98] As the U.S. Grand Prix in Watkins Glen struggled for survival against mounting odds around the globe, news from Los

Gilles Villeneuve won the October 7, 1979, U.S. Grand Prix at Watkins Glen driving a Ferrari 312T4. Rene Arnoux was second in a Renault. Didier Pironi was third for Tyrell. The time clock was winding down for the Formula One event in upstate New York. The podium of the 1979 U.S. Grand Prix would, however, contest the 1981 Caesars Palace Grand Prix in Las Vegas. Neither Villeneuve nor Pironi, though, would make it to the 1982 Caesars starting grid (courtesy International Motor Racing Research Center).

Angeles would catch the attention of New Jersey gambling investigators, as well as inform the negotiations for the Caesars Palace Grand Prix.

On December 17, 1979, citing "record first-quarter earnings," William McElnea and the forcibly-separated Clifford Perlman were "re-elected without opposition" to the board of Caesars World.[99] Within months, Clifford Perlman and Bernie Ecclestone would sign the contract for the Caesars Palace Grand Prix. The signing ceremony would be held in the underground board room of Caesars Palace, the bullet-proof structure constructed by Jay Sarno, Stanley Mallin, and Nathan Jacobson. "This is Bernie Ecclestone," read one account of the introduction by Clifford Perlman, "We want to have a Grand Prix here at Caesar's [sic] Palace and this is the guy who is going to fix it. Are you in favour?"[100] On a single affirmative voice, Clifford Perlman apparently called it, "Congratulations, gentleman. Done."[101]

Three days after Clifford Perlman and William McElnea were re-elected, Chris Pook of the Long Beach Grand Prix Association weighed in on the contemplated Las Vegas Formula One circuit. "It will be flat and uninteresting from the driver's point of view," suggested Pook, "But it will be a great course for spectators. And that's whom we have to please. After all, we're in the entertainment business."[102]

VIII

Trumpets and Tribunals

*The Caesars Palace Grand Prix That Wasn't,
the Final U.S. Grand Prix at Watkins Glen,
the Many Stains Upon Caesar*

There is one mind in all these men, and it is bent against Caesar. (*Julius Caesar* 2.4.5–6)

"The announcement by the shah of Formula One racing, Britisher Bernard Ecclestone, that Watkins Glen should be replaced by Las Vegas," rang the reports, "has raised quite a storm of protest in the colonies."[1] Indeed, international efforts to scuttle the U.S. Grand Prix at Watkins Glen in favor of an event at Las Vegas dominated the Formula One winter break headed into 1980. The global gambit also pointed up the futility of the ACCUS delegation to FISA, certainly with respect to the fortunes of the U.S. Grand Prix. Further, the potential loss of Watkins Glen as the east coast outpost of Formula One, incited one of the most acerbic voices in the annals of American automotive journalism.

"This pathetic urge for approval by our European peers has reached the point of absurdity," wrote Brock Yates. "We seem prepared to flagellate ourselves with a lunatic frenzy in order to receive the benediction from a tinhorn like Ecclestone."[2] At the same time, Yates, the incendiary editor of *Car and Driver*, saved some flame for the split state of affairs in homeland open-wheel racing. "Yet our so-called ruling authority, the ACCUS (Automobile Competition Committee of the United States)," continued Yates, "stands back in helpless disregard while USAC and CART render out the most prestigious form of domestic motorsport into small bits."[3]

An armada of stateside support then rallied the Watkins Glen cause. The gathering impetus also included the considerable influence of Mario Andretti. "I'd like to see both Watkins Glen and Las Vegas happen," reckoned the former Formula One champion. "But not one at the expense of the other. That shouldn't be."[4] Andretti was also tasked to consider a boycott of the emerging Las Vegas event, an exercise the Lotus-contracted driver simply could not entertain.

An American delegation of Mario Andretti, Tom Binford of ACCUS, and Malcolm Currie of the Watkins Glen Grand Prix Corporation then traveled to Paris on December 13, 1979, for a rare audience with the executive committee of FISA. There the American emissaries awaited the final decree of the international motorsport

Mario Andretti personally lobbied the executive committee of FISA to retain the 1980 U.S. Grand Prix at Watkins Glen on the Formula One calendar. At the same time, Andretti was being asked to "boycott" the concept of the Caesars Palace Grand Prix (author's collection).

body on the fate of the U.S. Grand Prix in the bucolic idyll of upstate New York. Clifford Perlman, William McElnea, and William D. Weinberger of Caesars Palace also awaited word from Paris on their own Formula One ambitions, while Perlman also awaited his fate with the New Jersey Casino Control Commission. Caesars World then closed the year-end trading above $18 per share, an 80 percent increase in 18 months, investors perhaps trafficking on whispers of aging mob kingpin Meyer Lansky, alleged heir-apparent Alvin Malnik—and the Caesars Palace Grand Prix.

***

"The [Caesars] Boardwalk Regency casino and hotel in Atlantic City," according to New Jersey gaming enforcement, "is owned or operated by principals who have a history of skimming profits, attempting fraud and dealing with organized crime figures."[5] The scathing report from New Jersey Attorney General John Degnan landed at the offices of the New Jersey Casino Control Commission on January 23, 1980. The results of the 17-month investigation by the State Division of Gaming Enforcement also spelled numerous areas of criminal concern to the Casino Commission.

The New Jersey investigation went well beyond the already-public Caesars Palace disclosures involving Lansky, Malnik, and Cohen, revealing, "credit lines of dubious collectability … extended to organized crime figures … by Caesars Palace credit manager Murray Gennis."[6] Further, Caesars Palace credit practices involved the complicit use of aliases for persons of unsavory reputation, including the notorious Frank Rosenthal. New Jersey investigators also took aim at Caesars Boardwalk Regency attorney Mark Geller, "an unethical lawyer."[7] Notably, it was Geller who was out in front of Caesars Boardwalk Regency construction updates, as well as the obligatory denials of organized crime influence while Caesars World ventured into the New Jersey market.

New Jersey investigators also explored vendor and lessee relationships at Caesars Palace in Las Vegas. One lessee of interest was the Caesars Palace art gallery of Leonard Rosen, who "has been convicted of failing to report $5.5 million in income."[8] The mention of Leonard Rosen in the New Jersey report, however, also circled the storyline back to the origins of Caesars Palace itself, and the relationship of Leonard Rosen, former Caesars Palace president Nathan Jacobson, and original Caesars Palace investor Irving Kovens in the Gulf American Land Corporation of Florida, an alleged billion-dollar land swindle.

The Caesars Boardwalk Regency in Atlantic City was developed from a former Howard Johnson's hotel. Anthony Marnell of Las Vegas was the architect. Marnell was also the architect for the Caesars Palace Grand Prix circuit. The Boardwalk Regency property opened at 2100 Pacific Ave. on June 26, 1979, with a temporary gambling license. Nearly one and a half years later, Clifford and Stuart Perlman were found not qualified to be licensed for the resort. New Jersey regulators also demanded that they vacate their positions at Caesars World and Caesars Palace (Library of Congress).

Fully expected though, New Jersey investigators duly explored the entangled relationships of Clifford Perlman with Alvin Malnik and, presumed in turn, with Meyer Lansky. News of the New Jersey report also appeared to finally perfect the purpose and positioning of the relationships. "The gaming enforcement division contends," read one post, "Caesars and Perlman knew Malnik was reputed to be an associate of Meyer Lansky."[9]

"Malnik's principal work for Lansky," furthered the abstract, "was to convert illegal cash by 'laundering' it in various real estate ventures—ventures for which Malnik obtained capital from Caesars World."[10] The financial mechanisms of Caesars

World—along with Alvin Malnik's tape-recorded tap into the apparent Caesars Palace take—thus appeared to provide the cash liquidity so vital to the operations of "the interwoven mobs which make up the national crime syndicate."[11]

The report of the New Jersey Division of Gaming Enforcement to the Casino Control Commission was a damning indictment of the Caesars World organizational structure, yet it contained no indictments, only information. Further, it offered no recommendations as to permanent licensure of the Caesars Boardwalk Regency resort. "While the commission might see fit to issue a license," suggested Attorney General Degnan, "it probably shouldn't be done without substantial conditions."[12]

The New Jersey Casino Control Commission would take the Gaming Enforce-

---

LAW ENFORCEMENT UNDERCOVER ACTIVITIES

HEARINGS

BEFORE THE

SELECT COMMITTEE TO STUDY LAW ENFORCEMENT UNDERCOVER ACTIVITIES OF COMPONENTS OF THE DEPARTMENT OF JUSTICE

UNITED STATES SENATE

NINETY-SEVENTH CONGRESS

SECOND SESSION

LAW ENFORCEMENT UNDERCOVER ACTIVITIES

JULY 20-22, JULY 27-29, AUGUST 18, SEPTEMBER 9, 14-16, 21, 28, AND 30, 1982

WEDNESDAY, SEPTEMBER 15, 1982

Errichetti, Angelo J., Camden, N.J., accompanied by counsel, Henry Furst, Esq..

Mayor Angelo Errichetti of Camden, New Jersey, delivered the FBI Abscam sting operation to politicians, government officials, gambling regulators, and Alvin Malnik. "Hundreds of pages of still secret tapes, including an hour-long session with Alvin Malnik, top money-mover for mobster Meyer Lansky," wrote Robert Greene, "bared inside details of how the mob, working with bought public officials and politicians, controlled the casino gambling industry in both Las Vegas and Atlantic City" (Greene, *Sting Man*, 9). Notably, Alvin Malnik was the owner of Caesars Pocono Resorts in Pennsylvania. The signage for the honeymoon resorts would be on full display during the run of the Caesars Palace Grand Prix (U.S. Government Printing Office).

ment investigative report of Caesars under advisement, while the Commission also considered additional review, formal hearings, and the unspecified "substantial conditions." Caesars World attorney Mark Geller was the first casualty of the report, resigning from Caesars Boardwalk Regency just days later. In the same week, the Abscam investigation began to dominate New Jersey and Atlantic City headlines. Angelo Errichetti, mayor of Camden, New Jersey, was famously caught on tape accepting cash and, in turn, was under withering public attack. Mayor Errichetti was also central to the introduction of the Abscam FBI operative to Alvin Malnik. Notably, Errichetti stated as well that mobster Gerardo Catena "owned Joseph Lordi, Chairman of the State Casino Control Commission."[13] Kenneth McDonald, vice-chairman of the New Jersey Casino Control Commission, then resigned amid allegations of accepting a $50,000 Abscam bribe.

The implication of Lordi and the resignation of McDonald engaged the direct attention of New Jersey Governor Brendan Byrne, while the Governor also closely observed the licensing process of Clifford Perlman and Caesars Boardwalk Regency. Publicly, Governor Byrne, the self-professed anti-mob reformer, "was 'surprised and disturbed' by the allegations."[14] Privately, the governor's "keep your filthy hands out of Atlantic City" message to the mob might have been simple code for "wash hands before entering." As the governor scrambled to tamp down Abscam, the Caesars Palace Grand Prix would then draw its own increasing criticisms, and the close, personal attentions of Bernie Ecclestone.

***

The functional relationship of FISA with the Formula One Commission mirrored that of the New Jersey Casino Control Commission and the New Jersey Division of Gaming Enforcement. The organizational structure was also true of the Nevada Gaming Commission and the Nevada Gaming Control Board. In each example, the governing bodies received non-binding recommendations from a fact-finding advisory body, after which they would conduct their own due diligence, consider further testimony, and—ultimately—make a binding determination of suitability. The respective cases of the Caesars Palace Grand Prix and Caesars Boardwalk Regency thus played out similarly. Due diligence of the governing bodies would lead to compromise rulings, each ruling eventually working against Caesars Palace, while each also sowed further controversy.

In Paris, the FISA overlords also heard the pleadings of Malcolm Currie and the American delegation, a collective wail to spare the U.S. Grand Prix at Watkins Glen. The response of FISA in compromise was to holdover Watkins Glen for 1980—albeit with a spring date—and to move forward with the Caesars Palace Grand Prix in the fall. The schedule thus moved the Long Beach Grand Prix from the first full weekend in April to the last full weekend in March. The U.S. Grand Prix at Watkins Glen was ordered to follow two weeks later on April 13, 1980. Recovering from a typical upstate New York winter, the April date would be a virtual non-starter, just as quickly placing the 1980 U.S. Grand Prix again in jeopardy. "Mal had no choice but to accept. It was either April or lose the race entirely," Henry Valent of the Watkins Glen Grand Prix

Corporation said. "Saving the race was our primary objective. Now we'll see if we can renegotiate the date."[15]

Across the country, the inaugural Caesars Palace Grand Prix was scheduled to run on the third weekend of October, effectively subverting the autumn colors of Watkins Glen, for a fair weather throw at the green felt of the Las Vegas tables. "[William D.] Weinberger said that the Grand Prix will probably be held Oct. 18, a Saturday," reported the *Las Vegas Review-Journal*. "Friday will likely be held for inspection of race cars and Sunday will likely be held for awards ceremonies."[16] Within days, though, the Las Vegas event was confirmed to run on November 2, 1980.

The apparent schedule commitment for the Formula One event sent Bill Weinberger and Caesars Palace scurrying to formalize approval of the event by local government, a push that aroused the naïve curiosities of Clark County officials. One county commissioner, in fact, was on record to demand an environmental study. "But on a track confined to a small area and an event which takes place only one time a year?" ran one Las Vegas op-ed piece. "You know, politicians and attorneys have one thing in common—they could both foul up the Lord's Prayer."[17] Meanwhile, the Watkins Glen promoters fervently prayed on hope for their own fall date, as they also pondered the near impossibility of preparing the frozen grounds of the stored upstate New York race course. From humble headquarters in downtown Watkins Glen, Malcolm Currie also contemplated the forming priorities of Formula One in North America.

"These are truly rich people and they're looking for suitable motels and restaurants. Unfortunately, we don't afford them quick access to a major city," lamented Currie of the Formula One crowd. "Long Beach, Las Vegas and Montreal all have civic centers and luxury hotels and facilities that these people want and need."[18] The comforts of privilege among the international wealthy had long outstripped the utility of the rural Watkins Glen complex, as well as of its unbridled crowd. Despite the promise of Watkins Glen to improve facilities and amenities in support of race teams and media, the traditions of the Glen infield would not go easily, "an infamous setting for rowdyism and violence nearly every year."[19]

Funding for the FISA-ordered improvements then tested the wherewithal of the Watkins Glen Grand Prix Corporation, particularly for a parcel of property that had been deeded a decade earlier to the Schuyler Industrial Development Corp as security for bond financing to improve the circuit. The Grand Prix Corporation took its case for financing to the State of New York, seeking official assistance in securing federal or other third-party loans. The call for funding also foretold the financial stresses of the Grand Prix Corporation. Ultimately, the 1980 U.S. Grand Prix at Watkins Glen would force the end game for the upstate New York classic.

As FISA met in Paris on February 23, 1980, to settle the latter half of the 1980 Formula One calendar, Watkins Glen was restored to its traditional early October slot. The U.S. Grand Prix West at Long Beach thus remained on its scheduled March 30, 1980, date, while the Caesars Palace Grand Prix was reiterated for November 2, 1980. With attendant bluster, FISA president Jean Marie-Balestre also set the expectations for the Watkins Glen Grand Prix Corporation. "If the Watkins Glen track is not improved, or its press and assembly facilities not adequate, or if spectator safety arrangements are deficient," cautioned Balestre, "the track would be permanently removed from Formula One racing competition."[20]

Balestre, however, failed to mention the requisite ability of the Grand Prix Corporation to fulfill its forthcoming payment obligations to Bernie Ecclestone and FOCA. Further, the words of Jean-Marie Balestre should serve as fair warning to Long Beach and Las Vegas. The Watkins Glen Grand Prix Corporation then scrambled through the summer of 1980 in pursuit of financing for the FISA ordered facility improvements, as well as to meet continuing bond obligations. Tenuous finances and tentative construction progress also remained at issue, through to the running of the U.S. Grand Prix at Watkins Glen on October 5, 1980.

The conditional confirmation of the Watkins Glen event then pivoted against the proposed Las Vegas round. Notably, the four-week lag between the newly rescheduled U.S. Grand Prix and the inaugural Caesars Palace Grand Prix came under

GRAND PRIX SCHEDULE

PARIS, FRANCE - The schedule for 1980 Grand Prix events on the Formula One automobile racing tour:

Jan. 13 - Argentina, Buenos Aires.
Jan. 27 - Brazil, Interlagos.
March 2 – South Africa, Kyalami.
March 30 - U.S. West, Long Beach, Calif.
April 13 – U.S. East, Watkins Glen, N.Y.
May 4 – Belgium, Solder.
May 18 – Monaco, Monte Carlo.
June 1 – Spain, Jarma.
June 29 – France, Castellet.
July 13 – Britain, Brands Hatch.
Aug. 10 – West Germany, Hockenheim
Aug. 17 – Austria, Oesterrichring,
Aug. 31 – Holland, Zandvoort.
Sept. 14 – Italy, Imola.
Oct. 5 – Canada, Montreal.
Nov. 2 – U.S. Las Vegas (subject to circuit being passed)

International news services confirmed the FISA Formula One race schedule in January of 1980. The U.S. Grand Prix at Watkins Glen, New York, was listed for April 13, 1980. The proposed Caesars Palace Grand Prix was listed for November 2, 1980, "subject to circuit being passed." Watkins Glen was then rescheduled to October 5, 1980, and would require passage of its own circuit. The proposed 1980 Caesars Palace Grand Prix, however, was canceled and then resurrected in 1981 (author's collection).

increased scrutiny, particularly regarding the constructors' post-season development schedules for their new 1981 machinery. Efforts to move the Las Vegas event to an October weekend following Watkins Glen then came into conflict with the domestic

Bernie Ecclestone (left) and Max Mosley (center) of FOCA appeared unified with Jean-Marie Balestre (right) of FISA in their quest to remove Watkins Glen from the Formula One series. At the same time, they were pitched in battle over technical regulations for the sport of Formula One. The three appeared no less quarrelsome at the 1981 Caesars Palace Grand Prix. Subversion of the resultant rules by Bernie Ecclestone and Brabham would impact the 1981 Formula One season of Mario Andretti and Alfa Romeo (John Blakemore, The Revs Institute).

racing schedule and SCCA-sanctioned Can-Am events at Laguna Seca and River-side on October 18, and October 26, 1980, respectively. "It sets the stage for a power struggle with Caesars Palace and Bernie Ecclestone who has made Las Vegas his special project, on one side," wrote Shav Glick for the *Los Angeles Times*, "and Les Richter, president of Riverside International Raceway on the other."[21] Opposition in the person of Les Richter also stood in marked contrast to the consultation offered by Richter 15 years before to the development of Stardust International Raceway in Las Vegas.

Despite the continued scheduling turmoil, the Clark County Commission voted on February 19, 1980, to approve the event,[22] lending their administrative agreement to the unzoned use of the Caesars Palace property for a Formula One program. Inevitably, the Commission vote also turned into a classic Las Vegas land grab. Unrelated to the Formula One venue at the north end of the property, the Commission requested that Caesars Palace dedicate a strip of land at the south end of the property for use in a future widening of Flamingo Road.

The property sought by county government would also be carved from a parcel of land that Steve Wynn had famously acquired in 1971 under curious circumstances, and then resold to Caesars Palace at a remarkable profit. That profit, in turn, became the bankroll from which Wynn began his decades-long acquisition and development

The original course concept for the Caesars Palace Grand Prix included this stretch of the world-famous Las Vegas Strip in front of Caesars Palace. Traffic concerns—as well as its status as U.S. Federal Route 91—scuttled the notion. Despite numerous subsequent efforts, Formula One has never raced along the Strip (courtesy LVCVA News Bureau).

program in the Las Vegas valley. Just as predictably, Caesars Palace brass bristled back at the notion of surrendering prime gambling real estate to the vagaries of Las Vegas valley government. "If you want to blow this race for the City of Las Vegas," Caesars Palace executive Harry Wald threatened, "we're willing to give it up. The request for the dedication has no bearing on the race track."[23]

Astride the somewhat besieged path to the inaugural Caesars Palace Grand Prix, Jean-Marie Balestre of FISA pressed the need for a preliminary race prior to unleashing the Formula One combatants on the Caesars circuit later in 1980. The advance test event requirement for Caesars Palace dropped Chris Pook into the discourse, as he also prepared for the March 30, 1980, U.S. Grand Prix West in Long Beach. "Chris Pook, founder of the Long Beach race and race director in Las Vegas," reported the

Los Angeles Times, "said he expects to comply by running a Formula Atlantic race 'several weeks before the Grand Prix.'"[24]

As Chris Pook engaged the Caesars Palace narrative, the build-up to the 1980 U.S. Grand Prix West was joined by an apparent build-up to the Caesars Palace Grand Prix. The actual date of the Caesars Palace inaugural, however, remained unstable. National reports still ranged from October 12, 1980, to November 2, 1980. Further, with Bill Weinberger's clock ticking, a Formula One circuit remained to be constructed. Indeed, although the Caesars Palace circuit would be routed primarily through the north parking lot of the resort, it was done so on a ribbon of deep-section, purpose-built, Formula One-worthy asphalt. Nonetheless, local odds-making—and optimism—sought to anchor the event. "It may be hard to picture," suggested a report on February 28, 1980, "but the Caesars Palace Grand Prix in October will prove to be the biggest sporting event ever to hit this town."[25]

Bullish Las Vegas opinion on the Grand Prix also ran concurrent with the swing of Caesars's scales, back across the country to Atlantic City. The gambling license of the Caesars Boardwalk Regency in Atlantic City, sidelined by the Abscam revelations, had received a lifeline. Further, the announcement in New Jersey press acknowledged the role that Abscam played in the Caesars World licensing process, while it conspicuously avoided direct mention of Alvin Malnik. "The [New Jersey] Casino Control Commission, in its first meeting since it was shaken by bribe and influence peddling charges in the FBI's Arab Scam probe," ran one report, "yesterday granted Caesars World's Boardwalk Regency a three-month extension of its temporary casino license."[26]

Reporting acknowledged the turmoil caused by the resignation of commission member Kenneth MacDonald in the wake of Abscam, as well as the efforts of Governor Brendan Byrne to stabilize the commission while he also quieted the state legislature. The intense public focus on Abscam and the New Jersey Casino Control Commission also tipped the apparently cozy relationship between the Governor and Clifford Perlman of Caesars World. "Byrne has frequently been associated with Perlman," reported New Jersey press, "and the two are regarded as personal friends."[27] Despite the accommodating nod from the Governor, Clifford Perlman remained severed from the Caesars World New Jersey operations pending disposition by the Casino Control Commission, citing only, "links with reputed organized crime figures."[28]

The public optimism for the 1980 Caesars Palace Grand Prix—as well as the temporary Atlantic City reprieve for Caesars World—belied intense maneuvering behind the scenes on the fate of Formula One in Las Vegas. Indeed, ongoing discussions over the Caesars Palace race date had devolved into acrimonious debate, with FOCA and Bernie Ecclestone pressing for an October date in Las Vegas, while FISA and the SCCA held firm for November 2, 1980. Bill Weinberger of Caesars Palace would simply have to straddle the outcome. With a pointed tease, Shav Glick of the *Los Angeles Times* then grabbed the lead of the 1980 Caesars Palace Grand Prix, as Glick also compiled his press notes for Long Beach. "Look for the Las Vegas Grand Prix, tentatively scheduled for Nov. 2 in the Caesars Palace parking lot," reported Glick on March 20, 1980, "to be scrubbed from the Grand Prix schedule."[29]

***

The U.S. Grand Prix West was the fourth race of the new decade and of the 1980 season. Formula One departed three early stops in the southern hemisphere, Argentina, Brazil, and South Africa, and—4 weeks later—made another ocean crossing to the fifth edition of Formula One on the streets of Long Beach, California. Originally scheduled on March 30, 1980, to consolidate logistics with the U.S. Grand Prix at Watkins Glen, the Long Beach event remained with the March date even after Watkins Glen was restored to October. The 1980 event was also rebranded, along with a three-year, $1 million sponsorship agreement with Toyota Motor Sales, USA. The Toyota Grand Prix of Long Beach was thus launched. "We are delighted to become close partners with such a major organization," Chris Pook said of the announcement. "Toyota

Advertising was produced for a 1980 Caesars Palace Grand Prix. The race, however, never materialized. The graphic appears to depict the #7 McLaren M29 of John Watson. Watson contested both the 1981 and 1982 Caesars Palace Grand Prix events (author's collection).

was the first sponsor to show interest in the Grand Prix here in Long Beach back in 1975 when we held our first Formula 5000 race."[30] The 1980 Toyota Grand Prix of Long Beach also marked its milestones, a first-time race winner, a new American driver in his inaugural season, and a horrific injury to a former Long Beach Grand Prix champion.

Pre-race reports for the Toyota Grand Prix of Long Beach inevitably pondered the demise of the Caesars Palace Grand Prix. Reporting also traced the Las Vegas developments from conjecture to confirmation. Citing issues with the unbuilt Caesars circuit, to the FISA demand for a preliminary event, to the lag of the scheduled November date, the 1980 Caesars Palace Grand Prix was *ad mortem* without turning a wheel. In fact, by week's end, William D. Weinberger of Caesars Palace was reportedly seeking an IndyCar event to replace the foregone departure of Formula One. "It seems that FISA (The Formula 1 governing body) couldn't attend the scheduled Nov. 2 date, so Weinberger has gone to work trying to secure Indy cars," ran one report. "A date has been proposed and Weinberger anxiously is awaiting a reply."[31]

Nelson Piquet was the class of the qualifying field for the 1980 Long Beach Grand Prix, taking a dominant pole in Bernie Ecclestone's Brabham-Ford. Piquet's 1:17.694 was nearly a second clear of second qualifier Rene Arnoux in a turbocharged Renault. Patrick Depailler then claimed third on the grid in an Alfa Romeo. Mario Andretti was mired in 15th, over two seconds back of Piquet's mark. Other notables included American Eddie Cheever in his inaugural Grand Prix season, qualified 19th in an Osella-Ford. The 1976 Long Beach winner Clay Regazzoni started 23rd in an Ensign-Ford. Twice Formula One champion Emerson Fittipaldi then anchored the field from 24th in his Fittipaldi-Ford, four seconds adrift of Nelson Piquet on pole.

Unchallenged from pole, Nelson Piquet would then lead the 1980 Toyota Grand Prix of Long Beach wire to wire. Patrick Depailler moved past Rene Arnoux at the start. A chain reaction of first-turn collisions in the mid-field, though, collected homeland hero Mario Andretti, along with Piquet's Brabham teammate Ricardo Zunino. Jean-Pierre Jarier in a Tyrell-Ford was also caught up and retired on lap 3. Jochen Mass in an Arrows-Ford continued on from the incident.

Piquet extended his position by nearly a second a lap over Depailler until Alan Jones in a Williams-Ford passed Depailler on lap 18 under braking at Queen's Hairpin. Alan Jones, however, retired on lap 47 after an incident with Bruno Giacomelli, striking the rear of Giacomelli's Alfa Romeo as Jones prepared to lap him. The departure of Jones moved Ricardo Patrese into second place, over a minute back of Nelson Piquet's blistering pace.

On lap 50, Clay Regazzoni in fourth position powered his Ensign-Ford down Shoreline Drive, the fastest section of the circuit. Much improved from his last-row start, the 1976 U.S. Grand Prix West winner was well inside the points and poised for a potential podium. Checking up for Queen's Hairpin, Regazzoni's Ensign suffered a catastrophic brake failure, sending him at full speed into the retired Brabham of Ricardo Zunino, though several "spherical elastic attenuators," and hard into a concrete barrier. Medical staff were quick to retrieve the badly injured driver. Clay Regazzoni survived, but suffered severe spinal trauma and was paralyzed from the waist down, the career of the five-time Grand Prix winner horribly ended.

Nelson Piquet in the Brabham-Ford then streaked across the finish line on lap 80 to win the 1980 Toyota Grand Prix of Long Beach. It was Piquet's first Grand Prix victory. Riccardo Patrese followed second in the Arrows, some 49 seconds behind. The Long Beach podium was the first for Patrese since the Swedish round in 1978, the year he was removed from the U.S. Grand after the death of Ronnie Peterson. Remarkably, Emerson Fittipaldi in his eponymous machine came through another 30

The 1980 Long Beach Grand Prix turned ugly on the third lap as the field approached Queens Hairpin at the end of the Shoreline straightaway. Jean-Pierre Jarier (#15 Renault) turns just ahead of the spinning Bruno Giacomelli (#23 Alfa Romeo). Jacques Lafitte ($26 Ligier) is immediately behind Giacomelli. Lafitte is followed by Keke Rosberg (#21 Fittipaldi) and Eddie Cheever (#31 Osella). John Watson (#7 McLaren) appears to be bearing straight toward Giacomelli. Clay Regazzoni (#14 Ensign) is inside Watson. Jochen Mass (#30 Arrows) trails the scene. Nelson Piquet won the event for Bernie Ecclestone and Brabham (Rick Lake collection).

seconds back, recovering 21 positions from last place on the starting grid. Fittipaldi was the final car on the lead lap. The third step on the Long Beach victory stand was also the final podium of Emerson Fittipaldi's decorated Formula One career.

The Long Beach podium and the finishing field also informed the starting grid of the 1981 Caesars Palace Grand Prix. Indeed, 15 of the Long Beach starters went on to take the green flag of the 1981 Caesars Palace event, including the great American race car driver, Mario Andretti. For Mario Andretti, though, 1980 represented another Long Beach lost, unclassified 23rd in the order. Forty-year-old Andretti now stood one for 13 in Grand Prix victories on his home soil. Twenty-two-year-old Eddie Cheever was top American in Long Beach with an unclassified 18th. The ascendance of 27-year-old Nelson Piquet on the Long Beach podium also heralded the perennial Formula One youth movement.

Forty-year-old Clay Regazzoni well understood the flower of youth in Grand Prix motorsport, as well as the risks of his profession. The uncontemplated risks of a stationary race vehicle and an English-language liability waiver, however, caused the paralyzed 1976 Long Beach winner to sue Chris Pook's Long Beach Grand Prix Association. Clay Regazzoni's lawsuit was dismissed in the fall of 1981, after a vigorous defense by attorney Cary Agajanian on behalf of the Long Beach Grand Prix Association defendants. "It is absurd to think that a professional driver who works all his life

Nineteen seventy-six Long Beach Grand Prix winner Clay Regazzoni qualified 23rd in an Ensign for the 1980 edition of the Long Beach race. Regazzoni would crash on lap 50 at the end of the high-speed Shoreline straightaway and suffer career-ending injuries. Regazzoni is trailed by 24th qualifier Emerson Fittipaldi in an eponymous machine. Fittipaldi improved remarkably to finish third, the final Formula One podium of his storied career (Rick Lake collection).

for the chance to participate in the fame, fortune, and danger involved in Grand Prix racing," protested the son of J.C. Agajanian, "would sue the people who make such racing possible because he is hurt by the very risks he gets paid to take."[32] Such black and white arguments, though, can tend to overlook parked Brabhams on the gray fringes at the high-speed pinnacle of motorsport.

Four days after the 1980 Toyota Grand Prix of Long Beach, another Long Beach court case was dismissed, one that punctuated the oft-curious symmetries of history. On April 3, 1980, a federal judge tossed a lawsuit by former Caesars Palace front man Jay Sarno against the Long Beach *Independent and Press-Journal*, claiming that the newspaper accused him "falsely and maliciously … of being associated with crime syndicates, organized crime figures, Mafia."[33] At issue, the Long Beach newspaper had asserted, "Sarno's attempt to gain control of amusement games aboard the Queen Mary could be a move to gain a business for laundering 'crime syndicate' money."[34] Fifteen years after the development of Caesars Palace, such a lawsuit by Jay Sarno might have been brushed away as an effort at proof against facts, Nonetheless, as with New Jersey reporting post–Abscam, the centurion phalanx of Caesar, Jerome Zarowitz, Jimmy "Blue Eyes" Alo, "Fat Tony" Salerno, Calvin Kovens, Sidney Korshak, Allen Dorfman, and Alvin Malnik, et al., were charitably omitted from print—allegedly.

***

Caesars World, Caesars Palace, and the saga of the 1980 Caesars Palace Grand Prix all broke cover amid the post-script of the Toyota Grand Prix of Long Beach. On April 10, 1980, the New Jersey Casino Control Commission scheduled hearings to consider the permanent gambling license for the Caesars Boardwalk Regency resort. The hearings were planned to commence on May 12, 1980. The product of extensive pre-negotiations, the hearings were also intended as a streamlined process to clear Caesars World, Inc. from the docket, certainly in contrast to the 7-month process required for the preceding Resorts International licensing. Despite apparent considerable application of licensing emollient, Clifford Perlman remained a board chairman occupying a very hot seat. "The state contends that Perlman," ran the latest reports, "had dealings … with at least two men with alleged ties to organized crime."[35] Curiously, the Casino Control Commission then voted unanimously to extend Caesars' temporary license to October 26, 1980.

Two weeks after the Commission action to schedule the Caesars World licensing hearings in May 1980, the professional patience of Caesars Palace vice president William D. Weinberger had run its own course. "I'm ruling out all types of racing for the foreseeable future," Weinberger stated. "We didn't get the cooperation from racing people in this country."[36] The report also posited the politics of the potential race dates for the 1980 Caesars Palace event. Indeed, two weekends following the October 5, 1980, date for the U.S. Grand Prix were considered. Potential October dates, however, ran into conflict with the SCCA-sanctioned Can-Am series, October 19, 1980, at Laguna Seca and October 26, 1980, at Riverside. "Riverside President Les Richter had told the SCCA that if Las Vegas ran a Grand Prix race on either October date," continued the report, "he would cancel all SCCA racing at his track."[37]

Alongside Bill Weinberger's comments, a replacement event at Caesars Palace for Indy Cars still floated. "Caesars Palace vice president William Weinberger," ran an Indiana source, "reportedly has struck a deal with USAC to run a championship event on the road course there in place of the Formula One event."[38] USAC, however—after initially agreeing to sanction the Indy Car championship jointly with CART—was enduring another truncated, cancellation-plagued season. Five events in—including the centerpiece Indianapolis 500—USAC crowned Johnny Rutherford as its champion on July 13, 1980, at the season-ending Red Roof Inns 150 on the Mid–Ohio Sports Car Course. The remainder of the post–July USAC events transitioned to the still running—and now *separate*—CART championship. Rutherford went on to win CART events at Michigan and Milwaukee. On November 9, 1980, in Phoenix, Johnny Rutherford was also crowned the 1980 CART PPG Indy Car World Series champion. The year of 1980 was a year that epitomized the debacle of the CART-USAC split. Further, it was a season that did not include a luxury-branded championship stop at Caesars Palace in Las Vegas.

As Bill Weinberger aired the frustrations of Caesar, the Formula One entrenchment of FOCA and FISA flared. Enacting rule changes for the 1981 season involving vehicle structures, aerodynamic effects, weights, and powerplants, FISA head Jean-Marie Balestre was certain to draw the fire of Bernie Ecclestone's FOCA. "They can invent all the rules they want," challenged Ecclestone consort Max Mosley, "but in the constructors federation we give the orders."[39] Notably, FISA also unveiled a

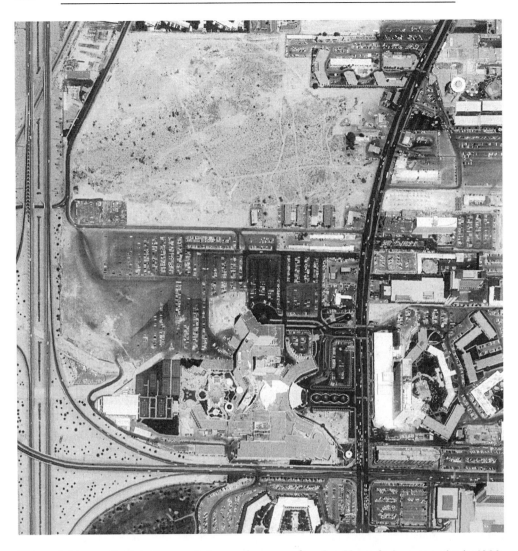

This aerial image depicts Caesars Palace and surrounding Las Vegas Strip properties in 1980. The Caesars Palace parking lot through which the Grand Prix circuit was constructed is at center. The Caesars Palace resort proper is directly below the parking lot. The world-famous Las Vegas Strip is the gently curving roadway to the right of Caesars Palace. Interstate 15 is to the left. Flamingo Road is below Caesars Palace. The Dunes hotel-casino is across (below) Flamingo Road from Caesars Palace. The Flamingo hotel-casino originally opened by Benjamin "Bugsy" Siegel in 1946 is at right, across the Strip from Caesars Palace. Some period 1946 structures still remained on the grounds of the Flamingo. Above the Caesars Palace parking lot is the vacant parcel owned by the former Howard Hughes Tool Company. Beyond the vacant dirt is the Castaways casino, also a Hughes holding. The Castaways property and vacant dirt parcel were developed by Steve Wynn as the Mirage in 1989 (courtesy HistoricAerials.com).

preliminary Formula One schedule for 1981 that listed the U.S. Grand Prix at Watkins Glen, but *not* the 1981 Caesars Palace Grand Prix.

Ultimately, the obvious bureaucracy of Grand Prix scheduling in the U.S. pointed up the coveted SCCA domestic sanction of Formula One, certainly much more so than the heft of Riverside Raceway or the Can-Am series. Neither entity, in fact, would survive the decade. Without naming Richter directly, Bill Weinberger was blunt. "[West Coast] promoters were afraid we'd cut into their crowds. The way we see it, we would have created more interest," Weinberger protested. "I feel we were cheated out of a race by the very people who are supposed to be guardians of the sport. They didn't give us a chance."[40] Given the storied offensive backfield of Caesars, cheating the Palace of chance might seem an undue risk for former Rams linebacker Les Richter. Nonetheless, Caesar stood down from the field while Richter held sway. William D. Weinberger of Caesars Palace and Bernard Ecclestone of FOCA, though, would quietly reconvene to race another day.

***

As Bill Weinberger's mettle was tested with the canceled 1980 Caesars Palace Grand Prix, so too was the patience of Clifford Perlman and Caesars World with the New Jersey Casino Control Commission. Hearings for permanent licensure originally slated to commence May 12, 1980, were pushed down the schedule to September 4, 1980. The schedule delay was ostensibly to provide time for the state to assemble an entirely new Commission panel, including the chair of Joseph Lordi, an effort spearheaded by Governor Brendan Byrne. Pending a newly seated panel, though, it was Abscam-tainted Commission Chairman Joseph Lordi who presided over the hearing schedule for Caesars World.

The apparent impasse erupted in July 1980 with a lawsuit filed by Caesars World seeking to force the hearings, as well as to reinstate Clifford Perlman to the Caesars World New Jersey operations. "The corporation and Mr. Perlman have been subjected to a period of uncertainty and interference," offered a Caesars World spokesperson in Los Angeles, "far beyond what was contemplated when…. Mr. Perlman voluntarily accepted the conditions of temporary disassociation."[41] Indeed, as of the filing, Clifford Perlman had been severed from New Jersey operations for over a year. The hiatus of Perlman could not have been productive for his business relationship with Alvin Malnik, both the posted public and the presumed private. Nonetheless, the deep concerns of the New Jersey Division of Gaming Enforcement remained. For that matter, so did Alvin Malnik's underlying ownership of the Caesars Pocono Resorts.

The stand-off between State and Caesar lasted through the summer, driven by New Jersey Governor Byrne's insistence that a new Commission be seated. On August 28, 1980, four new members were finally sworn into the new Jersey gambling body. "Members almost immediately will face the tough task," reported New Jersey press, "of reviewing an application for a permanent license for Caesars Boardwalk Regency."[42] Even still, Joseph Lordi—tainted by direct Abscam mention—retained the chairmanship of the new Commission, as well as direction of the Caesars World hearings.

On September 8, 1980, New Jersey press announced that the Casino Control Commission hearings on the Caesars World application for the Caesars Boardwalk Regency would finally commence. Eight months had now passed since the New Jersey Division of Gaming Enforcement issued its searing report on the Caesars applicants, Clifford Perlman principal among them. William McElnea of Caesars World was then quick to frame the corporate narrative. "We look forward to the hearings as a forum," McElnea said, "to dispel some of the myths and misconceptions that have circulated in the press over the last two years."[43] Rather, the Commission hearings would lay bare the dealings of Clifford Perlman with underworld elements, deal-making and deceptions with Alvin Malnik that were layered with intention. Further, the hearing process implicated William McElnea to some extent, either by tacit awareness or by failure to act. The hearings thus opened the bunker board room and the secret ledger of Caesar to the public. To William McElnea's comment, the hearings would also deliver Caesar to another murderous experience at the Forum.

***

Another announcement was also picked up on September 8, 1980, by New Jersey media. Some 300 miles northeast of Atlantic City, the 1980 U.S. Grand Prix at Watkins Glen was given the final approval for competition after inspection by representatives of the FISA Safety Committee. "The decision ends some 10 months of indecision about the future of the race," it was reported in Camden, New Jersey, "the oldest road-racing Grand Prix in the United States."[44] The decision by the FISA Safety Committee, however, was not without its own controversy, particular so with FISA-ordered track improvements commencing the same date as the initial FISA inspection.

The Watkins Glen Grand Prix Corporation struggled through much of the year to secure financing for the improvement program. Indeed, federal government assistance that offered early promise did not materialize. "Watkins Glen officials appealed to the federal Farmers Home Administration for a $750,000 loan guarantee to pay off old debts and to run this year's Grand Prix," it was reported, "They were turned down."[45] The office of New York Governor Hugh Carey then offered $500,000 for track improvements in funds from the Apalachin Regional Commission. The Apalachin funds were predicated first, though, on Watkins Glen raising $750,000 of their own.[46] Notably, Apalachin was the former home of Joseph Barbara, local Canada Dry bottler, genial La Cosa Nostra host, and departed crime lord.

In the week before the FISA inspection, Rochester, New York, financial consultant and amateur racer David Schlosser then offered a private promotion to raise $200,000 for track improvements, with continued efforts to raise the full $750,000. "Everyone in my group will become a limited partner, by legal definition, with the Watkins Glen Grand Prix Corporation," pitched Schlosser, "Because Watkins Glen is a non-profit corporation, this is a tremendous tax shelter."[47] On September 3, 1980, Schlosser announced that the initial $200,000 had been raised. Construction work was then scheduled to commence. The advance FISA inspector, however, arrived to find little more than the mobilization of construction equipment, rather than the completed improvements demanded seven months before by Jean-Marie Balestre of FISA.

The bucolic farmland table of Watkins Glen was thus set for sustained controversy. Nonetheless, a delegation including Grand Prix Drivers Association president Jody Scheckter inspected the Watkins Glen track-proper in late–September. "They just checked between the [Armco barrier] rails," clarified Currie to the local press.[48] On Scheckter's inspection, the 1980 U.S. Grand Prix at Watkins Glen would move forward on October 5, 1980. The financial salve of David Schlosser, however, was

The final U.S. Grand Prix at Watkins Glen would run on October 5, 1980. This vehicle plaque notes the event as the "27th Grand Prix of U.S." The number combined the U.S. Grand Prix at Watkins Glen and the U.S. Grand Prix West at Long Beach. The count also included the 1959 and 1960 "Grand Prix of the Unites States" at Sebring and Riverside respectively. The Formula Super Vee series at bottom of plaque raced at Caesars Palace in 1984 (author's collection).

soon to parch, later to dissolve away completely in a rinse of red ink. Further, whereas the Watkins Glen Grand Prix events of the recent past had been severely impacted by heavy rains and rowdyism, the 1980 event simply continued under a cloud.

Alan Jones, driving an FW07 for Frank Williams, arrived at Watkins Glen with the 1980 World Driving Championship already clinched over Nelson Piquet. Jones also took tenor for the assembled Formula One armada. "Sure, the Glen is a nice scenic track," Jones quipped, "but that doesn't mean we should have to live in the Stone Age."[49] The sentiment of new Formula One champion Alan Jones, was echoed by Nelson Piquet's Brabham boss Bernie Ecclestone. Ecclestone also carried the obvious heft of the FOCA fleet.

"The repaving job didn't quite do the trick, from what the drivers have told me," Bernie Ecclestone said from Watkins Glen. "They still complain that it's too bumpy and dangerous."[50] Despite the posting of Watkins Glen on the presumptive 1981 Formula One calendar, Ecclestone was not inclined to foregone conclusion. "I have no idea if we'll be back," was the rather rigid response.[51] Indeed, the financial closing of the 1980 U.S. Grand Prix at Watkins Glen would hit hardest at Bernie Ecclestone and FOCA. Further, the conclusion of the 1980 season brought sharpened focus to the accumulating issues standing between FOCA and FISA, issues that would also permeate the 1981 season and the 1981 Caesars Palace Grand Prix.

***

The 20th edition of the time-honored U.S. Grand Prix in Watkins Glen, New York, opened far differently than had its predecessors. From the subdued pre-race press to the absence of the Watkins Glen Grand Prix Corporation at local hospitality events, from the heavily-muddled finances to a new Schuyler County felony-vehicular arson law directed specifically at the race event, the pre-race narrative was curtailed in both scale and scope. The fanfare of Watkins Glen-past now played out as a distressed and dire dirge.

Apparent transitions at Watkins Glen were also accompanied by power shifts in Formula One. After nine seasons, 1979 Formula One champion Jody Scheckter announced his retirement from the pinnacle of motorsport. Emerson Fittipaldi, World Champion in 1972 and 1974, departed the seat of his eponymous driving team at year's end as well. Four years on with Colin Chapman's Team Lotus, Mario Andretti announced his departure from his 1978 Formula One championship squad for a seat at Alfa Romeo. "[Colin] Chapman and I had a frank conversation," Andretti said. "After the Toyota Grand Prix at Watkins Glen, I told him our partnership is over."[52] At the opposite end of the order, 19-year-old newcomer Michael Thackwell of New Zealand was added to the entry list of the U.S. Grand Prix, attempting the grid for Ken Tyrell in a companion machine to Jean-Pierre Jarier and Derek Daly.

Saturday qualifying for the 1980 U.S. Grand Prix marked yet another milestone. Bruno Giacomelli qualified on pole in his Alfa Romeo 179 with a new lap record of 1:33.291. Giacomelli's effort was also to be the only pole of his career. In fact, stateside stops provided the statistical highlights of Bruno Giacomelli's racing resume. Indeed, the 1981 Caesars Palace Grand Prix was to be Giacomelli's only podium finish. Nelson Piquet was second on the grid with a 1:34.080 for Bernie Ecclestone's Brabham works. Carlos Reutemann in a Williams and Elio de Angelis in a Lotus then formed the second row.

Alan Jones, the walk-off 1980 World Champion, followed next with a 1:34.216 in another Williams. In his swan song for Colin Chapman, Mario Andretti queued tenth at 1:35.243, over a second back of de Angelis, his ostensible junior teammate. Eddie Cheever slotted 16th in an Osella-Ford. Emerson Fittipaldi followed 19th on the grid for his Formula One send-off. In his own departure, reigning world champion Jody Scheckter struggled for the Scuderia Ferrari with a 1:38.149, 23rd on the grid. Formula One hopeful Michael Thackwell failed to qualify, his best time over 16 seconds off the new track record of Bruno Giacomelli.

Race day then dawned similarly to finances of the troubled Watkins Glen Grand Prix Corporation, clouded, accompanied by a pervasive chill. Bruno Giacomelli led the race from pole into the first corner. Alan Jones pressed hard from fifth on the grid to enter the first turn behind leader Giacomelli. Jones, however, overdrove the entry, ran wide, and was dispatched to the mid-field. Nelson Piquet and Carlos Reutemann settled in behind Giacomelli, followed by Didier Pironi in a Ligier.

Nelson Piquet and Carlos Reutemann then battled for second position for several laps, while Giacomelli widened his lead to a comfortable margin. As Piquet and Reutemann skirmished, Didier Pironi tightened the gap from fourth. Alan Jones—well behind the leaders on the first lap—was also mounting an incredible charge to move into fifth behind Pironi.

On lap 25, Nelson Piquet—under constant pressure by Carlos Reutemann—spun off in the first turn. At the same time, Alan Jones was closing in the mirrors of Didier Pironi and then moved past into third place. Williams' teammates Reutemann and Jones then circulated in tandem. Again, Alan Jones improved his position

The eccentric David Thieme of Essex Overseas Petroleum wishes Mario Andretti good luck on the starting grid of the October 5, 1980, U.S. Grand Prix at Watkins Glen. Lotus team principal Colin Chapman stands behind Thieme. The 1980 U.S. Grand Prix was Andretti's last start for Lotus. Thieme was arrested 6 months later by Swiss authorities. In 1981, the Essex livery was fully replaced by John Player tobacco branding before the Lotus squad reached Las Vegas. Grid positions visible around Andretti are, right to left, John Watson (McLaren), Hector Rebaque (Brabham), and Andrea de Cesaris (Alfa Romeo) (author's collection).

with a move past Carlos Reutemann into second, trailing leader Bruno Giacomelli by some 10 seconds.

Bruno Giacomelli was closing down on a potential inaugural Formula One win when his Alfa Romeo slowed on the 32nd lap. An electrical failure had spoiled a dominant day for the pole sitter. Alan Jones then unleashed his Williams from the lead of the race. On the 44th lap, Jones uncorked a resounding race lap record with an incredible 1:34.068, two tenths quicker than his qualifying time.

Alan Jones was unchallenged the rest of the way, streaking home on lap 59 to claim a dominant come-from-behind victory in the 1980 U.S. Grand Prix at Watkins Glen. Jones' margin over second place Carlos Reutemann was over 4 seconds. Jones also completed the race at a record average speed, 126.27 mph, nearly a 3-mph bump over the speed record set in 1978 by Carlos Reutemann. From the victory podium, race winner and World Champion Alan Jones was ebullient. "These cars are like aircraft, they're so smooth and sleek," Jones gushed. "I kind of messed up the liftoff … but then I got her under control, and it was a nice quiet flight in the country."[53] The jet age blast of Alan Jones thus thundered through the stone age-tranquil of Watkins Glen.

Emerson Fittipaldi made the final Formula One start of his career at the October 5, 1980, U.S. Grand Prix at Watkins Glen. Fittipaldi qualified 19th and retired on lap 15, his fourth retirement in a row to close his final campaign. Emerson Fittipaldi was in the starting field for the 1984 CART IndyCar Caesars Palace Grand Prix IV (author's collection).

Alan Jones' victory was his fifth of 1980, capping a forceful drive to the championship. Jones would also bring his championship *mojo* to the podium of the 1981 Caesars Palace Grand Prix. With second place at Watkins Glen, teammate Carlos Reutemann was classified third in the championship. Team owner Frank Williams also claimed the constructor's championship, 120 points to 66 for Guy Ligier's squad. Nelson Piquet was out of the points at Watkins Glen, but took third in championship points for Brabham and Bernie Ecclestone. Like Jones, both Reutemann and Piquet would figure prominently in the storyline of the 1981 Caesars Palace Grand Prix.

Mario Andretti finished a commendable sixth for Colin Chapman. Andretti's solitary lame duck point was his first in 15 races. Further, Mario Andretti's final season for Team Lotus resulted in a dismal 20th place position in championship points. Scuttled in Watkins Glen qualifying, the driving career of Michael Thackwell also arched forward to Caesars Palace. Thackwell notably subbed-in for an injured Rick Mears in Roger Penske's March 84C IndyCar at the 1984 Caesars Palace Grand Prix.

As in 1979, Alan Jones' Williams mount was sponsored by Saudia, the Saudi national airline. The Williams livery was joined in 1980 by TAG, a conglomerate company founded by Akram Ojjeh, a Syrian-born Saudi arms broker. Akram Ojjeh was, in turn, connected to the infamous Adnan Khashoggi, international arms merchant and decadent Las Vegas gambler. Despite the attractive green-on-white color scheme of the British-owned Williams race team, the Saudi sponsorships struck a certain dissonance in America, particularly against a backdrop of 52 hostages held in Iran in the waning days of the 1980 presidential campaign. Further, the active Saudi role in the 1973 Arab oil embargo could not be overlooked during a second oil crisis fueled by the 1979 Iranian Revolution.

The public pulpit of the 1980 U.S. Grand Prix at Watkins Glen would transcend the paddock and drive directly at the politics of the sport. The position of Bernie Ecclestone—Brock Yates' satirized "shah of Formula One racing"—was principal among the voices. "This was a very destructive year for Grand Prix racing," suggested Ecclestone. "FISA and Balestre … are in the demolition business. We (FOCA) are in the construction business. We've worked hard to build up this sport."[54] The solution of Ecclestone was a rebellion walkabout, a competing Formula One-platform series to commence in 1981. "We don't want a repeat of this year," continued the FOCA supreme, "so we'll probably stage our own series next season. We can project up to 16 races. I'd say we could supply 25 to 26 cars per race, too."[55]

The sentiments of Bernie Ecclestone were also echoed by two of the FOCA formation, notably representing the 1978 and 1980 World Champions. "After 25 years in Grand Prix racing," blasted Colin Chapman of Team Lotus, "I would rather stop than continue under Balestre."[56]

"The split was inevitable," added Frank Williams. "Under Balestre, FISA is no longer capable of administering professional motor sport."[57] The remarks of both gentlemen, typically circumspect in public statements, should be interpreted as highly provocative.

Stateside, Mario Andretti—then sizing a new Alfa Romeo ride for 1981—simply hoped that the escalation of hostilities into a combative split did not destroy the pinnacle of motorsport. The obvious parallel with the domestic CART-USAC open wheel racing split was not lost on the great American race car driver, then the only champion in both premier disciplines.

Simultaneously, Bernie Ecclestone teased the prospects of further expansion of the Formula One–based breakaway series in the American market. Noting the possibility of the rebel group appearing in 1981 at Watkins Glen, Ecclestone offered the prospects: "One here [Watkins Glen] if things work out, one at Long Beach, one at either Chicago or Las Vegas, and another at Indianapolis if they change their rules to allow our cars."[58] The invocation of Indianapolis Motor Speedway informed the long game of Bernie Ecclestone. Indeed, the U.S. Grand Prix would appear at the famed facility 20 years hence. By contrast, perhaps unknown to Ecclestone, the time clock of the Formula One Toyota Grand Prix of Long Beach was already winding down.

The expansion view of Bernie Ecclestone notably and neatly converged with the Saudi sponsorships of the 1980 world champion Williams team. Of note, Saudi Arabia was—and is—the largest exporter of oil and natural gas in the world. Ecclestone was soon to cast his colonization forces far beyond provincial Europe and the Americas, to the oil states of the Middle East, the oligarchs of the former Soviet Union, and more deeply along the petroleum-producing Pacific Rim. It was a global strategic

plan for sporting domination that had
much more in common with ExxonMo-
bil, Royal Dutch Shell, BP, and Vladimir
Putin's petro-*stroika*, than with the ven-
ue-captive fan base of Formula One. To
wit, the inaugural Malaysian Grand Prix
was underwritten with the title sponsorship of Petronas. Petronas was the
Malaysian-nationalized petroleum conglomerate that originated from Royal
Dutch Shell oil exploration concessions
in the 1960s and—not surprisingly—the
1973 Arab oil embargo.

The 1980 U.S. Grand Prix at Watkins
Glen was thus packed away amid signals
crossed, potential hope from the rebel
base, tainted with potential for financial failure from the post-race reckoning. Less than two months after the event
was won by Alan Jones, the struggling
enterprise pushed closer to closure. "The
Watkins Glen Grand Prix Corporation,"
ran news from nearby Ithaca, New York,
"defaulted today on a $104,000 bond
payment."[59] The failed payment was regular interest on the bond offering in 1971
by the Schuyler Industrial Development
Agency. It was the second such failed
bond payment of 1980.

Brabham owner and FOCA principal Bernie
Ecclestone assembled the World Federation
of Motor Sport in 1980, a breakaway from the
FISA Formula One series. Ecclestone teased
potential 1981 Federation race events at Watkins Glen, Long Beach, Chicago, Indianapolis, and Las Vegas. History, however, records
only a single World Federation of Motorsport
event, the rain-soaked and heavily asterisked
open of the 1981 season (Rick Lake collection).

Amid the disclosure, the former apparent savior of the U.S. Grand Prix and the
Grand Prix Corporation offered comment. "I don't have the foggiest idea of how to
unravel their (the corporation's) financial difficulties," stated a terse David Schlosser.
"We don't know how to work with these people if they're not straight with us."[60] The
comments by Schlosser were a remarkable departure from his infectious optimism
prior to the race. Further, the implied lack of transparency directed at the quasi-public Grand Prix Corporation recalled similar accusations in Long Beach just five years
before. Early in 1981, the Grand Prix Corporation would then descend into irrevers-
ible bankruptcy. One unsecured creditor of note was Bernie Ecclestone and FOCA,
then owed $800,000 for the appearances and expenses of their member teams at the
1980 U.S. Grand Prix, including Ecclestone's Brabham works, Chapman's Team Lotus,
and Williams Grand Prix Engineering.

The failed bond payment thus marked the point at which the Watkins Glen
Grand Prix Corporation nosed over into the inevitable death spiral, the venerable
post-war air bird doomed to auger in. The same corporate failure, however, marked
the definitive rebirth of the Caesars Palace Grand Prix concept. In 1981, the inaugural

Caesars Palace Grand Prix was to be held on the second weekend of October, the autumn splendor of upstate New York cast in hues of green and gold, to be supplanted by the unholy union of Czar and Caesar wagering at the felt of Las Vegas, behind tall *stacks*—of green and gold.

***

"Alvin I. Malnik, a Florida financier with alleged business connections to organized crime," read the opening reports from the New Jersey Casino Control Commission hearings, "tried to buy the Caesars Palace Casino in Las Vegas in 1975, the president of Caesars World, Inc. said."[61] Taken from the testimony of William McElnea on September 10, 1980, the suggestion of the alleged number two in the national organized crime syndicate purchasing a state-regulated Las Vegas gambling property should have sent a tremor through the mobster foundations of Caesar. Mention of Malnik as Las Vegas landlord to the concessionaire Caesar should also have rattled the desks of the Nevada and New Jersey gambling control bodies, let alone the underpinnings of the entire gambling industry. Rather, it was simply the overture of a command performance, the tragedy of Caesar performed for a rapt post–Abscam New Jersey audience, with national press in attendance to tally the stab wounds. Further, McElnea's testimony dovetailed precisely into the voice recordings of Alvin Malnik on the Abscam tapes. Further underscored was the essential premise that Meyer Lansky and the organized crime syndicate-controlled Caesars Palace from its inception, along with the various Caesars and their posturing praetorians.[62]

William McElnea testified as well that Caesars World "never seriously considered selling the casino to Malnik."[63] Nonetheless, McElnea confirmed that the sale-leaseback concept was not shelved until *after* the Caesars Pocono Resorts, Sky Lake, and Cricket Club arrangements were splashed public in 1975. The Casino Control Commission was thus troubled by the notion that the sale was considered—however lightly—and, further, that the information was withheld until five years later by the president of Caesars World, Inc.

Clifford Perlman, the much-maligned chairman of Caesars World, was next to provide the press fodder, admitting to the Commission panel that he knew Alvin Malnik and Sam Cohen "allegedly had ties to organized crime."[64] Rather than avoid improprieties, Perlman plunged headlong in the 1970s to formally connect himself and his state-regulated enterprise with those organized crime allegations. In the case of Cohen, Perlman acted to join an enterprise with a convicted felon. Further, Perlman did so contrary to the explicit demands of Nevada gambling regulators. Given the accumulated evidence, it might be supposed that Alvin Malnik and Clifford Perlman occupied proximate strata on the organizational chart of what writer Paul Coates described as "the interwoven mobs which make up the national crime syndicate."[65] One might also conjure an image of Malnik, Perlman, and Cohen, serving their terms on the requisite corporate planning committees.

Cliff Perlman further acknowledged that he intentionally withheld his awareness of the Malnik and Cohen allegations from the Caesars World board. "Business deals answerable to stockholders are different from personal involvement," as Perlman swung wild for the Commission. "Corporate deals were sound investments and the personal deals did not affect the corporation."[66] Perlman's logic was the gambler's tell of the wide-eyed, risk-prone crap shooter. Perlman bizarrely ignored the strict regulatory requirements of his massive gambling enterprise, even more so as he testified before a regulatory body. The comments also served up Clifford Perlman's ego. "They had an attitude," recalled Caesars World, Inc., counsel Bruce Aguilera of Clifford Perlman and Stuart Perlman. "'They're going to license us, we're the best.' They got a little cocky with [New Jersey regulators] and their attorneys got cocky."[67] Indeed, the daring and arrogance of Clifford Perlman eventually served up his own demise.

The Commission also learned of the failed efforts by Caesars World to extricate the corporation from its Caesars Poconos Resorts lease and Sky Lake contract obligations with Alvin Malnik. "A $15.25 million offer by Caesars World to get out of business deals with two alleged organized crime associates," read the reports, "was rejected."[68] The offer was rejected directly by Alvin Malnik, along with a demand for $18.75 million. Whether a lowball by Caesars World, or hardball by Malnik, the alleged number two in the national organized crime syndicate continued to own a Caesars-branded property, while he also derived a significant positive cash flow, and paid down the underlying mortgage from the Teamster Central State Pension Fund.

Perhaps sensing opportunity from the bombshell testimonies of McElnea and Perlman, the New Jersey Casino Control Commission then proceeded boldly into the Palace of Caesar. The Commission probed indelicately, and they also pressed names. The scope of the New Jersey hearings operated to mock the frequent flat-footing of Nevada regulators. On questioning, Perlman claimed not to be aware that Jerome Zarowitz held over $200,000 in current debentures in Caesars World, Inc. On the Zarowitz thread, the question then came, "What if you had accused the [former] owners of skimming?" "If I had accused them of stealing," Perlman replied weakly, "we would not have gotten Caesars Palace."[69]

Turning to the subject of Cal Kovens' role in the construction of the Cricket Club, "Did it occur to you Kovens might be ripping you off?" Again, Clifford Perlman offered a tone-deaf response: "I think he was just inept."[70] The Kovens question, however, tipped the Teamsters Pension Fund real estate fraud for which Kovens and Jimmy Hoffa were imprisoned. If only the Commission had requested that Clifford Perlman reconcile Irving Kovens as an original equity owner of Caesars Palace, with brother Calvin Kovens as the builder of the Cricket Club. A veritable coup at the Forum.

Alvin Malnik continued to stand as central specter for the interrogatories of the New Jersey Casino Control Commission. On prompt from his attorney, however, Clifford Perlman sought to distance himself from the alleged number two. "I defended him at first," bemoaned Perlman of Malnik. "I made a huge mistake. Public confidence in this industry requires a high degree of circumspection."[71]

The chairman of Caesars World, Inc., might well have been reading from note cards. Further, circumspection was an attribute that appeared largely lost on Perlman. Cliff Perlman's protest of Alvin Malnik, however, must also be reckoned with the Abscam tapes. "I know that as far as Cliff is concerned," Howard Criden stated, "they're partners."[72] Malnik and Perlman might then be presumed to have sorted his public plea over a fine meal at The Forge. Commission members were thus further alarmed, as they also made their own notes. "The New Jersey Casino Control Commission," sources said, "is likely to render trouble unto Caesars."[73]

One letter-writer to FBI director William Webster then summarized the stains of Abscam upon Caesar, however unintentionally. "The Roman Empire fell because of corruption," urged the hand-written note, "and we must seek out and remove corrupt members of our government."[74] Another simply wrote, "Hang them all."[75]

On November 13, 1980, the New Jersey Casino Control Commission published its decision on the permanent licensing application of Caesars Boardwalk Regency and its qualified directors, officers, and employees. "This Commission is not able to find by clear and compelling evidence that Clifford Perlman," concluded the finding, "possesses the good character, honesty, and integrity demanded by the Casino Control Act. Accordingly, Clifford Perlman is not qualified."[76] The voluntary hiatus of Clifford Perlman from Caesars' New Jersey operations was thus rendered

On November 13, 1980, the New Jersey Casino Control Commission ruled that Clifford Perlman and Stuart Perlman were not fit for a gambling license to operate the Caesars Boardwalk Regency casino. Names like Meyer Lansky, Alvin Malnik, Sam Cohen, and Jerome Zarowitz would plague their licensing applications. The Commission also ruled that, in order to allow the Caesars Boardwalk Regency to operate, Clifford Perlman must be removed from Caesars World, Inc. and Caesars Palace in Las Vegas. Perlman appealed to the New Jersey Supreme Court. Pending the outcome, though, Clifford Perlman would preside over the 1981 Caesars Palace Grand Prix (New Jersey Casino Control Commission).

State of New Jersey

In re Boardwalk Regency Casino Application
Cite as 10 *N.J.A.R* 295

IN THE MATTER OF THE APPLICATIONS
OF BOARDWALK REGENCY CORPORATION
AND THE JEMM COMPANY FOR CASINO
LICENSES

Decided: November 13, 1980
Approved for Publication by the Casino Control Commission
April 8, 1988

SYNOPSIS

Boardwalk Regency Corporation and the Jemm Company (lessor of the casino hotel operated by Boardwalk Regency) applied to the Casino Control Commission for casino licenses. Following a hearing by the Commission, a conditional license was granted to Boardwalk Regency and a limited owner-lessee license was granted to Jemm.

The main obstacle to licensure for Boardwalk Regency was the good character qualifications of four individuals required to be qualified. All were executives of Caesars World, Inc., parent company of Boardwalk Regency. The Commission, after consideration of the evidence, found that two of the individuals -- Clifford Perlman, Chairman of the Board of CWI, and Stuart Perlman, Vice-Chairman of the CWI board, and both major shareholders – did not establish their good character and were not qualified.

The Commission determined, however, that it had the authority to issue a casino license despite the disqualifying individuals, provided the license was conditioned s as to eliminate the influence of the unacceptable qualifiers. *N.S.J.A* 5:12-75 and -105. Such conditions must remove any unacceptable individuals from the categories of persons required to be qualified. In addition, there should be good reasons why the public interest would be better served through conditional licensure than through license denial and appointment of a conservator.

Accordingly, the Commission granted the license on the condition that Boardwalk Regency either separate the unqualified individuals from the corporation or withdraw from casino operations in New Jersey. The applicant was given a 30-day interim period in which to decide which of the two options it would elect.

permanent. The Commission issued the same determination for Stuart Perlman, Clifford's brother and vice-chairman of Caesars World, Inc.

The New Jersey report was distinctly devoid of spin. "Mr. Perlman in a very real sense," read the Perlman decision, "delivered his company into the hands of Mr. Malnik, Mr. Cohen, and Mr. Cohen's sons."[77] Unlike the State of Nevada—where regulators appeared to know much and did little—the New Jersey report was also devoid of a gambling license for Clifford Perlman. For William McElnea the decision was split, with one Commission member submitting a dissenting opinion. "Deliberate initiation, cultivation and maintenance of the relationships with Alvin Malnik, Sam Cohen, the Teamsters Pension Fund, Allen Dorfman and his insurance agency, in the face of this widespread official disapproval is evidence of a lack of good character," was the blunt dissent. "For all of the foregoing reasons, William H. McElnea is not qualified."[78]

New Jersey regulators also determined, despite the license rejection of the Perlmans, "that it had authority to issue a casino license despite the disqualifying individuals, provided the license was conditioned so as to eliminate the influence of the unacceptable qualifiers."[79] The conditional licensing of the Caesars Boardwalk Regency itself, then, might imply the good offices of New Jersey Governor Brendan Byrne.

Such conditional licensing of the Caesars gambling resort in Atlantic City also brought an ultimatum. "If Clifford Perlman and Stuart Perlman refuse to leave Caesars World and all subsidiaries, including those in Nevada," reported the *Associated Press*, "the state Casino Control Commission said their company would be denied a license and the 527-room Caesars Boardwalk Regency would be put under control of a state-appointed conservator."[80]

Knives thus delivered unto Caesar at the Forum, brothers Clifford and Stuart Perlman would pay heed to the line in the sand of the New Jersey shore, at least temporarily. The Perlman brothers accepted an unpaid leave of absence, while they also prepared to elevate potential legal remedies. Ensuing court actions hovered over Caesars World, Inc. and Caesars Palace for the next two years. In the meantime, though, Clifford Perlman would hover over the 1981 Caesars Palace Grand Prix. From the program, to the paddock, to the penthouse, and the podium, Clifford Perlman would be ever-present, while the trackside signage of Alvin Malnik's Caesars Pocono Resorts would provide backdrop, if not a hint of subtext.

IX

Course of Events

The Inaugural Caesars Palace Grand Prix, the End of the Emperor's Reign

Hail Caesar; read this schedule. (*Julius Caesar* 3.1.3)

The 1981 Formula One season opened precisely as Bernie Ecclestone had suggested at the 1980 season finale at Watkins Glen, an utter impasse between FOCA and FISA. To wit, the escalating war of words between Ecclestone as the head of FOCA, and Jean-Marie Balestre at the head of FISA, had turned to hostile actions in 1981. At stake between the boardroom combatants was quite simply the hearts, minds, soul—and control—of the pinnacle of motorsport.

In a protracted dispute over the propriety of technical regulations and the financial future of the sport, the flashpoint was symbolized by the aerodynamic side skirts pioneered in 1978 by Colin Chapman. FISA had removed their existence from the rulebook, a position largely supported by the membership of the Grand Prix Drivers Association. FOCA, conversely, demanded their technical inclusion, while it simultaneously endeavored to counter the voices of its contracted drivers. The skirts also struck at the "powerplant superiority" ideology of the manufacturers—Ferrari, Renault, and Alfa Romeo—versus the aerodynamic advantage of skirts afforded the constructors and their commoditized Ford-Cosworth engines, Brabham, Williams, Lotus, Tyrell, et al. Elimination of skirts could thus be presumed to restore a competitive advantage to the manufacturers. Finally, though, the clash was personified by the ego-play and intransigence of the principals themselves, Bernie Ecclestone and Jean-Marie Balestre.

With a debut to forget, FOCA and its rebel World Federation of Motor Sport sought to deliver the traditional season-opening South African Grand Prix on its own terms, with skirts in place—but without sanction by FISA. Reigning FISA Formula One world champion Alan Jones then played to the FOCA message, while he also drove a wedge in the rank-and-file of the drivers. Jones was adamant as well that the South African Grand Prix should count toward the 1981 world championship. "That's why I'm here. That's why my car is arriving," insisted Jones. "I am here to win at Kyalami on Saturday."[1] Once again, the livery of Jones' Williams machine was emblazoned with Saudi firms, Saudia Airlines, Albilad, and TAG, firms also connected to the Saudi royal family.

Carlos Reutemann (#2 Williams) won the World Federation of Sport South African Grand Prix on February 7, 1981, at the Kyalami circuit in South Africa. Nigel Mansell (#12 Lotus) finished eighth. The following Long Beach Grand Prix on March 15, 1981, was the official opening round of the 1981 FISA Formula One season. Essex Overseas Petroleum livery of Mansell's machine would transition to John Player tobacco over the course of the 1981 season (author's collection).

FOCA teams trotted 19 mounts to the gate for the South African Grand Prix, all of them powered by Ford. Notably, Ferrari, Renault, and Alfa Romeo refused to compete, delaying the highly anticipated debut of Mario Andretti alongside Bruno Giacomelli. Carlos Reutemann won the event over Nelson Piquet and Elio de Angelis, thus forming a Frank Williams, Bernie Ecclestone, and Colin Chapman rout of the podium. Notably, world champion Alan Jones retired in some irony on lap 62, with a failure to his skirt. Despite the bluster of Jones, the 1981 South African Grand Prix was documented with a non-championship asterisk, charitably described in some reports as a Formula *Libre* event, a descriptor recalling the seminal steps toward the 1961 U.S. Grand Prix at Watkins Glen.

The truncated South African Grand Prix did, however, force rapprochement of the warring factions. On March 5, 1980—in a peace brokered by Enzo Ferrari—FOCA and FISA agreed to a truce. "Sliding skirts would be banned, FOCA would control the financial side of Grand Prix racing but FISA would take a cut," reported United Press International, "and a joint FISA-FOCA-sponsors commission would be set up to oversee all Formula One races."[2] A prominent casualty of the hostilities, however, was the Goodyear Tire and Rubber Co. Disgruntled by international discord, Goodyear ended its 15-year run of supplying tires for international Formula racing at all levels. The Goodyear departure was not unlike the parting of PPG from the CART series as the CART-IRL battles raged 15 years hence. Goodyear, however, would return mid-season. Further, Goodyear rubber figured into the fortunes of the Caesars Palace Grand Prix.

Delays to the Argentinian Grand Prix then queued the Toyota Grand Prix of Long Beach as the formal opener of the 1981 Formula One season. Oddly, both Watkins Glen and Las Vegas were listed on the provisional 1981 Formula One calendar, either by way of the FISA regulars or by the thwarted FOCA rebellion. Long Beach thus marked the debut of Mario Andretti with Bruno Giacomelli and the Alfa Romeo team. The great American race car driver was optimistic after a dismal Lotus send-off. The near-runaway of Giacomelli at Watkins Glen further buoyed the performance hopes of the 1978 Formula One world champion. "The Alfa Romeo program is built with such positive attitude and enthusiasm," reflected Andretti of a season's promise. "It's really refreshing."[3] Andretti's homeland open in Long Beach, though, would not bear the marks of a Formula One championship run.

***

The gambling license case of Clifford Perlman, Stuart Perlman, and the Caesars Boardwalk Regency in Atlantic City was the first to pit the newly-enacted licensing laws of New Jersey against the time-honored rule-making in Nevada. The Perlman brothers were understandably determined, then, to wage battle in the New Jersey courts for the right to remain at the helm of Caesars World, Inc., in Los Angeles and their Caesars Palace resort in Las Vegas. Indeed, an appeal was filed with the New Jersey Appellate Court within days of their rejection by the New Jersey Casino Control Commission. With a 16 percent stake in Caesars World worth upwards of $50 million, Clifford and Stuart Perlman certainly had the attention of the investors. The stock implications of the Perlman case, though, struck not only the financial markets but the entertainment industry as well.

Jerrold Perenchio, partner in Tandem Productions, Inc., with famed television and film producers Norman Lear and Bud Yorkin, discussed the purchase of the Caesars World holdings with the Perlman brothers in early 1981. Initial negotiations appeared productive, headed toward a premium purchase of the Perlman stock. Perenchio, though, had a deep history with the origins of Caesars Palace. By his own account, Jerry Perenchio and his wife Robin separately purchased "two points at $50,000 each" of the original 1965 Caesars Palace investment promotion.[4] Although wife Robin Perenchio appears as an owner of record in the early Caesars Palace licensing, Jerry Perenchio does not, suggesting that his ownership may have been concealed by proxy.[5] Further, Jerry Perenchio was credited with making the introduction of the original Jay Sarno–led ownership coalition to the latter Clifford Perlman-Lum's ownership. It was a credit for which Perenchio received a reported $800,000 finder's fee.[6]

Such facilitation and consequent fee perhaps pointed up the rather thin pretense of business introductions, in which syndicated stakeholders were already acquainted. It was a system certainly modeled by Meyer Lansky, receiving a $200,000 finder's fee for "introducing" seller Albert Parvin to purchaser Sam Cohen when the Flamingo Hotel and Casino in Las Vegas was sold on in 1960. Parvin and Cohen certainly knew each other but, in the structure of the organized crime syndicate, someone must be credited with introduction, and that someone must also be paid. It was a cost of business already structured into the gambling deals but—at the same time—typically concealed from unwitting stockholders.

Jerrold Perenchio subsequently testified before the SEC in the wake of the 1969 Caesars Palace transaction to Lum's Inc., a sale from which the unlicensed Jerome Zarowitz collected $3.5 million. In his SEC testimony, Perenchio acknowledged a friendship with Zarowitz, but deflected the Zarowitz payday. "Mr. Zarowitz has never discussed his business with me," testified Perenchio. "He is a friend of mine, but we never discuss our personal business."[7] It should seem inconceivable that two unlicensed owners of Caesars Palace who pulled over $4 million from the same deal did not at least compare zeroes. Nonetheless, Perenchio's testimony stood, apparently uncontested. An ownership stake in Caesars World could thus cause Perenchio to

Jerrold Perenchio of Tandem Productions negotiated for the purchase of Clifford and Stuart Perlman's shares of Caesars World, Inc. in early 1981 amid the order of the New Jersey Casino Control Commission for the brothers to vacate their positions. Perenchio was reportedly paid an $800,000 finder's fee in 1969 for introducing Jay Sarno, Nathan Jacobson, and Stanley Mallin to Clifford Perlman. Perenchio claimed to have an ownership interest in the original Caesars Palace consortium, but did not appear to be documented as an owner-of-record by the Nevada Gaming Commission. Perenchio claimed a friendship with Jerome Zarowitz (author's collection).

be investigated much more deeply by both Nevada and New Jersey regulators as to his relationship with Jerome Zarowitz and potentially, as to Clifford and Stuart Perlman themselves. It was a subject that inevitably invoked the specter of Alvin Malnik and, by extension, Meyer Lansky. Perhaps also inevitable, sale negotiations appeared to terminate on the conjecture.

Concurrently, Alvin Malnik was reposted to the headlines. A $68 million amusement park development in Miami had reportedly ingratiated Malnik to Cricket Club resident Saudi Prince Turki bin Abdulaziz. The comparative irony of the living Saudi prince with the fictitious sheiks of the Abscam sting simply cannot be ignored. Published reports appeared to definitively link the Saudi royal—a *real* one—to the project. Alvin Malnik, however, insisted otherwise. "I have never," protested Malnik to the *Miami Herald*, "been involved in any meeting at any time or any place concerning any matter related to [the development]."[8]

Malnik's protest, however, followed a pattern, a theme deployed for years to deny alleged associations with Meyer Lansky. Nevertheless, Alvin Malnik enjoyed a close relationship with Prince Turki bin Abdulaziz. Ordered home in 1982 by the Saudi King, Prince Turki bin Abdulaziz was soon followed by Alvin Malnik and son Mark "Shareef" Malnik, "deserting South Florida, converting to Islam, adopting Arab names, and living among their wealthy, privileged Saudi friends."[9] For purposes of this Formula One study, such "friends" might have included names like Saudia Airlines, Albilad, and TAG.

As a Saudi deputy defense minister, Prince Turki also counted a well-documented relationship with Saudi arms merchant, international financier—and decadent Las Vegas gambler—Adnan Khashoggi.[10] "Khashoggi had a well-deserved reputation in town as a high roller and hedonist. He gambled from time to time at Caesars but he spread his business around," recalled William D. Weinberger of the international weapons broker. "He had a very *bad* reputation for not paying on time, or in the full amount."[11]

As national headlines splayed the news of Caesar and those Caesar-adjacent, another post emanated directly from the executive offices. On March 27, 1981, William McElnea tendered his resignation from Caesars World, Inc., effective upon a replacement. That replacement also came in a virtual weekend turn. On April 1, 1981, J. Terrence Lanni was elected president of the corporation. As William McElnea departed, though, he also tendered his 450,000 shares of the corporation to Clifford and Stuart Perlman.

Former investment banker William McElnea was credited on Wall Street with somewhat sanitizing the corporate image of Caesars World, Inc., certainly an improvement over the racketeered busts of Jay Sarno, Nathan Jacobson, and Jerome Zarowitz. Conversely, McElnea's performance before the New Jersey Casino Control Commission exposed his somewhat ineffectual oversight of the gambling institution. William D. Weinberger's former supervisor at Caesars World—and to some extent a progenitor of the Caesars Palace Grand Prix concept—thus departed the corporation.

Despite the professed personal reasons for William McElnea's change of pasture, Wall Street inevitably read into the transition. "It seems to indicate that the Perlmans have switched gears. It's clear that Bill [McElnea] has been working for years, raising money, meeting people, making speeches, and negotiating," suggested one gambling industry analyst. "If Cliff was stepping out, Bill would naturally move up. I think Caesars will be taking a dramatically different course."[12]

One month later, the SEC disclosed that Clifford Perlman and brother Stuart had acquired another 4.8 million shares of Caesars World.[13] The cumulative purchase of over 5 million shares—amid a regulatory order to divest—did not go unnoticed in New Jersey, one more ego-stroke of Clifford Perlman that did not play well beyond the proverbial Sky Lake Country Club. Further, Clifford Perlman's dramatically different course through the New Jersey appeals process was to be the path of *most* resistance, a path on which he was steadfast, even as he gazed down upon the construction of the Formula One racing circuit at Caesars Palace.

***

As the Toyota Grand Prix of Long Beach was the official open of the 1981 Formula One season, so too did Long Beach bear the definitive transitions of the U.S. Grand Prix at Watkins Glen, as well as the Caesars Palace Grand Prix in Las Vegas. The vernal equinox of 1981 also pointed up the tangled relationships of the American

Mario Andretti (#22 Alfa Romeo) leads Bruno Giacomelli (#23 Alfa Romeo), Nelson Piquet (#5 Brabham), and Eddie Cheever (#3 Tyrell) at the 1981 Long Beach Grand Prix. The race was won by Alan Jones driving a Williams. Jones' teammate Carlos Reutemann was second followed by Piquet. Mario Andretti qualified sixth and finished fourth. The Alfa machines would be less competitive as the season wore on (Rick Lake collection).

venues vying for Formula One theater. For Caesars Palace, a grand opening; for Watkins Glen, a grand closing. Further, the 1981 Long Beach event told the competitive fortunes of Mario Andretti, Bruno Giacomelli and their V-12 Alfa Romeo mounts.

Ricardo Patrese led Long Beach qualifying with a 1:19.399 in his Arrows-Ford. Alan Jones and Carlos Reutemann paired in qualifying for the Albilad Williams Racing team, second and third, respectively, at 1:19.408 and 1:20.149. Nelson Piquet was fourth on the grid for Bernie Ecclestone's Brabham works with a 1:20.289. From there, qualifying times dropped off noticeably. Mario Andretti was sixth at 1:20.476, over a second adrift of Patrese. Bruno Giacomelli—the qualifying darling of the 1980 U.S. Grand Prix—was ninth, another quarter-second off Andretti.

The 80-lap race then bore out similarly. Ricardo Patrese led through the quarter-mark until fuel feed issues dropped the Arrows pilot. Alan Jones, Carlos Reutemann, and Nelson Piquet then controlled the balance of the race, as well as the podium. Mario Andretti improved to fourth at the finish, albeit dropping nearly three quarters of a second per lap to Jones and the winning Albilad Williams. Andretti's three championship points on the day were to be the highlight of yet another frustrating season. Nearly 40 years removed, Mario Andretti recalled the disappointment of 1981.

"There was some cheating going on [in 1981] and it started with Brabham," recalled the 1978 Formula One world champion. "To reduce the downforce aspect of it, the cars had to be raised. Going out of the pits, you had to clear a square box, so the car would be a certain ride height. Coming back in the pits, you had to clear the same thing."[14] Brabham chief engineer Gordon Murray had indeed devised a hydraulic jacking system to lower the Brabham machines once they exited the pits. "The first time that it was deployed," continued Andretti, "Nelson Piquet lapped the field."[15]

Carlo Chiti, however—chief engineer for the Alfa-Romeo team—refused to follow the leader. "I said 'For God sakes, everybody's doing it!" reflected Mario Andretti. "We're getting our clock cleaned here."[16] Nearly 40 years on, Mario Andretti still cringes at the certain decline of his Alfa opportunity. "The reason I joined Alfa-Romeo from Lotus was because Giacomelli, the very last race of 1980 at Watkins Glen," Andretti concluded. "He led almost the whole race."[17]

Mario Andretti thus settled in for a long season of discontent. Andretti and Giacomelli combined for 13 retirements over the next 14 Formula One events. In fact, the two drivers would be tied on points headed into the season-ending Caesars Palace Grand Prix, three-to-three, Andretti's points at the Long Beach opener and Giacomelli's points at the penultimate round in Canada. It was a cruel summer indeed for the Alfa Romeo pairing.

From Long Beach, Bernie Ecclestone seized the soap box to champion the commercial opportunities of Formula One, boasting that 700 million people in Europe had watched the prior year's Long Beach offering. "I know they used to call the Indianapolis 500 the 'Brickyard Oval.' Well, for sponsors of successful Formula One teams, every Grand Prix track around the world is made of something much different than brick," claimed Ecclestone from California. "It's made of bricks cast in gold."[18]

Fact-check of the households notwithstanding, Ecclestone made his point. Going forward, Bernie Ecclestone's control of the broadcast feeds would become the foundation of his burgeoning wealth. The Albilad-Saudia-TAG Williams of reigning world champion Alan Jones then made its own point. Grand Prix sponsorship was fast becoming a weaponized nexus of gold, green, luxury brands, petro-dollars, international intrigue, unrepentant gamblers, and perhaps—fighter jets and anti-tank weapons.

At the same time, Bernie Ecclestone and FOCA posted their deadline to Watkins Glen for payment of the FOCA fees still owed from the 1980 U.S. Grand Prix. Henry Valent, Malcolm Currie, and the Watkins Glen Grand Prix Corporation thus had until May 1, 1981, to make good on the $800,000 debt. Three days removed from Long Beach, financial consultant David Schlosser of New York was sought for comment. "Our investor group has been out of the picture since a week or two after the race last October," offered Schlosser. "We told the Glen people that we're available, but they've never contacted us."[19] The relationship of the Watkins Glen Grand Prix Corporation and David Schlosser had clearly taken a hard turn.

State agencies were also reported with continued efforts to assist with supplemental funding, including the office of New York Senator Alphonse D'Amato, notably a name circulating real-time in the Abscam influence-peddling probe. Direct government assistance for the debts of the Watkins Glen Grand Prix Corporation to Bernie Ecclestone, however, were a virtually insurmountable sell. One state administrator appeared to share the same frustrations as David Schlosser. "We are awaiting a reorganization plan from the corporation," stated Bern Rotman of the State Commerce Department. "But at what price, is it an important attraction?"[20]

Less than two weeks before the Watkins Glen deadline, William D. Weinberger of Caesars Palace submitted a rather furtive plan to the Clark County Commission for a revised Caesars Palace Grand Prix concept. The newly-proposed 2.5-mile track would deploy the north parking lot of Caesars Palace, fallow property further to the north (owned by the Summa Corporation), and—remarkably—a one-quarter-mile stretch of the famed Las Vegas Strip. Badly disappointed in 1980, Weinberger refused to betray his hand. "I don't think we're ready for comment," hedged Weinberger. "I don't want to raise any false hopes or raise any undue excitement."[21] Nonetheless, details of the race package called for a section of the Las Vegas Strip to be closed for four hours a day over a three-day race weekend, tentatively scheduled for October 16–18, 1981.

For Watkins Glen, the FOCA deadline would come and go. For Bernie Ecclestone, the carry on close to $1 million supremely tested the supreme's patience. The Formula One Commission of FISA—steered by Ecclestone—then dropped the U.S. Grand Prix at Watkins Glen from the 1981 calendar. Bernie Ecclestone also fumed in public. "They'll never have another Grand Prix at the Glen while I'm still involved in Formula One racing, not in my lifetime," Ecclestone stated from London. "That track has been a plague upon our sport. Now that we finally got rid of it, there's no way we want it back, ever."[22] Leaving scant room for misinterpretation, Bernie Ecclestone once again made his point.

For William D. Weinberger, the failure of Watkins Glen triggered a phone call—from Caesars Palace in Las Vegas, to the London office of Bernie Ecclestone. "I told him," Weinberger recalled of the trans-Atlantic conversation, "'You know we both want to do this thing.'"[23] On May 5, 1981, news of the apparently resurrected Caesars Palace Grand Prix began to push around the globe. "Jean-Marie Balestre, president of the International Auto Sports Federation," reported a story from Monaco, "said the Formula One commission voted to recommend to FISA's executive committee that the [Las Vegas] race be held."[24]

Mario Andretti, suffering through a dismal season in Formula One, then set his sights for redemption at the May 24, 1981, running of the Indianapolis 500, and a contracted ride for CART director U.E. "Pat" Patrick. Excluded from contesting the pole due to Formula One commitments in Belgium, Andretti's STP-sponsored Patrick Wildcat was qualified eighth-fast by veteran Wally Dallenbach. Mario Andretti was thus relegated to start at the rear of the field, 32nd in the traditional field of 33.

Notably, the 1981 Indianapolis 500 was also excluded from the PPG CART Championship, contested solely as a leg of the 1981–1982 *USAC* championship. Like Caesars World chairman Clifford Perlman in New Jersey, the outcome of the 1981 Indianapolis 500 would be fiercely contested in hearings long after the event itself. As with the presence of Clifford Perlman, the conclusion of the 1981 Indianapolis 500 also hovered over the 1981 Caesars Palace Grand Prix.

***

Revelations from the FBI Abscam case continued to unfold in 1981 as the New Jersey Appeals Court considered the divestiture case of Clifford and Stuart Perlman and their Caesars World and Caesars Palace holdings. In the now-infamous FBI tape

Mario Andretti and his victorious #40 Patrick Wildcat pose with the world-famous yard of bricks at Indianapolis Motor Speedway on May 25, 1981. Andretti was declared the winner of the 1981 Indianapolis 500 after Tom Binford of USAC penalized Bobby Unser for passing cars during the final caution period. Bobby Unser's car owner Roger Penske, however, pushed back in protest. Final determination of the race winner was not made until the week before the 1981 Caesars Palace Grand Prix (author collection).

recordings, Clifford Perlman was implicated by attorney Howard Criden as being close to both Meyer Lansky and Alvin Malnik. Further, Criden offered definition to the presumed mentorship relation of Lansky toward Malnik, particularly as to the buying and selling of Las Vegas casinos. "He [Lansky] has been grooming Alvin for 100 years so-to-speak," stated Criden on tape, "OK? So, the message to me was 'Talk to Alvin.' That's all he [Lansky] said. He knows that I know Alvin and that Alvin trusts me."[25]

Howard Criden also explained the role of Meyer Lansky in the multi-million-dollar business of skimming gambling profits in Las Vegas, one of the most prodigious taps of liquidity in the gangster-economy of organized crime. "So early in the game, it was decided that they had to have somebody that everybody had implicit trust in," continued Criden to the FBI operative. "That guy became Meyer. Absolute, unequivocal law when it came to cutting up the pot."[26] Attorney Criden described the operations of the Las Vegas skim as run on a "very businesslike basis,"[27] no doubt checking the tactical boxes in the long-game strategic plan of the national crime syndicate.

The "cutting up the pot" in Las Vegas was of noteworthy controversy—and inquiry—in the days before and after the grand opening of Caesars Palace. "Raymond Patriarca, New England Rackets chief, and Gerardo (Jerry) Catena, leader of a Cosa Nostra gang in New Jersey," reported the *Los Angeles Times* in August of 1966, "each hold [*sic*] a 10% interest in Caesars Palace."[28] "Anthony (Fat Tony) Salerno" and "Vincent (Jimmy Blue Eyes) Alo" also received mention in the report.[29] The reader will also recall that the 1966 Nevada investigation retreated from Caesars Palace rather quickly and rather quietly.

Ultimately, Howard Criden delivered Alvin Malnik to the FBI sting operation, certainly bolstering the Lansky and Malnik bona fides of the middleman attorney. Understandably circumspect, Malnik nonetheless described deal points involving the Aladdin Hotel and Casino in Las Vegas for benefit of the fictitious Abscam oil millionaires. Malnik also positioned himself much more deeply inside the gambling industry than Nevada or New Jersey regulators wanted to fathom—allegedly.

"I'm persona non grata in [Nevada]," stated Malnik, "I mean, I can't be licensed. I can't even appear on the deal."[30] Alvin Malnik's command of Latin thus apparently ingratiated him to Caesar, just as he did to Middle Eastern business concerns, both real and imagined. Miamian Alvin Malnik as a persistent shadow figure in both Nevada and New Jersey also appeared to fortify context for his engagements with Clifford Perlman, the Sky Lake Country Club, the Cricket Club, the Caesars Pocono Resorts, and the Caesars Palace hotel-casino in Las Vegas.

Persistent headline mentions of Clifford Perlman and Alvin Malnik also served to undermine the Perlman cause in the New Jersey appeals court. One month after the latest Abscam splash, the verdict was delivered. "The top two officials of Caesars World Inc. must leave the corporation," a state appeals court ruled on July 21, 1981, "and its profitable Caesars Boardwalk Regency hotel casino in Atlantic City."[31] Once again, Clifford and Stuart were being shown the exit, this time by decree of the docket. Once again, the Perlmans were defiant, this time with a motion to the New Jersey Supreme Court.

J. Terrence Lanni, the newly-minted president of Caesars World, delivered the prepared response. "Today's appellate court decision intensifies the concern that our boards of directors have had for some time," Lanni said from Los Angeles, "about the

The banner signage of the Caesars Pocono Resorts owned by Alvin Malnik was a trackside fixture during the run of the Caesars Palace Grand Prix. Indeed, Malnik owned the properties while Caesars World leased and operated the honeymoon resort facilities (courtesy LVCVA News Bureau).

desirability of continuing operations in the state of New Jersey."[32] With such intense prepared remarks from his Caesars World president, Clifford Perlman could not resist inveighing from high to the national media.

"Suffice it to say New Jersey is an area that does not represent any economic opportunity today," stated Perlman on the ruling. "None."[33] Perlman's obvious ignorance of the issue in the mirror was served like a politician on parade. Further, the public jab at friend and governor Brendan Byrne, might have necessitated another reconciliation over dinner at The Forge in Miami. Cliff Perlman also compared the fortunes of the Atlantic City market to the long-standing economic engine of Caesars Palace in Las Vegas. "Since Caesars Palace earns more than five times what New Jersey earns," Perlman suggested, "there is a huge persuasion to not disturb the techniques of Caesars Palace. They are not easily replaceable."[34] Clifford Perlman's mention of "techniques" was instructive. It also underscored the compelling concerns of the New Jersey gambling bodies, as well as of the Las Vegas business model sketched by Alvin Malnik.

Clifford Perlman and Stuart Perlman moved forward in their appeal to the New Jersey Supreme Court. Meanwhile, the court of public opinion had already considered the evidence, as well as Cliff Perlman's ego. On the cumulative public statements of Lanni and Perlman, one New Jersey pundit leaned in. "That sounds like they are thinking about getting out," ran the opinion. "If so, good riddance."[35]

In the days after the New Jersey appeals court ruled against Clifford Perlman, the fate of the Watkins Glen Grand Prix Corporation appeared in parallel. "There will be no Grand Prix in Watkins this year," lamented Malcolm Currie. "We really have no more appeals. The governor's money is not forthcoming. As far as I know that's it."[36] Henry Valent and Malcolm Currie then huddled privately with the corporation lawyers to prepare for the public inevitable. On August 13, 1981, the Watkins Glen Grand Prix Corporation filed for bankruptcy protection under Chapter XI of the federal bankruptcy code, and the long downward spiral into the proverbial muck of the Watkins Glen infield was complete. In the bankruptcy filing, the debt to Bernie Ecclestone's Formula One Constructors Association was listed at $839,000.[37] With the fate of Watkins Glen sealed closed by the bankruptcy filing, it was finally time for William D. Weinberger of Caesars Palace to get excited.

* * *

"A long-standing bet will finally pay off for Caesars Palace and the City of Las Vegas this October 17th," heralded the deck of the national sports pages. "That's when the Caesars Palace Grand Prix will be run on a specially constructed track adjacent to the sprawling hotel."[38] The first pressers landed on the same date of Malcolm Currie's plaintive lament from the headquarters of the Watkins Glen Grand Prix Corporation. Notably, Bill Weinberger's launch of the press push for the Caesars Palace Grand Prix no longer danced around the perceived competition with Watkins Glen for a Grand Prix date. Nor was Caesars Palace relegated to third on the depth chart of the American Grand Prix events. With a race date in mid–October, William D. Weinberger's Caesars Palace Grand Prix was effectively the newly-struck United States Grand Prix.

"The biggest obstacle was that people didn't believe a corporate entity could

The groundbreaking ceremony for the 1981 Caesars Palace Grand Prix united gamblers, gears, gravel, and Greco-Roman goddesses. The attendees in business suits are identified as, from left, William D. Weinberger (Caesars Palace VP Casino Marketing), Harry Wald (Caesars Palace President and Chief Operating Officer), Ron Harris (Corrao Construction Project Manager), and Kevin Malley (Caesars Palace Sr. VP Hotel Operations). The caricaturized Caesar and his colleagues are not identified. Vehicle appears to be the Vel's–Parnelli Jones VPJ4 that Mario Andretti raced at the 1976 Long Beach Grand Prix (courtesy LVCVA News Bureau).

put on a race," stated Weinberger. "But we had confidence; we've been putting on sports events for years."[39] Indeed, Clifford Perlman and Weinberger's father, William S. Weinberger, had both championed premier-level professional sporting events at Caesars Palace for over a decade. The junior William D. Weinberger then picked up the sports promotions mantle as Caesars Palace vice president of casino marketing. Notably, William D. Weinberger would stage the penultimate match of Muhammad Ali's career, an eleventh-round technical knockout by Larry Holmes over the aging former heavyweight champion after Ali's trainer Angelo Dundee stopped the fight. The October 2, 1980, match was the only loss by stoppage ever suffered by "The Greatest."

The three-point sports marketing model employed by Bill Weinberger was that developed by his forebears; push the event extensively to the sports and gambling markets, engage the luxury-branded trappings of Caesar around the event, and make absolutely certain that event-goers must walk through the Caesars Palace casino pay zone to return to their rooms. Unencumbered access to the casino was, after all, the core value of the core business. The marketing campaign was also the same model used to great success for the showroom appearances of Frank Sinatra, a booking that always boosted the count room take, and the attendant *honoraria* to Miami and New York—allegedly.

In the marketing push from his office, Bill Weinberger also engaged the SCCA in coordinating the message. SCCA would indeed be present as the domestic sanctioning body for Formula One events. Further, the 1981 SCCA Can-Am series was scheduled to wrap its season in Las Vegas alongside the FISA-SCCA Formula One finale. SCCA press also quoted Weinberger on the prospects for the Caesars Palace Grand Prix, "world's greatest cars and drivers," "classic location," "one of the most prestigious sporting events in the world."[40] In a piece prepared prior to the Watkins Glen bankruptcy, Bill Weinberger also noted that he was "pleased to present the second Formula One event in the United States."[41] It was a sharp departure from Weinberger's two-year refrain, "but not at the expense of the Watkins Glen race."[42]

Pre-race publicity also engaged Chris Pook of the Long Beach Grand Prix Association, special "Grand Prix Consultant" for Caesars Palace and effectively, the producer of the event. "FISA granted the hotel a four-year run on the race and Caesars is spending $6 million in the inaugural event," Pook told the press, "half of that for construction of the 2.2-mile track. But that's nothing compared to the estimated $200 million that the city will get back in returns for this year alone."[43]

The Long Beach travel and pitch man was throwing big numbers, while he was also earning one, "a reputed $100,000 fee."[44] "When you mention the name Las Vegas and Caesars Palace," Pook continued on-message, "they're synonymous with promotion, with the leisure world, with activities with marketing."[45] The gush was as if lifted from a glossy Caesars Palace travel brochure in the Long Beach offices of "Western Promotions & Marketing, Inc."[46]

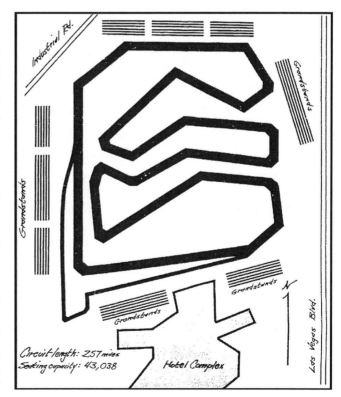

Crude early sketch of the Caesars Palace Grand Prix Formula One circuit depicts the essential layout of five tight fingered turn configurations. Las Vegas Strip is at right. Caesars Palace resort buildings are at bottom (author's collection).

Mention of the 2.2-mile course by Chris Pook also pointed up one of the few remaining obstacles confronting the Caesars Palace Grand Prix. Specifically, there was no Formula One race circuit on which to conduct a Formula One race event. In fact, as of mid–June 1981, ground had not yet been broken for the Grand Prix construction project. "We're hoping to have the drawing completed by the third week of this month," Corrao Construction of Las Vegas indicated, "and start construction by the first of July. It's going to be a push."[47] The construction project then pointed up the plentitude of pacts struck by William D. Weinberger.

Renowned gaming and hospitality architect Anthony Marnell provided the design proper of the Caesars Palace Grand Prix circuit. "We were the Palace architect," recalled Marnell. "We did all those sporting events for Cliff Perlman and the gang."[48] Marnell had notably designed the Caesars Palace Fantasy Tower as well as the Abscam-stained Caesars Palace Boardwalk Regency. Anthony Marnell's Formula One circuit design, though, was required to be approved by FISA, the international sanctioning body of Formula One. "We didn't know very much about the physical requirements of a Grand Prix track. So, Caesars sent me to Europe," continued Marnell. "I met Bernie [Ecclestone] in London and I met him at Monza and we went over all the requirements. We went back and forth with our architects and theirs and came up with a track layout and the specifications that it had to be built to."[49]

"The original thought," suggested Anthony Marnell, "was to have it go out onto the strip as part of the race. That meant rebuilding part of the strip and that is part of a federal highway. Even back then there were permissions that no one was going to get in time."[50] The notion of Formula One racing along the world-famous Las Vegas Strip thus began a 40-year unrequited crusade that continues to this day.

FISA reviewed not only the length of the circuit, but configurations of the turns, estimated speeds of the straightaways, calculated qualifying times, race-average speeds of the track, safety run-off areas, pit and paddock facilities, and—to the point of Watkins Glen—hospitality offerings and host amenities. Naturally, Caesars Palace could anticipate superlative marks for the latter. FISA analysts, though, also reviewed the composition and thickness of the asphalt paving.

Indeed, contrary to popular notion, the Caesars Palace Grand Prix was not contested over a series of mall-spaced drive aisles. Nonetheless, that popular notion loomed large, particularly among the international press. Some 40 years later, veteran Las Vegas sports reporter Ron Kantowski quoted Jackie Stewart on the subject. "You can't hold a Grand Prix," the former world champion was reported to have said, "in a bloody car park."[51] To the wisdom of Jackie Stewart, nor could Caesars Palace include a length of the Las Vegas Strip in the layout of the circuit.

Corrao Construction, longtime building partner of Anthony Marnell, was then contracted for the excavation, grading, paving, and special facilities construction. Corrao crews would break and remove existing asphalt parking paving all along the track layout, excavate to a depth prescribed by a geotechnical engineer to meet FISA specifications, and then construct a new roadbed to include the specific asphalt paving section of the racing surface. A similar approach was taken to construct the continuation of the track on the vacant dirt parcel to the north of the Caesars Palace parking lot.

Crews of Corrao Construction worked during the summer of 1981 to build a FISA-approved Formula One asphalt surface through the existing Caesars Palace north parking lot and the unimproved parcel to the north. Vacant lot to north was owned by the Summa Corporation, the successor to the Howard Hughes Tool Company. Interstate 15 is at the left and stretches across to the right. Mt. Charleston area is in far-left background. Sheep Mountains are in far-right background (courtesy LVCVA News Bureau).

Remarkably, the Caesars Palace Grand Prix circuit straddled two heritage Las Vegas properties across 75 acres, the south section originally owned by Kirk Kerkorian, the seminal Caesars Palace landlord, and the north section previously owned by Howard Hughes. By 1981, the northerly property was held by the Summa Corporation, the Howard Hughes successor gambling and property development company. Further, the Caesars Palace Grand Prix site was bordered to the west by Interstate 15, the only interstate freeway system in the Las Vegas valley. To the east, though, the circuit grounds were sited directly adjacent to the world-famous Las Vegas Strip, still dotted with mid-century gas stations in front of the track proper. Perhaps best of all, the Caesars Palace Grand Prix drivers would compete for international fame and fortune just a few hundred yards from the Fabulous Flamingo Hotel and Casino, opened 35 years earlier by the infamous Benjamin "Bugsy" Siegel. Perhaps oddly, though, construction of the Caesars Palace Grand Prix would be supervised entirely by Chris Pook, the originator of the Long Beach Grand Prix.

The four-year odyssey of William D. Weinberger—Caesars' public-facing VP of casino marketing—was thus near fruition. Caesars' centurions of organized crime, however, had been playing the Las Vegas long-game for decades, from deep in the shadows. The underpinnings of Caesars Palace only intensified the complexity and

character of the Cae-
sars Palace Grand Prix,
truly the first luxury-
branded competition in
the United States at the
pinnacle of motorsport.
Finally, the inaugural
Caesars Palace Grand
Prix stands in his-
tory with the personal
imprint of William D.
Weinberger, decidedly
not the casino draw of
Holmes-Ali, but a much
better bout.

On August 16, 1981,
the *Los Angeles Times*
reported that Clifford
Perlman, "Chairman
of the Board of Caesars
Palace," had announced
that renowned actor

Clifford Perlman named actor Paul Newman as the Chairman of the Caesars Palace Grand Prix. Newman (right) joined Mario Andretti (left), Al Unser, and William D. Weinberger of Caesars Palace on August 30, 1981, at the Plaza Hotel in Manhattan for the first stop of a cross-country press tour. To the dismay of Paul Newman, his acting career and the push of photograph seekers dominated the event. Bill Weinberger was just out of frame to the left (ZUMA Press Inc. / Alamy Stock Photo).

Paul Newman was named as "Chairman of the Caesars Palace Grand Prix."[52] "Newman—with Perlman," continued the *Times*, "will co-host a black-tie party to be held
in the hotel the evening before the competition."[53] The report came less than two
weeks after Clifford Perlman's comments about the vacuous state of economic opportunity in the otherwise great state of New Jersey. In black tie, the respective chair-fel-
lows might then recall the famous pose of Nathan Jacobson with Jimmy Hoffa at the
August 5, 1966, opening night extravaganza of Caesars Palace.

The simultaneous gladiator games and Roman chariot races of Emperor Clifford
Perlman—as he hastened to the New Jersey Supreme Court *and* to the podium celebration of the 1981 Caesars Palace Grand Prix—were thus declared underway.

***

Both spurred and supervised by Chris Pook, the crews of Corrao Construction
endeavored throughout the sweltering summer of 1981 to complete the Caesars Palace Grand Prix circuit in time for the October race event. High air temperatures at
nearly McCarran Airport approached 115 degrees. High temperatures on the curing black asphalt of the Caesars Palace parking lot, though, tipped 150. Nevertheless,
it was the standard fare of property development in the global capital of gambling,
especially so with a bold new attraction to put to market, one with such high stakes
for the pay zone. Spend money to make money. Just be sure to bring water.

"We have had ample time to prepare," explained Ron Harris of Corrao Construction. "We built the Desert Inn in six months, so to build a race track like this
and provide the safety features necessary wasn't as difficult as outsiders may think."[54]

The mention by Ron Harris of the Desert Inn hotel-casino was instructive, pointing up the captive gambling construction marketplace enjoyed by firms such as Corrao Construction and Taylor Construction. Mention of the Desert Inn also recalls the mob-adjacent curtain of Las Vegas development legacy: Bugsy Siegel, Del Webb, Marion Hicks, Clifford Jones, Moe Dalitz, and Albert Parvin.

By August 15, 1981, a complex ribbon-candy of asphalt appeared across the former Kerkorian and Hughes properties on the Las Vegas strip, barely time for the 60-day asphalt curing period, certainly sufficient though for three-time Indianapolis 500 winner Al Unser to provide hot laps for the gathered press caravan. Unser was also a race veteran of the former Stardust International Raceway, shuttered 10 years before just six miles due west of the Caesars Palace circuit. Al Unser, doing press stints in a sponsoring Datsun 280ZX turbo, was keen to praise the undertaking. "When you hear somebody is going to build a race track, it usually ends up to be a Mickey Mouse low-dollar deal," Unser was quoted as saying by *Las Vegas Review-Journal* sports reporter Mike Henle, "This one is not. They're working very

This sweeping view from the 27-story Caesars Palace Fantasy Tower looks roughly east across the Las Vegas valley. Turn one of the Caesars Palace Grand Prix circuit is the center of the image. World-famous Las Vegas Strip is just beyond turn one, running from top-left to mid-right. Las Vegas Strip resorts immediately visible are, from right, the low-rise north end of the Flamingo Hilton, Ralph Engelstad's Imperial Palace, Holiday Inn casino-hotel (currently Harrah's) and the Rat Pack–era round tower of the Sands hotel-casino. The Landmark tower and Las Vegas Hilton (currently the Westgate) are visible beyond the Sands tower. The Las Vegas Hilton was originally developed by Kirk Kerkorian as the International. From right to left, Shell, Texaco, Standard, and Mobil gas stations still dot the Las Vegas Strip. Sir Jackie Stewart complained that the Caesars Palace Grand Prix circuit lacked backdrop. Sir Jackie may have been looking in the wrong direction (courtesy LVCVA News Bureau).

hard to make this a successful track."[55] Nearly 40 years on, however, the "Mickey Mouse" reference was used explicitly by its most prominent driver to describe the circuit of the Caesars Palace Grand Prix.

Al Unser's interview with Mike Henle also struck a lightning rod in domestic open wheel auto racing, specifically, whether brother Bobby Unser—or Mario Andretti—was the rightful winner of the 1981 Indianapolis 500. "Unser's brother Bobby won this year's Indianapolis 500," wrote Henle, "only to find out one day later that he lost the title to Mario Andretti for allegedly passing other cars while leaving the pits."[56] The highly contentious issue progressed from the ranks of the Indianapolis Motor Speedway, through to the USAC appeals board process. Tom Binford, chief steward of Indianapolis Motor Speedway—and the head of ACCUS—levied the originating penalty against Unser and declared Andretti the winner. Bobby Unser and team owner Roger Penske, however, pushed back and filed an appeal to the sanctioning USAC. As of Henle's writing, the appeal was not concluded. "My own opinion," explained Al Unser, "is that they [USAC] won't give it back to him [brother Bobby]. It's wrong when they tell you can cheat a little bit, but you can't cheat all the way."[57]

Two weeks later, Al Unser then continued his media duties for the 1981 Caesars Palace Grand Prix at the historic Plaza Hotel in New York City. In a press conference presented by Bill Weinberger on August 30, 1981, Unser was joined at the dais by the esteemed Chairman of the Grand Prix, Paul Newman. Al Unser, however, was also joined by Mario Andretti. The appearance of Newman, the revered Academy Award nominated actor, dominated the time and tenor of the event, to the disappointment of the reluctant celebrity. "There were about six notebooks in the crowd," reported the *Boston Globe*, "but about 60 cameras. The sound of the shutter clicking was constant and only ended, temporarily, when the exasperated Newman called a halt."[58] Paul Newman did, however, explain his interest in motorsport competition, an interest that arose from his 1969 auto racing film with wife Joanne Woodward, *Winning*.

Newman also described the origins of his relationship with Mario Andretti, a nod to the ill-fated Holman & Moody "Honker II" race vehicle that Mario Andretti contested in the 1967 Can-Am series, including at Stardust International Raceway. "The car wouldn't perform," Newman stated of his unpaid sponsorship on the nose of the Honker II. "Nothing went right. Mario finally said, 'I'll put my name on the car and let Newman drive it.'"[59] The close relationship of Paul Newman and Mario Andretti continued forward, including Andretti's win at the 1983 Caesars Palace Grand Prix, driving a Newman-Haas Racing Lola T-700 in the debut year for the team.

As William D. Weinberger continued to push the message, he also made efforts to explain the *premium*, in the premium brand of the Caesars Palace Grand Prix. "Formula One is the highest echelon, the most snobbish and the most extravagant. That is in keeping with the Caesars Palace image," Weinberger was quoted as saying by Shav Glick for the *Los Angeles Times*. "Everything we do is designed to bring in gamblers and we have found that major sports events bring in good customers—high rollers—to Las Vegas."[60] Major sporting events were always a premier Las Vegas gambling attraction, along with some requisite Frank Sinatra.

"Our high rollers like an excuse to come to Las Vegas," explained Weinberger.

"They like to tell their friends, 'I'm going to see the Leonard fight,' or, in this case, 'I'm going over to see that Grand Prix.'"[61] Indeed, the welterweight title unification fight between "Sugar" Ray Leonard and Thomas "The Hitman" Hearns, "The Showdown," was held one month before the inaugural Caesars Palace Grand Prix. "Hitman" jokes notwithstanding in Las Vegas, Leonard took the unified title by TKO over Hearns.

"Boxing and gambling go together," Caesars senior vice-president Murray Gennis said of the Leonard-Hearns fight. "Big fights attract the biggest players."[62] Among the Caesars Palace-*adjacent*, big fights also attracted players like Anthony Salerno, Jerome Zarowitz, Frank Rosenthal, William Fugazy, and Roy Cohn. Two weeks after the inaugural Caesars Palace Grand Prix, Gennis, who catered to the needs of the wealthiest high rollers, was also snared in a Pacific Rim gambling scrum involving $280,000, five suitcases, international air customs, and an arrest.

"If they're [high rollers] on our VIP list (the $20,000 group)," continued Bill Weinberger, "we'll send a plane for them, set them up in a suite, and give them meals, show tickets, and $250 seats for the race."[63] For Weinberger, the premium prices on the best seats for the race were designed to create a perception of value to the comped high rollers. By contrast, the most expensive seat for the preceding Long Beach Grand Prix was $50, the high-water mark in 1981 for premier-level stateside motorsports events not named the Indianapolis 500. The $250 price tag thus stood as a potential deterrent to the domestic race fan, typically not cut from high roller cloth and wholly unaccustomed to "the most snobbish and the most extravagant."[64] Weinberger's four-year odyssey was thus beginning to present a pre-race pivot. Further, despite the presence of Paul Newman, the 1981 Caesars Palace Grand Prix would not enjoy a colorful Hollywood billing like "The Showdown."

"Formula One is the thoroughbred of auto racing and we wanted a segment of the sport that deals with a world championship," Bill Weinberger continued in the week before the Caesars Palace Grand Prix, "and we wanted a segment of the sport that deals with a world championship as opposed to a national championship like CART or NASCAR."[65] Weinberger clung to that premise during his tenure over the Grand Prix, a notion that his successors walked back in 1983 as Caesars Palace hosted the CART IndyCar series *and* a NASCAR event. Perhaps weary from two years of Watkins Glen conjecture, Bill Weinberger also leaned in on the misfortune—or mismanagement—of the upstate New York classic. "We have the dollars available for purses and promotion," Weinberger said, "something Watkins Glen lacked—and hopefully we'll recover those dollars."[66] Bill Weinberger's closer, however, might have foretold the pre-race gate, as well as the Caesars Palace casino take.

With a FISA-sanctioned Formula One circuit complete, the run-up to the Caesars Palace Grand Prix turned from the press to the pavement. The 14-turn track involved 1,350,000 square feet of asphalt weighing 23,100 tons. Another 25,000 tons of select rock material was used to compact the new track base below. Over 7,000 cubic yards of sand were spread beyond the fringes of the paved corners. "The sand is just a long line of safety precautions at each turn," suggested Ron Harris of Corrao Construction. "It serves as a buffer before drivers reach other safety barriers."[67] "Other safety barriers" would naturally include tire barriers, the "spherical elastic attenuators" pioneered by Chris Pook and the Long Beach Grand Prix Association.

This image from the October 16, 1981, Caesars Palace Grand Prix Can-Am event depicts the proximity of the circuit to the Interstate 15 freeway corridor. Competitors are in turn 14, the final corner before proceeding onto the front straightaway. Event signage is affixed to the Caesars Palace freeway marquee at left. Side-by-side Nissan and Datsun signage points up the branding shift of the Japanese manufacturer in the early 1980s. Chris Pook and the Long Beach Grand Prix Association were responsible for erection and dismantling of track-adjacent facilities, fencing, barricades, grandstands, and fencing (courtesy LVCVA News Bureau).

"More than 4.5 miles of barriers (5,466 cubic yards of concrete)," continued the report, "will be used as the next to last line of protection."[68] The concrete barriers also recall the formative years of the Long Beach Grand Prix, and their monetized importance as a lease-back lifeline. At Caesars Palace, though, Chris Pook oversaw the production of new concrete barriers in Las Vegas, rather than the prohibitive costs of transport from California. Just as in Long Beach, the concrete barriers proved ideal for three-foot-tall banner advertising. Chris Pook's team thus draped the barriers with sponsoring signage, including that of the beleaguered Caesars Boardwalk Regency and Alvin Malnik's Caesars Pocono Resorts.

The "last line of protection" installed around the circuit was a series of catch fences designed to protect the 45,000 anticipated spectators from the on-track—and potential off-track—action. Race fans also recall that the 15-foot-tall fence line imparted a certain *detention*-like quality to the event grounds along the world-famous Las Vegas Strip. Indeed, unlike the early Long Beach Grand Prix events, there would be no walk-ins. Further, the Caesars Palace security guards were armed, just like Sanford Waterman addressing Frank Sinatra's Caesars Palace gambling debt in 1970.

Pre-race coverage of the Caesars Palace Grand Prix introduced another Long Beach player to the Caesars Palace promotions and management team. Jack Long, sponsorship consultant for the inaugural Long Beach Grand Prix, was posted to a similar role for the Las Vegas race. As vice president of casino marketing for the Caesars Palace Grand Prix, Long touted promotional contracts with boldface names like Datsun, Coca-Cola, Goodyear, Coors, and Moet champagne for the Caesars

Palace Grand Prix. Jack Long also lauded $1.5 million in television advertising for the broadcast of the race by NBC. "You can see why this (the race) is so important," offered Long, "why television makes this race a big one."[69] One more holdover from the Long Beach echelon was the role of medical consultant for the inaugural Caesars Palace Grand Prix. Indeed, plucked from the headlines of the day, Dr. Jeffrey R. MacDonald—medical consultant for the Long Beach Grand Prix and convicted *Fatal Vision* murderer—also pitched his medical tent for the Caesars Palace event. Notable as well, Jeffrey MacDonald staffed for Caesar while his murder convictions awaited the appeal docket of the US Supreme Court.

NBC, covering its first-ever Formula One race, dispatched Paul Page and Charlie Jones to voice the event. The NBC broadcast booth was assembled on the 17th floor of the Caesars Palace Fantasy Tower. The third figure in the booth would be none other than Roger Penske, car owner in the CART series for Bobby Unser, and still an appellant before the USAC board. The NBC *Sportsworld* broadcast was directed by NBC legend Don Ohlmeyer. Mark Thatcher, son of British Prime Minister Margaret Thatcher, handled the microphone duties on the pit crawl. Two of NBC's 16 cameras were positioned to provide the international feed to 13 countries, duly levied by Bernie Ecclestone as the preeminent of FOCA. Stationed on a broadcast scaffold stand high above turn 10 was Gary Gerould.

As the protest of the 1981 Indianapolis 500 continued, Roger Penske joined the NBC broadcast team for the October 17, 1981, Caesars Palace Grand Prix. The Indianapolis 500 decision was finalized in the week before the Caesars Palace event. Roger Penske returned to Caesars Palace for the CART IndyCar events in 1983 and 1984 (Rick Lake collection).

"NBC was trying to make a splash there with Roger [Penske]," recalled longtime motorsports and NBA broadcaster Gary Gerould, "who I had known from various Indy events."[70] Gerould, early in his booth experience in motorsports, marveled at the preparation of relative novice Penske. "I was frankly jealous because he had one of his vice presidents prepare all kinds of background information. Roger walks into a production meeting and he's got all these pages and cards ... about every driver," reckoned Gerould. "I figured, whoa, it must be nice to be Roger Penske!"[71]

On Thursday, October 8, 1980, advance teams from the Formula One fleet and NBC started to arrive in Las Vegas to prepare for the inaugural Caesars Palace Grand Prix. The Caesars Palace tennis sports pavilion was converted to the Formula One paddock. Hospitality kiosks were erected. Pedestrian wayfinding from the Grand Prix perimeter to the casino proper was positioned. Contingency parking plans at the Dunes hotel-casino to the south and Summa's Castaways hotel-casino to the north were put into place. Hors d'oeuvre, cocktail, and dining creations for the celebrity-laden formal hosted by Clifford Perlman and Paul Newman were finalized. Even mustachioed LeRoy Neiman—modern impressionist painter of the Caesars Palace Grand Prix program and poster art—knew his marks.

The same day, the USAC appeals board ruled that Tom Binford of the Indianapolis Motor Speedway had improperly penalized Bobby Unser after the conclusion of the 1981 Indianapolis 500. The race win was thus restored to Bobby Unser, and summarily *removed* from Mario Andretti. Andretti's first path of recourse was an appeal to ACCUS, of which Tom Binford was president, a veritable doom loop.

"Do I blame Bobby? Do I blame Penske? No. I blame USAC 100%," reflected Mario Andretti, still wearing his 1981 Indianapolis 500 winner's ring. "It's as simple as that. I'll never relinquish that. [Unser] beat it, and they got away with it. That's the absolute fact. Period."[72] Mario Andretti, however, would not disparage his former IndyCar team owner. Rather, Andretti was left to marvel at the maneuvering. "Roger Penske," continued Andretti, "he'll go through whatever he has to, to try and prevail."[73]

Mario Andretti—the great American race car driver—rolled away one week later at the inaugural Caesars Palace Grand Prix as the *second*-place trophy of the preceding Indianapolis 500. Meanwhile, Roger Penske—Bobby Unser's winning car owner—was positioned in the NBC broadcast booth on the 17th floor of the Caesars Palace Fantasy Tower—well-prepared to provide his own color commentary.

***

The 15-year history of Caesars Palace—like any sustained business model—was underscored by constants, while it was also punctuated with change. "Preserve the core" was the mantra of Stanford business researchers Jim Collins and Jerry Porras, "and stimulate progress."[74] Caesars Palace may have been the Frankenstein-archetype of the Stanford researchers' wisdom, yet the resort certainly flourished, especially at the bottom line. The hotel-casino opened on August 5, 1966, with 700 hotel rooms. By 1981, Caesars Palace had morphed into a mega-resort of 1,800 rooms—with no small debt of alleged thanks to Alvin Malnik and the pervasive "we" of the Abscam recordings. Further changed were the sports offerings. Premier-level world

Fine artist Leroy Neiman and actress Morgan Fairchild attend the October 8, 1980, pre-race reception for the 1981 Caesars Palace Grand Prix hosted by Clifford Perlman and Paul Newman. The Grand Prix reception was a celebrity-studded affair that mixed Hollywood, gamblers, and prominent race car drivers. Fairchild was then starring in the TV drama *Flamingo Road*. The program was notably produced by the Lorimar TV production company of Merv Adelson, Irwin Molasky, and Lee Rich. Irwin Molasky also constructed Stardust International Raceway in Las Vegas. Leroy Neiman created the impressionistic art pieces for the 1981–1983 Caesars Palace Grand Prix events (courtesy LVCVA News Bureau).

championship boxing had given way—at least for a long Las Vegas weekend—to the premier-level pinnacle of motorsport, the Formula One world championship.

Other aspects of the Caesars Palace hotel-casino operation, though, remained standing as apparently immovable objects. Harry Wald was on the ground in 1966 during the construction of the resort and was also in the original gambling license consortium with Jay Sarno, Stanley Mallin, and Nathan Jacobson. Wald was still on the grounds of Caesars Palace in 1981, as president and chief operating officer. In fact, Harry Wald was number three on the depth chart of the 1981 Caesars Palace Grand Prix program, behind only Clifford Perlman and Paul Newman. Wald's courageous silver coiffure would also make for easy mane-spotting through the festivities of the Caesars Palace Grand Prix. International authorities would also observe Harry Wald coming from afar to extricate Caesars Palace casino executive Murray Gennis from $280,000 worth of unusual circumstances.

The program of the 1981 Grand Prix then illuminated the stable state of sloganism at the 15-year-old resort. Jay Sarno's caricaturized Caesar invited grand opening revelers to an orgy of excitement in Caesar's Palace of Pleasure. In 1981, the ever-expanding echelon of Caesars World lawyerdom had given the tagline little more than a tepid rinse, watering it no further than "Caesars Palace—Where every fantasy comes true."[75] Preserve the core—Stimulate progress.

Program pages for the 1981 Caesars Palace Grand also introduced the Las Vegas gathering to the names, faces, and machinery of the Formula One racers and their teams, as well as to their respective point standings in the 1981 Formula One drivers and constructors' championships. Indeed, the long-awaited and much-ballyhooed 1981 Caesars Palace Grand Prix was not only the

Mario Andretti learned his fate in the appeals process of the 1981 Indianapolis 500 one week before the 1981 Caesars Palace Grand Prix. Andretti was stripped of the race win, yet still wears the winner's ring presented at the 1981 Indianapolis 500 victory banquet. Mario Andretti was a master of compartmentalizing the politics of motorsport—and his contract responsibilities in the office of his race car (Bruce Aguilera collection).

finale of the season, it would also determine the Formula One world driving champion. World championship bragging rights thus belonged to William D. Weinberger. It was a coveted play that most Grand Prix organizers and events could never boast, including Chris Pook and the Long Beach Grand Prix.

Carlos Reutemann, driving a TAG-Williams FW07 for Frank Williams, led the championship chase with 49. Reutemann's season, however, was not exactly peaking, scoring only six points over the previous five rounds. Nelson Piquet followed with 48 points in a Brabham BT49 for Bernie Ecclestone. Piquet's late-season form was also in marked contrast to the decline of Reutemann, surging with 22 points over the same five-round run. Coming off a win at the preceding Canadian Grand Prix, Jacques Lafitte trailed in third for Guy Ligier and the Talbot-Ligier squad. Further, with 43 points, Lafitte and Ligier still had a shot at the championship.

Reigning world champion Alan Jones followed with 37 points in a companion machine to Reutemann. Alain Prost was tied in points at 37 in his turbocharged Renault RE30. With nine points on offer for the win and six points for second, the first two positions in the championship would be decided between Carlos Reutemann, Nelson Piquet, and Jacques Lafitte. Alan Jones and Alain Prost were certainly gunning to close the season with a win, but were otherwise fighting for third place at

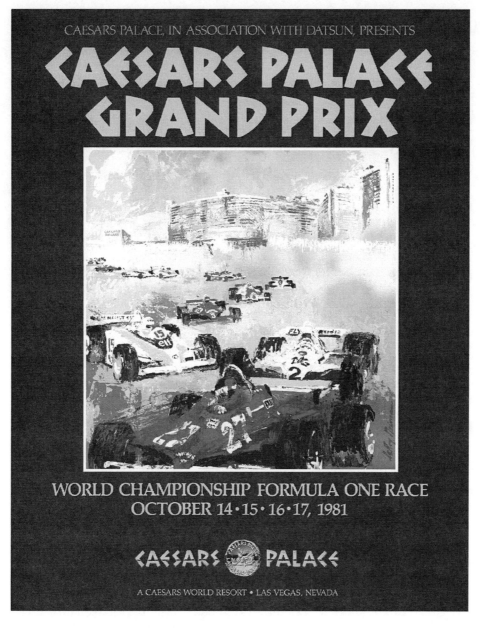

Poster art by Leroy Neiman for the 1981 Caesars Place Grand Prix creates an impressionistic ribbon of Formula One vehicles in the foreground of the luxury-branded Caesars Palace resort. Notably depicted are Gilles Villeneuve (#27 Ferrari), Carlos Reutemann (#2 Williams), Alain Prost (#15 Renault), Eddie Cheever (#3 Tyrell), and Andrea de Cesaris (#8 McLaren) (Bruce Aguilera collection).

best in the driving championship. Alan Jones also announced his retirement headed into Las Vegas. Seven years on the politically contentious circuit, as well as a soured relationship with Carlos Reutemann, had taken their toll. Mario Andretti, with an administrative second place in the Indianapolis 500, still sat on three points in the Formula One championship. Andretti was also tied on points with teammate Bruno

Nelson Piquet (#5 Brabham) leads teammate Hector Rebaque through turn three at the October 17, 1981, Caesars Palace Grand Prix. Piquet finished fifth and claimed the 1981 Formula One world championship. Rebaque retired on lap 20 and was classified 18th. Banner signage of the embattled Caesars Boardwalk Regency in Atlantic City is visible just left of Rebaque's rear wheel (author's collection).

Giacomelli, the Alfa Romeo fleet clinging to 16th and 17th place in the championship standings.

Coming into Las Vegas, the constructors championship of the 1981 Formula One season was long decided. With three wins and six second-place finishes between them, Carlos Reutemann and Alan Jones clinched the constructors laurels for Frank Williams and the Saudia-TAG sponsored team. Saudi royal petro-currency was obviously suitable for the pursuit of topline military aircraft, as well as pursuit of the occasional Formula One world championship crown. By contrast, Bernie Ecclestone's Parmalat-sponsored Brabham works finished second in the constructors race with a commendable 61 points, but to an utterly dominant 95 points for Williams. The Williams rout of Brabham clearly proved how difficult it can be to take on the largest petroleum export economy in the world with a herd of Parmalat-branded dairy cows. Petro-cash was also anticipated to be exchanged for petro-chips at the Caesars Palace tables. "We knew well the affinity the Saudis had for F1," William D. Weinberger reflected some 40 years on, "and frankly were counting on a whole gaggle of them attending the race and gambling."[76]

Hovering among the backmarkers in the drivers championship, Mario Andretti took pause at the Caesars Palace Grand Prix trappings, his new homeland race destination. "It's always exciting to see a new venue coming up and especially when you talk about Vegas," reflected Mario Andretti of the new Caesars Formula One circuit.

"The only problem there at Caesars is that they were somewhat restricted. You know, the track was a little bit of a Mickey Mouse layout because there was not enough real estate to cover it, to stretch your legs."[77] Despite looking way up in the points at two Lotus drivers, Andretti efforted a smile on home soil, certainly when the cameras were clicking.

Qualifying for the inaugural Caesars Palace Grand Prix practice brought the Williams machines of points leader Carlos Reutemann and defending champion Alan Jones to the front of the grid. Reutemann was on pole with a quick lap of 1:17.821, Jones a tick back at 1:17.995. The Williams machines of both Reutemann and Jones were notably shod with Goodyear tires. Gilles Villeneuve followed his third-place finish at Canada with third on the grid in Las Vegas, a quick 1:18.060. Second on points, Nelson Piquet qualified fourth at 1:18.161. The championship contender, though, complained of neck strain due to the counterclockwise direction of the high-speed corners. Piquet was not alone in his concerns. It was a counter-intuitive malaise in the wisdom of the domestic race fan, much more accustomed to simply seeing race cars simply turn left.

Piquet was followed in qualifying by Alain Prost, John Watson in a McLaren, and Patrick Tambay in another Ligier. Bruno Giacomelli became the hope of the Alfa Romeo team, timed eighth-quick with a 1:18.792. Mario Andretti slotted 10th for Alfa Romeo, over a second off the pole at 1:19.068. Championship contender Jacques

Reigning Formula One world champion Alan Jones led the October 17, 1981, from start to finish. Jones collected a reported $89,000 for the victory in his Williams FW07C machine. The identity crisis of Nissan and Datsun in background created an interesting juxtaposition. The speed limit signage of the Caesars Palace parking lot is noteworthy, "Speed Limit 10" (author's collection).

Lafitte was off to a miserable final round, mired in the sixth row with a 1:19.167. American Eddie Cheever rolled off 19th in a Tyrell. Eliseo Salazar anchored the field with 1:21.629 in his Ensign-Ford, nearly four seconds off of Reutemann's pole.

In addition to complaints of neck exertion, history records Formula One drivers taking exception to the Las Vegas heat during practice and qualifying. Notably, though, history also records a high temperature of 65 degrees for the qualifying session. Notable as well, Formula One drivers were prone to complain about the fall weather in upstate New York.

As Formula One qualifying wrapped on Friday, the Caesars Palace Grand Prix circuit was taken by the SCCA Can-Am series and the Caesars Palace Coors Can-Am Challenge. Shuttered after the 1974 season, the Can-Am series was rebooted in 1977. The new Can-Am series also used familiar iron, largely Formula 5000 tubs put to pasture with the demise of the SCCA Formula 5000 in 1976. Can-Am mounts retooled from F5000 chassis were required to run full bodywork—as opposed to open wheel—and generally deployed the same 5-liter V-8 Chevrolet power as their forebears. The full bodywork also served to distinguish the wherewithal of the competitors, the front-runners with all-new streamlined moldings, the backmarkers often festooned with shop-made closures stitched to the former F5000 fuselage. Some of the same Formula 5000 tubs also traced their lineage through the starting field of the 1975 Long Beach Grand Prix.

The new Can-Am series also incorporated an under-two-liter class, a nod in structure to the former SCCA United States Road Racing Championship of the 1960s. Remarkably, the season champions in the first four seasons of the reboot were drawn directly from the ranks of Formula One, Patrick Tambay, Alan Jones, and Jacky Ickx. Amid the chaos of USAC and CART, the Can-Am series surged in renaissance, to wit, a season finale in Las Vegas alongside the pinnacle of motorsport. Further, the Can-Am fields of Caesars Palace informed the starting grid of the Caesars Palace IndyCar events to come, as well as showcased future winners of the Indianapolis 500. Finally, the appearance of Can-Am at Caesars Palace recalled the last premier-level road racing event in the Las Vegas valley, the finale of the 1968 SCCA Can-Am series at Stardust International Raceway won by Denis Hulme in a McLaren M8A, and the horrific demise of the high-winged Chaparral 2G and driver Jim Hall's sports racing career.

Danny Sullivan qualified on pole for the Caesars Can-Am event in a Frissbee-Lola-Chevrolet. In fact, Sullivan's pole time of 1:22.751 was within one second of the tail end of the Formula One field. Points leader Geoff Brabham—son of former Formula One world champion Jack Brabham—was alongside Sullivan in a bright red VDS 001. Teo Fabi followed driving a Budweiser-liveried March for Paul Newman. Bobby Rahal qualified fourth in another of Paul Newman's March machines. Notably, Rahal joined the Newman team with the departure of Al Unser from the Can-Am series in August.

The Caesars Palace Can-Am grid also started such recognized road racing talents as Al Holbert, John Morton, and Randy Lewis. Playing to the locals, Graham McRae competed in an eponymous entry, lavishly emblazoned with sponsorship from the Circus-Circus hotel-casino. McRae's white and pink racer was thus a

Danny Sullivan steers his Frissbee through the apex of turn 14 of the Caesars Palace Grand Prix circuit. Sullivan won the October 16, 1981, Can-Am event for Garvin Brown Racing and returned for the 1982 Caesars Palace Can-Am race. Danny Sullivan would sit on the pole of the November 11, 1984, CART IndyCar Caesars Palace Grand Prix IV (author's collection).

tangible testament to the temples of Jay Sarno, Caesars Palace at the south end of the Las Vegas Strip, Circus-Circus at the far north.

Danny Sullivan also dominated the race action of the 38-lap Caesars Can-Am event. Sullivan crossed the line in 54 minutes with an average speed of 94.912 mph. As with qualifying, the race pace of Sullivan was near that of the Formula One machinery, a potential top-10 equivalent against the pinnacle of motorsport. Teo Fabi followed Sullivan some two seconds back. With four wins on the season for Paul Newman, Teo Fabi scored second in the final 1981 Can-Am points. Geoff Brabham trailed Fabi in third. Brabham counted two wins on the season and was crowned the 1981 Can-Am series champion. Bobby Rahal finished fourth for Paul Newman.

For Danny Sullivan, his Can-Am experience propelled him to a handful of starts in the 1982 CART IndyCar series, then to Formula One in 1983 with Ken Tyrell and a points-paying finish at Monaco. Returning to the CART series in 1984, Danny Sullivan would contest the Caesars Palace Grand Prix IV, qualifying on pole. The following year, Danny Sullivan survived his famous "Spin and Win," improbably entering the winner's circle at the famed Indianapolis Motor Speedway. Can-Am champion Geoff Brabham also enjoyed a path through the CART IndyCar series—and noble recognition as the son of the legendary Jack Brabham—certainly as opposed to the co-opted use of the Brabham name by Bernie Ecclestone. Teo Fabi went forward to straddle the demands of Formula One *and* the CART IndyCar series in a single season, contesting 25 events between the two schedules in 1983. Fabi racked up four

Carlos Reutemann came into Las Vegas with the points lead in the 1981 Formula One world championship standings, 49 to 48 over Nelson Piquet. Reutemann started on pole but went backward, allowing Piquet to prevail. As Reutemann negotiates turn eight, the Castaways hotel-casino is visible beyond the circuit while the Las Vegas Hilton towers in the distance. The NBC Sports banner is noteworthy (author's collection).

John Gunn (#39 Lola) and John Graham (Ralt RT-1) pitch the battle of the backmarkers during the October 16, 1981, SCCA Can-Am race at the Caesars Palace Grand Prix. Gunn qualified 13th and finished 15th. Graham qualified 18th, last on the grid, and finished just ahead of Gunn. Gunn and Graham were the last two finishers, four laps down to winner Danny Sullivan. The defined fuselage of Gunn's Lola belies its Formula 5000 heritage. Gunn raced the same Lola in its original open-wheel configuration at the September 28, 1975, Long Beach Grand Prix (photograph by Marc Nelson).

IndyCar wins in 1983, and—inevitably—suffered the wrath of Bernie Ecclestone. Bobby Rahal contested the 1981 Can-Am season with two Formula One Grand Prix events already under his belt in 1978. Rahal also joined the CART IndyCar series in 1982, a career trajectory that included top-10 finishes at Caesars Palace Grand Prix events III and IV, his win at the 1986 Indianapolis 500, as well as three CART IndyCar series championships.

The top finishers of the October 16, 1981, SCCA Caesars Palace Coor Can-Am Challenge thus proved the mettle of the medium. Ascending to the main Las Vegas stage the next day was the Formula One event, the absolute pinnacle of motorsport. The inaugural Caesars Palace Grand Prix was indeed the first premier-level motorsports event held in the Las Vegas Valley since the vaunted SCCA Johnson Wax Canadian-American Challenge Cup series concluded their 1968 season six miles due west of Caesars Palace. With Carlos Reutemann on pole, 24 screaming Formula One machines were set to take the standing start of the 1981 Caesars Palace Grand Prix. Just as on November 10, 1968, at Stardust International Raceway, Mario Andretti— the great American race car driver—was in the Caesars Palace show.

***

"Argentina's Carlos Reutemann is the favorite in [the] million-dollar Caesars Palace Grand Prix," ran the late-week betting line, "Las Vegas bookmakers have rated him an 8–5 favorite."[78] By the morning of the race, the title contenders of Reutemann, Nelson Piquet, Jacques Lafitte were all even at 2–1 odds. The level picks pointed up the dearth of stateside awareness of the vagaries of the sport, as well as the utter absence of book influence by someone like Frank Rosenthal. Remarkably, Caesars Palace took no action on its own event. It was likely not a good look to take action on Nelson Piquet for the win, while Brabham team owner Bernie Ecclestone was lavishly ensconced nearby in the Caesars Palace baccarat parlor. Further, the local sports books were busy that day with the lines for the first game of the 1981 World Series, the epic marquee matchup of the New York Yankees versus the Los Angeles Dodgers, Ron Guidry and Reggie Jackson taking on Fernando Valenzuela and Steve Garvey.

As both the championship leader and the pole sitter, Carlos Reutemann was the focal point of the pre-race press parade, and the strategy for the race. "There's not that much difference in cars or drivers, really," offered the Williams driver. "Any edge is crucial. It probably will come down to whose car is in the best shape and who makes a mistake."[79] "I'm going to drive the limit of the tires, the limit of the car and myself," continued the polesitter. "I think I need to go for the win. Alan [Jones] can't win the championship, but he is going to try and win this race."[80]

Race morning for the inaugural Caesars Palace Grand Prix dawned pleasant with temperatures in the 60s, climbing into the 70s by the time the race approached. Winds, though, had picked up overnight, gusting up to 15 mph from the northeast. The direction of the gusts then created the occasional dust path from the unimproved Summa Corporation property, across to the all-paved Caesars Palace property. Again, the sunshine and the utter lack of precipitation created obvious contrast to the often weather-impacted U.S. Grand Prix at Watkins Glen. Fair weather, an armed

Surrounded by Caesars and their centurions, singer Tom Jones lofts a methuselah of Moët & Chandon to christen the opening ceremonies of the inaugural October 14–17, 1981, Caesars Palace Grand Prix. From left of flag, Clifford Perlman (Caesars Palace Chairman of the Board) presides as the ruling Caesar. First supporting Caesar Harry Wald (President and Chief Operating Officer of Caesars Palace) stands to the left of Perlman. At far left, the ceremonial Caesar in costume balances the platform. Clifford Perlman was still embroiled in his licensing battle with New Jersey gambling regulators. Both Perlman and Wald stood for the podium celebrations as well (Bill Weinberger collection).

force, and the associated decrease in illegal inebriants, might also ensure a reduction in Grand Prix–related car torchings.

The standing start of Formula One also created contrast, certainly for the domestic race fans accustomed to a rolling queue. In a contest of the continents, Argentinian Carlos Reutemann, started from pole, taking the outside position headed into the first turn. Australian Alan Jones was alongside with Canadian Gilles Villeneuve and Brazilian Nelson Piquet tucked immediately behind. As the starting lights went green, though, Carlos Reutemann went backward, his winning strategy apparently derailed before it was even deployed.

Alan Jones accelerated immediately into the lead, followed down the main straight by Gilles Villeneuve and a surging Alain Prost from the third row. Championship leaders Reutemann and Piquet were immediately under attack. Bruno Giacomelli came past from the fourth row as did John Watson in a McLaren from sixth on the grid. Remarkably, Jacques Lafitte improved from his 12th starting position to

Mario Andretti at left shares a pit lane laugh at the October 17, 1981, Caesars Palace Grand Prix with entertainer Sammy Davis, Jr., in center. At right in jacket is Harry Wald, President and Chief Operating Officer of Caesars Palace. The nose of Andretti's Alfa Romeo 179 can be seen between Davis Jr. and Wald. Mario Andretti qualified 10th for the event and retired on lap 22 with a rear suspension failure. Two weeks after the Grand Prix, Harry Wald was embroiled in an international scandal involving Caesars Palace casino executive Murray Gennis and the smuggling of casino marker collections from Australia. Crew members are not identified (courtesy LVCVA News Bureau).

circulate sixth in the early going. On the second lap, Patrick Tambay hit the concrete barriers hard with the front of his Ligier machine virtually shorn away. Miraculously, Tambay exited the destruction of the incident under his own power with only minor injuries. "It was an incredible accident," exclaimed Chris Pook. "He is so lucky that he's still got his legs."[81]

Alan Jones was then on a march, separating from his pursuers by over one second per lap. Alain Prost moved past Gilles Villeneuve on the third lap. Villeneuve, Giacomelli, Watson, Lafitte followed while Reutemann and Piquet were mired in seventh and eighth, out of the points positions vital to their respective championship hopes. Mario Andretti circulated in ninth directly behind Piquet, showing a dash of homeland form for the partisan crowd. Gilles Villeneuve then started to retreat, moving steadily backward in his Ferrari. Jacques Lafitte passed both Bruno Giacomelli and John Watson to move into third and—on track—only one championship point behind Nelson Piquet, two points behind Carlos Reutemann. Piquet, however, moved past Reutemann to take over seventh, only one position out of the points. Nelson Piquet then went around John Watson, into sixth and an on-track points tie with Carlos Reutemann. When Villeneuve retired with engine problems on lap 22, Piquet took over the presumptive points lead. Carlos Reutemann then passed John Watson to once again tie the points as they ran. The homeland hopes of Mario Andretti were put to rest on lap 29 as he retired with a rear wishbone failure.

At the midpoint, Alain Prost pitted from second place to replace worn Michelin rubber on his Renault. The pit move of Prost put the championship contenders of Lafitte, Piquet, and Reutemann into second, third, and fourth positions, respectively, separated by no more than two points as they circulated. Carlos Reutemann, however, started to fall off and was overtaken by Nigel Mansell in a Lotus. Alain Prost and Bruno Giacomelli also followed past the hapless Reutemann.

Racing effortlessly out front, Alan Jones built on his formidable lead, stretching

Derek Daly (#17 March) and Nigel Mansell (#12 Lotus) on the back straightaway between turns 11 and 12 at the October 17, 1981, Caesars Palace Grand Prix. Unimproved dirt parcel was owned by Summa Corporation, the former Howard Hughes Tool Company. The EZ Wider sponsorship of Daly's March and the John Player Special branding of Mansell's Lotus exemplify the presence of tobacco dollars at the pinnacle of motorsport. Notably, Mansell's Lotus was sponsored early in the 1981 season by David Thieme's Essex Overseas Petroleum. The riverboat-themed front of the Holiday Inn hotel-casino is visible across the Las Vegas Strip (photograph by Marc Nelson).

it to 50 seconds before throttling back in his Saudia-TAG Williams machine shod with Goodyear rubber. As Reutemann trailed away, Nelson Piquet also started to slow. Nigel Mansell came past, although Piquet remained in a crucial points-paying position. When Michelin-shod Jacques Lafitte pitted for fresh rubber, the 1981 Formula One world championship became Nelson Piquet's to lose. As the laps dwindled, however, Piquet struggled to hold position over the returning Lafitte.

A dominant Alan Jones and his Williams FW07 then streaked past the flag position on the 75th lap of the inaugural Caesars Palace Grand Prix. Jones' margin of victory over second-place Alain Prost in the Renault was 20 seconds. Bruno Giacomelli and his Alfa Romeo were in the frame with Prost, less than one-half of a second behind. In his first full season for Colin Chapman's Team Lotus, Nigel Mansell took fourth. Nelson Piquet then brought his Brabham to the flag fifth, another 20 seconds behind Mansell, but less than two seconds ahead of Jacques Lafitte in the Ligier. John Watson in the McLaren was seventh, filling the mirrors of Lafitte.

So decisive was the performance of Alan Jones that he put a lap into polesitter and teammate Carlos Reutemann. Strategy vanquished, Carlos Reutemann was posted with an eighth-place finish, out of the points and relegated to runner-up in the world championship.

From the pits, new world champion Nelson Piquet had to be assisted from his Brabham. "Piquet was so exhausted that he blacked out and vomited," reported Jep Cadou for *National Speed Sport News*. "He had to be half carried into the press room a full hour after the race for intervewing."[82] The Formula One crown, though, belonged undeniably to Piquet, and to Brabham team owner Bernie Ecclestone.

Carlos Reutemann labored to explain away his performance from the pole of the race, and against teammate Alan Jones. "He knew he'd lost the title when, due to a balky gearbox," it was reported of Reutemann. "Alain Prost passed him during the race."[83] Carlos Reutemann also noted that he had not spoken with Frank Williams about renewing their contract arrangement for 1981.

The friction between the Williams teammates, simmering since the third round in Argentina, was on full boil in the post race. Alan Jones, jovial with winning his final start for Frank Williams, could not resist throwing barbs at his 1981 teammate, along with any notion that he might have helped Carlos Reutemann win the championship. "It was like a choice between TB [tuberculosis] and cancer," Jones said bluntly. "I couldn't care a damn."[84]

Both Alan Jones and Nelson Piquet were lavishly feted in the various podium celebrations. Clifford Perlman and Harry Wald of Caesars Palace also took their turns smiling for the cameras in their luxury-branded satin inaugural event jackets. William D. Weinberger, by contrast, played to the sidelines. Frankly, it might have played better in New Jersey if it was Weinberger that was captured in the press images.

For Bruno Giacomelli of the Alfa Romeo team, finishing on the third step of the Caesars Palace podium was the high point of a Formula One driving career. Notably muted on the day, teammate Mario Andretti would take his leave of the Alfa Romeo squad, although he would return for the 1982 Caesars Palace Grand Prix. At the end of a long campaign, newly-crowned Formula One world titleholder Nelson Piquet put the champion's stamp on the inaugural Caesars Palace Grand Prix event. "It was a

From right front, Harry Wald, Clifford Perlman, Alan Jones, and Alain Prost share the victory celebration of the inaugural Caesars Palace Grand Prix on October 17, 1981. Bruno Giacomelli is behind and between Perlman and Wald. Jones won the inaugural Caesars Palace Formula One event driving a Williams. The centurion helmet winner's trophy is in the foreground. Prost was second for Renault. Mario Andretti's teammate Bruno Giacomelli finished third for Alfa Romeo. It was the only podium finish of Giacomelli's career. Notably, all three drivers wore Marlboro patches on their racing suits. On November 1, 1981, Alan Jones attended a reception in Sydney, Australia, at which Caesars Palace casino executive Murray Gennis was under surveillance by Australian authorities. Gennis was arrested and charged with currency smuggling two days later. Person between Jones and Prost is not identified (John Blakemore Photograph Collection, The Revs Institute).

fantastic job by Caesars Palace," stated Piquet from the festivities, "I think it is a very, very hard circuit. I think it is a circuit we can race on for many years."[85] By contrast, Bernie Ecclestone avoided the press circus altogether, departing the race course—as was his custom—before Nelson Piquet crossed the finish line.

Despite the endorsement of the new world champion and his employer, international motorsport press forced the last word on the experience of the inaugural Caesars Palace Grand Prix, and the portent for the future of Formula One. "Slot cars winding around the city centre car parks of the world," posted *Motorsport Magazine*, "rather like hapless rats caught in a complicated and fruitless trap."[86] One need only look, however, at such sterile oil-state stadia as the modern Abu Dhabi or Mexico City circuits to see how that worked out. At least Caesars Palace had the world-famous Las Vegas Strip in its pocket.

*** *** ***

Nelson Piquet, center, joins the champagne celebration of the October 17, 1981, Caesars Palace Grand Prix, while NBC captures the action from left front. Driving a Brabham for Bernie Ecclestone, Nelson Piquet finished fifth in the race event and won the 1981 Formula One world driving championship by one point over Carlos Reutemann. Piquet is flanked by Alain Prost at left, Alan Jones and Bruno Giacomelli at right. Race fuel for the 1981 Caesars event was purchased from Union Oil. Accordingly, Union Oil publicist Bill "Hat Man" Brodrick is visible at far left (Bruce Aguilera collection).

"It's back to reality," wrote Mike Henle the morning after the Caesars Palace Grand Prix. "The race course is a parking lot again. The press room is again a maintenance warehouse and the garage is the Sports Pavilion."[87] It should also be noted that the local sports books were once again at full strength; San Francisco versus Green Bay and Cincinnati versus Pittsburgh were key gridiron matchups that week. Thirty-five years removed from conspiring to fix the national championship football game, Jerome Zarowitz would be all over the football lines.

On the ground, Chris Pook and his Long Beach Grand Prix Association staff had survived their first Formula One venture beyond the familiar laps around the city center of Long Beach. "It went the way it was supposed to go," Mike Henle quoted Pook as saying, "and that was proper."[88] The Long Beach Grand Prix Association and their subcontractors held over to remove the remaining effects of the inaugural Caesars Palace Grand Prix, catch fences, grandstands, concrete barriers, "spherical elastic attenuators," and the banner signage of Alvin Malnik's Caesars Pocono Resorts.

In fact, three days after the Caesars Palace Grand Prix, the Malnik-stained

license appeal of Clifford Perlman and brother Stuart returned to the national discourse. Astride their case before the New Jersey Supreme Court and—by October
of 1981—their annual license renewal of the Atlantic City resort, Caesars World and
the Perlman brothers appeared to be stonewalling the New Jersey Casino Control
Commission. New complaints were then lodged by the commission against Caesars
World. "William H. McElnea," it was reported in New Jersey, "failed to return phone
calls to investigators about his sale of 450,000 shares of stock to the Perlman's."[89] Caesars World also ignored requests by New Jersey investigators for the minutes of board
and audit committee meetings as well as an internal audit report, subjects sought
by officials over six months prior. "The division [of gaming enforcement] respect-
fully submits," wrote director G. Michael Brown, "that these questions should be fully
explored before any license renewal is issued."[90]

One week later, in an apparent Hail Mary, Caesars World announced that the
corporation intended to repurchase the shares held by Clifford Perlman and Stuart
Perlman. Once again, J. Terrence Lanni delivered the spin, "a major step in resolving

This 1981 Caesars World, Inc., stock certificate marks transition at the corporate parent of Caesars Palace. With a date of November 2, 1981, the certificate carries the facsimile signatures of
Bruce Aguilera as corporate secretary and J. Terrence Lanni as corporate president. Former
Caesars World president William McElnea tendered his resignation shortly after the November 1980 gambling license ruling from the New Jersey Casino Control Commission. Lanni was
named as Caesars World president days later. Bruce Aguilera was elected corporate secretary
in May 1981, amid the buildup to the Caesars Palace Grand Prix. Aguilera later served as president of the 1983 CART IndyCar Caesars Palace Grand Prix III. Caesars Palace casino executive
Murray Gennis was arrested by Australian authorities on smuggling charges one day after this
certificate was issued (author's collection).

the problems between the company and the New Jersey regulators."[91] Once again, the images in the mirror—and the images from the Caesars Palace Grand Prix—were ignored. Incredibly, the proposed repurchase would pay the Perlmans $20 per share, an $11 per share premium over valuation. Further, the plan called for Clifford Perlman to remain as chairman of Caesars Palace for another five years. While expressing concerns off the record, New Jersey officials committed publicly, to "determine if this constitutes compliance with the casino commission's order."[92]

The standing order of the New Jersey Casino Control Commission, though, was clear, requiring specifically that the person of Clifford Perlman be stricken from Caesars World, along with its New Jersey and Nevada operations. A half-measure at best then, the Caesars World plan allowed Clifford Perlman "to continue running the company's principal asset (Caesars Palace)."[93] Further, the indulgence of the 120 percent premium in the repurchase represented a seller's windfall to the Perlman brothers of some $50 million. The resultant harvest might spell observers to conclude that the plan was another point of entry into the cash count of the company, a supplemental tap of liquidity in service to masters elsewhere.

On November 3, 1981—two days after the Caesars World repurchase announcement—news began to reverberate from Australia. The reports also came as a hard left hook to Caesars Palace, much like Australian Alan Jones and his strong move to the first turn at the Caesars Palace Grand Prix two weeks prior. "Vegas Casino Official Seized in Australia," reported the *Los Angeles Times*, "Police Say Man Had $280,000, Thought to Be Gaming Funds."[94] Murray Gennis, Caesars Palace senior vice-president, was being detained by Australian officials. "In Las Vegas, a spokesman for Caesars World," continued the *Times*, "said there would be no immediate comment on the arrests."[95]

X

Continuum and Controversy

The 1982 Caesars Palace Grand Prix,
the Arrest of Caesars' Centurion,
the Departure of Formula One from Las Vegas

There was more foolery yet, if I could remember it. (*Julius Caesar* 1.2.299)

The 1981 Caesars Palace Grand Prix was the first of its kind, a purpose-built circuit fully branded in the name of a corporate promoter. The luxury-branded offerings of the resort along the world-famous Las Vegas Strip added a truly inimitable cachet to the event, along with some brilliant neon Nevada nuance. William D. Weinberger and Caesars Palace had produced a world-class entertainment event, completely resetting expectations for a Formula One competition, at least beyond the yacht crawl in the harbor at Monte Carlo. The event also engaged the supremes of Formula One, both international and domestic. Indeed, Bernie Ecclestone, Jean-Marie Balestre, and Chris Pook all appeared to pull on the same end of the rope for benefit of the event, at least in public. Further, Bernie Ecclestone found a working partner in William D. Weinberger of Caesars Palace. At the same time, the presence of Clifford Perlman on the victory podium of the 1981 Caesars Palace Grand Prix unified the thesis, the converged influences of Las Vegas, organized crime, and the pinnacle of motorsport.

For Caesars Palace itself, though, the Grand Prix event was measured solely at the bottom line. Like the complex backstory of the resort property itself, the subject requires some dissection. Headed into the Caesars Palace Grand Prix, Harry Wald reported that the preceding Holmes-Ali fight at Caesars Palace churned $123 million through the Las Vegas economy. The pending Grand Prix inevitably contrasted against boxing, then the ultimate Las Vegas sporting draw. "Boxing is a gambler's sport," stated John Romero, a Las Vegas publicist and sportswriter. "Auto racing is not. Boxing has its roots in betting and intrigue and mystery and payoffs and dives."[1] Stated as if a proclamation from Caesar himself. The roots of the fight game also included some Caesars-adjacent figures, Anthony "Fat Tony" Salerno, Vincent "Jimmy Blue Eyes" Alo, Ruby Lazarus, Jerome Zarowitz, Elliott Paul Price, Ash Resnick, and Frank Rosenthal. William Fugazy of the Long Beach *Queen Mary* project

The reigning Caesar looks down upon his domain from a penthouse deck on the 27th floor of the Caesars Palace Fantasy Tower at the October 17, 1981, Caesars Palace Grand Prix. In foreground from right, Clifford Perlman (Chairman of the Board of both Caesars Palace and the corporate parent, Caesars World, Inc.), actor Paul Newman (Grand Marshal of the Grand Prix), and Cam-Am driver Danny Sullivan. Sullivan would drive for Paul Newman in the 1982 SCCA Can-Am series. Sullivan also drove briefly for Gerald Forsythe and Paul Newman during the 1982 CART IndyCar season. Paul Newman joined with Carl Haas in 1983 to create Newman-Haas Racing, the team for which Mario Andretti won the 1983 Caesars Palace Grand Prix III. Clifford Perlman, on the other hand, resigned from Caesars Palace before the 1982 Caesars Palace Grand Prix (courtesy LVCVA News Bureau).

and the infamous attorney Roy Cohn also dabbled in boxing promotions, notably right alongside Anthony Salerno.

In the months before the Caesars Palace Grand Prix, consultant Chris Pook estimated a $200 million bump to the Las Vegas economy. As Chris Pook spirited away to Long Beach, however, the Las Vegas Convention and Visitors Authority delivered the hard numbers, reporting an economic impact of $158 million to the gambling city. The authority also noted that 38,000 of the 45,000 grandstand seats were filled for the Grand Prix. "In the last two weeks, interest in the race drastically increased," stated Rossi Ralenkotter of the Visitors Authority. "We received an enormous amount of publicity from the event."[2] Ralenkotter further reported a 98.6 percent hotel occupancy rate for the three-day Grand Prix event.

"Rogers & Cowan, Paul Newman's PR firm and one of the largest in the world," recalled William D. Weinberger, "estimated the value of the PR at $50 million."[3] The exercise was not unlike the constant conjectures of Chris Pook, the Long Beach City Council, and the woebegone Long Beach Convention and News Bureau, involving the somewhat intangible marketing benefit of the Long Beach Grand Prix. Theirs, however, was often a futile and tangled exercise. For Bill Weinberger and Caesars Palace, the true measure was not occupancy rates, local economic impact, or the vagaries of international public relations. The dominant metric was pure and simple—in gold and green—the casino drop, the essential reason for the very existence of the 15-year-old resort. By contrast to Long Beach, Caesars Palace simply counted the millions of dollars in bills and coins extracted from the sweaty fists of Caesars Palace casino gamblers and delivered to the underground casino count room—where the core value of the core business became measurable.

"As a casino event," Bill Weinberger reflected after four decades, "the Grand Prix was total failure. Gamblers just weren't interested in making a special trip to LV for an F1 race."[4] Despite the years-long buildup and ballyhoo, the inaugural Caesars Palace Grand Prix did not match the gambling, drinking, and celebrity-driven party of the Holmes-Ali fight, of Leonard-Hearns, or the occasional Frank Sinatra appearance, singing "Luck Be a Lady" in the Caesars Palace *Circus Maximus* showroom. The Grand Prix event might not even have matched the casino drop of Jimmy Connors and the Alan King Tennis Classic organized by Weinberger's father in 1977.

"Paul Newman, our race chairman, was very generous with his time and that was a big draw," continued Weinberger, "but not for gamblers."[5] Perhaps if Newman had appeared in the guise of "Fast Eddie Felson" from his breakout film *The Hustler*. "Our big hope," Weinberger recalled, "was we would draw a whole new crowd of European and other foreign gamblers which never materialized."[6] Indeed, even the anticipation of a Saudi contingent cheering Alan Jones Saudia Williams FW07 and stacking petrochips on Caesars Palace tables evaporated. Bill Weinberger was particularly vexed by the absence of the Saudi Formula One fans. "It never happened," pondered the former Caesars Palace vice president, "and we never knew why."[7]

The inaugural Caesars Palace Grand Prix thus joined the 1959 Sebring, 1960 Riverside, and early Long Beach events in the Formula One financial loss column, while the 20-year experience of Formula One at Watkins Glen had devolved into its own contentious bankruptcy. The comparative financial wherewithal of Caesars Palace, though, nudged the Las Vegas event forward, certainly under the stewardship of William D. Weinberger and later, Bruce Aguilera. The heavily politicized landscape of professional motorsports, however, invited further incursions into the standing agreement between Bernie Ecclestone of FOCA and Bill Weinberger.

Planning for the 1982 Caesars Palace Grand Prix would thus commence. Chris Pook and the 1982 Toyota Formula One Grand Prix of Long Beach were set to roll for another year. Clifford Perlman and Stuart Perlman were unlicensed in New Jersey, while their Nevada lifeline was in peril. On the same date that Rossi Ralenkotter released the impact numbers for the Caesars Palace Grand Prix, though, Murray Gennis—senior vice president of Caesars Palace and a colleague of William D. Weinberger—sat in an Australian jail.

∗∗∗

As the Formula One fleet decamped Caesars Palace for their return to Europe, the rumor mill of premier-level motorsport began to churn wildly. Notably, prospects for the 1982 Caesars Palace Grand Prix occupied a position at the pivot. "The fun rumor ... is that the soon-to-be-announced Championship Auto Racing Teams schedule will include a race at Las Vegas," reported the *Associated Press* on November 10, 1981. "The talk is that the race would outstrip the Indianapolis 500 as the richest purse in auto racing."[8] The purse was further rumored at "close to $2 million."[9] What was omitted, however, was exactly how the domestic CART IndyCar series was intended to network at Caesars Palace with the recently departed Formula One circus, let alone how the paperclip maze of the Caesars Palace road course would accommodate the IndyCar machines themselves.

Two weeks later, the formal 1982 schedule of the CART PPG IndyCar series splashed. The CART Caesars Palace Grand Prix 200 was indeed scheduled on October 17, 1982, as the 11th event of a 13-race season. Schedule notes also indicated that Formula One would return to Caesars Palace on October 16, 1982, for an unprecedented premier-series double header spectacular. "This has never been done before," stated CART board chairman John Frasco, "running Indy cars and Formula One cars on the same weekend at the same facility, so you can imagine the sizable hurdles there were to get over." [10] Frasco also noted that the IndyCar event would run on one of three "tri-oval" variations being considered for the 2.2-mile Caesars Palace road course.

"Frasco said the Las Vegas twin bill," continued the reporting, "was put together under the direction of Bill Weinberger."[11] The invocation of Weinberger implied the continued rope-pulling of Bernie Ecclestone and FOCA, despite the inevitable side-by-side performance contrasts of the premier open-wheel formulae. That comparison of premier domestic and international open-wheel racing disciplines certainly stoked the interest of the competing fan bases. It was a direct comparison, however, that the sanctioning bodies and producers of the respective series had assiduously avoided over the years. Finally, though, the introduction of John Frasco to the discourse would drive the promotion of the final Caesars Palace Grand Prix into the courtroom.

The Formula One fortunes of Mario Andretti also accompanied the conjectures of the 1982 Caesars Palace Grand Prix twin-bill. Andretti, soured after a dismal 1981 season for Alfa Romeo, was apparently offered a Saudi-sponsored Williams seat for 1982 after the retirement of Alan Jones. As year-end approached, though, Andretti deferred announcement of his plans for 1982. Mario Andretti did, however, offer favorable comment on the prospects for the 1982 Caesars Palace Grand Prix. "The addition of the Indy cars, without question, will make this the most exciting and complete weekend of racing ever," Andretti said. "If anyone can accomplish this, it's Caesars Palace."[12] As the extraordinary Caesars Palace twin-bill took form, Mario Andretti also embodied the spectacle lain before Caesar himself, Andretti the heritage product of the originating Roman Empire state, directing the order of battle between the warring factions—FOCA versus FISA, and CART versus USAC.

Jean-Marie Balestre and FISA then reclaimed the upper hand in the emerging 1982 double booking at Caesars Palace. One week after John Frasco launched the 1982 CART schedule, FISA rescheduled the Formula One Caesars Palace Grand Prix to September 25, 1982. The rescheduled date was in direct conflict with a CART IndyCar

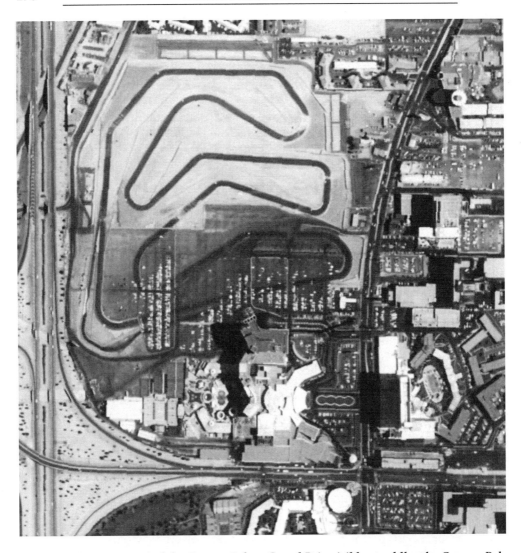

The Formula One course of the Caesars Palace Grand Prix visibly straddles the Caesars Palace north parking lot and the fallow land of the Summa Corporation to the north. The parking lot returned to normal duty as soon as Chris Pook and the Long Beach Grand Prix Association dismantled the race barriers and grandstands. When 170 mph race vehicles were not on the premises, the speed limit of the parking lot was 10 mph (courtesy HistoricAerials.com).

event at Michigan International Speedway, notably owned by Roger Penske. FISA also went in on the apparently unsavory notion that the CART IndyCar series might be perceived as a co-equal—or even *superior*—to Formula One, at least for a long Las Vegas weekend. "It [FISA] also passed a rule at its Paris meeting," ran the stateside report, "that no open-wheel racing with engines of two liters or more could be raced as a 'secondary event' to a Grand Prix."[13] Converted five-liter open-wheel machines of the rebooted Can-Am series notwithstanding, the path forward to the ambitious 1982 Caesars Palace twin-bill Grand Prix had just been pillaged.

John Frasco and CART were then forced to walk back the 1982 schedule, vacating the October 17, 1982, Las Vegas date completely. Simultaneously, Mario Andretti

PRESENTED BY DATSUN

WORLD CHAMPIONSHIP FORMULA ONE RACE
COORS CAN-AM • MOTORCYCLES • SEPTEMBER 23-26, 1982

A CAESARS WORLD RESORT • LAS VEGAS, NEVADA

The poster art of Leroy Neiman for the September 23–26, 1982, Caesars Palace Grand Prix further elevated the impressionistic style. Indeed, all of the Formula One vehicles are fictitious. The poster notes the return of the SCCA Can-Am series and the addition of a motorcycle event (Bruce Aguilera collection).

made the decision to return stateside to contest the 1982 CART IndyCar series full-time. Andretti, naturally, contemplated an opportunity for redemption at the Indianapolis Motor Speedway and the 1982 running of the Indianapolis 500. "The Formula One situation was becoming a bit too much in the way of travel required," Andretti said. "I just wasn't enjoying it the way I should have been."[14] Mario Andretti also chose to stay with Pat Patrick's Wildcat team for 1982, resuming the ride that took him to the hotly disputed second place trophy in the 1981 Indianapolis 500. Prospects for another entertaining Formula One presser with Paul Newman at the Plaza Hotel in Manhattan thus dimmed considerably.

One week after Mario Andretti rendered his decision unto the CART series, national headlines pivoted back to Caesars Palace. "Caesars World, Inc. stockholders," ran the national reports, "have approved a proposal to purchase the 4.8 million shares belonging to company founders Clifford and Stuart Perlman."[15] The repurchase agreement was a direct result of the order by the New Jersey Casino Control Commission that the Perlman brothers be severed. Approval of the stockholders was not without an uprising, though, particularly as the agreed price per share would indebt the corporation at a 100 percent premium over market value. The agreement also confirmed Clifford Perlman atop the organizational chart of the flagship Caesars Palace hotel-casino in Las Vegas. "Clifford Perlman is to be hired as chief executive of Caesars Palace," continued the reports, "His contract can be terminated if New Jersey officials rule he cannot be employed by the Nevada subsidiary."[16] Clifford Perlman thus entered the second year of his personally protracted stand-off with the New Jersey Commission.

Amid the voices of the stockholders, one Caesars World investor stood to inquire about Caesars Palace senior vice president Murray Gennis, released back to Las Vegas but still awaiting trial in Australia on currency smuggling charges. J. Terrence Lanni was prepared with the corporate response. "Lanni said it was 'a stupid and foolish mistake' and a violation of company policy," continued the reporting, "when Senior Vice President Murray Gennis failed to take the cash to a bank in Australia for transfer to this country. Lanni said the money was collected as casino gambling debts and was 'quite legal.'"[17] Lanni's tortured analysis of international currency law aside, the smuggling of six-figures in suitcases rather recalled the compendium of the House Select Committee on Assassinations, "Lansky and [Dino Cellini] are kingpins of a gambling empire extending to every casino in the free world."[18] Further, the specter of Murray Gennis acted as the pin prick to the appeal balloon floated by Caesars World and Clifford Perlman toward the New Jersey Supreme Court. It just went pop.

***

While Caesar sorted centurions and smugglers, Chris Pook and the Long Beach Grand Prix Association were restored to their familiar Long Beach city-center, the trusted Grand Prix branch of Harbor Bank, and an inspired ocean view framing Abram Pritzker's Hyatt Queen Mary Hotel. The 1982 edition of the Toyota Grand Prix of Long Beach would be restored as well. The Long Beach event was scheduled to run on its traditional first weekend in April. Further, the race was not the opener of the 1982 Formula One season, as happened during the aberration of the 1981 schedule.

Chris Pook, "one of the more active racing entrepreneurs in the world,"[19] had also expanded his pay zone in 1982. Nearly a decade on the streets of Long Beach transitioned to a well-paid consultancy for Pook at the 1981 Caesars Palace Grand Prix. Pook, in turn, was now a feasibility consultant for the emerging Detroit Grand

Prix, the third scheduled Formula One event in the United States for 1982. "It's all in the planning stage," Chris Pook said of his work for Robert McCabe of the Detroit effort. "We have done some preliminary work. We have been retained to assist."[20] Amid the bankruptcy proceedings of the Watkins Glen Grand Prix Corporation, Chris Pook was also forced to deny reports that the Long Beach Grand Prix Association was attempting to acquire the Watkins Glen circuit.[21]

Chris Pook and Bernie Ecclestone then presented something of a united front for the 1982 Detroit Grand Prix. Notably, however, negotiations between Robert McCabe and Bernie Ecclestone had sputtered in 1981, just as the Formula One car carriers descended on Caesars Palace. Ecclestone's purse demand of an unprecedented $2.5 million would naturally be at issue. Bernie Ecclestone reportedly also sought organizational control of the event. "We just couldn't see eye to eye," McCabe said. "I had four months of negotiating which was not pleasing."[22]

Headed into the 1982 Long Beach event, Bernie Ecclestone struck a pronounced and positive tone for the scheduled Detroit Formula One event. "It's a natural, isn't it?" Ecclestone said. "It's the auto capital of the world and now Detroit gets a Grand Prix. We're happy to be coming."[23] The purse demand of 1981 went largely unmentioned by McCabe and Ecclestone in 1982. Nonetheless, the happiness measure of Bernie Ecclestone was calibrated in green, gold, and zeroes. Further, the Motor City event was to be a decidedly foreign affair. Even the esteemed Ford Cosworth Formula One powerplant knew that its rightful lineage was a construct of Britain's Colin Chapman works, as opposed to American industrialist Henry Ford.

Bernie Ecclestone was also on the move in New York, although steering well clear of certain time-worn upstate pastures. Rather, Ecclestone, "czar of Formula One racing,"[24] was seeking a new Formula One event in New York City. It was another bold Ecclestone overture, one that involved a temporary Grand Prix circuit at Flushing Meadows in the borough of Queens in New York City. Flushing Meadows was the site of the 1939 and 1964 World Fair events, as well as of F. Scott Fitzgerald's "valley of ashes" in the 1925 classic *The Great Gatsby*. Ecclestone might not have grasped the historical significance—much less the literary—but was determined in his pursuit. "We are ready and willing," Ecclestone said before the 1982 Long Beach Grand Prix, "to do anything it takes to make it go in New York."[25]

Scheduled on April 4, 1982, the Toyota Grand Prix of Long Beach was the third event of the season. With the retirement of Alan Jones, Frank Williams and his Saudi TAG-sponsored squad were represented by the returning Carlos Reutemann and newcomer Keke Rosberg, father of modern Formula One driver Nico Rosberg. Reutemann, though, retired abruptly after the preceding Brazilian Grand Prix. With 1 week to land a replacement, Frank Williams enlisted the aid of Formula One retiree—and great American race car driver—Mario Andretti. One week removed from a contracted CART IndyCar commitment in a Ford Cosworth-powered Wildcat for Pat Patrick on the one-mile paved Phoenix oval, Andretti slid into Carlos Reutemann's Ford-Cosworth powered FW07 for Frank Williams on the streets of Long Beach. After a two-year retirement, Niki Lauda also returned to Formula One competition in 1982. Lauda was paired with John Watson on the venerable Marlboro-sponsored McLaren team.

Gilles Villeneuve and his Ferrari 126C2 crossed the finish line of the April 4, 1982, Long Beach Grand Prix third behind winner Niki Lauda and Keke Rosberg. The #27 Ferrari, however, was disqualified for an illegal rear wing. Sadly, Gilles Villeneuve would not make it to the season finale in Las Vegas (Rick Lake collection).

Starting from the fourth row, Niki Lauda then drove a brilliant race to win the 1982 Long Beach Grand Prix. It was only the third start of Lauda's newly resurrected career. Keke Rosberg trailed 15 seconds back in second for Frank Williams. Gilles Villeneuve in a Ferrari followed Rosberg but was disqualified by FISA for the rear wing configuration of his machine. Riccardo Patrese showed form for Bernie Ecclestone and Brabham, trailing Rosberg by over a minute but advanced to third on the podium. Michele Alboreto was classified fourth in a Tyrell. Reigning world champion Nelson Piquet, no fan of the Long Beach circuit, retired from a shunt into the barriers on lap 25. Mario Andretti fared no better in his one-off in the TAG-Williams FW07, retired back to the CART IndyCar series with an accident on lap 19. Eddie Cheever was the top American on the day, out on lap 59 with gearbox issues in his Ligier.

The early season form of Keke Rosberg informed his 1982 Formula One campaign, while his ascendance at Williams in the departure of Carlos Reutemann informed the 1982 Caesars Palace Grand Prix. Michele Alboreto leveraged his Long Beach finish to mark a year of constant improvement, six points-paying finishes and a season-ending payday in Las Vegas. Eddie Cheever similarly marked his new opportunity with Guy Ligier, three finishes in the points including two podiums in America. Mario Andretti, on the other hand, drew a summer of CART IndyCar duty in 1982. Andretti also endured another controversial Indianapolis 500, shunted on a first-lap accident involving Kevin Cogan. Cogan, who infamously drove for Roger

Penske at Indy in 1982, was picked up by George Bignotti for 1983. Kevin Cogan's mount for the 1983 Indianapolis 500 would be rather *famously* sponsored—by Caesars Palace.

Remarkably, Mario Andretti returned to the Formula One grid late in the 1982 season, driving in the final two events for Enzo Ferrari. Andretti then scored the final points of a storied Formula One career in the penultimate 1982 round at Monza, an extremely popular pole position and third-place finish behind Rene Arnoux in a Renault and Patrick Tambay in a companion Ferrari. The Ferrari machines of Tambay and Andretti, though, were emblazoned with numbers 27 and 28, respectively, the numbers assigned to Gilles Villeneuve and Didier Pironi for the 1982 season. Sadly, Pironi had suffered career-ending injuries in the German Grand Prix on August 6, 1982. Gilles Villeneuve, though, was tragically killed during qualifying for the Belgian Grand Prix one month after Long Beach.

The Formula One series soldiered on to Monaco after the loss of Gilles

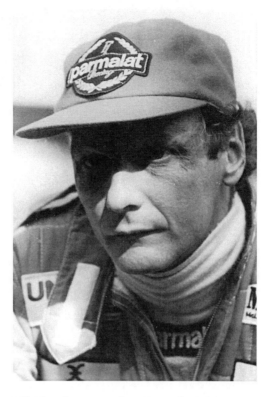

Niki Lauda returned to Formula One competition in 1982. Driving a McLaren MP4, Lauda won the April 4, 1982, Long Beach Grand Prix in only his third start after emerging from retirement. Niki Lauda also raced in the 1982 Caesars Palace Grand Prix in Las Vegas, Nevada (Bruce Aguilera collection).

Villeneuve. Riccardo Patrese claimed the following Monaco Grand Prix for Bernie Ecclestone and Brabham, the pinnacle at the pinnacle. The next round of the Formula One campaign was the inaugural Detroit Grand Prix. Robert McCabe's Detroit vision marked the first time that a single country had hosted three Grand Prix events in a Formula One season. Detroit also marked a discreet seven-figure fee for Bernie Ecclestone and FOCA. It was out with Watkins Glen and welcome to Las Vegas, Detroit, and—potentially—New York City.

John Watson won the 1982 Detroit round, vaulting the 36-year-old McLaren driver to the mid-season World Championship points lead. "I suppose it (the victory) was somewhat unexpected," Watson offered from the victory celebration. "Now we just have to keep working as hard as we have been to see that it keeps happening all year."[26] With two wins through Detroit—and for the first time in his career—John Watson was in the championship conversation. Watson's mid-season surprise kept the McLaren racer in that discussion all the way to the final Formula One event at Caesars Palace.

Much like the 1981 Caesars Palace Grand Prix being held over on the Formula

American Eddie Cheever joined the Ligier team after spending 1981 with Tyrell. Cheever drove the Ligier-Matra to a fine second place at the inaugural Detroit Grand Prix on June 6, 1982. Cheever also landed on the podium of the 1982 Caesars Palace Grand Prix. French cigarette brand Gitanes was a long-time sponsor of the Ligier team (author's collection).

One schedule for 1982, so too would the Detroit Grand Prix make another run in 1983. In fact, the Detroit Grand Prix would run through 1988 until being scuttled. As always, the Detroit Grand Prix events included the considerable Formula One influences—and fees—of Bernie Ecclestone. In 1984, though, the Detroit Grand Prix

also involved Jack Long in the promotional efforts for the race. Long was notably posted to the corporate Las Vegas masthead for the 1981 Caesars Palace Grand Prix. As well, in another mid-season surprise, the 1984 Detroit Formula One Grand Prix would engage William D. Weinberger of Caesars Palace. Even more curious, both Long and Weinberger were punching the clock for Bernie Ecclestone.

***

John Watson won the June 6, 1982, Detroit Grand Prix driving for McLaren. Watson also won the Belgian Grand Prix and had a total of seven points-paying finishes headed to the season finale 1982 Caesars Palace Grand Prix. John Watson would enter Las Vegas in a position to force a championship tiebreaker (Bruce Aguilera collection).

Originally from the Shaker Heights area of Cleveland, Murray Gennis joined Caesars Palace in Las Vegas in 1972 under the supervision of William S. Weinberger, father of William D. Weinberger. In the post-war period, Murray and brother Ed Gennis worked in the Midwest distribution network for Emerson Radio and Television, plying their wares at trade shows and dealerships in the Great Lakes states and along the East Coast. "A table model television receiver with a sixteen-inch direct view cathode ray rube, giving a picture 13 inches by 10 inches," ran the Emerson pitch in 1948. "The set will retail for less than $500."[27] Cathode tube television was an expensive way to watch Ed Sullivan and *Toast of the Town* in 1948. Early television hardware—and some apparent side hustle—also made the Gennis brothers wealthy. "I'm not sure what he might have done in addition to selling TV's and radios," suggested the junior William D. Weinberger, "but he knew a lot of bookmakers and gamblers."[28] Murray Gennis was also a regular visitor to Miami, "on business plus pleasure."[29] In fact, by 1969, Murray Gennis called Miami his home.

The path of Murray Gennis to Caesars Palace was further defined at his next stop. In 1970, Gennis was named "president and treasurer of the Skyways Motel of Miami."[30] The Skyways presented a distinctive Miami style, lavish pool garden, convention facilities, and air conditioning. Directly across the road from Miami Airport—gateway to the Caribbean—the Skyways Motel also held an almost mythical quality in mid-century mob lore. CIA-trained Cuban counter-revolutionaries gathered at the Skyways Motel. The FBI also observed Meyer Lansky and Santo Traffi-cante meeting at the Skyways in the heyday of Lansky's Cuban gambling resorts.

"The Skyways is largely owned by Sam Tucker," it was reported in 1965, "one of the charter members of the Cleveland Syndicate."[31] Sam Tucker, it should be noted, was also a co-owner of the Desert Inn and Stardust hotel casinos in Las Vegas along with Moe Dalitz. Dalitz, in turn, was the principal owner of Stardust International Raceway. Sam Tucker also held mutual business interests with Calvin Kovens.[32] Not surprisingly, Sam Tucker was further connected to mob kingpin Meyer Lansky.[33]

When the Skyways Motel was sold by Sam Tucker in 1972 to a syndicated investment group, Miami news could not resist the backstory. "A major motel that was developed by, and for years operated by, figures identified with organized crime investment activity here," reported the *Miami Herald*, "has been sold."[34] Shortly after the sale, Murray Gennis was announced at Caesars Palace in Las Vegas. "Mr. Gennis has more than 25 years of business experience," the senior Weinberger said in Las Vegas. "He has a fine background and we are very glad to have him with our organization."[35] Murray Gennis of Shaker Heights thus joined William S. Weinberger of Shaker Heights in the luxury brand of Caesars Palace in Las Vegas. Ultimately, it was the "fine background" of Murray Gennis that would drive the headlines.

As William S. Weinberger moved from Caesars Palace to Bally's in New Jersey, son William D. Weinberger moved from Caesars World in Los Angeles to Caesars Palace in Las Vegas. The Las Vegas posting was the junior Weinberger's introduction to the much older Gennis. "Murray Gennis and I had equal stature on the Caesars organizational chart," recalled Bill Weinberger. "He was specifically in charge of the hosts, which meant he often had the last word on giving out credit to customers which made him a very important person in the casino."[36] Bill Weinberger

Murray Gennis of Shaker Heights, Ohio, was the president of Sam Tucker's notoriously-connected Skyways Motel in Miami prior to being posted as a casino executive at Caesars Palace. Tucker was notably a member of the Cleveland Syndicate that included Moe Dalitz, Morris Kleinman, Ruby Kolod—and deep connections to Meyer Lansky (author's collection).

and Murray Gennis thus collaborated on numerous events in the three years prior to Gennis' arrest in Australia. As Weinberger describes it, "it was not a match made in heaven."[37]

While Bill Weinberger held a very public role as vice president of Caesars Palace casino promotions, the arrest of Murray Gennis in Australia would, to some extent, divine the dark arts of Las Vegas casino credit and—in this case—casino collections. When Gennis was arrested on November 3, 1981, he was in the company of Reg Andrews, a retired Australian businessman. Andrews was self-described "as a public relations officer for Caesars Palace."[38] Reg Andrews was certainly a regular gambler at Caesars Palace, but well outside the crease of the official corporate organizational chart.

"Reg was a bookmaker in Australia," described Bill Weinberger, "and he would bring in or send in players from time to time."[39] "One of the things Reg did for us was move money," continued Weinberger. "I'm not sure how. He had his ways."[40] When Andrews' "ways" failed him in 1981, the "retired businessman" found himself in trouble with Australian authorities. Andrews' legal difficulties then conjured a deal. "He [Andrews] would give them a much bigger fish than he," according to Weinberger. "He would give them Caesars Palace."[41]

Coordinating with Murray Gennis in Las Vegas for a cash collection, Andrews then alerted Australian investigators. Gennis landed in Australia less than two weeks after the 1981 Caesars Palace Grand Prix. Once on the ground, Murray Gennis—the host of hosts—presented a celebration of invited high rollers befitting Caesar, "some 100 guests, including Alan Jones," winner of the October 17, 1981, Caesars Palace Grand Prix.[42] While under surveillance at the gathering of VIP gamblers, Gennis also harvested cash.

When Gennis was arrested at Kingsford Smith International Airport in Sydney, his suitcases divulged a six-figure smuggle. Murray Gennis, however, had declared no more than $4,000 in cash. Murray Gennis was subsequently bargained back to the United States by a Caesars Palace lawyer, along with a $100,000 bail bond. J. Terrence Lanni then minimized the Gennis arrest at the Caesars World annual shareholder's meeting on December 29, 1981, claiming "the money was … 'quite legal.'"[43] In April of 1982, though, Murray Gennis failed to show for a court appearance guaranteed by the bond. "His lawyer contended that Gennis," it was reported, "was suffering from a heart condition."[44] Gennis played the classic Meyer Lansky lament. Unmoved, Australian officials issued an arrest warrant.

"Don't go down to Australia, Murray," Frank Sinatra advised the Caesars Palace vice president. "They'll throw you in the jug."[45] On advice of counsel, however—and with his Nevada gambling license in peril—Murray Gennis returned on July 27, 1982, to face Australian authorities. Silver-coiffed Harry Wald was at his side. The presiding judge "showed a keen interest in Caesar's Palace."[46] The judge also questioned Harry Wald directly. Later that same day, Gennis pled guilty to charges of "attempting to take currency out of Australia."[47] Murray Gennis could have faced a five-year prison sentence. Instead, the criminal lawyers for Caesars Palace and Murray Gennis bargained it down to a $30,000 fine.

The legal appeal of Clifford Perlman and Stuart Perlman in New Jersey also turned concurrent with the case of Murray Gennis in Australia. With a 5–1 vote, the New Jersey Supreme Court upheld the order of the New Jersey Casino Control Commission that the Perlman brothers be severed from Caesars World and Caesars Palace. On July 30, 1982, three days after Murray Gennis pled guilty, Clifford Perlman submitted his resignation during a board meeting at Caesars Palace.

Murray Gennis of Caesars Palace, left, poses with Reg Andrews of Australia at a reception in Sydney, Australia, on November 1, 1981. Notably, Caesars Palace Grand Prix winner Alan Jones was also in attendance. Reg Andrews was a self-described public relations officer for Caesars Palace. Andrews was also informing Australian police on the trans-pacific gambling marker collections of Gennis. Murray Gennis was arrested two days later at the Sydney airport for currency smuggling (author's collection).

"After the (state) Supreme Court decision," Perlman reflected from his vacated office, "I realized that there would be a termination of my contract."[48] Perlman's moment of contemplation, however, quickly gave way to the ego-play that ran through the New Jersey licensing process. "If I was operating in gaming in New Jersey, it would elevate that state considerably in my opinion," continued Perlman. "What they did demeaned that state, there's no question in my mind about that. I was a pawn in that political game."[49]

Clifford Perlman, apparent political refugee and departed Emperor, then took leave from his $305,000 annual salary at the Palace of Caesar. Perlman's exit from Caesars World and Caesars Palace, though, was hardly a haircut. Clifford and Stuart Perlman were still sitting on a $30 million down payment from Caesars World, Inc. for the repurchase of their shares. The Perlman pay zone thus preserved, the brothers were also slated to receive some $10 million annually from Caesars World for the next six years. "The board of directors of Desert Palace, Inc, the operating company of Caesars Palace," it was reported in Las Vegas, "accepted the resignation 'with deep regret.'"[50] Going forward, the Perlman brothers were shackled to the Palace only by a non-compete clause scheduled to expire on February 1, 1983. J. Terrence Lanni was then named as chairman of Caesars Palace. Lanni was also appointed as the head of Desert Palace, Inc., the gambling entity of Caesar created in 1965 by Jay Sarno, Stanley Mallin, Nathan Jacobsen, and controlled for organized crime interests from behind the corporate curtain by Jerome Zarowitz—allegedly.

At the same time, Terrence Lanni seemed to downplay the notion that Caesars World had considered vacating the New Jersey gambling market in order to retain Clifford Perlman. "The good thing about it," Lanni commented, "is one man doesn't make an entire company."[51] Terrence Lanni, in turn, proclaimed the elevation of Harry Wald in the Caesars Palace operation. "It's a Harry Wald show," announced Lanni one week after the resignation of Perlman. "Harry Wald is the number one officer in Caesars Palace. He reports to me."[52]

Going forward, Perlman's former appellation of "chief executive officer" was to be stricken from the lexicon of Caesar. The official portrait of Clifford Perlman was also stricken from the page layout for the official program of the 1982 Caesars Palace Grand Prix just six weeks away. Finally, nor would Clifford Perlman preside over the podium celebration of the 1982 Grand Prix, his ensemble of satin jacket, designer jeans, and tennis kicks to be replaced by Harry Wald, resplendent in brilliant coiffe, wide-collared shirt, and bold print tie.

One week before the 1982 Caesars Palace Grand Prix, Harry Wald attempted to place a period after Murray Gennis and the handling of international debt collections under the regime of Clifford Perlman. "In past years, Caesars Palace has found you to be one of its very important and loyal customers," Harry Wald wrote in a remarkable letter to Australian gambling customers of Caesars Palace. "As you no doubt are aware, Mr. Murray Gennis, our senior vice-president, encountered some difficulties in Australia during the past year. Those problems have now been resolved."[53] "From time to time one of our customers would bring payments for other customers from Australia to us," continued Wald, without mention of Reg Andrews. "In the future, we would appreciate that any payments be remitted directly to us and not through other individuals who might claim to represent Caesars Palace."[54]

As the letter of Harry Wald hit the post boxes of Sydney, Australia, the Formula One circus caravan once again departed Europe for its return pilgrimage to the splendor of Caesars Palace and the luxury-branded trappings of Las Vegas. As in 1981, the Caesars Palace Grand Prix would close the season, as well as decide the 1982 world championship. Keke Rosberg entered the Caesars Palace finale holding the points lead, 42 points to the badly injured Didier Pironi's 39. John Watson of McLaren was third on points with 33, in a position to force a tie with Rosberg. Notably, Keke Rosberg also occupied the William race seat vacated by Alan Jones of Australia. Alan Jones, however—1980 world champion, winner of the 1981 Caesars Palace Grand Prix, and guest of Murray Gennis at the Sydney soiree—would not be in the Caesars Palace starting field.

***

"If a Formula One world championship Grand Prix on a 'parking lot' course next to the Las Vegas strip was considered a gamble in 1981," read the deck of the *Las Vegas*

Review-Journal, "the odds have shifted dramatically in 1982."[55] Indeed, the 1981 Caesars Palace Grand Prix had crowned Nelson Piquet as the Formula One world champion. Further, despite the dismal report from the Caesars casino count room, the race stood as the largest sporting event in Nevada history. In fact, the Caesars Palace Grand Prix pulled nearly double the attendance of the last premier-level motorsport championship decider in Las Vegas, the 1968 Stardust Can-Am Grand Prix. William D. Weinberger of Caesars Palace thus continued with the formula for 1982. Murray Gennis was even on hand to host the international high rollers, if any bothered to make the trip.

"We were confident, of course, that we had constructed a competitive track of world caliber," Bill Weinberger said in 1982, "but you really don't know for sure until it is tested under fire."[56] Grumblings from the combatants at the pinnacle of motorsport were thus subdued as they returned for the 1982 event. The Caesars Palace circuit was indeed the fastest of the three American Formula One circuits contested in 1982, up to 170 mph as the screaming Grand Prix machines hit the speed trap on the long back straight across the Summa property. "We realize that while speed is the common denominator of auto racing, it is not the total measure of competitiveness," continued Weinberger, "but in our case it exceeded predictions in speed and performance, particularly those made by people who had not actually seen the course."[57]

Jack Long, vice president of marketing for the Caesars Palace Grand Prix, also offered comment in the name of Caesar. "We (Caesars) have only wanted to do super class events," proclaimed Long, "and we'll try and keep that trend, always offering something new and improved."[58] It was a stump speech that Jack Long would also carry with him to his difficult and short-lived run atop the Indy Racing League.

To some extent, Mario Andretti had played both advocate and adversary in 1981. Andretti's presence with Paul Newman at Bill Weinberger's Manhattan presser certainly bolstered the star power of the event. As a race car driver, however, Mario Andretti was not a fan of the low-speed hairpin turns of Caesars, nor of their lateral-force demands on Formula One drive trains. Headed into the 1982 Caesars Palace Grand Prix, though, Andretti again played to the promotion. "I think the Caesars Palace track surprised a lot of people in a very positive way," Andretti said before the 1982 event. "I see the event becoming a tremendously big happening."[59]

Mario Andretti also rolled into Las Vegas in 1982 driving a bright red Ferrari F126. "I always maintained a very good relationship with Ferrari. Mr. Ferrari asked me if I would do Monza and Las Vegas. I said absolutely, at least if I can get a good test," recalled Mario Andretti. "He had 2 full days setup at the test track at Ferrari. At the end of the first day, I broke the track record. I said I'm fine, I don't need until Sunday, give everyone a day off."[60]

By contrast with Mario Andretti's championship run in 1978, the former Formula One number-one went one-off amid a full CART IndyCar schedule for 1982. With only two Formula One events on the docket, Andretti nonetheless held four championship points after a remarkable third place for the Scuderia Ferrari at the penultimate round in Monza. That Monza miracle then set up a Roman homecoming for the final Formula One start in the career of the great American race car driver.

Mario Andretti (in T-shirt with helmet in hand) stands alongside his #28 Ferrari 126C2 at the September 25, 1982, Caesars Palace Grand Prix. The #27 Ferrari of Patrick Tambay is beyond to the left. Andretti and Tambay were posted to the Ferrari team after the death of Gilles Villeneuve at the Belgian Grand Prix and the career-ending injuries to Didier Pironi at the German Grand Prix. Mario Andretti qualified on pole and finished third at the Italian Grand Prix two weeks before Las Vegas. The 1982 Caesars Palace Grand Prix was Andretti's final Formula One start. Crew members are not identified (courtesy LVCVA News Bureau).

The Formula One points battle of 1982 had otherwise produced a rather flattened curve. In fact, 11 different drivers had crested the podium in the 15 events contested prior to the Caesars Palace finale. Rene Arnoux, Niki Lauda, and Alain Prost held two victories apiece. With his triumph in Detroit, John Watson also had two wins to his credit. Sadly, the sidelined Didier Pironi was twice victorious as well. So strong was Pironi's season through the 12 rounds before his injuries that he was only three points out of the championship lead headed into Las Vegas. On the strength of a single win and a string of points finishes, Keke Rosberg of Williams and his 42 points held the advantage for the Caesars Palace finale. With Pironi out of the cockpit, Rosberg's closest challenger was John Watson of McLaren, a full race's worth of

Derek Warwick (#35 Toleman) leads Andrea de Cesaris (#22 Alfa Romeo), Derek Daly (#5 Williams, and Niki Lauda (#8 McLaren) into turn one at the September 25, 1982, Caesars Palace Grand Prix. The drivers were classified 17th, ninth, sixth, and 15th, respectively, at the finish. Diagonal Caesars Palace parking lot striping is noteworthy (courtesy LVCVA News Bureau).

points back at 33 markers. If Watson could muster the Caesars Palace victory and the nine championship points on offer—and if Rosberg finished seventh or worse—the McLaren driver would force the tie. Further, with two wins in his pocket to Rosberg's single, Watson firmly held the tiebreaker advantage.

Formula One qualifying for the second annual Caesars Palace Grand Prix set the order of battle for the Roman repatriation of Mario Andretti. Andretti also showed form in his Ferrari, qualifying seventh with a 1:17.921, over one second quicker than his 1981 time in the Alfa Romeo. As well, Mario Andretti split the championship contenders on the time sheets. Keke Rosberg was just ahead of Andretti with a 1:17.886. John Watson followed ninth at 1:17.986. Streaking to the leading edge of Caesars Palace qualifying, though, were the distinctive turbocharged Renault RE30 machines of Alain Prost and Rene Arnoux. Prost was on pole with a scorching 1:16.356, pulling well over a second from the pole time of Carlos Reutemann at the 1981 Caesars Palace Grand Prix. In fact, Prost's pole mark was over two seconds clear of his own 1981 qualifying time. Rene Arnoux pulled alongside Prost on the all-Renault front row with his own mark of 1:16.786. Tucked behind Alain Prost and Rene Arnoux was Michele Alboreto driving a Tyrell. In his first full season in Formula One, Alboreto's qualifying effort was a revelation. In fact, despite six points-paying finishes thus far in his 1982 campaign, Alboreto had only twice cracked the top five in qualifying. Alboreto's time was also a remarkable turnaround from 1981, in which the Tyrell

Eddie Cheever (#25 Ligier) leads Manfred Winkelhock (#9 ATS) down the front straight at the 1982 Caesars Palace Grand Prix. Chico Serra (#20 Fittipaldi) trails just right of pit lane. Car exiting turn 14 is not identified. Pit lane exit is visible in center of image. Open-air hospitality suites at left of Caesars Palace Grand Prix sign are noteworthy (courtesy LVCVA News Bureau).

machines were mired in the back of the pack. From third-quick on the grid, Michele Alboreto was thus poised for his own Roman holiday.

The 1982 Caesars Palace Grand Prix returned its companion series for the second annual event. The SCCA Can-Am competition once again supported the Formula One round on the Las Vegas circuit. Unlike 1981, though, the 1982 Can-Am series continued on to Riverside and Laguna Seca after the Las Vegas stop. Further, the star power of Can-Am was diminished in 1982. Geoff Brabham, 1981 series champion, made the jump to the CART IndyCar series. Teo Fabi was on the ground at Caesars Palace but had jumped from Can-Am to the Candy-Toleman Formula One squad, a backmarker of the 1982 field. Indeed, Teo Fabi did not make the Formula One qualifying cut for the 1982 Caesars Palace event, over five seconds adrift from polesitter Alain Prost. Bobby Rahal, fourth in the 1981 Caesars Palace Can-Am event, had also moved to the 1982 CART IndyCar series with Jim Trueman. Nonetheless, 1981 Caesars Palace Can-Am winner Danny Sullivan—although dabbling in IndyCar for Gerald Forsythe—returned to contest the entire 1982 Can-Am season.

Notably, Danny Sullivan rolled into Las Vegas driving a resplendent Budweiser-liveried March 827, owned by Caesars Palace Grand Prix pitchman Paul Newman. Amid the drop-off in driver appeal, though, the 1982 SCCA Can-Am series arrived with a remarkable new talent, Al Unser, Jr. Unser, the son of three-time Indy 500

Goodyear tires crowd the Williams pit area at the 1982 Caesars Palace Grand Prix. Goodyear, Michelin, Pirelli, and Avon all provided tires for the 1982 Formula One season. Caesars Palace 27-story Fantasy Tower beyond provided observation areas and the NBC broadcast booth (courtesy LVCVA News Bureau).

winner Al Sr., was astride a streamlined Frissbee machine entered by Rick Galles, Unser's later IndyCar benefactor. In an oddity of Formula One scheduling, the 1982 Caesars Palace Can-Am also rolled off as the *de facto* main event. Indeed, the booming Chevrolet V-8's of the Can Am series thundered off the starting line on Sunday, September 26, 1982, the day *after* the Formula One race had run its course.

While the Formula One drivers of the 1981 Caesars Palace Grand Prix complained of "neck exertions" and the 65-degree heat, the 1982 event brought a legitimate late summer sweat. Indeed, when Jean-Marie Balestre and FISA moved the Caesars Palace Grand Prix two weeks earlier, from October to September, the infamous Las Vegas heat was prepared to oblige the autocracy. Formula One teams were greeted early Saturday morning by temperatures in the 80s. As the grid formed on

Saturday afternoon, the air temperature climbed to over 90 degrees, on scorching black asphalt, in the middle of the great southwestern desert. A field of the world's best race car drivers would then swelter in their unventilated race suits for a throw at a hot Caesars Palace table, while the autumnal chill of Watkins Glen must have felt like a far-away friend.

The turbocharged Renault duo of Alain Prost and Rene Arnoux commanded the start of the 1982 Caesars Palace Grand Prix, accelerating smartly and hurtling toward the Las Vegas strip at 120 mph. The hard left of turn one then steered the leaders around a full hairpin. Seconds later, the field transitioned from the paved parking area of the original Kirk Kerkorian property, to the undeveloped desert scrub of the original Howard Hughes property. By the time they rounded turn 14 to complete the first lap, Rene Arnoux had slipped around teammate Alain Prost and streaked past the start-finish line and pit lane as the new leader of the race.

The early laps found Arnoux continuing to hold Prost at bay. Michele Alboreto was a solid third in the Tyrell but was being gapped by the Renault machines. Eddie Cheever driving for Ligier, Riccardo Patrese in a Williams, and Keke Rosberg in the Williams rounded out the top six. Homeland hopes and a thunderous cheer arose when Mario Andretti passed Keke Rosberg for sixth. After a lackluster start, though, championship chaser Watson was bogged in 12th. John Watson, however, was soon to mount his own charge for the crown.

Rene Arnoux gave way to polesitter Alain Prost by lap 15. At the same time, John Watson moved forward, passing Riccardo Patrese, Mario Andretti, Keke Rosberg, Derek Daly, and Nelson Piquet in three short laps. When John Watson passed Eddie Cheever, he trailed only Michele Alboreto and the Renaults of Prost and Arnoux. By lap 20, Arnoux was off with gearbox issues in his machine. Alain Prost remained at the point although Alboreto began to close. Watson, meanwhile, moved closer to Alboreto. On the 26th lap, Mario Andretti was delivered his swan song, out with a wishbone failure, just as in 1981. With Andretti retired, Keke Rosberg was restored to fifth. As the 1982 Caesars Palace Grand Prix moved past the halfway mark, though, there was soon a change at the front.

While Michele Alboreto chased Alain Prost, the Prost Renault developed a tire-induced vibration. Prost slowed while Alboreto filled his mirrors. On lap 53, Michele Alboreto managed past the struggling Prost to lead his first Formula One Grand Prix. John Watson also improved past Prost four laps later. Michele Alboreto then set the fastest lap of the race, a strong 1:19.629 on lap 59. Alain Prost drifted further back until he settled in fourth, nearly a minute behind Alboreto but just in front of Keke Rosberg. On track, the championship advantage remained with Rosberg, 44 points to 39 for John Watson. John Watson continued solidly in second but, with tire issues of his own, could not close on leader Alboreto.

At the end of 75 laps, Michele Alboreto streaked past the flag stand on the Caesars Palace front straight to claim his very first Formula One victory. The 1982 Caesars Palace Grand Prix was Michele Alboreto's day. Behind Alboreto, the order of the closing laps remained John Watson, Eddie Cheever, Alain Prost, and Keke Rosberg. Alboreto's inaugural triumph was the first victory in four years for team owner Ken Tyrell. For John Watson, it was his fifth podium of the season. Tied on points with the

The field of the September 25, 1982, Caesars Palace Grand Prix leaps forward from their stand-ing start and approaches turn one adjacent to the world-famous Las Vegas Strip. Alain Prost (#15 Renault), Rene Arnoux (#16 Renault), Michele Alboreto (#3 Tyrell), Eddie Cheever (#25 Ligier), Keke Rosberg (#6 Williams), Riccardo Patrese (#2 Brabham), Mario Andretti (#28 Fer-rari), John Watson (#7 McLaren), Derek Warwick (#35 Toleman), and Nelson Piquet (#1 Brab-ham) form the top ten of the emerging arrowhead formation. Alboreto, Watson, and Cheever finished 1–2–3. Keke Rosberg finished fifth and claimed the 1982 Formula One world champi-onship. Mountain wall in far background is Blue Diamond Ridge. The Blue Diamond forma-tion created a huge amphitheater effect in the west Las Vegas valley (courtesy LVCVA News Bureau).

badly injured Didier Pironi, Watson was classified third in the world driver's champi-onship. From third place, American Eddie Cheever stood on his third podium in the 1982 campaign.

Replacing Alan Jones on the Williams team, Keke Rosberg claimed his first For-mula One race win and the championship in the same season. More wins would await, but the 1982 world drivers championship was the high point of Rosberg's career. Thirty-four years later, son Nico Rosberg claimed his own world drivers

Derek Warwick (#35 Toleman) leads the line through turn 11 at the September 25, 1982, Caesars Palace Grand Prix. Hotel-casino towers along the Las Vegas Strip are, from left, the Holiday Inn, Imperial Palace, Flamingo Hilton, and Kirk Kerkorian's MGM. Kerkorian was also the original landlord of Caesars Palace as well as a gambling licensee (courtesy LVCVA News Bureau).

championship for Mercedes AMG Petronas Motorsport. Like his father before him, the junior Rosberg's team was underpinned by millions of dollars in petro-wealth. For Frank Williams, it was the fourth world drivers championship in a portfolio that now includes seven, along with nine constructors championships and 114 total race victories.

From the confines of the paddock, Mario Andretti offered a final toast to his Formula One driving career, making Enzo Ferrari proud with gritty performances to close his truncated 1982 effort. Departing Las Vegas from McCarran International Airport the same day, though, Andretti jetted to Michigan for another commitment to Pat Patrick and the CART IndyCar series. Mario Andretti's departure from Caesars Palace came 20 years after Graham Hill won his first world drivers championship. It was also 20 years after Alvin Malnik, Jay Sarno, and Stanley Mallin first appeared in their respective FBI dossiers. One day after pushing a turbocharged Ferrari 126 in Las Vegas to the point of failure, Andretti tucked into a Patrick Wildcat IndyCar at over 200 mph on the high banks of Roger Penske's Michigan International Speedway. From 25th on the grid, the great American race car driver brought the Wildcat home in second place behind winner Bobby Rahal. Second place at Michigan, however, was likely of no greater comfort to Mario Andretti than a drivetrain failure during his final Formula One start at the 1982 Caesars Palace Grand Prix.

Notably, the 1982 Caesars Palace Grand Prix marked 15 years since Mario Andretti was presented the Martini and Rossi "Driver of the Year" award in 1967 at the Stardust Hotel and Casino, owned by notorious Cleveland racketeer Moe Dalitz. The 1982 Caesars Palace Grand Prix, however, also marked the high point of the entire Formula One exercise in Las Vegas. Indeed, Mario Andretti would be back in 1983 to lead the CART IndyCar program at a newly configured Caesars Palace "roval."

***

On September 26, 1982, the Formula One teams, officials, and hangers-on were left to repack the caravan for the return to the long off-season in Europe. As the posh of the pinnacle queued down the Las Vegas strip toward McCarran Airport, the Caesars Palace grandstands refilled for more action. Indeed, the Caesars bill posted two additional race events to cap the Grand Prix weekend. The Sunday afternoon SCCA Can-Am event was preceded by a two-wheel thriller, the AFM-PRO Coors Caesars Palace Formula One Motorcycle Grand Prix. "The bikes should provide a spectacular show," pitched Bill

Michele Alboreto won the September 25, 1982, Caesars Palace Grand Prix driving a Tyrell 011. The Las Vegas event was Alboreto's first Formula One victory. On the strength of his win in the season finale and seven point-paying finishes, Michele Alboreto finished eighth in the final Formula One points standings. International singing star Diana Ross (left) served as grand marshal alongside actor Paul Newman. Miss Ross also performed at Caesars Palace during the Grand Prix weekend. Diana Ross also returned for the November 11, 1984, Caesars Palace Grand Prix IV (Bruce Aguilera collection).

Weinberger. "With engines producing over 160 horsepower, these bikes are capable of speeds of up to 190 mph, same as Formula One cars."[61] For many of the spectators, the full-throttle, tucked-in motorcycle road racers were the high point of the weekend.

David Aldana of Santa Ana, California, one of the stars of the seminal Bruce Brown movie *On Any Sunday*, qualified toward the front of the Coors Motorcycle Grand Prix riding a works 1000cc machine for Team Honda. Harry Klinzmann on a Kawasaki, though, was on pole with a 1:47.913. Privateer Nicky Richichi was alongside on a Yamaha TZ750 with a 1:48.209. To the delight of the southwestern crowd, David Aldana led from the start and leaned his Honda into the first turn along the Las Vegas strip. Nicky Richichi was soon past though, followed by Thad Wolff, Klinzmann, and Aldana.

Nicky Richichi then gapped the field, leading lap after lap on his screaming water-cooled Yamaha. David Aldana was out by the mid-point, the loose exhaust system of his Honda sapping power and sending him to the paddock. By halfway though, Miles Baldwin—another Yamaha TZ750-mounted privateer—was closing on Richichi. As Baldwin set his sights on Richichi, the race leader uncorked the fastest lap of the race of the lap with a 1:46.454. One lap later, Nicky Richichi was off and Miles Baldwin was through to the lead. "I could see him (Richichi) slowing down. I knew it was his tire," offered Baldwin. "Right then he fell down."[62] Miles Baldwin held on over the final two laps to take the checkered flag of the 1982 Coors Caesars Palace Motorcycle Grand Prix.

An estimated 20,000 fans watched Miles Baldwin take the popular victory. Baldwin was followed across the line by John Woo on another Yamaha and Harry Klinzmann on the Kawasaki. "On the cool-off lap the crowd was going crazy," remarked Klinzmann from the podium, "so I was doing wheelies to keep 'em going."[63] Miles Baldwin's share of the reported $20,000 purse was $5,000. The motorcycle payday was definitely not Formula One money. Michele Alboreto likely pocketed six-figures for his Saturday afternoon at the Caesars Palace pass line. Nor was Baldwin's first-place effort anything approaching the Can-Am prize. Indeed, the winner of the 1982 Caesars Palace Can-Am event was slated to take home over $25,000.

The AFM-PRO event of the 1982 Caesars Palace Grand Prix combined two-stroke and four-stroke motorcycles representing the major Japanese manufacturers, Honda, Yamaha, Kawasaki, and Suzuki. The formula was the forerunner of the modern superbike. Identified are, from right, Vincent Hill #64, Kerry Bryant #23, Rich Oliver #35, Jeff Heind #67. Canadian Miles Baldwin won the event on a Yamaha TZ750. Rich Oliver finished seventh (courtesy LVCVA News Bureau).

What the motorcycle contingent did take with them on their way out of town were shots from the local press. "The motorcycles were pitiful. The bikes were dirty and the riders looked like they had just climbed out from underneath a 50-gallon drum of axle grease," wrote Mike Henle of the *Las Vegas Review Journal*. "They were not in the same class as Caesars Palace."[64] As history records, both the pinnacle of motorsport and the daring field of professional motorcycle road racers then took their permanent leave of Caesars Palace.

With the two-wheelers and their axle grease stilled, it was left to the dwindling bill of the SCCA Can-Am series to cap the 1982 Caesars Palace Grand Prix. "In this town," suggested the *Los Angeles Times*, "Can-Am racing can be expected to draw fewer spectators than a crap table and case less excitement that a $5 jackpot on a nickel slot machine."[65] Rather, with its morning motorcycle lead-in and residual from the Formula One championship closer, the 1982 Caesars Palace Can-Am event pulled a reported 28,000 spectators though the gates. By contrast, the 1968 Stardust Can-Am Grand Prix at Stardust International Raceway drew 21,320.

Unlike the inaugural 38-lap sprint in 1981, the 1982 edition of the Caesars Palace Can-Am event had the feel of an afternoon enduro, 66 laps and two mandatory pit stops to spice the competition. The 90-degree temperatures of Saturday also eased for the Sunday Can-Am event. Wind gusts above 30 mph, however, pushed the sand of the Summa property across the track. Starting from pole, Sullivan and his Budweiser March 827 were chased by the career-surging Al Unser, Jr., in a Galles Frissbee. Unser Jr., born on April 19, 1962, was notably well under the legal Nevada gambling age of 21. Undeterred, Al Unser, Jr., took the pass line around Sullivan on lap four and held point until the halfway mark when he dipped into the pits for a mandatory stop. Danny Sullivan remained on track for another 10 circuits and built a 12 second lead over the trailing Al Unser, Jr. When Sullivan rejoined the track after his mandatory stop on lap 39, he managed to slot in ahead of Unser Jr. The Frissbee and Al Unser, Jr., then battled back and came around the March of Danny Sullivan on the front straightway two laps later. On the next circuit, Danny Sullivan passed back with authority and would not be challenged. Al Unser, Jr., then struggled on his final mandatory pit stop. With spins on lap 48 and lap 59, Unser Jr. was out of contention.

Danny Sullivan and his March 827 powered down the front straightaway on lap 66 and to the checkered flag, taking his second consecutive SCCA Caesars Palace Can-Am victory. Al Unser, Jr., and his Galles Frissbee trailed through nearly a minute later. Al Holbert, the seventh-place finisher in 1981, was elevated to third on podium in 1982, albeit nearly a lap down to Sullivan. Danny Sullivan collected the obligatory $25,500 for the win. "The sand would cover the apex (of the turn) and we had to run on radar," remarked Sullivan from the celebration. "If the car got a little loose, the wind would move the car around."[66] With two spins on the day, Al Unser, Jr., had to concur. Sitting on three wins in the 1982 Can-Am season, though, Al Unser, Jr., stretched his points lead. A second-place at Riverside and the win at the Laguna Seca finale carried Al Unser, Jr., to the 1982 SCCA Can-Am championship.

For 1983, Danny Sullivan received the call-up to Formula One. Danny Sullivan leveraged his Caesars Palace auditions to pair with Michele Alboreto on Ken Tyrell's new Benetton-sponsored team. Danny Sullivan's 1981 Caesars Palace Can-Am

The SCCA Can-Am series returned to Las Vegas for the 1982 Caesars Palace Grand Prix. Along pit lane from far end, Al Unser, Jr. (#15 Frissbee), John Kalagian (#9 Frissbee), and Eddie Wachs (Ralt RT2). The machines of Unser Jr. and Kalagian were powered by five-liter Chevrolet engines. Wachs' Ralt was powered by a two-liter Hart engine and classified separately. The September 26, 1982, Can-Am event of the Caesars Palace Grand Prix was won by Danny Sullivan, followed by Al Unser, Jr., and Al Holbert. Unser Jr. was the 1982 Can-Am champion and would also compete in the 1983 and 1984 CART IndyCar Caesars Palace Grand Prix events. The domed structure visible beyond pit lane is the Caesars Palace OmniMax theater, open from 1979 until 2000 (courtesy LVCVA News Bureau).

performance, in particular, could be measured favorably against the Formula One field. Danny Sullivan scored points in 1983 at Monaco for Ken Tyrell before returning stateside in 1984 for a very successful season in CART IndyCar. Al Unser, Jr., on the other hand, launched directly from his 1982 Can-Am championship into the premier American open-wheel series, continuing with Rick Galles as his team owner.

The 1982 Caesars Palace Can-Am event was the fifth appearance in Las Vegas of the once-vaunted series, commencing with the finale of the inaugural 1966 season

The elevated flag stand of the September 25, 1982, Caesars Palace Grand Prix is visible along the pit lane wall in center of image. Race control booth is at far right. Dated event signage covers the Caesars Palace marquee along Interstate 15. Silhouette of Spring Mountains is apparent in distance. Datsun pylon to right of Caesars marquee marks turn 14. Chris Pook and the Long Beach Grand Prix Association dismantled the race facilities upon completion of the Grand Prix (courtesy LVCVA News Bureau).

won by John Surtees at Stardust International Raceway. Like the Formula One finale and the AFM-PRO motorcycle event before it, though, the 1982 Caesars Palace Grand Prix was the last appearance of Can-Am in Las Vegas.

The Can-Am series itself continued forward for another 5 years, albeit in incremental decline to its certain point of oblivion. By 1987 the Can-Am series relied on cast-off rebodied March 85C IndyCars to seed its marginal fields. The championship of the original 1966 Canadian-American Challenge Cup was won by the 1966 Stardust Raceway victor, former Formula One world champion John Surtees. That inaugural season received notable supporting performances from Bruce McLaren, Denny Hulme, Mario Andretti, Mark Donohue, Jim Hall, Phil Hill, Chris Amon, Dan Gurney, Graham Hill, Peter Revson, and George Follmer. As a point of contrast, the concluding 1987 SCCA Can-Am championship was won by Bill Tempero.

***

William D. Weinberger of Caesars Palace had cause for caution headed into the 1982 Caesars Palace Grand Prix, particularly after the resignation of chairman Clifford Perlman and the disposition of charges against vice-president Murray Gennis. The second annual Formula One event was now under the marketing *macro-scope* of Caesars Palace and Caesars World, Inc. Weinberger had also challenged his competing Las Vegas gambling operators to join in a coordinated marketing push to bolster the event. "Well, let's put it this way," cautioned Weinberger. "We can't do this by ourselves. We expected this thing to grow every year."[67] In its most publicly measurable indicator of growth, however, the 1982 Caesars Palace Grand Prix found itself in recession. To wit, the 1982 ticket gate fell from 38,000 to 32,000, a drop off of 15 percent.

On the Monday after the race weekend, Caesars Palace president Harry Wald played it close. "I know it was a loser as far as Caesars was concerned," assessed Wald of the Grand Prix take. "We did not recoup our costs as far as the event was concerned."[68] Harry Wald was, however, careful to disassociate the fortunes of the casino itself from the Grand Prix balance sheet. "You can't mix the two together," continued Wald. "The casino might lose or it might win, but it's not part of the [Grand Prix] event."[69] The public comments by the original Caesars Palace investor somewhat further divined the myriad mysteries of the casino business. The casino was the core reason for the existence of all that surrounded it. An annual Grand Prix event that might otherwise impede the flow of cash through the casino would be doubtful, if not altogether disposable.

Neither Bill Weinberger not Harry Wald would be rushed into comment on the prospects for continued premier-level racing alongside the famed Las Vegas Strip. "[Caesars officials will] come out with a statement as to what our ... thoughts are," concluded Harry Wald, "as far as the loss we sustained on this."[70] As the 1982 Caesars Palace Grand Prix wilted from the news pages, the proposed New York Grand Prix appeared to gather momentum.

Tightlipped with respect to the Caesars Palace Grand Prix event, Bill Weinberger nonetheless commented in support of Formula One at Flushing Meadows. "There will be a two-week interval between the races at Las Vegas and New York," suggested Weinberger, "giving Europeans and Latin Americans 17 days of a racing vacation."[71] Rather like Chris Pook, Bill Weinberger was developing his own national reputation as a motorsports organizer worthy of reckon. Weinberger's comments also tipped his growing relationship of trust with Bernie Ecclestone. As well, Bill Weinberger's lean toward the eastern seaboard foretold his own fate under the umbrella of Caesars World, Inc.

On Friday night, November 12, 1982, Caesars World, Inc., acted swiftly to reset the upper echelon of its centurion structure. Accordingly, executives across the Caesars Palace operation were terminated with immediate effect. "In the past few weeks, we have wanted to streamline our management," Harry Wald said. "We have taken positive steps to improve profitability of the hotel."[72] Among those being streamlined, there was one notable promotion. Bruce Aguilera, corporate counsel and secretary of Caesars World, received a parallel assignment at the Caesars Palace gambling resort as "vice president—law, administration and secretary."[73] "Wald would not say," concluded the reporting, "if other terminations or changes were being considered."[74]

On the same day as the bombshell report of the Caesars Palace shakeup, the notion of a Formula One and CART IndyCar doubleheader at Caesars Palace was resurfaced. "I rather think it might develop," Jackie Stewart said from the 1982 SEMA convention in Las Vegas. "I think it's fairly logical to try and maximize the weekend to attract the broadest amount of spectators."[75] One auto industry executive at the SEMA convention suggested that Bernie Ecclestone had already blessed the concept.[76] It remained to be determined, however, if Roger Penske, Pat Patrick and John Frasco of CART were similarly inclined.

On reports once again of the massive premier-series double header in Las Vegas, Bill Weinberger of Caesars Palace was eagerly sought for comment. Weinberger, though, offered only a reticent "We're hoping."[77] Later the same day, Bill Weinberger learned of his own fate in the streamlining of Caesar's centurion guard. "William D. Weinberger, a Caesars Palace vice president," ran the report, "will be leaving the Las Vegas resort to become an executive at Caesars Boardwalk Regency in Atlantic City."[78] The junior Weinberger thus joined the father in high-profile Atlantic City gambling operations. With a quick presser from Caesars World, the Caesars Palace

William D. Weinberger, Caesars Palace VP of casino marketing, was transferred to the Caesars Boardwalk Regency casino in Atlantic City, New Jersey, two months after the 1982 Caesars Palace Grand Prix. Father William S. Weinberger of Bally's Park Place was thus joined by his son in Atlantic City gambling. One of the junior Weinberger's first assignments was the Caesars redevelopment program of the century-old Hotel Traymore property along the Boardwalk. After demolition, the former Traymore site was used as a parking lot, providing some tinge of irony for the progenitor of the Caesars Palace Grand Prix. William D. Weinberger returned to Las Vegas for the CART IndyCar Caesars Palace Grand Prix IV (Library of Congress).

Grand Prix had just lost its founder. Bill Weinberger, however, would continue in Formula One promotions elsewhere. On the newly unveiled Caesars Palace organizational chart, though, the task of shepherding the 1983 Caesars Palace Grand Prix had just been assigned to the legal desk of Bruce Aguilera.

Less than two weeks later, national news struck the strategic plan of the national organized crime syndicate, directly at the pinnacle of the alleged "gambling empire extending to every casino in the free world."[79] "Mobster Meyer Lansky, 80, was checked out of Mt. Sinai Hospital," reported the *Miami Herald*, "after a two-week stay for examinations of a stomach ailment."[80] Word on the street, however, was that cancer had returned after surgery two years earlier to remove a tumor from his left lung.

As strategic planning of the national crime syndicate tilted closer to succession, street speculation naturally ran to the presumed preeminence of Alvin Malnik in the Lansky syndicate structure. Two weeks after Meyer Lansky returned home, Clifford Perlman and brother Stuart signed a $185 million agreement to purchase the Dunes Hotel and Casino in Las Vegas, directly south across Flamingo Road from Caesars Palace.[81] The Dunes was notably controlled by Morris Shenker, Jimmy Hoffa's long-time criminal attorney. Kirk Kerkorian had once owned a slice of the Dunes as well. On news of the Dunes purchase agreement, one might also suspect some updates to the strategic plan, at least involving the Las Vegas profit center.

Amid the news of Meyer Lansky and Clifford Perlman, Henry Valent of Watkins Glen, New York, passed away. "Mr. Valent," it was reported, "had been suffering from cancer for several months."[82] Henry Valent, the long-time president of the bankrupt Watkins Glen Grand Prix Corporation, was 67 years old at his passing. The threads of history through American organized crime and organized American Grand Prix motorsport were thus at forced transition. It would be left to two remaining Caesars Palace Grand Prix events to write the legacy of their overlap in Las Vegas, on properties formerly owned by Kirk Kerkorian and Howard Hughes. Like Elvis Presley famously departing the showroom of Kirk Kerkorian's International Hotel, though, Formula One had already left the building. Nearly 40 years later, the pinnacle of motorsport has yet to return to the pinnacle of world-class entertainment, hospitality, and gambling.

XI

Running in Circles

The Caesars Palace Grand Prix III Goes IndyCar,
the Departure of Meyer Lansky,
the Reemergence of the Emperor

Was the crown offered him thrice? (*Julius Caesar* 1.2.238)

The New Year of 1983 rang in with some fanfare for aging mob kingpin Meyer Lansky. Despite his ailments and recent discharge from Mt. Sinai hospital in Miami, the frail 80-year-old mobster found himself recognized on two national lists of repute. *Forbes* magazine named Lansky as one of the 400 wealthiest people in America. "Lansky, whose occupation is given by Forbes as 'mob moneyman,'" read the report, "comes in at around $100 million."[1] The *Forbes* editors would have struggled to produce a more accurate net worth for the aging mobster. Alleged interests in "gambling, pornography, prostitution, labor racketeering, and extortion"[2] simply did not lend themselves to traditional accountancy. Nor were the trustees of myriad Swiss and Bahamanian offshore bank accounts inclined to disclose zeroes for attribution—allegedly.

On the same day that the *Forbes* list splashed, Meyer Lansky was also named on a roster of celebrity Miami residents. "They're here and they're there, securely tucked away in the sundry corners of South Florida," it was reported in Miami, "neighbors with names like Isaac Singer and Calvin Klein and Alan King."[3] To those names of the Nobel laureate, the famed clothing designer, and the comedic actor who emulated Allen Dorfman in the movie *Casino* was added the infamous Meyer Lansky. "Lansky, Prohibition-era bootlegger and now the ailing financial wizard for the underworld," continued the Miami report, "makes his home on the beach."[4] With the exception of Lansky, the 1983 list of noteworthy Miamians was in sharp contrast to the list of Miami hoodlums published in 1963. That 1963 list included any number of notorious Meyer Lansky-connected and Caesars Palace-adjacent sobriquets: Dino Cellini, Santo Trafficante, Anthony "Fat Tony" Salerno, Jerome Zarowitz, Ruby Lazarus, Marvin Krause, and Al Mones.

Simultaneous with the New Year names of note, however, Meyer Lansky was readmitted to the hospital. Lansky was reportedly in satisfactory condition at Mt. Sinai while being treated for dehydration. "He is old and he is sick and there are a lot of things wrong with him," offered the hospital spokesperson.[5] On that sweeping diagnosis, however, Meyer Lansky descended into his departure, finally succumbing on January 15, 1983. The official cause of death was lung cancer. As with Joseph Barbara in Apalachin before, the most closely guarded secrets of the national crime syndicate may have been buried with Meyer Lansky.

The passing of the most popularly known mobster in modern American history brought the spectrum, from scorn on the street corners to tribute in the temples. Even law enforcement officials bestowed respect to one of the most elusive targets they had ever trailed. "He was the most powerful member of organized crime as we know it," remarked former FBI agent Ralph Hill. "He was stronger than even the Italian figures. He's responsible, primarily, for all of the casino gambling as it's known on this country."[6]

Meyer Lansky was the alleged financial genius of the national organized crime syndicate for nearly four decades. Lansky, in turn, was also the alleged mentor of Alvin Malnik, partner with Caesars World and Clifford Perlman in Pennsylvania and Miami properties. In early 1983, Meyer Lansky made the Forbes 400 list, a list of celebrity Miami residents—and the obituaries (Library of Congress).

"He wound up beating everybody," added Patrick Healy of the Chicago Crime Commission. "He was the grandfather of it all, almost up until the very time of his death. The heir apparent—that's really a much bigger question that anything else."[7] The departure of Meyer Lansky indeed intensified speculation around his succession. Sources indicated that the Chicago outfit and their Las Vegas enforcer Anthony Spilotro were poised to penetrate the Lansky structure.[8]

Government accounts, however, leaned toward Alvin Malnik, perhaps already positioned in control of Lansky's real estate holdings, hotels, golf courses, and international accounts. Allegedly mentored by Meyer Lansky, Alvin Malnik might also oversee the more salacious side of the syndicate, the aforementioned "gambling, pornography, prostitution, labor racketeering, and extortion."[9] In Lansky's decline, the standoff between Chicago and Miami must then be presumed. To wit, one of Alvin

Malnik's Rolls-Royce auto-mobiles was bombed in the months prior to Lansky's passing. With Meyer Lansky passed on, Alvin Malnik departed Miami to pursue his Saudi Arabian sojourn.

Five days after the passing of Meyer Lansky, the infamous Allen Dorfman was shot execution-style in Chicago. Dorfman, the powerful former insurance consultant to the Teamsters Central States Pension Fund, was convicted one month prior with Teamsters president Roy Williams and Chicago mobster Joseph "Joey the Clown" Lombardo in a conspiracy to bribe Nevada senator Howard Cannon and to defraud the pension fund. Joseph Lombardo, it should be noted, was alleged by federal authorities to be, "a high-ranking member of organized crime in Chicago and a cold-blooded killer."[10] The bribery trial was also not the first joint venture of Allen Dorfman and Joseph Lombardo. A prior case involving the two ended when the key witness was shot to death. "Authorities say," reported the *Chicago Tribune*, "Lombardo 'controlled' Dorfman's contacts with organized crime."[11]

Once again, Patrick Healy of the Chicago Crime

Alvin Malnik of Miami was alleged to be the heir apparent of Meyer Lansky in the financial structure of the national organized crime syndicate. Malnik is well-known as an attorney, investor, property developer, and philanthropist. Alvin Malnik was also a business partner of Clifford Perlman and Caesars World, Inc., in the Caesars Pocono Resorts and Sky Lake development in Miami. Malnik owned the Forge Restaurant in Miami, location of at least one meeting with FBI operatives in the Abscam sting operation. The Forge is now owned by son Shareef "Mark" Malnik. Alvin Malnik is pictured here in 2016 at a Friars Club event in New York honoring Tony Bennett with the Entertainment Icon Award (WENN Rights Ltd. / Alamy Stock Photo).

Commission was sought for comment on the most recent departure from the ranks of the rackets. "There's no doubt in my mind that Mr. Dorfman was killed to keep him quiet," Healy said. "A lot of people in the criminal world will sleep better tonight

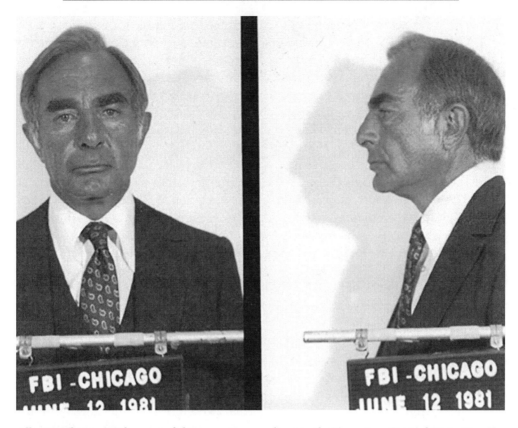

Allen Dorfman was the powerful insurance consultant to the Teamsters Central States Pension Fund. Dorfman was the direct overseer of pension fund loans while Jimmy Hoffa was in prison. Further, Dorfman was a partner with Jay Sarno in the company seeking the gaming concessions aboard the *Queen Mary* as the Long Beach City Council was also approving the Long Beach Grand Prix concept. In 1983, Allen Dorfman was executed in Chicago five days after the passing of Meyer Lansky (Federal Bureau of Investigation).

knowing that Dorfman is silenced."[12] Allen Dorfman was deeply connected to the Las Vegas gambling industry and its multi-million-dollar appetite for Teamsters loans. Dorfman was also inextricably linked to Jay Sarno, Stanley Mallin, Nathan Jacobson, and the development of Caesars Palace. In Miami, Allen Dorfman left an unmistakable mark on the transactions between Clifford Perlman and Alvin Malnik. In the southland, Allen Dorfman and Roy G. Lewis of Riverside International Raceway held mutual interests in the Beverly Ridge development in Santa Monica. Further in the southland, Jay Sarno and Allen Dorfman made a run at the Long Beach City Council for control of the gaming concessions aboard the *Queen Mary*, even more notable for its proximity to Chris Pook and the approval of the Long Beach Grand Prix. Despite the obvious prowess of Allen Dorfman, the longtime racketeer appeared to have been forcibly confronted by the limits of his own usefulness.

Perhaps not coincidentally, on January 21, 1983—the same day that Allen Dorfman was executed—the Nevada Gaming Commission approved a $10 million cash infusion to the Dunes Hotel and Casino by former Teamsters borrowers Clifford and Stuart Perlman, pending the closing of their purchase and their gambling license approval. The venerable Dunes was situated somewhere between "Mob-influenced" and "Mob-controlled" since it opened in 1955. Connected with colorful characters like Morris Shenker, "Icepick Willie" Alderman, Charles "Kewpie" Rich and now, Clifford Perlman in its lineup, the legacy of the Dunes in the lore of Las Vegas was a lock. Post-Meyer Lansky, the Dunes perhaps also appeared as a leading economic indicator. The national organized crime syndicate clearly had some sorting to do, while the Las Vegas profit center of its economic engine appeared very much in play.

***

"The fate of this year's Caesars Palace Grand Prix," ran national headlines, "is up in the air."[13] The resurrected premier-series twin bill in 1983 at Caesars Palace had inevitably devolved into more stand-off than celebration. First pitched by Bill Weinberger in early 1982, the ambitious event was originally conceived to emulate the 1971 Questor Grand Prix at Ontario Motor Speedway. "I thought an unsanctioned, unlimited race with both CART and F1 Cars on the track at the same time would be a hoot and draw a lot of attention," recalled Weinberger some 40 years later. "I was told that would never happen because though to the untrained eye the cars looked similar there was too much of a difference between them to make for a fair race. I thought the Caesars track would be a good site to even out those differences."[14] John Frasco and CART were interested, Bernie Ecclestone perhaps less so. "We did all meet that year at the Indy 500," relished Bill Weinberger, "and turned quite a few heads when we were all seen together. The rumor mills were really churning."[15]

Indeed, rumors involving the Caesars Palace Grand Prix would run the annual cycle over its entire history. "Bernie liked the spectacle it would make," continued the former Caesars Palace VP, "John [Frasco] wanted to do it because he had nothing to lose and [CART] could bury USAC if we pulled it off."[16] A definitive conclusion to the protracted CART-USAC war would have rewritten domestic open-wheel history. The conclusion of hostilities might also have prevented the even more damaging CART-IRL split.

Even though Ecclestone and FOCA embraced the spectacle of the 1971 Questor event—and solidly trounced the IndyCar contingent—the czar of Formula One perhaps sensed more to lose than to gain. "It never really went very far toward reality though," lamented Bill Weinberger.[17] Nonetheless, the prospect of the CART-Formula One double-header lingered through the spring of 1983 and served as the lead-in to the 1983 Toyota Grand Prix of Long Beach. The open-wheel twin-bill also landed on Bruce Aguilera's desk, while it pressed the Caesars World corporate attorney to the microphone.

"No determination has been made whether we will or won't have the race," Bruce Aguilera was quoted as saying in a report March 24, 1983.[18] Aguilera also confirmed continued negotiations with Bernie Ecclestone and FOCA, hopeful that they could be concluded by the weekend of the Long Beach Grand Prix. The Caesars VP of law and administration, however, also indicated that he was in talks with John Frasco and CART. "We could do both," continued Aguilera. "There's a lot of options out there. We would prefer having Formula One and CART."[19]

Like so many Ecclestone productions, the Caesars Palace Grand Prix event

The Leroy Neiman art for the 1983 Caesars Palace Grand Prix III depicted the Caesars Palace-sponsored March IndyCar driven by Kevin Cogan for George Bignotti at the 1983 Indianapolis 500. Cogan brought the same livery to the 1983 Caesars Palace Grand Prix III. The world-famous Caesars Palace fountains extend from the hotel-casino plaza to the Las Vegas Strip. The original 14-story hotel tower opened in 1966 is beyond the fountains. The 27-story Fantasy Tower stands at right. The obvious guest room expansion points up the comments of Alvin Malnik to the FBI operatives in the Abscam sting (Bruce Aguilera collection).

might thus turn on the figurative dime. "Bernie's sanctioning fee was what, $2.5 million?" Bruce Aguilera pondered years later. "CART's fee was a third of that."[20] As the attention of international motorsport turned toward Long Beach, though, the Caesars Palace Grand Prix was still on the Formula One schedule.[21] CART, on the other hand, was not. In Long Beach, Chris Pook then pondered dimes of his own, and the Toyota Grand Prix of Long Beach was preparing to turn as well.

"The biggest news to come out of Friday's opening round of qualifying for the eighth annual Long Beach Grand Prix concerned Indy cars," reported longtime Indy-Car scribe Robin Miller. "After Rene Arnoux posted fast time in the 60-minute Formula One qualifying session, Caesars Palace announced that Championship Auto Racing Teams would be coming to Las Vegas October 8."[22] As a matter of the race calendar, the announcement placed the CART IndyCar show on Saturday, with Formula One to close the weekend on Sunday. Bruce Aguilera was also quoted by Miller, confirming that negotiations with Bernie Ecclestone and FOCA were ongoing. Aguilera also assured that there would be a companion event to the IndyCar opener, but did not commit to the presence of Formula One in Las Vegas. "Of course, the G.P. boys performed on a 2.2-mile, 14-turn road course," continued Robin Miller, "and CART will contest its 200-miler on a 1.5-mile oval with five flat corners."[23]

With Caesar sorted, the Long Beach cameras and microphones took aim at Chris Pook. "Pook confirmed Friday he would hold a post-race press conference," read national accounts, "but declined comment on what he would say."[24] Speculation ran toward a complete makeover of the Long Beach Grand Prix, something along the lines of cutting sanctioning fees by a factor of three. The 1983 Toyota Formula One Grand Prix of Long Beach then went off as an absolutely thrilling race event. McLaren-mounted John Watson and Niki Lauda recovered from their miserable 22nd and 23rd starting positions, to finish first and second, respectively.

John Watson's triumph was an unprecedented move forward through the field to the top step of a Formula One podium. Watson's margin over third-place Rene Arnoux in a Ferrari was well over a minute. Homeland partisans enjoyed two Americans in the field, Eddie Cheever for Renault and Danny Sullivan for Ken Tyrell's Benetton team. In fact, Danny Sullivan finished one position ahead of teammate and 1982 Caesars Palace Grand Prix winner Michele Alboreto. The old guard also witnessed Alan Jones in a short-lived reemergence from retirement. Jones made it to lap 58 before he exited the race due to fatigue.

Chris Pook then delivered as promised on his post-race presser and confirmed the rumors. The Toyota Grand Prix of Long Beach was going to become part of the PPG CART IndyCar World Series in 1984. "I regret to say that this year's race will be the last event for Formula One cars here," echoed Bernie Ecclestone of FOCA, "The factors involved in the decision are purely economic."[25] In the years from 1975 to 1984, the economic engine of the Long Beach Formula One Grand Prix recorded losses totaling $1.88 million. In the next column, those events that turned a profit put only $554,265 into the coffers of the Long Beach Grand Prix Association.

"It is indeed sad that our European colleagues have not seen fit to share more equitably in the costs of the World Championship," Chris Pook said, adding punctuation to the presser. "I believe that unless they address this problem quickly they will be

Marc Surer (#29 Arrows) leads Jacques Lafitte (#2 Williams), Keke Rosberg (#1 Williams), Patrick Tambay (#27 Ferrari), Riccardo Patrese (#6 Brabham), and Rene Arnoux (#28 Ferrari) down Shoreline Drive at the 1983 Long Beach Grand Prix. The 1983 event was the last Formula One event on the Long Beach street circuit. Like the Caesars Palace Grand Prix, Chris Pook and the Long Beach Grand Prix Association would transition to the CART IndyCar series (Rick Lake collection).

facing merely a European championship rather than a true World Championship."[26] Rather, Bernie Ecclestone moved on from Long Beach to chase monarchs, oligarchs, kleptocrats, broadcast contracts, and petro-wealth around the planet to create a multi-billion-dollar global sporting brand. Chris Pook, meanwhile, once again raised the ire of Les Richter of Riverside International Raceway. Statements by Richter also recalled his departure in 1975 as a director of the Long Beach Grand Prix Association.

"When they decided they wanted to run racing in Long Beach," Richter said, "I had no problem with it as long as they agreed not to compete. They would run road course events with Formula One and that was it."[27] The new direction of Chris Pook ostensibly steered the Long Beach Grand Prix straight to the same race calendar as Richter's 500-kilometer CART IndyCar race held in August. "They're [Long Beach Grand Prix] coming in now and have a race for no rent … and no taxes," continued Richter, "and they'll be competing with people like me who do. Some will go to Long Beach and some will come here and some will go to Las Vegas, but everybody will be hurt."[28] The Budweiser 500 CART IndyCar event would run at storied Riverside

Chris Pook of the Long Beach Grand Prix Association, left, and Bernie Ecclestone of FOCA would part ways after the 1983 Long Beach Grand Prix. Ecclestone and FOCA continued with the Detroit Grand Prix for 1984 and also added a Dallas Formula One Grand Prix. Bernie Ecclestone hired Jack Long and William D. Weinberger to promote both American rounds of Formula One in 1984. Chris Pook and the Long Beach Grand Prix Association continued with their production services contract for the 1983 Caesars Palace Grand Prix III (Rick Lake collection).

International Raceway on August 29, 1983, for the last time. Dropped from the 1984 CART schedule, Les Richter could protest no more.

***

The murder of Allen Dorfman on January 20, 1983, did little to deter the presentencing hearings for the remaining convicts in the conspiracy trial to bribe U.S. Senator Howard Cannon. Teamsters president Roy Williams, alleged Chicago mobster Joseph Lombardo, and their co-conspirators were due in federal court in Chicago on February 10, 1983. Concurrently, Clifford Perlman and Stuart Perlman prepared their pitch to the Nevada Gaming Control Board for permanent licensing as new owners of the Dunes Hotel and Casino in Las Vegas. The respective hearings in Chicago and Las Vegas both twisted on testimony and tape recordings. Remarkably, the name of Alvin Malnik was heard aloud on both pieces of FBI audio file. Adding to his long-standing relationship with Clifford Perlman and Caesars World, Alvin Malnik was now also linked specifically to Allen Dorfman and Joseph Lombardo.

"You know," the voice of slain Allen Dorfman was heard in Chicago, "that (expletive) Malnik never called back."[29] The recording was made by FBI agents on May 22, 1979, in the office of Allen Dorfman by court-authorized wiretap. The voice on the end of the line informed the federal conspiracy case, as well as underscored the criminal relationship of Allen Dorfman with the Chicago mob.

"Well, we'll have to walk in on him," Joseph Lombardo replied to Dorfman.

"We'll just walk in on him."[30] Allen Dorfman had by then been involved with Joseph "Joey the Clown" Lombardo for years, while the national crime syndicate pillaged the coffers of the Teamsters Central States Pension Fund to which Dorfman was a consultant. The discourse between Allen Dorfman and Joseph Lombardo also revealed that the two had prior dealings with Alvin Malnik.

In Las Vegas, the Nevada Gaming Control Board was treated to the infamous Abscam tapes, captured in an FBI sting operation in October of 1979, tapes featuring the voice of Alvin Malnik. "Malnik is a reputed associate of the late organized crime king," reported Nevada press. "In the tape Malnik implied with the use of the word 'we' that he had a piece of Caesars Palace."[31] The Perlman brothers were capably represented at their license hearing by former Nevada Governor Grant Sawyer. It is perhaps instructive that Grant Sawyer was a guest at the grand opening of Caesars Palace on August 5, 1966. In fact, then-Governor Sawyer presided over the Caesars Palace ribbon cutting ceremony with Jay Sarno and Nathan Jacobson, flanked in turn by former Bugsy Siegel employee Abe Schiller.[32]

Under withering questions from Nevada regulators about his dealings with Alvin Malnik, Clifford Perlman attempted to invoke the name of Allen Dorfman in defense. "Perlman told the board that he canceled a request from murdered Teamsters associate Allen Dorfman," ran the Nevada account, "for complimentary memberships in a Miami country club in which he was involved."[33] As guarantor of the Teamster loans for the Cricket Club in which he partnered with Alvin Malnik, Perlman described his stand-off with Dorfman as "an act of courage and foresight."[34]

Despite the common thread of Alvin Malnik and Allen Dorfman in the Chicago and Las Vegas hearings, the outcomes played much differently. On April 1, 1983, Teamsters president Roy Williams was sentenced to 55 years in federal prison. Co-conspirator Joseph "Joey the Clown" Lombardo received a sentence of 15 years. Allen Dorfman, of course, was sentenced to death. "Mr. Williams, you sold the working man out," stated U.S. District Court Judge Prentice Marshall from the bench. "You were willing to take the working man's pension and use it. Yes, use it for your own aggrandizement."[35]

One week after the Chicago sentences were meted out, Clifford Perlman was approved in Las Vegas by a 3–1 vote as a licensed gambling operator of the Dunes Hotel and Casino. Brother Stuart was unanimously approved. The Perlman brothers then moved forward to manage the gambling property in anticipation of the sale closing. In the days that followed, though, Clifford Perlman set about firing over two dozen Dunes executives, including Morris Shenker's personal assistant. Notably gone as well was Charles "Kewpie" Rich, a well-connected consultant holdover from the original ownership of the resort. Eight months later, unable to close with Morris Shenker, Clifford and Stuart Perlman sold their option on the Dunes. Their $10 million bridge loan to the property was forfeited. The Dunes, however, continued in operation until 1993 when it was purchased—and then demolished—by Steve Wynn. The former Dunes property then gave way to the magnificent Bellagio, notably the location of a later Formula One query between Steve Wynn and Bernie Ecclestone, with Bruce Aguilera in tow.

With the Dunes tent folded, the Perlman brothers then redoubled their efforts on Regent Air, a start-up luxury air carrier funded from their Caesars World stock buyout. Former Caesars World executive William McElnea joined the brothers in the airline venture. Promising "*all*-frills," Regent Air's three-plane fleet of Boeing 727 jetliners commenced air operations on October 14, 1983. Like the act of Clifford Perlman in New Jersey, however, the Civil Aeronautics Board refused to continue the operating certificate until the mob-tainted Perlman brothers were gone. Regent Air was then leveraged on to an investment group and quickly flew further south, losing $10 million per year over its first three years. By 1987, Regent Air relinquished its certificate to the Civil Aeronautics Board and declared Chapter VII bankruptcy. Notably, the bulk of the purchase price was still owed to Clifford and Stuart Perlman.

The following year, Stuart Perlman died of a heart attack in Miami. In late 1989, brother Clifford joined original Caesars Palace landlord Kirk Kerkorian as chairman and CEO of the new MGM Grand Hotel and Theme Park in Las Vegas. Perlman, however, resigned just three months later, reportedly to focus on the affairs of his late brother's estate. At the time of Clifford Perlman's resignation, however, the state of New Jersey had opened an investigation into a bankrupt title company owned by the Perlman brothers. "Former workers at Chelsea Title Agency," it was reported in New Jersey, "claim the company failed to put money deducted from their paychecks toward health- and life-insurance premiums, state unemployment, state and federal taxes."[36]

From his continued vantage point in the Caesars World organization, Bill Weinberger witnessed the downfall of the former Caesar. "I saw Cliff shortly after the Dunes deal went upside down," recalled Weinberger. "He and Stu had walked away from Caesars with almost $100 million. He told me if he did a couple more deals he would be broke as everything he had invested in after Caesars had gone down the tubes."[37] For Clifford and Stuart Perlman, Regent Air was the deal too far, the failed back end of which likely also scuttled their title company venture. Clifford Perlman, as well, endured his own personal bankruptcy. The greatest Caesar of the Palace had duly taken the blade.

Nonetheless, the banners proclaiming the might of Caesar remained, ready to herald their collective luxury-branded message along Chris Pook's concrete track barriers at the 1983 Caesars Palace Grand Prix III. Once again, "Caesars Palace" signage was accompanied by "Caesars Tahoe," "Caesars Boardwalk Regency," and—of course—Alvin Malnik's "Caesars Pocono Resorts."

***

Chris Pook shifted forward after the final Formula One event in Long Beach. Regardless of format or formula, Pook was still under contract with Caesars Palace as "Grand Prix Consultant."[38] Preceding the 1983 Indianapolis 500, Chris Pook then jumped aboard the promotional efforts for the 1983 Caesars event, "Caesars Palace Grand Prix III." "The more familiar Indy cars and drivers will provide 'considerable excitement and interest,'" promised Pook. "We firmly believe that Indy car racing will be an exciting spectacle."[39] Pook's comments were accompanied by emerging details of the Caesars Palace CART IndyCar event. Turn one and turn 10 of the Formula One circuit were connected to form a five-turn "roval," a *portmanteau* of "road course"

Kevin Cogan finished fifth in the 1983 Indianapolis 500 driving a Caesars Palace–sponsored March for George Bignotti. Bignotti teammate Tom Sneva won the event. Both Cogan and Sneva competed at the 1983 CART IndyCar Caesars Palace Grand Prix III (Bruce Aguilera collection).

and "oval." IndyCar practice would commence on Thursday, October 6, 1983. Qualifying to seed the 22-car event would follow on Friday. As with the preceding Caesars Palace Formula One events, NBC Sports provided a domestic telecast of the Caesars Palace Grand Prix III.

The media avails of the 1983 Indianapolis 500 also provided Bruce Aguilera an opportunity for some luxury-branded Caesars Palace promotion of his own. Aguilera organized a Caesars Palace casino night on Friday, May 27, 1983, at Abram Pritzker's Hyatt Regency Hotel in downtown Indianapolis. The Caesars casino party was rendered complete with Caesars Palace-branded tables, chips, and staff, all appropriately delivered by corporate jet. "I had to get the approval of the governor," recalled the corporate lawyer, "because, of course, gambling is not legal in Indiana."[40] The smoke-filled boiler room of the 1957 Terre Haute gambling syndicate, however, might have taken exception.

The Caesars casino party was a hit, as was the Caesars Palace sponsorship of Kevin Cogan's March 83C, entered by Dan Cotter and George Bignotti for the Indianapolis 500. Cogan qualified the luxury-branded racer in 24th. On race day, Kevin Cogan soldiered home admirably in fifth. Cogan's Texaco-sponsored teammate Tom Sneva, however, won the 1983 Indianapolis 500 in dominant fashion over Al Unser and Rick Mears, leading nearly half of the event before drinking the ceremonial milk of victory lane. Tom Sneva would also bring his Texaco-sponsored swagger to the Caesars Palace Grand Prix III and IV.

The attentions of Caesar then turned to Bernie Ecclestone and his international game of high intrigue, huge dollars, and hardball. One week after the Indy 500, Formula One took to the streets of Detroit once again. From a lavish suite high atop the Detroit Renaissance Center, Ecclestone sought to diminish the path of Formula One through the United States of America. "Formula One never was designed to have more than one race in this country," proclaimed Ecclestone from his Detroit pulpit. "The second U.S race just came along and the third and fourth races were just accidental."[41]

Ecclestone's hit could also be fairly interpreted to mean that his negotiations with Bruce Aguilera of Caesars Palace had stalled. Nonetheless, Bernie Ecclestone played good faith for benefit of the press, "we have a contract with Las Vegas that goes two more years."[42]

Sir Jackie Stewart had taken aim at the fortunes of the Caesars Palace Grand Prix as well. "I'm not knocking Las Vegas," posited the three-time world champion, "but it's run on a vacant lot of ground rather than through the streets. There's no backdrop like there is at other races."[43]

From Detroit, Bernie Ecclestone also squared off with the CART IndyCar series and offered his recollection of an incredible exchange with Roger Penske and John Frasco. "Ecclestone says he approached CART executives John Frasco and Roger Penske ... about a consolidation of the two circuits into a 'mutual formula,'" ran a report from the Detroit Grand Prix, "but Penske rejected the idea."[44]

"We proposed something like 25 races," claimed Bernie Ecclestone, "16 to count toward the championship, with 11 of them mandatory and, I think, three of them to be run in the United States."[45] For his part—nearly 40 years on—Roger Penske declined to comment on Ecclestone's fantastic—perhaps imaginary—master series.[46] Ecclestone also saved some snark for the structure of his American racing series rival. "In CART, two people write the rules and don't tell anyone what they are," Ecclestone further said. "If it doesn't suit, they change the rules. The people at CART are consistent, they've never done anything they said they were going to do."[47]

Bernie Ecclestone boasted from the 1983 Detroit Grand Prix that he had once pitched to Roger Penske (pictured) a unified Formula One-CART IndyCar racing series. Ecclestone also took aim at the CART power structure, including John Frasco (author's collection).

On that shutdown, the cancellation of the 1983 Formula One event at the Caesars Palace Grand Prix was presumptive. Two weeks after the Detroit Grand Prix, reports in the press appeared to render it a formality.[48] By early July, three months before the 1983 Caesars Palace Grand Prix, the prospect of Formula One in Las Vegas was no more. "A CART race, again with television, was scheduled for Saturday, relegating that Sunday's [Formula One] Grand Prix to secondary status," according to a New York report. "Instead of second billing, Ecclestone and FOCA decided no billing was better and the Grand Prix was cancelled."[49] In the same report, the proposed New York Grand Prix was purportedly postponed to 1984.

Bernie Ecclestone, FOCA, and the entire sport of Formula One were thus removed forever from the grand marquee of Caesars Palace on the famed Las Vegas Strip. The domestic PPG CART IndyCar World Series officially became the headliner of the Caesars Palace Grand Prix, while Bruce Aguilera and Chris Pook cast about for a suitable companion event to flesh out the October race weekend. Corporate lawyer Aguilera enjoyed the immediate reduction in the cost column afforded by the CART IndyCar event. Further, in contrast to Ecclestone, it was far more likely that CART would take a check. Thrust into event promotion in the departure of Bill Weinberger, Bruce Aguilera was also encouraged by the name recognition of the American Indy-Car drivers, Andretti, Unser, Mears, Sneva, et al. "The Formula One names," Aguilera reflected years later, "were just not recognized by the American public."[50]

***

"The world's most prominent personalities in race car driving," ran the pre-race pressers, "will converge on Caesars Palace, Las Vegas, for the third annual Caesars Palace Grand Prix."[51] Gone forever were the exotic Formula One driver names and race teams hailing from points around the globe. Rather, the September 1983 press piece from the desk of Caesars Palace president Harry Wald was pushing racing personalities who had cut their teeth turning left on American dirt ovals in Offenhauser-powered roadsters. Nonetheless, the recognizable brand names of the PPG CART IndyCar World Series epitomized the gathering exodus of American interests from the Formula One series toward the pinnacle of domestic open-wheel motorsport. In 1983, the race organizers of Caesars Palace and Long Beach also punctuated the marked pivot away from the exorbitant fees of Bernie Ecclestone and FOCA. Even Watkins Glen—sullied by Ecclestone and crippled by insolvency—hosted a round of the CART IndyCar series in 1981. The October 4, 1981, CART IndyCar Watkins Glen 200 was the historic circuit's last event of note before emerging from bankruptcy proceedings in 1984.

The announcement from Harry Wald of Caesars Palace also tidied other matters around the 1983 Caesars Palace Grand

Headed into the 1983 CART IndyCar Caesars Palace Grand Prix III, Caesars president Harry Wald pitched "the world's most prominent personalities in race car driving" (*San Francisco Examiner*, September 4, 1983). Wald may not have been aware that the cream of the CART Indy-Car series cut their teeth turning left in Offenhauser-powered roadsters on fairgrounds dirt ovals (Bruce Aguilera collection).

Prix III. Bruce Aguilera was finally formalized as the president-proper of the Grand Prix. The companion events to the CART IndyCar headliner also came into view. The depleted Can-Am series would not make a return to Las Vegas. Rather, the finale of the 1983 SCCA Trans-Am season was scheduled to run at Caesars Palace on Saturday, October 8, 1983. The Trans-Am event was the first of its formula in Las Vegas since a 1967 outing at Stardust International Raceway won by Mark Donohoe driving for Roger Penske.

The Trans-Am race also moved Paul Newman over, from the celebrity receptions of Caesar to the confines of the race course. Newman was scheduled to compete in his turbocharged Bob Sharp Racing Datsun 280ZX. Gone too was the AFM-Pro motorcycle road race. With a stained send-off by the local media, there was no danger of a reappearance in black leather and axle grease. The intrepid two-wheel troupe showcasing the daring, dynamic David Aldana was being replaced with a NASCAR Winston West stock car event, featuring 55-year-old Herschel McGriff.

Caesars Palace Grand Prix president Bruce Aguilera joined the promotional pitch as well. "Those of you who have been here before will recognize the different Caesars Palace Grand Prix track," proclaimed the corporate attorney, "and, of course, the replacement of Formula One … with the thrilling Indy Cars."[52] Indeed, the contrast of the 1982 road course and 1983 "roval" was dramatically apparent in fly-over imagery.

Once again, architect Tony Marnell was engaged in the further development of the Caesars Palace Grand Prix facilities. Marnell's course conversion replaced the maze of hairpin turns with a single gently-curved swoop running alongside the Las Vegas Strip. The conversion also pulled over a mile of distance from the race circuit. The effect would produce a marked increase in speed and sound between the international Formula One contingent and the domestic IndyCar field.

"I was working television news at the Las Vegas ABC affiliate just a few miles away from Caesars Palace. I will never forget walking outside the newsroom and hearing the unmistakable whine of the turbocharged Indy cars during practice," recalled longtime action sports broadcaster Rick Lake. "It was like they were right across the street."[53] With some 800 horsepower in a 1,500-pound package, versus 550 horsepower and 1,200 pounds for Formula One, the CART IndyCar series was going to produce a pointed contrast in performance alongside the Las Vegas Strip.

As a fully-fledged championship event on the PPG CART IndyCar trail, the Caesars Palace Grand Prix III figured in the points positions of the title contenders. Unlike 1981 and 1982, the 1983 Las Vegas event would not have the cachet of the finale in a top billed championship. The 1983 Caesars Palace CART IndyCar event did, however, have Mario Andretti. Further, Mario Andretti was driving for Paul Newman, one of the Trans-Am contenders. "I was not very happy with the Patrick team and I wanted to have a little more control of what was going on," reflected Mario Andretti. "That was always my style."[54] Andretti also recalled the origins of Paul Newman and Carl Haas in IndyCar ownership. "I had developed a relationship with Carl Haas because [son] Michael had driven for him," continued Andretti. "Paul Newman, I had kept a relationship with him since the [Holman-Moody] Honker days in 1967. I'm the one who put the two parties together. It was a marriage made in Heaven."[55]

The five-turn roval for the CART IndyCar rounds of the Caesars Palace Grand Prix was created by connecting Formula One turn one with Formula One turn 11. Formula One turn 11 is at top-center of image. A gently-curved straightaway was constructed to link the two corners. The disconnection points of Formula One turns five, six, and 10 are evident. The portions of the Caesars Palace circuit through the north parking lot have once again been overtaken by Caesars Palace guests and employees. Tennis courts are prominent at the left edge of the resort. The Caesars Palace Sports Pavilion used as the covered race paddock is at the extreme left bottom corner of the resort property (courtesy HistoricAerials.com).

With a throw to the controversial finish of the 1981 Indianapolis 500, Andretti's nemesis Bobby Unser would be in the Caesars Palace Fantasy Tower broadcast booth alongside Paul Page to provide color commentary for the NBC coverage of the event. Brother Al Unser, VIP hot lap pilot for the 1981 Caesars Palace Grand Prix, was entered in the Caesars Palace Grand Prix III. With a win in Cleveland—and a remarkable run of points in every single race—three-time Indy 500 winner Al Unser was also in the points lead of the PPG CART IndyCar World Series.

The collective Andretti and Unser IndyCar champions then formed the front end of the 1983 Caesars Palace storylines. Their progeny, however, formed part of the IndyCar starting field. Michael Andretti, the 20-year-old son of the great American race car driver, was poised to make his IndyCar debut at Caesars Palace. In fact, the younger Andretti marked his 21st birthday just three days before the Caesars Palace event. Michael joined the team of Kraco Enterprises founder Maurice Kraines for his first at bat alongside his father.

Al Unser, Jr., the 21-year-old son of Al Unser, was competing in his first full season of IndyCar racing. Unser Jr. was entered in a Gurney Eagle chassis branded as the Coors Light Silver Bullet. The junior Unser was notably recorded with his IndyCar debut in the same Coors Light livery at Atlanta Motor Speedway on April 17, 1983, 2 days *before* his 21st birthday. The extremely young, supremely talented second-generation drivers then received their baptism in the pinnacle of domestic open-wheel motorsport, in the pinnacle city of world-class entertainment, hospitality, and gambling.

Al Unser, Sr., entered the 1983 Caesars Palace Grand Prix with a commanding

Al Unser driving for Roger Penske entered the 1983 Caesars Palace Grand Prix as the CART IndyCar points leader. The three-time winner of the Indianapolis 500 maintained his points lead at Caesars Palace. Teo Fabi, though, tightened the points race headed to the season finale at Phoenix (Bruce Aguilera collection).

point lead over second-place Teo Fabi. Fabi joined the CART IndyCar series for Forsythe Racing after his 1981 SCCA Can-Am campaign and a miserable 1982 season in Formula One. Despite winning two IndyCar events to Unser's one, Teo Fabi trailed Al Unser by nearly a full race of points, 106 to 125. Nonetheless, Fabi had put together his two wins and another pair of podiums in the last four races. With 60 points on offer for the remaining three races, Teo Fabi still had a strong chance to run down Unser for the 1983 CART IndyCar championship.

The 1983 CART IndyCar points standings trailed off after Al Unser and Teo Fabi. Rick Mears stood third for Roger Penske with 92. Mears was also fresh from an IndyCar win at Penske's Michigan International Speedway, while Penske himself returned to the familiar luxury-branded trappings of Caesars Palace from his 1981 Formula One NBC broadcast stint.

Opposite: **Michael Andretti made his CART IndyCar competition debut on October 8, 1983, at the 1983 Caesars Palace Grand Prix III. Andretti turned 21 just three days before. Driving the Kraco March for owner Maurice Kraines, Andretti qualified 15th and retired on lap 74 (courtesy LVCVA News Bureau).**

Al Unser, Jr., joined father Al for his debut season in the 1983 CART IndyCar series. The junior Unser drove the Coors Light Silver Bullet Gurney Eagle for car owner Rick Galles. The Roman Wheels sponsorship on the engine cowl was a holdover from the 1982 Can-Am campaign. Unser Jr. and Galles brought the same livery to the 1983 CART IndyCar Caesars Palace Grand Prix III. Unser qualified 11th and was recorded with a 10th place finish after a spin on lap 171 (author's collection).

Bobby Rahal was in his second full season on the CART IndyCar trail. After three successive podiums—including a win at the Budweiser 500 at Riverside—Rahal was fourth in points with 84 for owner Jim Truman. Indy-Car veteran Tom Sneva was fifth in the points standings at 82 for George Bignotti. Sneva was also sitting on the big one, taking home over $350,000 for his resounding win at the 1983 Indianapolis 500. Notably, 43-year-old Mario Andretti held the sixth position in the points battle with 80. Andretti also claimed one win thus far in the 1983 campaign, the Provimi Veal 200 at Road America in Elkhart Lake, Wisconsin.

CART IndyCar qualifying for the 1983 Caesars Palace Grand Prix III would be a statistical rewrite for the Caesars circuit. Qualifying also produced times that were some 40 seconds quicker per lap than the 1982 Formula One pole. John Paul, Jr., produced the first lap record for the roval with a time of 34.888 seconds in his VDS Penske PC10, averaging 116.086 mph around the 1.25-mile track. John Paul was also

CART IndyCar rookie John Paul, Jr., qualified on pole for the 1983 Caesars Palace Grand Prix III in his VDS Penske PC-10. Paul was extremely competitive on the day and ultimately finished second to race winner Mario Andretti driving for Newman-Haas (Bruce Aguilera collection).

the only time under 35 seconds. Paul came into Caesars Palace fresh from his win at the Norton Michigan 500 in only his fourth IndyCar start. John Paul, Jr., also won an SCCA Trans-Am event in a DeAtley Motorsports Camaro just one month before Caesars Palace.

Teo Fabi was second-quick around the roval circuit with a 35.124 in his Skoal March for Gerald Forsythe. The championship hopeful would have a running start from the front row in his championship quest over Al Unser. To the delight of the crowd, Mario Andretti qualified third in his Newman-Haas Budweiser Lola at 35.169. Derek Daly moved on from a sixth-place Formula One finish for Frank Williams at the 1982 Caesars Palace Grand Prix, to put his Provimi March on the Caesars Palace IndyCar grid in 1983. Daly trailed Andretti to the second row by less than one tenth at 35.261.

Bobby Rahal crashed his Red Roof Inns March hard during Thursday practice and was transported to the hospital. Rahal nevertheless returned to the track on crutches for Friday qualifying and put his machine in the show, seventh-quick with a 35.829. Al Unser followed tenth to the grid in his Hertz Penske. Unser, with a 35.966, was nearly a full second off of points challenger Teo Fabi. Kevin Cogan was 15th on the time sheets but was disqualified after qualifying for using "left front tire compound on the right front."[56] Cogan, however, was playing with house money. The Caesars Palace-sponsored driver was predictably added to the rear of the field as a "promoters' option."[57] Cogan teammate Tom Sneva was remarkably slow in his qualifying attempt, nearly three seconds adrift of polesitter John Paul. Sneva, veteran Johnny Rutherford, and Roger Mears were also added to the rear of the Caesars Palace grid for benefit of the show.

The SCCA Trans-Am opener of the Caesars Palace show brought a field of purpose-built race chassis cloaked in the guise of American V-8 powered Pony cars, Chevrolet Camaros, Corvettes, Pontiac Trans-Am Firebirds, Mercury Capris, and Ford Mustangs. The domestics were joined by the occasional weight-to-power equalized import. Paul Newman—winner of the 1982 Trans-Am round in Brainerd, Minnesota—was entered in his distinctive red, white, and blue Bob Sharp Datsun 280ZX turbo. The 55-year-old Newman was joined at the seniors table by 45-year-old David Hobbs. Hobbs, a former Formula One driver, was leading the Trans-Am points championship as the pack of punched out Pony Cars descended upon Las Vegas. Joining Paul Newman from the celebrity circles was Bruce Jenner. Jenner, winner of the decathlon at the 1976 Olympic Games, was indeed a motorsport convert. Jenner was also a roving reporter for the NBC broadcast team. Bruce Jenner was entered for the Trans-Am event in a Ford Thunderbird. Newman, Hobbs, and Jenner were joined by a field of hard chargers, many of them determined to leverage the Trans-Am series for a claim on some next level race seats.

While David Hobbs commanded the points battle, teammate Willy T. Ribbs held a puncher's chance to overtake the veteran driver for the 1983 Trans-Am championship. Ribbs would go for the win and the 22 points on offer. Hobbs was then left to defend, and bargain for a dreaded 13th place finish or better to clinch. When the Trans-Am qualifying clock wound down, Willy T. Ribbs left no doubt where he stood, at the head of the Trans-Am field with a 40.912 lap. Ribbs' qualifying time in his Chevrolet Camaro, in fact, nipped at the heels of the CART IndyCar field.

Willy T. Ribbs and his DeAtley Motorsports Camaro then went on a desert march, dominating the 89-lap event to win wire to wire. Dave Watson was second in a Pontiac Firebird, Tom Gloy third in a Mercury Capri. Fourth went to David Hobbs, the point leader. Wally Dallenbach, Jr., son of the CART IndyCar race steward, was fourth. "I couldn't go too much faster," commented Ribbs from the podium. "The tires were about used up."[58]

Along with Willy T. Ribbs, Wally Dallenbach, Jr., was also in his first year of frontline professional competition. "I mean, here I am in Las Vegas driving a race car," recalled Dallenbach, Jr. "We could've been on the moon, though. and I don't know that I would been impressed with where I was at. I was just trying to make sure I was going to be in the car the next week."[59]

Like Ribbs and Dallenbach, Lyn St. James was in her first year of Trans-Am competition. St. James was partnered with Tom Gloy on the Lane Sports team. St. James qualified her Mercury Capri in 20th at the Caesars Palace Grand Prix Trans-Am and brought it home in 12th. The introduction of Lyn St. James in Las Vegas, however, brought a certain simile to the Palace of Caesar, a female race

The SCCA Can-Am series was replaced by the SCCA Trans-Am series for the 1983 Caesars Palace Grand Prix III. Willy T. Ribbs (#28 Chevrolet Camaro) qualified on pole and led from start to finish. Tom Gloy (#8 Mercury Capri) qualified second and finished third. David Hobbs won the 1983 Trans-Am championship (photograph by Ernie Ohlson).

car driver among the Greco-Roman goddesses of Jay Sarno's grandiose resort vision.

"I've never been a fan of Las Vegas," recalled the barrier-breaking sportscar and open-wheel race car driver. "It was one of the few times ever that I would just stay in my race suit. I would be walking through the massive lobbies and the casino section because you have to walk through the casino section to get anywhere in a hotel in Vegas. I'd get on the elevator wearing this crazy race suit and no one even batted an eye. Because Vegas is just crazy."[60]

The celebrity racers found their troubles during the Trans-Am event at the 1983 Caesars Palace Grand Prix. Paul Newman started his Datsun 280ZX from third on the grid but was shunted by another driver on lap 11 and moved backward. Newman finished the race 11 laps off the lead in 18th place. Bruce Jenner retired on lap 73 with an oil leak and was credited with 21st in the final order, right where he started.

The hard chargers of Willy T. Ribbs, Tom Gloy, Wally Dallenbach, Jr., and Lyn St. James parlayed their Trans-Am experiences into later opportunities in IndyCar. For 1983 Trans-Am champion David Hobbs, sports endurance racing would soon be his swan song before becoming a fixture in the broadcast booth. Nonetheless, all four would return to Las Vegas in 1984 for another throw at the Trans-Am opener of the Caesars Palace Grand Prix IV.

***

The long lenses of the NBC sports team were posted high atop the Caesars Palace Fantasy Tower for the broadcast of the October 9, 1983, Caesars Palace Grand Prix III. The camera panned from the mountain vista in the north to the world-famous Las Vegas Strip and then drew down Las Vegas Boulevard toward Caesars Palace. For those with a keen eye, the NBC cameras also offered a glimpse of the banner signage of Alvin Malnik's Caesars Pocono Resorts.

Paul Newman served as chairman of the 1982 and 1982 Caesars Palace Grand Prix events. In 1983, Newman contested the SCCA Trans-Am event in a turbocharged Datsun 280ZX at the Caesars Palace Grand Prix III. Newman returned to contest the 1984 Caesars Palace SCCA Trans-Am event (Bruce Aguilera collection).

"It's time for the IndyCars to race in Las Vegas for the first time," continued Page as he introduced broadcast partner Bobby Unser. "The last time the Indy 500 drivers raced here as a group was 1957."[61] Paul Page, however, was quite incorrect. The Indianapolis 500-based AAA Championship trail competed at the long-demolished Las Vegas Park thoroughbred oval on November 14, 1954, an event won by the late Jimmy Bryan. Remarkably, Page also overlooked Bobby Unser's Las Vegas IndyCar victory in 1968. Indeed, Bobby Unser won the USAC Championship Stardust 150 at Stardust International Raceway on March 30, 1968, an event in which Mario Andretti finished second. "But Bobby," Page turned it over to Unser, "when they come here today, it's a whole, clean sheet of paper."[62]

"We have here what I term as a parking lot race track," Bobby Unser leaned in, "and it's got nothing but a parking lot and cement barriers all over the place and a lot of grandstands and a lot of people."[63] For purposes of the continued NBC contract with Caesars Palace, Bobby Unser's wheels were slightly off-course. "Truthfully," continued Unser, as if corrected by an earpiece producer, "I think it's going to make for a very interesting and good race. And it's more like a road course than anything else but you always turn left here."[64] As Bobby Unser brought his comments back to the center of the circuit, Bruce Aguilera and the corporate legal department must have exhaled in unison.

"Lady and gentlemen," comedian Joan Rivers gave the command to the drivers, "start your engines."[65] The gender nod of Joan Rivers was to Desire Wilson of England, posted on the grid in 18th position in a March 83C. The rolling start of

Polesitter John Paul, Jr. (#12 VDS Penske) leads Teo Fabi (#33 Skoal Bandit March), Mario Andretti (Budweiser Lola), and Derek Daly (#90 Provimi Veal March) down the front straightaway during the first caution period of the October 8, 1983, CART IndyCar Caesars Palace Grand Prix III. Fabi dropped out of the race once the field resumed green. Andretti and Paul finished first and second respectively (photograph by Ernie Ohlson).

the CART IndyCar Caesars Palace Grand Prix III offered a dramatic departure from the standing start of the prior Formula One events. Fast qualifier John Paul, Jr., and his VDS Penske 10B led an amassed 20,000 horsepower down the front straight of the Caesars Palace roval to control the start of the race. Mario Andretti and his Newman-Haas Lola, however, had a clear run at Paul as the field hit the green flag. Andretti then pulled ahead of the IndyCar rookie as their cars cleared the stripe. Paul, though, with the inside line, drove hard into turn one and managed past Andretti as the field raced north just yards from the Las Vegas Strip.

CART IndyCar rookie John Paul, Jr., then built a lead over Derek Daly and Teo Fabi as Mario Andretti slipped back. A caution flag on lap eight bunched the field as Andretti mulled his move. When the race returned green on lap 17, Andretti closed on leader John Paul. One lap later, points contender Teo Fabi was off with a broken throttle cable. Mario Andretti, with a huge roar of approval from the crowd, then moved past John Paul, Jr., for the lead on lap 19.

Indy 500 winner Tom Sneva in George Bignotti's Texaco March was out with a spin on lap 30. Sneva's miscue turned him against traffic on the high-speed front straight and once again unfurled the yellow flag. Pit stops under caution reset the

Roger Mears (#9 Master Mechanic March) leads Michael Andretti (#99 Kraco March) on the front straightaway of the Caesars Palace Grand Prix III. Al Unser, Jr. (#17 Coors Light Gurney Eagle) is visible at right of image. Others are not identified. Mears is the brother of four-time Indy 500 winner Rick Mears. Mears, Andretti, and Unser Jr. were recorded with finishes of seventh, 19th and 10th respectively (courtesy LVCVA News Bureau).

order with Bobby Rahal leading as the race returned green. A quick caution for Dick Simon then allowed Pancho Carter to pass Rahal for the lead. Mario Andretti trailed fourth followed by Al Unser, Sr., Chip Ganassi, and the Caesars Palace-sponsored Kevin Cogan. Pancho Carter then ticked off 23 laps out front before another caution flag appeared when Geoff Brabham spun his Kraco-sponsored March in turn five.

Pancho Carter turned for the pits under yellow and, as the race resumed green, Mario Andretti once again took the lead. Kevin Cogan, however, was around Andretti one lap later. Cogan and his Caesars Palace March then led for a dozen laps before caution waved once again for spins involving Michael Andretti and Bobby Rahal. On the lap 77 restart, John Paul, Jr., took command for a single lap before he was passed by Mario Andretti. The 43-year-old Andretti then put on a master class for the 23-year-old rookie, leading for nearly 100 laps.

On lap 171, Mario Andretti locked his brakes steering into turn one. John Paul, Jr., seized the opportunity, tucked under Andretti, and grabbed the lead. "After passing Mario, I thought it was going to be nice," later commented Paul.[66] John Paul, Jr., however, was sorely mistaken. As Paul led Andretti down the long back straight and around turn 4, the great American race car driver set his sights. Mario Andretti found his opening at the inside of turn 5 and powered by Paul. Former Formula One champion Mario Andretti then held his advantage over IndyCar rookie John Paul, Jr.,

for the next seven laps to take the checkered flag of the Caesars Palace Grand
Prix III by a scant two seconds over the
young chaser.

"I just about handed it to him there
at the end," Andretti mused from the
victory celebration. "My brakes locked
up going into turn one and [Paul] got
by."[67] Andretti's tenacity triumphed over
the trainee, while the master collected
his 36th win in an IndyCar career that
already spanned two decades. Mario
Andretti also collected $69,291 at the
pay window from the reported $434,000
purse.[68] "Paul drove a clean, calculated
race," offered Mario Andretti of John
Paul, Jr. "I definitely gained respect for
him today."[69]

For a hard-earned runner-up, John
Paul, Jr., posted a Las Vegas payday of
nearly $55,000. The fine finish for the
23-year-old IndyCar rookie boosted his
1983 race winnings to over $250,000.
Paul also marveled at the racecraft and
road clinic of Mario Andretti. "Mario
went by me," lamented Paul, "before I
knew he was there."[70] Despite his Michigan win and three podium finishes, John

Kevin Cogan and his Caesars Palace-sponsored George Bignotti March made the cover
of the program for the October 8, 1983, Caesars Palace Grand Prix III. Cogan was disqualified for a tire infraction after Caesars
qualifying but was added to the field by promoter's option. Kevin Cogan led over Mario
Andretti at the mid-point but retired on
lap 132 after an accident. Cogan was credited with a 16th place finish (Bruce Aguilera
collection).

Paul, Jr., finished behind Teo Fabi in the PPG CART IndyCar World Series rookie of
the year standings.

Teo Fabi left Caesars Palace as he came in, second place in the championship
chase behind Al Unser, Sr. Fabi's retirement on lap 18, however, left the championship
contender out of a points-paying position. Al Unser, Sr., on the other hand, brought
his Penske PC10B home in fourth, padding his points lead by another 12 markers
over Fabi. Moving on from the Caesars Palace Grand Prix, Teo Fabi would win out,
posting victories at Laguna Seca and Phoenix to nearly steal the crown away from Al
Unser, Sr. Unser could not match the pace of Fabi down the stretch but remained solidly in the points, clinging to his lead to win the 1983 PPG Cart IndyCar World Series
championship. It was the second IndyCar crown for the 44-year-old Unser. It was not
to be his last.

One week after the Caesars Palace Grand Prix III, the Formula One series was
camped in South Africa for the finale of the 1983 world championship. The 1983
season had produced a very tight points battle. Alain Prost of Renault entered the
final round sitting atop the points at 57. Nelson Piquet was close behind for Bernie
Ecclestone and Brabham with 55. Piquet and Prost qualified close, less than one half

Mario Andretti drove the resplendent red and white Budweiser Lola T-700 for Paul Newman and Carl Haas at the 1983 Caesars Palace Grand Prix. In the debut year for the team, Andretti notched two wins including a very popular victory in Las Vegas. Mario Andretti also claimed three second-place finishes and was a very close third overall in the final 1983 CART IndyCar points standings behind Al Unser and Teo Fabi (author's collection).

second separating the contenders. Nelson Piquet led convincingly in the opening laps. Alain Prost, though, was out before halfway with a turbocharger failure in his Renault. Piquet then needed to finish only fourth or better to clinch his second world championship for Bernie Ecclestone. Brabham teammate Riccardo Patrese won the event while Nelson Piquet brought his machine home third. Like Al Unser, Sr., the 1983 Formula One world championship would also not be the last for Nelson Piquet. For Bernie Ecclestone and Brabham, however, the 1983 drivers championship was the last recorded for the Formula One marque started by Jack Brabham in 1962.

While Nelson Piquet savored his second world championship and Riccardo Patrese his race win, Bernie Ecclestone was apparently shopping. On October 20, 1983, the *Los Angeles Times* reported that Ecclestone extended to Al Unser, Jr., "an offer to drive in Formula One for Bernie Ecclestone's Brabham-BMW team."[71]

"Bernie (Ecclestone) called me," Unser later recalled of the exchange. "I don't know how he got my home number, but he called me. He asked me to come and drive his car."[72] Unser Jr., fresh from his debut IndyCar season, begged off. "I told him thanks a lot," Unser said, "but I haven't done well at Indy and that's where I want to be and that's what I want to do."[73] Bernie Ecclestone sold the once-proud Brabham Formula One constructor team on just five years later.

Al Unser, Jr., would then return to the 1984 Caesars Palace Grand Prix IV to compete in the CART IndyCar event. Between the years of 1984 and 1992, Unser went on to collect seventeen IndyCar victories. On May 24, 1992, Al Unser, Jr., collected the biggest of all, winning the 76th Indianapolis 500 by .043 seconds over Scott Goodyear. "You don't know what Indy means," Unser Jr. famously stated from victory lane.[74] Three months after Al Unser, Jr.'s, watershed victory in the Indianapolis 500, the Brabham works officially shut their doors.

***

Attendance figures for the 1981 and 1982 Caesars Palace Grand Prix events certainly cast a trend, from 38,000 in 1981 to 32,000 in 1982. The 1983 Caesars Palace Grand Prix III then trailed further, with a reported "25,000 people in attendance."[75] Notably, the SCCA Can-Am support event of the 1982 Caesars Palace Grand Prix had soundly outdrawn that number with 28,000 fans reported in the stands. Names like Andretti, Unser, Rutherford, and Sneva notwithstanding, it should be presumed that the 1983 casino take to the underground Caesars Palace cash cave followed the curve of the decreasing spectator count.

The NASCAR Winston West Coors 200 closer of the 1983 Caesars Palace Grand

The CART IndyCar pinnacle of domestic open-wheel motorsport was contrasted at the 1983 Caesars Palace Grand Prix III by the cars and stars of the NASCAR Winston West series. The IndyCar times were nearly 10 seconds quicker per lap than the NASCAR racers. Jim Robinson won the NASCAR event in an Oldsmobile with an average race speed of just over 55 mph (courtesy LVCVA News Bureau).

Prix weekend provided nothing of note to reset the casino fortunes. Headliner Herschel McGriff recorded a 24th place finish. Coors 200 winner Jim Robinson collected $5,450 for a long afternoon in a comparatively slow NASCAR saddle. Scott Brayton, the last-place competitor in the Saturday CART IndyCar Caesars Palace Grand Prix, collected nearly twice as much. Further, the caution-plagued NASCAR event finished with an average speed of 55 mph, left looking up at the disinterested travelers driving the national speed limit on Interstate 15 immediately to the west.

Despite the 30 percent drawdown from 1981 to 1983, the Las Vegas CART IndyCar event was renewed for 1984. "The Caesars Palace Grand Prix at Las Vegas on Nov. 11 [1984]," it was reported, "will conclude the season."[76] The 1984 event also drew on the naming of its 1983 predecessor, simply dubbed the Caesars Palace Grand Prix IV. As a season finale, the Caesars Palace box office would never pull the numbers of the U.S. Grand Prix that it effectively replaced. Nonetheless, the Las Vegas event stood to determine the champion of its respective discipline for three years of the four-year run.

Formula One also announced their 1984 race schedule shortly after the Caesars Palace Grand Prix III. Once again, FISA, Bernie Ecclestone, and FOCA had drawn up plans for an ambitious three-event tour of the United States. The Detroit Grand Prix was slated to return to the schedule on June 24, 1984. A Grand Prix stop in Dallas was planned two weeks after Detroit. In fact, ticket packages were already being offered for the Dallas Grand Prix. The race itself, however, was "yet 'to be confirmed.'"[77] Finally, the New York Grand Prix planned for Flushing Meadows returned to the discourse, scheduled for September 24, 1984. The New York Grand Prix, however, was also clouded in controversy.

"The [New York] Department of Investigations," it was reported on November 10, 1983, "is conducting an investigation of the proposed New York Grand Prix auto race."[78] The inquiry by New York officials was the latest in a series of investigations that beset the New York venture. Indeed, the proposed New York Grand Prix was fraught from its inception with charges of political maneuvering, conflicts of interest, and worse.

Promoted by former New York mayoral aide and Queens Borough administrator Daniel Koren, the New York Grand Prix could have served Bernie Ecclestone's dream of Formula One Grand Prix racing along the great metropolitan skylines of the world. "I'm delighted that at last this is going to happen in New York," pitched Ecclestone. "It's happening 10 years later than it should have. The three proposed sites are all excellent, close to transportation and restaurants, a factor that was missing at Watkins Glen."[79] Even Bernie Ecclestone, though, did not have a handle on the backroom intrigues of New York City politics.

Investigators leaned in on allegations of inappropriate political influences involving the Grand Prix from Queens Borough president Donald Manes. Manes, notably, was Daniel Koren's former borough boss as well as a continued benefactor. Donald Manes seemed every bit the New York counterpart to Long Beach city manager John Mansell. At the same time, the financial wherewithal of Grand Prix promoter Koren appeared uncertain. By 1984, community groups were amassed against

The New York Grand Prix was planned in 1984 to run through Flushing Meadows, site of the 1939 and 1964 New York World's Fair. The New York Grand Prix was also under investigation virtually since its inception. Nearly four decades on, Formula One has yet to turn a wheel within sight of the New York metropolitan skyline (Library of Congress).

the Grand Prix project at Flushing Meadows as well. "Support for the race dwindled and the promoters are now having trouble raising funds," it was reported. "The race is not dead yet but efforts to get it under way have been slowed considerably."[80] Further, the planned Formula One event was effectively being supplanted by the CART Indy-Car Meadowlands Grand Prix in New Jersey.

Protracted investigations and community dissent then brought the New York Grand Prix to a standstill. By late 1985, the financial partnerships of the Grand Prix imploded in lawsuits.[81] The lawsuits appeared to be the beginning of the definitive end. Two months after the investor lawsuits, the federal government rolled in. In fact, just as in Long Beach, the New York Grand Prix case was first referred to the Federal Organized Crime Strike Force.[82]

"The inquiry was focused on the role of [Daniel Koren], on campaign contributions made to [Donald] Manes," according to a federal official, "and on 'the flow of money from outside the United States.'"[83] Federal investigators were also looking into charges of kickbacks and bribes to Donald Manes involving Queens Borough parking concessions, a play that might also have been embedded in the Grand Prix promotion. "An executive of one collection agency used by the PVB [Parking Violations Bureau]," read one report, "said he paid bribes ... at Manes' direction."[84]

On February 10, 1986, Manhattan District Attorney Robert Morgenthau issued subpoenas to New York city agencies, seeking to unravel the extortion scheme.[85] Donald Manes resigned his Queens Borough post one day later. Two weeks after the subpoenas were issued, the deputy director of the Parking Violations Bureau was indicted on charges of extorting $410,000 from city-contracted collection agencies.

The indictment was announced by U.S. Attorney Rudy Giuliani. On March 13, 1986, Donald Manes of Queens, New York, was found dead of an apparent self-inflicted stab wound to his heart.

Some 50 years after the Vanderbilt Cup races at Roosevelt Raceway on Long Island, the New York Formula One Grand Prix passed on with the death of Donald Manes. Daniel Koren, promoter of the Grand Prix, appeared to lie low after the death of Donald Manes, finally surfacing over two years later in a retail establishment on Madison Ave.[86] It was a certain tumble for the former political operator and promoter of a never-to-be multi-million-dollar international Formula One Grand Prix. The New York Grand Prix dream of Daniel Koren and Bernie Ecclestone thus concluded its troubled history somewhere between race cars and racketeering. The role of the organized crime syndicate perhaps tipped by "the flow of money from outside the United States" was not revealed. Further, there were no public assertions of participation by Bernie Ecclestone in the extortion schemes of Donald Manes.

In the mid–1980s, the New York Grand Prix was also another example of the domestic CART IndyCar series stealing the thunder—and the venues—from the international Formula One show. Indeed, the inaugural CART IndyCar Meadowlands Grand Prix in East Rutherford, New Jersey, was held on July 1, 1984. The Meadowlands Sports Complex—one of three potential Formula One sites considered by Koren and Ecclestone—offered a compelling view of the metropolitan New York skyline. The inaugural Meadowlands CART event was also won by Mario Andretti for Newman-Haas Racing.

Formula One, FISA, Bernie Ecclestone, and FOCA thus limped into the United States in 1984. The Detroit and Dallas Grand Prix events remained on the Formula One calendar. Rather oddly, Bill Weinberger of Caesars Palace and promoter Jack Long would be involved in both races. "[The] Detroit race was perhaps," recalled Weinberger, "the biggest cluster f**k in which I have ever been involved."[87] One might also imagine that the former centurion of Caesar had a variety of cluster f**ks from which to choose.

The emerging CART open-wheel advantage was also building momentum for an international assault, reportedly seeking race promotions in Europe, Asia, and Canada. On the heels of the announced 1984 Formula One schedule, FISA then went on a CART offensive. "The world governing body directed its 63 member clubs," reported the *New York Times*, "to suspend the licenses of drivers, entrants, officials, and race organizers who participate in any series that conflicts with a world championship."[88] One such club was the decades-old Sports Car Club of America, the domestic sanctioning body of Formula One and the recent Trans-Am round of the Caesars Palace Grand Prix III. FISA secretary general Yvon Leon minced no words: "the order was aimed at preventing the Championship Auto Racing Teams from adding international dates."[89] The worldwide gambling domination of the Meyer Lansky organization was thus rivaled perhaps only by the command and control apparatus of FISA—allegedly.

"I think that it's hurt them to lose those races [Long Beach and Caesars Palace] in this country," countered John Frasco of CART, "but Formula One problems in North America aren't related to CART. It all boils down to economics and names."[90]

The PPG Cart IndyCar series would indeed run at both Long Beach and Caesars Palace in 1984. Chris Pook—in the first year of his Long Beach CART contract—then found himself pitted against John Frasco in the Caesars Palace promotion, all an apparent matter of "economics and names."

**

The 1984 Toyota Grand Prix of Long Beach was the 10th edition of the modern classic originated in 1975 by Chris Pook. The 1975 inaugural was built around an SCCA Formula 5000 open-wheel race that featured Al Unser and Mario Andretti. In 1976, the event transitioned to a championship stop on the international Formula One calendar, a format that survived until 1983. The 1984 Long Beach Grand Prix, though, was the first year of the new CART IndyCar contract for Chris Pook and his California motorsports production. CART IndyCar opened the 1984 season in Long Beach by unleashing 800-horsepower turbocharged open-wheel rockets around the city-center. The 1984 Toyota Grand Prix of Long Beach would also feature Al Unser and Mario Andretti.

Mario Andretti won the first CART IndyCar event at the Long Beach Grand Prix on April 1, 1984. Andretti is the only driver to win both Formula One and IndyCar events at the Long Beach street circuit. Andretti's win also informed a strong season in his second year with Newman-Haas Racing, a season that concluded at the final Caesars Palace Grand Prix (Rick Lake collection).

Motorsports storylines inevitably emerge each year between the vernal equinox of the Sebring 12-Hour endurance race and the first weekend of April in Long Beach. One lead-in to Long Beach, in particular, engaged the Caesars Palace Grand Prix. "Caesars Palace has signed an agreement," read the Las Vegas dateline, "to bring Indy auto style racing to the Las Vegas resort for the next five years."[91] The announcement also confirmed the date already posted on the CART race calendar, November 11, 1984.

"[Bruce] Aguilera said CART indicated it wanted to have Caesars on the schedule," continued the report, "and would do the marketing of the race."[92] The marketing arrangement, however, also appeared to place John Frasco and CART in certain overlapping responsibilities with Chris Pook and the Long Beach Grand Prix Association. "With CART assuming the responsibility for the $454,000 race," concluded the announcement, "Caesars could devote its energy to other areas."[93] Rather, with $500,000 of skin in the Las Vegas game, John Frasco appeared to be pitted directly against Chris Pook.

For Mario Andretti, the 10th visit to the Long Beach street circuit would be a strong launch to his 1984 campaign. Andretti's Long Beach stop also picked up where the 1983 Caesars Palace Grand Prix left off, with a resounding win in a Newman-Haas Lola for the great American race car driver. Andretti carved the quickest qualifying lap on the newly shortened CART IndyCar Long Beach circuit. Mario Andretti then went wire to wire, finishing nearly a full lap ahead of second-place Geoff Brabham. By contrast, the fortunes of newly-crowned CART IndyCar champion Al Unser, Sr., served to anchor the Long Beach order. Unser and Penske teammate Rick Mears debuted the new Penske PC12 machine to qualify in the bottom third of the starting grid. Both Penske drivers then retired with mechanical issues on lap 27. For Mario Andretti and Al Unser, Sr., the Long Beach Grand Prix then set up a divergence of fates that would play throughout the year, all the way through to the CART IndyCar season finale at the Caesars Palace Grand Prix IV.

XII

Requiem and Reprise

The Final Caesars Palace Grand Prix and the Many Returns of Bernie Ecclestone

Here was a Caesar. When comes such another? (*Julius Caesar* 3.2.266)

"I don't call motor racing a sport any more," Bernie Ecclestone declared at the 1984 Monaco Grand Prix. "It's all part of the commercial entertainment business now. It's Hollywood."[1] The unfolding failure of the New York Grand Prix aside, Ecclestone's comment was a fair assessment, certainly against the glitzy backdrop of Monaco's Hotel de Paris, Casino de Monte-Carlo, and the yacht harbor. "We need a glamorous image," continued the Formula One impresario, "And if people are going to go on watching, we need a few heroes and a lot of razzmatazz."[2] To the point of the New York Grand Prix then, Formula One could have used fewer corrupt politicians and less shameless racketeering.

Less than a week after Bernie Ecclestone's comments were published in a Chicago newspaper, his talking points were punctuated by a passage in Las Vegas, a departure that bore directly on the legacy of Caesars Palace. "Jay Sarno, a founder of Caesars Palace," it was reported, "has died at that casino-hotel in Las Vegas."[3] Jay Sarno, inveterate impresario from the Atlanta Cabana to Caesars Palace and beyond, died of a heart attack on July 21, 1984, at the age of 63.

Jay Sarno had cultivated the essential, garish flair of the Caesars Palace resort; in Ecclestone's words, "a lot of razzmatazz." Sarno then curated the glamorous assemblage of stars, singers, politicians, wags, and hangers-on in an elevated but inimitably Las Vegas style; to Ecclestone's point, "It's Hollywood." Clifford Perlman then burnished the Caesars Palace image further with the addition of high-profile sporting events on the Caesars campus. Finally, William D. "Bill" Weinberger called the trifecta of the luxury brand with the development of the Caesars Palace Grand Prix, at the same time introducing Bernie Ecclestone directly to the style house of Sarno.

Jay Sarno, however, financed the splendor of Caesar with the heavily-encumbered patronage of Jimmy Hoffa, Allen Dorfman, and the Teamsters Central States Pension Fund. The passing of Allen Dorfman 18 months before Sarno, though, might thus have clouded the beneficiary payout on the Jay Sarno life insurance policies. The brass play of Jay Sarno and Allen Dorfman in 1974 with the Long Beach City Council for the gaming concessions on the *Queen Mary* then certainly extended their influence, if not their pay zone. Sarno's front for Allen Dorfman in Long Beach also steered down the same corridors of power—*at the same time*—as the 1974 city approval of Chris Pook's Long Beach Grand Prix.

"Jay Sarno died the way every man wished he could," a biographer wrote, quoting a Sarno anecdote. "He departed this life in the most fantastic suite inside the most gorgeous hotel in the world with a beautiful girl, owing the IRS a million bucks."[4] Indeed, Jay Sarno's final moments played out in the Caesars Palace Fantasy Tower, broadcast home for the NBC coverage of the Caesars Palace Grand Prix. The collocation warrants the question. Did Jay Sarno ever attend the Caesars Palace Grand Prix?

"If my dad did go to [the Grand Prix], he never told me," recalled Jay Sarno, Jr. "I doubt it would be his sort of thing. The most important attribute to him of a car was not speed, but air conditioning."[5] The younger Sarno then related a tale about the elder's penchant for Cadillacs, and the utter absence of scheduled maintenance upon them. "[I] asked my dad if he ever changed the oil in his then 1-year old Cadillac. He said he had not, but he should," recalled Sarno. "The next day he took the car to the dealer (Cashman) to have the oil changed."[6] Jay Sarno, with time on his hands, visited the Cashman Cadillac showroom and took a fancy to the latest offerings. With the vehicle still on the service lift, the older Cadillac was traded in on the spot for a minty-crisp showroom model. "This became one of my favorite jokes about my dad: How does Jay Sarno change the oil in his car?" related Jay Sarno, Jr. "He just gets a new car, because it comes with new oil."[7]

The passions and proclivities of Jay Sarno thus shaped the skyline and swagger of Las Vegas, while the power plays and privileges of Bernie Ecclestone shaped the future and finances of Formula One. The overlap of their influences in Las Vegas would be also be felt in the decades to come. Indeed, Jay Sarno was departed. Bernie Ecclestone, however, returned to Las Vegas long after the final Caesars Palace Grand Prix.

***

"Former Gaming Control Board member Jeff Silver," read the scroll of Caesar, "has been named senior vice president of marketing at Caesars Palace."[8] The former gambling regulator, turned gambling executive, had famously shut down the attempts of the notorious Frank Rosenthal to obtain a Nevada gambling license as a key employee of the Stardust Hotel and Casino. Jeff Silver now changed his jacket to join one of the most racketeered gambling properties on the Las Vegas Strip— allegedly. As a marketing executive, Silver somewhat also acquired the portfolio of Bill Weinberger, including the forthcoming Caesars Palace Grand Prix IV.

"As a marketing concept, the race was expensive," recalled Silver, "and the drivers, support crews and assorted supporters were quite demanding."[9] With licensure in accountancy and law, Jeff Silver was also struck by the partialities of the Palace praetorians. "Caesar's bosses, such as Henry Gluck and Terri Lanni, who lived in Los Angeles," continued Silver, "were more interested in creating a kinship with the European moneyed-elite, as they had nurtured with the Hollywood personalities living in their neighborhood."[10]

Despite the departure of Formula One from the Caesars Palace Grand Prix, the

The poster art for the 1984 edition of the Caesars Palace Grand Prix was the first to feature photography rather than a Leroy Neiman painting. 1983 Caesars Palace Grand Prix III winner Mario Andretti peered upon the Palace from his 1984 Newman-Haas chariot with the steely gaze of a Roman gladiator. Indeed, it was time to move the Caesars Palace Grand Prix along—from impressionism to realism (Bruce Aguilera collection).

kinships of Nevada gambling kingpins also included Bernie Ecclestone and Adnan Khashoggi. While the eccentric business tycoons were both unrepentant high-stakes gamblers in Las Vegas, Khashoggi was perhaps the greater risk to the credit line. "[Khashoggi] has had markers in Las Vegas," read a 1984 report, "that have totaled in the millions."[11] Ecclestone and Khashoggi conducted business between themselves as

Global arms merchant and unrepentant gambler Adnan Khashoggi was a nexus figure, thread-ing Las Vegas, dubious criminal connections, Saudi Formula One sponsors, and Bernie Eccle-stone (Roland Godefroy, Wikimedia Commons).

well. In 1987, Ecclestone bought the London mansion of Adnan Khashoggi, convert-ing it into his FOCA headquarters.[12] The billionaire bettors also shared the pinnacle of bargains gone bad, two of the most expensive divorces in history.

Jeff Silver thus inherited the sharp dichotomy of Caesars Palace and its captive promotion, the Caesars Palace Grand Prix. It was the proverbial pit and the pinnacle, a divergence of high-roller *haute couture*, against a diminishing motorsports event that bought T-shirts off the rack. "There were no illusions that this was a Caesar's casino promotion rather than a sporting contest," surmised Silver, "which explains why the other resort hotels wanted nothing to do with it. There was no way they would send their good customers to Caesars [for the Grand Prix] when the only entrance, VIP seating and exit was through the Caesar's Palace casino!"[13]

***

Formula One returned to North America in 1984 with three consecutive events. The Canadian Grand Prix won by Nelson Piquet was run on June 17, 1984, at Circuit Gilles Villeneuve in Montreal, Quebec. One week later, the Formula One tents trav-eled around Lake Ontario and Lake Erie to set up the circus in downtown Detroit for the third annual Detroit Grand Prix. Two weeks after the Detroit show, it was over 1,000 miles southwest to the Cotton Bowl in Dallas for the inaugural Dallas Grand Prix. Remarkably, both William D. Weinberger and Jack Long were involved in the Detroit and Dallas operations.

For Jack Long, the Detroit and Dallas Formula One rounds were part of his three-race premier-level business portfolio for 1984. Ironically, the third event was the Caesars Palace Grand Prix IV. "Jack had signed contracts to operate three races that year," recalled Bill Weinberger, "Dallas F1, Detroit F1 and Caesars CART."[14] In an odd turn of relationships, Jack Long's wife was also the former secretary to Bill Weinberger at Caesars World, Inc. in Los Angeles. Mrs. Long, unfortunately, was suffering from cancer. "[Jack Long] was overwhelmed to say the least," continued Bill Weinberger, "and asked me to join him in working those three races."[15] Weinberger and Long formed a partnership for their 1984 venture. There would be no need, however, for a 1985 renewal.

"For the Detroit race we worked for Bernie [Ecclestone]," continued Weinberger, "who, in order to get the race on, became the de facto promoter. We were in charge of getting all sponsors and handling race operations."[16] Weinberger, accustomed to the relative autonomy of his various Caesars World and Caesars Palace positions, bristled at the pecking order. "[Ecclestone] was a total absentee boss. Jack [Long], with his personal problems adding to the mix, was in completely over his head," Weinberger reflected, "and I had no authority to do anything."[17]

Chaos behind the scenes notwithstanding, the third annual Detroit Grand Prix proceeded forward on June 24, 1984. After losing a reported $1.2 million in 1982 and 1983, the Detroit franchisee was optimistic for a turnaround. "We should nearly break even this year," offered Robert McCabe of Detroit Renaissance. "Next year we should make money."[18] Detroit Renaissance also held a contract with Bernie Ecclestone and FOCA to stage the Detroit Formula One Grand Prix through 1988. McCabe was thus hopeful that the vagaries of the Detroit turnstiles could outpace the escalating guarantees demanded by Ecclestone. "FOCA will walk away from this year's event," it was reported, "some $2 million to $3 million richer."[19]

A reported 75,000 fans then turned out to witness Nelson Piquet make it two in a row in North America, winning the 1984 Detroit Grand Prix in a Brabham for Bernie Ecclestone. Elio de Angelis was second in a Lotus some 30 seconds back. Teo Fabi, splitting time in 1984 between Formula One and CART, was third for Bernie Ecclestone. Only six of the 26 starters were still running on the final lap. Fourth in the 1984 final order, Alain Prost of McLaren was quite blunt about the Detroit circuit. "It's too bumpy, too narrow, has too many surface changes, too many manhole covers, and too many dangerous corners," complained Prost. "It's just a lousy course."[20]

Bernie Ecclestone too joined the chorus of driver complaints to pivot Formula One away from the downtown streets of Detroit. Indeed, the Detroit Grand Prix would run out its FOCA contract in 1988 before joining the CART IndyCar series in 1989. Robert McCabe of Detroit Renaissance finally raised the flag of financial surrender as Formula One steered into Detroit for the final time in 1988. McCabe's capitulation in 1988 was in obvious contrast to his fiscal confidence in 1984. "We're not in the racing business," McCabe finally admitted, "to make money."[21]

The much-maligned 1984 Dallas Grand Prix featured miserable heat, mangled asphalt, and a missing bankroll. William D. Weinberger and Jack Long soldiered under contract with Bernie Ecclestone to manage the event and collect the money. The one-and-done Formula One race was won by Keke Rosberg over Rene Arnoux and Elio de Angelis. Race leader and pole sitter Nigel Mansell was punted back to sixth (author's collection).

Money matters also drove both the pre-race and the post-script of the 1984 Dallas Grand Prix. Founded by Don Walker of DRW Investments, Ltd., the Dallas Grand Prix paired racing legend Carroll Shelby with the popular culture of the television show *Dallas* to create its own version of a celebrity-driven Formula One festival. "It was a race being held," suggested a former partner of Walker, "as an excuse to hold a party."[22] Walker also signed an agreement with Bernie Ecclestone and FOCA to stage the Dallas Formula One event through 1988. Whereas the Detroit Grand Prix appeared to pay its bills, the 1984 Dallas Grand Prix on July 8, 1984, would add financial failure to its long list of on-track issues. Payment of the FOCA guarantee, in fact, nearly derailed the entire Dallas exercise.

"Bernie gave me a copy of the contract he had with Don for the 1984 race," related Bill Weinberger. "These contracts were super-secret and each one was different depending on what Bernie felt he could get from the promoter and how anxious Bernie was to do the race."[23] Indeed, Bernie Ecclestone was legendary for holding his dollars close, and his contracts closer. "There was something like a $125,000 progress payment due Bernie (FOCA) on a certain date," continued Weinberger. "When the payment didn't show up as expected Bernie called me. He asked me to drop everything and immediately talk to Don to find out where the money was."[24] The former Caesars Palace casino executive called on the collection, while Don Walker was apparently playing Texas Hold 'Em. "Don pleaded ignorance of any payment due and then produced his copy of the contract showing the schedule of payments and when they were due," concluded Weinberger. "I then produced my copy of the contract which showed the correct due dates and amounts. My understanding is Bernie received the call and the money shortly after that."[25]

Friday and Saturday track sessions in high temperatures quickly deteriorated the poorly prepared racing surface around the Cotton Bowl circuit. Concrete crews then worked throughout the night to make emergency repairs for the Formula One start. The hastily redressed paving, however, prompted a call for a driver boycott. "Bernie had to have a meeting with them," Bill Weinberger recalled, "and read them the riot act."[26]

The cultural convergence of Texas oil money and Saudi conglomerate wealth also drove the discord headed into race day. "F1 drivers are the biggest prima donnas in sport," commented Larry Waldrop, a partner of Don Walker. "They bitch about everything."[27]

Bernie Ecclestone, however, returned fire from the Formula One contingent. "It's bad enough to come here and have the worst facilities. They're really the worst in the world," retorted the Formula One czar. "I mean we're not accustomed to working out of cow sheds."[28] Despite the bickering, the grid was formed at the insistence of team managers and Bernie Ecclestone.

A crowd estimated at over 100,000 then watched Keke Rosberg survive a hot day in a Williams FW09 to take the Dallas Grand Prix victory over Rene Arnoux and Elio de Angelis. "The track didn't offer any grip," commented winner Rosberg. "It was broken up quite badly."[29]

"The track is a joke," added Nelson Piquet after a crash on lap 46. "Coming off the corners, you couldn't believe it. It was like driving in icy conditions."[30] In Dallas, only eight cars out of 25 starters survived to take the checkered flag. Rene Arnoux was the only other car on the lead lap after Rosberg.

Agricultural accommodations and icy conditions congregated the complaints for Bernie Ecclestone as Formula One departed Watkins Glen in 1981. Nonetheless, the Formula One impresario pronounced that "the conditions in Dallas would be righted for a return in 1985. Rather, Bernie Ecclestone and Formula One were troubled in Dallas no more. On March 25 [1985]," it was reported, "[Don] Walker placed Dallas Grand Prix of Texas Inc. in Chapter 11 bankruptcy."[31]

"The Dallas race," recalled Bill Weinberger, "was an unmitigated disaster as an event."[32] The bankruptcy filing of Don Walker completely engulfed his nearly 100 syndicated enterprises. The bankruptcy also revealed hundreds of bank accounts, commingled funds, diverted profits, and "concurrent investigations by the FBI and the U.S. Securities and Exchange Commission."[33] It was a backdrop befitting the Palace of Caesar, however unsettling to Weinberger, perhaps its most superlative centurion.

The 1984 Dallas Grand Prix thus entered American Grand Prix history as did the 1959 Sebring and 1960 Riverside events before it, one and done, along with a ledger of financial fiasco in its flume. "All in all, the six weeks I spent in Dallas leading up to the race," concluded Bill Weinberger, "were probably among the worst of my life on any number of levels."[34] The 1984 Dallas Grand Prix checked all manner of undesirable boxes for the former Caesars Palace executive. The two U.S. Grand Prix rounds for 1984 thus concluded under the collective umbrella of Bernie Ecclestone, Jack Long, and Bill Weinberger. For Bill Weinberger and Jack Long, though, they would transition from chaos to CART. Indeed, the 1984 CART IndyCar Caesars Palace Grand Prix IV still lay before them. In Las Vegas, Weinberger and Long would also umbrella alongside John Frasco.

***

The 1984 CART IndyCar season produced several dynamic storylines headed toward the finale at Caesars Palace. Mario Andretti's win at Long Beach was followed by victories at the Meadowlands Grand Prix, the Michigan 500, the Provimi Veal 200 at Road America, the Escort Radar Warning 200 at Mid–Ohio, and the Detroit News Grand Prix. Roger Penske parked his newly launched PC12 chassis after the second round at Phoenix, plugging Rick Mears and Al Unser instead into off-the-rack March 84C IndyCar machines. Rick Mears made good on the transition to March machinery to capture the 1984 Indianapolis 500. Mears, however, was seriously injured on September 7, 1984, during practice for the Molson Indy round at Sanair in Quebec. Roger Penske then called on sometime Formula One driver Michael Thackwell to pilot Mears' Pennzoil March for the Caesars Palace Grand Prix IV.

Also marking 1984 was the phoenix rise of the boutique IndyCar constructor, a throwback to the independent IndyCar chassis builders of the 1960s. Three such efforts, in fact, would come from the ranks of Bernie Ecclestone's FOCA. Teddy Yip entered Bruno Giacomelli in a Theodore T83 chassis at the Long Beach round. Giacomelli—the former Alfa Romeo teammate to Mario Andretti—was out on lap six in Long Beach. Record industry executive Mike Curb also entered a bespoke machine at Long Beach, placing Kevin Cogan in a Ligier LC02 powered by a Cosworth engine. Cogan—the former Caesars Palace-sponsored driver for George Bignotti—was the only driver to finish behind Giacomelli at Long Beach, retired on lap three. "The Ligier chassis was a huge failure," read one report, "and the French effort was history."[35]

Gary Gerould, left, and Paul Page, right, voiced all four years of the Caesars Palace Grand Prix for NBC Sports, Page on play-by-play and Gerould as roving color commentator. On November 11, 1984, Paul Page provided the final sign-off for the Caesars Palace Grand Prix concept (Bruce Aguilera collection).

With the CART IndyCar season winding down, Robin Miller of the *Indianapolis Star* reported a boutique bombshell. Al Unser, Jr., was signing with Lotus for the 1985 CART IndyCar season. "I know I'm taking a helluva gamble," commented Unser. "If it is a bad car I'm stuck with it and if it's a good car, nobody else will have one."[36] Rather than a full works effort, the 1985 Lotus IndyCar was effectively a commission from former Formula 2 team owner Roy Winkelmann. Winkelmann had notably campaigned Jochen Rindt in Formula 2 before Rindt joined forces with Bernie Ecclestone.

"It's like losing your girlfriend," lamented Rick Galles, Unser's Coors Light car owner. "I think we're a lot better than this Lotus deal and I don't think it's as much of a factory deal as Al believes."[37] The suspicions of Galles were proven correct. Plagued by money woes and a lack of sponsorship, the Winkelmann Team Lotus 96T IndyCar project was over before it ever hit an American test track. By January of 1985, Al Unser, Jr., quit the Winkelmann effort to drive for Doug Shierson in the Domino's Pizza Lola. Unser and Galles, though, would soldier together through the 1984 CART IndyCar finale at the Caesars Palace Grand Prix IV. The pair would later reunite in 1988, continuing forward to a memorable triumph at the Indianapolis Motor Speedway in 1992.

***

Michigan labor attorney John Frasco was the chairman of CART from 1980 until 1989. Frasco, though, was also the promoter of several race events on the CART IndyCar calendar, including the 1984 Caesars Palace Grand Prix IV. The apparent conflict of negotiating events for CART—and for himself—became a metaphoric blade unto Caesar as Frasco was removed from the CART board (Bruce Aguilera collection).

Promotions and operations of the 1984 Caesars Palace Grand Prix IV would reunite the principals of the 1981 and 1982 Caesars Palace Formula One events while drawing them into the power center of CART and John Frasco. The new management structure indeed returned one of Caesar's own centurions to Las Vegas. The coalition of the final Caesars race event, however, also created its own Palace intrigue, with the original Grand Prix Consultant deemed disposable. That intrigue also played out in court. Years later, it would pitch the recollections of the departee, against that of his former Caesars Palace Grand Prix colleagues.

"Caesars had agreed to give promotional rights exclusively to CART rather than promote the race itself," the *Las Vegas Review-Journal* reported. "With that agreement, Long Beach Grand Prix promoter Chris Pook, involved with the first three events here, was released."[38] Indeed, Chris Pook was informed that his services were no longer required. Pook, however, pushed back, still in possession of a four-year race consulting agreement through 1984 with Caesars Palace.

"CART [and] John Frasco took over the event," recalled Chris Pook, "and basically 'fired' the [Long Beach Grand Prix Association] stating that he did not need us to operate it and instead hired [Jack Long] directly!"[39] John Frasco's hard turn against Chris Pook somewhat positioned the Long Beach Grand Prix founder against Jack Long, his *own* marketing consultant for the first Long Beach event. The termination of Chris Pook's Caesars Palace agreement also drove Pook to huddle with his lawyers.

"This led to a lawsuit between [Long Beach Grand Prix Association] and Caesars which after 18 months of acrimony was settled in [our] favor!" continued Chris Pook. "[It was] all very tenuous because [Long Beach Grand Prix Association] was by then in the first year of its new CART Contract!"[40] Chris Pook was further complimentary of Bruce Aguilera and the response of his Caesars Palace office to the lawsuit.

"Bruce [Aguilera], I believe, was very embarrassed about the whole thing and drove the settlement," Chris Pook furthered the subject. "Aguilera was not only a very good attorney but a fair and upstanding individual who played a very important role in the entire event."[41] While Chris Pook steadfastly invoked the name of Caesar, executive centurions William D. Weinberger and Bruce Aguilera did not recall the lawsuit. Ultimately, Chris Pook believed the driver of discontent to simply be John Frasco, certainly as opposed to Caesars Palace or perhaps, CART.

Period reports provided context to the engagement of Bill Weinberger with Jack Long, while also adding subtext for the personal role of John Frasco in the Caesars Palace Grand Prix IV. "[Bill] Weinberger, formerly the vice president of Caesars Palace," according to the *Las Vegas Review-Journal*, "is now an associate of Jack Long. Together, the pair did the Detroit and Dallas grand prix races."[42] "Long and Weinberger are tied to another four years of a five-year agreement with Caesars to stage auto race events," continued the *Review-Journal*. "The promoter—John Frasco—also is the director of CART."[43]

The reported 4-year tail of Bill Weinberger and Jack Long, however, did not bear out, certainly not at Caesars Palace. In fact, their agreement effectively concluded with the 1984 Caesars Palace Grand Prix. Further, the days of Michigan labor attorney John Frasco at CART were numbered.

On October 30, 1989, the 10-member CART board was dissolved, and John Frasco removed as chairman. A new board was then formed to include each of the 24 team owners. Further, each member would have an equal vote. From cabal to collective, temperament then turned against the former chairman. "Frasco, a Detroit attorney who had been CART chairman since September, 1980," wrote Shav Glick for The *Los Angeles Times*, "was removed after discontent reached groundswell proportions."[44] "Under Frasco's administration the rich teams—primarily those of Penske and Pat Patrick—were getting richer," Glick paraphrased a team manager, "while the rest picked up the crumbs."[45]

Elsewhere, it was reported that the personal role of John Frasco in race events was of considerable concern. "Some owners believed there was a conflict of interest with Frasco," reported the *Chicago Tribune*, "who negotiated a [CART] contract for a race ... while also serving as promoter of the race."[46] Sidney Korshak, the infamous Chicago labor attorney to the rackets—as well as a former consultant to Caesars Palace—might have respected the Midwest moxie of John Frasco—allegedly.

***

Mario Andretti brought a dominant point lead into Las Vegas for the CART IndyCar season finale at the Caesars Palace Grand Prix IV. The 1984 Indianapolis 500, though, was another in the loss column for Andretti, shunted on pit lane by Josele Garza while running inside the top 10. Nonetheless, with six race wins and points in four other events, Mario Andretti and his Newman-Haas Budweiser Lola led the championship points convincingly over Tom Sneva and the Texaco March, 160 to 143. Sneva had played tough in 1984, though, claiming two wins and three other podium finishes. Tom Sneva also upped his road racing game considerably, enough so that he finished a commendable third in the season opener at Long Beach. The championship decider at Caesars Palace had come down to Andretti and Sneva. If Tom Sneva won, Mario Andretti needed to finish ninth or better to clinch the championship. Bobby Rahal in Jim Truman's March was already a lock on third. No one else was even close.

Michigan oilman U.E. "Pat" Patrick was a long-time IndyCar team owner. Patrick provided the STP-sponsored Wildcat VIII in which Mario Andretti was ultimately declared second in the 1981 Indianapolis 500. Pat Patrick and Roger Penske were the race team owners of wealth and influence wrangling with their lawyers over that controversial 1981 Indy crown. Patrick and Penske were thus the powers of their own palace, epitomizing for many the protracted CART versus USAC and CART versus IRL splits in premier-level American open-wheel racing (Bruce Aguilera collection).

Danny Sullivan, winner of the 1981 and 1982 Caesars Can-Am events, had joined the 1984 CART IndyCar series with Doug Shierson after spending 1983 on Ken Tyrell's Benetton Formula One team. Remarkably, Sullivan garnered three race wins in his first full IndyCar season. Danny Sullivan also stood fourth in points with 110, tied with Rick Mears. With Mears sidelined, Sullivan could then separate himself at Caesars Palace. Bobby Rahal, though, would remain out of points reach.

The SCCA Trans-Am series also returned for the 1984 Caesars Palace Grand Prix. Willy T. Ribbs and Greg Pickett each stood on four wins for the season headed to Las Vegas. With two wins and remarkable consistency, Tom Gloy held the points lead and had already clinched the 1984 Trans-Am title. Wally Dallenbach, Jr., though, was the Trans-Am driver on the rise. Driving for a homegrown team dubbed "The Colorado Connection," Dallenbach had seven finishes inside the top five and was

After his CART IndyCar debut at the 1983 Caesars Palace Grand Prix, Michael Andretti ran his first full year of premier-level IndyCar competition in 1984. The CART IndyCar rookie returned to Las Vegas for the 1984 CART IndyCar Caesars Palace Grand Prix holding a respectable seventh in points with five podium finishes (courtesy LVCVA News Bureau).

also fifth in points. In fact, Dallenbach and his family-friendly Camaro finished second to Darin Brassfield's Budweiser-sponsored DeAtley Motorsports Corvette at the Riverside Trans-Am round one month prior to Caesars Palace. Dallenbach could not press Gloy for the title, but he was poised to step up in Las Vegas.

"The second year it really sunk in. I thought, man, we're here with IndyCars, we're here in Las Vegas," reflected Dallenbach. "That's when I remember how good it was."[47] In only his second year of professional competition, Wally Dallenbach also recalled the origins of the family Trans-Am team. "We bought a couple of the old DeAtley cars. My sister's boyfriend, my sister, and myself," continued Dallenbach. "Just three knuckleheads doing most of the heavy lifting on this Trans-Am deal. I think a lot of teams felt sorry for us."[48]

Gone from the Caesars Palace Grand Prix IV was the NASCAR Winston West event, to be replaced by the screaming Robert Bosch Super Vee open-wheel series. Departed too were the names of the lower tier stock cars, handles like Herschel McGriff, Clive Skilton, Buddy Boys, John Krebs, and Harry Goularte to be replaced

The SCCA Trans-Am competition at the 1984 Caesars Palace Grand Prix points up the proximity of the easterly leg of the Caesars Palace roval to the Las Vegas Strip. Gary Schons (#31 Pontiac Firebird) fights oversteer into turn one of the Las Vegas race circuit behind Craig Carter (#56 Chevrolet Camaro). The Holiday Casino and the Holiday Inn high-rise hotel is directly across the Strip. Dunes hotel-casino sponsorship on left bumper of Schon's race car is noteworthy. The Dunes was immediately south of Caesars Palace (photograph by Ernie Ohlson).

by open-wheel stars in the making, Roger Penske., Jr., Arie Luyendyk, Mike Follmer, Mike Groff, and Jeff Andretti. Notably, the Bosch Super Vee feeder series launched its 1982 champion to the pinnacle of domestic motorsport, Jeff Andretti's older brother Michael.

Qualifying for the Caesars Palace Grand Prix IV obliterated the one-year-old track record of John Paul, Jr. Widening of the exit of turn-five was credited with a remarkable spike in speed down the long Caesars Palace front straight. In fact, nearly three quarters of the field would break Paul's 1983 mark of 34.888 seconds. Danny Sullivan grabbed the pole with a scorching 32.952 in his Domino's Pizza Lola, nearly two seconds quicker than John Paul the year before. A 2-second gap seemed like a lifetime on a short loop like the Caesars Palace roval.

Mario Andretti was alongside Sullivan with a 33.293 for Paul Newman and Carl Haas, nearly two seconds below his own 1983 time. John Paul, Jr., then made good on the time charts, recording a time of 33.411 in the Provimi Veal March. Bobby Rahal squared next to Paul with the same qualifying time, another 33.411 in Jim Trueman's 7-Eleven March.

Tom Sneva remained in a Texaco Star March Cosworth in 1984 but had taken the Texas oil money to a new team, joining former McLaren Formula One team manager

Mike Follmer (#16 Ralt RT5) competed in the Robert Bosch Super-Vee series at the 1984 Caesars Palace Grand Prix IV. Follmer is the nephew of 1972 Can-Am champion George Follmer. Mike Follmer joined Al Arciero and Roger Penske, Jr., on the three-car team in Las Vegas. Al Arciero (#96 Ralt RT5) is beyond Follmer. The event was won by Ludwig Heimrath, Jr., over Arie Luyendyk and Penske (Mike Follmer collection).

Teddy Mayer. Teddy Mayer, in fact, had stood six miles west exactly 16 years earlier on the starting line of the former Stardust International Raceway in support of Bruce McLaren and Denny Hulme. Hulme won the 1968 Stardust Can-Am Grand Prix that day, along with the 1968 Canadian-American Challenge Cup. Mayer's newest driver Tom Sneva dropped a four-second improvement on his 1983 qualifying time around the Caesars roval to slot fifth on the grid. Alongside Sneva in the starting order was Mayer's former McLaren driver, former Formula One world champion—and CART IndyCar rookie—Emerson Fittipaldi.

Geoff Brabham was sixth on the grid for in a March 84C for Maurice Kraines. Brabham was making his third start at the Caesars Palace Grand Prix, notably crowned the 1981 Can-Am champion atop the Caesars podium. PPG CART IndyCar World Series champion (1983) Al Unser was having a dismal season for Roger Penske but was an admirable seventh on the time sheets. Unser, too, had a Stardust Raceway event in his portfolio, the 1968 Stardust 150 USAC IndyCar race won by brother Bobby.

In his first full CART IndyCar season, Michael Andretti qualified ninth with a 34.178. Michael Thackwell, subbing for injured Indy 500 winner Rick Mears, slotted 10th for Roger Penske. Al Unser, Jr., though, was already second-guessing his

Danny Ongais (#25 Interscope March) leads Al Unser, Sr. (#1 Miller High Life March) out of turn five of the Caesars Palace roval at the 1984 Caesars Palace Grand Prix. Danny Ongais unifies the racing line, from the popular funny car win for Mickey Thompson at the 1969 NHRA Stardust National Open in Las Vegas, to the wretched weather of the 1977 U.S. Grand Prix at Watkins Glen in an Interscope-Penske, to the 1984 Caesars Palace Grand Prix IV. Al Unser, Sr., notably competed at the 1968 USAC IndyCar Stardust 150 at Stardust International Raceway. Reigning CART IndyCar champion Unser also raced hard for the win at the 1984 Caesars Palace Grand Prix. Both Ongais and Unser, Sr., retired from the 1984 event (author's collection).

Winkelmann Team Lotus deal by the finale at Caesars Palace. Unser placed his Coors Light Silver Bullet March 84C 16th on the grid for Rick Galles. Three slots behind Unser was 42-year-old Danny Ongais. Ongais had carried the Interscope colors of Ted Field from Formula One to CART IndyCar in 1979. Danny Ongais also stood third on the podium of the 1984 Detroit News Grand Prix behind Mario Andretti and Tom Sneva. Few in the crowd of the 1984 Caesars Palace Grand Prix IV, though, could have recalled that Danny Ongais also won the funny car final of the 1969 Stardust NHRA National Open in a Mickey Thompson Mustang at Stardust International Raceway.

The grid of the Caesars Palace Grand Prix also threw back to the first four-time winner of the Indianapolis 500. A.J. Foyt was running select oval-only appearances in the 1984 CART IndyCar season. Foyt was off the pace in qualifying with a 36.224, nearly 11 mph slower than Danny Sullivan. A.J. Foyt, though, was added to the back of the field as a promoter's option, presumably a pitch in from John Frasco himself. Foyt, too, had a Stardust Raceway credential. A.J. Foyt qualified seventh for the 1968 Stardust 150 USAC road race.

The SCCA Trans-Am leg of the 1984 Caesars Palace Grand Prix would be the

John Morton (#64 Jet Engineering March) leads Ed Pimm (#98 Dubonnet Gurney Eagle), and Randy Lewis (#34 Wysar Racing March) during a caution period at the November 11, 1984, CART IndyCar Caesars Palace Grand Prix. Cars on pit lane are not identified (courtesy LVCVA News Bureau).

anomaly in the four-year run of the Las Vegas event. In each prior year that Caesars Palace hosted a season finale, the event also determined the annual champion. Tom Gloy, though, had already sewn up the 1984 Trans-Am championship. Caesars Palace then quite literally served up the victory lap for Tom Gloy.

In a weekend of record resets, fast Trans-Am qualifier Dave Watson dropped Willy T. Ribbs' Trans-Am track record from a 40.912 to 39.594. Watson then led out to cover the field for the first 16 laps in his Trick Gasoline Chevrolet Camaro. On lap 17, Wally Dallenbach, Jr., went past in the Colorado Connection Camaro and into the lead. Twenty-one-year-old Dallenbach commanded the 1984 Caesars Palace Trans-Am event for the next 14 laps, finally surrendering to Tom Gloy on lap 31.

Tom Gloy in the factory-supported 7-Eleven Mercury Capri and Wally Dallenbach in the privateer Camaro then dueled for the next 50 circuits of the Caesars Palace roval. Gloy uncorked a fast lap during the race of 38.00 flat, an incredible two seconds better than his qualifying effort. It was also within breathing distance of A.J. Foyt's CART IndyCar time. "Dallenbach battled Gloy side-by-side and bumper-to-bumper," reported the *Associated Press*, "until [Dallenbach] spun into one of the sand pits just six laps from the end."[49] Dallenbach recovered from the excursion but it was too late. Tom Gloy crossed the start-finish line of the Caesars Palace Grand Prix roval to place an exclamation point on the 1984 SCCA Trans-Am championship. Wally Dallenbach, Jr., followed Gloy some nine seconds back.

The Las Vegas victory was Gloy's third Trans-Am win of the season. Wally Dallenbach used his hard-earned second-place finish to vault past Willy T. Ribbs in the

Paul Newman (#33 Nissan 300ZX) trails in this image from SCCA Trans-Am action at the 1984 Caesars Palace Grand Prix. Dave Watson (#37 Chevrolet Camaro) leads Bob Lobenberg (#55 Pontiac Trans Am), Darin Brassfield (#3 Chevrolet Corvette), and David Hobbs (#1 Cherolet Corvette). The event was won by Tom Gloy over Wally Dallenbach, Jr. Hobbs was third. Paul Newman retired on the first lap of the race (author's collection).

final points standings. Dallenbach improved to fourth while Ribbs dropped to fifth. Trans-Am champion (1983) David Hobbs finished third in the race to join Gloy and Dallenbach on the Caesars Palace Trans-Am podium. Hobbs, however, finished a distant eighth in the championship. Greg Pickett followed Hobbs across the finish line and claimed second in the final points standings.

Paul Newman, despite qualifying eighth, was out of the race before the first turn. David Hobbs and fifth qualifier Paul Miller tangled going into turn one. As the field collapsed toward the apex, Newman and his Diet Coke Nissan 300ZX caught the Porsche 924 of Miller. From 13th on the grid, Larry Park in a Corvette plowed hard into Newman. The world-famous actor and part-time auto racing hobbyist was done for the day, credited with a 33rd-place finish.

Amid the disappointment of Paul Newman's Trans-Am outing, Newman publicist Tom Blattler summarized the actor's four-year experience at the Caesars Palace Grand Prix. "He feels certain people here burned him in the past," Blattler explained. "They named him race chairman, then used him to bring in other celebrities."[50] The comments by Tom Blattler could only be directed at Clifford Perlman, the disgraced—and deposed—Caesars World and Caesars Palace chief executive. The disenchantment of Paul Newman might also offer framework in the weeks ahead on the fate of the entire exercise of the Caesars Palace Grand Prix. Notably, Blattler spoke within view of the banner signage of Alvin Malnik's Caesars Poconos Resorts.

***

"The eight-month battle for the national championship is about to come to an end," opened Paul Page for the NBC broadcast of the November 11, 1984, CART IndyCar Caesars Palace Grand Prix. "The divers stand at this moment, alone with their thoughts."[51] The eight-month battle for the 1984 championship had been dominated by Mario Andretti. Mario Andretti only needed to finish ninth or better to take home the championship laurels and the cash harvest that went with it. On camera, Andretti presented consummate professional poise and total focus.

"This race is that important. It's going to decide a national champion," offered Andretti, the 1978 Formula One world champion. "If it goes our way, obviously it's going to represent the only reward that's really meaningful for us this year."[52] Rather, it was the only reward *remaining* for the Newman-Haas team, especially with Paul Newman and Carl Haas posted on pit lane. Further, with Andretti's domination of the CART IndyCar statistics, a collapse in the finale was simply not an option. As Mario Andretti offered those words

Much like Mario Andretti, Paul Newman endured four years of the Caesars Palace Grand Prix, as grand marshal in 1981 and 1982, SCCA Trans-Am competitor in 1983 and 1984. According to Newman's publicist, the venerable actor felt burned and used during his Las Vegas experience (Bruce Aguilera collection).

from the grid walk, though, the great American race car driver could not foresee how close it would all come to slipping away.

"We've got to win the race and the car is capable. We're happy with the way the car is working," Tom Sneva commented just feet away from Andretti. "After we win the race we'll just have to see what happens to Mario."[53] As Sneva boasted, though, the Texaco Star driver could not anticipate how close he had just called the race.

Singing star Diana Ross took center stage in 1984 to offer the most famous words in motorsports, "Gentlemen, start your engines."[54] Thirteen rows of two race cars each then took an opening stroll before queuing up for the pace lap. CART starter Nick Fornoro watched the field intently as they exited turn-five of the Caesars Palace roval. Polesitter Danny Sullivan tightened the front rows as he built speed headed toward Fornoro's green flag. As Nick Fornoro unfurled green, John Paul, Jr., sprang from the third starting position and—just like Mario Andretti in 1983—dove for the inside advantage headed into turn one just yards from the famed Las Vegas Strip.

Tom Sneva drove his Texaco Star March 84C to a victory over Mario Andretti at the 1984 CART IndyCar Caesars Palace Grand Prix IV. Sneva's car owner Teddy Mayer notably shepherded Denny Hulme to the win in the 1968 Stardust Can-Am Grand Prix at the former Stardust International Raceway, some six miles west of Caesars Palace (author's collection).

John Paul, Jr., pushed Danny Sullivan wide on the exit, pinching Mario Andretti. Bobby Rahal came past Sullivan before he could get his Dominos Pizza Lola righted. Mario Andretti was then around Sullivan as well. Danny Sullivan, however, fought back on the north side of the course and managed past Andretti. Tom Sneva was lurking behind Sullivan. As the screaming turbocharged CART IndyCar machines emerged from turn five and back onto the long front straight, John Paul, Jr., led the first lap followed by Bobby Rahal, Danny Sullivan, and Mario Andretti.

Bobby Rahal took over in the early going, leading until lap 31 when Jacques Villeneuve inherited the lead. Jacques Villeneuve, younger brother of the late Gilles Villeneuve, commanded the event until the one-third point when he turned to the pits. Howard "Howdy" Holmes, driving another March 84C for Teddy Mayer, led until lap 65 when Bobby Rahal once again raced into the lead. Mario Andretti also took a turn at the front, leading the Caesars Palace Grand Prix IV until Jacques Villeneuve went to the point on lap 103. Villeneuve remained out front for 20 laps until getting tagged by Geoff Brabham, into the wall and out of the race on lap 123.

Tom "The Gas Man" Sneva moved to the front after the retirement of Jacques Villeneuve. Sneva, though, was soon joined by Al Unser. Unser, the defending CART IndyCar national champion, was reportedly cut loose by Roger Penske just the day before. Unser, then, might have had something to prove in the latter stages of the CART IndyCar finale. Tom Sneva and Al Unser battled for nearly 30 laps, Unser often diving to an advantage into turn one, with Sneva then powering past on the back side of the course. Theirs was the duel of the day, with Mario Andretti observing close behind from third.

While Tom Sneva and Al Unser battled for the lead, John Paul, Jr., re-emerged to challenge Mario Andretti for third. On lap 147, Andretti and Paul touched in turn-five and spun around. The heart-stopping synchronized spin appeared that it was going to send both into the sand runoff. Andretti, though, righted his machine in the center of the track and continued toward the CART IndyCar championship from third position. Paul recovered as well to remain in fourth.

On lap 148, Al Unser attempted another inside pass of Tom Sneva into the braking zone of turn three. As Unser moved abreast of Sneva, Sneva turned in sharply on Unser and closed the approach hard. As Tom Sneva's left side pod bore down on Al Unser's right-front tire, the Miller High Life March 84C snapped around, shooting across the outside sand trap and landing hard into the tire barriers. Al Unser was out for the day. "I was right alongside of him and he drove into me," protested Unser. "I was far enough up and he had no right to do that to me."[55] Unser was visibly angry, Sneva's metaphoric gas can pouring fuel on the apparent flames of Unser's relationship with Roger Penske. "I'm damned mad about it," continued Unser. "I could have won that race."[56]

Tom Sneva, whose championship strategy demanded a race win, understandably played off what appeared as deliberate. "We'd been running side by side for three or four laps. I didn't see him there and we ran our racing line," demurred Sneva. "He knew what I'd been doing, and I knew what he'd been doing."[57] Recovered from the destroyed Miller March, Unser stepped out and wagged a finger at Tom Sneva as the Texaco Star came by on a caution lap. "I thought he was indicating," joked Sneva afterward, "what position I was in."[58]

Nick Fornoro returned the field to green on lap 153. Tom Sneva remained at the front followed by Mario Andretti. Two late race caution periods for Emerson Fittipaldi and Pancho Carter put Mario Andretti within striking distance of leader Tom Sneva. Andretti seemed uncomfortable taking the championship from second place and started to charge. Andretti, though, backed off into lapped traffic to preserve the larger prize. Tom "The Gas Man" Sneva then powered his Texaco Star March 84C down the Caesars Palace front straight on lap 178 and streaked under Nick Fornoro's checkered flag to win the Caesars Palace Grand Prix IV. Mario Andretti followed through 6.47 seconds later. John Paul, Jr., completed the 1984 Caesars Palace podium in third, the last car on the lead lap. Al Unser, Jr., showed well in his swan song for Rick Galles with a fourth-place finish.

"We did our part," Tom Sneva reflected from his victory celebration, "but unfortunately, [Andretti] did his."[59] Tom Sneva collected race winnings of $52,340 from the $470,000 purse. Tom Sneva could do no more, closing out a strong 1984 campaign in second place with 163 points to 176 points for Mario Andretti.

From the Newman-Haas pits, Mario Andretti was able to savor the 1984 CART IndyCar championship. "It's the only reward that means anything for us for this season. And it's due," contemplated Andretti. "This championship just ranks right at the top."[60] From second place, Mario Andretti took home $46,523. As the new PPG CART national champion, though, Andretti's pay zone was just unfolding.

In his second year of CART IndyCar competition, Al Unser, Jr. (#7 Coors Light March) leads the venerable A.J. Foyt (#14 Gilmore March) and Howdy Holmes (#41 Jiffy Mixes March). Foyt's March is noticeably shorn of its right front wing, the victim of a skirmish in the early laps. Unser finished fourth, one lap behind winner Tom Sneva. Foyt retired on lap 56 with a spectacular fire. Holmes led laps in the early going but retired after a crash on lap 102 (author's collection).

"The first $1 million point fund in motorsports history," trumpeted Chris Economaki's *National Speed Sport News*, "was distributed at the sixth annual [CART] banquet in the Las Vegas Hilton Grand Ballroom."[61] Mario Andretti collected $300,000 from the PPG CART IndyCar point fund to boost his 1984 winnings to nearly $1 million. "You should see the two trophies that I have for the IndyCar race. They are helmets from the Romans, from Julius Caesar's era and they're solid bronze," Mario Andretti reminisced of his Las Vegas fortune. "Each helmet weighs probably 40 pounds. I couldn't lift it over my head!"[62]

Andretti also marked the 15th anniversary of his last national championship, his 1969 triumph during which he recorded his only win in the Indianapolis 500. By contrast with his 1984 pay day, Mario Andretti harvested some $360,000 of winnings in 1969. Andretti could also be forgiven for appearing to push for the win in 1984 at Caesars Palace. Indeed, Mario Andretti had punctuated his 1969 USAC IndyCar championship with a win at the season-ending Rex Mays 300 road race at Riverside International Raceway.

"Well as the sun now sets on the Las Vegas Strip, the racers go away to dream for the winter, of an even bigger and better year for CART in 1985," concluded the NBC broadcast of the 1984 Caesars Palace Grand Prix. "This is Paul Page. For Johnny Rutherford, Gary Gerould, and Bruce Jenner, so long from Las Vegas."[63]

***

The broadcast sign-off from Paul Page at the 1984 Caesars Palace Grand Prix IV trumpeted the new year for CART but served no hint of a return of the CART IndyCar series to Las Vegas. The largest Las Vegas daily published its race coverage the following day yet offered no further clarity. "No official announcement has been made," reported the *Las Vegas Review-Journal*, "regarding next year's event in Las Vegas."[64] The fate of the Caesars Palace Grand Prix then played as its own Palace plot, while it continued to engage Bill Weinberger, the former Caesars Palace vice president of casino marketing.

"Bill Weinberger remembers how he and two associates," continued the *Review-Journal*, "drew up the first Caesars Palace Grand Prix on the back of a placemat while sitting in their favorite eatery."[65] Weinberger, as a marketing consultant with Jack Long for the event, also had the word from the turnstiles: "We were far ahead of last year in pre-race sales."[66] The gate for the 1984 Caesars Palace Grand Prix was then announced at 38,000, drawing even with the spectator count for the inaugural 1981 Formula One event. The 1984 head count was a remarkable 50 percent improvement over 1983.

One month later, however, reports began to surface that the Caesars Palace Grand Prix was in peril. "Caesars Palace and the Championship Auto Racing teams—thought to be best buddies," reported the *Las Vegas Review Journal*, "are throwing hints of divorce."[67] CART, the sanctioning savior of the last two Caesars Palace events, appeared to imply that Caesars Palace sought an exit. The impasse also pitted Michigan attorney John Frasco of CART, the promoter-in-fact of the 1984 Caesars Palace Grand Prix, against Bruce Aguilera, corporate counsel of the luxury-branded host resort.

"[John] Frasco says he has received formal notice from Caesars Palace saying the classy Las Vegas resort wants out of future races," continued the report. "Caesars Palace Grand Prix President Bruce Aguilera says the resort is simply involved in normal negotiations."[68] John Frasco notably refused to release a copy of the letter he claimed from Caesars Palace. John Frasco, however, was also believed to be negotiating with Miami interests for a late season CART race, an event in which Frasco would likely have a financial interest. "This also comes after the second year of what was supposed to be a five-year agreement between Caesars and CART," the report furthered. "So much for contracts."[69]

On December 27, 1984, CART offices in Michigan released a 15-event race schedule culminating on October 27, 1985. The finale of the 1985 CART IndyCar season was slotted simply as "Miami, Fla; race name and length to be announced."[70] The Caesars Palace Grand Prix did not appear. CART offices offered context the next day, as word of the passing of Caesar spread from coast to coast.

"It's for sure," a CART spokesperson explained the removal of the Caesars Palace event. "The hotel is building a new entrance in conjunction with its sports book and the addition would have stretched into the first turn. The course would have been redone, but neither side wanted to spend the money."[71] The CART announcement, however, was not accompanied by reaction from Caesars Palace. "Caesars Palace executives refused comment on the future of the race," read another report, "and expressed surprise that CART, which had sanctioned the Indy-car race the past two years, had dropped the race from the schedule."[72]

The CART IndyCar series returned on April 14, 1985, for its season opener on the street circuit of the Long Beach Grand Prix. There would be no return of the series, however, to Las Vegas. Nonetheless, Danny Sullivan (#4 Miller High Life March) and Mario Andretti (#1 Beatrice Lola) picked up in Long Beach rather where they left off at Caesars Palace in 1984, nose to tail in the early laps. As in 1984, Mario Andretti took the win in Long Beach. The next event on the 1985 IndyCar calendar was the Indianapolis 500. Danny Sullivan and Mario Andretti figured together at Indy as well, with an historic spin and win for Sullivan and a second place for Andretti (Rick Lake collection).

On the same day that the 1985 CART schedule was released, CART chairman John Frasco was en route to Miami to meet Ralph Sanchez.[73] Sanchez, president of Miami Motorsports, Inc., had been negotiating vigorously for either a Formula One or CART IndyCar event in Miami. Ralph Sanchez, in fact, entertained Bernie Ecclestone of FOCA and John Frasco of CART as early as 1983. Miami Motorsports had already hosted two street races in Miami for IMSA endurance sports cars. The well-attended shows featured Emerson Fittipaldi, Brian Redman, Hurley Haywood, John Paul, Jr., and Danny Ongais. In fact, A.J. Foyt teamed with Bob Wollek in the 1984 event to finish fourth in a Porsche 935.

On December 28, 1984, John Frasco and Ralph Sanchez confirmed their agreement to run a CART IndyCar event in Miami. The finale of the 1985 CART season was going to run on a $2 million semi-permanent oval track that was yet to be constructed. "It'll be a very fast track," proclaimed Frasco.[74] John Frasco, it was later confirmed, "had a money interest as a promoter of the Indy car event at Miami."[75]

Ten years after the inaugural 1985 CART IndyCar event in Miami, Ralph Sanchez opened the $70 million Homestead-Miami Speedway some 30 miles south of the former CART IndyCar race site. Homestead-Miami Speedway would also host another prominent South Floridian. On October 8, 2000, Mark "Shareef" Malnik—son of Alvin Ira Malnik—raced an IMSA Barber Dodge race at Homestead. Shareef Malnik was, by then, also the owner of The Forge restaurant in Miami, "a dining and entertainment venue that rivals the best in world."[76] The Forge, former luxury-branded host to Meyer Lansky,[77] Abscam operatives, and the name of Caesar, was thus the pinnacle of its respective milieu—allegedly.

On February 24, 1985, Miami Motorsports, Inc., held the third annual IMSA Grand Prix of Miami. The event was won by Al Holbert and Derek Bell in a Porsche 962. David Hobbs and Darin Brassfield—Caesars Palace Trans-Am contestants of note—were second in a March 85G for DeAtley Motorsports. Two days later, the threads of this Caesars Palace saga would knot even more tightly.

"William H. Webster, Director of the Federal Bureau of Investigation, announced today the indictment of nine individuals, charged with violations of the Racketeer Influenced and Corrupt Organizations Statute with predicate offenses of Hobbs Act, Extortion, Murder, and Labor Racketeering," read the February 26, 1985, press release. "The indictment charges the following individuals to comprise a group associated in fact and also known as the 'Commission' of La Cosa Nostra."[78] The first name listed in the indictment was "Anthony Salerno, Boss, Genovese Family."[79]

The naming of Anthony "Fat Tony" Salerno thus recalls the November 1957 gathering of organized crime figures at the estate of Joseph Barbara in Apalachin,

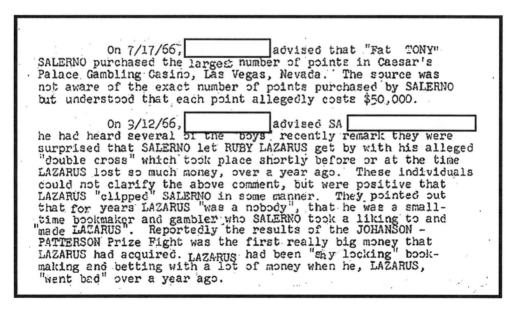

On 7/17/66, [ ] advised that "Fat TONY" SALERNO purchased the largest number of points in Caesar's Palace Gambling Casino, Las Vegas, Nevada. The source was not aware of the exact number of points purchased by SALERNO but understood that each point allegedly costs $50,000.

On 3/12/66, [ ] advised SA [ ] he had heard several of the "boys" recently remark they were surprised that SALERNO let RUBY LAZARUS get by with his alleged "double cross" which took place shortly before or at the time LAZARUS lost so much money, over a year ago. These individuals could not clarify the above comment, but were positive that LAZARUS "clipped" SALERNO in some manner. They pointed out that for years LAZARUS "was a nobody", that he was a small-time bookmaker and gambler who SALERNO took a liking to and "made LAZARUS". Reportedly the results of the JOHANSON - PATTERSON Prize Fight was the first really big money that LAZARUS had acquired. LAZARUS had been "shy locking" book-making and betting with a lot of money when he, LAZARUS, "went bad" over a year ago.

Anthony "Fat Tony" Salerno—boss of the Genovese crime family—was indicted on February 26, 1985, for violations of the RICO act. Salerno was sentenced on January 13, 1987, to 100 years in prison. Anthony Salerno was a persistent presence, weaving the story forward from 1959. Along the way, Anthony "Fat Tony" Salerno crossed the many influences of Caesar and the Caesar-adjacent, William Fugazy, Dino Cellini, Calvin Kovens, Jimmy "Blue Eyes" Alo, Jerome Zarowitz, and Alvin Malnik—allegedly (Federal Bureau of Investigation).

New York, a collective widely believed to be organized by crime boss Vito Genovese. The Apalachin crime retreat was also a pleasant hill-and-dale drive from the Grand Prix circuit in Watkins Glen.

For Anthony Salerno, 1985 was also the 20-year anniversary of his "Little Apalachin" gathering in Palm Springs with Jerome Zarowitz, Vincent "Jimmy Blue Eyes" Alo, Elliott Paul Price, and Ruby Lazarus. The Palms Springs gathering was documented to involve the split of ownership points in the Caesars Palace hotel-casino, then under development in Las Vegas by front-pieces Jay Sarno, Stanley Mallin, and Nathan Jacobson. From Salerno to Jacobson and all in between, the interests of Caesar engaged the Teamsters Central States Pension Fund and Allen Dorfman, as well as such curious actors as Alvin Malnik and Calvin Kovens. For the lot of them, there was their alleged participation in the infrastructure and apparatus of Meyer Lansky's worldwide gambling syndicate, a syndicate to which Bernie Ecclestone and Adnan Khashoggi would be best advised to clear their markers.

The path of American Grand Prix and the path of Caesars Palace had thus come full circle. From the first U.S. Grand Prix in Florida in 1959—along a route that ultimately led to Caesars Palace—that same thread had now returned to Miami. Similarly, the phalanx of Miami-connected organized crime elements pushed forward to their beachhead development in Las Vegas, the luxury-branded Caesars Palace. Clifford Perlman and Alvin Malnik, both of Miami, cemented their notorious Abscam-bolstered relationship with their sale-leaseback arrangement of the Caesars Pocono Resorts. The presence of Clifford Perlman and the banner signage of Malnik's Pocono properties, then became the visible manifestation of their bond as the Caesars Palace Grand Prix played.

The 25-year parallel odyssey had culminated in only four Grand Prix events at Caesars Palace, Formula One in 1981 and 1982, CART IndyCar in 1983 and 1984. Post-Caesar, Formula One would never return to the proximity of the Las Vegas Strip. Bernie Ecclestone, however, would return to Las Vegas many times over, the reprise of the Formula One czar to restore the pinnacle brand of international motorsport, to the pinnacle city of unlimited gambling, lavish hospitality, and world-class entertainment.

***

The layout of the Caesars Palace Grand Prix circuit was notable for its contrast of paved parking lot and parched desert sand. Properties once owned respectively by Kirk Kerkorian and Howard Hughes provided the raw earth upon which the race course was designed by architect Anthony Marnell and constructed by Corrao Construction. The relative modernity of the evolving Caesars Palace resort also stood in sharp contrast to the low-rise Castaways Hotel-Casino owned by Howard Hughes to the north. It was the proverbial Las Vegas casino divergence of carpet joint cash versus sawdust joint coin.

Owned by the renamed Summa Corporation after Howard Hughes' passing, the fallow Castaways dirt north of the Caesars Palace parking lot offered the necessary acreage to create the FISA-length circuit required for Formula One competition. Caesars Palace struck an affordable short-term lease with Summa executives for the encroachment of the race course upon the Hughes dirt. Clifford Perlman and Caesars Palace, however, could not package the financing for an outright purchase of the Summa land.

Two years after the cancellation of the Caesars Palace Grand Prix, Las Vegas casino mogul Steve Wynn made an offer that was too good for the Summa Corporation to refuse. "Legal records on file with Clark County," it was reported, "indicated it was a deal in the neighborhood of $50 million."[80] Clifford Perlman and Caesars Palace had begged off at $20 million.

While Steve Wynn and his attorneys negotiated with the Summa lawyers, the Caesars Palace Grand Prix circuit was still largely intact. On November 22, 1989, five years after the Caesars Palace Grand Prix IV, Steve Wynn opened the 3,044 room Mirage resort and casino. The north end of the Caesars Palace Grand Prix circuit was thus consumed. At the time of its opening, the Mirage was the largest hotel in the world. The Mirage is regarded to this day as the progenitor of modern Las Vegas.

While Steve Wynn descended upon the Summa property, Caesars Palace was also considering a higher use for its north parking lot, the homestand from 1981 to 1984 of the front straightaway, pit lane, and hospitality suites of the Caesars Palace Grand Prix. "Plans for a $150 million Roman-themed shopping complex have been announced by Caesars Palace officials," it was reported in Nevada. "The complex, to be known as the Forum at Caesars, would cater to the 4.5 million people who visit the plush Las Vegas Strip resort annually."[81] Three months after the opening of Steve Wynn's Mirage resort, Caesars Palace executive Henry Gluck announced the formal ground-breaking of the luxury-branded Forum shopping mall.[82]

When the Forum mall finally opened on May 11, 1992, motorsports writer Mike Henle had a chance for a big splash from the grime of his former motorsports beat. "In a city with a hectic 24-hour pace," Henle wrote for the *New York Times*. "Caesars Palace has converted a failed auto race track into a $100 million fantasy land that it calls the Forum Shops at Caesars, part mall and part entertainment center."[83]

Even Irwin Molasky, constructor of Moe Dalitz's long-shuttered Stardust International Raceway, played to the theme. "The Forum takes us light years into the future," proclaimed the longtime Las Vegas property developer and Dalitz business partner. "It's like an adult Disneyland."[84]

From four embedded weekends at the Caesars Palace Grand Prix, Mike Henle also had a rare perspective of the significance of the former Kerkorian land. "Caesars Palace is noted for its sponsorship of major boxing and tennis matches. In the early 1980's Caesars Palace Grand Prix also had major auto races," continued Henle. "But in 1984, the track lost $3 million and Mr. Gluck shut it down in November of that year."[85] The comments may have been revisionist in hindsight. Nonetheless, 8 years on, it was time for some racing reflection. As Steve Wynn's Mirage and the Forum Shops at Caesars Palace forever entombed the ruins of the Caesars Palace Grand Prix, though, Bernie Ecclestone would soon make his return to Las Vegas.

***

"One afternoon in March 1991, Ayrton Senna swept past the chequered flag at the corner of Jefferson and Third Avenues in Phoenix, Arizona to become the first driver in history to win five US Grands Prix," wrote David Phillips for *Motorsport Magazine* in the December 1996 issue. "As it now stands, Senna may also have the distinction of being the last driver to win a US Grand Prix."[86] Phillips' piece for *Motorsport* pointed up the utter vacuum of Formula One in the United States in the wake of the 1991 Phoenix event. Indeed, the successive departures of Bernie Ecclestone and Formula One from Watkins Glen, Caesars Palace, and Long Beach were well-documented. The Detroit Grand Prix ran from 1982 to 1988 before transitioning to the CART IndyCar series. The Dallas Grand Prix was an abject one-and-done footnote.

"Dallas had the potential for being a tremendous event," Chris Pook was quoted by Phillips as saying. "It's just unfortunate that [Don] Walker couldn't abide by the rules, which resulted in his taking a vacation in the Big House and of course the event went away."[87] Chris Pook also ventured out on the Caesars Palace Grand Prix, his signature promotion after stabilizing the Long Beach Grand Prix. "Caesar's Palace was in principle a good concept," continued Pook. "It's just that the American public who go to watch motor races don't gamble. Phoenix was a very sad set of circumstances. There was never a chance."[88]

"Jack Long, who along with Bernie Ecclestone formed a corporation to promote the Phoenix race," read an Arizona report, "says there will be a Formula One event in Phoenix for 'at least' the next five years, which is the length of their contract."[89] The gamble by Jack Long and Bernie Ecclestone in the Arizona desert fell two years short. So much for contracts indeed.

For Jack Long, the Formula One vacuum deposited the venerable motorsports promoter in the American open-wheel vortex. In December of 1995, Jack Long was hired as the executive director of the Indy Racing League, the IRL. The IRL was formed in 1994 by Indianapolis Motor Speedway chairman Tony George to counter the growing impact of the CART IndyCar series. The counter-offensive by the IRL spearheaded the second phase of "The Split" in American open-wheel racing with immediate and corrosive effect. The absence of Formula One in America and the devaluation of American open-wheel racing were also accompanied by a rapid rise in the popularity of American NASCAR stock car competition. Amid the divergence of American spectator interest—and sponsorship dollars—Bernie Ecclestone attempted another colonial incursion.

"The concept of F-1 returning to Las Vegas went public past year," reported the *Las Vegas Review-Journal*, "when a splashy two-page ad depicting a race course wending through the MGM Grand property appeared in the 1995 Indianapolis 500 program."[90] The ad proudly proclaimed the debut of the "United States Grand Prix—Las Vegas."[91] In fine print directly below, however, was the note "Provisional." A small color logo in the ad then checked the paper claim of the promotional entity, "US/GP LV."[92] Billed as the "1996 Formula One season finale,"[93] the pitch also depicted a fantastic conceptual course running down the Las Vegas Strip, around the massive pyramid of the Luxor hotel-casino and down Tropicana Avenue, turning north to engage the property of the MGM Grand Adventures theme park and a starting grid just east of the MGM parking structure.

The prospect of a Formula One Grand Prix on the grounds of the MGM Grand might have offered another timeless image of MGM developer Kirk Kerkorian posed

(PROVISIONAL)

...1996 Formula 1 season finale...roaring through the streets of the Entertainment Capital of the World.
To receive your illustrated pamphlet for advance ticket and room reservation packages call 1-800-794-4449.

The proposed 1996 United States Grand Prix at Las Vegas would have marked the return of Formula One to America after a five-year absence. Pitched in the program of the 1995 Indianapolis 500, the race circuit was designed to include the world-famous Las Vegas Strip. The starting grid is positioned in the foreground, running from left to right. The dark monolith in the center is the MGM Grand Las Vegas developed by Kirk Kerkorian and opened in 1993. It is the largest hotel in the United States with 6,852 rooms. The pyramid-shaped structure at upper left is the Luxor. The long-shuttered Stardust International Raceway was six miles in the distance to the west (author's collection).

atop a piece of heavy earthmoving equipment, just as at Caesars Palace in 1965. Further, a podium celebration to include the Wizard of Oz, Dorothy, and Toto from the MGM theme park would have been a heartstring Hollywood touch. A corporate shakeup at MGM in late 1995, however, appeared to still the notion of an MGM-anchored U.S. Grand Prix in Las Vegas. Notably, the corporate restructuring was presided over by J. Terrence Lanni, hired away from Caesars World earlier that year. Indeed, rather than Formula One on the world-famous Las Vegas Strip, Las Vegas received the debut of the woebegone Indy Racing League on September 15, 1996, at the newly opened Las Vegas Motor Speedway.

Steve Wynn and his newest Las Vegas Strip resort development, the Bellagio, then entered the Las Vegas Formula One picture. "Opening his new Bellagio property with an F-1 race in spring of '98," it was reported, "was an intriguing possibility."[94] The Bellagio was being constructed on the former grounds of the Dunes hotel-casino, directly south across Flamingo Road from Caesars Palace. Bruce Aguilera, then chief counsel of Wynn's Mirage, Inc., holding company, recalled the visit of Bernie Ecclestone to discuss the proposal.

"Steve wanted something spectacular for the opening of the Bellagio," recounted the former president of the Caesars Palace Grand Prix. "We'd get the big press and international, Bellagio, Italy, Monte Carlo type of stuff."[95] Steve Wynn, certainly a fan of fast cars and fast company, envisioned a majestic concept. "Steve called me in his office one day. He said Bernie's coming out. We're going to talk about a Grand Prix," continued Aguilera. "I almost said, 'No you don't want to do that.' But I bit my tongue."[96] "Bernie Ecclestone came in, we greeted each other and hugged," the corporate lawyer went on, as though being deposed. "Steve's dog was in the office and when Bernie bent down the dog bit him on the nose. I thought, 'Oh my God,' this is horrible. Thankfully, Bernie didn't sue."[97] An international legal crisis thus averted, planning for a Bellagio-based Las Vegas Grand Prix would thus unfold.

The grand plan of Steve Wynn would engage the world-famous Las Vegas Strip, a concept that Bruce Aguilera knew well had failed for Caesars Palace in 1981: "Steve wanted to go out to the Strip, through the Bellagio porte cochere, around the fountain and everything."[98] The combined Formula One vision of Bernie Ecclestone and Steve Wynn, though, also involved the U.S./GP-LV Partnership and its president, promoter Tommy Baker.

"[Tommy] Baker says that both Wynn and Ecclestone insist that the race be held on The Strip," it was reported in early 1997. "The provisional track layout is three miles in length and involves a half a mile straight."[99] Baker also noted that the Las Vegas Strip Grand Prix circuit would be devoid of "wiggles through car parks."[100] Obvious jabs at the former Caesars Palace Grand Prix just never grow old.

The Bellagio proposal, however, was faced with considerable opposition from neighboring Las Vegas Strip gambling operators. The proposed weekend of Grand Prix competition was regarded much less as a Las Vegas marketing opportunity, and much more as a deterrent to the hardened path of hardcore gamblers to the gambling tables, truly the core value of the core business.

Tommy Baker, "a likeable fellow who talked as fast as those F-1 cars,"[101] next proposed a purpose-built circuit on 160 acres of undeveloped acreage fronting the Las Vegas Strip, some two miles south of Caesars Palace. The proposal, however, came with strings attached. "Baker said if the Las Vegas Convention and Visitors Authority will ante up $9 million to finance construction of a temporary circuit, the race essentially would be on for 1998," reported the *Las Vegas Review-Journal*. "A slot on the F-1 calendar has already been set aside for a U.S. Grand Prix."[102]

"I think Las Vegas is good for us and we would be good for Las Vegas," Bernie Ecclestone said after touring the Las Vegas property in early 1998. "It's one of those situations where it's a good marriage—but we shouldn't have got divorced the last time we were here."[103] The notion of a Las Vegas divorce also united Steve Wynn with Bernie Ecclestone and Adnan Khashoggi. Eventually those giants of their respective industries would document *three* of the most expensive divorces in history.

While Tommy Baker and Bernie Ecclestone contemplated a run at the south Las Vegas strip, Chris Pook and the Long Beach Grand Prix Association contemplated their payday. "Dover Downs Entertainment, Inc, … agreed to buy Grand Prix Assn. of Long Beach," it was reported on March 28, 1998.[104] The reported $90 million deal involved stock and cash. It was also a deal that "would make Dover one of the biggest operators of motor sports in the U.S."[105] Dover Downs Entertainment, Inc., it should be noted, also owned and operated an 80,000 square foot video lottery

Las Vegas gambling and development magnate Steve Wynn proposed a 1998 United States Grand Prix from the base of his new Bellagio resort. The Bellagio was developed on the site of the former Dunes hotel-casino immediately south of Caesars Palace. The three-mile circuit would have included the Las Vegas Strip and a loop through the Bellagio porte cochère entrance and around the massive fountains. Caesars Palace hotel tower expansion is visible at right of image (Library of Congress).

casino in Dover, Delaware. It is perhaps instructive then, in a Dover Downs transition report to the SEC for the year 2000, the Dover casino was managed by "Caesars World Gaming Development Corporation."[106]

In Las Vegas, Tommy Baker and his Formula One pitch with Bernie Ecclestone were one of several proposals being considered by regional government for use of the vacant south Strip land. A championship golf course, however, prevailed over the proposed Las Vegas Grand Prix circuit and its $9 million public price tag. By late 1998, Baker's sputtering prospects for a U.S. Grand Prix were met by competition across the country. Indeed, new proposals from San Francisco, Dallas, and the Indianapolis Motor Speedway were being floated for a new Formula One event in 2000. The race for the 2000 U.S. Grand Prix was ultimately decided in favor of Indianapolis and Tony George, founder of the IRL.

Perhaps also instructive, one year later Chris Pook was named as the president and CEO of Championship Auto Racing Teams. "Pook said he was released from his contract with Dover Downs Entertainment," the *Associated Press* reported, "which owns the Long Beach association."[107] The tenure of Chris Pook with CART, though, concluded with the bankruptcy of the racing series in 2003. The former CART faction and the IRL series of Tony George would finally reunite in 2008, to go forward simply as IndyCar.

The various pitch angles of Tommy Baker and Bernie Ecclestone in Las Vegas eventually went the way of the MGM tease in the 1995 Indy 500 program, all tabloid and no track. By the early 2000s, the motorsports appetite of the Las Vegas market was being sufficiently served by Las Vegas Motor Speedway—LVMS. The appetite of Bernie Ecclestone for the Las Vegas market, however, was not. An exchange between Bernie Ecclestone and LVMS owner Bruton Smith in 2005 then steered the Formula One conversation to Las Vegas Motor Speedway.

"[Bruton] Smith said his company has been approached by F1 representatives," it was reported, "about a possible race at their Las Vegas track."[108] Bruton Smith, however, did not see the oval-based LVMS as a viable Formula One venue. Further, the speedway was located nearly 20 miles north of the Las Vegas Strip, in the far desert of the Las Vegas valley. Bernie Ecclestone would not have been inspired by the lack of neon nuance and casino clang in the northern reaches.

"If they put up the money, we'd consider that," Bruton Smith said, "but not Las Vegas."[109] Rather, Smith envisioned a Formula One festival at the Infineon Raceway road course in Sonoma County, California. The former Sears Point Raceway had now been considered at least twice for Formula One, over the span of some 35 years. "It depends on what [Bernie Ecclestone] wants to do," Smith continued. "(It would take) a lot of commas. If he's got that kind of net worth, he ought to be able to make a deal with me. Money talks."[110] Despite the obvious attraction of the Northern California wine country and proximity to San Francisco, the Infineon Raceway notion gathered no further traction. Money indeed talks, but for Bernie Ecclestone, the payday appeared to talk more with a "Las Vegas" in front of it.

While the Formula One fates in Las Vegas frittered, Las Vegas Strip resorts were undergoing their own entertainment revolution. That revolution marked a sea change in the desert of Las Vegas, while it also captured the imagination of Bernie Ecclestone. International entertainment giant *Cirque du Soleil* opened *Mystère* at Steve Wynn's Treasure Island resort in December of 1993. *Mystère* was the first resident show of its type in Las Vegas. The show also runs to this day. By 2014, the *Cirque du Soleil* production company had opened an incredible nine resident stage shows along the Las Vegas Strip.

The emergence of the avant-garde Cirque-style shows also marked a hard shift away from the proverbial Hollywood headliner marquee of brand name singers, actors, and comedians that had anchored the Las Vegas entertainment offerings for decades. In fact, *The Beatles Love* Cirque show plays in the Mirage Love Theatre, over the former north section of the Caesars Palace Grand Prix. Oddly, another Las Vegas Formula One venture in 2014 informed the thought processes of Bernie Ecclestone, and the engagement of *Cirque du Soleil*.

"Formula One's chief executive Bernie Ecclestone has revealed that a blockbuster race on the streets of Las Vegas," it was reported on October 18, 2014, "is 'ready to go.'"[111] The report raced around the globe, once again tantalizing Formula One fandom while it also invoked comparisons to the Caesars Palace Grand Prix. The 2014 report also smacked of a retread of the failed efforts fronted by Tommy Baker originating in 1996. Reports in 2014, however, also tipped a potential new interest, an interest that might overlap the Formula One circus with the Circus of the Sun.

"In 1996 I met Bernie in Montreal for breakfast ... and the introduction was done by the guy who was trying to organise the Las Vegas Grand Prix," Guy Laliberté of *Cirque du Soleil* said. "Bernie had visited Las Vegas a couple of months before and met Steve Wynn. He saw the show *Mystère* and fell in love with it, really liked it, his family liked it and the introduction was done."[112] The introduction of entertainment billionaires Bernie Ecclestone and Guy Laliberté was made by the apparently fast-talking Tommy Baker. The introduction, however, also led to an invitation for Laliberté to invest in Baker's U.S./GP-LV Partnership.

As the various Formula One proposals of Tommy Baker foundered, so did the enthusiasm and investment of Guy Laliberté. "My reporting to Bernie on the [1998] Vegas Grand Prix," Guy Laliberté continued, "was that I had my reservations about the people on the team and eventually I stepped out of it."[113] The wisdom of both Grand Prix and gambling in 2014, however, was that Guy Laliberté was somehow engaged in the new Las Vegas Formula One venture. Reports further confirmed that Formula One track designer Hermann Tilke was dispatched to Las Vegas to consider the circuit layout.[114]

Formula One plans in 2014 also introduced future McLaren CEO Zak Brown to the Las Vegas discourse. Brown, then the sponsorship agent for Formula One, also played a familiar trumpet. "Vegas would be a fantastic addition to the F1 calendar and would be successful for so many people involved," Brown said in 2014. "It's a great fit for the F1 brand and would draw a lot of interest from sponsors in one of the most important strategic markets for F1."[115]

Las Vegas, however, was a strategic market for Formula One only to the extent that the sport served the core value of the core Las Vegas business, delivering wealthy unrepentant gamblers from around the globe to the gambling tables along the Las Vegas Strip. "A race on a street track which includes The Strip," pondered the 2014 reporting, "would put F1 on the doorstep of the world's wealthiest entertainment magnates and would dramatically boost its visibility in the States."[116] Again, though, Formula One was a foregone failure if the weekend festival blocked the endless flow of gamblers to those same doorsteps, doorways to the true corridors of power in Las Vegas, those that eventually lead to the casino count rooms.

The potential overlap of the two circuses nonetheless lent a measure of Las Vegas mystique. Las Vegas would then furnish the eternal carousel, along with an apparently endless supply of clowns. Jay Sarno—developer front of both Caesars Palace and Circus-Circus in Las Vegas—might have approved, especially if he could receive his commission for a facade wrapped in Sarno block.

Reports of Formula One in Las Vegas then transitioned to Farid Shidfar, a tech entrepreneur credited with—among numerous global ventures—the production for the 2010 grand opening of The Cosmopolitan hotel-casino in Las Vegas. "[Shidfar] claimed he had secured a promise of $150 million from unnamed Chinese investors in Beijing," it was reported in Las Vegas. "He was also given an official go-ahead from the Las Vegas Convention and Visitors Authority."[117] Farid Shidfar was also reported to hold a contract with Bernie Ecclestone. Then, as with the MGM pitch and the protracted pursuit by Tommy Baker, the efforts in 2014 to bring Formula One back to Las Vegas appeared to fizzle. Once more, so much for contracts.

Twenty years after Guy Laliberté and Cirque du Soleil revolutionized entertainment along the Las Vegas Strip, the sport of Formula One braced for profound change of its own. On January 23, 2017, American entertainment and broadcasting giant Liberty Media acquired the commercial rights to the sport of Formula One. The deal was reported to be worth $8 billion. Liberty Media was now the owner of such diverse entertainment brands as Formula One, SiriusXM, and the Atlanta Braves. It is worth noting that, in 1971, the majority stockholders of the heavily racketeered Parvin-Dohrmann Corporation were also the majority stockholders of the Atlanta Braves. It is truly a small world among the 1 percent.

As Liberty Media took control of an entire sport, Bernie Ecclestone was then removed from his former position. "I was dismissed," Ecclestone stated on the day of the purchase. "This is official."[118] Bernie Ecclestone also proclaimed his accomplishments, detected though with a hint of humility, perhaps even contrition. "I'm proud of the business that I built over the past 40 years and all that I have achieved with Formula 1," Ecclestone continued. "I would like to thank all of the promoters, teams, sponsors and television companies that I have worked with."[119]

Bernie Ecclestone was thus sacked from the sport over which he ruled as czar for nearly four decades. The specter of Ecclestone, though, would certainly linger around the sport of Formula One. The fantasy of Formula One in Las Vegas lingered as well. In December 2017, it was reported that Formula One Licensing BV, a company of the Liberty Media Formula One Group, submitted trademark applications with the U.S. Patent and Trademark Office.[120] The official application sought exclusive merchandising trademarks for a proposed Las Vegas Grand Prix.

"We have made no secret that we are looking for destination cities, and regarding the U.S.," Ron Kantowski of the *Las Vegas Review-Journal* quoted a Formula One official, "Las Vegas has been mentioned alongside Miami and New York."[121] Once again, the reporting invoked the Caesars Palace Grand Prix. The incursion of Formula One Licensing BV into the Las Vegas landscape also marked the 35th anniversary of the 1982 Caesars Palace Formula One event. Thirty-five years on, the notion of Formula One in Las Vegas was no closer, the Caesars Palace Grand Prix existing in popular culture only as parking lot trope, while Caesars Palace itself celebrated 50 years in existence. From the feast of Caesar, though, the storyline would soon pivot once again to Miami.

"Miami is considering a 10-year deal with international auto racing giant Formula One," the *Miami Herald* reported on May 3, 2018, "to host a Grand Prix."[122] Like the former Las Vegas ventures, the proposed Miami event transitioned from a street circuit concept to a purpose-built temporary race course. The latter also invoked Hermann Tilke and his typical sterile stadium-style track designs. "Then again," ran one complaint from Formula One fandom, "what can you expect from a track built in a parking lot?"[123] The 40-year refrain of Formula One at Caesars Palace was thus struck once again. Further, the juxtaposition of Las Vegas and Miami in the Formula One licensing application was instructive, just as those two constituencies informed the development of Caesars Palace.

Some 60 years removed from the very first U.S. Grand Prix and the concurrent origins of Caesars Palace, this study brings the question: Did motorsports endeavors lock onto the draft of gambling or rather, was it the other way around? Was organized crime seeking to tap the liquidity of the cash business of motorsports or, were motorsports promoters and venues indebted to the prodigious lending apparatus of organized crime? There are no easy answers from the respective pay zones. Roy Gene Lewis of Riverside International Raceway certainly appeared to check the latter. Further, the layered dynamic of the Long Beach *Queen Mary*, the Long Beach Grand Prix, and the attempted Long Beach infiltration of Jay Sarno and Allen Dorfman appeared somewhat similarly—and truly strange. The victory celebration of the 1981 Caesars Palace Grand Prix then placed Las Vegas, organized crime, and the pinnacle of motorsport on the same podium. Perhaps it is all simply the boundless quest in the trajectory of the 1 percent, with the newly-minted then drafting others 100 percent of the time. "Hoodlums have always enjoyed rubbing elbows with the elite. It imbues them with a sense of respectability," wrote Ed Reid and Ovid Demaris of that bargain in *The Green Felt Jungle*. "And conversely, many of the so-called elite are imbued with a sense of evil."[124]

This is a story in which certain antagonists arose. "Bernie [Ecclestone] is the ultimate entrepreneur," suggested William D. Weinberger. "He would do whatever it took to get a race on if he wanted it."[125] Whatever it took, indeed. During this research, though, similar comments were directed toward Meyer Lansky, Allen Dorfman, Jay Sarno, Clifford Perlman, and Alvin Malnik. Further, if those accumulated actors had not done "whatever it took," there would have been no Caesars Palace Grand Prix—*allegedly*. For that matter, the same sentiment was offered along the way of Chris Pook and Roger Penske.

An extraordinary *protagonist* also emerged from the research, Mario Andretti, the great American race car driver. Andretti occupies his own rarefied thread, traversing from his first Formula One start in 1968 on pole at Watkins Glen, to the 1978 Formula One world championship, to the starting grid of the four premier events of the Caesars Palace Grand Prix. Along the way, Mario Andretti won the 1969 Indianapolis 500, the 1971 Questor Grand Prix, the 1977 Long Beach Grand Prix, the 1983 Caesars Palace Grand Prix, the 1984 Long Beach Grand Prix, and the 1984 CART IndyCar championship. Mario Andretti then kept on going.

Like so much of the storyline, though, the legacy of the Caesars Palace Grand Prix is clouded. Was it all simply a parking lot and a dirt field waiting to be torn asunder for redevelopment to its full Las Vegas real estate potential? Over 35 years of nearly constant efforts to return Formula One to the world-famous Las Vegas Strip might suggest otherwise. On the other hand, the billions of dollars invested in Steve Wynn's succeeding Mirage hotel-casino and the Forum Shops at Caesars will likely meet their own point of dramatic implosion some two decades hence. In that regard, Las Vegas is truly unlike any other market in the world. The core value of the core business simply must be preserved.

In a resort destination city that balances the bargain solely at the bottom line then, the Caesars Palace Grand Prix might mirror the late-model Cadillac of Jay Sarno, the public-facing front of the resort at its inception, who also perished in one of its lavish suites before the final Caesars Palace Grand Prix. Jay Sarno's late model Cadillac was the luxury-branded chariot of the first Caesar himself, dispatched to the lube rack, stuck in neutral, and then abruptly abandoned by its owner.

During the run of the Caesars Palace Grand Prix, Mario Andretti proudly proclaimed the promise of the Palace. With a racing career sorted and settled, though,

Mario Andretti was more contemplative. "Everything was big, enormous, and interesting because that's Vegas. I loved that part for sure. I'm happy that I was able to experience both layouts," concluded Andretti. "I didn't think the Caesars Palace Grand Prix had much of a life because of the restricted real estate, to lay out a proper road course. It was an experiment, just like Stardust International Raceway."[126] Andretti thus put his own period on the providence of the Caesars Palace Grand Prix.

Caesars Palace vice president Murray Gennis offered his own view of the core business of the luxury-branded former Formula One host resort. "The thing I tell people before they gamble is this," Gennis explained in 1987 from his executive office in Caesars Palace. "You see this beautiful hotel here? The beautiful grounds? The beautiful casino? The beautiful pools? The beautiful statues? The beautiful chandeliers? All this beautiful stuff here—it didn't come from winners."[127] With the exclamation point of Murray Gennis well pinned, the Caesars Palace Grand Prix was thus the luckless loser, never meeting its promise to stack the underground casino count room of the Caesars Palace host resort, let alone clear its considerable markers. Just a simple, lowly discard to the luxury-branded landfill—of the way Las Vegas used to be.

Mario Andretti—the great American race car driver—was the only racer to compete in the four premier-level events of the Caesars Palace Grand Prix, Formula One in 1981 and 1982, CART IndyCar in 1983 and 1984. Further, Andretti won the 1983 Caesars Palace Grand Prix III and clinched the CART IndyCar championship at the 1984 Caesars Palace Grand Prix IV. Notably, Mario Andretti also contested the three Can-Am events and the lone USAC IndyCar race at the former Stardust International Raceway in Las Vegas, NV. "I remember in those days, we were like, what the hell happened to Stardust?" Andretti would recall of his 1981 foray at Caesars Palace, "That would have been a much better place to have the F1 races, but by then it was all over" (Mario Andretti interview) (Rick Lake collection).

Chapter Notes

Chapter I

1. Greene, *The Sting Man*, 216.
2. *Star-Gazette* (Elmira, NY), October 31, 1919.
3. *New York* (NY) *Daily News*, December 14, 1946.
4. *Star Gazette* (Elmira, NY), April 9, 1948.
5. *Ibid.*
6. *Edinburg* (IN) *Daily Courier,* June 26, 1948.
7. *Ibid.*
8. *Star-Gazette* (Elmira, NY), September 28, 1948.
9. *Ibid.*
10. *Berkshire Eagle* (Pittsfield, MA), October 1, 1948.
11. *Star-Gazette* (Elmira, NY), September 28, 1948.
12. *Star-Gazette* (Elmira, NY), October 4, 1948.
13. *Star-Gazette* (Elmira, NY), October 29, 1948.
14. *New York* (NY) *Daily News*, December 19, 1946.
15. *Democrat and Chronicle* (Rochester, NY), December 1, 1948.
16. *Press and Sun Bulletin* (Binghamton, NY), September 22, 1952.
17. Bill Green interview.
18. *Oneonta* (NY) *Star*, May 15, 1956.
19. *Democrat and Chronicle* (Rochester, NY), September 16, 1956.
20. *Elmira* (NY) *Advertiser,* June 17, 1957.
21. *Star-Gazette* (Elmira, NY), October 6, 1957.
22. *New York Times*, November 15, 1957.
23. *Ibid.*
24. *Star-Gazette* (Elmira, NY), November 15, 1957.
25. *Ibid.*
26. *Ibid.*
27. *Ibid.*
28. *Star-Gazette* (Elmira, NY), November 25, 1957.
29. *Democrat and Chronicle* (Rochester NY), June 18, 1959.
30. *Press and Sun-Bulletin* (Binghamton, NY), November 15, 1957.
31. *Ibid.*
32. *Asbury Park* (NJ) *Press,* June 28, 1995
33. *Reno* (NV) *Gazette-Journal,* November 15, 1957.
34. *Ibid.*
35. *Los Angeles Times,* November 15, 1965.
36. *Las Vegas* (NV) *Review-Journal,* November 15, 1965.
37. *Journal News* (White Plains, NY), September 25, 1958.
38. *Democrat and Chronicle* (Rochester, NY) September 29, 1958.
39. *Ibid.*
40. *Atlanta* (GA) *Constitution,* June 5, 1957.
41. *Atlanta* (GA) *Constitution,* November 1, 1958.
42. *Atlanta* (GA) *Constitution,* January 22, 1959.
43. *Ibid.*
44. *Ibid.*
45. *Tampa* (FL) *Tribune,* January 22, 1959.
46. *Ibid.*
47. *Democrat and Chronicle* (Rochester, NY), October 19, 1959.
48. *Democrat and Chronicle* (Rochester, NY), December 13, 1959.
49. *Terre Haute* (IN) *Tribune,* November 30, 1957.
50. *Ibid.*
51. *Anderson* (IN) *Daily Bulletin,* August 19, 1958.
52. *Terre Haute* (IN) *Tribune,* August 20, 1958.
53. *Oakland* (CA) *Tribune,* February 10, 1960.
54. *Ibid.*
55. *Fort Lauderdale* (FL) *News,* April 11, 1972.
56. *Miami* (FL) *News,* November 23, 1960.
57. *Observer* (London, Greater London, England), April 17, 1960.
58. *Miami* (FL) *News,* May 27, 1960.
59. *San Francisco Examiner,* June 15, 1960.
60. *Pasadena* (CA) *Independent,* June 16, 1960.
61. *San Francisco Examiner,* July 20, 1960.
62. *Democrat and Chronicle* (Rochester, NY), October 10, 1960.
63. *Boston Globe*, October 20, 1960.
64. *Los Angeles Times,* November 21, 1960.
65. *Ibid.*
66. *Ibid.*
67. *Ibid.*
68. *Independent* (Long Beach, CA), December 17, 1960.
69. *Ibid.*
70. *Star-Gazette* (Elmira, NY), January 9, 1961.

71. *Ibid.*

72. *Las Vegas* (NV) *Review-Journal,* October 17, 1961.

73. *Ibid.*

74. *Ibid.*

Chapter II

1. Weisberg, Harold, Press Conference, November 13, 1967.

2. FBI Record No. 124–90068–10116, August 27, 1958.

3. *Miami* (FL) *News,* July 13, 1970.

4. Weisberg, Harold, Press Conference, November 13, 1967

5. *Oakland* (CA) *Tribune,* January 4, 1961.

6. *Ibid.*

7. *Ibid.*

8. *Los Angeles Times,* February 5, 1961.

9. *Miami* (FL) *News,* March 16, 1961.

10. *Miami* (FL) *News,* July 9, 1961.

11. FBI New York FO File 92–1099, June 13, 1963, 4.

12. FBI New York FO File 92–1099, October 4, 1963, 2.

13. FBI New York FO File 92–1099, September 12, 1961.

14. FBI Los Angeles FO, Case: Vincent Alo, August 9, 1967, 4.

15. FBI New York FO File 92–1099, August 31, 1961, 10, 17.

16. FBI New York FO File 92–1099, August 14, 1961, 2.

17. *Daily News* (NY), December 23, 1947.

18. FBI New York FO File 92–1099, August 31, 1961, 54.

19. *Orlando* (FL) *Sentinel,* June 11, 1964.

20. *San Francisco Examiner,* June 6, 1961.

21. *Ibid.*

22. *Democrat and Chronicle* (Rochester, NY), August 4, 1961.

23. *San Francisco Examiner,* September 6, 1961.

24. *Democrat and Chronicle* (Rochester, NY), August 4, 1961.

25. *Ibid.*

26. *San Francisco Examiner,* September 6, 1961.

27. *San Francisco Examiner,* September 8, 1961.

28. *San Bernardino County* (CA) *Sun,* September 11, 1961.

29. *Los Angeles Times,* September 11, 1961.

30. *Ibid.*

31. *San Bernardino County* (CA) *Sun,* September 12, 1961.

32. *Roseville* (CA) *Press-Tribune,* September 12, 1961.

33. *San Bernardino County* (CA) *Sun,* September 12, 1961.

34. *Las Vegas* (NV) *Review-Journal,* October 17, 1961.

35. *Atlanta* (GA) *Constitution,* March 6, 1962.

36. *Ibid.*

37. *Ibid.*

38. DOJ Memorandum, AAG-Criminal Division Herman Miller to Director-FBI, October 15, 1962.

39. Brill, *The Teamsters,* 218.

40. DOJ Memorandum, AAG-Criminal Division Herman Miller to Director-FBI, October 15, 1962.

41. FBI Chicago FO File 62–2020, November 29, 1962.

42. *Ibid.*

43. FBI Chicago FO File 122–60, February 7, 1963.

44. *Ottawa Citizen* (Ottawa, Ontario, Canada), October 3, 1961.

45. *Star-Gazette* (Elmira, NY), October 9, 1961.

46. *Democrat and Chronicle* (Rochester, NY), October 9, 1961.

47. *Gazette* (Montreal, Quebec, Canada), October 13, 1961.

48. *Elmira* (NY) *Advertiser,* October 24, 1961.

49. *Daily Sentinel* (Grand Junction, CO), October 13, 1961.

50. *Ibid.*

51. FBI Miami FO File 92–515, April 2, 1962.

52. *Ibid.*

53. FBI New York FO File 166-New, May 23, 1969.

54. *Miami* (FL) *News, September 30, 1962.*

55. *Reno* (NV) *Gazette-Journal,* December 19, 1970.

56. FBI Miami FO, Agency File No. 62–9–29–585, September 28, 1965.

57. *St. Louis* (MO) *Post-Dispatch,* January 16, 1983.

58. *Indianapolis* (IN) *News,* August 20, 1958.

59. Roberts and Wright, *American Desperado,* 245.

60. *Edmonton Journal* (Edmonton, Alberta, Canada), October 25, 1962.

61. *Los Angeles Times,* October 22, 1962.

62. *Ibid.*

63. *Ibid.*

64. *Huntsville* (AL) *Times,* May 14, 1961.

65. *Times Colonist* (Victoria, British Columbia, Canada), October 22, 1962.

66. *Los Angeles Times,* October 22, 1962.

67. *Las Vegas* (NV) *Review-Journal,* May 10, 1963.

68. *Los Angeles Times,* January 17, 1964.

69. *San Bernardino County* (CA) *Sun,* October 28, 1965.

70. *Ibid.*

71. *Los Angeles Times,* June 14, 1959.

72. *Pasadena* (CA) *Independent,* January 16, 1960.

73. *Oakland* (CA) *Tribune,* January 15, 1960.

74. *Reno* (NV) *Gazette-Journal,* March 27, 1965.

75. *Ibid.*

76. *Ibid.*

77. *Ibid.*

78. *San Bernardino County* (CA) *Sun,* June 26, 1966.

79. *Ibid.*

80. *Oakland* (CA) *Tribune,* June 5, 1970.

81. *Orlando* (FL) *Evening Star,* February 4, 1967.

82. *Observer* London, Greater London, England), December 12, 1982.

83. *Oakland* (CA) *Tribune,* June 5, 1970.

84. *Ibid.*

85. *Ibid.*

86. *Oakland* (CA) *Tribune,* January 28, 1970.

87. *Ibid.*

88. *Ibid.*

89. *Congressional Record,* September 26, 1972, 29644.

90. *Los Angeles Times,* January 29, 1973.

Chapter III

1. *Bakersfield* (CA) *Californian,* January 28, 1965.

2. *Los Angeles Times,* January 27, 1965.

3. *Ibid.*

4. Schwartz, *Grandissimo,* xiii.

5. *Reno* (NV) *Gazette-Journal,* March 8, 1974.

6. Southern Nevada Jewish Heritage Project, Interview with Stanley and Sandy Mallin, January 7, 2015, 13.

7. *Baltimore* (MD) *Sun,* August 21, 1968.

8. *Ibid.*

9. Schwartz, 56.

10. *Tampa Bay* (FL) *Times,* January 23, 1966.

11. *Fort Lauderdale* (FL) *News,* April 22, 1972.

12. *Miami* (FL) *News,* January 27, 1965.

13. *Ibid.*

14. *Tallahassee* (FL) *Democrat,* November 4, 1957.

15. *SEC News Digest,* December 17, 1970.

16. *San Francisco Examiner,* January 27, 1965.

17. *Civil Aeronautics Board,* Docket 16207, Kirk Kerkorian et al., Interlocking Relationships, September 23, 1965.

18. FBI Airtel, SAC-Las Vegas to Director-FBI, February 18, 1966, 3–4.

19. *Las Vegas* (NV) *Review-Journal,* May 19, 1966.

20. *Ibid.*

21. *Nevada State Journal,* May 19, 1966.

22. *Star-Gazette* (NY), October 7, 1968.

23. John Surtees interview.

24. Sir Jackie Stewart interview.

25. *Ibid.*

26. *Miami* (FL *News,* August 7, 1963.

27. FBI Miami FO File 92–515, October 21, 1965

28. *Daily News* (NY), December 23, 1947.

29. *Miami* (FL) *News,* January 21, 1963.

30. FBI Miami FO File 92–515 Sub II, September 16, 1963.

31. FBI Miami FO File 92–515, November 12, 1963.

32. FBI Miami FO File 92–515, December 20, 1963.

33. *Ibid.*

34. Thompson, *Shadowland,* Chapter 12.

35. Cannon & Gerry, *Stardust International Raceway,* 171.

36. *Las Vegas* (NV) *Review Journal,* January 6, 1964.

37. FBI New York FO File 137–9551, November 1, 1964.

38. *Akron* (OH) *Beacon-Journal,* July 11, 1966.

39. *Las Vegas* (NV) *Sun,* November 1, 1965.

40. *Ibid.*

41. *Ibid.*

42. *Las Vegas* (NV) *Israelite,* December 2, 1965.

43. *Los Angeles Times,* January 17, 1964.

44. *Los Angeles Times,* November 15, 1965.

45. *Los Angeles Times,* December 23, 1966.

46. Watkins, *Bernie,* 75.

47. Bower, *No Angel,* 44.

48. Bower, 27.

49. Thompson, Chapter 12.

50. Boyer Las Vegas Early History Project, Stuart Mason, November 9, 2006.

51. *Ibid.*

52. Desert Palace, Inc., Articles of Incorporation, December 2, 1964.

53. *Salt Lake City* (UT) *Tribune,* November 24, 1964.

54. *Chicago Tribune,* January 29, 1965.

55. Schwartz, 69.

56. Watkins, 245.

57. vintagelasvegas.com, August 4, 2019.

58. *Los Angeles Times,* April 17, 1974.

59. *Miami* (FL) *News,* January 29, 1965.

60. Messick, *Lansky,* 192.

61. *Tennessean* (Nashville, TN), June 16, 1974.

62. *Miami* (FL) *News,* March 22, 1966.

63. *Detroit* (MI) *Free Press,* May 8, 1972.

64. Messick, 199.

65. *Republic* (Columbus, IN), April 8, 1968.

66. *Ibid.*

67. *San Francisco Examiner,* July 21, 1966.

68. *Ibid.*

69. *Nevada State Journal* (Reno, NV) August 4, 1966.

70. *Los Angeles Times,* August 4, 1966.

71. *Ibid.*

72. *Ibid.*

73. *Las Vegas* (NV) *Review-Journal,* September 23, 1966.

74. *Los Angeles Times,* August 4, 1966.

75. *Ibid.*

76. *Ibid.*

77. *Oakland* (CA) *Tribune,* August 4, 1966.

78. *Press and Sun-Bulletin* (Binghamton, NY), August 17, 1966.

79. *Albuquerque* (NM) *Journal,* August 18, 1966.

80. *Nevada State Journal* (Reno, NV), August 18, 1966.

81. *Ibid.*

82. *Los Angeles Times*, August 18, 1966.

83. *Baltimore* (MD) *Sun,* September 7, 1966.

84. *Ibid.*

85. *Nevada State Journal* (Reno, NV), September 9, 1966.

86. *Herald-News* (Passaic, NJ), August 4, 1966.

87. Watkins, 84.

88. Watkins, 85.

89. *SEC News Digest*, September 19, 1969.

90. *Ibid.*

91. *Los Angeles Times,* December 18, 1966.
92. *Ibid.*
93. *Ibid.*
94. *Ibid.*
95. Schwartz, 112.
96. FBI Los Angeles FO, Case: Vincent Alo, August 9, 1967.
97. *Ibid.*
98. *Ibid.*
99. *Los Angeles Times,* November 17, 1967.
100. *United States v. Lazarus,* United States Court of Appeals, Ninth Circuit, June 18, 1970, 425F.2d 638 (9th Cir. 1970).
101. Southern Nevada Jewish Heritage Project, Interview with Stanley and Sandy Mallin, January 7, 2015.
102. *Ibid.*
103. *Ibid.*
104. *Ibid.*
105. Brill, 213.
106. Southern Nevada Jewish Heritage Project, Interview with Stanley and Sandy Mallin, January 7, 2015.
107. *Las Vegas* (NV) *Sun,* June 23, 1968.
108. Southern Nevada Jewish Community Digital Heritage Project, Interview with Gary Sternberg, February 15, 2015.
109. *Las Vegas* (NV) *Sun,* June 23, 1968.
110. *Los Angeles Times,* July 12, 1968.
111. *Los Angeles Times,* September 26, 1968.
112. *Ibid.*
113. *Los Angeles Times,* December 28, 1968.
114. *Reno* (NV) *Gazette-Journal,* January 13, 1969.
115. *Miami* (FL) *News,* April 28, 1969.
116. *Ibid.*
117. *Ibid.*
118. *Nevada State Journal* (Reno, NV), April 24, 1969.
119. *Ibid.*
120. Bower, 121.
121. Greene, 221.

Chapter IV

1. eventmanagerblog.com, November 27, 2018.
2. *Santa Cruz* (CA) *Sentinel,* January 19, 1969.
3. *Ibid.*
4. *Star-Gazette* (Elmira, NY), October 3, 1969.
5. *Ibid.*
6. *Ithaca* (NY) *Journal,* October 6, 1969.
7. *Democrat and Chronicle* (Rochester, NY), October 8, 1969.
8. *Ibid.*
9. *Ithaca* (NY) *Journal,* October 6, 1969.
10. *Ibid.*
11. Bower, 47.
12. *Tampa* (FL) *Tribune,* October 20, 1969.
13. *Tallahassee* (FL) *Democrat,* October 22, 1969.
14. *Miami* (FL) *News,* July 24, 1970.
15. *Miami* (FL) *News,* March 26, 1970.
16. miamibeachvisualmemoirs.com, October 13, 2017.
17. *Tampa Bay* (FL) *Times,* July 22, 1970.
18. *Reno* (NV) *Gazette Journal.* June 13, 1969.
19. *Independent* (Long Beach, CA), June 13, 1969.
20. *Reno* (NV) *Gazette Journal.* June 13, 1969.
21. *Reno* (NV) *Gazette Journal.* June 16, 1979.
22. *Reno* (NV) *Gazette Journal.* June 13, 1969.
23. *Arizona Daily Star* (Tucson, AZ), October 8, 1969.
24. *Reno* (NV) *Gazette-Journal.* June 13, 1969.
25. *Independent* (Long Beach, CA), August 13, 1969.
26. *Reno* (NV) *Gazette-Journal.* August 14, 1969.
27. *Reno* (NV) *Gazette-Journal.* August 22, 1969.
28. *Reno* (NV) *Gazette-Journal.* August 14, 1969.
29. Watkins, 89.
30. *Honolulu* (HI) *Star-Bulletin,* October 29, 1967.
31. *Akron* (OH) *Beacon-Journal,* July 17. 1970.
32. *Ibid.*
33. *Press Democrat* (Santa Rosa, CA), April 24, 1970.
34. *Times* (San Mateo, CA), May 7, 1970.
35. *San Francisco Examiner,* May 2, 1970.
36. *Los Angeles Times,* May 7, 1970.
37. *San Francisco Examiner,* May 2, 1970.
38. *San Francisco Examiner,* April 29, 1970.
39. Watkins, 90.
40. *Times* (San Mateo, CA), May 14, 1970.
41. *Press Democrat* (Santa Rosa, CA), May 14, 1970
42. *Ibid.*
43. Watkins, 90.
44. *Las Vegas* (NV) *Sun,* April 24, 1970.
45. *Ibid.*
46. insiderlv.com, August 1998.
47. *Fort Lauderdale* (FL) *News,* November 29, 1965.
48. *Reno* (NV) *Gazette-Journal.* August 22, 1969.
49. New Jersey Casino Control Commission Boardwalk Regency Corporation and the Jemm Company, In the Matter of the Applications for Casino Licenses, November 13, 1980, 295.
50. *Ibid.,* 304.
51. Greene, 230.
52. *Ibid.*
53. *Los Angeles Times,* November 11, 1981.
54. Watkins, 91.
55. *Sydney* (New South Wales, Australia) *Morning Herald,* June 11, 1972.
56. *Ibid.*
57. Bower, 54.
58. *Reno* (NV) *Gazette-Journal,* September 7, 1970.
59. *Honolulu* (HI) *Star-Bulletin,* December 23, 1970.
60. *Akron* (OH) *Beacon-Journal,* November 2, 1970.
61. *Ibid.*
62. *Reno* (NV) *Gazette-Journal,* November 13, 1970.
63. *SEC Digest,* December 3, 1970.
64. *Honolulu* (HI) *Star-Bulletin,* December 3, 1970.

65. *Ibid.*

66. *Miami* (FL) *News*, January 25, 1965.

67. *Atlanta* (GA) *Constitution*, December 8, 1970.

68. Southern Nevada Jewish Heritage Project, Interview with Stanley and Sandy Mallin, January 7, 2015.

69. *Ibid.*

70. *Ibid.*

71. *Green Bay* (WI) *Press*, December 10, 1970.

72. *Atlanta* (GA) *Constitution*, December 8, 1970.

73. *Napa* (CA) *Register*, August 15, 1970.

74. *Ibid.*

75. *Ibid.*

76. *Los Angeles Times*, September 7, 1970.

77. *San Francisco Examiner*, November 29, 1970.

78. *Ibid.*

79. *Ibid.*

80. *Ibid.*

81. *Fort Lauderdale* (FL) *News*, December 13, 1970.

82. *Ibid.*

83. *Los Angeles Times*, December 15, 1970.

84. *Santa Cruz* (CA) *Sentinel*, December 13, 1970.

85. *Los Angeles Times*, December 15, 1970.

86. *Ibid.*

87. *Record* (Hackensack, NJ), December 20, 1970.

88. *Reno* (NV) *Gazette-Journal*, December 19, 1970.

89. *Green Bay* (WI) *Press*, December 19, 1970.

90. *San Francisco Examiner*, January 12, 1971.

91. *Ibid.*

92. *Ibid.*

93. *Los Angeles Times*, January 13, 1971.

94. *Ibid.*

95. *San Bernardino County* (CA) *Sun*, March 19, 1971.

96. *Ibid.*

97. *Independent* (Long Beach, CA, March 26, 1971.

98. *Los Angeles Times*, March 29, 1971.

99. Bower, 58.

100. *Los Angeles Times*, March 29, 1971.

101. *San Francisco Examiner*, March 30, 1971.

102. *Ibid.*

103. *San Bernardino County* (CA) *Sun*, April 19, 1971.

104. *Ibid.*

105. *Detroit* (MI) *Free Press*, July 1, 1964.

106. *Hartford* (CT) *Courant*, September 3, 1960.

107. *Los Angeles Times*, July 15, 1970.

108. *Pocono* (PA) *Record*, March 26, 1971.

109. FBI Las Vegas FO File 87–8351, August 3, 1971.

110. *Ibid.*

111. *Ibid.*

112. DOJ Press Release, October 22, 1971.

113. *SEC Digest*, December 8, 1971.

114. *New York Times*, December 7, 1971.

115. Greene, 216.

116. Southern Nevada Jewish Heritage Project, Interview with Stanley and Sandy Mallin, January 7, 2015.

117. *Reno* (NV) *Gazette-Journal*, September 22, 1975.

118. *Philadelphia* (PA) *Inquirer*, November 28, 1971.

119. Bower, 63.

120. *Philadelphia* (PA) *Inquirer*, November 28, 1971.

121. *Ibid.*

122. *San Bernardino County* (CA) *Sun*, January 28, 1972.

123. *Times* (San Mateo, CA), February 3, 1972.

124. *Arizona Daily Star* (Tucson, AZ), February 20, 1972.

125. *Ibid.*

126. *Democrat and Chronicle* (Rochester, NY), October 9, 1972.

127. *Reno* (NV) *Gazette-Journal*, October 2, 1980.

128. *Independent* (Long Beach, CA), July 16, 1973.

129. *Independent Press-Telegram* (Long Beach, CA, August 11, 1974.

Chapter V

1. *Santa Maria* (CA) *Times*, October 29, 1973.

2. *Argus* (Fremont, CA), November 28, 1973.

3. *Daily Messenger* (Canandaigua, NY), October 15, 1973.

4. *Post-Standard* (Syracuse, NY), November 20, 1974

5. *Longview* (WA) *Daily News*, December 3, 1974.

6. *Post-Standard* (Syracuse, NY), November 20, 1974.

7. *Ibid.*

8. *Independent* (Long Beach, CA), November 20, 1974.

9. *Ibid.*

10. *Los Angeles Times*, November 20, 1974.

11. *San Francisco Examiner*, October 15, 1975.

12. Official Program, United States Grand Prix West, March 28, 1976, 18.

13. *Star-Gazette* (Elmira, NY), October 7, 1974.

14. *Ibid.*

15. *San Francisco Examiner*, October 7, 1981.

16. *Independent Press-Telegram* (Long Beach, CA, August 11, 1974.

17. *Ibid.*

18. *Ibid.*

19. *Ibid.*

20. *Ibid.*

21. *Ibid.*

22. *Ibid.*

23. *Los Angeles Times*, December 14, 1976.

24. *Independent Press-Telegram* (Long Beach, CA), August 11, 1974.

25. *Independent* (Long Beach, CA), November 15, 1974.

26. *Ibid.*

27. *Pomona* (CA) *Progress Bulletin,* November 20, 1974.

28. *Los Angeles Times,* July 10, 1974.

29. *Los Angeles Times,* November 21, 1974.

30. *Los Angeles Times,* November 26, 1974.

31. *Los Angeles Times,* November 20, 1974.

32. *Independent Press-Telegram* (Long Beach, CA), November 17,1974.

33. *Independent* (Long Beach, CA), November 20, 1974.

34. *Independent Press-Telegram* (Long Beach, CA), November 23,1974.

35. *Ibid.*

36. *Independent* (Long Beach, CA), December 19, 1974.

37. *Daily Oklahoman* (Oklahoma City, OK), April 23, 1975.

38. *Independent* (Long Beach, CA), December 19, 1974.

39. *Independent* (Long Beach, CA), December 17, 1974.

40. *Independent* (Long Beach, CA), September 30, 1975.

41. *Independent Press-Telegram* (Long Beach, CA), December 17, 1974.

42. *Independent* (Long Beach, CA), December 17, 1974.

43. *Ibid.*

44. *Independent* (Long Beach, CA), August 23, 1967.

45. *Ibid.*

46. *Star Tribune* (Minneapolis, MN), May 22, 1960.

47. *Chicago Tribune,* April 11, 1961.

48. *Independent* (Long Beach, CA), March 27, 1968.

49. *Los Angeles Times,* April 22, 1968.

50. *Edwardsville* (IL) *Intelligencer,* July 7, 1976.

51. Russo, *Supermob,* 436.

52. *Los Angeles Times,* March 10, 1971.

53. Russo, 436.

54. *Ibid.,* 310.

55. *Palm Beach* (FL) *Post,* October 21, 1973.

56. *Fort Lauderdale* (FL) *News,* June 4, 1969.

57. *Palm Beach* (FL) *Post,* October 21, 1973.

58. *Independent* (Long Beach, CA), July 14, 1977.

59. *Ibid.*

60. *Ibid.*

61. *Democrat and Chronicle* (Rochester, NY), January 10, 1979.

62. *News-Herald* (Franklin, PA), September 27, 1967.

63. *SEC News Digest,* June 10, 1975.

64. *Miami* (FL) *News,* October 10, 1972.

65. William D. Weinberger interview.

66. *Ibid.*

67. *Reno* (NV) *Gazette-Journal,* April 19, 1974.

68. William D. Weinberger interview.

69. *Independent* (Long Beach, CA), March 20, 1975.

70. *Independent Press-Telegram* (Long Beach, CA), February 2, 1974.

71. *Los Angeles Times,* June 30, 1975.

72. *Ibid.*

73. *Naples* (FL) *Daily News,* July 28, 1975.

74. *Ibid.*

75. *Los Angeles Times,* September 25, 1975.

76. *Ibid.*

77. *Los Angeles Times,* June 30, 1975

78. *Independent* (Long Beach, CA), August 13, 1975.

79. *Democrat and Chronicle* (Rochester, NY), August 4, 1975.

80. Bower, 77.

81. *Ottawa Journal* (Ottawa, Ontario, Canada), September 3, 1975.

82. *Ibid.*

83. *Los Angeles Times,* November 13, 1975.

84. *Ibid.*

85. *Ibid.*

86. *Tribune* (Scranton, PA), February 28, 1975.

87. *Orlando* (FL) *Sentinel,* February 21, 1971.

88. *Ibid.*

89. *Miami* (FL) *News,* February 21, 1974.

90. *Arizona Republic* (Phoenix, AZ), July 23, 1972.

91. *Indianapolis* (IN) *News,* June 10, 1975.

92. *Ibid.*

93. *Los Angeles Times,* November 13, 1975.

94. *Ibid.*

95. *Ibid.*

96. *Ibid.*

97. *Times* (San Mateo, CA), November 14, 1975.

98. *Los Angeles Times,* March 19, 1976.

99. *News-Press* (Fort Myers, FL), December 7, 1975.

100. *Los Angeles Times,* September 19, 1975.

101. *Los Angeles Times,* September 15, 1975.

102. *Ithaca* (NY) *Journal,* May 6, 1975.

103. *Independent Press-Telegram* (Long Beach, CA), September 28, 1975.

104. *Los Angeles Times,* September 28, 1975.

105. Bobby Unser interview.

106. *Los Angeles Times,* September 28, 1975.

107. *Independent* (Long Beach, CA), September 29, 1975.

108. *Ibid.*

109. *Ibid.*

110. *Los Angeles Times,* September 30, 1975.

111. *Independent* (Long Beach, CA), September 30, 1975.

112. *Ibid.*

113. *Ibid.*

114. *Independent Press-Telegram* (Long Beach, CA), February 7, 1976.

115. *Ibid.*

116. *Ibid.*

Chapter VI

1. *Star-Gazette* (Elmira, NY) October 5, 1975.

2. *Democrat and Chronicle* (Rochester, NY), September 25, 1975.

3. *Star-Gazette* (Elmira, NY) October 24, 1975.

4. *Star-Gazette* (Elmira, NY) October 23, 1975.

5. *Orlando* (FL) *Sentinel,* October 12, 1975.

6. *Independent Press-Telegram* (Long Beach, CA), February 7, 1976.

7. *Independent Press-Telegram* (Long Beach, CA), March 21, 1976.

8. *Ukiah* (CA) *Daily Journal,* December 3, 1975.

9. *Independent Press-Telegram* (Long Beach, CA), March 27, 1976.

10. *Ibid.*

11. Official Program, United States Grand Prix West, March 28, 1976, 45.

12. *Independent Press-Telegram* (Long Beach, CA), March 27, 1976.

13. *Ibid.*

14. *Los Angeles Times,* March 7, 1976.

15. *Independent* (Long Beach, CA), March 19, 1976.

16. *Ibid.*

17. *Independent* (Long Beach, CA), March 29, 1976.

18. *Ibid.*

19. *Ibid.*

20. *Ibid.*

21. *Times* San Mateo, CA), March 29, 1976.

22. Bower, 81.

23. *Times* San Mateo, CA), March 29, 1976.

24. *Independent Press-Telegram* (Long Beach, CA), April 10, 1976.

25. *Evening Times* (Sayre, PA), April 10, 1976.

26. *Central New Jersey Home News* (New Brunswick, NJ), May 20, 1976.

27. *Brattleboro* (VT) *Reformer,* February 14, 1977.

28. *Orlando* (FL) *Sentinel,* May 20, 1976.

29. *Miami* (FL *News,* August 7, 1963.

30. *Independent* (Long Beach, CA), April 14, 1976.

31. *Independent* (Long Beach, CA), April 21, 1976.

32. *Ibid.*

33. *Independent* (Long Beach, CA), April 14, 1976.

34. *Ibid.*

35. *Independent* (Long Beach, CA), June 14, 1976.

36. *Los Angeles Times,* May 14, 1976.

37. *Independent* (Long Beach, CA), February 24, 1976.

38. Official Program, United States Grand Prix West, March 13–15, 1981, 55.

39. *Independent* (Long Beach, CA), May 20, 1976.

40. *Independent* (Long Beach, CA), May 19, 1976.

41. *Los Angeles Times,* June 17, 1976.

42. *Ibid.*

43. *Independent Press-Telegram* (Long Beach, CA), April 16, 1977.

44. *Ibid.*

45. *Independent* (Long Beach, CA), June 18, 1976.

46. *Independent Press-Telegram* (Long Beach, CA), July 17, 1976.

47. *Los Angeles Times,* June 18, 1976.

48. *Independent Press-Telegram* (Long Beach, CA), August 7, 1976.

49. *Los Angeles Times,* December 16, 1979.

50. Official Program, United States Grand Prix West, March 26–28, 1976, 74.

51. *Los Angeles Times,* August 27, 1976.

52. *Ibid.*

53. *Ibid.*

54. *Independent* (Long Beach, CA), July 7, 1976.

55. *Los Angeles Times,* August 27, 1976.

56. *Independent Press-Telegram* (Long Beach, CA), September 26, 1976.

57. *Independent* (Long Beach, CA), September 16, 1976.

58. *Independent Press-Telegram* (Long Beach, CA), July 17, 1976.

59. *Independent Press-Telegram* (Long Beach, CA), September 4, 1976.

60. *Philadelphia* (PA) *Inquirer,* April 8, 1976.

61. *Ibid.*

62. *Ibid.*

63. *Ibid.*

64. *Star-Gazette* (Elmira, NY) October 5, 1975.

65. *Democrat and Chronicle* (Rochester, NY), July 12, 1976.

66. *Ibid.*

67. *Ibid.*

68. *Ithaca* (NY) *Journal,* October 9, 1976.

69. *Star-Gazette* (Elmira, NY) October 7, 1976.

70. *Democrat and Chronicle* (Rochester, NY), October 12, 1976.

71. *Ibid.*

72. *Ibid.*

73. *Press and Sun-Bulletin* (Binghamton, NY), October 25, 1976.

74. Ithaca (NY) Journal, October 25, 1976.

75. *Guardian* (London, Greater London, England), January 8, 1977.

76. *Times Colonist* (Victoria, British Columbia, Canada), October 26, 1976.

77. *El Paso* (TX) *Times,* November 4, 1976.

78. *Democrat and Chronicle* (Rochester, NY), November 19, 1976.

79. *Democrat and Chronicle* (Rochester, NY), January 8, 1977.

80. *Ibid.*

81. Bower, 85.

82. *Ibid.*

83. *Post-Star* (Glen Falls, NY), April 23, 1976.

84. *Independent* (Long Beach, CA), September 22, 1976.

85. *Ibid.*

86. *Ibid.*

87. *Los Angeles Times,* March 22, 1977.

88. *Ibid.*

89. *Independent* (Long Beach, CA), September 22, 1976.

90. *Ibid.*

91. *Ibid.*

92. *Los Angeles Times,* March 22, 1977.

93. *Ibid.*

94. *Ibid.*

95. William D. Weinberger interview.

96. *Ibid.*

97. *Ibid.*

98. *Las Vegas* (NV) *Review-Journal,* April 2, 1977.

99. *Ibid.*

100. *Independent Press-Telegram* (Long Beach, CA), April 2, 1977.

101. *Ibid.*

102. *Independent Press-Telegram* (Long Beach, CA), April 3, 1977.

103. *Ibid.*

104. *Ibid.*

105. *Ibid.*

106. *Motorsport Magazine,* May 1977.

107. *Ibid.*

108. *Southern Illinoisan* (Carbondale, IL), April 4, 1977.

109. *Ibid.*

110. *Independent* (Long Beach, CA), April 4, 1977.

111. *Ibid.*

112. *Ibid.*

113. *Ibid.*

114. *Independent* (Long Beach, CA), April 7, 1977.

115. *Independent* (Long Beach, CA), June 10, 1977.

116. *Star-Gazette* (Elmira, NY) October 6, 1957.

117. *Independent* (Long Beach, CA), June 10, 1977.

118. *Independent* (Long Beach, CA), June 3, 1977.

119. *Ibid.*

120. *Independent* (Long Beach, CA), May 20, 1976.

121. *Independent* (Long Beach, CA), June 10, 1977.

122. *Ibid.*

123. *Ibid.*

124. *Independent* (Long Beach, CA), April 4, 1977.

125. Bower, 91.

126. *Ibid.* 115.

127. *Nevada Evening Gazette* (Reno, NV), May 14, 1977.

128. *Star-Gazette* (Elmira, NY), May 15, 1977.

129. *Bakersfield* (CA) *Californian,* April 10, 1977.

Chapter VII

1. *Independent* (Long Beach, CA), June 3, 1977.

2. *Record* (Hackensack, NJ), June 3, 1977.

3. *Ibid.*

4. *Pittsburgh* (PA) *Press,* February 19, 1978.

5. *Pittsburgh* (PA) *Press,* February 20, 1978.

6. *Asbury Park* (NJ) *Press,* August 23, 1976.

7. *Congressional Record,* June 18, 1969. 16464.

8. New Jersey Casino Control Commission, in the Matters of the Application of Bally's Park Place, Inc., a New Jersey Corporation, for a Casino License, March 16, 1981, 374.

9. *Ibid.,* 370.

10. *Philadelphia* (PA) *Daily News,* March 7, 1979.

11. *Ibid.*

12. *Philadelphia* (PA) *Inquirer,* April 22, 1979.

13. *Los Angeles Times,* March 30, 1978.

14. *Ibid.*

15. *Ibid.*

16. *Ibid.*

17. *Ibid.*

18. *Springfield* (MO) *Leader and Press,* April 2, 1978.

19. *Los Angeles Times,* April 15, 1999.

20. *Los Angeles Times,* April 3, 1978.

21. *Ibid.*

22. *Ibid.*

23. *Los Angeles Times,* April 5, 1978.

24. *Las Vegas* (NV) *Review-Journal,* April 3, 1978.

25. *New York Times,* April 17, 1978.

26. *Ibid.*

27. *Ibid.*

28. *Ibid.*

29. *Ibid.*

30. House Select Committee on Assassinations, Chicago Police Department Files, May 22, 1978, 7.

31. *Ibid.,* 19.

32. *Ibid.,* 16.

33. Hearings before the Permanent Subcommittee on Investigations, Organized Crime Activities, October 24–25, 1978, 754.

34. *Ibid.,* 722–724.

35. State of California, Organized Crime Control Commission, May 1978, 83.

36. *Record* (Hackensack, NJ), May 26, 1978.

37. *Ibid.*

38. *Poughkeepsie* (NY) *Journal,* May 27, 1978.

39. *Democrat and Chronicle* (Rochester, NY), August 20, 1978.

40. *Democrat and Chronicle* (Rochester, NY), September 29, 1978.

41. *Ibid.*

42. *Democrat and Chronicle* (Rochester, NY), September 30, 1978.

43. *Ibid.*

44. *Democrat and Chronicle* (Rochester, NY), September 29, 1978.

45. *Star-Gazette* (Elmira, NY), October 2, 1978.

46. *Ibid.*

47. *Star-Gazette* (Elmira, NY), October 5, 1978.

48. *Ibid.*

49. *Star-Gazette* (Elmira, NY), October 4, 1978.

50. *Indianapolis* (IN) *Star,* November 19, 1978.

51. Brill, 218.

52. *Chicago Tribune,* September 24, 2006.

53. *Miami* (FL) *Herald,* August 5, 1978

54. *Ibid.*

55. *Hartford* (CT) *Courant,* August 4, 1978.

56. *Oshkosh* (WI) *Northwestern,* April 7, 1979.

57. New Jersey Casino Control Commission, in the Matters of the Application of Bally's Park Place, Inc., a New Jersey Corporation, for a Casino License, March 16, 1981, 296.

58. *New York Times,* May 31, 1979.

59. *SEC News Digest,* July 24, 1979.
60. *Ibid.*
61. Official Program, Toyota Grand Prix of Long Beach, March 13–15, 1981, 45.
62. *Ibid.*
63. *Berkeley* (CA) *Gazette,* February 13, 1979.
64. *Ibid.*
65. *Los Angeles Times,* March 15, 1979.
66. *Los Angeles Times,* November 20, 1974.
67. *Los Angeles Times,* March 15, 1979.
68. *Los Angeles Times,* March 22, 1979.
69. *News-Pilot* (San Pedro, CA), April 7, 1979.
70. *Los Angeles Times,* April 6, 1979.
71. thenational.ae/sport, November 12, 2011.
72. *Los Angeles Times,* June 14, 1979.
73. *Ibid.*
74. *Ibid.*
75. *Los Angeles Times,* April 12, 1979.
76. *Los Angeles Times,* June 18, 1981.
77. *San Bernardino County* (CA) *Sun,* July 18, 1979.
78. *Ibid.*
79. *Ibid.*
80. *Ibid.*
81. Chris Pook e-mail, October 10, 2019.
82. *San Bernardino County* (CA) *Sun,* July 18, 1979.
83. *Los Angeles Times,* March 22, 1977.
84. *Las Vegas* (NV) *Review-Journal,* July 21, 1979.
85. *Times-Tribune* (Scranton, PA), July 29, 1979.
86. *Ibid.*
87. Greene, 229.
88. *Ibid.* 228.
89. *Ibid.*
90. *Ibid.,* 221.
91. *Ibid.,* 222.
92. *Las Vegas* (NV) *Review-Journal,* October 11, 1979.
93. *Star-Gazette* (Elmira, NY), September 29, 1979.
94. *Ibid.*
95. *Democrat and Chronicle* (Rochester, NY), October 7, 1979.
96. *Democrat and Chronicle* (Rochester, NY), October 8, 1979.
97. *Star-Gazette* (Elmira, NY), November 20, 1979.
98. *Los Angeles Times,* December 11, 1979.
99. *Asbury Park* (NJ) *Press,* December 12, 1979.
100. Lovell, *Bernie Ecclestone—King of Sport,* Chapter 7.
101. *Ibid.*
102. *San Bernardino County* (CA) *Sun,* December 12, 1979.

Chapter VIII

1. *Decatur* (IL) *Daily Review,* December 11, 1979.
2. *Ibid.*
3. *Ibid.*
4. *Star-Gazette* (Elmira, NY), November 30, 1979.
5. *Central New Jersey Home News* (New Brunswick, NJ), January 24, 1980.
6. *Ibid.*
7. *Ibid.*
8. *Courier-News* (Bridgewater, NJ), January 24, 1980.
9. *Central New Jersey Home News* (New Brunswick, NJ), January 24, 1980.
10. *Ibid.*
11. *Los Angeles Times,* November 15, 1965.
12. *Courier-News* (Bridgewater, NJ), January 24, 1980.
13. Greene, 217.
14. *Courier-Post* (Camden, NJ), February 5, 1980.
15. *Star-Gazette* (Elmira, NY), December 14, 1979.
16. *Las Vegas* (NV) *Review-Journal,* December 13, 1979.
17. *Las Vegas* (NV) *Review-Journal,* February 6, 1980.
18. *Press and Sun-Bulletin* (Binghamton, NY), February 3, 1980.
19. *Ibid.*
20. *Press and Sun-Bulletin* (Binghamton, NY), February 23, 1980.
21. *Los Angeles Times,* February 23, 1980.
22. *Las Vegas* (NV) *Review-Journal,* February 20, 1980.
23. *Ibid.*
24. *Los Angeles Times,* February 13, 1980.
25. *Las Vegas* (NV) *Review-Journal,* February 28, 1980.
26. *Paterson* (NJ) *News,* February 28, 1980.
27. *Courier-Post* (Camden, NJ), April 6, 1980
28. *Republican and Herald* (Pottsville, PA), May 22, 1980
29. *Los Angeles Times,* March 20, 1980.
30. *Monrovia* (CA) *News-Post,* March 2, 1980.
31. *Las Vegas* (NV) *Review-Journal,* March 27, 1980.
32. *San Bernardino County* (CA) *Sun,* September 25, 1981.
33. *Reno* (NV) *Gazette-Journal,* April 3, 1980.
34. *Ibid.*
35. *Asbury Park* (NJ) *Press,* April 11, 1980.
36. *Democrat and Chronicle* (Rochester, NY), April 27, 1980.
37. *Ibid.*
38. *Star Press* (Muncie, IN), April 27, 1980.
39. *Hartford* (CT) *Courant,* April 19, 1980.
40. *Ibid.*
41. *Daily Journal* (Vineland, NJ), July 2, 1980.
42. *Millville* (NJ) *Daily,* August 29, 1980.
43. *Paterson* (NJ) *News,* September 8, 1980.
44. *Courier-Post* (Camden, NJ), September 8, 1980
45. *Courier-Post* (Camden, NJ), September 28, 1980
46. *Star-Gazette* (Elmira, NY), March 18, 1981.
47. *Courier-Post* (Camden, NJ), September 28, 1980
48. *Star-Gazette* (Elmira, NY), September 25, 1980.

49. *Democrat and Chronicle* (Rochester, NY), October 5, 1980.

50. *Ibid.*

51. *Ibid.*

52. Official Program, Toyota Grand Prix of Long Beach, March 13–15, 1981, 45.

53. *Democrat and Chronicle* (Rochester, NY), October 6, 1980.

54. *Democrat and Chronicle* (Rochester, NY), October 5, 1980.

55. *Ibid.*

56. *Star-Gazette* (Elmira, NY), October 31, 1980.

57. *Ibid.*

58. *Democrat and Chronicle* (Rochester, NY), October 5, 1980

59. *Ithaca* (NY) *Journal*, December 1, 1980.

60. *Ibid.*

61. *Record* (Hackensack, NJ), September 11, 1980.

62. Greene, 229.

63. *Record* (Hackensack, NJ), September 11, 1980.

64. *Central New Jersey Home News* (New Brunswick, NJ), September 19, 1980.

65. *Los Angeles Times,* November 15, 1965.

66. *Central New Jersey Home News* (New Brunswick, NJ), September 19, 1980.

67. Bruce Aguilera interview.

68. *Central New Jersey Home News* (New Brunswick, NJ), September 24, 1980.

69. *New York Times,* September 28, 1980.

70. *Ibid.*

71. *Ibid.*

72. Greene, 222.

73. *Asbury Park* (NJ) *Press,* October 20, 1980.

74. FBI, Citizen's Letter to Director William Webster, February 4, 1980.

75. *Ibid.*

76. New Jersey Casino Control Commission, in the Matters of the Application of Bally's Park Place, Inc., a New Jersey Corporation, for a Casino License, March 16, 1981, 315.

77. *Ibid.*

78. *Ibid.,* 335.

79. *Ibid.,* 295.

80. *Daily Record* (Morristown, NJ), October 24, 1980.

Chapter IX

1. *Indianapolis* (IN) *News,* February 2, 1981.

2. *Hartford* (CT) *Courant,* March 6, 1981.

3. *Hartford* (CT) *Courant,* January 24, 1981.

4. *Philadelphia* (PA) *Inquirer,* December 12, 1981.

5. *Las Vegas* (NV) *Review-Journal,* February 11, 1967.

6. *Herald-News* (Passaic, NJ), December 13, 1981.

7. *Philadelphia* (PA) *Inquirer,* December 22, 1981.

8. *Miami* (FL) *Herald,* February 10, 1981.

9. *Miami* (FL) *Herald,* May 1, 1983.

10. *Central New Jersey Home News* (New Brunswick, NJ), September 18, 1975.

11. William D. Weinberger interview.

12. *New York Times,* March 27, 1981.

13. *SEC News Digest,* April 27, 1981.

14. Mario Andretti interview.

15. *Ibid.*

16. *Ibid.*

17. *Ibid.*

18. *Democrat and Chronicle* (Rochester, NY), March 15, 1981.

19. *Star-Gazette* (Elmira, NY), March 18, 1981.

20. *Ibid.*

21. *Las Vegas* (NV) *Review-Journal,* April 18, 1981.

22. *White Plains* (NY) *Journal, May 10, 1981.*

23. William D. Weinberger interview.

24. *San Bernardino County* (CA) *Sun,* May 30, 1981.

25. *Miami* (FL) *Herald,* June 15, 1981.

26. *Ibid.*

27. *Ibid.*

28. *Los Angeles Times,* August 4, 1966.

29. *Ibid.*

30. *Miami* (FL) *Herald,* June 15, 1981.

31. *Reno* (NV) *Gazette-Journal,* July 21, 1981.

32. *Herald-News* (Passaic, NJ), July 22, 1981.

33. *Herald-News* (Passaic, NJ), August 3, 1981.

34. *Ibid.*

35. *Herald-News* (Passaic, NJ), July 24, 1981.

36. *Burlington* (VT) *Free Press,* June 26, 1981.

37. *Democrat and Chronicle* (Rochester, NY), August 15, 1981.

38. *San Bernardino County* (CA) *Sun,* June 26, 1981.

39. *Ibid.*

40. *SCCA News,* June 25, 1981.

41. *Ibid.*

42. *San Francisco Examiner,* August 2, 1981.

43. *San Bernardino County* (CA) *Sun,* June 26, 1981.

44. *Los Angeles Times,* October 11, 1981.

45. *Ibid.*

46. *Independent* (Long Beach, CA), July 16, 1973.

47. *Las Vegas* (NV) *Review-Journal,* June 3, 1981.

48. Anthony Marnell interview.

49. *Ibid.*

50. *Ibid.*

51. *Las Vegas* (NV) *Review-Journal,* December 8, 2017.

52. *Los Angeles Times,* August 16, 1981.

53. *Ibid.*

54. *Las Vegas* (NV) *Review-Journal,* October 8, 1981.

55. *Las Vegas* (NV) *Review-Journal,* August 19, 1981.

56. *Ibid.*

57. *Ibid.*

58. *Boston Globe,* September 2, 1981.

59. *Ibid.*

60. *Los Angeles Times,* October 11, 1981.

61. *Ibid.*

62. *Record* (Hackensack, NJ), September 15, 1981.

63. *Los Angeles Times,* October 11, 1981.

64. *Ibid.*

65. *Dispatch* (Moline, IL), October 4, 1981.

66. *Ibid.*

67. *Las Vegas* (NV) *Review-Journal,* October 8, 1981.

68. *Ibid.*

69. *Las Vegas* (NV) *Review-Journal,* October 16, 1981.

70. Gary Gerrould interview.

71. *Ibid.*

72. Mario Andretti interview.

73. *Ibid.*

74. Collins and Porras, *Built to Last,* 17.

75. Media Information, Caesars Palace Grand Prix, October 14–17, 1981.

76. William D. Weinberger interview.

77. Mario Andretti interview.

78. *Chicago Tribune,* October 13, 1981.

79. *Town Talk* (Alexandria, LA), October 15, 1981.

80. *Reno* (NV) *Gazette-Journal,* October 17, 1981

81. *Las Vegas* (NV) *Review-Journal,* October 19, 1981.

82. *National Speed Sport News,* October 21, 1981.

83. *Ibid.*

84. *Los Angeles Times,* October 20, 1981.

85. *San Francisco Examiner,* October 19, 1981.

86. *Motorsport Magazine,* November 1981.

87. *Las Vegas* (NV) *Review-Journal,* October 19, 1981.

88. *Ibid.*

89. *Courier-Post* (Camden, NJ), October 20, 1981.

90. *Ibid.*

91. *Daily Register* (Red Bank, NJ), November 1, 1981.

92. *Ibid.*

93. *Ibid.*

94. *Los Angeles Times,* November 3, 1981

95. *Ibid.*

Chapter X

1. *Miami* (FL) *News,* October 13, 1981.

2. *Las Vegas* (NV) *Review-Journal,* November 4, 1981.

3. William D. Weinberger interview.

4. *Ibid.*

5. *Ibid.*

6. *Ibid.*

7. *Ibid.*

8. *Pensacola* (FL) *News Journal,* November 11, 1981.

9. *Ibid.*

10. *Indianapolis* (IN) *Star,* November 24, 1981.

11. *Ibid.*

12. *Boston Globe,* November 29, 1981.

13. *Los Angeles Times,* December 24, 1981.

14. *Reno* (NV) *Gazette-Journal,* December 19, 1981.

15. *Asbury Park* (NJ) *Press,* December 30, 1981.

16. *Ibid.*

17. *Los Angeles Times,* December 20, 1981.

18. House Select Committee on Assassinations, Chicago Police Department Files, May 22, 1978, 16.

19. *Ithaca* (NY) *Journal,* January 7, 1982.

20. *Indianapolis* (IN) *Star,* May 14, 1981.

21. *Star-Gazette* (Elmira, NY), Mar 20, 1981.

22. *Lansing* (MI) *State Journal,* October 15, 1981.

23. *Johnson City* (TN) *Press,* February 26, 1982.

24. *San Francisco Examiner,* June 2, 1989.

25. *New York* (NY) *Daily News,* March 14, 1982.

26. *Democrat and Chronicle* (Rochester, NY), June 7, 1982.

27. *Detroit* (MI) *Free Press,* July 18, 1948.

28. William D. Weinberger interview, October 10, 2020.

29. *Miami* (FL) *Herald,* June 7, 1966.

30. *Miami* (FL) *News,* July 3, 1970.

31. *Miami* (FL) *Herald,* September 13, 1965.

32. *Miami* (FL) *Herald,* January 22, 1967.

33. *Miami* (FL) *Herald,* January 9, 1972.

34. *Ibid.*

35. *Las Vegas* (NV) *Review-Journal,* June 26, 1972.

36. William D. Weinberger interview.

37. *Ibid.*

38. *Los Angeles Times,* November 3, 1981.

39. William D. Weinberger interview.

40. *Ibid.*

41. *Ibid.*

42. *Sydney* (New South Wales, Australia) *Morning Herald,* July 31, 1982.

43. *Asbury Park* (NJ) *Press,* December 30, 1981.

44. *Miami* (FL) *Herald,* July 30, 1982.

45. *Sydney* (New South Wales, Australia) *Morning Herald,* July 31, 1982.

46. *Ibid.*

47. *Miami* (FL) *Herald,* July 30, 1982.

48. *Las Vegas* (NV) *Review-Journal,* July 31, 1982.

49. *Ibid.*

50. *Las Vegas* (NV) *Review-Journal,* July 30, 1982.

51. *Las Vegas* (NV) *Review-Journal,* August 9, 1982.

52. *Ibid.*

53. *Sydney* (New South Wales, Australia) *Morning Herald,* September 17, 1982.

54. *Ibid.*

55. *Las Vegas* (NV) *Review-Journal,* September 21, 1982.

56. *Ibid.*

57. *Ibid.*

58. *Ibid.*

59. *Ibid.*

60. Mario Andretti interview

61. *Las Vegas* (NV) *Review-Journal,* September 21, 1982.

62. *Cycle News,* October 6, 1982.

63. *Ibid.*

64. *Las Vegas* (NV) *Review-Journal,* May 15, 1983.

65. *Los Angeles Times,* September 26, 1982.

66. *National Speed Sport News,* September 29, 1982.

67. *Reno* (NV) *Gazette-Journal,* September 23, 1982.

68. *Las Vegas* (NV) *Review-Journal,* September 27, 1982.

69. *Ibid.*

70. *Ibid.*

71. *Star Press* (Muncie, IN), October 31, 1982.

72. *Las Vegas* (NV) *Review-Journal,* November 17, 1982.

73. *Ibid.*

74. *Ibid.*

75. *Ibid.*

76. *Ibid.*

77. *Ibid.*

78. *Las Vegas* (NV) *Review-Journal,* November 18, 1982.

79. House Select Committee on Assassinations, Chicago Police Department Files, May 22, 1978, 16.

80. *Miami* (FL) *Herald,* November 30, 1982.

81. *Record* (Hackensack, NJ), December 15, 1982.

82. *Star-Gazette* (Elmira, NY) December 21, 1982.

Chapter XI

1. *Edmonton Journal* (Edmonton, Alberta, Canada), January 2, 1983.

2. *Miami* (FL) *News,* January 17, 1983.

3. *Miami* (FL) *Herald,* January 2, 1983.

4. *Ibid.*

5. *Miami* (FL) *News,* January 5, 1983.

6. *Miami* (FL) *Herald,* January 16, 1983.

7. *Ibid.*

8. *Miami* (FL) *News,* January 17, 1983.

9. *Ibid.*

10. *Chicago Tribune,* December 16, 1982.

11. *Ibid.*

12. *Reno* (NV) *Gazette-Journal,* January 21, 1983.

13. *Reno* (NV) *Gazette-Journal,* March 24, 1983.

14. William D. Weinberger interview, October 10, 1983.

15. *Ibid.*

16. *Ibid.*

17. *Ibid.*

18. *Reno* (NV) *Gazette-Journal,* March 24, 1983.

19. *Ibid.*

20. Bruce Aguilera interview.

21. *Gazette* (Montreal, Quebec, Canada), December 20, 1982.

22. *Indianapolis* (IN) *Star,* March 26, 1983.

23. *Ibid.*

24. *Detroit* (MI) *Free Press,* March 26, 1983.

25. *Santa Maria* (CA) *Times,* March 29, 1983.

26. *Ibid.*

27. *San Bernardino County* (CA) *Sun,* April 8, 1983.

28. *Ibid.*

29. *St. Louis* (MO) *Post-Dispatch,* February 27, 1983.

30. *Ibid.*

31. *Reno* (NV) *Gazette-Journal,* April 7, 1983.

32. *Nevada State Journal* (Reno, NV), August 7, 1966.

33. *Reno* (NV) *Gazette-Journal,* April 7, 1983.

34. *Ibid.*

35. *Southern Illinoisan* (Carbondale, IL), April 1, 1983.

36. *Courier-Post* (Camden, NJ), February 22, 1990.

37. William D. Weinberger interview.

38. Official Program, Caesars Palace Grand Prix III, October 5–9, 1983.

39. *Journal and Courier* (Lafayette, IN), May 28, 1983.

40. Bruce Aguilera interview.

41. *Province (*Vancouver, British Columbia, Canada, June 5, 1983.

42. *Windsor Star* (Windsor, Ontario, Canada), June 1, 1982.

43. *Detroit* (MI) *Free Press,* June 5, 1983.

44. *Ibid.*

45. *Ibid.*

46. Mary Lou Pernicano e-mail, August 21, 2019.

47. *Detroit* (MI) *Free Press,* June 5, 1983.

48. *Miami* (FL) *Herald,* June 29, 1983.

49. *Democrat and Chronicle* (Rochester, NY), July 7, 1983.

50. Bruce Aguilera interview.

51. *San Francisco Examiner,* September 4, 1983.

52. Official Program, Caesars Palace Grand Prix III, October 5–9, 1983.

53. Rick Lake interview.

54. Mario Andretti interview.

55. *Ibid.*

56. *Indianapolis* (IN) *Star,* March 26, 1983.

57. *Ibid.*

58. *Las Vegas* (NV) *Review-Journal,* October 9, 1984.

59. Wally Dallenbach, Jr., interview.

60. Lyn St. James interview.

61. NBC Sports, Caesars Palace Grand Prix III, October 9, 1983.

62. *Ibid.*

63. *Ibid.*

64. *Ibid.*

65. *Ibid.*

66. *National Speed Sport News,* October 12, 1983.

67. *Indianapolis* (IN) *Star,* October 9, 1983.

68. *National Speed Sport News,* October 12, 1983.

69. *Los Angeles Times,* October 9, 1983.

70. *Indianapolis* (IN) *Star,* October 9, 1983.

71. *Los Angeles Times,* October 20, 1983.

72. *Auto Week,* June 12, 2015.

73. *Ibid.*

74. *Star Press* (Muncie, IN), May 26, 1992.

75. *Indianapolis* (IN) *Star,* October 9, 1983.

76. *Arizona Republic* (Phoenix, AZ), November 16, 1983.

77. *Fort Worth* (TX) *Star Telegram,* December 12, 1983.

78. *New York* (NY) *Daily News,* November 10, 1983.

79. *New York Times*, October 28, 1982.

80. *New York* (NY) *Daily News*, January 1, 1984.

81. *Kamin v. Koren*, 621 F. Supp. 444 (S.D.N.Y. 1985)

82. *New York Times*, January 31, 1986.

83. *Ibid.*

84. *Asbury Park* (NJ) *Press*, February 25, 1986.

85. *Post-Star* (Glenn Falls, NY), February 25, 1986.

86. *New York* (NY) *Daily News*, July 28, 1988.

87. William D. Weinberger e-mail, March 3, 2020.walker

88. *New York Times*, December 25, 1983.

89. *Ibid.*

90. *Ibid.*

91. *Star-Gazette* (Elmira, NY) March 31, 1984.

92. *Ibid.*

93. *Ibid.*

Chapter XII

1. *Chicago Tribune,* July 15, 1984.

2. *Ibid.*

3. *Los Angeles Times,* August 4, 1984.

4. Schwartz, 266.

5. Jay Sarno, Jr., e-mail, October 3, 2019.

6. *Ibid.*

7. *Ibid.*

8. *Reno* (NV) *Gazette-Journal,* September 5, 1984.

9. Jeff Silver e-mail, September 10, 2019.

10. *Ibid.*

11. *Las Vegas* (NV) *Review-Journal,* July 3, 1984.

12. *Arizona Republic* (Phoenix, AZ), June 2, 1989.

13. Jeff Silver e-mail, September 10, 2019.

14. William D. Weinberger interview.

15. *Ibid.*

16. *Ibid.*

17. *Ibid.*

18. *Detroit* (MI) *Free Press,* June 25, 1984.

19. *Ibid.*

20. *Los Angeles Times,* June 18, 1988.

21. *Ibid.*

22. *D Magazine,* July 1985.

23. William D. Weinberger e-mail, May 4, 2020.

24. *Ibid.*

25. *Ibid.*

26. *Ibid.*

27. *Motorsport Magazine,* August 1984.

28. *Fort Worth* (TX) *Star Telegram,* July 8, 1984.

29. *Fort Worth* (TX) *Star Telegram,* July 9, 1984.

30. *Ibid.*

31. *D Magazine,* July 1985.

32. William D. Weinberger e-mail, May 4, 2020.

33. *D Magazine,* July 1985.

34. William D. Weinberger e-mail, May 4, 2020.

35. *Indianapolis* (IN) *Star,* September 30, 1984.

36. *Ibid.*

37. *Ibid.*

38. *Las Vegas* (NV) *Review-Journal,* November 13, 1984.

39. Chris Pook e-mail, August 21, 2019.

40. *Ibid.*

41. *Ibid.*

42. *Las Vegas* (NV) *Review-Journal,* November 13, 1984.

43. *Ibid.*

44. *Los Angeles Times,* January 8, 1990.

45. *Ibid.*

46. *Chicago Tribune,* October 31, 1989.

47. Wally Dallenbach, Jr., interview.

48. *Ibid.*

49. *Daily Oklahoman* (Oklahoma City, OK), November 12, 1984.

50. *Las Vegas* (NV) *Review-Journal,* November 12, 1984.

51. NBC Sports, Caesars Palace Grand Prix IV, November 11, 1984.

52. *Ibid.*

53. *Ibid.*

54. *Ibid.*

55. *Indianapolis* (IN) *Star,* November 12, 1984.

56. *National Speed Sport News,* November 14, 1984.

57. *Ibid.*

58. *Indianapolis* (IN) *Star,* November 12, 1984.

59. NBC Sports, Caesars Palace Grand Prix IV, November 11, 1984.

60. *Ibid.*

61. *National Speed Sport News,* November 14, 1984.

62. Mario Andretti interview.

63. NBC Sports, Caesars Palace Grand Prix IV, November 11, 1984.

64. *Las Vegas* (NV) *Review-Journal,* November 12, 1984.

65. *Las Vegas* (NV) *Review-Journal,* November 13, 1984.

66. *Ibid.*

67. *Las Vegas* (NV) *Review-Journal,* December 17, 1984.

68. *Ibid.*

69. *Ibid.*

70. *Palm Beach* (FL) *Post,* December 28, 1984.

71. *Las Vegas* (NV) *Review-Journal,* December 28, 1984.

72. *San Bernardino County* (CA) *Sun,* December 28, 1984.

73. *Ibid.*

74. *Miami* (FL) *Herald,* December 29, 1984.

75. *Akron* (OH) *Beacon-Journal,* July 6, 1987.

76. *South Beach Magazine,* April 29, 2006.

77. Hearings before the Permanent Subcommittee on Investigations, Organized Crime Activities, October 24–25, 1978, 724.

78. Department of Justice, Press Release, February 26, 1985.

79. *Ibid.*

80. *Santa Maria* (CA) *Times,* October 31, 1986.

81. *Reno* (NV) *Gazette-Journal,* April 30, 1987.

82. *Reno* (NV) *Gazette-Journal,* February 17, 1990.

83. *New York Times,* July 12, 1992.

84. *Ibid.*

85. *Ibid.*

86. *Motorsport Magazine,* December 1996.

87. *Ibid.*

88. *Ibid.*

89. *Arizona Republic* (Phoenix, AZ), May 28, 1989.

90. *Las Vegas* (NV) *Review-Journal,* September 23, 1996.

91. Official Program, Indianapolis 500, May 28, 1995.

92. *Ibid.*

93. *Ibid.*

94. *Las Vegas* (NV) *Review-Journal,* September 23, 1996.

95. Bruce Aguilera interview.

96. *Ibid.*

97. *Ibid.*

98. *Ibid.*

99. grandprix.com, January 27, 1997.

100. *Ibid.*

101. *Las Vegas* (NV) *Review-Journal,* August 13, 2016.

102. *Las Vegas* (NV) *Review-Journal,* September 23, 1996.

103. *Reno* (NV) *Gazette-Journal,* April 11, 1998.

104. *Los Angeles Times,* March 28, 1998.

105. *Ibid.*

106. SEC, Transition Report for the transition period from July 1, 2000 to December 31, 2000, Commission file number 1–11929, Dover Downs Entertainment, Inc.

107. *Associated Press,* December 19, 2001.

108. *Indiana* (PA) *Gazette,* June 25, 2005.

109. *Ibid.*

110. *Ibid.*

111. forbes.com/sites/csylt, October 18, 2014.

112. *Ibid.*

113. *Ibid.*

114. *Ibid.*

115. *Ibid.*

116. *Ibid.*

117. knpr.org/desert-companion, March 26, 2018

118. bbc.com/sport/formula1, January 23, 2017.

119. *Ibid.*

120. *Las Vegas* (NV) *Review-Journal,* December 8, 2017.

121. *Ibid.*

122. *Miami* (FL) *Herald,* May 3, 2018.

123. apexoff.com, October 15, 2019.

124. Reid and Demaris, *The Green Felt Jungle,* 73.

125. William D. Weinberger interview.

126. Mario Andretti interview.

127. *Miami* (FL) *News,* April 6, 1987.

Bibliography

Books

Bernstein, Carl, and Woodward, Bob. *All the President's Men.* New York: Warner Books, 1974.

Blum, William. *The CIA: A Forgotten History.* London: Zed Books, Ltd., 1986.

Bower, Tom. *No Angel: The Secret Life of Bernie Ecclestone.* London, England: Faber & Faber Limited, 2011.

Brandt, Charles. *I Heard You Paint Houses: Frank "The Irishman" Sheeran & Closing the Case on Jimmy Hoffa.* Lebanon, NH: Steerforth Press, 2016.

Brill, Steven. *The Teamsters: The Men, the Money, the Mob, and the Murder of Jimmy Hoffa.* New York: Pocket Books, 1978.

Cannon, Randall, and Gerry, Michael. *Stardust International Raceway: Motorsports Meets the Mob in Vegas, 1965–1971.* Jefferson, NC: McFarland, 2018.

Collins, Jim, and Porras, Jerry. *Built to Last: Successful Habits of Visionary Companies.* New York: Harper Business, 1994.

Davidson, Donald C. *1968 Indianapolis 500 Mile Race Yearbook.* Los Angeles: Floyd Clymer Publications, 1968.

Denton, Sally, and Morris, Roger. *The Money and the Power: The Making of Las Vegas and Its Hold on America.* New York: Alfred A. Knopf, 2001.

Friedman, Dave. *Indianapolis Racing Memories, 1961–1969.* Osceola, WI: Motorbooks International, 1997.

Granatelli, Anthony. *They Call Me Mister 500.* Chicago: Henry Regnery Company, 1969.

Greene, Robert W. *The Stingman: Inside Abscam.* New York: Elsevier Dutton Publishing, 1981.

Hersh, Seymour M. *Dark Side of Camelot, The.* New York: Little, Brown, and Company, 1997.

Hungness, Carl. *Indianapolis 500 Yearbook.* 1969–1972. Speedway, IN: Carl Hungness Publishing, 1973.

Hungness, Carl. *Indianapolis 500 Yearbook.* Speedway, IN: Carl Hungness Publishing, 1981.

Kennedy, Robert F. *The Enemy Within: The McClellan Committee's Crusade Against Jimmy Hoffa and Corrupt Labor Unions.* New York: Harper, 1960.

Libby, Bill. *Champions of the Indianapolis 500: The Men Who Have Won More Than Once.* New York: Dodd, Mead, and Company, 1976.

Lovell, Terry. *Bernie Ecclestone: King of Sport.* London: John Blake Publishing, 2008.

Maheu, Robert, and Hack, Richard. *Next to Hughes: Behind the Power and Tragic Downfall of Howard Hughes by His Closest Advisor.* New York: HarperCollins, 1992.

Manchester, William. *The Death of a President.* New York: Harper & Row, 1967.

Messick, Hank. *Lansky: The Shocking Untold Story of the Most Powerful Figure in the American Underworld Today—Meyer Lansky, Chairman of the Board of the National Crime Syndicate.* G.P. Putnam Sons, 1971.

Moehring, Eugene P. *Resort City in the Sunbelt: Las Vegas, 1930–1970.* Reno, NV: University of Nevada Press, 1989.

Nye, Doug. *McLaren: The Grand Prix, Can-Am, and Indy Cars.* Richmond, Surrey: Hazelton Publishing, 1984.

Pileggi, Nicholas. *Casino: Love and Honor in Las Vegas.* New York: Simon & Schuster, 1995.

Puzo, Mario. *Mario Puzo: Inside Las Vegas.* New York: Grosset & Dunlap, 1976.

Reid, Ed, and Demaris, Ovid. *The Green Felt Jungle: The Truth About Las Vegas.* New York: Trident Press, 1963.

Roberts, Jon, and Wright, Evan. *American Desperado: My Life—From Mafia Soldier to Cocaine Cowboy to Secret Government Asset.* New York: Crown Publishing Group, 2011.

Russo, Gus. *Supermob: How Sidney Korshak and His Criminal Associates Became America's Hidden Power Brokers.* New York: Bloomsbury USA, 2006.

Sawyer, Grant. *Hang Tough: An Activist in the Governor's Mansion.* University of Nevada Oral History Program, 1993.

Scalzo, Joe. *The Unbelievable Unsers.* Chicago: Henry Regnery Company, 1971.

Schumacher, Geoff. *Sun, Sin, and Suburbia.* Las Vegas: Stephens Press, LLC, 2004.

Schwartz, David. *Grandissimo: The First Emperor of Las Vegas, How Jay Sarno Won a Casino Empire, Lost It, and Inspired Modern Las Vegas.* Las Vegas: Winchester Books, 2013.

Shakespeare, William. *Julius Caesar.* New York: Simon & Schuster, 2011.

Sheehan, Jack. *The Players Who Made Las Vegas.* Reno, NV: University of Nevada Press, 1997.

Sheehan, Jack. *Quiet Kingmaker of Las Vegas: E. Parry Thomas.* Las Vegas: Stephens Press, 2009.

Smith, John L. *Running Scared: The Life and Treacherous Times of Steve Wynn.* New York: Barricade Books, 1995.

Talbot, David. *The Hidden History of the Kennedy Years.* New York: Free Press, 2007.

Thompson, Douglas. *Shadowland: The Untold Story of the Mafia's Global Gambling Conspiracy.* Edinburgh, Scotland: Mainstream Publishing, 2012.

Turner, Wallace. *Gambler's Money: The New Force in American Life.* Boston: Houghton Mifflin Company, 1965.

Watkins, Susan. *Bernie: The Biography of Bernie Ecclestone.* Somerset, United Kingdom: Haynes Publishing, 2010.

Wyden, Peter. *Bay of Pigs: The Untold Story.* New York: Simon & Schuster, 1979.

Young, Eoin S. *McLaren: The Man, the Cars, & the Team.* Newport Beach, CA: Bond, Parkhurst Publications, 1971.

Magazines

Brown, Joseph. "Shareef Malnik & The Forge Dynasty." *South Beach Magazine,* April 29, 2006,

"Forlorn in the USA?" *Motorsport Magazine,* December 1996.

Henry, Alan. "1984 Dallas Grand Prix race report." *Motorsport Magazine,* August 1984.

Henry, Alan. "The United States Grand Prix west." *Motorsport Magazine,* May 1977.

Hutchinson, Peter L.V., "Inside the Sports Racers." *Car and Driver,* November 1967.

Kovacik, Bob. "USRRC: Vegas, Riverside, and Laguna." *Sports Car Graphic,* July 1967.

Kramer, Michael. "Manes, the Mess, and the Mayor." *New York Magazine,* February 10, 1986.

Lyons, Pete. "Caesars Palace Grand Prix—The trivialization of Grand Prix Racing!" *Car and Driver,* February 1982.

Lyons, Pete. "Can-Am." *Vintage Motorsport,* November/December 1996.

Manney, Henry N. "Can-Am Championship." *Road & Track,* February 1967.

"A Place to Run in the Sun." *Motor Trend,* August 1966.

Roebuck, Nigel. "A gamble that didn't pay off." *Motorsport Magazine,* January 2012.

"Rumbles under the roulette wheel." Motorsport Magazine, November 1981.

Tosches, Nick. "The Man Who Kept the Secrets." *Vanity Fair,* April 6, 1997.

Tremayne, David. "I know how fast good luck can turn back on you. And I've had some good fortune this summer." *Motorsport Magazine,* August 2010.

Wright, Angela, and Jarvis, Jan. "Grand Prix, Grand Scam-Grand Jury?" *D Magazine,* July 1985.

Yates, Brock. "You Ain't Seen Nuthin' 'Til You've Seen Vegas." *Car and Driver,* November 1967.

Ephemera

Boyer Las Vegas Early History Project, Interview with Stuart Mason, November 9, 2006.

Caesars Palace Grand Prix Press Release. "Andretti Will Race in Caesars Palace Grand Prix." September 25, 1982.

Caesars Palace Grand Prix Press Release. "Auto Racing and Las Vegas? Caesars Palace Made it Work." October 20, 1981.

Caesars Palace Grand Prix Press Release. "Caesars Palace—A Matter of Image." September 25, 1982.

Caesars Palace Grand Prix Press Release. "How Fast is Caesars Palace Grand Prix? No. 1 Among U.S. Formula One Courses." September 25, 1982.

Caesars Palace Grand Prix Press Release. "Newman Returns as Race Chairman of Caesars Palace Grand Prix." September 25, 1982.

Media Information, Caesars Palace Grand Prix, October 17, 1981.

Media Information, Caesars Palace Grand Prix, September 25, 1982.

Official Inaugural Program, Caesars Palace Grand Prix, October 14–17, 1981.

Official Program, Caesars Palace Grand Prix, September 23–26, 1982.

Official Program, Caesars Palace Grand Prix III, October 6–9, 1983

Official Program, Caesars Palace Grand Prix IV, November 9–11, 1984.

Official Program, Grand Prix of the United States, Watkins Glen, NY, October 8, 1961.

Official Program, Grand Prix of the U.S., Riverside International Raceway, November 19–10, 1960.

Official Program, Inaugural Long Beach Grand Prix, September 28, 1975.

Official Program, Indianapolis 500, May 28, 1995.

Official Program, Long Beach Grand Prix, April 1–3, 1977.

Official Program, Lubri Lon Long Beach Grand Prix, April 8, 1979

Official Program, Questor Grand Prix, Ontario Motor Speedway, March 28, 1971.

Official Program, Toyota Grand Prix of Long Beach, 1983.

Official Program, Toyota Grand Prix of Long Beach, April 2–4, 1982.

Official Program, Toyota Grand Prix of Long Beach, March 13–15, 1981.

Official Program, Toyota Grand Prix of Long Beach, March 30, 1980.

Official Program, Toyota Grand Prix of Long Beach, March 30–April 1, 1984.

Official Program, United States Grand Prix West, Long Beach, CA, March 26–28, 1976

Southern Nevada Jewish Community Digital Heritage Project, Interview with Gary Sternberg, February 15, 2015.

Southern Nevada Jewish Heritage Project, Interview with Stanley and Sandy Mallin, January 7, 2015.

Weisberg, Harold, Press Conference, November 13, 1967.

Newspapers

Akron (OH) *Beacon-Journal,* 1966–1987.
Albuquerque (NM) *Journal,* 1966.
Anderson (IN) *Daily Bulletin,* 1958.
Argus (Fremont, CA), 1973.
Arizona Daily Star (Tucson, AZ), 1969–1972.
Arizona Republic (Phoenix, AZ), 1972–1989.
Asbury Park (NJ) *Press,* 1976–1995.
Associated Press, 2001.
Atlanta (GA) *Constitution,* 1957–1970.
Auto Week, 2015.
Bakersfield (CA) *Californian,* 1965–1977.
Baltimore (MD) *Sun,* 1966–1968.
Berkeley (CA) *Gazette,* 1979.
Berkshire Eagle (Pittsfield, MA), 1948.
Boston Globe, 1960–1981.
Brattleboro (VT) *Reformer,* 1977.
Burlington (VT) *Free Press,* 1981.
Central New Jersey Home News (New Brunswick, NJ), 1976–1980.
Chicago Tribune, 1961–2006
Courier-News (Bridgewater, NJ), 1980.
Courier-Post (Camden, NJ), 1980.
Cycle News, 1982.
Daily Journal (Vineland, NJ), 1980.
Daily Messenger (Canandaigua, NY), 1973.
Daily Oklahoman (Oklahoma City, OK), 1975.
Daily Record (Morristown, NJ), 1980.
Daily Register (Red Bank, NJ), 1981.
Daily Sentinel (Grand Junction, CO), 1961.
Decatur (IL) *Daily Review,* 1979.
Democrat and Chronicle (Rochester, NY), 1948–1983.
Detroit (MI) *Free Press,* 1948–1984
Dispatch (Moline, IL), 1981.
Edinburgh (IN) *Daily Courier,* 1948
Edmonton Journal (Edmonton, Alberta, Canada), 1962–1983.
Edwards (IL) *Intelligencer,* 1976
El Paso (TX) *Times,* 1976.
Elmira (NY) *Advertiser,* 1957–1961.
Evening Times (Sayre, PA), 1976.
Fort Lauderdale (FL) *News,* 1965–1972.
Fort Worth (TX) *Star Telegram,* 1983.
Gazette (Montreal, Quebec, Canada), 1961.
Green Bay (WI) *Press,* 1970.
Guardian (London, Greater London, England), 1977.
Hartford (CT) *Courant,* 1960–1981.
Herald-News (Passaic, NJ), 1966–1981.
Honolulu (HI) *Star-Bulletin,* 1967–1970.
Independent (Long Beach, CA) 1960–1977.
Independent Press-Telegram (Long Beach, CA, 1974–1984.
Indiana (PA) *Gazette,* 2005.
Indianapolis (IN) *News,* 1958–1981.
Indianapolis (IN) *Star,* 1978–1984.
Ithaca (NY) *Journal,* 1969–1982.
Johnson City (TN) *Press,* 1982.
Journal and Courier (Lafayette, IN), 1983.
Journal News (White Plains, NY), 1958.
Lansing (MI) *State Journal,* 1981.

Las Vegas (NV) *Israelite,* 1965.
Las Vegas (NV) *Review-Journal,* 1965–2017.
Las Vegas (NV) *Sun,* 1965–1970.
Longview (WA) *Daily News,* 1974.
Los Angeles Times, 1965–1998.
Miami (FL) *News,* 1960–1987.
Millville (NJ) *Daily,* 1980.
Monrovia (CA) *News-Post,* 1980.
National Speed Sport News, 1981–1984.
Nevada Evening Gazette (Reno, NV), 1977.
Nevada State Journal, 1966.
New York (NY) *Daily News,* 1946–1988.
New York Times, 1957–1992
News-Herald (Franklin, PA), 1967.
News-Pilot (San Pedro, CA), 1979.
News-Press (Fort Myers, FL), 1975.
Oakland (CA) *Tribune,* 1960–1970.
Observer (London, Greater London, England), 1960–1982.
Orlando (FL) *Evening Star,* 1967.
Orlando (FL) *Sentinel,* 1964–1976.
Oshkosh (WI) *Northwestern,* 1979.
Ottawa Citizen (Ottawa, Ontario, Canada), 1961–1975.
Palm Beach (FL) *Post,* 1973–1984.
Pasadena (CA) *Independent,* 1960.
Paterson (NJ) *News,* 1980.
Pensacola (FL) *News Journal,* 1981.
Philadelphia (PA) *Daily News,* 1979.
Philadelphia (PA) *Inquirer,* 1971–1981.
Pittsburgh (PA) *Press,* 1978–1979.
Pocono (PA) *Record,* 1971.
Pomona (CA) *Progress Bulletin,* 1974.
Post-Standard (Syracuse, NY), 1974.
Post-Star (Glen Falls, NY), 1976–1986.
Poughkeepsie (NY) *Journal,* 1978.
Press and Sun-Bulletin (Binghamton, NY), 1952–1980.
Press Democrat (Santa Rosa, CA), 1970.
Province (Vancouver, British Columbia, Canada), 1983.
Record (Hackensack, NJ), 1970–1982.
Reno (NV) *Gazette-Journal,* 1957–1998.
Republic (Columbus, IN), 1968.
Roseville (CA) *Press-Tribune,* 1961.
St. Louis (MO) *Post-Dispatch,* 1983.
Salt Lake City (UT) *Tribune,* 1964.
San Bernardino County (CA) *Sun,* 1961–1984.
San Francisco Examiner, 1960–1983.
Santa Cruz (CA) *Sentinel,* 1969–1970.
Santa Maria (CA) *Times,* 1973–1986.
SCCA News, 1981.
SEC News Digest, 1969–1981
Southern Illinoisan (Carbondale, IL), 1977–1983.
Springfield (MO) *Leader and Press,* 1978.
Star Press (Muncie, IN), 1980.
Star Tribune (Minneapolis, MN), 1960.
Star-Gazette (Elmira, NY), 1919–1984.
Sydney (New South Wales, Australia) *Morning Herald,* 1972–1982.
Tallahassee (FL) *Democrat,* 1957–1969.
Tampa (FL) *Tribune,* 1959–1970.
Tampa Bay (FL) *Times,* 1966–1970.

Tennessean (Nashville, TN), 1974.
Terre Haute (IN) *Tribune,* 1957–1958.
Times (San Mateo, CA), 1970–1976.
Times Colonist (Victoria, British Columbia, Canada), 1962–1976.
Times-Tribune (Scranton, PA), 1979.
Town Talk (Alexandria, LA), 1981.
Tribune (Scranton, PA), 1975.
Ukiah (CA) *Daily Journal,* 1975.
Windsor Star (Windsor, Ontario, Canada), 1982.

Official Sources

Civil Aeronautics Board, Docket 16207, Kirk Kerkorian et al., Interlocking Relationships, September 23, 1965.
Commonwealth of Massachusetts, Legislative Research Bureau, Report Relative to Casino Gambling, April 13, 1983.
Congressional Record, June 18, 1969.
Congressional Record, March 8, 1967.
Congressional Record, September 26, 1972
Desert Palace, Inc., Articles of Incorporation, December 2, 1964.
DOJ Memorandum, AAG–Criminal Division Herman Miller to Director-FBI, October 15, 1962.
DOJ Press Release, October 22, 1971.
FBI Airtel, SAC–Las Vegas to Director-FBI, February 18, 1966, 3–4.
FBI Chicago FO File 122–60, February 7, 1963FBI New York FO File 92–1099, June 13, 1963.
FBI Chicago FO File 62–2020, November 29, 1962.
FBI Las Vegas FO File 87–8351, August 3, 1971.
FBI Los Angeles FO, Case: Vincent Alo, August 9, 1967.
FBI Miami FO, Agency File No. 62-9-29-585, September 28, 1965.
FBI Miami FO File 92–515, April 2, 1962.
FBI Miami FO File 92–515, December 20, 1963.
FBI Miami FO File 92–515, November 12, 1963.
FBI Miami FO File 92–515, October 21, 1965
FBI Miami FO File 92–515 Sub II, September 16, 1963.
FBI New York FO File 137–9551, November 1, 1964.
FBI New York FO File 166-New, May 23, 1969.
FBI New York FO File 92–1099, August 14, 1961.
FBI New York FO File 92–1099, August 31, 1961.
FBI New York FO File 92–1099, October 4, 1963.
FBI New York FO File 92–1099, September 12, 1961.
FBI Record No. 124–90068–10116, August 27, 1958.
Hearings before the Permanent Subcommittee on Investigations, Organized Crime Activities, October 24–25, 1978.
House Select Committee on Assassinations, Chicago Police Department Files, May 22, 1978, 7.
Kamin v. Koren, 621 F. Supp. 444 (S.D.N.Y. 1985)
New Jersey Casino Control Commission, in the Matters of the Application of Bally's Park Place, Inc., a New Jersey Corporation, for a Casino License, March 16, 1981, 374.
New Jersey Casino Control Commission Boardwalk Regency Corporation and the Jemm Company,

In the Matter of the Applications for Casino Licenses, November 13, 1980, 295.
Pennsylvania Crime Commission, Report on Organized Crime, July 2, 1970.
SEC, Transition Report for the transition period from July 1, 2000 to December 31, 2000, Commission file number 1–11929, Dover Downs Entertainment, Inc.
State of California, Organized Crime Control Commission, May 1978.
United States v. Lazarus, United States Court of Appeals, Ninth Circuit, Jun 18, 1970, 425F.2d 638 (9th Cir. 1970).

Television

NBC Sports, Caesars Palace Grand Prix III, October 9, 1983.
NBC Sports, Caesars Palace Grand Prix IV, November 11, 1984.

Websites

apexoff.com
archives.gov
bbc.com/sport/formula1
champcarstats.com
eventmanagerblog.com
forbes.com/sites/csylt
grandprix.com
insiderlv.com
jfklibrary.org
knpr.org/desert-companion
loc.gov
miamibeachvisualmemoirs.com
newspapers.com
oldracingcars.com
f1.fandom.com
petelyons.com
racer.com
racing-reference.info
racingarchives.org
racingsportscars.com
revsinstitute.org
sec.gov
thehenryford.org
themobmuseum.org
ultimateracinghistory.com
unlv.edu
vintagelasvegas.com
wikipedia.org

Interviews and Correspondence

Aguilera, Bruce, in-person interview with Randall Cannon, August 22, 2019.
Andretti, Mario, telephone interview with Randall Cannon, January 27, 2016, and August 22, 2019.
Dallenbach, Jr., Wally, telephone interview with Randall Cannon, August 21, 2019.
Gerould, Gary, telephone interview with Randall Cannon, August 21, 2019.

Green, Bill, telephone interview with Randall Cannon, June 17, 2020.

Henle, Mike, e-mail to Randall Cannon, July 25, 2019.

Lake, Rick, telephone interview with Randall Cannon, May 13, 2020.

Long, Jack, telephone interview with Randall Cannon, September 16, 2019.

Marnell, Anthony, telephone interview with Randall Cannon, August 28, 2019.

Pernicano, Mary Lou, e-mail to Randall Cannon, August 21, 2019.

Pook, Christopher R., e-mail to Randall Cannon, August 21, 2019, and October 20, 2019.

St. James, Lyn, telephone interview with Randall Cannon, August 20, 2019.

Sarno, Jay, Jr., e-mail to Randall Cannon, October 3, 2019.

Scodwell, Tony, in-person interview, August 20, 2019.

Silver, Jeff, e-mail to Randall Cannon, September 10, 2019, and September 11, 2019.

Stewart, Sir Jackie, telephone interview with Randall Cannon, March 23, 2016.

Surtees, John, telephone interview with Randall Cannon, February 25, 2016.

Unser, Al, telephone interview with Randall Cannon, September 6, 2019.

Unser, Bobby, interview with Randall Cannon, January 29, 2016.

Weinberger, William D., e-mail to Randall Cannon, March 3, 2020, and May 4, 2020.

Weinberger, William D., in-person interview with Randall Cannon, October 10, 2019.

Index

Numbers in **bold italics** indicate pages with illustrations